SURVIVOR'S GUIDE TO
SMALL BUSINESS

Maria Townsley

THOMSON
━━━━━━
SOUTH-WESTERN

Australia · Canada · Mexico · Singapore · Spain · United Kingdom · United States

SOUTH-WESTERN
™
THOMSON LEARNING

Survivor's Guide to Small Business
by Maria Townsley

Vice President/Executive Publisher: Dave Shaut
Team Leader: Karen Schmohe
Executive Editor: Eve Lewis
Project Manager: Enid Nagel
Production Manager: Patricia Matthews Boies
Editor: Darrell E. Frye
Executive Marketing Manager: Carol Volz
Channel Manager: Chris L. McNamee
Consulting Editor: settingPace
Marketing Coordinator: Sharon Turner
Manufacturing Coordinator: Kevin L. Kluck
Art and Design Coordinator: Tippy McIntosh
Cover Design: Paul Neff
Internal Design and Composition: settingPace
Editorial Assistant: Linda Keith
Production Assistant: Nancy Stamper
Printer: Edwards Brothers, Ann Arbor

About the Author

Maria Townsley has been an educator and a professional writer in the business and educational arenas since 1984. Her corporate business activities include creating marketing materials and designing and implementing software documentation and training courses. Active in adult education and business training programs, Ms. Townsley has been a member of the Society for Technical Communication for many years.

Photo Credit: cover © Barton Stabler/Artville, all others © Getty Images/PhotoDisc

ISBN: 0-538-72573-7

Printed in the United States of America
1 2 3 4 5 6 07 06 05 04 03 02

For more information, contact South-Western, 5191 Natorp Boulevard, Mason, OH 45040.
Or you can visit our Internet site at www.swep.com.

YOUR COURSE PLANNING JUST GOT EASIER!

The *Survivor's Guide to Small Business* is a text like no other! Designed for professionals and managers who need to know the basics, this text will guide you through the world of small business development. Using a conversational style, *Survivor's Guide to Small Business* provides the most current topics and issues in entrepreneurship in an easy to understand manner.

Looking for other career-enhancement titles for today's professional? Explore these additional Survivor's Guides from South-Western!

Survivor's Guide to Finance
by Bergeron
Finance is the universal language of business! *Survivor's Guide to Finance* makes financial decision-making clear and concise to managers of all levels. Users with no formal training in accounting or finance will find this book as a solid source of financial understanding.

Text/CD Package   0-538-72517-6

Survivor's Guide to Technical Writing
by Ingre
A comprehensive, easy-to-use guide for key workplace communication skills is found in the *Survivor's Guide to Technical Writing*. Integrating the most current technology, this book reflects the most current topics and issues in technical communication.

Text/CD Package   0-538-72578-8

Survivor's Guide to the Legal Environment
by Adamson
Success in the workplace often depends on your ability to understand the basics of contracts, business organizations, and other day-to-day legal issues. Join us as we guide you in exploring the essentials and foundations of the law.

Text/CD Package   0-538-72523-0

SOUTH-WESTERN

THOMSON LEARNING

Join us on the Internet at www.swep.com

HOW TO USE THIS BOOK

Establishing a successful business requires more knowledge, skill, and effort than hanging a sign that says, "Lemonade 5¢" in your front yard. How do you know where to start?

The idea of starting a business can seem overwhelming. However, the goal becomes more attainable when the process is broken down into individual steps. That's what *Survivor's Guide to Small Business* does; it tells you (1) what you need to do, (2) when you need to do it, and (3) how you can accomplish each task.

Pour a cup of coffee (or a glass of 5¢ lemonade) and sit down with the *Survivor's Guide to Small Business*. Dog-ear the pages. Highlight the items you want to remember. Write notes in the margin. Use the worksheets, review the sample documents, and use the contact information on the CD. In other words, here are the tools—use them.

The approach in the *Survivor's Guide to Small Business* is logical. It walks you through developing your business idea, producing your product or service, and establishing your business. The eight units cover broad topics such as evaluating the current business environment, steps to complete before you start your business, hiring and managing employees, acquiring and managing financial resources, marketing activities, communicating effectively in the business environment, and methods of expansion for your successful business.

Each chapter in a unit focuses on a specific step in the process. For example, individual chapters address developing and manufacturing your product, obtaining licenses, writing a business plan, selecting suppliers, setting prices, selecting a financial institution, and developing your advertisements. Details such as guidelines for delivering an effective presentation and performing introductions aren't forgotten. When it is appropriate, specific information has been provided for retail, manufacturing, service, and home-based businesses.

In the end, success in the business world is the result of your decisions and actions. The *Survivor's Guide to Small Business* is a valuable tool that can help you succeed.

FIGURES AND TABLES Throughout the text figures and tables provide a quick overview of the material under review.

HYPOTHETICAL SCENARIOS A generous supply of hypothetical scenarios within the chapters provides understandable applications of small business issues under discussion.

TECHNOLOGY INSIGHTS Features highlighting the impact that new technology has on small business are given for each chapter. Technology Insights features cover the topics of PDAs (Personal Digital Assistants), business planning software, customer loyalty cards, speech recognition software, and telecommuting employees, among others.

END-OF-CHAPTER EXERCISES Each chapter ends with material to help you review the chapter concepts and assess the strength of your knowledge. Your knowledge of business terms is assessed in Use Business Terms. Test Your Reading assesses your retention of the facts. Your critical thinking skills and ability to apply the concepts covered in the chapter are measured in Think Critically About Business.

REAL-LIFE BUSINESSES The Real-Life Businesses at the end of the chapters have been selected for their involving nature and their potential to both integrate and project the nature of current business practices. Therefore, often there is no "right" answer to the questions that follow each business profile.

DATA CD The CD packaged with your textbook contains documents that enhance your knowledge of business in general. Samples of common business forms, such as a General Partnership Agreement, a Fictitious Business Name Statement, Employee Handbook, a Start-up Period Worksheet and many others, are included on the CD.

INTRUCTOR'S RESOURCE CD Provided on the CD to support the text is an Instructor's Manual that supplies solutions to all end-of-chapter questions. This CD also includes PowerPoint slides to help instructors present the material in class.

EXAMVIEW® PRO CD This CD provides an electronic test bank for each chapter to allow instructors to customize the testing program, edit questions, and create different versions of the same test.

REVIEWERS

Jack D. Cichy
Professor of Management
Grand Rapids, MI

Todd A. Finkle
Fellow, Fitzgerald Institute for Entrepreneurial Studies
Akron, OH

Don Friis
Instructor, Business Administration
Coeur d'Alene, ID

Cheryl Gracie
Instructor
Ann Arbor, MI

Len Middleton
Professor
Ann Arbor, MI

Michael B. Ryan
Attorney at Law
Bakersfield, CA

Jeffrey P. Shay
Assistant Professor
Missoula, MT

TABLE OF CONTENTS

Unit Eight   The Growth and Expansion of Your Business

UNIT 1

Evaluate the Business Environment

CHAPTERS

CHAPTER 1

Business Environment

GOALS

♦ Define entrepreneurship
♦ Describe how the economy affects the business environment
♦ Evaluate the current economic environment
♦ Explain the impact of small businesses

Sara Metsger could be described as successful. After earning a Bachelor of Science in Information Systems five years ago, she started her career as an entry-level programmer for a company that specializes in providing financial services for other businesses. During the last five years, Sara has been promoted twice. She is currently the lead programmer for a group of four programmers who are responsible for supporting a small accounting software application. Although Sara enjoys her job, she feels that many of her skills are not utilized. She spoke to her supervisor about the situation during her last performance review. Sara received a good raise, but her supervisor told her that there would not be any opportunities for advancement in the foreseeable future. Sara could look for a job at another company, but she likes the idea of operating her own business. After encouragement from her family and friends, Sara decided to investigate the possibility of starting a business.

Entrepreneurship

The decision to establish and operate your own business will impact every aspect of your life. It will require dedication, time, and most of the money you can scrape together. In return, the experience will encompass almost every descriptive word you can use—rewarding, exhausting, terrifying, and exhilarating—to name only a few. Every year, many new businesses are started but the failure rate is high. Only 20 percent of new businesses survive five years or more. However, every successful small business and large corporation started the same way—an individual with an idea.

What Is an Entrepreneur?

An **entrepreneur** is an individual who owns, manages, and assumes the financial risk of a business enterprise. Entrepreneurs are not as rare as you may think. Tax returns show that every year in the last decade, the number of new businesses established by American entrepreneurs has increased. According to the U.S. Small Business Administration, more than 21 million Americans are entrepreneurs.

Why Become an Entrepreneur?

The reasons for establishing a new business are different for everyone. You may be tired of working for someone else or you feel that your current job is not challenging or satisfying. You want to be your own boss and make the business decisions your current employer has not made successfully. You might want additional income to make your life more comfortable. You could have a passion for a hobby or activity that can be turned into a successful business, enabling you to spend every day doing something you truly enjoy.

Entrepreneurship in America

In addition to personal reasons, your environment and culture also contribute to your decision to start a business. **Culture** is an integrated pattern of behavior, knowledge, and beliefs that are acquired from a group and passed on to future generations. As an American citizen, you are influenced by American culture.

American culture values innovation, individuality, and advancement based on ability. This creates an environment that encourages entrepreneurship. Throughout America's history, tales of success and the American dream attracted individuals from many different countries. New Americans brought their own unique ethnic cultures with them which they passed on to the generations that followed them. Many of their values, such as hard work and a desire for personal achievement, have encouraged their children and grandchildren to strive for personal and financial success. This is evident in the number of businesses owned by ethnic minorities, including Americans of Asian, African, and Hispanic descent. According to the Small Business Administration, ethnic minorities owned 3.25 million businesses by 1997. Figure 1.1 identifies the percentage of businesses owned by ethnic minorities in 1997. The number of businesses owned by ethnic minorities is increasing 20 to 40 percent every year.

FIGURE 1.1   1997 Business Ownership

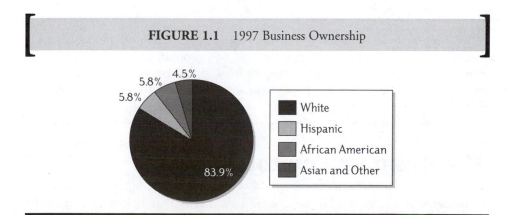

Characteristics and Skills of an Entrepreneur

Many of the tasks involved in running a business are the same, regardless of the type of business. For example, a steel manufacturer and a florist shop pay taxes, hire employees, and purchase materials. However, successful entrepreneurs are not all alike. They don't have the same personal characteristics or skills. They have different interests and experiences. Personal characteristics such as perseverance, integrity, and ingenuity are not common to all entrepreneurs. These qualities, however, can be helpful in achieving success in business or other career fields.

Operating a business successfully requires a variety of skills. Useful skills can be placed in three broad categories—logical, creative, and communicative. Logical skills require the ability to plan, evaluate, and calculate. Creative skills require the ability to design and create new products and methods. Communicative skills require the ability to listen to others, present your thoughts in a way that can be easily understood, and persuade others to agree with you. Table 1.1 identifies specific activities an entrepreneur may perform in each skill category.

TABLE 1.1 Entrepreneurial Skills

Logical	Creative	Communicative
◆ Perform legal tasks to establish business	◆ Create new product or service	◆ Negotiate with suppliers
◆ Manage business finances	◆ Design business location	◆ Provide customer service
◆ Set prices	◆ Select merchandise	◆ Hire employees
◆ Schedule jobs, workers, and tasks	◆ Market product or service	◆ Prepare business correspondence

Every entrepreneur does not have all the skills required to run a business. However, these tasks are necessary for a business to succeed. Therefore, an entrepreneur must acquire the skills through training, establish the business with one or more partners who have the missing skills, or hire employees or consultants with the needed skills.

Hypothetical Scenario

Sara Metsger has a college degree in Information Systems and some work experience managing a small group of programmers within a larger company. Based on her background, list the entrepreneurial skills that Sara may possess. Identify the skills that may be missing. Is it possible for Sara to acquire any missing skills by keeping her current job? What steps should she take to prepare herself for the role of an entrepreneur?

The Business Environment

The existing business environment affects purchasing decisions made by **consumers,** individuals who use goods. This means that before you decide to establish a business, you need to analyze the current business environment. This knowledge will help you make many decisions as you start and operate your company. Decisions such as the type of product or service you sell to consumers, the number of employees you hire, and the location you select are only a few of your choices that are affected by the current business environment. To run a business, it is not necessary to be an **economist,** a specialist who studies the economy. However, understanding the economy will help you notice the signs of change in the prosperity of your customers and adapt your business decisions accordingly.

In today's world, countries affect each other on an economic level. Dips in the American economy are quickly reflected by dips in the economies of other countries. Economic decisions made by individuals or a business group in one country can affect millions of people in another part of the world. OPEC (Organization of Petroleum Exporting Countries) is a clear example. Members of OPEC include countries with large reserves of crude oil such as Saudi Arabia, Iran, Iraq, and Indonesia. OPEC sets the price for the oil sold and exported to other countries. When OPEC increases the price of a barrel of crude oil, the price of gasoline increases at gas stations all across America. Paying more for gasoline affects Americans' behavior and economic decisions. They travel less and spend less on luxury items.

To manufacture and produce items, a business must use resources. **Resources** are natural sources of materials or wealth. Resources include naturally occurring items such as oil, trees, and minerals. The way a nation uses resources to produce goods and services is its **economic system.** Resources are limited within any geographic area, such as within a nation's borders. Therefore, a nation's economic system affects a citizen's opportunities and success in business. There are two major types of economic systems—command and free market.

Command Economy

In a **command economy,** the government owns most of the nation's resources and commands businesses to produce specific items or perform specific jobs. The government controls the business environment within the country's boundaries. It determines the product and the quantity that a business will produce. The type and quantity of products manufactured are not directly determined by any actual need for the products or the rate at which consumers purchase the product. Therefore, a business does not necessarily make a profit. Figure 1.2 demonstrates the relationship between the basic economic components in a command economy. The consumer has little impact on the business decisions made by the manufacturers. For example, a government agency could determine that 6,000 chairs are needed. It selects three manufacturers, who will each make 2,000 chairs. The government distributes the resources needed to make the chairs to each of the manufacturers. The manufacturers will make a total of 6,000 chairs. If 8,000 consumers actually want to buy chairs, 2,000 consumers will not be happy. If only 4,000 consumers want to buy chairs, there will be 2,000 extra chairs that no one will buy.

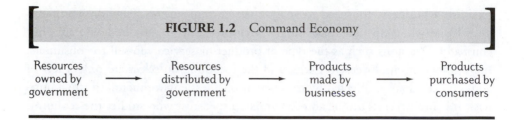

FIGURE 1.2   Command Economy

Resources owned by government → Resources distributed by government → Products made by businesses → Products purchased by consumers

Free Market Economy

Most industrial nations, including the United States, have a free market economy. In a **free market economy,** resources are privately owned and each business determines the products or services it will produce and sell. The market for a product, which defines the number of items that can be sold, determines the product and quantity of the product that a business will produce. The purpose of each business in a free market economy is to earn a profit. Every business decision is based on the potential profit that can be earned or lost from the action. Through the economic factors of demand, supply, and scarcity, consumers have a major impact on the success of any business in a free market economy. Figure 1.3 explains the relationship between consumers and manufacturers in a free market economy.

   Law of Demand   The economic **law of demand** states that consumers will buy more of a product at a lower price than at a higher price. For example, if Sally's

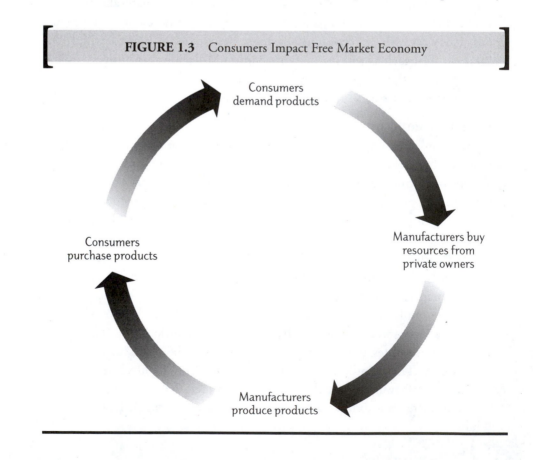

FIGURE 1.3   Consumers Impact Free Market Economy

Consumers demand products

Manufacturers buy resources from private owners

Manufacturers produce products

Consumers purchase products

Seashore Sweets advertised double-dipped ice cream cones for $0.10 on the hottest day of summer, the line of customers waiting to buy a cone would be a block long. If Tim's Treats, a competitor located across the street, advertised the same cone for $5, it probably wouldn't sell a single cone. Consumers will buy more cones for $0.10 than they will for $5. Figure 1.4 illustrates that the demand for the cheaper cones is higher than the demand for the more expensive cones and demand drops as the price increases.

FIGURE 1.4   Law of Demand

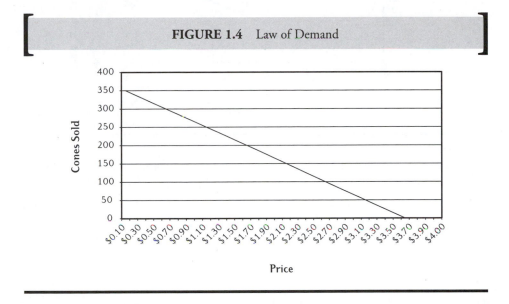

Law of Supply The economic **law of supply** states that producers are willing to sell more of a product at a higher price than at a lower price. Although Sally's Seashore Sweets can sell hundreds of cones for $0.10, Sally is not willing to sell hundreds of cones for such a low price. The store would quickly go out of business. Rather than making a profit, Sally's Seashore Sweets would be losing money because it costs more than $0.10 to make the cone. It could not continue to sell cones at this price. Because businesses operate to earn a profit, they want to sell more products at a higher price to earn the most profit possible. For example, Sally's Seashore Sweets would rather sell the double-dipped ice cream cones for a higher price to cover the cost of making the cones and earn a profit on each sale. After the sale, if a customer asked to buy a cone for $0.10, Sally would refuse to sell the cone. If a customer offered $5 for each cone, Sally would be happy to sell the customer as many ice cream cones as possible. Figure 1.5 illustrates how Sally's desire to sell cones increases as the price increases.

Equilibrium In a free market economy, supply and demand determine the price of a product or service. The **equilibrium price** for a product is the price at which the quantity supplied exactly equals the quantity demanded of that product. If you place the data for supply and demand on the same line chart, the lines intersect at the equilibrium price. At the equilibrium price, the consumer is willing to pay a price that is acceptable to the business. The business earns a profit and the

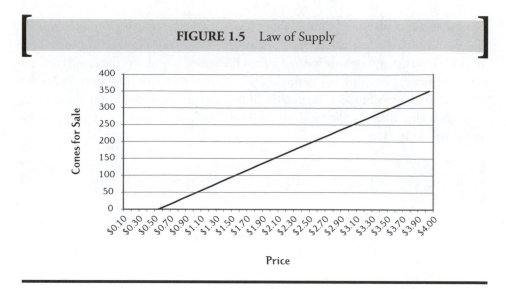

FIGURE 1.5   Law of Supply

consumer does not feel cheated. Figure 1.6 illustrates the equilibrium price for ice cream cones at Sally's Seashore Sweets. The equilibrium price for Sally's double-dipped ice cream cone is $2.10. Sally is willing to sell a cone for $2.10 and enough consumers are willing to pay $2.10 for the cones that Sally can earn a profit on her sales. Consumers that want to pay less will buy their ice cream cones from a different store or won't buy any cones at all.

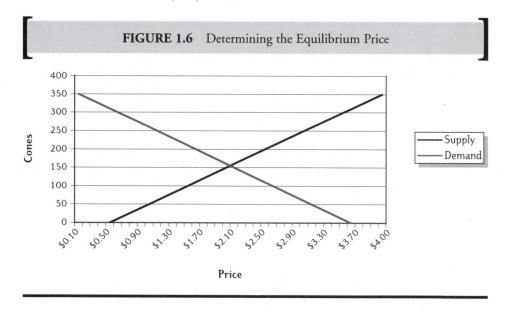

FIGURE 1.6   Determining the Equilibrium Price

Scarcity When a product is manufactured, resources are consumed. For example, if wood is used to make a chair, the tree is consumed. As resources are consumed, the resources that remain become more valuable and the products made from those resources become more expensive. **Scarcity** occurs when consumers want more than the available resources. Some resources, such as trees, can be replaced by businesses that use the resource. However, it takes time to replenish the resource. Planting a new tree does not immediately replace the tree that was used. A 100-foot tree takes many years to grow. Resources that are very limited, useful, and cannot be replenished, such as gold and gems, are valuable. Supply and demand assign value to products. The value of each resource is derived from the availability of the material and its usefulness.

Business Cycles

Occasionally, the economic conditions within a free market economy fluctuate. Although these fluctuations are known as cycles, the occurrence of these changes is not regular or predictable. A **business cycle** is a time period identified by a specific level of economic activity. It is marked by changes in economic activity measured by economic factors such as employment levels, prices, and production. Although conditions in the economy never change as smoothly or as regularly as the example in Figure 1.7, which shows three complete business cycles, you can identify the four parts of the business cycle. The economy goes through periods of expansion and contraction separated by a peak or a trough. A business cycle usually takes several years to complete.

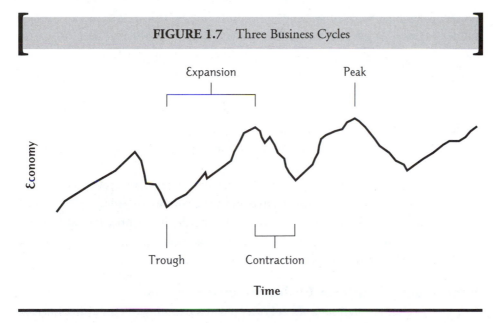

FIGURE 1.7   Three Business Cycles

The economy constantly experiences minor fluctuations without entering a new phase in the business cycle. Local disasters such as tornadoes or poor harvests cause prices to increase because the supply of some items goes down while the demand remains steady. Local surpluses can cause prices to decrease because the supply of some items increases while the demand remains steady. Because of the constant shifts in the economy, it is difficult to determine the turning point that marks the change from one phase to the next. Often, the change can only be identified by economists in hindsight, well after the change has occurred.

During a time of **expansion,** a period of general economic improvement, business is booming. The value of most companies increases, proven by the increase of stock prices for companies that are traded publicly in the stock market. Large and small businesses expand. They increase production, develop new products, open additional stores or offices, and hire additional employees. Unemployment is low. Consumers feel confident about their economic future and spend money freely. Prices rise because consumers are willing and able to pay the higher prices.

The economy continues to expand, sometimes for several years, before it reaches its peak. A **peak** is the end of an expansion phase in a business cycle. It is not a single moment when everything is great just before the economy suddenly falls apart. Indicators such as unemployment and stock prices change gradually, beginning to show weakness. Companies stop hiring new employees and begin to show caution in their spending.

During a time of **contraction,** a period of general economic decline, personal and business income and consumption drop. Companies cut back production because they have surplus items in their inventories. They not only stop hiring new employees; they may also reduce their current workforce. Consumers begin to feel that their jobs are in danger. Consumers reduce spending, resulting in a lower income for many businesses. Businesses continue to reduce spending. The stock prices of publicly traded companies drop. Consumers are not only worried about their job security, they begin to lose money in their investments and stock purchases. These additional losses force consumers to reduce spending even more. Weak companies may be forced out of business. Based on severity and duration, a contraction may be classified as a recession or a depression. A **recession** is a period of significant decline in trade, employment, and income. A recession usually lasts from six months to a year. A **depression** is a recession that is major in scale and duration. It can last several years.

A **trough** is the end of a contraction phase in a business cycle. Like a peak, it is easier to identify after it has occurred and the economy is beginning to recover. Consumers begin to buy more products, reducing the inventories stored in many company warehouses. As product demand increases, manufacturers increase production. The expansion phase of the next business cycle will begin.

Importance of Business Cycles to Entrepreneurs

Current economic conditions affect entrepreneurs planning to establish a business or operate an existing business. During a period of expansion, conditions are favorable for establishing or expanding a business.

- Consumers are willing to spend money.
- Business loans are easy to obtain.
- The interest rate on loans is low.
- Materials needed for products are easily available.

A period of contraction is not the best time to launch a new business venture. Consumers are cautious and unwilling to try new products or new business establishments. The money needed to start a new business is difficult to obtain. The chance for success is much lower during a contraction than during a period of expansion. The more severe the contraction and the longer it extends, the more difficult it will be to establish a successful business before the economy recovers.

The economic environment also affects existing businesses. It may be necessary to put any plans for expansion on hold. Small businesses, defined as businesses with fewer than 500 employees, may be hit harder than larger businesses by a dip in the economy.

Evaluate the Current Business Environment The importance of the current business environment to your success means that you should evaluate the environment before you invest your time and money in a business venture. There are many economic indicators that can be used to take a snapshot of the current environment. Some indicators move before the economy changes. Other indicators move after the economy changes. **Leading economic indicators** are statistics that reliably move up or down before the general economy follows. They are often used to predict the behavior of the general economy. The leading economic indicators shift direction three to 12 months before the economy follows, leading the change in direction. *The Wall Street Journal, Investor's Business Daily,* and *BusinessWeek* are among many sources that publish leading economic indicators.

Examine the leading economic indicators to evaluate the current economic environment before you prepare to start a new business venture. Although there are a variety of indicators, the commonly used leading economic indicators in Table 1.2 can help you analyze current conditions. Identify the current rating and recent trend for the economic indicators in the table to predict the economic environment for your business.

TABLE 1.2   Leading Economic Indicators

Economic Indicators	Description	Current Rating	Recent Trend
Unemployment claims	Number of initial claims for unemployment insurance		
S&P 500	Standard & Poor's 500 Stock Price Index represents the price movements of common stocks in the stock market		
Consumer Price Index (CPI)	Measures the average change in the price urban consumers pay for a specific list of goods and services		
Producer Price Index (PPI)	Measures the average change in price from the perspective of the sellers, domestic producers of goods and services		
Average workweek	Average hours worked by personnel in one week in a manufacturing business		
New building permits issued	Number of new residential building permits issued		

TABLE 1.2   Leading Economic Indicators (continued)

Economic Indicators	Description	Current Rating	Recent Trend
Money supply (M2)	Measure of U.S. money supply that includes currency held by the public, traveler's checks, demand deposits, checkable accounts, savings deposits, time deposits less than $100,000, and balances in money market mutual funds (other than those limited to institutional investors)		
Vendor performance	Percentage of companies receiving slower deliveries from suppliers		
Durable goods orders	Orders placed by manufacturers for durable goods, such as cars, that last more than three years		
Consumer sentiment index	Measures consumers' confidence in the economy		
Plant and equipment orders	Orders placed for manufacturing equipment		

Contributions of Small Businesses

The economy affects the success of small businesses. However, the relationship goes both ways. Small businesses also affect the economy. Although the economy is made up of many businesses, both large and small, small businesses are responsible for much of the stability and growth of the American economy. Although the success or failure of one small business will not change the national economic environment, the success or failure of many small businesses can have a tremendous impact on the economy. Many individuals are employees of American small businesses. The following statistics demonstrate the impact of small businesses on the economy:

- More than 99 percent of employers are small businesses.
- Almost all of the individuals who are self-employed are classified as small businesses.
- Small businesses conduct 47 percent of all sales in America.
- Small businesses are more likely to hire workers who are younger or older than average workers because they are more flexible in accommodating employees that prefer to work part time.
- Most workers receive their initial on-the-job training in basic skills from small businesses.
- Businesses that specialize in high technology products are usually small businesses. Ninety-four percent of these businesses have fewer than 500 employees.

Small businesses affect more than the economy. Their innovative ideas and experimentation have led to many technological advances. Small biotech firms have discovered medical advances that have helped many individuals, possibly family or friends who are close to you. Small businesses are responsible for many products or services that make your life easier or more enjoyable, such as a variety of timesaving household appliances, floral arrangements, and computer games. As a consumer, you frequently purchase products or services from small businesses. Many retail stores that you visit, veterinarians who care for your pets, and restaurants where you meet your friends for dinner are small businesses.

Technology Insights

Using the Internet

Many individuals surf the Internet every day. They play games, exchange e-mail with business associates, and chat with distant friends and relatives. For entrepreneurs, however, the Internet is a powerful business tool. Accurate and timely information is critical to making decisions that could lead to the success or failure of your business venture. Details about current economic conditions, existing products, competitors, and other helpful information can be found on the Internet. To locate this information, it is important to become familiar with web sites that will help you search the Internet for specific words or phrases. Visit several of the following web sites to become familiar with the search process and the syntax you should use to perform an efficient search that will provide relevant and helpful information. These web sites provide additional search tools:

- www.google.com
- www.yahoo.com
- www.go.com
- www.excite.com
- www.metacrawler.com

Think Critically   Use one or more of the Internet search tools to locate information about Coldwater Creek. How would this information help a potential competitor? Make a list of the useful information you think an entrepreneur could find on the Internet.

CHAPTER REVIEW

Many individuals have what it takes to be entrepreneurs. In fact, statistics from the Small Business Administration show that the number of successful entrepreneurs increases every year. People decide to establish a business for a variety of reasons. Your reasons for pursuing a new business venture are unique to you. The environment in America is ideal for entrepreneurs. The American culture encourages independence, resourcefulness, and the personal achievement that results from fully using your skills. Entrepreneurial skills can be divided into three groups—logical, creative, and communicative. All of these skills are required to establish and operate a successful business.

The free market economic system in the United States provides the ideal environment for entrepreneurs. It is driven by consumers' demands for specific products or services. Businesses must use privately owned resources to produce the items demanded by consumers. The economy is driven by the laws of supply and demand. The law of demand identifies the quantity that consumers want to purchase. The law of supply identifies the quantity that businesses want to sell. The demand equals the supply when the business sets a price that is satisfactory to both the seller and the buyer.

In a free market economy, business conditions fluctuate, forming business cycles. A business cycle, which could last several years, goes through four stages—expansion, peak, contraction, and trough. A period of expansion is the best time to establish a new business. Consumers are more willing to buy new products and visit new stores during times of economic prosperity.

Leading economic indicators can help you evaluate the current stage of the business cycle. Use the economic information to select a good time to establish a business and make decisions for an existing business.

Small businesses have a major impact on the economy and living conditions. They employ a majority of American workers and produce a high percentage of American goods. They are also responsible for many innovations and advances in technology and other products.

USE BUSINESS TERMS

Fill in the blanks with the appropriate term.

business cycle

command economy

consumer

contraction

culture

depression

economic system

economist

entrepreneur

equilibrium price

expansion

free market economy

law of demand

law of supply

leading economic indicators

peak

recession

resources

scarcity

trough

1. The ____?____ signifies the lowest point of a business cycle.
2. The economic system in the United States is a(n) ____?____ .
3. A(n) ____?____ can be classified as a recession or depression.
4. ____?____ affects an individual's interest in becoming an entrepreneur.
5. Everyone is a(n) ____?____ .
6. ____?____ determines the value of a useful resource.
7. Entrepreneurs should examine the current values and trends of the ____?____ before beginning a business venture.

TEST YOUR READING

8. How many American citizens are entrepreneurs?
9. How does culture affect entrepreneurship in America?
10. Describe the skills an entrepreneur should have or acquire.
11. Why is it important to understand the economy?
12. How are resources handled in a nation with a command economy?
13. Describe the consumer's impact on business in a command economy.
14. How are resources handled in a nation with a free market economy?
15. Describe the consumer's impact on business in a free market economy.
16. Explain the laws of supply and demand. Provide an example.
17. Describe the environment during a period of expansion and a period of contraction.
18. What is a small business?
19. Why are business cycles important to entrepreneurs?

THINK CRITICALLY ABOUT BUSINESS

20. Examine your personal characteristics and skills. Evaluate your potential as an entrepreneur.
21. Describe the role of culture for individual entrepreneurs and entrepreneurship in America. How has your culture affected your interest in entrepreneurship?
22. Describe the effect of current economic conditions on a local business establishment.
23. Evaluate the leading economic indicators. Would this be a good time to establish a new business?

Economic Indicators	Current Rating	Recent Trend
Unemployment claims		
S&P 500		
Consumer Price Index (CPI)		
Producer Price Index (PPI)		
Average workweek		
New building permits issued		
Money supply (M2)		
Vendor performance		
Durable goods orders		
Consumer sentiment index		
Plant and equipment orders		

REAL-LIFE BUSINESS

Coldwater Creek

In 1984, Dennis and Ann Pence established Coldwater Creek in a single room equipped with a telephone, a pile of merchandise, and the dream of becoming successful entrepreneurs. Today, Coldwater Creek is one of the leading catalog retailers in the country. It took more than a dream to develop the small business with only two owners into a large company with almost 2,000 employees.

The first Coldwater Creek catalog was 18 pages long. It was mailed to about 2,000 consumers. The products in the catalog were selected carefully to appeal to their chosen market—professional women 35–55 years of age who are comfortable shopping through a catalog or web site. In the year 2000, Coldwater Creek mailed approximately 180 million catalogs. The mailing list for the four Coldwater Creek catalogs consisted of more than 10 million customers.

Coldwater Creek passed several milestones as it grew into a major catalog retailer. Each step was the result of careful consideration that prepared the way for future growth.

- 1984—Coldwater Creek was established.
- 1985—Northcountry, the company's core catalog featuring a variety of clothing, accessories, and gift items, was introduced.
- 1993—Spirit of the West, a catalog carrying similar upscale items, was introduced.
- 1999—Coldwater Creek Home, a catalog specializing in home accessories that fit the company's image, was introduced.
- 1997—Coldwater Creek began trading on the NASDAQ under the symbol CWTR.
- 1999—Coldwater Creek established an Internet retail site— www.coldwater-creek.com.
- 2000—Natural Elements, a catalog featuring women's clothing, was introduced.

As the company grew, it established brick and mortar retail locations in several states. The retail locations attract customers that are more comfortable examining merchandise before making a purchase.

Coldwater Creek is still selective about the products it sells. It chooses items that not only appeal to the customer but also fit its requirements of high-quality products and designs inspired by nature and the western atmosphere. Customer satisfaction was one of the original priorities of the company's founders, and the company continues to receive high ratings from loyal customers.

Think Critically

1. Why did Coldwater Creek select professional women for their primary market?
2. Visit the company's web site at www.coldwater-creek.com. Evaluate the products and selection available on the site.
3. Analyze the growth of Coldwater Creek. Why did the company choose these avenues of growth? What would you have done differently?
4. Identify the current stock price for the company. Summarize the evaluations given by several stock analysts who have examined the company.

CHAPTER 2

Types of Businesses

GOALS

- ◆ Identify the basic types of businesses
- ◆ Define how businesses are categorized
- ◆ Describe four critical factors that affect your business success
- ◆ Compare the three methods of becoming a business owner

Tony Jiminez is tired of working for someone else. Since he was a child, Tony has dreamed of opening his own business and becoming a millionaire by the age of 30. Tony just celebrated his 29th birthday. Although he probably won't become a millionaire in the next year, Tony does hope to open a business. In the past 10 years, Tony has saved $25,000. He is ready to begin researching the different business types he could operate.

Business Types

After you decide to establish a business, you will have to choose the type of business that you want to operate. You are surrounded by examples. Drive through your city. There are small businesses that provide many products or services.

You visit some types of businesses on a regular basis. One small business cuts your hair. A second is a small gourmet coffee shop that sells mouthwatering pastries. A third cleans your teeth every six months. Some businesses are more unusual. These businesses include one that cleans semi-trucks and trailers, one that delivers "bouquets" of cookies to hospital patients, and another that transports children to after-school activities. There are even businesses that earn a profit by telling other businesses how to earn a profit! Regardless of the type of product a business sells, any company can be identified as a specific type of business—manufacturing, retail, service, or nonprofit.

Manufacturing Business

The process of making products from raw materials by hand or machinery is **manufacturing.** When you think of manufacturing, you probably picture a large mill, factory, or plant that employs thousands of workers who manufacture products on long assembly lines. However, manufacturing also includes many small businesses. Businesses that make and sell products from a single location are also manufacturers. These businesses include bakeries, small shops that grind prescription lenses for glasses, and other manufacturers that produce street signs. These small manufacturing businesses often employ fewer than five workers.

Manufacturing is responsible for many of the goods used in America and exported to other countries. American manufacturers currently employ about 17 million workers. In 1997, manufacturers shipped almost $4 trillion in products. American manufacturers have a reputation for high-quality products throughout the world. Aided by their reputation, major growth has recently occurred for manufacturers in the areas of electronic devices and other electrical equipment.

Retail Business

The sale of goods or services directly to the final customer is **retail.** A retail business gathers products to sell to consumers. For example, a grocery store buys oranges from an orchard in Florida, corn from a farm in Iowa, and soft drinks from a bottling company in Georgia. The grocery store sells these items to you and other local consumers. Without retail businesses, many products would not be available to the average consumer. You would have to visit several states or countries just to gather the ingredients for one meal.

American retailers made sales valued at a total of $3 trillion in 1999. There are currently more than 1 million American retailers that employ more than 21 million workers. Retailers purchase products from manufacturers, employ local workers, and pay taxes.

Service Business

Businesses that sell services to consumers and other businesses are the largest and fastest-growing type of business in America. **Service** is useful labor that does not produce a tangible product. Rather than selling a physical product or object, service businesses perform activities for their customers. Customers pay for the time, labor, and skill provided by the business. Service businesses with individual customers include automotive repair, dating services, and funeral homes. Service businesses that have other businesses as customers include cleaning services, temporary personnel suppliers, and some businesses that provide specialized functions such as accounting or software programming.

In 1997, service companies earned $2.4 trillion. The demand for service businesses continues to grow. For many businesses, it is more cost-effective to pay a service business to perform specialized tasks than to hire, train, and maintain their own employees.

Nonprofit Business

Some businesses are not conducted or maintained for the purpose of making a profit. These are known as **nonprofit** or not-for-profit businesses. Nonprofit businesses are often established to raise funds for a specific cause such as medical research, homeless children, or literacy programs. Regardless of the "nonprofit" label, nonprofit businesses actually do earn a profit. If the business didn't earn a profit, it would not be able to continue to operate. No business can operate for long when it is losing money. The difference between a nonprofit business and a regular business is the way that the profit is used. A nonprofit business cannot engage in ongoing commercial or fund-raising activities that provide profit to individuals or interests outside the organization's area of specialization, the chosen social cause. Individuals who establish nonprofit businesses may be known as **social entrepreneurs.**

Although a nonprofit business can earn a profit, these funds are applied to the organization's social cause. This benefits the target group and all of American society. Therefore, nonprofit organizations may receive federal tax benefits. A nonprofit business must meet specific requirements to be granted tax exemption.

Business Categories

All businesses can be placed into categories. A standard method of categorizing businesses was developed in 1997 by the U.S. Census Bureau with the assistance and cooperation of Canada and Mexico. Every five years, the U.S. Census Bureau conducts an economic census to provide in-depth information about the current status and future trends in the American economy. To present and analyze the collected data, the Census Bureau uses the North American Industry Classification System (NAICS).

The **NAICS code** consists of five or six digits. The first five digits have the same meaning in all three nations. The meaning of the sixth digit is defined by each nation. The digits of the code, displayed in Figure 2.1, identify the main business activity of each **establishment,** a single location where a business operates. Each portion of the NAICS code provides additional information about the business activities performed at each establishment.

FIGURE 2.1   NAICS Code

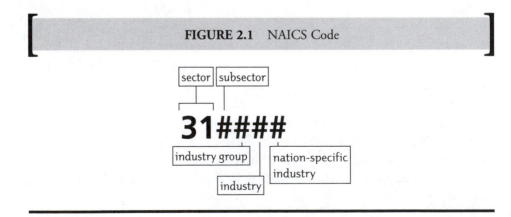

The Census Bureau also provides performance statistics and **benchmark ratings,** standard expectations of company performance, based on business activities. This enables a business to measure its performance against the performance of businesses that are similar in size and compete in the same industry. An **industry** is composed of companies that perform similar business activities that are distinct from those performed by other businesses. This information is useful to entrepreneurs. When you are researching the type of business you want to open, you'll find information about similar companies that can help you establish estimates of potential production and income.

To begin your research, use Table 2.1 to identify the sector that fits your business.

TABLE 2.1   NAICS Sectors

Sector Code	Sector Titles	Sector Code	Sector Titles
11	Agriculture, Forestry, Fishing, and Hunting	55	Management of Companies and Enterprises
21	Mining	56	Administrative and Support and Waste Management and Remediation Services
22	Utilities		
23	Construction	61	Educational Services
31–33	Manufacturing	62	Health Care and Social Assistance
42	Wholesale Trade	71	Arts, Entertainment, and Recreation
44–45	Retail Trade	72	Accommodation and Food Services
48–49	Transportation and Warehousing	81	Other Services (except Public Administration)
51	Information		
52	Finance and Insurance	92	Public Administration
53	Real Estate and Rental and Leasing		
54	Professional, Scientific, and Technical Services		

For more information about NAICS codes, log on to the Census Bureau's web site at www.census.gov/epcd/www/naics.html.

Hypothetical Scenario

Tony Jiminez began looking around his community for any ideas about a business that might succeed. Although he enjoys playing on a softball team with his coworkers, he doesn't have any particular interests or hobbies that could be developed into a business. After some investigation, he realized that he would rather be engaged in a business that sells products rather than a service, but he still can't identify a business category that promises success in his geographic area.

Path to Business Success

There are many ways to achieve success in business. To evaluate the choices on your path to entrepreneurial success, examine the most critical factors, including cost, opportunity cost, risk level, and potential reward.

Cost

Every business choice you make will cost something. The price may be money or materials. It may be the time and effort it will require to perform a specific task. You have to evaluate the situation and decide if you are willing to pay the price in order to achieve success. Answer the following questions. Be realistic in your answers. Underestimating your costs or overestimating your resources can doom your business to failure before it gets off the ground.

- **How much time will it require to establish your business?** Think in terms of hours per week and the length of time you will work to establish the business. For example, "I can work 20 hours a week for the next year to set up my business."

- **How much money will it require to establish your business?** Think of the cost of the items you need to purchase for the business. If you plan to quit your current job to concentrate on your business venture, include all of the living expenses covered by your current salary. You will still need to pay for housing, food, utilities, and other recurring expenses.

- **What materials are needed to establish your business?** Include items such as equipment, location, and raw materials. The materials you need and the cost of the different materials will vary widely from business to business. A pool cleaning service will require equipment that is different from a freelance software programmer. Include only those items that you must have for the business. Luxury items or items that would be nice to have aren't necessary when you start the business.

Next, you will have to identify the resources that are available for your use. If you know that other individuals will help you by contributing their skills or resources, identify and list their contributions with your own.

- **How much time can you spend to achieve your business goals?** Again, think in terms of hours and length of time. If you don't want to spend your evenings or weekends working, don't include those hours. If your business has not succeeded in one year, do you want to continue your efforts? How long will you be willing to put time and money into the business?

- **Do you have to work another job while you try to establish your business?** Use this question as a reality check. If you have to maintain a fulltime job while you are working to establish your new business, you could quickly become physically and emotionally drained. How many hours a week do you *really* want to spend working? If you work 40 hours a week for a regular income, you probably don't want to work another 40 hours a week for your business. When you do open for business, when will you be able to meet with clients or customers? Will your customers want to meet with you during the time you have available? A freelance architect can easily meet with clients in the evening. However, if your clients are businesses, you will have to be available, on some type of regular schedule, during normal business hours.

- **How much money do you have available for this purpose?** Most potential entrepreneurs don't have several hundred thousand dollars in a sock under the mattress. You may have some money saved for a particular purpose, such as buying a car or sending yourself or your children to college. Don't include any funds that you don't want to risk. If the loss of these funds would create a severe hardship for you, don't risk them.

- **Identify the materials available to meet your business needs.** Many businesses start as hobbies. Individuals with hobbies may already own some of the equipment they need for a small business. For example, an individual that designs and creates pottery as a hobby may already own a kiln and a potter's wheel. Your business may not require the newest and best version of everything. If you have a computer that runs the accounting software package you select and a word processing application, you may not need a new computer for the business. You can upgrade your materials or purchase additional items later.

After you know the resources that you need and the resources that are available, you can begin to calculate the additional resources you need. How will you overcome any shortfalls?

Opportunity Cost

Success in business is the result of making good decisions. Making a decision means that you are choosing between two or more alternatives. If you choose alternative A, you can't reap the benefits that would have happened if you chose alternative B. For example, if you choose to rent 552 Boohoo Street for your business office, you can't also rent 123 Main Street. The benefit that you sacrifice by pursuing an alternative is the opportunity cost. Choosing to establish a business can have a high **opportunity cost.** You may sacrifice income from your regular job if you quit to establish your business. You may give up time spent on hobbies or time with your family and friends. You might sacrifice money you would spend on vacations or other purchases. You have to decide if the opportunity cost of your business is one you want to pay. Use the following questions to evaluate the opportunity cost of establishing your business.

- **What do you do with your free time now?** If you maintain your regular fulltime job and work to establish a new business at the same time, free time may become a distant memory. You will have to establish your priorities before you start. Set rules and make schedules. This will help you set some time aside that you don't spend working. However, the bulk of your current free time will probably still be spent working.

- **What would you have done with the money you are investing in the business?** What did you plan to do with the funds you will spend on your business? Going on vacation, buying a new computer, and redecorating your home are activities that may have to wait until you earn a profit from your business.
- **Are there any activities or plans that you don't want to give up to start your business?** If you can't work around these activities, you may want to reconsider your business plan or change the timing of your business venture. For example, you may choose to wait until your car loan has been paid or your youngest child starts school.

Risk Level

For many entrepreneurs, the risk level may be one of the most important factors. **Risk level** identifies the probability of losing the money, time, or materials invested in the business. Even though you don't plan to fail, you should not enter a business situation that risks more than you are willing to lose. Ask yourself the following questions.

- **Do you feel that the time spent on a business project is wasted if the project does not succeed?** Every business attempt is not successful. You can anticipate your potential reaction by your past experience in similar situations. If your business does not succeed, you will be disappointed. You may feel that the time you spent on the business was wasted. If you enjoy the activities or learn something from the experience, you may feel that the business venture was valuable, regardless of whether the business succeeds or not.
- **Are you willing to lose the materials you use in the business project?** If the business fails, you may need to sell the equipment purchased for the business or other property to repay any loans you took when you established the business.
- **How would your life be affected if you lost all of the funds invested in the business venture?** If the failure of this business would put you in line at the local soup kitchen, you may want to think twice or modify your plans to incur less risk. Reevaluate your plans. You may be able to scale down your plans to minimize the risk or limit your potential loss.

Potential Reward

Some people think of success in monetary terms. "When I have $1 million, I'll quit working." Others may feel they are successful if they have a job they enjoy that covers their expenses. Another may want 20 retail locations and a million-dollar income every year. To recognize success when you reach it, you should identify your goals.

- **What is the annual income you want to earn from your business?** This isn't the initial amount you expect your company to earn to cover expenses and break even. This is the amount you would like to earn when the business is firmly established, consistently earning a steady income that is more than the cost of operating the business.

- **Do you want to manage employees?** If your business really takes off, this is a decision you will have to make. Do you want to expand your business by hiring employees? If you don't want to manage others, your business will be naturally limited to the work you can do alone.

- **How long do you want your business to operate?** If you plan to work alone, the business will close when you retire. If you create a family business, it can be passed down to your children and perhaps your children's children and beyond. Many small family businesses have been passed down for generations. A company that expands to many business establishments and thousands of employees can easily become a company that outlives its founder and affects thousands of lives.

There is no standard for what defines success. You have to determine what success means to you. Write your personal definition of business success. Use as many criteria as necessary to make your definition complete. You'll want to recognize the moment when success arrives.

Hypothetical Scenario

After one of their regular Sunday afternoon softball games, Tony's team gathered at the local diner. Tony overheard the owner talking to someone in the next booth about retiring and moving to Arizona. Tony looked around the crowded diner, wondering how much work the diner would be to operate and how much income the diner could generate. Although Tony does not have a passion for cooking, he does want to operate a successful business. The diner seems to fill a need in the community. He decided to prepare some questions for the current owner.

Becoming a Business Owner

Research and planning will set the stage for success. However, to become a successful entrepreneur, you have to own a business. There are several ways to become a business owner:

- You can acquire an existing business.
- You can purchase a franchise.
- You can establish a new business.

There are similarities between acquiring an existing business and purchasing a franchise. In both situations, the business has a track record that will help you predict how the business will perform for you.

Buying an Existing Business

Small businesses are often sold by owners for a variety of reasons. An owner may sell the business because he or she wants to retire, the business has grown too big, or the entrepreneur wants to cash in on the hard work of establishing the business. An owner could also choose to sell the business because it is losing money, the area in which the business is located has become depressed, or the business has internal problems. Before you decide to buy an existing business, you should gather as much information as possible.

Finding a Business Business owners don't usually hang a "For Sale" sign to advertise that the owner is looking for a buyer. This would discourage any current suppliers, employees, and customers. You can use several sources to identify businesses that are for sale. Excellent sources include bankers, lawyers, accountants, business brokers, trade magazines, and product suppliers.

- Bankers, lawyers, and accountants often form solid professional relationships with their clients. When an owner decides to sell, he may suggest that these professionals can discreetly begin to look for a buyer. If you have previously contacted the professional, your name will probably be mentioned.

- Business brokers are similar to real estate agents. However, they work with individuals or companies selling businesses rather than residential real estate. **Business brokers** introduce qualified buyers to an owner planning to sell a business. Usually, the business broker represents the interests of the owner, an important thing to remember in any discussions or negotiations. While representing the seller, the business broker can have the seller's business appraised to ensure that the seller sets an appropriate price, represent the seller in price negotiations, protect the seller from any unwanted publicity, and smooth the legal process. In return, the broker receives a commission of 10 to 12 percent of the sale price, another reason that brokers try to negotiate the highest possible selling price.

- **Trade magazines** are publications that contain information about a specific industry or interest. Most trade publications carry classified advertisements in the back of the magazine. Owners hoping to sell a business involved in the industry will place an advertisement in a trade magazine. Advertisements provide basic data about the company and contact information for interested buyers.

- Suppliers know a great deal about their customers. They often know if an owner is planning to sell. Generally, they share this information only with other customers. This source is more useful for owners planning to expand by purchasing a smaller business than for first-time buyers.

Investigating an Existing Business When you are investing your time and money, there is no such thing as asking too many questions or getting too much information. When you buy a house, you examine every part of the house. You look in every closet, run the water, and look up the chimney. Experts are called to examine the structure and check the heater. You find out about neighborhood rules and city regulations. Tax records also provide vital information. The taxes on the property should be paid in full and the deed for the property should be clear so the house can be sold. You should go through many of the same steps before you buy a business.

- **Ask why the business is for sale.** No one is going to sell the perfect business for no reason at all. Be wary of vague answers or answers that don't seem reasonable. The seller could be hiding a problem affecting the company.

- **Ask how the price of the business was determined.** The price may include the value of the property owned by the business, the inventory in storage or on order, the annual income, the debts owed by the business, the amount customers owe to the business, and expenses such as taxes and fees. Be cautious if projections of future growth were used to set the current price for the business.

- **Ask to view at least three years of financial statements and income tax returns.** The business should show a history of growth. Be cautious of any business that shows a downward trend, particularly if the economy or industry is not slowing during the same time period. Ask an accountant to review these records.

- **Ask to view information about any debts owed *by* the business and any debts owed *to* the business.** Some debts may be owed by or to the current owner. These will not be sold with the business.

- **Ask to view information about any legal issues associated with the business.** This can include lawsuits, permits, licenses, regulations, and environmental issues. Ask a lawyer to review this information. Use the library or Internet to view any issues that may affect the business. If the city plans to build a highway nearby, the location could lose a lot of business from customers that stop in on their way to or from work.

- **Ask to view information about the owner's projections about the company's finances and plans for future growth.** The owner's plans for future growth may provide insight into some current conditions within the business. Ask a banker to look over any financial projections of future performance.

- **Ask for a list of business references.** This list should include customers, creditors, and suppliers. Check all the references the owner provides before agreeing to any purchase.

- **Ask if the company's name, logo, and signs are included in the purchase.** This is an important point if the company's name and logo have a high recognition factor. Changing the name of a business instantly alerts customers to the change in ownership, impacting any customer loyalty the business currently inspires.

Before you make any purchase, consult your lawyer, accountant, and banker. If you haven't already established a working relationship with these professionals, this is the time to do so.

Do some additional research. If you are not familiar with the industry, investigate current trends and projections for its future. You don't want to become involved in an industry that is on a permanent downward trend.

Contact the local Better Business Bureau. Ask if any complaints have been filed against the business. If you are buying the company's name and logo, you are also buying the company's reputation. Don't deal with owners who have several complaints lodged against them. A tarnished reputation is difficult, if not impossible, to repair. A small business relies heavily on the opinion of its customers. Satisfied customers will tell their friends, bringing in more business. Dissatisfied customers will tell anyone who will listen, discouraging them from visiting the establishment.

You may want to include a non-competition clause in the purchase agreement. A **non-competition clause** prevents the seller from opening a similar business within a specific geographic area. This is intended to prevent the seller from opening a competing business across the street from your new business. The seller would lower the value of the business you just purchased by retaining customer and supplier relationships. Be aware that non-competition clauses are not enforced in all states. Consult a lawyer for information about the laws in your state.

Buying a Franchise

Operating a franchise is an excellent opportunity for many entrepreneurs. It is less risky than establishing a new business or purchasing an existing one. A **franchise** is a commercial relationship in which you, the franchisee, are permitted to use the licensed trademark and marketing plan of the trademark owner, the franchiser, in exchange for an initial fee and possible ongoing royalty payments. The terms of the relationship between the franchiser and franchisee are described in the **franchise agreement,** a contract between the two parties. Depending on the franchise agreement, the franchiser may supply training, procedure manuals, equipment, and other items or support.

You probably shop and eat at several franchises. Fast-food restaurants, in particular, have a large number of franchise establishments. There are a number of advantages to purchasing a franchise. The name and product of the franchiser have a high recognition value among consumers. The franchiser has already developed a proven method of doing business. You also gain the benefit of any advertising created and distributed by the franchiser.

Of course, there are disadvantages as well. You are required to follow the franchiser's business plan. You can't make any creative changes to the look or feel of the business. Pricing is usually determined by the franchiser. The franchiser may select your suppliers. Depending on the terms in the franchise agreement, the franchiser could allow another franchisee to open an establishment near your location, cutting into your profits and customer loyalty.

Finding a Franchise Many large and reputable companies offer the opportunity to purchase a franchise. If you are interested in a particular business, visit a local establishment and speak to the owner. If the business is a franchise, the manager can provide contact information for the corporate office. If there isn't a nearby location, use the Internet to find contact information. In response to your query, franchisers will send detailed information.

A **franchise broker** is an individual who sells or arranges for the sale of a franchise. A franchise broker could work independently, representing several different franchisers.

Investigating a Franchise All franchise agreements are not the same. The Federal Trade Commission (FTC) requires that franchisers give a disclosure document to any potential franchisee at least 10 days before the franchise agreement is signed. The FTC requires that the franchiser prepare a document called the **franchise disclosure statement** that contains required information about the franchiser and franchisee. Details include the franchiser's financial statement that has been verified by an outside auditor, the fees and payments required to be a franchisee, and the relationship between the franchiser and the franchisee. The disclosure statement is intended to protect potential franchisees from taking unreasonable financial risks. However, you are responsible for your business decisions. Be sure to find answers to the following questions and consult your lawyer and accountant before you agree to purchase a franchise:

◆ **Ask for information about the products or services the franchise sells.** The primary product of the franchise should be the goods or services it sells, not the franchises. Examine the products or services for quality and value. Research the need for these products or services in your geographic area. If the products are not appropriate for your area, the income expected for the franchise may not materialize. For example, a software engineering consulting firm that provides on-site technical assistance for large networks would be very successful in many large cities. However, the same business would not be profitable in a small winter resort town in Montana.

◆ **Ask for a complete list of the items covered by the initial fee.** The franchiser might provide training, operation manuals, standard fixtures for the establishment, signs, and the initial inventory. All franchisers do not provide the same items.

◆ **Ask for a complete list of any ongoing fees and expenses.** The franchiser can charge an ongoing royalty payment. The amount of the payment could be fixed or based on the franchisee's profits. The franchiser could require franchisees to pay for all or part of the advertising costs. Franchisees could be required to buy all of their supplies from the franchiser. This could be more expensive than finding a local supplier that meets the franchiser's quality standards.

◆ **Ask if the franchiser will provide financing.** If the franchiser provides financing, you will have alternatives to a bank loan. Before financing through the franchiser, compare the interest rates and terms to those you can get through other sources.

◆ **Ask how a franchisee's geographic territory is protected.** The franchiser should place some type of geographic limitations on new franchises. For example, if you purchase a franchise that sells ice cream, the company should not sell another franchise that would be located across the street from you.

◆ **Ask how the franchise rights are handled if you want to sell your franchise in the future.** You may not want to operate the franchise forever. It is important to know now what restrictions you will face if you want to sell the franchise in the future.

♦   **Ask about the financial consequences if your franchise fails.** Although the success rate of franchises is higher than the success rate of other small businesses, they can fail. Verify that you can financially survive any penalties or consequences.

♦   **Ask the Federal Trade Commission about any complaints filed against the franchiser.** Mark the envelope and letter with "FOIA Request." The letter to the FTC should include your contact information and the name and address of the franchiser. The service is usually free. Send the request to:

> Freedom of Information Act Request
> Federal Trade Commission
> Washington, D.C. 20580-0002

Don't rely only on the disclosure statement and franchise agreement. Contact other franchisees for the same business. Ask about their satisfaction level with the business arrangement. If they have had any problems, ask how they were resolved. For the sake of comparison, contact one or two other franchisers. Compare the franchise agreements and disclosure statements. How does the franchiser you have selected compare to the others?

Before you sign any purchase agreement, ask an attorney to review the contract. To locate an attorney, contact your state bar association. Franchise law is an area of specialization. Ask the bar association for a list of members that specialize in franchise law. (Refer to the CD for contact information for the bar association for each state.)

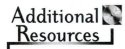

Starting a New Business

In many ways, purchasing an existing business or buying a franchise is easier than starting a new business. The framework and procedures are already in place. An existing business or franchise already has established methods of doing business, combinations of products, and consumers that are familiar with the business and its product selection. The business already has a reputation and consumer expectations are already set.

When you start a new business, you have to create or select the products or services you will sell. You will have to identify the consumers that might purchase your products and invent new methods of selling your products to them. Through trial and error, you will create methods of doing business that work for your venture.

There are many questions that you will have to answer before you establish your business. To start on the right foot, you will have to research as many aspects of your business plan as possible. The success of your business relies on the foundation you create before you open your doors for the first time.

◨ Hypothetical Scenario

Tony prepared a list of questions and went back to the diner Monday evening to talk to the owner. Although he liked the answers to his questions, Tony decided he needed more information and an evaluation by an accountant and lawyer before making an offer on the diner.

◪ Technology Insights

Using Your Computer

A computer is one piece of equipment that every business should own, regardless of the product or service the business sells. The computer should be capable of running all the basic business software, including applications that perform word processing, accounting, and desktop publishing.

If you already have a computer, select your business software carefully. The minimum requirements for the computer needed to run every application are printed on the side or back of the software packaging. Consult these requirements before making any purchases.

Before you select any software, spend some time deciding how you can use your computer to help your business succeed. A word processing application will be useful in writing your business correspondence. An accounting application will help you track your inventory, expenses, and income. A desktop publishing application can help you create flyers, newsletters, and brochures.

Consult your accountant before you select an accounting package. Many accountants will prefer one program over another. It will simplify the exchange of data if your accountant selects your accounting package. Before you begin using your computer for business purposes, purchase a reliable data backup method such as a writable CD drive or a Zip® drive. Back up your data regularly and keep a copy of your most recent backup in an off-site location such as your home.

Think Critically   How would you use a computer to help your business succeed? Make a list of the business software you would purchase.

CHAPTER REVIEW

Businesses can be classified as one of four types. A manufacturing business makes products from raw materials by hand or machinery. A retail business gathers products to sell to consumers. Service businesses perform activities for their customers. Nonprofit businesses raise funds for social causes.

Businesses can be further categorized by codes. Used throughout North America, this code is known as the North American Industry Classification System or NAICS code. Each digit in the five- or six-digit code provides information about a business establishment and its activities.

To evaluate your business choices, you must weigh several critical factors. The cost of each choice is the time and effort required to complete a task. The opportunity cost is the benefit that you sacrifice by choosing a different alternative. The risk level of an alternative measures the chance of failing and losing anything you have invested in the venture. Of course, all entrepreneurs keep their eyes on the potential reward for all the time and effort they put into their business activities.

Entrepreneurs can become business owners by purchasing an existing business, purchasing a franchise, or establishing a new business. The alternative that presents the least risk is purchasing a franchise. Buying an existing business is next in risk level. The business already has an established mix of products and a loyal customer base. The entrepreneur who chooses to establish a new business is taking the most risk. This entrepreneur must create the framework for the new business, forming a solid foundation based on research and careful decisions.

USE BUSINESS TERMS

Fill in the blanks with the appropriate term.

benchmark rating	NAICS code
business broker	non-competition clause
establishment	nonprofit
franchise	opportunity cost
franchise agreement	retail
franchise broker	risk level
franchise disclosure statement	service
industry	social entrepreneur
manufacturing	trade magazine

1. The buyer decided to add a(n) ___?___ to prevent the seller from opening a similar business in the same city.
2. A(n) ___?___ usually represents the individual selling the business.
3. The Federal Trade Commission requires franchisers to provide a(n) ___?___ .

4. A large company may do business in more than one ___?___.
5. The ___?___ consists of five or six digits.
6. All plumbers are in the same ___?___.
7. Less time to enjoy your hobbies could be part of the ___?___ of operating your business.

TEST YOUR READING

8. Identify a manufacturer in your geographic area. Describe the business.
9. Which manufacturing areas have shown recent growth?
10. Describe the business activity of a retailer.
11. How do retailers fit into the economy?
12. What is the fastest-growing type of business?
13. Describe how a nonprofit business is different from other businesses.
14. Identify the parts of the NAICS code.
15. Describe the cost of establishing your business.
16. Why do businesses not advertise that they are for sale?
17. Describe the duties of a business broker.
18. What does the franchisee purchase from the franchiser?
19. Create a table that compares buying an existing business, buying a franchise, and establishing a new business.

THINK CRITICALLY ABOUT BUSINESS

20. Describe the business you would consider opening. What is the business type?
21. Identify the NAICS code that is appropriate for your business.
22. Describe the cost, opportunity cost, risk level, and potential reward for your business venture by answering the questions in each section. Are they acceptable? Explain your answer.
23. Identify a franchise that would fit into your geographic area. Contact the franchiser for information. Request a package of information, including the disclosure statement and franchise agreement.

REAL-LIFE BUSINESS

AAMCO Transmissions, Inc.

Not all successful franchises sell fast food. AAMCO Transmissions was among the first franchisers of auto care services. AAMCO was established in 1963 in Philadelphia, Pennsylvania. In the same year, the first AAMCO franchise opened, doubling the number of establishments.

Today, there are more than 700 establishments in the United States and Canada that bear the AAMCO name. Each location is owned and operated by franchisees. More than 50 locations are operated by the sons or daughters of the original franchisees. The franchise was passed down to the next generation like a family business. Additionally, more than 150 franchisees are former employees of other AAMCO franchises. This creates a positive image of AAMCO Transmissions, Inc. as a successful franchiser.

Among consumers, AAMCO is an easily recognized name. AAMCO has a reputation for high-quality service and a warranty that demonstrates the quality of the work performed.

AAMCO offers a great deal of support to its franchisees. Training includes lessons about marketing, recruiting employees, and providing customer service. Even after a franchise is operational, franchisees can receive optional support and training. The franchiser operates technical support and customer support hotlines. AAMCO will also help franchisees select and analyze the location for the new franchise. Nationwide advertising campaigns assist all the franchisees.

Automotive service is a growing industry. The number of vehicles in operation and the average age of the vehicle has increased steadily. In 1999, there were more than 201 million vehicles in operation. The average age of these vehicles was nine years. Older vehicles require more service. The future of the automotive service industry is rosy.

In 2001, the initial investment for an AAMCO franchise was less than $200,000. Among other items, this amount covered license fees, necessary equipment, inventory, and dealer training.

Think Critically

1. Why would someone be interested in purchasing a franchise from AAMCO Transmissions, Inc.?
2. Visit the company's web site at www.aamcotransmissions.com. Can you find any additional information that would affect your interest in purchasing a franchise?
3. Contact an AAMCO franchisee owner. Describe any additional information you discover. How does this information affect your interest in purchasing a franchise?
4. Use your phone book. Locate any local AAMCO franchise establishments. How far apart are the locations? Could another AAMCO franchise be established in your city? Explain your answer.

CHAPTER

Your Product

GOALS

- ◆ Select products and services to sell
- ◆ Create a unique characteristic that sets your business apart from others
- ◆ Perform a study to test the marketability of your product
- ◆ Manufacture your product
- ◆ Protect your products and business with patents, copyrights, and trademarks

Miranda Martin loved anything and everything about television and big screen movies. She watched television for hours every day and went to the theater every weekend. She only wished that she could spend her days doing something connected to the television or movie industry rather than her current job as a software engineer. When she received a small inheritance, she decided to open a retail business in a local mall that would use her knowledge of television and movies.

Select Products to Sell

Every business sells something. A successful business sells products that consumers will buy. Determining which products or services you want to sell is one of the first critical business decisions you will make. Some product selections are obviously wrong, some are questionable, and others are winners. The trick is to pick more winners than losers and choose the right combination of winners. For example, when Tim Ribbon decided to establish a business, the product selection seemed obvious. He named the business Tim's Ribbons and stocked ribbons of every size and color. After the first few consumers wandered through without making any purchases, Tim asked a passing shopper why no one was buying anything. She seemed surprised he would even ask such a question. She looked around the store and exclaimed, "All you sell is ribbon!" Clearly, Tim's product selection was wrong.

Consumer Needs and Wants

Every day, consumers use, eat, or consume a variety of products. When they shop, they replace products they have consumed and purchase new products. Consumers spend almost 98 percent of their net income—the amount that remains after taxes are paid—on their needs and wants.

Needs are the items you can't live without, such as food, water, clothing, and shelter. **Wants,** on the other hand, are items you would like to have but can live without. A sports car, computer, and television are wants. Any item that goes beyond filling the most basic needs is a want.

Factors Affecting Consumers' Wants   To sell the right products, you have to know what consumers want. A consumer's wants are affected by factors such as culture, social class, gender, and individuality.

Culture comes from your social and family environment. It is inherited from your ancestors and will be passed to your children. Your culture affects your beliefs and values. It is reflected in the clothes you wear and the traditions you celebrate. Culture determines which foods you can eat with your fingers and how you will celebrate your holidays. It also affects your purchases. American culture encourages purchases for activities like Little League baseball and Fourth of July celebrations. Your ethnic culture inspires additional purchases based on traditions or special occasions.

Your **social class** is a group that shares the same economic or social status. In America, social class is determined mainly by income, education, and occupation. However, these three items can be changed. Generally, a higher level of education, usually a college degree or technical certificate, leads to a more prestigious career that earns more money. Therefore, social class in America is not set in stone. In fact, children often rise to a higher social class than their parents because they have a higher level of education. Members of the same social class share many similarities in lifestyle and possessions.

Although **gender** had a more important role in the past, it still affects product selection in areas such as clothing and jewelry. For many products, including such items as sports equipment and tools, there are gender-neutral items or a different version for males and females.

Regardless of any other factors that influence a consumer's purchase, each purchase is a personal choice. **Individuality,** the distinctive characteristics that make each individual unique, affects each consumer's purchasing decisions. Individuality explains why Tina buys a blue dress and Lisa buys a red dress, even if both dresses are the same popular style.

Types of Goods

As an entrepreneur, you will have to select the types of products your business will sell. **Merchandise** are any products that are bought and sold in business. Physical goods can be categorized as staple goods, fashion goods, seasonal goods, and convenience goods.

Staple goods are merchandise that are constantly demanded by customers. Most consumers keep a variety of staple goods in their homes. Examples include grocery items such as milk, bread, and sugar. Personal hygiene products and cleaning products are also staple goods. Consumers will replace staple goods when they run out, if not earlier. In fact, running out of a staple good like milk or eggs can trigger a quick trip to the store for a replacement. Because these items are replaced as they are used, businesses can predict the rate at which they are sold. This means the business can plan its purchases to keep enough of the items in inventory.

Fashion goods are merchandise that follow changes in style and thus change constantly. Hemlines go up or down. Colors become popular for a season, then fade away. To be in style, individuals purchase clothing frequently. Items such as couches, dinnerware, and home decorating accessories are also influenced by fashion. Manufacturers of these products frequently release new styles and designs.

Changes in fashion follow a predictable pattern, displayed in Figure 3.1. A creative individual designs a new style. People are attracted by the style and begin to wear or use the items. The crowd adopts the style as it gains popularity. A creative individual designs another new style, starting a new cycle. As the new style becomes more popular, the previous style loses popularity and its sales begin to decline as the sales of the new style increase.

FIGURE 3.1   Fashion Cycle

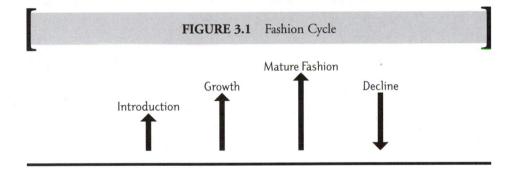

Seasonal goods are merchandise that are popular only during certain times of the year. Skis and snow boots are used in winter activities. Therefore, they are sold during the fall and winter months. Swimming and gardening are summer activities. Therefore, swimsuits and gardening tools are sold during the spring and summer months. Seasonal goods also include items sold for holidays such as Christmas ornaments and Halloween costumes.

Convenience goods are merchandise that are purchased frequently by consumers. These are usually small, inexpensive items. Convenience goods are often displayed near the checkout counter where customers can make impulsive purchases. Newspapers, batteries, and film are convenience goods sold by a variety of stores.

Types of Services

Like goods, services sold by businesses can be categorized. Services can be identified as staple services and seasonal services.

A **staple service** is useful labor that does not produce a tangible product but is constantly demanded by customers. Employment agencies and cleaning services are two examples of staple services.

A **seasonal service** is useful labor that does not produce a tangible product and is popular only during certain times of the year. Customers can be businesses or individuals. Seasonal services include pool cleaning, skiing lessons, and landscaping. Clever entrepreneurs that provide seasonal services will offer a variety of seasonal services to keep their business income more stable throughout the year. For example, a landscaping service that cares for the grounds of a business in the summer months by spreading mulch and mowing grass can also clear snow from the parking lot and salt the sidewalks in the winter months.

Merchandise Mix

Craft stores sell material, paint, and thread. Toy stores sell red wagons, bicycles, and electronic games. Department stores sell clothing, major appliances, and furniture. The **merchandise mix** is the variety, breadth, and depth of merchandise a store carries.

Most businesses carry a **variety** of merchandise. The number of different merchandise types and the quantity of each merchandise type determine the merchandise mix. The **breadth** is the number of merchandise lines carried by a business. The **depth** is the number of items in various colors, sizes, styles, and price ranges offered within a merchandise line. As Figure 3.2 shows, a department store carries a wide breadth of items, from socks to refrigerators, but not much depth. They may have only one or two types of refrigerators. An electronics store carries much less breadth, but a deeper selection of products within product lines. The electronics store doesn't sell socks, but it does have 10 different types of refrigerators and keeps several of each type in stock.

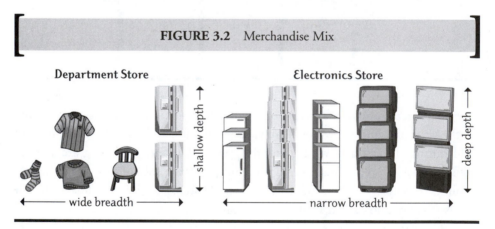

FIGURE 3.2   Merchandise Mix

Factors in Selecting Your Merchandise Mix Factors that affect the products or services a business chooses to sell include: the wants and needs of the customer, customer expectations, the space available to display or keep merchandise, and the financial limitations of the business.

The wants and needs of the customers are the primary factors a business uses to choose a successful merchandise mix. The merchandise mix creates an identity for the business, which attracts a specific type of customer or customers searching for a particular type of item. For example, an employment service that specializes in technical personnel, including programmers and engineers, will attract high-tech businesses that use these skills. A retailer that sells clothing will attract customers that prefer the clothing styles stocked by that retailer.

Customers expect businesses to carry certain products. A toy store will sell board games. A grocery store will sell lightbulbs. A landscaping service will mulch gardens in the spring. If a business does not provide a product or service that customers expect, customers will go to a business that does meet their expectations.

The space available to display merchandise may limit some retailers. However, it has more influence on an existing business that wants to add products than it does on new businesses. A new business would obtain the space needed to display and sell the items they intend to sell when it is established. If the business could not afford the space, it would choose to sell different or fewer items. A business that initially planned to sell furniture, for example, would obtain enough space to display and store the furniture. A business that originally planned to sell decorative accessories might not have the additional space to display couches or chairs if the store decided to add them to its existing merchandise mix.

The financial limitations of a business determine the products that the business can afford to purchase. If the business cannot acquire merchandise to sell, it will not be able to earn income by selling the merchandise. Products that are above the business's price range cannot be added to its merchandise mix.

Difference Between Goods and Services

Consumers purchase both goods and services. However, as shown in Table 3.1, the product that you sell and the expectations of the customer are different for goods and services. Some of the differences are obvious. Others are more subtle.

TABLE 3.1   Goods Versus Services

Goods	Services
Physical object	No physical object
Ownership transferred	Ownership not transferred
Object can be reused or consumed	Labor, time, or skill cannot be reused
Quality between manufacturers is similar	Quality depends on the individual worker

When consumers purchase goods, they purchase physical objects they can touch and manipulate. They can set the item on a shelf, use it, or store it in the garage. The ownership of the object is transferred. The consumer can point to the object and say, "That's mine." After the ownership of the object is transferred, the object can be used and reused until it is consumed or worn out and thrown away. The quality and value of the object is similar between retailers and manufacturers. If you pay $20 for a watch, you purchase a watch that has approximately the same quality as any other $20 watch, regardless of the manufacturer or the retailer.

When consumers purchase services, they receive the worker's labor, time, and skill. However, they don't receive a physical object. No ownership is transferred. The labor, time, or skill of the worker can't be reused. There is no way to possess the worker's skill. The quality of the service varies from one worker to another, depending on the characteristics of the individual worker.

Hypothetical Scenario

Miranda Martin knew that she wanted her business to focus in some way on television programs and movie releases. She considered several options, including a video rental franchise. One day, she was in a video store when a young girl asked the clerk if they sold posters of her favorite television show. Miranda realized that there was a mix of products that she couldn't recall seeing in any store. She decided that her merchandise mix would include videos of television pilots and movies, posters, and television and movie memorabilia such as autographs and props. She realized that keeping up with the new television shows and movie releases would be challenging, similar to following fashion trends.

Unique Business Idea

If every restaurant sold nothing but cheeseburgers, it wouldn't matter where you decided to eat lunch. However, restaurant menus vary widely.

Some restaurants are different because of the atmosphere they provide rather than a specific dish. For example, a small restaurant was opened in an old-fashioned fire station. The pizza served was not original, but the unique location attracted a steady crowd. Another restaurant installed video games and dancing characters in costumes. It quickly attracted a loyal following of children who demanded birthday parties in the child-friendly atmosphere.

Every successful business is based on a unique idea that makes it different from its competition. That difference could be based on a new product, a new service, a unique product assortment, a different way of selling your products, or a unique location.

New Products

How many times have you seen a new product at the store and said, "I thought of that!" Your favorite coffee cup chips, so you drink out of the other side. Sometimes you overcome the problem by using a solution someone else developed. You can't get the lid off the jar of peanut butter, so you reach for a round rubber gripper that increases your grip on the lid, enabling you to open the jar. Sometimes you develop a unique solution to the problem. If the problem is common, as you see in Figure 3.3, your unique solution could become the basis for a profitable business.

FIGURE 3.3 Business Opportunity

Problem ➡ Solution ➡ Business Opportunity

Every day, people develop new products to meet specific needs. Now you want to create an idea for a new product. To create a solution, you first need to identify a problem. Identify problems that need solutions in your present environment. If you can't find problems on your own, people will be happy to point out problems for you. Sometimes, they can also give you clues to possible solutions. These clues often start with the phrase, "I wish that there was a way to . . ." As Table 3.2 shows, many solutions are the foundation for a profitable manufacturing or retail business.

TABLE 3.2 Business Success Based on a Product

Product	Description	Business
Stop Stick	Tire deflation device used by law enforcement agencies	Stop Stick, Ltd.
Polymer coating for ceramics	Coats ceramics for the sublimation and photo mug industries	Cactus Coatings, Inc.
Specialty soap	Soap in special shapes and packaging for individuals or businesses	Mary Ellen's Sweet Soaps
Lindita's Salsa	Dehydrated salsa mix	Lindita's Inc.

New Service

Just as the solution to a problem could be a new product, the solution could be a new service. If the service is popular and consumers are willing to pay for it, your service could be turned into a business. Although some services seem viable, consumers might not be willing to pay enough for the service to support a business. For example, it would be nice if someone would wash your car every week, but you probably would not pay $20 a week for workers to come to your house to wash it for you. Some services cannot be turned into a business because they do not require any special skill and do not have enough value to the consumer. There are many services, as shown in Table 3.3, that have value to consumers but don't require an advanced degree or special training to perform.

TABLE 3.3 Basic Service Businesses

Service	Description	Consumer
Driver	Transport children to after-school activities such as sporting events, doctor appointments, or lessons	Parents
Catering	Provide hot meals to senior citizens living independently	Adult children (purchased for their parents) and elderly citizens
Genealogist	Research family tree and family history	Adults
Bed and Breakfast	Provide meals and lodging to travelers	Vacationing adults
Cleaning	Clean residences or offices	Adults and businesses

Other services, shown in Table 3.4, require special skills, knowledge, or training. Many of these service businesses are started by individuals. Often they remain small businesses run only by the individual without any additional permanent employees.

TABLE 3.4   Skilled Service Businesses

Service	Description	Consumer
Architect	Design residences or office buildings	Adults and businesses
Software instructor	Teach the elderly to use e-mail and Internet software	Senior citizens
Accountant	Assist small businesses in tracking finances and filing income tax returns	Small businesses
Web page designer	Design and create web sites for small businesses	Small businesses
Plumber	Install or repair plumbing fixtures	Adults and businesses

Unique Product Assortment

As a consumer, you probably visit some retail establishments just because you like the combination of products they sell. Many retailers have created successful businesses based not on a single product but on a unique collection of products that follow a single theme. They attract consumers interested in a particular activity or type of product. Table 3.5 identifies several popular retailers that base their merchandise mix on a single unique theme.

TABLE 3.5   Businesses with a Unique Merchandise Mix

Business	Merchandise Mix
Bath and Body Works	Personal care products
Sharper Image	Innovative products
Williams-Sonoma	Kitchen accessories
Crate and Barrel	Home and kitchen products
Pottery Barn	Home furnishings

Selling Method

Some businesses sell an ordinary product or collection of products. However, they sell the products in a unique atmosphere or use a method that is unique. This may create a reputation that attracts additional consumers. Table 3.6 identifies several retailers that base their sales on the presentation or selling methods they use.

> **TABLE 3.6** Businesses with a Unique Presentation or Sales Method

Business	Presentation
Starbucks Coffee	Café atmosphere occasionally includes events such as live music or coffee tasting
Dave & Buster's, Inc.	Combination of restaurant and interactive entertainment, including billiards, shuffleboard, and simulators
Amazon.com	Uses web site for selling books, music, and other products

Unique Location

The location of some businesses is not important at all. A single owner that sells products through a web site could work out of her living room. If a consumer hires an architect to design a home, they could meet at the architect's home, consumer's home, or building site. Other businesses rely on the physical location as the only unique feature to attract customers. Gas stations are very much alike. You might choose one gas station over another just because it's on the right side of the street or it's easier to get back onto the highway from the selected location after pumping gas.

Hypothetical Scenario

Miranda knew that her merchandise mix of videos of television pilots and movies, posters, and other television and movie memorabilia would be unique, but she wanted something extra that would draw in more customers. She decided to set an area aside in the back of the store where she would show a popular movie once a week, then invite the viewers to stay and discuss the film after the screening. The screening and refreshments would be free, but she planned to have copies of the film, associated posters, and other memorabilia related to the movie displayed near the screening area. If she chose the films carefully, she thought she could attract and develop a core group of customers.

Market Research

Before you commit your resources to creating your business, determine that the business has a good chance of succeeding by researching and consulting several sources. Although your family and friends can provide some feedback about your business idea, there are several other sources that provide additional and more informed insight.

The Purpose of Market Research

Market research is the systematic collection of information about your customers, your competition, and the business environment. Use the data you discover to target your potential customers, identify business opportunities, increase your potential for success, and identify weaknesses in your plans.

Target Your Customers Identifying general characteristics about the consumers who might purchase your products allows you to tailor your product offerings and advertising to transform these potential consumers into customers. Additionally, doing this type of research may reveal that you are targeting the wrong group of consumers or that your product is not reasonably priced. For example, if they spend $25 on hobbies each month, but your hobby-related product is priced to sell at $200, you may not be able to sell your product successfully. Your market research should answer some of the following questions about the consumers who are interested in your product.

- What is the average age of consumers interested in your product?
- What is their gender?
- What is their income?
- What is their education level?
- What is their occupation?
- What are their hobbies and interests?
- How many children do they have and what are their ages?
- Where do they shop?
- Why do they choose a specific product?
- How do they spend their disposable income?
- What type of materials do they read?
- What media do they listen to and watch?

Examine Your Competition Information about your competition is very valuable because it can provide some good ideas and help you avoid costly mistakes. Comparing sales and product characteristics will help you refine the goods and services you provide. It could also indicate that the competitors have filled all of the consumers' needs for a product like yours and your business would probably not succeed. Your market research should answer some of the following questions.

- Who are your competitors?
- How much do consumers spend on products similar to yours each month?
- How much do they buy at one time?
- How often do consumers buy a product similar to yours?
- How much do consumers pay for a similar product?
- What is the quality of the competitor's product?
- What services do your competitors offer?
- Do your competitors earn a profit?
- What advantages does your business have over the competition?
- Are there any untapped areas of the market that you could fill?
- How do the competitors communicate with consumers?
- What makes your business different from your competitors' businesses?

Examine the Environment Several factors can lead to changes in the demand for your product. This could include changes in the consumers, fashions, or the economic environment. Your market research should answer some of the following questions.

- What is the current trend in the age of the population where you will draw customers?
- Will any changes in the political environment affect your business?
- Will the market for your product increase, decrease, or remain steady?

Conducting Market Research

There are many ways to perform market research. **Primary research** is performed by gathering information directly from the source for a specific purpose. **Secondary research** is performed by reading information that was previously gathered. (Refer to the CD for a list of secondary research sources.) To conduct secondary market research, you can locate information at the library or on the Internet. General information about population trends and fashion can easily be found through secondary resources. The information is up-to-date and the process is quick and inexpensive.

Additional Resources

For information that is specific to your product, geographic area, or business needs, you may have to conduct primary research. Primary research is more time-consuming and, therefore, more expensive. Large companies often hire an outside business to conduct primary market research on an ongoing basis as well as before they invest in a new product. Ongoing market research provides a constant check on the success of the company's activities before the results hit the bottom line financially. This enables companies to halt unsuccessful activities before they lose too much money and to foster activities that increase their profits. As a small business, you may have to conduct your own primary research through personal interviews, focus groups, surveys, personal observation, or experimentation.

Personal Interviews Because of the time involved in conducting one-on-one personal interviews—usually about one hour per interview—you will be limited to results from a very small sampling of potential customers. Often, only 50 interviews may be conducted during a research study. However, the information you receive will be detailed and will help you discover attitudes and opinions shared by your customers. Use visual aids such as product samples or product packaging if they are available. Use the following suggested format for questions.

- Ask open-ended questions such as, "Why are you attracted to Product A?"
- Follow up their answers with probing questions such as, "Why do you feel that the product may be reliable, valuable, helpful, and so forth?"

Focus Groups A moderator usually guides a focus group of eight to 10 participants in a single meeting that lasts one to two hours. The moderator may follow a script of open-ended questions similar to those used in personal interviews. Like personal interviews, give the focus group visual aids such as product samples or product packaging if they are available. The moderator should encourage group members to support any ambiguous or general answers with specific details. The moderator must also keep the group focused on the research topic. Don't let the group stray into discussions that are not related, such as plans for the weekend or favorite recipes.

Surveys Surveys are one of the most common methods of gathering information. You've probably seen workers with clipboards haunting the halls of your favorite shopping mall and asking shoppers if they have a few minutes to answer some questions. Surveys are intended to be fairly quick, requiring about 10 minutes to complete. Respondents may be anonymous. They often answer only yes or no, or choose an answer from several alternatives provided. Because you supply the possible choices for the respondents' answers, you must be careful with the wording of the questions. Your bias should not affect the respondents' selections. Ask someone to review your survey questions before you use them. Use the following suggested format for questions.

- Ask for any necessary general information before you ask for specific details. For example, ask if the respondent has a computer before asking about the software the respondent uses.
- Ask close-ended questions such as, "How many hours a week do you spend exercising? A. 0–1 hour; B. 1–2 hours; C. 2–5 hours; D. More than 5 hours"
- Make each question as short as possible.
- Be careful that the wording of the question, the order of the possible answers for each question, or the order in which the questions are asked do not influence the respondents' answers. For example, the question, "How many hours of television do your children watch during the week?" will generate a different response than "How many hours of television do you *allow* your children to watch on *school nights?*"
- If the survey is written, include complete instructions for filling out and returning the survey.

Personal Observation In some cases, you can gather information by observing consumer behavior that you could not gather in a survey or discussion. Count the foot traffic that passes by a certain store in the mall, the number of shoppers that enter the store, and the number of shoppers that make a purchase in the store. This simple activity will give you some idea of consumer interest in a particular retailer and satisfaction with the retailer's merchandise mix, signified by a purchase. Interest in a particular product can be gauged by the number of consumers that examine the product rather than pass by without a second glance.

Experimentation Test marketing a new, inexpensive product is easier for established businesses. They can easily offer samples to existing customers to receive feedback on its popularity, quality, or other characteristics. For example, a bakery can easily test a new cookie recipe. Test marketing more expensive products or alterations to existing products is costly and difficult. For new entrepreneurs selling goods, experimentation may not be a realistic option. However, service businesses that don't require any special equipment and operate out of the home may be able to offer their services to a limited number of potential customers. This gives them an opportunity to "get their feet wet" and test the market before quitting their day jobs or investing too much in a business idea that doesn't have much of a chance of succeeding.

Hypothetical Scenario

Miranda wanted to find out if her business would have a chance to succeed. Since the business would carry merchandise focused on television and movies, she wanted to identify a specific type of consumer that would purchase her products. She decided to write some survey questions that would narrow down the age group, gender, and amount that a potential customer would spend on her merchandise.

Making Your Product

Many businesses may use products they invent to perform a service, but manufacturing the product is not the primary purpose of the business. You may want to start a business that is based on a product that you can't manufacture in your kitchen or garage. It may require specialized equipment or components that are not available to the general public. To see your idea turned into a physical object and manufactured in large quantities for sale, you will have to develop your idea, produce a design, make a prototype, select a manufacturer, and design the product packaging.

Develop Your Idea

Develop your idea as thoroughly as possible before you begin to develop the design. Keep detailed records of your concept and changes to the concept. The following steps will guide you in developing your product idea:

♦   Make a list of all the product's capabilities.
♦   Define the features that will make it perform the tasks you have listed.
♦   Define the advantages that this product will have over any existing products.
♦   Describe the composition of the parts and how the parts will fit together.
♦   Draw a basic sketch of the finished product. If it is an accessory for an existing product, show how it works with the existing product or attaches to the existing product.

Produce a Design

Unless you are a design engineer, you will have to find a qualified design engineer to produce your design. A **design engineer** converts concepts and information into detailed plans and specifications that are used to manufacture a product. The engineer's expertise enables him or her to consider the cost of manufacturing the product, availability of materials, ease of production, and performance requirements when creating the design document. A mechanical drawing for an object is similar to blueprints for a house. Using the design document and mechanical drawings produced by the design engineer, a manufacturer can make the product. The specifications define the materials to be used, the measurements of each piece in the object, how the pieces fit together, and drawings of the completed object as the design engineer envisions it.

Finding a design engineer may be as simple as looking in the local phone book or local business-to-business phone book. If you can't find one in the phone book, you may need to work backward by finding a manufacturer first and asking the manufacturer to recommend a design engineer to create the specifications.

Many design engineers will work with individual inventors. You should ask if the engineer has worked on products similar to yours in the past. Experience with a similar product will improve the quality of work you receive and decrease the amount of time needed, lowering your cost.

Nondisclosure Agreement When you reveal information about your product, you are giving others a chance to use your ideas to gain profit. In other words, someone will likely try to steal your idea. From this point forward, you should ask anyone that becomes involved to sign a nondisclosure agreement, sometimes called a confidentiality agreement. This includes your design engineer.

A **nondisclosure agreement** is a contract in which the individuals promise to protect the confidentiality of any secret information that is revealed during business transactions or employment. If the other party reveals any information to an unauthorized party, you have the right to sue for damages. Do not rely on a nondisclosure agreement provided by the other party. They may try to protect themselves rather than you, or the document may actually waive your rights to any confidentiality. It is your invention that you want to protect. Use your own nondisclosure agreement. Because of variations in the law from state to state, consult an attorney in your state. A nondisclosure agreement that is valid in one state may not be valid in another state.

Make a Prototype

The first full-size functional model of your invention is a **prototype.** The prototype proves that your invention works. In the process of making a prototype, improvements may be made to the design that will smooth the manufacturing process or lower the cost of manufacturing.

You may be able to find a business in your local phone book or business-to-business phone book that makes prototypes. Listings could be under the heading "Prototypes," "Model Maker," or "Machine Shops." Another good source is the design engineer who created the mechanical drawings of your product. A referral from the design engineer will also ensure that the prototype maker has worked with the design engineer before and is familiar with products similar to yours. If you are satisfied with the work of the design engineer, you will probably be happy with the work of the selected prototype maker. Ask the prototype maker to sign a nondisclosure agreement.

Select a Manufacturer

Before you reveal any confidential information about your product, ask the manufacturers that you talk with to sign a nondisclosure agreement. Request quotes from two or three manufacturers. Ask about the lead time required to manufacture your product. If you enter into a manufacturing contract, ask a lawyer to review the contract before you sign it. Be sure that the contract identifies the consequences if the goods are not produced and delivered on schedule. No matter how good the contract seems, how high the quality of their work looks, and how accommodating the company acts, check references before you sign a contract with the manufacturer.

Identifying manufacturers that have experience in your industry is fairly easy. Take the NAIC code that identifies your business to the library. Use one of the directories that contains listings of industrial businesses. These references include *Dun and Bradstreet* and *Standard and Poor's*. Manufacturers involved in your specific industry will be listed. This is your list of possible manufacturers. Narrow the list down by criteria such as location, personal meetings, membership in a trade association, and references.

Design the Product Packaging

The final piece of the manufacturing puzzle is the product packaging. For your first product, you may be tempted to cut costs by spending only a minimal amount of time and money on the product packaging. Doing so would be a mistake.

In a retail situation, consumers will often judge a product by its packaging. If you place an excellent product in a plain box with only a faded photocopy on the box, consumers may never discover the product. On the other hand, an average product placed next to it may leap off the shelves because its packaging is colorful and innovative.

Examine the packaging of the products that will compete with your product. You need to create an image that sets your product apart from others, creating a unique identity. Consult a graphic designer to design your packaging, but keep a tight rein on the design. Remember that the packaging will create the image for your company and your product.

FDA Approval

The **Food and Drug Administration (FDA)**, an agency under the U.S. Department of Health and Human Services, regulates a variety of products, including food, drugs, medical devices such as pacemakers and hearing aids, biologics such as vaccines, animal feed and drugs, cosmetics, and radiation-emitting products. If your new product falls into one of these categories, you will have to investigate the regulations that affect your product. Your product may have to receive approval from the FDA before you can sell it. Other products must meet regulatory standards or may require special labeling. Check with the FDA for further information.

Hypothetical Scenario

Although Miranda wasn't manufacturing a product, she did want to keep her movie screening idea and merchandise mix secret until she was ready to establish her business. Therefore, she asked several people, including one of her cousins who works for a local video store franchise, to keep her secret. After some thought, she asked them to sign a nondisclosure agreement.

Protect Your Products

If your business produces written documents, invents products, or manufactures products, you want to protect your right to continue your activities and prevent other businesses or individuals from copying your products. The type of products your business makes will determine the type of protection you need. Legal protection is provided by patents, copyrights, trademarks, and servicemarks.

Patent Your Product

Every unique product you invent should be patented. A **patent,** which is issued by the United States Patent and Trademark Office (USPTO), grants property rights to the inventor, for a limited time, that prevent others from making, using, offering for sale, or selling the invention in the United States or importing the invention into the United States from another country. A patent does not grant you the right to make, use, or sell a product. It grants you the right to *exclude* anyone else from making, using, or selling the product for the specified time period.

There are three types of patents. A **utility patent** is based on the *functionality* of the product. A utility patent is appropriate if you invent or discover a new and useful process, machine, article of manufacture, composition of matter, or any new and useful improvement of these items. A **design patent** is based on the *look* of the product. A design patent is appropriate if you invent a new, original, and ornamental design for a manufactured item. A **plant patent** is appropriate if you invent or discover and asexually reproduce any distinct and new variety of plant.

A utility patent is granted for 20 years from the date of *filing* for the patent. A design patent is granted for 14 years from the date the patent is *issued.* When a patent expires, others are free to make, use, or sell the product. The protection granted by a utility patent is much broader, making it more popular and more useful than a design patent. If your modifications to an existing product affect its functionality at all, apply for a utility patent rather than a design patent. Every year, approximately 200,000 patent applications are filed. Most of the applications are for utility patents.

A patent not only protects your product, it increases the value of your business. Patents are business assets that are valued by banks and potential buyers if you decide to sell your business. You can *sell* your patent to another party for an agreed cash price. You can *license* your patent to one or more individuals or businesses to manufacture and sell the product in exchange for a percentage of the product's sale price. You can *keep* all your patent rights and be the exclusive manufacturer of your product, selling your product yourself or through other retailers.

Steps in Getting a Patent

◆ **Keep records in a bound notebook as you work on your invention.** The records that you keep as you move through each step of the development process are important to applying for your patent. As you work, use as much detail as possible when you record your concept, test results, and changes to your design. Sign, date, cross-reference, and attach any loose documents to your bound notebook. Ask all participants to sign and date entries about any activities in which they were involved. If possible, ask a witness or notary public to sign the entry. A **notary public** is a licensed public officer who certifies that writings are authentic. Many banks and other financial institutions have a notary public on staff. The information in the bound notebook can be used to prove the **conception date,** the date of the invention. This may be needed to prove that your invention can be patented if a similar patent request is filed at the same time.

- **File your records with the USPTO as "disclosure documents" in the Disclosure Document Program.** This does not mean that the information about your invention can be freely disclosed to anyone. Continue to use a nondisclosure agreement for anyone involved in your product. This action will not affect the date of any patent that you file for later. It is valuable because it can be used to prove the invention's date of conception if there is a conflict with any other patent application filed around the same time as you file your patent application. Continue to keep records after filing your disclosure document. Check with the USPTO for guidelines, forms, and fees for filing a disclosure document.

- **Consult a patent attorney.** An attorney who specializes in patent law will be helpful for the following steps. The bar association for your state will be able to provide contact information for patent attorneys who practice in your state.

- **Perform a patent search.** Before you apply for a patent, you will have to verify that you are not infringing on an existing patent. Your patent attorney will hire an independent patent searcher to manually search existing patents that may be related to your patent application. Your patent attorney will compare the identified patents to your product and give you an informed opinion of your product's chances for receiving a patent.

- **File a patent application with the United States Patent and Trademark Office.** A prototype is not necessary to file a patent. If your patent attorney suggests that you request a design patent rather than a utility patent, get a second opinion. The USPTO should respond within 8–14 months.

- **Receive the patent for your product.** After a patent has been granted, information about the product can be publicly disclosed. Information about any patented product can be obtained from the USPTO by anyone who requests it.

- **Pay maintenance fees for your patent.** To keep your utility patent for the full time period of 20 years, you must pay a maintenance fee at predetermined times. The maintenance fee is due 3.5, 7.5, and 11.5 years from the date the patent is granted. If maintenance fees are not paid, the patent will expire.

For more information about obtaining a patent, go to the USPTO web site at www.uspto.gov.

Register Your Copyright

If you have put your thoughts into a tangible form by writing, drawing, painting, photographing, or filming them, you own the way that your thoughts are expressed. You cannot copyright an idea, but you can copyright the way that the idea is expressed in any media. Products created by your mind, rather than made by your hands, are considered to be **intellectual property.** In the United States, your creative work is automatically copyrighted as you produce it. A **copyright** grants the author the exclusive right to copy, modify, publish, perform, display, and sell the creative work. The author can sell all or some of these rights to a third party. In some situations, the copyright may belong to a business rather than an individual author. For example, documents such as software manuals, marketing presentations, and brochures written by an employee in the course of normal business are known as a **work for hire.** The copyright is owned by the employer, not the employee.

Register a Copyright   Although a creative work is automatically copyrighted without any further effort by the creator, there is a good reason to register your copyright. If you want to sue someone for infringing on your copyright, a copyright registered with the Copyright Office, a branch of the U.S. Library of Congress, proves your copyright ownership and date of creation without doubt. It provides a public record of your copyright. To register your copyright, perform the following steps.

- **Complete an application for registering your copyright.** Applications are available from the Copyright Office.
- **Mail the application, registration fee, and the necessary copies of your work to the Copyright Office at the following address.** (This address is also listed on the CD.) Check the requirements with the Copyright Office. Requirements will vary, based on the type of work you are registering and the publication status of the work.

    Library of Congress
    Copyright Office
    Register of Copyrights
    101 Independence Avenue, S.E.
    Washington, D.C. 20559-6000

- **Receive your certificate of registration.** Your copyright is registered on the date that the Copyright Office receives your complete registration package. However, it may be several months before you receive your certificate. The Copyright Office receives more than 600,000 applications each year.

Copyrights and the Internet   The Internet is a vast storehouse of fact, fiction, creative prose, pictures, sound, film, and more. The temptation to copy and paste items from a web site to your own site or into your own school or business documents is strong. Copying material infringes on the owner's legal rights.

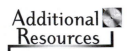

Additional Resources

However, the Internet can be a wonderful resource. Facts cannot be copyrighted. It is the way that a fact is expressed that is copyrighted. If you need to know the path hummingbirds follow when they migrate, the statistics for a specific baseball player, or the number of square miles in Louisiana, that data is probably somewhere on the Internet. Use the facts. Don't use the material, however, without the author's permission. Increasingly, individuals who copy materials are sued by the copyright owners, both businesses and individuals. Software programs on the Internet can automatically compare the materials found in two locations making it easier to find and prosecute copyright violators.

Register Your Trademark or Servicemark

If you watch a few minutes of commercials on television or thumb through a magazine, you will see several trademarks and servicemarks that you easily recognize. A **trademark** is a symbol used to identify the source of a *physical product* and distinguish it from any other products that may be similar. A **servicemark** is a symbol used to identify the source of a *service* and distinguish it from any other service that may be similar. The symbol may be a word, name, design, or a combination of letters and design.

Some of the marks may have been designed when you were still a child. Many have been used heavily in advertising campaigns. You recognize these marks and associate them with a particular company, product, or service. Familiarity with a company's mark can instill confidence in the company and its products. Advertising encourages you to associate a specific image with the mark that you will also associate with the product. For example, you may think that a particular product is innovative, traditional, or sexy based on the image evoked by the company's mark.

Large companies would contact a marketing company to design a trademark. An entrepreneur establishing a small business could consult a graphic designer. To find a graphic designer, simply look in your local phone book or business-to-business phone book. Another source could be a local art school. Students or instructors might be interested in creating your trademark as a "real" project or class assignment.

A trademark is not required, and not all businesses use a trademark or servicemark. However, if you use a trademark or servicemark and sell the identified items or services in different states or countries, you gain legal advantages when you register your mark with the USPTO. You publicly claim the mark and the right to use it to identify your goods or services.

Before you receive federal registration for your mark, you may be able to use the symbol ™ for your trademark and ﹕ᴹ for your servicemark. Regulations governing the use of ™ and ˢᴹ vary from state to state, so you should consult the laws for your state. After you receive notice that your mark is registered by the USPTO, you can use the symbol ® with your mark. You cannot use ® while your registration is pending.

- **Although you aren't required to perform a search to verify that your mark doesn't conflict with one already registered, you may want to perform the search.** An attorney familiar with trademark law or an independent trademark search company can have the search performed for you.
- **You can use the Internet to file the application to register your mark.** The Trademark Electronic Application System is located at www.uspto.gov. Be sure that you register your mark as a trademark or servicemark, whichever is correct. If you try to register it incorrectly, the registration may not be valid. You can file a *use* application, meaning you have already used the mark, or an *intent-to-use* application, meaning that you haven't used the mark yet but intend to use it in the future. If there are no conflicts, the USPTO should respond in six to seven months and your mark should be registered in a year.
- **Maintain your right to use your mark.** The registration is valid for 10 years. To maintain your trademark registration, you must file an Affidavit of Use between the fifth and sixth year after registration and during the ninth year. You must renew your registration every 10 years.

Hypothetical Scenario

Miranda decided that she wanted a logo that could be printed on T-shirts, hats, or other items that she could give away or sell at her movie screenings. She didn't have a lot of cash set aside for the logo design, so she decided to talk to the local art academy. She made an appointment with one of the instructors. After a few minutes of discussion, he decided to create an assignment for his upper-level graphic design class. Miranda would come to class on Monday to describe the type of image she wanted for her store. By Friday, she would have several designs to choose from, each design completed by a senior-level graphic design student.

Technology Insights

Market Research

One of the first problems that a business encounters when it is ready to perform market research is finding subjects that are willing to try new products and provide feedback. You know they're out there, you just can't find them. Like many other things, willing test subjects can be found on the Internet. Not only can they be found on the Internet, enterprising businesses have already gathered them in one place, ready and eager to try your latest product and provide detailed feedback that can answer your product development questions. Does it taste too sweet? Was the product packaging attractive? Would you buy the product for yourself?

Several businesses saw the potential of the Internet for market research in the late 1990s. They formed partnerships with companies that needed market research and found individuals who were willing to participate. To encourage individuals to participate, they provide free samples, offer rewards, and conduct contests. The participants volunteer to try a sample of the product. They receive the product through the mail or via a delivery service, try the product, and log on to a specified web site to provide feedback. The company that provided the samples receives the participants' feedback, neatly totaled and summarized.

Think Critically

1. What type of products benefit from this service?
2. How would you use a service like this to help you develop your product?

CHAPTER REVIEW

Consumers purchase products that fill their needs and wants. Needs are items that you can't live without such as food, water, clothing, and shelter. Wants are items you would like to have but can live without. Wants include everything but the barest necessities. Consumer wants are affected by their culture, social class, gender, and individual characteristics and preferences. Entrepreneurs have to select merchandise that consumers will purchase. Physical goods can be classified as staple goods, fashion goods, seasonal goods, and convenience goods based on the demand for the items. Services can be classified as staple or seasonal, also based on consumer demand. The merchandise mix identifies the variety, breadth, and depth of the products the business carries. Most businesses sell products that fill consumers' wants rather than needs.

A business needs a unique characteristic that makes it different from its competition. The difference could be based on a new product, a new service, a unique product assortment, a different way of selling your products, or a unique location. New goods and services are constantly developed to solve problems and meet specific needs. For a business to earn a profit, it must sell a product that solves a problem and takes full advantage of its unique characteristic.

Before you invest too much into your business idea, you should conduct market research to evaluate your chance for success. The information you gather will help you target your customers, identify opportunities, increase your success, and identify weaknesses in your plans. You can conduct your research by interviewing consumers, holding focus groups, surveying consumers, observing consumer behavior, and experimenting with different products and options.

There are several steps to developing a new product:

1. Develop your idea thoroughly before you attempt to complete its design.
2. Produce a design and create mechanical drawings that can be used to manufacture the product.
3. Ensure that your product works by building a prototype.
4. Identify a manufacturer that will make your product.
5. Finally, design your product packaging.

Protect your products and your business by acquiring patents, copyrights, trademarks, and servicemarks when they are appropriate. A patent can protect you by preventing others from making, using, or selling your product for the specified time period. A copyright protects your creative products, such as a fictional story or a photograph, by preventing others from copying, modifying, publishing, performing, displaying, or selling your creative work. Registering your trademark or servicemark protects your business by ensuring that your products can be distinguished from any products made by other companies. This protects your company's public image and profits.

USE BUSINESS TERMS

Fill in the blanks with the appropriate term.

breadth
conception date
convenience goods
copyright
culture
depth
design engineer
design patent
fashion goods
Food and Drug Administration (FDA)
individuality
intellectual property
market research
merchandise
merchandise mix
needs
nondisclosure agreement

notary public
patent
plant patent
primary research
prototype
seasonal goods
seasonal service
secondary research
servicemark
social class
staple goods
staple service
trademark
utility patent
wants
work for hire

1. ___?___, which comes from your social and family environment, is inherited from your ancestors and will be passed to your children.
2. ___?___ are merchandise that are constantly demanded by customers.
3. The ___?___ is the number of merchandise lines carried by a business.
4. ___?___ can help you target your potential customers, identify business opportunities, increase your potential for success, and identify weaknesses in your plans.
5. Focus groups are a method of performing ___?___.
6. Ask individuals or businesses to sign a ___?___ to protect information about your product until it is patented.
7. Written stories, photographs, and films are examples of ___?___.

TEST YOUR READING

8. Identify retailers that sell products that satisfy your needs.
9. Describe how your culture, social class, gender, and individuality affect the products you want.
10. Categorize the products you purchased during your last shopping trip.
11. Use a retailer's merchandise mix to explain why you would select the retailer to purchase a specific item you want.
12. Describe the difference between goods and services.
13. Use an example to explain how you can turn a problem into a business opportunity.
14. Describe several products that would be found at one of the retailers listed in Table 3.5. Why do these products fit into its merchandise mix?
15. Why should you study your competition?
16. Describe the information you can gather during a personal interview.
17. What is the purpose of a mechanical drawing?
18. Why is a utility patent recommended over a design patent?
19. List the types of items that can be copyrighted.

THINK CRITICALLY ABOUT BUSINESS

20. What did Tim Ribbon do wrong when he opened his store? Describe how he could fix his mistake.
21. Create a chart that describes a reasonable merchandise mix for your business.
22. Describe how you will make your business unique.
23. Describe an original service that might be turned into a successful business. Explain why it might succeed.
24. Write a survey containing 15 to 20 questions that will reveal important information for your business.

REAL-LIFE BUSINESS
Boston Duck Tours

Some business ideas are more unusual than others. Who would have thought that touring Boston in an amphibious vehicle from World War II would become a successful small business? In 1994, Andy Wilson borrowed over $1 million, firmly believing that people would flock to his doors to take a Duck Tour through the city of Boston. He was right. In 1994, the company had four Ducks and 15 employees. In an average day, they gave tours to 600 people. By 2000, the company had 17 Ducks, 90 employees, and was giving tours to an average of 2,700 customers a day.

A Duck is actually a DUKW, an amphibious truck that first saw military service with the marines during World War II. They were used to transport soldiers and supplies between ship and shore. They travel at a speed of 6.4 miles per hour on the water and 50 miles per hour on land. Manufactured in 1942, each DUKW cost $10,800 to produce. The name is based on the code used by General Motors: "D" identifies 1942 as the first year of production, "U" indicates that the vehicle is an amphibious utility truck, "K" indicates that the vehicle has front-wheel drive, and "W" indicates that the vehicle has a tandem axle.

Although you wouldn't think so at first glance, the DUKW is a perfect vehicle for a tour of a city with both land and water scenic areas. Rather than boarding a ferry, the DUKW can simply launch into the water. When it reaches the other side, it drives up and out of the water.

Boston Duck Tours has made excellent use of the vehicle's capabilities. The 80-minute tour route passes many of the historic landmarks in Boston and plunges into the Charles River to see the city from a different angle. The tour conductors are known as ConDUCKtors. Each ConDUCKtor dresses in a unique costume and presents a unique version of information about the sites they pass. The variation in ConDUCKtors encourages tourists to take more than one tour because each experience is unique. You can find more information about the company at www.ducktours.com.

Think Critically

1. If you were a banker, would you have loaned Andy Wilson the money to start his business? Explain.
2. Why did Andy Wilson name his business Boston Duck Tours?
3. Describe Andy Wilson's product.
4. Would scenic tours in DUKWs work in your city? Explain your answer. Draw a map that describes the route the tour would follow.

UNIT 2

Before You Start Your Business

CHAPTER  4

Legal Structure and Financial Resources

GOALS

♦   Choose a legal structure for your business
♦   Register a name for your business
♦   Calculate your start-up costs
♦   Acquire start-up capital

Jim Soga is a college student who works at a local pizza restaurant. One day, Jim and four of his friends were telling stories about delivering pizza and reminiscing about "real food," food that didn't come from the school cafeteria or fast-food restaurants. They realized that several of the nearby fast-food restaurants made a sizable profit delivering fast food to students who were unable or unwilling to leave the campus. From their own experience and an informal survey of other students, they concluded that many students would be willing to pay a delivery fee for menu items from local sit-down restaurants that didn't offer a delivery service.

Legal Structures

There are four general structures you can follow for your business—sole proprietorship, partnership, corporation, and limited liability company. You can find examples of each structure in your local phone book. Choose the structure that fits your situation and the individuals involved in your business. Within each general structure, there are some standard alternatives that you can use to tailor the structure to fit your business.

Sole Proprietorship

The most simple business structure is the sole proprietorship. By default, unless you file papers with your state authority, your business is a sole proprietorship. A **sole proprietorship** is a business owned by a single individual that is not registered with your state as any other form of business. In fact, if you have performed any freelance tasks, such as landscaping or photography, accepted a commission for a product you made, or accepted a contract for your work, you are already a sole proprietor. Almost 75 percent of existing businesses are sole proprietorships, businesses owned by single individuals with entrepreneurial spirits.

There are significant legal and financial consequences of owning a sole proprietorship. You are your business, and your business is you. You are personally responsible for all of the actions your business performs. This includes any debts the business may incur. If necessary, you will have to sell your personal possessions to repay a business debt. This means that you are not only risking the money you actually invest in your business, you are also risking your personal possessions, including your house, car, and collection of baseball cards. This is true regardless of whether your business uses these possessions or not. You do not have to operate your business in your home to risk losing your house if you are a sole proprietor.

You are also personally liable for any lawsuits filed against your company. If an employee feels that you have discriminated against him, if a customer falls because the floor is wet, or a child chokes on a small part that breaks off your product, you can be sued. If the business is held responsible, you will be required to pay any damages from your business and personal resources.

The business structure has other consequences as well. Because your business is a sole proprietorship, your business will cease to exist when you retire or die. If you want to create a family business that can be passed on to your children, choose a different legal structure.

Choosing to establish your business as a sole proprietorship will limit the money and resources you have available for purchases and expenses. Limited funds is one reason for the failure of many sole proprietorships. Proprietors are limited to the funds they can raise from loans or savings. With limited financial resources, the entrepreneur may not be able to establish the business and run it for several months or more until it can survive on the profit it generates.

Taxation for Sole Proprietors Taxation is also affected by your business structure. The taxation method for the business proceeds for a sole proprietor is known as **pass-through taxation.** The business is not taxed. The profit from your business is passed through to your personal income tax returns. Business profit is treated as personal income for the sole proprietor. Pass-through taxation is much easier to calculate and requires fewer forms, simplifying the taxation process. Be aware of the following information when you file income tax for a sole proprietorship. Consult the Internal Revenue Service for the most recent forms and regulations for

Additional Resources

filing federal and state income tax returns for your business. (Refer to the CD for contact information for tax agencies for each state.)

- **Report profit or loss from your business on Schedule C when you file your personal tax forms.**
- **Report your self-employment taxes on Schedule SE when you file your personal tax forms. Self-employment taxes** are contributions to the social security and Medicare programs. Sole proprietors pay twice as much in self-employment taxes as employees pay in social security and Medicare taxes. This happens because employers pay half of the total amount owed for each employee. Without an employer, you have to pay the entire amount yourself.
- **You will be taxed on all profit (sales – expenses) earned by your business, even if you choose to reinvest those profits in your business or save the funds for future business needs.**
- **You may need to make estimated tax payments.** Because an employer does not withhold income taxes from your income, you should estimate the amount of tax you will owe at the end of the year on your business profit. Based on this amount, you can make estimated tax payments every quarter to federal and state tax agencies.
- **If you hire employees, you will be required to file additional tax forms.**

Owning a sole proprietorship has many advantages. You're the boss. You determine how the business will operate. If the business is failing or you decide to do something else, you can easily discontinue a sole proprietorship, keeping in mind that you are still responsible for any debt or legal obligations incurred by the business. Finally, after expenses are paid, you receive all the profits.

Partnership

Many businesses are established as partnerships. A **partnership** is a business owned by two or more individuals that has not been incorporated. There are two types of partnerships—a general partnership and a limited partnership.

The most common, and the one usually identified as a partnership, is a general partnership. In a **general partnership,** all partners are equally involved in operating the business and all partners have unlimited liability for company debts. Except for the fact that more people are involved, a general partnership is very similar to a sole proprietorship.

A limited partnership is less common. In a **limited partnership,** one or more of the partners is a limited partner and one or more of the partners must be a general partner. Like partners in a general partnership, **general partners** are equally involved in operating the business, indicated by participation in business decisions, and have unlimited liability for company debts. Every partnership must have at least one general partner to operate the business and accept liability. A **limited partner** has only limited personal liability for the company's debts and no voice in company decisions. **Limited personal liability** means that the partner's financial risk is limited to the amount invested in the business. A limited partner's personal property is not at risk if the business fails or closes with unpaid debt. In exchange for limited liability, a limited partner is not allowed to make any day-to-day management decisions concerned with operating the business. A limited partner who becomes involved in operating the business could be treated as a general partner in any legal proceedings regarding the business, placing the partner's personal assets at risk.

A limited partner is often an investor in a business that sells a product that the investor is not familiar with or the investor has little interest in the product or operating the business. Usually, a limited partner provides cash or other valuable resources but not skill or knowledge. The limited partner invests in the business with the hope of earning a financial return on the investment. If the business succeeds, the share of the profits that the limited partner receives will be determined by the amount the partner invested in the business. If the business fails, the limited partner loses no more than the amount invested.

Like a sole proprietorship, general partners are personally liable for any lawsuits filed against the company. If your business is sued and the business is held responsible, general partners may have to sell personal assets to pay any damages. Limited partners may lose only the money or resources invested in the business.

Also like a sole proprietorship, your business will cease to exist when a partner dies or withdraws from the partnership. A written partnership agreement should be created between or among all the partners to determine what will happen to the business in various situations such as the death or retirement of a partner. The legal agreement can enable your business to continue after a partner leaves the business.

Partnerships are based on the theory that there is strength in numbers. The business benefits from the money, resources, knowledge, and skill contributed by all the partners. All of the general partners, using all of their combined experience and business knowledge, make the business decisions. The additional information input by the partners may result in better decisions.

Taxation for Partnerships   Like a sole proprietorship, the taxation method applied to a partnership is pass-through taxation. The business is not taxed. The profit from the partnership is passed through to the personal income tax returns of the partners. Partners pay taxes on their share of the company's profit or deduct their share of the losses. Be aware of the following information when you file income tax for a partnership. Please consult the Internal Revenue Service (IRS) for the most recent forms and regulations for filing federal and state income tax returns for your business.

- **The partnership must file a Form 1065.** The IRS will use the information on this form to verify the partners' tax returns.
- **The partnership must provide a Schedule K-1 to the IRS and to each partner.** The Schedule K-1 identifies each partner's share of the company's profit or loss.
- **Report profit or loss from your partnership, identified on Schedule K-1, on Schedule E when you file your personal tax forms.**

- **Like a sole proprietor, partners must pay self-employment taxes.** Report your self-employment taxes on Schedule SE when you file your personal tax forms. Self-employed individuals, including sole proprietors and partners, pay twice as much in self-employment taxes as employees pay in social security and Medicare taxes. This happens because employers pay half of the total amount of these taxes for each employee.

- **You will be taxed on all profit earned by your partnership, even if you choose to reinvest those profits in your business or save the funds for future business needs.**

- **You may need to make estimated tax payments.** Because an employer does not withhold income taxes from your income, you should estimate the amount of tax you will owe at the end of the year on your business profit. Based on this amount, you can make estimated tax payments every quarter to the federal and state tax agencies.

- **If you hire employees, you will be required to file additional tax forms.**

Choosing Your Partners The individuals you choose to go into business with will have a profound effect on your business and the pleasure that you take from going to work every day. You don't want to be involved in a business with someone who doesn't follow through on a decision or leaves you to do all the work. You don't plan to end up in court when you start a business with your best friend. Sometimes these things happen anyway. There are several things you should consider before you choose your business partners.

- **Compatibility**—Partners will spend a great deal of time together establishing and operating a business. Any little personality quirks that bother you now may become major irritants in the future. If you don't think her jokes are funny or his constant chatting drives you up the wall, don't expect things to get better in the future. Ask yourself if you really want to tie yourself to this individual in critical areas such as business interests and financial resources.

- **Ability to cope with stress**—Starting a business can be very stressful. How does your potential partner handle stress? If she is going to spend the day at the beach relaxing while you face the IRS audit or fire the employee who isn't working out, you may want to reconsider. A partner who is only around when things are going well may be missing too often or at critical times.

- **Decision-making methods**—Examine how your partner makes decisions. A game of "paper, scissors, rock" or flipping a coin may be a fun way to choose a movie, but it isn't the best method for selecting a business location or committing your business to a contract valued at several hundred thousand dollars.

- **Spending**—Observe your partner's spending habits. A business plans its purchases and manages its finances carefully. A partner who spends money easily and comes up short when the rent is due does not have good spending habits. Remember that the profits from the business will be distributed to the partners. If one of the partners spends money from the business foolishly, it impacts all of the partners' pocketbooks.

- **Reliability**—Individual partners are usually responsible for a particular area of the business such as ordering merchandise or keeping the books. You must be able to rely on that individual to perform the tasks. If the partner is unreliable, your store will run out of merchandise or bills and receipts will pile up, unpaid and unrecorded.

- **Risk-taking behaviors**—Taking risks is not necessarily a bad thing. Starting a business is inherently risky to some extent. However, you should be comfortable with the same level of risk as your partner. Your comfort level with risk will impact many of the decisions you make.

- **Work habits**—Establishing a business is a lot of work. You and your partners will need to work until tasks are complete. This may require more than the regular 8:00 to 5:00 workday. Self-control and dedication are required to run a business when it's the first day of summer and you would rather be outside in the sunshine.

- **Attention to detail**—Many business tasks are monotonous and require attention to detail. Sloppy paperwork or inattention could result in costly mistakes.

- **Ethics**—You probably don't plan to start a business with a criminal. However, behavior doesn't have to be criminal to be unethical. Dealing ethically with customers and suppliers is important in creating a good reputation for your business.

- **Experience**—If experience is a good teacher, then a partner who has learned from previous experience can be very valuable. A partner who has run a successful business in the past will give your business an advantage.

Partnership Agreement If you plan ahead and follow the advice of a good lawyer, you can avoid some of the pitfalls that other businesses have encountered. If you can learn from the mistakes made by someone else, you won't have to make the same mistakes yourself. A **partnership agreement** is a legal document that describes the rights and responsibilities of each partner in a partnership. It establishes the ground rules for the role of every partner in the group and determines what will happen when conflict arises. If you don't have a partnership agreement, the laws concerning partnerships in your state will be used if any disagreement or other conflict sends your business to court. This may cause consequences that are not advantageous to you or your partners. Partnership agreements should cover some of the following topics. (Refer to the CD for an example of a partnership agreement.)

Additional Resources

- **Define each partner's contributions to the business.** A partner could contribute money, resources, skill, or knowledge. For example, if three partners establish a restaurant, one partner may contribute the financing, the second contributes a building to serve as the restaurant's location, while the third partner may have limited financial resources but does have 10 years of experience managing a restaurant for another company.

- **Define the percentage owned by each partner.** The percentage owned by each partner does not have to be equal. It could be determined by the value of each partner's contributions to the business or by the role each partner takes in operating the business on a daily basis.

- ◆ **Allocate the percentage of profits and losses.** The percentage of profit or loss allocated to each partner does not have to be equal. Many businesses allocate profit and loss based on the percentage owned by the partners.

- ◆ **Define the timing and method used to distribute profits.** Each partner will have different financial needs, so it is important to agree on when and how profits will be distributed. It is common for profits to be distributed annually. However, you may want to specify guidelines for allowing a partner to withdraw cash from the business.

- ◆ **Define the authority of each partner in committing the business to any legal agreements.** Unless specified in your partnership agreement, a single partner has the authority to commit the business to a binding agreement of any type. You may want to require that all or a majority of partners must agree before committing the company to any course of action.

- ◆ **Define the role of each partner in making business decisions.** One option may be allowing individual partners to make commitments valued at less than a specific dollar amount and require a majority agreement for commitments over the dollar amount. You don't want to make it difficult to accomplish any task. For example, you don't want to require a majority vote to order a head of lettuce if you own a restaurant. However, you might want a majority decision to select your supplier or sign a contract purchasing 100 heads of lettuce every day. You must define the dividing line between decisions that require a vote and decisions that can be made individually. Limited partners are not involved in the day-to-day management decisions.

- ◆ **Define the responsibilities of each partner.** Many businesses divide responsibilities among the general partners. If Jill can multiply numbers without a calculator and maintain accurate records, she might be interested in keeping the financial records for the business. If Jack can charm the whiskers off a cat, ask him to handle negotiations with suppliers and complaints from customers. Consider the strengths of each partner and the needs of your particular business.

- ◆ **Define the method used to add new partners to the partnership.** Professional groups such as doctors and lawyers often expand by admitting new partners to the group. Many partnerships require a unanimous vote to admit a new partner. New partners may bring additional resources or customers to the business.

- ◆ **Define what will happen if a partner withdraws from the partnership or dies.** This section of your partnership agreement is known as a buy-sell agreement. A **buy-sell agreement** defines who can buy a partner's interest in the business, the situation that activates the buy-sell agreement, and the price to be paid for the partner's interest. Typically, a buy-sell agreement is activated when a partner receives a purchase offer from someone who is not currently a partner, a divorcing spouse of a current partner receives an interest in the business as part of the settlement, a creditor forecloses on a debt secured by a partner's interest in the business, a partner declares personal bankruptcy, or a partner dies or suffers an incapacitating injury. You can limit potential buyers to the current partners or require a unanimous vote for the potential partner, limiting the options for a partner who wishes to leave the business but protecting you from being in business with an individual you cannot work with or don't like. (Refer to the CD for an example of a buy-sell agreement form.)

Additional Resources

- **Define how disputes between partners will be settled.** You must define a course of action to be followed if your partners cannot agree on a significant issue. Duels at dawn have been illegal for quite some time, and if you don't want to hire a lawyer and go straight to court, you may prefer to take your dispute to a mediator or an arbitrator. A **mediator** is a neutral third party, with no power to enforce a decision, who meets with the two parties to resolve a dispute without going to court. Mediation is usually fairly informal and does not follow any formal rules governing evidence or procedure. An **arbitrator** is a neutral third party who meets with the two parties to resolve a dispute without going to court. The arbitration process is more formal than mediation. However, although arbitration uses the laws of evidence and procedure, they are less formal than those used in court proceedings. If the parties agree to **binding arbitration,** the arbitrator can impose a decision on the opposing parties. If the parties agree to **nonbinding arbitration,** the arbitrator can recommend a solution, but not force the parties to agree.

If you always received a minus in the "ability to work well with others" column on your report card and performance evaluations, a partnership may not be the right legal structure for your business. Carefully consider the advantages and disadvantages of your proposed partnership, your business situation, and your personal preferences.

Corporation

The most complicated business structure is the corporation. A **corporation** is a business structure, created and regulated by state law, that functions as an independent legal entity. The legal standing of a corporation as a separate entity from the people that own the corporation has many repercussions. On its own, a corporation can borrow money, enter into business contracts, pay taxes, and be sued.

One of the most important reasons that an entrepreneur would choose to establish a business as a corporation is the advantage of gaining limited personal liability. Limited personal liability protects the entrepreneur's personal assets by limiting the potential loss to the amount invested in the business. The entrepreneur's personal assets are not at risk if the business fails or closes with unpaid debt.

Another important characteristic of the corporation business structure is also the result of the corporation's status as a separate legal entity. Its existence is not tied to the individuals who established or operate the company. Regardless of whether the owners who establish the corporation sell their interests, withdraw from the business, or die, the corporation will continue to exist. In exchange for these important advantages, however, the acts of establishing and operating a corporation are more complicated than the simpler sole proprietorship or partnership.

Corporations may be owned by the entrepreneurs who establish and operate the business or they can be owned by millions of individuals, strangers who may never meet the corporations' founders or each other. Corporations are owned by **shareholders,** individuals who own shares of the corporations. Shareholders have specific rights granted by the state and the corporations. Shareholders have the right to attend shareholders' meetings, vote to elect the corporations' directors, and receive a share of the corporations' profits.

A **public corporation** trades its shares, also called stock, publicly on a stock market. Any individual who can afford to purchase a share of the corporation can become a shareholder. A public company usually follows a typical hierarchy. The shareholders elect **directors,** who make major decisions affecting the corporation, such as deciding to purchase a location and hiring or appointing officers, particularly the chief executive officer. **Officers** supervise the day-to-day administration and management tasks and hire managers and other employees to manage and complete the tasks associated with the corporation's business purpose. Most states insist that a corporation have a president, secretary, and treasurer. In most states, one individual can wear several hats and fill all of the required officer positions. Although the specific tasks of each individual may vary between corporations, the general hierarchy of a public corporation will be similar to the hierarchy pictured in Figure 4.1.

FIGURE 4.1   Hierarchy of a Public Corporation

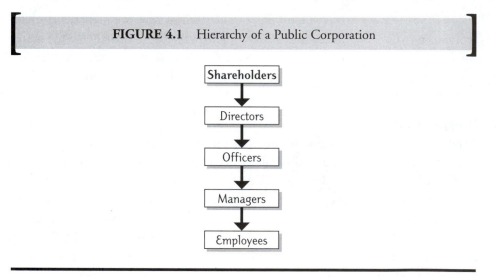

A **private corporation** does not trade its shares publicly. To purchase shares of a private corporation, you must purchase the shares directly from a current shareholder, an activity that is usually governed by the rules established by the corporation. A private corporation usually has only a few shareholders. For example, family members establishing a family business may create a private corporation. In a private corporation, shareholders may perform several roles, acting as directors and officers as well as shareholders and managers.

Establishing a Corporation A single individual can form a corporation. In fact, in some industries, it is a common practice. In some instances, if you work as an independent contractor, some businesses may refuse to hire you unless you are incorporated. State regulations and requirements for establishing and operating a corporation may vary.

A corporation is considered to be a foreign corporation in any state other than the state where it is incorporated. This may require you to register in other states before you do business in them. Each state handles the description of doing business and the requirements for foreign corporations differently. Check the requirements in your state.

Filing articles of incorporation is an essential step in establishing a corporation. **Articles of incorporation** is a document filed with the state to establish a corporation. The document usually includes information about the corporation such as the company's main business purpose, the location of the home office, the names of the directors, and the type of stock that the corporation will issue. The steps below are some common guidelines for establishing a corporation. The process is determined by the state where you incorporate.

- **Identify the individuals who will be the directors for your corporation.** You will need the names of your directors to file the articles of incorporation, so you must agree on the directors before you file the paperwork.

- **File the articles of incorporation with the proper state authority.** In most states, this is usually the secretary of state or the corporations commissioner. If you are the only individual involved, you will sign the articles of incorporation. If several individuals are involved, they can all sign the articles or appoint one person, known as the **incorporator,** to sign the articles.

- **Identify the registered agent for the corporation.** When you file your articles of incorporation, you will be asked to identify your **registered agent,** the individual who will be the point of contact for the corporation. This enables the state, IRS, or any member of the public to contact your business.

Operating a Corporation After filing the articles of incorporation, your new corporation will have several tasks to perform. One of the first tasks is writing the bylaws for your corporation. **Bylaws** define the internal regulations and procedures a corporation follows. They are usually adopted by the shareholders at the first shareholders' meeting. Bylaws can include the normal procedures for corporate activities such as holding meetings, electing directors, and choosing officers. The responsibilities of the corporation's officers and directors are also in the corporation's bylaws. Only shareholders can amend the bylaws after they are adopted.

One of the next tasks is issuing stock to the corporation's shareholders. Refer to the ownership percentages you agreed to before establishing the corporation. Be sure to record the distribution of shares.

To retain your status as a corporation, your business has to fulfill specific requirements. If these requirements are not met, you may lose the advantage of limited liability. Many of these responsibilities involve paperwork, recording the actions of the corporation, its shareholders, directors, and officers.

◆ **Hold annual meetings for the directors and shareholders.** Record the issues discussed, votes taken on the issues, and actions taken by the shareholders and directors.

◆ **Formally issue shares to the initial shareholders.** The shareholders own an interest in the corporation, a separate business entity. Issuing the stock formalizes your earlier agreement concerning the percentage that each corporation shareholder will own. You must record the names of the corporation's initial shareholders, the number of shares each shareholder purchases, and the method each shareholder uses to pay for the shares. In most states, private stock sales that are offered to individuals who will also operate the company do not have to be registered with the Securities Exchange Commission. Check the rules in your state.

◆ **Documents must be signed in the name of the corporation, not the individual director or officer.** This is part of the corporation's existence as a separate entity, protecting shareholders from liability. The corporation, not the individual, is committing itself to an action.

◆ **The corporation must maintain a separate bank account.** Again, this is part of the corporation's existence as a separate entity, paying its own bills and using the money it earned. You cannot use this as a personal account without risking the loss of the protection of limited liability.

◆ **Maintain financial records of all the corporation's activities.** The corporation's financial records should clearly demonstrate that the corporation is a separate entity from its shareholders, officers, and managers.

◆ **File a separate income tax return for the corporation.** As a separate entity, the corporation files income tax returns that are separate from any shareholder, director, or manager.

◆ **Record any actions that require participation or approval by the shareholders or directors.** Most of these actions are ones that require a substantial financial commitment by the corporation. This includes activities such as issuing additional stock, approving a long-term lease, authorizing a loan, and adopting an employee retirement plan.

Shareholders' Agreement Shareholders have several important responsibilities. They vote to elect or remove directors. They vote to approve the bylaws. After the bylaws are approved, they can vote to approve amendments to the bylaws. Shareholders vote to approve the corporation's sale of any major assets and to approve a merger with another business. Finally, they can vote to dissolve the corporation.

The shareholders' agreement restricts the shareholder's options when choosing to sell shares of the corporation. It defines who can buy a shareholder's interest in the business and the price to be paid for the shareholder's interest. You can limit potential buyers to the current shareholders or require a unanimous vote for the potential shareholder, limiting the options for a shareholder who wishes to leave the business but protecting you from being in business with an individual you cannot work with or don't like. A shareholders' agreement can require that employees leaving the company who own stock must sell their shares to a current shareholder. This practice keeps shares of the business within the corporation.

S Corporation Status An S corporation offers two valuable advantages sought by many entrepreneurs—limited liability and pass-through taxation. However, some states choose to tax an S corporation as they do a regular corporation, not allowing pass-through taxation. Check the regulations to determine how S corporations are taxed in your state.

To establish your business as an S corporation, you can't have more than 75 shareholders and all of the shareholders must be residents or citizens of the United States. You can change your business to a regular corporation in the future. In the past, corporations were established as an S corporation initially so the losses experienced by a new business could be passed through to the shareholders' tax returns. Later, when the business began to earn a sizeable profit, shareholders would change the business to a regular corporation so they would not be taxed on the profits that the corporation retained.

Taxation for Corporations Corporations do not use the pass-through taxation method. Corporations are taxed as an entity on their profits, filing an income tax return that is separate from those filed by shareholders. Shareholders pay income tax on any salary they draw from the corporation as an employee. A **dividend** is a portion of the corporation's profit that is paid to shareholders. A dividend distributed by a public corporation encourages investors to buy the corporation's stock in the stock market.

A corporation pays taxes, at a special corporate rate, on the profit that remains after paying salaries, bonuses, and expenses. The taxed profit includes any money the corporation keeps for future expenses. This explains why dividends are often described as being taxed twice. The corporation pays a tax on the money as a profit and the shareholder pays a tax on the dividend as income.

Completing the appropriate tax forms is more complicated for a corporation than for a sole proprietorship or partnership. Seek assistance from a qualified accountant or other tax professional who is experienced in corporate tax requirements. A corporation could be the ideal structure for your business or it could bring complications you really don't need until your business has been firmly established and needs the structure to help it expand.

Limited Liability Company

Combining some of the best features of a sole proprietorship or partnership with the advantages of a corporation, the limited liability company is a business structure that is gaining in popularity. A **limited liability company,** usually known as an LLC, is a business structure that features pass-through taxation and limited personal liability. It can be more complicated to set up and operate an LLC than a partnership, but not as difficult as a corporation. Because an LLC is less complicated than a corporation, the LLC business structure has virtually replaced the S corporation.

In most states, you can be the sole owner of an LLC. You should consider the LLC business structure if the sole proprietorship or partnership structure is right for you, but you are concerned about personal liability. It is important to remember that any business can be sued at any time. The reason for the lawsuit doesn't have to be an error you made. Your business could be sued if a person slips and falls in your parking lot or a child is injured playing with a toy sold by your business, even if another company manufactures it.

Establishing an LLC While any type of business can be a sole proprietorship or partnership, some states limit the types of businesses that can be structured as an LLC. For example, businesses in the financial industry and healthcare industry, as well as some professionals such as accountants and architects, may not be able to form an LLC in your state. Check the regulations in your state. The following steps may be required to establish your LLC.

- **Some states require that you publish your intention to form an LLC.** If this is a requirement in your state, you can publish your intention in your local newspaper.
- **File articles of organization with your state's LLC filing office.** In most states, this is usually the secretary of state. The document usually includes information about the LLC such as the name of the business and the names of the members.
- **Identify the registered agent for the LLC.** When you file your articles of organization, you will be asked to identify your registered agent. Like the corporation's registered agent, this individual will be the point of contact for the LLC. This enables the state, IRS, or any member of the public to contact your business.

Operating an LLC The management requirements for an LLC are less formal than those for a corporation. It is not necessary to hold formal meetings for members, but if the members discuss an issue significant to your business or vote on a course of action, it is a good practice to record the process in writing. This will prevent later disputes and record your decision.

Although all the members of an LLC can participate in managing and operating the business, you can choose to designate specific members to run the business or hire an individual who will manage the business. This is known as *manager management.* This enables some members to invest money without actively participating in the business, similar to a limited partner in a partnership. This may occur if family members invest in your business but prefer that you manage the business on a day-to-day basis.

Establish a separate bank account for the business. If you use funds from the business for your personal expenses or constantly pay business expenses from your personal account, you are risking your limited personal liability because you are treating the business as a sole proprietorship or partnership.

Operating Agreement In some states, an LLC is required to have an operating agreement. Even if your state does not require an operating agreement, it is still a good idea to have one. Similar to a partnership agreement or corporate bylaws, an **operating agreement** is a legal document that describes the rights and responsibilities of each member in an LLC. Your operating agreement sets the rules for the role every member will perform in your LLC and determines what will happen when members have serious business disagreements. If you don't have an operating agreement, the laws concerning an LLC in your state will be used if any disagreement or other conflict sends your business to court. This may cause consequences that are not advantageous to you, the other members, or your business. Operating agreements should cover some of the following topics.

- **Define the percentage owned by each member.** The percentage owned by each member is usually determined by the value of each member's contribution to the business.

- **Allocate the percentage of profits and losses.** The percentage of profit or loss allocated to each member is often based on the percentage owned by each member.

- **Define the timing and method used to distribute profits.** You should agree on when and how profits will be distributed or if a portion of the profit will be retained by the business to pay for future growth. If profits are distributed, they are usually distributed annually. However, you may want to specify different procedures for your business. Before a member encounters critical financial needs, set guidelines for allowing a member to withdraw cash from the business. This may prevent disputes during a member's financial crisis.

- **Define the voting power of each member.** Most LLCs allocate voting rights by the percentage of the company each member owns. If you own 35 percent of the business, your vote is worth the same percentage. This method means that your single vote worth 35 percent easily overrules Joe, who owns 2 percent, and Vicki, who owns 5 percent, even if they both vote against you. Alternatively, every member's vote can count equally. In this scenario, Joe, who owns 2 percent, and Vicki, who owns 5 percent, will overrule your vote if they both vote against you.

- **Define what will happen if a member withdraws from the LLC or dies.** This is similar to the buy-sell agreement in a partnership agreement. Without a buy-sell agreement, the laws in your state will determine if your LLC will automatically be dissolved when a member dies or withdraws from your LLC. Use the buy-sell agreement to define who can buy a member's interest in the business, the situation that activates the buy-sell agreement, and the price to be paid for the member's interest.

- **Define how disputes between members will be settled.** You must define a course of action to be followed if the members absolutely cannot agree on a significant course of action. If you are deadlocked, you can choose to solve your problem by meeting with a mediator or an arbitrator. Mediation is usually fairly informal and does not follow any formal rules governing evidence or procedure. The arbitration process is more formal than mediation, following rules that are less restrictive than court proceedings.

Taxation for an LLC For tax purposes, an LLC is not a separate entity. It utilizes pass-through taxation for federal taxation, the same taxation method used by a sole proprietorship or partnership. However, some states do tax the LLC separately or charge a tax fee to the business.

An LLC can choose to be taxed as a corporation. This protects owners from paying tax on the profit left in a business for future growth. However, you will be required to use corporate taxation rules for five years before you can return to pass-through taxation, so choosing this route is a serious decision that will impact your taxes and the taxes of the LLC for several years. Consult a tax professional and verify the tax regulations in your state.

- **If you are the sole owner, report the profit or loss from your business on Schedule C and file it with your personal income tax returns as a sole proprietorship would.**
- **If there are several owners, the business must file a Form 1065.** The IRS will use the information on this form to verify the members' tax returns.
- **The LLC must provide a Schedule K-1 to the IRS and each partner.** The Schedule K-1 identifies each partner's share of the company's profit or loss.
- **Report profit or loss from your LLC, identified on Schedule K-1, on Schedule E when you file your personal tax forms.**
- **Like a sole proprietor, members must pay self-employment taxes.** Report your self-employment taxes on Schedule SE when you file your personal tax forms. Self-employed individuals, including sole proprietors and partners, pay twice as much in self-employment taxes as employees pay in social security and Medicare taxes. This happens because employers pay half of the total amount of these taxes for each employee.
- **You will be taxed on all profit earned by your LLC, even if you choose to reinvest those profits in your business or save the funds for future business needs.**
- **You may need to make estimated tax payments.** Because an employer does not withhold income taxes from your income, you should estimate the amount of tax you will owe at the end of the year on your business profit. Based on this amount, you can make estimated tax payments every quarter to the federal and state tax agencies.
- **If you hire employees, you will be required to file additional tax forms.**
- **A few states tax an LLC on the income it earned.** Check the tax regulations in your state for forms and procedures.
- **A few states charge an annual fee to each LLC that may be labeled as a tax.**

Like a partnership, how you work with and relate to the members of your LLC is critical to the success of your business and your personal satisfaction. Although you can have members in your LLC that invest in your business without participating, it is common for all the members to actively participate in operating the business.

Choose the Right Legal Structure for Your Business

Establishing your business with the right structure and the right people will improve your chances for success and increase the enjoyment you get from the experience. Choosing a legal structure for your business is a key decision that affects many areas of your business. It determines the taxes you pay, the way your business relates to customers and other businesses, the amount of authority you will have to speak for your company, and the weight of your opinion in any internal business discussions. You will have to consider the advantages and disadvantages of each business structure, the tax structure you want to use, the number of active and inactive owners, and the importance of limiting your personal liability. Table 4.1 and the questions that follow it will help you choose the general structure that is right for your business.

TABLE 4.1   Compare Business Structures

	Sole Proprietorship	Partnership	Corporation	LLC
Advantages	Easy to establish	Easy to establish	Limited personal liability	Limited personal liability
	Sole authority for making decisions	Partners combine resources to establish the business	Separate legal identity	Members combine resources to establish the business
	Easy to dissolve	Easy to dissolve	Not affected by withdrawal of individual shareholder	Easy to dissolve
	Pass-through taxation	Pass-through taxation	Hired managers make day-to-day decisions	Choose pass-through or corporate taxation
Disadvantages	Unlimited personal liability	Unlimited personal liability for general partners	Extensive record-keeping required	More complicated than sole proprietorship or partnership
	Limited resources for establishing the business	Potential for serious disagreements between partners	Activities affected by government regulations	Potential for serious disagreement among members
	Business closes when you retire	Without partnership agreement, closes when partner withdraws	Most difficult and expensive structure to establish and dissolve	Without operating agreement, closes when member withdraws
	Owners taxed on profits retained by the business	Owners taxed on profits retained by the business	Major decisions require a vote by shareholders or directors	Must keep corporate taxation method for five years if selected

- **Do you have all of the knowledge and skill necessary to perform the primary purpose of your business?** If you know how to perform the functions that are the main purpose of the business, you can hire consultants, including accountants and lawyers, to perform business activities. A sole proprietorship might work for you.
- **Do you need additional funds to establish your business?** If you can't raise the funds, even through loans, you will need partners. This eliminates the sole proprietorship, but leaves the other options open.

- **Is it important to limit your personal liability?** Although it is always good to limit your risk, some products or businesses are more likely to need protection than others. For example, a dude ranch may be sued if a guest falls off a horse but a fabric store may not encounter as many opportunities for injury or liability for the injury of others.

- **Do you want to establish a business with your spouse?** Obviously, this would eliminate the sole proprietorship option. Make sure that you identify how the interest in the business will be distributed if you or your spouse withdraw, divorce, or die.

- **Do you want to establish a family business that you can pass to your children?** Do not establish a sole proprietorship. If you do not want to establish a corporation, use a partnership or operating agreement with a buy-sell agreement that will be triggered when you retire or withdraw from the business.

- **Which taxation method will benefit you the most?** Pass-through taxation is the simplest. Corporate taxation eliminates the tax you pay for the corporation's retained earnings. The amount of earnings the corporation retains is a determining factor in the best taxation method. The corporation will pay its own taxes for its earnings.

- **How much paperwork do you want?** The simpler business structures require the least amount of record keeping.

Hypothetical Scenario

> Jim Soga and his friends made a list of the local sit-down restaurants that didn't offer a delivery service. They thought they could earn a profit in two ways: (1) Charge the students a delivery fee; (2) Negotiate a lower price for each item with the restaurant. They believed that restaurant owners would accept a lower price for each item because the restaurant could not make these sales without Jim and his friends. The students, of course, would pay the full price listed on the menu. Since Jim had the best "people skills," the group nominated him to negotiate with the owners of the restaurants on the list. After being rejected by the first five restaurants on the list, he asked the last owner why she was not willing to discuss the possibility. She explained, "It sounds like a good idea, but you're just a college kid. I can't risk my time and effort if you don't show any sign of commitment to the idea. If you were a business, I would be more interested."

Register a Name

Many ancient civilizations believed that a name had power, defining the form, substance, and characteristics of an object, a place, or a person. Even today, expectant parents spend months reading through books of possible names for their child. Almost as anxious, entrepreneurs scribble combinations of words, letters, and sometimes numbers, hoping to find just the right combination that will spell magic for their fledgling companies.

There are all kinds of theories when it comes to naming a business. (1) Use your last name. (2) The first letter should be an "A" so it's listed first in the phone book. (3) The name should tell you what the company does. (4) The name should be abstract so your business can create an image for the name. (5) The name should be concrete so that the name creates an image for the business. Obviously, there isn't a consensus on how to create the perfect name for your business. There are a few guidelines to follow.

- **The name of your business must be unique, distinct from any existing business.** You can't register a name that is the same as the name of an existing business or a name that is so similar to the name of an existing business that it would confuse consumers.
- **Depending on your business structure, you may have to include a specific word or abbreviation in the name.** Examples include words such as "Corporation," "Incorporated," "Limited," or an abbreviation such as Corp., Inc., or Ltd. These words or abbreviations identify the structure of the business.
- **The name can't contain specific words prohibited by the state.** This usually includes words such as Bank, Cooperative, Federal, National, United States, or Reserve.

If you have been working as a freelance professional, you have probably used only your own name. Although you operate as a sole proprietorship, you have not created a name for your business. You can continue to operate this way indefinitely, without ever creating a name, simply operating under your own name.

If you establish your business as a partnership, you and your partners will probably want to create a name for your business. **Doing business as** (DBA) identifies the business situation in which a business operates under a name that is different from the real name of the owner. Sole proprietors can also use a fictitious name in the same way.

Registration Requirements

Depending on the type of business structure you select, you may be required to register your name with local, state, or federal agencies. If your sole proprietorship or general partnership has a name that *contains* all the owners' last names, you are *not required* to register the name of your business. For example, if your name is Chuck Smith and you establish a sole proprietorship called Smith's Stores, you will not be required to register the name. If your business is a sole proprietorship or general partnership and the name of your business *does not contain* all the last names of the owners, you are *required* to register the fictitious name. Limited partnerships, corporations, and LLC business structures are required to register the name of the business, but this is usually performed automatically when you file the articles of organization or the articles of incorporation.

A "fictitious name statement" is usually filed with your county or state. This registers the name in the geographic area in which you file the statement. It also identifies the owners of the business and makes this information publicly available. After registering the name, owners are authorized to act in the name of the business. This includes legal activities such as opening a separate bank account for the business, signing contracts, and borrowing money. (Refer to the CD for an example of a fictitious name statement.)

Additional
Resources

Although registering your fictitious name is usually performed at the county level, registration in some states is conducted at the state level with the secretary of state. The following steps will walk you through the general procedure of registering a fictitious name for your sole proprietorship or general partnership. Check with your county or state for specific fees and requirements for your business.

- **Create a name for your business.** Remember that the name can't include some specific words and it may need to include a word or abbreviation that identifies your business structure.
- **Verify that the name is not already in use.** Most states maintain this information in a database that you can easily search by typing in your proposed business name. It may even be available on the Internet site for the office.
- **File the fictitious name statement.** This will register your business name.
- **In some states, you may be required to publish your fictitious name, informing the public that you are doing business as your fictitious business name.** You may have to submit proof that you met this requirement to the county or state office where you registered your business name.

Hypothetical Scenario

Jim and his friends decided that the food delivery service idea had enough potential to pursue. They decided to form a partnership, fill in some details about their plans for the business, and approach the restaurant owners again. They performed a search and registered the name of their business, Real Food Express, in their state.

Calculate Costs for Your Start-up Period

Any business can start off with a bang if it has unlimited financial resources. Most entrepreneurs aren't that lucky. In fact, many entrepreneurs start with very limited resources and have to acquire the necessary funding. Before you can begin to acquire the funds, it's a good idea to calculate how much you need. Why ask Aunt Ethel for a loan if it isn't necessary?

For some businesses, it is easy to calculate the cost of establishing the business. If you want to work as a freelance consultant operating as a sole proprietorship, you may only need to purchase a computer and some business software to track your additional income. If you establish a franchise, the franchiser can tell you the amount you will need. Other businesses require more work to calculate your start-up cost.

Start-up Period

According to the Small Business Administration, one of the leading causes of business failure is the lack of sufficient start-up capital. The start-up period is the length of time between the date you open for business and the date your business earns a profit. Your start-up capital should get you through the time period of opening and operating your business until it generates a profit.

The IRS defines **start-up costs** as any amount paid for creating your business before you begin operating the business. Most start-up costs are one-time expenses. This can include purchasing furniture for the office, a down payment on a building, and purchasing manufacturing equipment.

However, when you estimate the funds you will need to start your business, you have to think of a longer time period. Just because you open your doors for business does not mean that your business will automatically begin to earn a profit. You will need to consider many other expenses before your business begins to earn enough to support itself. Many of these expenses, known as **operating expenses,** are ongoing and recurrent expenses involved in operating the business. Operating expenses can include rent for your business location, utilities, and salaries for your employees.

The final expense that you will have to consider in your financial planning is cost of goods sold. **Cost of goods sold** is the amount you pay to manufacture or acquire a single unit of the items you sell. If you sell a service, it is the amount you spend to provide service to one customer. For example, if you pay $5 to manufacture a product you sell for $7, the cost of goods sold is $5.

Using the Start-up Period Worksheet

The key to correctly estimating your start-up cost is your list of expenses. If you list everything you need to purchase and your monthly business expenses, but forget that you will have to make monthly payments for rent, your estimates will be too low. Use a separate sheet to list all of the items. Research to determine reasonable amounts for each item. Add the items and place the subtotals on the worksheet. Follow the instructions on the worksheet (Figure 4.2 on page 83) to calculate the total amount of your costs.

Start-up Costs

- **Cost of location**—This start-up expense is the amount you spend to purchase the location or pay a down payment for the land or the building where your business will operate. If you haven't investigated locations, call a Realtor for an estimate on the type of location you need.

- **Cost of equipment**—This start-up expense includes any equipment, such as manufacturing equipment and computers, your business needs. Investigate the possibility of purchasing used equipment to keep your expenses down. You can buy new equipment with all the bells and whistles later.

- **Delivery and installation**—Labor costs for delivery, set up, and installation of your equipment can be quite high.

- **Site preparation**—Preparing your site for business could include remodeling, repair, and decoration costs.

- **Deposits for utilities**—Most services require a deposit when you initiate service.

- **Fees for professional services**—This includes fees paid to attorneys, accountants, and other consultants before your business opens.

- **Business licenses and permits**—This includes any fees for setting up your business structure and local fees for opening your specific type of business.

- **Advertising**—Any advertising fees paid before your business opens are start-up costs.
- **Initial inventory**—Use your cost of goods sold and determine the quantities you want in stock to calculate the cost of your initial inventory.
- **Miscellaneous**—Include any start-up costs that don't fit in any other category. This can include items such as office supplies and travel expenses.
- **Other**—Include any start-up costs specific to your business.

Operating Expenses

- **Rent/mortgage**—If you did not purchase your location with cash, you probably pay rent or make a mortgage payment every month.
- **Repairs and maintenance**—Many businesses hire cleaning companies to maintain the store or office. Even if you don't pay someone else to clean your location, you will still need maintenance supplies such as lightbulbs. Repairs to your equipment or facility can be expensive. Set aside a budgeted amount every month for minor repairs to keep your business running smoothly.
- **Inventory**—Use the cost of goods sold to determine the cost of restocking the products you sell.
- **Supplies**—Office supplies include paper clips, envelopes, and paper. It can also include tape for the cash register, sales receipts, and food for the fish in the office aquarium.
- **Telephone**—Phone service is necessary for every business.
- **Utilities**—Electricity, water, and waste collection are necessary.
- **Advertising**—Any advertising after the business is open is an operating expense.
- **Insurance**—Your business property should be insured. Depending on the risks that are faced by your business, you may need additional coverage.
- **Salaries**—Employees expect to be paid regularly.
- **Benefits**—This includes health insurance for your employees and any additional perks such as dental insurance and maternity leave.
- **Taxes**—As a business, you pay taxes on the income the business earns.
- **Fees for professional services**—Depending on the needs of your business, you may pay a consultant to perform accounting services rather than hiring a full-time accountant or doing it yourself. Legal fees also fit into this category.
- **Shipping**—Some businesses may never ship anything. Others ship all of their products directly to customers.
- **Internet service**—Many businesses use the Internet to sell products or attract customers. Others use the Internet for research to keep up with industry trends or as a communication tool.
- **Miscellaneous**—Minor expenses that don't fit into any other category can be placed here. Minor expenses could include postage, photocopying, or a summer picnic for employees.
- **Other**—Include any operating expenses specific to your business situation.

Owners' Salary/Draw/Dividends

- **Salaries**—Include any salaries regularly paid to the business owners.
- **Draws**—Owners may have the right to withdraw cash from the business at specific times. This is usually defined in the partnership agreement or operating agreement.
- **Dividends**—Most companies do not pay dividends during the start-up period. They spend their profit on expanding the business rather than distributing it to owners or shareholders.

Loan Payments

- **Loans**—Identify any loans taken by your business and the amount of the payments.

FIGURE 4.2   Start-up Period Worksheet

Start-up Period Worksheet

Start-up Costs	Amount	Operating Expenses (continued)	Amount
Location	____	Insurance	____
Equipment	____	Salaries	____
Delivery and installation	____	Benefits	____
Site preparation	____	Taxes	____
Deposits for utilities	____	Fees for professional services	____
Fees for professional services	____	Shipping	____
Business licenses and permits	____	Internet service	____
Advertising	____	Miscellaneous	____
Initial inventory	____	Other:	
Miscellaneous	____	_____	____
Other:		_____	____
_____	____	_____	____
_____	____		
_____	____	**Owners' Salary/Draw/Dividends**	
		Salaries	____
Operating Expenses		Draws	____
Rent/mortgage	____	Dividends	____
Repairs and maintenance	____		
Inventory	____	**Loan Payments**	
Supplies	____	Loans:	
Telephone	____	_____	____
Utilities	____	_____	____
Advertising	____	_____	____

Hypothetical Scenario

Jim and his partners sat down to calculate the expenses for their new business, Real Food Express. Jim suggested they would need to print and post fliers around campus and purchase a computer and business software to track their business activities. Other partners added items to the list such as promotional items for the restaurant owners, a telephone line for the business, and professional advice from a lawyer about contracts with the restaurant owners.

Acquire Start-up Capital

When you were growing up, your parents probably told you that money didn't grow on trees. Although it's true that money doesn't grow on trees, it isn't impossible for a clever entrepreneur with a good business idea to acquire enough money to start a business. In fact, there are several sources of financing. After you know how much money you need, you will have to make some decisions about where you will acquire the funds. The most common sources of capital for new businesses include personal savings, friends and family, financial institutions, venture capital firms, and angel investors.

Personal Savings

The easiest place to look for money is your own pockets. Financing your business alone gives you complete control. If you need additional skills, you can hire employees or pay consultants for their expertise without giving up any of the ownership of your business.

If you have personal assets such as a home, jewelry, or investments, you may be able to sell these possessions or use them to obtain more money. Unfortunately, you may not be able to fund a business on your own, no matter how much change you find between the couch cushions or under the seats in your car. Even if you can't fund the business alone, investing your own funds does convince potential investors that you are committed to the success of the business. Also, if you form a business with other individuals, your voice in company decisions may be determined by the ownership percentage you were able to finance.

Friends and Family

Relatives and friends can be an excellent source of funds. However, it is important to treat any loan from your friends or family members in a professional manner. Don't accept any loans without a **promissory note,** a legal contract in which you promise to repay the debt. The promissory note should identify the amount of the loan, the interest rate, the payment terms, and the borrower's possessions that can be sold or claimed by the lender, if necessary, to repay the loan. Regardless of the lender's attitude, a promissory note will prevent any future disagreements over the terms of the loan. (Refer to the CD for an example of a promissory note.)

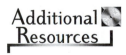
Additional Resources

Although you may be able to get a lower interest rate for the loan than a bank would give you, borrowing from family or friends can affect a relationship forever. You can be sure that Uncle Louis will ask about your business every time he sees you.

He may attempt to give "advice" that you don't need or want. Whether your business venture succeeds or fails, it will be a tale that is retold at every family gathering.

Financial Institutions

Banks and credit unions are the most popular source of business loans. When you apply for a business loan from a financial institution, you will have to convince the loan officer that your business has a good chance of succeeding. If you are not well prepared with plans, facts, and numbers, your loan request may be denied. The loan officer needs to know how much money you need, how you plan to use the money, and why your business will succeed.

The banker is looking for a borrower with experience and commitment. Experience managing a similar business is ideal. Experience successfully managing any business in any industry or participating in a business in the same industry is also valuable. Investing your personal funds in the business will go a long way toward convincing the loan officer of your commitment to making your business a success. (Refer to Chapter 13 for ideas about writing a loan proposal.)

Venture Capital

Another source of business financing is a venture capital firm. As the name suggests, a **venture capital firm** is a business that invests in small, emerging companies in exchange for partial ownership. Venture capitalists prefer companies that will show a high rate of return within five to seven years. However, you don't receive the investment without involvement from the venture capital firm. The firm will lend its expertise in management and strategic plans for the company.

Individuals can also provide venture capital to emerging companies. These individuals, known as **angel investors,** are often wealthy or experienced business-people who want to exchange their money for the opportunity to become involved in your business. Although venture capital firms and angel investors can offer you funds and expertise, you are giving up some control of your company by allowing them to actively participate in the management of your company.

Venture capitalists do not remain with your company forever. Typically, they withdraw three to five years after making the initial investment, after accruing a profit and placing your company on the road to success.

Outside the Box

There are methods of gathering funds for a new business that aren't as traditional as more familiar sources. For example, customers or potential customers may be so eager for your service or product that they will offer to prepay or pay a large deposit, enabling you to deliver the order and providing extra cash to finance additional business activities. There are also rumors of small enterprises financed through personal credit cards belonging to the business owners. There are high interest rates on many personal credit cards, so this is not a good long-term solution for business purchases. Personal credit cards can be a resource if the money can be repaid before the interest charges become too high.

Hypothetical Scenario

Jim and his partners reviewed the list of expenses. Although each single expense seemed small, together they added up to more capital than the group could easily raise. A quick vote determined that they didn't want to go into debt to establish Real Food Express. They decided to prioritize the items and make the deliveries themselves until the business was able to earn enough to hire delivery drivers.

Technology Insights

Printing

A century ago, if you wanted a high-quality printed document, you had to take a sample of the document to a professional printing business. The printer would create the real document by laboriously placing all of the letters in a tray, inking the tray, and pressing the paper to the letters to print the document. Today, most desktop printers have capabilities that would have made those early printing professionals green with envy.

Before you go to the store to select a printer for your business, you should consider how you want to use the printer. This will identify the characteristics you should prioritize and determine the price range of the printer you should buy.

♦ **Speed**—Identify the number of pages the printer can print in a single minute. This is important if you are constantly printing very long documents. For most small businesses, it isn't necessary to get the fastest printer available.

♦ **Quality**—Resolution, measured in dots per inch (dpi), is one way of evaluating the quality of a printed page. The more dots per inch, the more realistic an image will appear. This is more important if you print images for documents such as catalogs, coupons, or newsletters.

♦ **Paper tray**—Most printers today have paper trays that hold anywhere from several sheets of paper to a ream of paper. This is important only if you print long documents.

♦ **Color**—If you will always print only black-and-white documents, color isn't important. However, the lower end of color capability may cost only $100 more. If you have the option, you probably will occasionally use color.

Think Critically Visit a nearby computer store. Identify and price a printer that would meet the needs of your business.

CHAPTER REVIEW

There are four general structures you can follow for your business—sole proprietorship, partnership, corporation, and limited liability company. The sole proprietorship is the easiest to establish, maintain, and dissolve. The biggest disadvantage of establishing a sole proprietorship is unlimited personal liability for the owner. Partnerships can be established as general partnerships or limited partnerships. Limited partnerships protect the limited partners by limiting their liability for the company's actions. Every partnership must have at least one general partner to make business decisions and accept unlimited personal liability. A corporation is the most complex business structure. It exists as a legal entity, separate from its owners. Limiting their liability for the corporation's actions protects all shareholders. Public corporations sell shares of the company through a stock market. Limited liability companies offer the advantages of limited liability for the owners and the ability to choose between pass-through or corporate taxation.

The name you give your company becomes an important part of your company's image. Create a name that is unique, verify that the name is not already in use, and file the fictitious name statement to begin operating your business under its new name.

Many companies fail because the owners do not acquire sufficient funds to keep the business operating until it earns a profit. In your financial planning, you need to consider start-up costs, operating expenses, salaries for the owners, and loan payments if any money is borrowed.

You can acquire financing for your business from a variety of sources. Investing your personal resources may keep you out of debt and convince lenders of your commitment if you need to apply for loans. Family and friends may be able to loan you money but the debt could affect your relationship. Financial institutions are the most common lenders for entrepreneurs. Finally, venture capital firms and angel investors may be willing to loan your business money. In exchange, they expect to have input into your management decisions and strategic planning.

USE BUSINESS TERMS

Fill in the blanks with the appropriate term.

angel investor
arbitrator
articles of incorporation
binding arbitration
buy-sell agreement
bylaws
corporation
cost of goods sold
directors
dividend
doing business as (DBA)
general partner
general partnership
incorporator
limited liability company (LLC)
limited partner
limited partnership
limited personal liability

mediator
nonbinding arbitration
officer
operating agreement
operating expenses
partnership
partnership agreement
pass-through taxation
private corporation
promissory note
public corporation
registered agent
self-employment taxes
shareholder
sole proprietorship
start-up costs
venture capital firm

1. To form a corporation, you need to file ___?___ with your secretary of state.
2. A partnership will dissolve when a partner withdraws unless the partners have a(n) ___?___ .
3. ___?___ supervise the day-to-day administration and management tasks for a corporation.
4. The point of contact for a corporation is the ___?___ .
5. A(n) ___?___ is a portion of the corporation's profit that is paid to shareholders.
6. An operating agreement is used by a(n) ___?___ .
7. ___?___ are ongoing recurrent expenses involved in running a business.

TEST YOUR READING

8. Describe pass-through taxation.
9. What are the advantages and disadvantages of being a limited partner?
10. What topics should be covered by a partnership agreement?
11. Why would an entrepreneur choose to establish a business as a corporation?
12. Describe the hierarchy within a corporation.
13. What is the difference between a public corporation and a private corporation?
14. Why is the limited liability company business structure popular?
15. Describe the benefits of having an operating agreement.
16. How do you create a name for your business?

17.   How do you determine the start-up costs of opening a franchise?
18.   Describe the cost of goods sold.
19.   List the potential sources of start-up capital.

THINK CRITICALLY ABOUT BUSINESS

20.   Choose a legal structure for your business. Explain why the structure you selected is right for your business.
21.   Create a name for your business. Describe the image you want to create for your business. How will the name you select affect that image?
22.   Calculate the start-up costs for your business. Research to find accurate prices for the location and equipment you will need.
23.   Identify sources of start-up capital for your business. Write a sample promissory note.

REAL-LIFE BUSINESS

Kinko's

From a single room that measured 100 square feet in September 1970, Kinko's has become a private corporation that now has more than 1,100 branch offices throughout the world. Paul Orfalea borrowed the money to open the first Kinko's right after he graduated from college. In the single location, he had one copying machine and an offset press. The shop also offered film processing, stationery, and school supplies. The success of the first shop may have been helped by its location near the University of California at Santa Barbara.

Kinko's has grown steadily over the years, incorporating new technology into its business as it became available. By 1979, Kinko's had 80 branches in 28 states. Kinko's continued to grow. In 1983, it opened its first international branch in Canada. In 1985, a branch office in Chicago began staying open 24 hours a day. In 1987, Kinko's expanded its service by adding mailing and faxing capabilities in all of its stores. Again utilizing technological advances, Kinko's had more than 130 videoconferencing centers. In 2000, Kinko's, with kinkos.com, enabled customers to send electronic documents to be printed. The copies can then be picked up at any Kinko's location. Kinkos.com also enables customers to print, bind, and ship documents for next-day delivery throughout the country.

Think Critically

1.   How has Kinko's use of technology affected the company?
2.   Visit the company's web site at www.kinkos.com. Evaluate the products and selection available on the site.
3.   Analyze the growth of Kinko's. Why did the company choose these avenues of growth? What would you have done differently?
4.   How has the business structure of a private corporation affected the company?

CHAPTER 5

Write a Business Plan

GOALS

- ◆ Explain the purpose of a business plan
- ◆ Identify components of a business plan
- ◆ Outline your business plan
- ◆ Write your business plan

Carmen Aponte's husband, Vincent, is a veterinarian in a small town in Indiana. A few weeks ago, the retail space next to her husband's animal clinic became available. Carmen decided to jump in with both feet. She quickly signed a lease for the space before she took the time to perform any research or make any plans. When she met with an accountant, he agreed that her idea of opening a pet supply store next to her husband's clinic might work, but he recommended that she write a business plan to help her investigate the potential for her store.

The Business Plan

Traveling from New York City to Los Angeles without a map simply isn't wise. A map helps you select the shortest route, saving you time, resources, and irritation. A business plan is a map for your business, helping you take your business to the success that you want it to be without wasting time and resources caused by a lack of planning.

A **business plan** is a document that describes your company's purpose, objectives, and methods for achieving its objectives. Your business plan may be one of the most important documents you write. It should map out in detail the company's preferred future for the next three to five years. It isn't a one-time task. You will need to revisit your business plan periodically, updating it as the business and the business environment change. In fact, many businesses update their business plans annually, making them more valuable in providing ongoing guidance for the company. (Refer to the CD for an example of a business plan for a small business.)

Purpose of a Business Plan

The finished plan serves as a guide for your business decisions. It gives you a realistic idea of the steps involved in starting and operating your business. Before making any major decisions, you can evaluate the consequences of each choice against your business objectives, determine which choice will help you reach your goals, and proceed confidently.

Potential creditors use the finished plan to determine the risk involved in loaning money to your business. A business plan that is poorly thought out and shows little understanding of the process of establishing a business and making it a success will raise warning flags for any creditor. An entrepreneur's lack of resources or skills will be evident in the business plan.

In the process of writing your business plan, you may discover information that will put the potential success of your business in question. You could discover that there isn't a large demand for your product or that the competition is just too successful or too large to challenge. For example, you don't want to open a toy store just down the street from a large national toy store chain. You may discover that your idea works, but you should focus on a different type of customer. Writing the business plan can improve your business idea and help you avoid potentially fatal business decisions.

Although potential investors may use your business plan, obtaining a loan is not the primary purpose of the plan. As you write your plan, you will set goals for your business and determine how you will reach those goals. The plan helps you determine the resources you will need to start the business, the risks that your business will face, and the success level you can achieve.

Determine Resources A business plan helps you determine the resources that you have available and the resources that you need. Resources include tangible items such as money, equipment, supplies, and location. Resources also include intangible items such as skill and experience. In the business plan, you evaluate the resources you have and determine the resources that you need. After you know which items you need, you can make plans to acquire the resources that will help you attain your business goals and focus your available resources on a specific course of action.

Identify Risks Fires, earthquakes, and tornadoes aren't the only risks a business encounters. A business faces many different types of risk. There are risks associated with almost every aspect of operating a business. You could choose products that won't sell. Your competition could open a larger store in the same area. You may not have the knowledge you need of the industry you selected. Customers may not be located near your site. Employees who are trained and knowledgeable may be difficult to find. The cost of the supplies may be too high to make a profit from the price customers are willing to pay. All of these are risks that businesses face every day. An honest risk assessment contained in your business plan will take these types of risks into account to determine if your business can succeed. You should consider these risks when setting your business objectives and planning your success.

As you determine the risks that your business will encounter, you will be able to identify your company's strengths and weaknesses. You can turn these characteristics into advantages when you face the competition in your industry or geographic area.

Set Goals Unrealistic expectations will lead to discouragement and failure. Realistic goals may be less satisfying, but the success you achieve at each step will help you achieve the larger objectives later. The goals for your business might refer to the number of sales, the number of new customers, the number of loyal customers, income, or combinations of these values. In your initial business plan, you should set objectives that will be filled when your business begins to earn a profit. Later goals will identify how you want the business to grow, such as adding a web site or opening another location.

Hypothetical Scenario

After the discussion with her accountant, Carmen Aponte decided that she needed more information about writing a business plan. She realized that there is a lot of information she needs to learn about starting and operating a business in a retail environment and selling the products she plans to stock. She started her search for information on the Internet.

Components of a Business Plan

A thorough business plan has several parts. Each component of the document helps it fulfill its purpose of determining resources, identifying the risks, and setting reasonable goals for your business. A business plan written with potential investors or creditors in mind includes many details—particularly about the financial aspects of your business that may be described in the plan and included as supporting documents.

Writing a business plan requires time, effort, and many hours of research. This process discovers information to create strategies that will make your business thrive. As shown in Figure 5.1, a business plan consists of four major parts—the executive summary, information about your business, information about the company's finances, and supporting documents. Later, you will add an introduction to the front of the document. The introduction enables you to introduce yourself and your company, explain why you created a business plan, and inform readers of how your document is organized. The finished business plan should not be more than 30 to 50 pages in length.

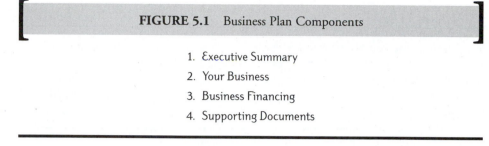

FIGURE 5.1   Business Plan Components

1. Executive Summary
2. Your Business
3. Business Financing
4. Supporting Documents

Executive Summary

The **executive summary** summarizes the information contained in the rest of the document. Reading only the executive summary should give the readers a good idea of the information in the rest of the document. The rest of your business plan should contain the details that support your statements and conclusions in the executive summary. The executive summary ranges from several paragraphs to a maximum of four pages.

Your Business

The second part of the business plan contains detailed information and analysis about your product, business structure, customers, competition, location, managers and leadership of your business, personnel, and organization. It describes the type of business you operate and the way in which you do business. This section requires the most time because you need to research your competition and the current business environment. Although you want your business to look like an attractive investment, you must write a realistic evaluation of its prospects. This section of the document will be several pages in length.

Business Financing

The third part of the business plan describes your business finances. The goal of this section is to convince potential investors and creditors that the company is a good financial risk and has the potential to earn money. Potential employees should feel that the company would be a stable employer with a good future.

This section needs to provide information about your **cash flow,** the movement of cash in and out of your business. As a new business, you will have to create a **cash flow projection,** a forecast of the funds you expect to receive and pay out during a specific time period. A cash flow projection tells you how much cash your business needs and the source of the cash. This section of the document will be several pages in length.

Supporting Documents

The final part of your business plan contains any separate documents that support the information and conclusions in your plan. Include résumés of the business owners, credit information, legal documents related to the business, and marketing statistics for the geographic area. This section of the document could be several pages in length.

Hypothetical Scenario

As Carmen discovered new information about retail activities and the pet industry, she began to keep track of good resources. She saved the addresses of web sites, read magazines that advertised or reviewed pet products, visited local stores that sold any pet products, volunteered at an animal shelter, and observed obedience training classes at a local club, carefully noting the products recommended and used by the trainers.

Outline Your Business Plan

Identifying the objectives and audience for your business plan before you begin to outline the document helps you determine the level of detail that you need to include in each topic and the information that should be emphasized or played down. An **outline** is a listing of the primary parts of a document. A good outline makes it easy to identify the topic of each section. Your outline defines the structure and content of your business plan. It's similar to a detailed table of contents. Your outline doesn't need to include every detail that will be in your final business plan. Only the headings, a few comments under each heading, and the source of the information are needed. Use complete sentences or brief phrases to identify the information in each section. However, the more information you include in your outline, the easier the task of writing the plan will become. Use the following guidelines to write your outline.

- **List the headings and subheadings of your business plan.** Headings and subheadings identify the importance of each piece of information. Headings are more important than subheadings. Details fit under the subheadings. This provides the structure of your business plan.

- **Place main headings at your left margin.** Subheadings will be indented so that headings at the same level will be easy to locate.

- **Use at least two subheadings at each level.** If the information can't be divided into two subheadings, you do not need this heading level. Simply place your information in paragraphs under the heading that is one level higher.

- **The information under each heading should fit into the topic identified by the heading.** If the information does not support the heading, your business plan will not be well organized, regardless of the properly organized headings. Putting information under the wrong heading makes it difficult for the reader to understand your business plan or find the information they need. It's like putting your socks in the drawer with your T-shirts instead of putting them in the sock drawer where they belong.

- **Identify any sources in the outline.** This will help you locate the information again when you actually write your business plan.

- **Be accurate.** Remember that your readers may be familiar with your industry, type of business, or product. Any mistakes or inaccuracies in your document will probably be caught by at least one reader—probably the one you wanted to impress the most.

◆ **Review your outline.** Verify that all the information you want in your business plan is in your outline and has been properly placed under the correct heading. Move any items if necessary.

Note: Many of the topics included in a business plan will be covered more thoroughly in future chapters of this book. It is a good idea to prepare the outline of your business plan now and return to the plan after completing each chapter. Write the final draft of your business plan when you complete the entire book. This will give you a more complete understanding of your business, methods of operating a business, and the strategies that you can implement to make your business more successful.

As you prepare your outline, refer to the following checklist in Figure 5.2. Place a check before each item as you include it in your outline. Every item may not belong in your business plan, but think carefully before you eliminate any item in the list.

FIGURE 5.2 Checklist for Business Plan

❒ Mission statement
❒ Legal business structure
❒ Business history or milestones
❒ Strategic objectives
❒ Tactical objectives
❒ Business location
❒ Business hours
❒ Product description
❒ Benefit to customer
❒ Unique characteristic of business
❒ Product packaging
❒ Product sales method
❒ Product delivery method
❒ Additional product services
❒ Product quality
❒ Product price range
❒ Average price in the industry
❒ Price discounts
❒ Product warranty
❒ Geographic location
❒ Use of business space
❒ Market trends
❒ Customer characteristics
❒ Market size
❒ Market surveys
❒ Competitors

❒ Competitors' products
❒ Competitors' annual sales
❒ Competitors' share of market
❒ Competitors' sales methods
❒ Competitors' services
❒ Competitors' delivery methods
❒ Competitors' strengths
❒ Competitors' weaknesses
❒ Competitors' pricing strategies
❒ Marketing strategy
❒ Marketing media
❒ Key personnel description
❒ Organizational chart
❒ Job descriptions
❒ Support services description
❒ Manufacturing process
❒ Lead time
❒ Product costs
❒ Make or buy strategy
❒ Development budget
❒ Employees—hiring
❒ Employees—training
❒ Funds invested by owner
❒ Funds needed by business
❒ Future financial plans
❒ Date business earns profit

❒ Start-up costs
❒ Operating expenses
❒ Cost of goods sold
❒ Cash flow statement
❒ Income statement
❒ Balance sheet
❒ Financial projections
❒ Legal documents
❒ Patents
❒ Licenses or permits
❒ Contracts
❒ Market research studies
❒ Letters of intent from customers
❒ Real estate or equipment lease agreements
❒ Product sample or photograph of the product
❒ Credit history for the owners or business
❒ Résumés for key personnel
❒ Résumés for companies providing professional services
❒ Employee handbook
❒ Customer policies

Executive Summary

Although the executive summary is the first major part of your business plan, it is the last part you will write. After you have outlined the entire business plan, return to this section. Include the highlights of all the sections in the document outline in your executive summary. When you write the executive summary, choose the information you want to include that will be the most meaningful for your audience.

Your Business

This section is the heart of your business plan. Research these topics through several sources, analyze the information, and predict its effect on your business. By the time you have completed this section of your business plan, you will have an excellent understanding of your business, its potential, and the steps that will help it reach its full potential.

Business Activities As the owner, you should be knowledgeable about your business. Most of the information in this section should not require a lot of research. Describe your company and its characteristics. Explain its purpose and its legal organization. Describe your product or service and the location you have selected for the business. Together, this information should present an accurate picture of the business you plan to start.

◆ **Include the mission statement for your business.** A **mission statement** is a brief description of your company's purpose. It should set expectations for your customers and employees. A mission statement, as shown in Figure 5.3, is brief, limited to only one or two sentences. However, it should contain several pieces of information, including: (1) the product or service your company provides, (2) a description of the company's customers, (3) the geographic area you service, (4) your company's unique business idea, (5) your methods of doing business, and (6) your vision for the future of the company.

FIGURE 5.3   Sample Mission Statement for Harrison Cookie Bouquets

To provide fresh, creative bakery arrangements with thoughtful, pleasant, high-quality service for our local customers and same-day delivery for local hospitals and long-term health care facilities.

◆ **Describe the legal business structure.** Identify the business structure of your company as a sole proprietorship, partnership, corporation, or limited liability company.

◆ **Describe the type of business you will operate.** Classify the business as a retail, manufacturing, or service business.

◆ **Identify the product or service you will sell.** This should be only a brief description. There will be more details about your product in the next section.

- **Describe the history or background of your company.** If this is a new business, describe how the product or concept was developed and when your business was established. If this is a new franchise, describe the history of the franchiser. If you bought an existing business from someone else, describe the history of the business. When you update this section in the future, you will have more history to talk about. When you have been in business for several years, you should include only milestones, the significant events in the development of your company.

- **Explain why your business will be profitable.** Profitability is the result of having the right product at the right time in the right place for the right people at the right price. With this in mind, explain why you think your business meets these criteria.

- **Set strategic and tactical objectives for your business and describe how your business will meet those objectives.** Each objective should include a value that can be measured, the method used to measure the results, and a reasonable time period in which the objective should be achieved. A **strategic objective** is a goal that a business plans to achieve in three to five years. The time period of three to five years makes a strategic objective a long-term goal. Strategic objectives can be grouped into key business areas that all companies hope to improve. These areas include increasing revenue, improving efficiency, performing better than the competition, using technology to improve business operations, improving customer relations, and enhancing the product or service the business sells. To achieve strategic objectives, you will usually have to accomplish several smaller tasks as well. These short-term goals that are necessary to reach a strategic objective are known as **tactical objectives.** Tactical objectives should also include a value that can be measured, the method used to measure the results, and a reasonable time period in which the objective should be achieved. For example, tactical objectives might include purchasing a specific software package and a computer to reach the strategic objective of reducing expenses by 10 percent by preventing errors in ordering inventory and customer shipments.

- **Identify your business location and hours.** This needs only a brief description. There will be more details about your location later in the document. The hours that your business is open will attract or deter potential customers. A grocery store that is open only from 10 A.M. to noon would not attract many customers.

Your Product Describe the product that you sell. Explain how your product benefits your customers. The benefit the customers receive is the reason they buy your product. Understanding their motivation will help you sell more of the same product and develop additional products and services to sell.

Describe the characteristics of your product that make it different from any product offered by the competition. Characteristics could include the product's functionality, appearance, packaging, sales method, delivery method, quality, price, and warranty.

The way that your product is packaged, sold, and delivered can attract or deter customers. For example, you might buy a book from a web site so you don't have to go to a store. Rather than picking the book up at the store, it can be shipped to your address or delivered directly to your friend's house in time for her birthday. Additional services such as gift wrapping and delivery can create a positive image of the company and the product.

The quality and price range of your product will attract a specific type of customer. The price of a product usually reflects the quality of its components and the manufacturing process used to make the item. A customer can't buy high-quality diamond earrings for a few dollars. On the other hand, customers won't be willing to pay a high price for a low-quality product.

If you offer a warranty for your products or services, you have to decide what you will cover with the warranty. A **warranty** is a guarantee of the integrity of a product that usually ensures the buyer that the business will take responsibility for repair or replacement of defective parts or the entire product. More expensive items usually offer a better warranty than cheaper products. Warranties are primarily offered by the manufacturer. However, it is becoming more common for retailers and service providers to offer warranties as well. Retailers will often offer an **extended warranty,** a warranty that lasts longer than the warranty offered by the product's manufacturer. Customers pay a fee for the extended warranty.

Your Location Any Realtor can tell you how important the right location can be for your business and how catastrophic the wrong location can be. Explain how your location and any special characteristics of your location will help your business. For example, if your restaurant is the only Italian restaurant within a 45-minute drive in a well-populated middle-class area, your location will attract customers. However, if your restaurant has no nearby competition because you are located in the middle of the desert and no one lives within the 45-minute drive area, your location is a disaster for your business.

Describe how you will use your business space. If it is a retail business, describe how much space will be used to display products. If it is a restaurant, identify the number of customers you can serve at one time. The space outside your building can be just as important. Adequate parking encourages more customers to visit. Easy access from busy streets will also encourage shoppers to visit your location.

If you plan to operate your business from your home, explain how this benefits your business. Benefits could include lower costs and flexible work hours. If there are obvious disadvantages, such as space or equipment needs, explain how you will overcome them.

Product Market Research will enable you to document the demand for your product. Analysis of the information you gather can produce exciting strategies for attracting more customers and increasing your sales. The information you provide should give only a broad picture of your customers and the market for your products.

You can find information about your market and potential customers from a variety of sources. Trade associations, industry journals, and magazine articles can provide important details that will demonstrate that you are well informed and knowledgeable about your industry and its market. You may want to cite your sources. Include a copy of any articles or other sources in the supporting documents section at the end of your business plan if it is appropriate.

There is a wide diversity in the people who live and work in the area around your business. Not all of them are potential customers. You will have to identify characteristics that are common to the individuals who are most likely to purchase your product. For example, young couples commonly purchase baby strollers for their first child. Some clothing brands target consumers of a specific age range, gender, and income level.

Research will help you know the size of the market, or the quantity of products that could be sold. To identify your share of the market, you can divide the number that you plan to sell by the total number that will be sold. Describe how you will increase the quantity that your business sells, increasing your share of the market. Predict changes in your industry and how your product or service is prepared for these changes.

Market analysis is obviously more complicated than the information you will include in your business plan, but you need to provide enough information here to give the big picture. If you conducted surveys or performed other actions to collect information about your market, you can include details in the supporting documents section at the end of your business plan.

Competition Businesses that sell similar products compete for sales. Never say that you don't have competition. Even if your product is innovative, consumers always have alternatives. Consider what consumers did before your product became available. For example, the first automobiles were innovative, but they competed with horses. Knowing who your competitors are and how they do business is critical. Use the information you gather about your competitors to evaluate or predict the performance of your business. As a new business owner, you should collect enough information about other companies to predict why and how your business will be profitable, regardless of your competitors.

Identify five businesses that are your most successful competitors. Write a paragraph about each competitor. If possible, provide information about their annual sales. Describe each business and the marketing methods they use. Compare their methods to yours. Explain how their products and services are different from your products and services. Identify the strengths and weaknesses of your competitors.

Pricing is one of the major areas in which businesses compete. Examine the pricing strategies of your competition. Explain how your prices compare to your competitors' prices and the average price of similar products in the same industry. Include any discounts that you plan to offer regularly such as bulk discounts or discounts for prompt payment. Describe how your pricing strategy will help your business succeed.

At the end of this section, you may want to place the information about your competitors in a table. Place the information for your business in the first or last column. As you see in Table 5.1, this provides a clear and simple method of presenting the information and comparing your business to the competition.

TABLE 5.1	Competition					
	Little Bells	Big Bells	Just Bells	Little Whistles	Big Whistles	All the Bells and Whistles
Annual Sales						
Share of Market						
Marketing Methods						
Products						
Services						
Pricing						

Advertising and Public Relations To attract customers, you need to let them know that you exist and why they should buy your product or service. This section does not need to include too many details. In fact, it shouldn't be more than a few paragraphs in length. If you have samples of items such as brochures or magazine advertisements, you can include them in the supporting documents section at the end of the business plan.

If you operate a franchise, you probably don't need to worry about advertising. The franchiser usually controls any advertising for all the franchises. Depending on the type of advertising the franchiser uses, you may have the option of inserting your business location into the advertising to promote your franchise.

If you operate an independent business, you will have to create a marketing strategy. After you choose your target market, you can select a method of communicating with these potential customers. Radio and television advertisements can easily target consumers who are in a similar age range and geographic area. Other methods of communication may include billboards, newspapers, direct mail, and the Internet. New methods of reaching your customers are constantly developing.

Key Personnel For any business, leadership is important. For a new business, leadership is critical. Good leaders with experience can create success from the right components. Poor leaders may not be able to build a successful company, regardless of how good the business concept may be. You must present each member of your management team as a successful professional.

There are critical areas in every business, including marketing and sales, financial management, product development, and administration. Although you don't need a separate individual to manage each area, a member of your management team should be assigned responsibility for each area. In a sole proprietorship, of course, the proprietor is responsible for all areas.

Write a brief description of each of your key personnel. Identify their areas of responsibility and emphasize their most relevant and most recent experience. Explain how these skills can be applied to your business.

If a critical business area is not covered, explain how you will fill the need. This could be a description of a manager you will hire or a consultant with the necessary experience. For example, you could hire a freelance accountant to maintain financial records and make financial recommendations, leaving you with the responsibility of making or approving any financial decisions.

Organizational Structure   An **organizational chart,** shown in Figure 5.4, is a graphic representation of the hierarchy of the company's managers and employees. The chart usually shows each individual's name and job title. The lines between the individuals or departments indicate the relationships between the two connected parties. Managers are placed above the individuals or groups that report to them.

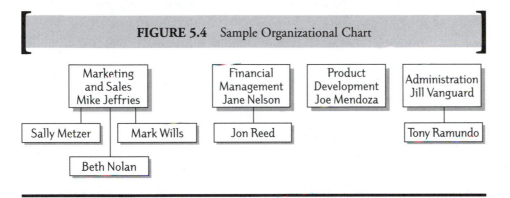

FIGURE 5.4   Sample Organizational Chart

Write a brief description of each of the main positions in the company. Base the description on the function the employee performs and the requirements for the job. For example, a technical consulting firm may need to hire programmers with specific skills.

Provide a brief description of the support services you have engaged. Support services include legal services, accounting services, and advertising agencies. In the description, identify the strengths of the service providers that will help your business succeed.

Operations   The day-to-day tasks of running your business are the components of your business operations. For a manufacturer, this includes the steps in the manufacturing process. For a retailer, this includes acquiring the products to sell and interactions with customers.

For a new business that isn't operating yet, this section will describe how you are developing your product or service. If you have already started developing your product, you should describe the steps in the development process and your current progress. Identify the remaining steps you need to complete. Investors reading your plan will look at your progress and the thoroughness of your planning. Include steps such as obtaining patents and acquiring a location.

Describe the production process for making your product or providing your service. If the product or service requires **lead time,** the amount of time between ordering and receiving the item, identify the normal amount of lead time and explain why it is needed. Explain the costs involved. For example, to operate a restaurant, you need to purchase ingredients, pay the chef, and pay a serving staff. You should justify your decision to manufacture your own components rather than purchasing them from a supplier. If you decide to purchase components, you should justify this reasoning as well. This is known as your **make or buy strategy.** Your decision might be based on convenience, lack of equipment, or product quality. Basically though, it always comes down to money. Defend your make or buy strategy by explaining its effect on your business income.

Present your development budget. Include any expenses, such as salaries, manufacturing materials, and professional fees involved in developing, prototyping, and manufacturing your product. If your business provides a service rather than a physical item, include the cost of hiring and training your employees as well as the cost of materials they will need to provide the service.

Identify the number of employees you will need and how you will recruit them. Evaluate the local labor pool for the skills and expertise you need to employ. If they do not have the needed skills, describe how you will train them. Estimate the cost of hiring and training your personnel.

Financial Overview Information about the finances for your company is important to any audience, but potential investors will be particularly interested in the data. For a start up business, investors will want to know several things.

- **The amount of money invested by the owners indicates their commitment to the business and the financial risk assumed by the owner and the business.** Describe how these funds have been used.
- **The amount of money still needed by the business identifies the financial risk the business may have to assume in debt if other alternatives aren't available.** Describe how these funds will be used and when they will be needed.
- **Describe any plans that will affect your company's financial future.** This could include plans to sell shares in the stock market, sell the business to a new owner, or purchase another company.
- **Identify the date when you expect the business to earn a profit.** Use your expenses and expected business income to calculate this date.
- **Identify the funds required during the start-up period.** Explain any start-up costs the business will incur.
- **Identify the operating expenses your business incurs regularly.** List and explain the operating expenses.
- **Include the cost of goods sold.** This information helps readers evaluate your sales levels.

Business Financing

Three financial statements should be included in any business plan. Together, these three documents—a cash flow statement, an income statement, and a balance sheet—provide an accurate picture of the health of your business. An established business may include three to five years of these financial statements. Newer businesses should include data for the time period they have been operating. It is a good idea to ask an accountant to prepare the financial statements. If you use your business plan to attract investors, an experienced accountant may be able to recommend actions your business can take to make it a more attractive investment.

Cash Flow Statement A cash flow statement is used to analyze your cash inflows and outflows. It identifies the source of any cash entering your business, such as sales, loans, or investments. It also identifies the reason for any cash leaving your business, such as loan payments, equipment purchases, and salaries.

Income Statement An income statement may be referred to as a profit/loss statement. It shows your profit or loss for a specific time period. This information is used to evaluate your company's performance.

Balance Sheet A balance sheet is a snapshot of the current value of your business. It details everything your business owns, known as assets, and everything your business owes, known as liabilities. Assets include equipment, cash, and inventory. Liabilities include amounts owed to suppliers, amounts owed on loans, and mortgages.

Financial Projections In this section of the business plan, you create projected financial statements for the next three to five years. Investors will study your projections carefully. Most investors expect projections to be overly optimistic. To avoid this, you can prepare three scenarios for your projections. Worst case, expected, and best-case scenarios will create realistic expectations for you and any potential investors.

For existing businesses, realistic expectations should be based on past performance. For example, if your income has increased 10 percent every year for the last three years, you shouldn't project a 30 percent increase next year without some major business event that impacts your expectations.

Supporting Documents

As you write your business plan, make a list of the documents you use to analyze information and write the text. Attach these documents in the main part of the business plan if they are used to support your conclusions. Several documents may be attached. Consider attaching the following documents:

- Legal documents created when the company was established such as articles of incorporation, a partnership agreement, or a buy-sell agreement
- Patents
- Licenses or permits
- Contracts
- Market research studies
- Letters of intent from customers

- Real estate or equipment lease agreements
- Product sample or photograph of the product if it applies to your product
- Credit history for the owners or business
- Résumés for the key personnel
- Résumés for companies providing professional services
- Employee handbook
- Customer policies

Outline Template

Placing the right information in the right location makes it easier for a reader to understand and evaluate your business plan. The outline template in Figure 5.5 will help you create the outline for your business plan.

FIGURE 5.5   Business Plan Outline Template

I. **Executive Summary**
II. **Your Business**
   A. Business Activities
      1. Mission statement
      2. Legal business structure
      3. Product or service
      4. History
      5. Objectives
      6. Location
   B. Your Product
      1. Description
      2. Warranty
   C. Your Location
      1. Geographical location
      2. Use of business space
   D. Product Market
      1. Demand
      2. Customers
   E. Competition
      1. Competitors
      2. Pricing

II. **Your Business** (continued)
   F. Advertising and Public Relations
      1. Advertising
      2. Marketing strategy
   G. Key Personnel
   H. Organizational Structure
      1. Employees
      2. Support services
   I. Operations
      1. Current status
      2. Production process
   J. Financial Overview
      1. Funds used
      2. Funds needed
III. **Business Financing**
   A. Cash Flow Statement
   B. Income Statement
   C. Balance Sheet
   D. Financial Projections
IV. **Supporting Documents**

Hypothetical Scenario

Carmen spent several weeks researching her business plan. By the time she finished the outline, she was confident that her business would succeed. She discovered that location is one of her biggest advantages. The nearest store that carries a full line of pet products is a 40-minute drive from her location. Also, the proximity of her husband's animal clinic means that potential customers will be passing her store every day. Her husband agreed to send a letter to his clients announcing the store opening. To encourage customers to take advantage of her location, Carmen plans to give a 10 percent discount to new customers who bring a copy of the letter into the store.

Write Your Business Plan

Your business plan is a document that represents your business. Therefore, you want to put your best foot forward. The design, content, and presentation of your business plan should reflect the professional image that you want to project. Use the following guidelines when you prepare your business plan.

- **Use a desktop printer or type your document on high-quality 8.5" × 11" paper.** Your business plan should look as professional as your personal résumé. Do not use colored paper.

- **Use an attractive professional format.** Use headings and subheadings so the organization of your document is obvious. Don't use more than two or three different fonts in the entire document, usually one font for the headings and a different font for the text. Too many fonts will make your document look like a ransom note. If you want to use color, confine it to graphs or charts. Color in the text of the document tends to emphasize the "look" of the document rather than the content.

- **Bind the document.** Don't staple or tie the pages together. Use a report binder with a cover. Use the appropriate-size binder for the length of your document.

- **Check your spelling and grammar.** An error in spelling or grammar does not present a good image of your business. A simple spelling mistake can make your document look careless and sloppy, no matter how much time you spent researching and writing the business plan.

- **Use language that is professional.** Don't use slang terms. If a term is unique to your product or industry, define it when you use it the first time. Don't leave the reader wondering what you are talking about.

- **Write in a style that is clear and easy to understand.** If readers cannot understand what you are trying to accomplish with your business, you will not gain their support. Don't be "chatty." This isn't a letter to your best friend. It is a business document that will be read by business professionals. Avoid excess words. Be brief.

- **Organize your document logically.** Create a table of contents that identifies the location of each major heading.

- **Prioritize the information in each section.** Place the most important information in each section at the beginning of the section. Readers that only scan through your document should be able to locate your key points. Don't make your readers search for information by burying an important point in the last paragraph of a section.

- **Ask someone to review your business plan.** Ideally, you will be able to ask someone who is experienced in preparing business plans to review your document. Your reviewer should be able to point out items that are missing or incomplete as well as errors in presentation, spelling, and grammar. A content review performed by a reviewer who is familiar with your industry or product will also be valuable. This reviewer may suggest items that you did not consider or identify errors in your analysis and conclusions.

You did most of the necessary research when you developed your outline. Now it's time to fill in the gaps with text that flows smoothly.

Step 1—Write About Your Business

Although the information about your business is not the first section in your business plan, it is the first section you write. Follow the outline you prepared. As you fill in the details about your business, make a list of supporting documents that you want to include in the supporting documents section at the end of your business plan. Verify your information by checking the sources you listed as you prepared your outline. You don't want to introduce errors into your document because you remembered something incorrectly and were too lazy to check the facts.

Step 2—Write About Your Business Financing

Prepare the financial statements for your business. Make reasonable projections or create scenarios for the best, average, and worst possibilities. Scenarios are most likely to impress your audience. Knowledgeable readers will recognize inflated projections.

Step 3—Gather Your Supporting Documents

Refer to the list of supporting documents you created as you wrote about your business. Arrange them in the same order as the references are encountered in the business plan. Don't use any low-quality photocopies.

Step 4—Write the Executive Summary

Write the executive summary last, just before you create the table of contents. This enables you to summarize your plan and highlight your most important data. Summarize the main points that appear under each heading. If your executive summary is properly written, many readers will be able to get the information they need from the executive summary without reading the main section of your business plan. The executive summary should not be more than four pages long. Include the following information:

- **Summarize your business concept.** Include a description of the unique characteristic of your business that makes it different from the competition.
- **Identify the legal structure of the company.** Include a brief description of the key personnel.
- **Describe the current status of your business.** If it is a start-up business, describe significant steps you have accomplished in the start-up process. If the business is already operational, describe significant milestones in its history.
- **Describe the source and use of your business funding.** If it is a start-up business, identify the source of any current funding and how it has been spent.
- **Request additional funding if necessary.** If this business plan was prepared to attract investors or request loans, identify the amount of money the business needs and the way that it will be spent. Describe how these funds will help the business succeed.
- **Provide a financial overview.** Summarize your current financial status and your projected financial performance for the next three to five years.

Step 5—Prepare the Introduction

The purpose of the introduction is to identify yourself and your business, explain why the business plan was written, and identify the location of specific information in the plan. The introduction includes a cover sheet, the purpose statement, and the table of contents.

Cover Sheet Several pieces of information belong on the cover sheet. Contact information for you and your business will enable readers to reach you. This is particularly important if the audience is comprised of potential investors. Under the heading "Business Plan," include the following information on your cover sheet:

◆ Your name

◆ Business name

◆ Address

◆ Telephone and fax number

◆ E-mail address

◆ Web site address

◆ Company logo

◆ Date the plan was prepared

◆ Copyright information

◆ Number the pages: "Page 1 of ___"

◆ Number all copies, and label them "Copy 1 of ___"

◆ Prominently display a confidentiality agreement on the front of the plan. Keep copies of signed and dated confidentiality agreements in company records.

Purpose Statement Identify the reason you prepared the business plan. You may want to attract investors, inform shareholders, or educate employees. For new businesses, the business plan sets goals and establishes a path to success, providing a measurement standard for evaluating achievements and guidance for making critical decisions.

Table of Contents Readers may be seeking a single piece of information. Help them find the information by including a table of contents that is thorough and accurate. Be sure to include all your headings and subheadings in the table of contents. Create the table of contents last so that all page numbers are accurate.

Hypothetical Scenario

After reviewing the financial data and projections produced by her accountant, Carmen has to decide how to gather additional funds to help her establish the business. She has already decided that she does not want to add a partner, but she believes that she can attract one or two investors who would be able to lend her the funds she needs. Carmen plans to make several copies of her recently completed business plan for submitting requests for funding to local banks and lending institutions.

Technology Insights

Business Plan Software

There are several commercial software packages that can help you prepare your business plan. Many provide templates and sample documents. If you decide to purchase a software program to help you write your business plan, make a chart, such as the one below, comparing the various programs. This will help you evaluate the programs and choose the one that will work best for your business. However, it is important to remember that you will still need to perform the research. A standard business plan package cannot analyze your specific situation. Only you know the details that affect your product, your location, your skills, and your potential for success.

	Package 1	Package 2	Package 3	Package 4	Package 5
Word processing tool					
Chart tool					
Outline tool					
Sample plans					
Publish plan to web site					
Format options					
Help tool					
Collaboration tool					
Export plan to standard word processor					
Price					

Think Critically Make a list of the business planning software available. Evaluate each package using the criteria in the table above.

CHAPTER REVIEW

Your business plan is one of the most important business documents you will write. It will guide your business for the next three to five years, providing direction that will affect your decisions. The business plan helps you determine the resources you will need to start the business, the risks that your business will face, and the goals you can achieve. Resources include tangible and intangible items such as cash, equipment, and skill. Risks come in a variety of forms. Competition, changes in product demand, and economic downturns are only a few of the risks faced by businesses every day. A business that uses its resources well and faces risks successfully will achieve its goals and increase its chances of becoming successful.

There are four main components of a business plan. The executive summary contains the highlights from the rest of the document and provides analysis and conclusions about the business. The second section describes your business, your product, and your plans for the future. The third section provides information about your business finances by including financial statements and financial projections. The last section contains documents that support the information in the business plan, including contracts, customer letters of intent, and market surveys.

You do most of the work in writing a business plan when you write the outline. You perform any necessary research, set the goals for your business, and make decisions about the business opportunities you will pursue. Based on the details you discover as you write the outline, you will be able to project your potential for success. If the projections don't look good, you may decide that the business has no chance of succeeding and choose to pursue other activities.

Finally, you write the business plan. The more effort and details you put into the outline, the easier it will be to write the business plan. You assemble the main headings and subheadings with the details you researched to produce a business plan that will impress investors and employees while providing practical guidance for your business decisions.

USE BUSINESS TERMS

Fill in the blanks with the appropriate term.

business plan	mission statement
cash flow	organizational chart
cash flow projection	outline
executive summary	strategic objective
extended warranty	tactical objective
lead time	warranty
make or buy strategy	

1. You can create a(n) ___?___ to forecast the funds you expect to receive and pay out during a specific time period.
2. Prepare a(n) ___?___ to define the structure and content of your business plan.
3. A(n) ___?___ will set expectations for your customers and employees.
4. ___?___ must be achieved to accomplish your strategic objectives.
5. The company's ___?___ indicates the relationship between individuals or departments.
6. When customers order some specialty items, the ___?___ may be longer than required for standard items.
7. Many manufacturers provide a(n) ___?___ that guarantees the integrity of a product.

TEST YOUR READING

8. What time period should be covered in a business plan?
9. How do potential creditors use a business plan?
10. How does a business plan benefit a business owner?
11. Identify the main components of a business plan.
12. How does a business owner use a cash flow projection?
13. Make a flowchart that shows the sequence to follow when you write your business plan.
14. Explain the relationship between a strategic objective and a tactical objective.
15. Why is your make or buy strategy important?
16. Why is it important to gather information about your competitors?
17. Who controls advertising for franchise owners?
18. Describe the physical appearance of a good business plan.
19. Identify the information that should be on your cover sheet.

THINK CRITICALLY ABOUT BUSINESS

20. Identify the resources you will use to write a business plan for your business.
21. Begin to prepare your business plan. Identify at least five resources where you can find information for items in your business plan.
22. Write the mission statement for your business. Explain the statement.

23.   Identify the key personnel in your business. Explain what these individuals offer your business.

REAL-LIFE BUSINESS

Skyline Chili, Inc.

Although it is often known as Cincinnati-style chili, the recipe for this unique product is actually a family secret passed down through generations in Kastoria, Greece. Nicholas Lambrinides came to America to fulfill his dream of opening a family restaurant based on his family's secret recipe. In 1949, Lambrinides opened his first restaurant at a location with a view of the Cincinnati, Ohio, skyline.

More than 75 percent of Skyline's sales are based on their unique foundation products—3-way, 4-way, and 5-way chili dishes and cheese coneys. The 3-way consists of spaghetti topped with the secret-recipe chili and cheese. Options include diced onions or beans. Cheese coneys are special hot dogs with chili. Every day, the chili is made in a single location in Cincinnati and shipped to the restaurants and franchises. This ensures that the quality and flavor of the product are consistent. The atmosphere at Skyline Chili is also different from most restaurants. The food is prepared at an open steam table, visible from every booth and table in the restaurant. These two features—unique product and unique delivery—have made Skyline Chili a successful business.

Growth was not always easy. Skyline made some wrong moves in its early expansion attempts. In the 1970s and 1980s, Skyline opened single restaurant units in locations such as Atlanta, Pittsburgh, and Washington, D.C. Without the support of surrounding Skyline restaurants and a market familiar with the product, the single units usually struggled and failed. Based on these results, Skyline Chili now plans to expand outward from its Cincinnati headquarters. There are currently more than 100 locations, two-thirds of which are franchises, operating in Ohio, Indiana, Kentucky, and Florida. Individual franchisees in this geographic area know what to expect in sales and volume. In 1999, average unit volume was $875,000 while the average check was $6.50.

Nicholas and his four sons maintained the secrecy of the family recipe over the years, even though they opened many restaurants. Today, the chili is also sold at grocery stores in canned and frozen forms. Although Skyline Chili is no longer owned by the Lambrinides family, the chili recipe is still a secret, stored in a safe, and the chili is still made only in the commissary in Cincinnati.

Think Critically

1.   What is unique about Skyline Chili's product and delivery?
2.   What are the unique characteristics of Skyline Chili's business that have led to its success?
3.   Why did early expansion attempts fail?
4.   How has a business plan affected Skyline Chili's business decisions? Explain your answer.

CHAPTER 6

Select and Acquire a Location

GOALS

- ◆ Explain the importance of location in achieving success
- ◆ Compare the types of business sites
- ◆ Determine your facility needs
- ◆ Select a business site
- ◆ Acquire a business site

Several years ago, Michael Windfeather discovered a hobby that took advantage of his artistic and mechanical skills. For the last three years, he has been designing and making jewelry with a Native American flair. He has sold enough pieces that Windfeather Designs has become a recognized name with several local jewelers. Recently, a major jeweler offered him a contract for a number of new designs and the delivery of the unique jewelry items. Although Michael will create the designs, he will hire others to follow the designs to make the jewelry. Michael needs to find a location where he and his employees can work.

Importance of Location

The site you select for your business can determine its success or failure. A restaurant that is an hour's drive from any residences will have a hard time attracting customers. A restaurant located near a busy shopping mall, on the other hand, may be full to capacity during the mall's shopping hours.

As a business owner, you have several requirements for your ideal location. These requirements include employees, customers, amount of available space, and access for suppliers and customers. The type of business you plan to establish will determine your location requirements. For example, retail establishments require access for customers. Manufacturing establishments do not require customer access but may need shipping facilities to receive large quantities of supplies and ship the finished materials to retailers or customers. Other businesses require a large number of employees with specific skills who must be drawn from the local workforce.

The location of your business is not only important to its success, it's also a major decision that is difficult to change if you choose badly. One of the major expenses in establishing and operating a business is the lease, rent, or mortgage that you pay every month. When you rent or lease a business location, you usually sign a contract for at least a year. If you purchase or build your business location, you will be required to make a large cash payment, thus committing yourself to the location for many years.

The key to selecting a good location for your business is knowing what you need and performing research to find it. Use every possible resource to identify the location that will contribute to the success of your business. Potential resources include census data, Realtors, your local chamber of commerce, local media, and visits to the potential business sites.

Census Data

The U.S. Census Bureau collects information from businesses and individuals in every geographic area of the United States. The statistics they compile are available for your use. You can find information that is specific to your state and county, including the number of high school and college graduates, median household income, ethnic background, gender and age mix in the community, authorized housing units, and some business statistics. Armed with this information, you can identify a county or community that is likely to fulfill your requirements for local employees and customers. (The U.S. Census Bureau web site address is available on the CD.)

Realtors

Like many professionals, Realtors specialize in specific categories. Commercial real estate agents specialize in business properties. A good Realtor does more than provide a list of available sites. He or she will attempt to match your list of requirements to available properties. Realtors can also provide you with information about the surrounding area, valuable information that can help you select the right location. The Realtor's knowledge of existing businesses, growth trends, and future developments planned for the geographic area can provide important input into your decision-making process. Commercial Realtors are also familiar with the cost involved in renting, building, or repairing a business site in your geographic area. A Realtor who specializes in your particular type of business will be more prepared to assist you and may be able to think of items you did not consider in choosing a location.

When a residential property is purchased or rented, the Realtor usually represents the seller, not the buyer. The seller pays the fee earned by the Realtor. However, the business arrangement for commercial Realtors is different. The sales and rental prices for commercial properties are generally higher than the prices paid for residential properties. Therefore, the commission earned by the Realtor is higher. When dealing with commercial properties, the Realtor's fees may become part of the negotiated price and both the buyer and seller may contribute to the Realtor's fee.

Unlike residential properties, commercial properties may be listed with only one Realtor. To find the property you want, you may have to contact a large number of Realtors. To avoid this, you can retain a **buyer's agent.** A buyer's agent is a real estate agent who represents the buyer, not the seller. As your representative, the buyer's agent can save time by finding available properties and limiting the properties based on your requirements. This is a valuable service because there are fewer commercial properties than residential properties and the available properties are listed with many separate Realtors.

Do not depend entirely on the Realtor. Spend some time studying maps of the surrounding area. Become familiar with local streets, neighborhoods, businesses, restaurants, and educational facilities. This will help you evaluate access to the site, local customers or employees, competition, the availability of food services for your employees and customers, and the skills that are taught by the local schools.

Chamber of Commerce

Your local chamber of commerce can provide services and information to help you choose a location, gather information about the local workforce, and identify establishments and customers who need your services or products. It also enables you to network with other businesses that supply services or products you need.

Local Media

Local media outlets contain valuable information about the geographic area, its citizens, and its future. The media also provide information about an area's past, current conditions, and any planned changes. For example, plans for a new highway or subdivision may affect a commercial property by improving access or increasing the number of potential customers. News about forthcoming legislation may affect taxes or regulations for your business.

Visit the Site

Before you make the final commitment, visit and carefully examine the proposed site. Examine the property several times. You want to know what the conditions are during your proposed business hours, on weekends, in the evenings, and in the afternoon. A site that seems perfect for a video rental store could have plenty of traffic as commuters travel to and from work. However, commuters might be traveling on your side of the street in the morning, when renting a video is the last thing on their minds. In the afternoon, commuters are on the other side of the street and the traffic is too congested to get to the video store.

Hypothetical Scenario

Michael Windfeather has already sold many of his designs to local jewelers. Therefore, he is confident that the local demographics are promising if he decides to open his own retail site. However,

Michael doesn't really want to sell his jewelry directly to consumers. He enjoys creating the designs and seeing them take shape in the hands of a skilled craftsperson. For his purposes, Michael will use the demographics to help him locate employees who can do justice to his designs and perform the highly specialized tasks. He plans to contact the chamber of commerce and a local art school.

Types of Business Locations

Each business operates in a unique location. Communities determine where businesses can operate, limiting them to specific areas that do not conflict with community residences or recreational areas. Counties and cities have **zoning ordinances,** laws that regulate the use of private land by limiting development and business activities within specific geographic areas.

The intention of zoning ordinances is to protect residents, homes, property, and businesses that exist in an area and to encourage the growth of the community. Zoning laws enable communities to balance the needs of its citizens with the needs of local businesses. Zoning ordinances can also prevent businesses from operating in an area. For example, zoning restrictions will prevent a steel manufacturer from opening next to a clothing store. This protects the interests of the clothing store. Their customers would be intimidated by shopping in an environment dominated by the steel manufacturer.

Zoning laws also limit the business activities of companies that operate in an area. It is common for zoning laws to regulate details and activities such as parking, landscaping, signage, noise levels, and the appearance and size of the building. A small town that wants to attract tourists to its antique stores may prohibit parking on the street and require landscaping that screens parking lots from the street. Zoning laws may require a particular architectural style or specify building materials such as brick or stucco. A small coastal town that relies heavily on income from tourists may specify that businesses stay within the colors and styles of a New England harbor town.

Before you assume that any site is appropriate for your business, verify the zoning regulations that apply to that particular site. To investigate the zoning regulations for your area, contact the city clerk's office. Your local library may also maintain a copy of the zoning regulations for your area. Local government web sites are also good sources of information about local ordinances. Zoning laws identify agricultural, residential, commercial, industrial, and mixed-use areas.

Agricultural Zone

A zone that has been designated an **agricultural zone** is occupied by farms that perform farming or ranching activities. Farming activities include growing and harvesting crops. Ranching activities include raising livestock. A single-family dwelling can be located on the property, but building additional residences is not permitted in most agricultural zones. Permitted buildings may include a roadside stand to sell the farm's products.

Residential Zone

A zone designated as a **residential zone** includes areas that provide housing, public services, and facilities for the residential population. Housing includes single-family homes, apartment buildings, and mobile home parks. Public areas include parks, green-belt areas around some neighborhoods, and public recreational sites. Facilities needed for the residential population include police stations, fire stations, and health care facilities such as hospitals. Day care facilities, churches, schools, and cemeteries are also found in residential zones. Some small businesses are located in homes. However, the community usually places strict restrictions on businesses operated from private residences.

Residential Location Many sole proprietorships are operated from the owners' homes. Professionals such as freelance writers, architects, and accountants may operate in a separate room of the house designated as an office or perform paperwork on a corner of the dining room table. Unless a steady stream of customers arrives all day or a large truck backs into your driveway to deliver supplies, your neighbors may have no idea that you operate a business in your home.

This does not mean that a business operated in your home is not required to meet zoning requirements. Zoning regulations for businesses operating in private residences usually specify details such as the size and location of a sign identifying the business, parking for customer vehicles, limitations on the number of employees, and the storage of inventory on the property. Complaints from neighbors receive prompt attention from zoning inspectors.

Commercial Zone

A zone that has been designated a **commercial zone** may include areas that provide retail sales, services, professional offices, and other commercial activities for your neighborhood or community. Buildings in a commercial zone might include a clothing store, dentist's office, bank, and restaurant. Often, businesses are grouped together in business districts or shopping centers.

Business District Due to zoning ordinances, businesses are often established in a **business district,** an unplanned grouping of businesses in a single location. The specific businesses and retailers who operate in a business district are established by chance. There is no planned mix of businesses. A business district may have two shoe stores, a consulting firm, and a radio station. Businesses succeed or fail based on their individual business practices. The lack of an organized approach, which would include selecting a mix of retailers and businesses that complement each other and meet the community's needs, makes it more difficult for each business to succeed. There are three types of business districts—a neighborhood business district, a secondary business district, and a central business district.

Neighborhood Business District The smallest business area, the **neighborhood business district,** is an unplanned business area that is usually located on a major road near a residential area. It meets the basic needs of the nearby residents. For shoppers, the neighborhood business district has a grocery store, pharmacy, and video store.

Specialty stores and businesses will not find enough customers in a neighborhood business district.

Secondary Business District A **secondary business district** is an unplanned business area that grows around a major intersection. The businesses in a secondary business district draw customers from several surrounding neighborhoods. For shoppers, a secondary business district usually contains at least one department store and several smaller specialty retailers. Stores and businesses that are very specialized will not find enough customers in a secondary business district.

Central Business District The downtown area of many communities is a **central business district.** It is an unplanned shopping area created where the community's public transportation system is centered. The central location enables consumers from various parts of the community to shop in the central business district.

Although the central location and the presence of public transportation provide easy access for consumers, there are also disadvantages. Often, central business districts suffer from older buildings in poor repair, lack of parking, and congested streets. The unplanned nature of the business mix means that consumers often can't find everything they need in one trip. For example, consumers in a shopping center know that there will be a mix of retailers that will enable them to purchase clothing, shoes, and accessories in a single trip. In a downtown shopping district, stores may be located far apart, if they are available at all. Table 6.1 describes the characteristics of the three types of business districts.

TABLE 6.1 Business Districts

Business District	Location	Population Served	Contains
Neighborhood	Major road	Neighborhood	Meets basic needs
Secondary	Major intersection	Several neighborhoods	Meets basic needs plus several small specialty stores
Central	Downtown	Entire community	At least one department store plus specialty stores

Shopping Centers Planning is one of the main differences between a business district and a shopping center. The other major difference is the businesses located in a shopping center. A shopping center contains only retailers. Although a business district may have an office for a Realtor or a public accountant, a shopping center will only have retail establishments. A **shopping center** is a shopping district owned, planned, and managed by a single individual or business. The developer who planned the shopping center selected the site for easy access by customers, the amount of space available for the shopping center, and a parking area that is sufficient for the number of stores and shoppers. A shopping center contains at least one **anchor store,** a major store that attracts customers to the shopping center. The mix of retailers in a shopping center is carefully planned and chosen to meet the needs of the customers served by the shopping center. When an opening occurs, the developer selects a retailer who sells products not already sold by other retailers in the shopping center.

For retailers, there are several advantages to operating in a shopping center. Most shopping centers have customer traffic. It is much easier for a retailer, particularly a specialty retailer, to attract customers who are already in the shopping mall for other reasons than it is to attract customers who are passing by in a car on their way to another destination. For shoppers, there are many advantages to visiting a shopping center rather than a single store operating alone. The carefully selected mix of retailers means that the customer will find a large variety of products. The customer will also find easy access to the shopping center from major roads, often highways. Adequate parking means that consumers will not have to circle the lot searching for parking spaces. Most shopping centers have security officers who protect both retailers and customers, providing a safe environment for shoppers.

There are also several disadvantages for retailers in a shopping center. Although there is heavy customer traffic, the customers may not be interested in your products. Attracted by the shopping center's anchor store, customers may not visit specialty stores that are not located near the anchor store. A retailer might be limited in the products the store can carry because other retailers in the shopping center already sell them. This removes some of the control a proprietor has over his or her store. The hours of operation are determined by the shopping center, not the individual retail proprietors. Finally, most shopping centers have a **merchant association,** which establishes rules that regulate the appearance of the stores, such as the store front, window displays, and signs. They may also share the cost of maintenance and security for the shopping center. Based on size and functionality, there are four types of shopping centers—a neighborhood center, a community center, a regional center, and a super-regional center.

Neighborhood Center The smallest shopping center, the **neighborhood center,** meets the basic product and service needs of a neighborhood. The planned nature of a neighborhood center sets it apart from a neighborhood business district. Retailers in a neighborhood center sell groceries, small gift items, and personal services that are frequently purchased such as dry cleaning and beauty salon treatments. The anchor store is usually a grocery store, home improvement center, or discount store. The neighborhood center is built on 3 to 10 acres and has approximately 50,000 square feet that can be leased by businesses. It requires a population of 2,500 to 40,000 to support a neighborhood center. Specialty businesses may not find enough customers in a neighborhood center.

Community Center Next in size, the **community center** meets the basic needs of a neighborhood and provides a few additional products such as clothing and appliances. A community center might have two anchor stores, usually a grocery store, home improvement center, or discount store, and a junior department store. It is located on 10 to 30 acres and has approximately 100,000 to 300,000 square feet that can be leased to businesses. It requires a population of 40,000 to 150,000 to support a community center. Specialty businesses may not find enough customers in a community center.

Regional Center Larger than the community center, a **regional center** contains retailers who sell products such as general merchandise, clothing, and furniture. The anchor stores for a regional center will consist of at least two full-line department stores. The site is located on 30 to 50 acres and has approximately 300,000 to 1,000,000 square feet that can be leased. Major roadways, usually highways, provide access to a regional center. Each anchor store is approximately 100,000 square feet. It requires a population of 150,000 or more to support a regional center. Most specialty businesses will find enough customers in a regional center.

Super-Regional Center Largest of all, a **super-regional center** has more than 750,000 square feet of retail space. Three or more full-line department stores, each approximately 100,000 square feet, anchor the super-regional center. It is located on a minimum of 50 acres. A highway almost always provides access. Like a regional center, it requires a population of 150,000 or more to support a super-regional center. Most specialty businesses will find enough customers in a super-regional center. Table 6.2 describes the characteristics of the four types of shopping centers.

TABLE 6.2 Shopping Centers

Shopping Center	Anchor Store	Size (Square Feet)	Area (Acres)	Population Served
Neighborhood	1	50,000	3–10	2,500–40,000
Community	2	100,000–300,000	10–30	40,000–150,000
Regional	2+	300,000–1,000,000	30–50	150,000+
Super-regional	3+	750,000+	50+	150,000+

Business Incubator Establishing a new business is difficult. Sharing expenses and resources among several small businesses can help the businesses survive and succeed. This is the basic idea of a business incubator. Business incubators provide inexpensive space, dispense business advice, and share equipment and office expenses to assist new businesses. They are primarily used by new businesses for the first two to three years. **Business incubators** are a method of promoting economic growth by encouraging individuals to launch new businesses.

The incubator concept began in the early 1980s and grew rapidly. The National Business Incubator Association (NBIA) estimates that there were only 12 incubators in the country in 1980. By the year 2000, there were more than 900 business incubators in operation. The community establishes some incubators. Individuals, educational institutions, and private businesses sponsor others. An incubator may be established to foster general businesses or could specialize in areas such as high technology, medical research, or manufacturing. Business incubators supported by physical facilities and educational programs have a success rate as high as 80 to 90 percent. This is much higher than the average success rate for new businesses.

There are three types of business incubators. Local governments usually establish *mixed-use incubators*. They are meant to encourage economic growth and decrease unemployment rates. *Micro-enterprise incubators* are aimed at economically depressed areas with a low-income population. *Technology incubators* encourage the development of high-technology companies that have the opportunity to grow rapidly.

Industrial Zone

A zone that has been designated an **industrial zone** is occupied by manufacturers of various products. Industrial businesses can be divided into light industrial and heavy industrial businesses based on their activities and by-products. Activities in a light industrial zone include light manufacturing, research and development, and business park offices. Laboratories, automobile repair garages, and manufacturers who do not create too much noise or waste by-products may also be considered light industrial businesses. Businesses in heavy industry include sheet metal plants, plastics fabricators, and paper mills.

Freestanding Location Unless they are very well known, a retailer will not be found in a **freestanding location,** a retail site not connected to other buildings or in a shopping center. It is too difficult for small retailers with a limited product selection to attract customers to a freestanding building where they cannot visit other stores or businesses. However, many other types of businesses will thrive in a freestanding location. Manufacturers and other industrial businesses often require a building that stands alone, isolated by their need for space and regulations that require them to operate a certain distance from other buildings because of noise, pollution, or business activities.

Freestanding locations have several advantages and disadvantages. Advantages include the lack of direct competition, the possibility of lower rent, the ability to modify the building, and the easy availability of parking space. The disadvantages include the lack of other businesses to attract customers, higher promotional and maintenance costs because they are not shared with other tenants, and community regulations that affect the construction of your building or your planned operations.

Mixed-Use Zone

A zone that has been designated a **mixed-use zone** includes residential housing and facilities mixed with commercial businesses. Mixed-use zones make it easier for citizens to access retailers, professionals, and services they need.

▌ Hypothetical Scenario

After reviewing the zoning regulations for his city, Michael has determined that his business can be categorized as light industrial. His lack of interest in selling directly to consumers means that he is not operating a retail establishment. This avoids many of the strict zoning requirements for retailers and provides many more options in location.

Determine Your Facility Needs

Before you begin to shop for a specific site or open a business in your living room, you should decide exactly what you need. For example, do you need access for customers?

If all of your products are sold on the Internet or your services are performed at the customer's site, customer access is not important to you. The priority that you set on each characteristic of your business site will determine the number of available sites that meet your requirements and the price that you will pay for the site.

General Factors

Selecting a business site is easier for some businesses than for others. Businesses that require special facilities will find it more difficult to find a business site. Each type of business requires different features and facilities. Regardless of the type of business, all businesses must examine several factors before they are able to select a site. These factors include demographics, taxes, zoning regulations, local laws, security, community growth, building, and cost.

Demographics Businesses draw employees and customers from the surrounding areas. Therefore, the characteristics of the local population are important to businesses. **Demographics** are the statistical characteristics of human populations. When analyzing the demographics of an area, the age and income of the local population are two of the most important characteristics. When you hire employees from the surrounding area, you must be sure that they have the education to perform the necessary tasks. Often, there are groupings of similar businesses in a particular area that have a common set of specialized skills. For example, Silicon Valley is an area in California where a large portion of the population has technological and computer skills. Because of the grouping of skills in the area, many software companies operate in Silicon Valley. This occurred because many colleges in the area produced graduates with specific degrees in technological and computer areas. This same method of specialization has occurred in many areas of the country, creating an area dominated by a particular type of business that requires the specialized skill.

If your business requires a specific skill set that is not common, identify the schools that teach the skills you need. Establishing your company near one of these schools may ensure a steady supply of employees for your business.

Taxes Because taxes are a necessary expense for companies that earn a profit, consider the tax rate in a specific location before you decide to establish your business there. The tax rate between different locations can vary considerably. Your Realtor should be able to tell you the amount of property taxes paid every six months for any existing building you are considering. If you build a new building on land that was previously zoned for other use, such as agricultural land that is being developed for the first time, the amount paid previously will not reflect the amount that you will be charged. In this situation, investigate the current tax rate and ask your Realtor for information about the average property tax paid by other businesses in the area.

Zoning Regulations Do not establish a business in an area that has not been zoned for your business activity. The penalties for operating a business in the wrong zone vary for different locations. Penalties may include a fine and you may be required to move your business. The expense of the fine and the move is often enough to shut down a small business. This can still occur even if the business that previously occupied the space performed the same business activity that you intend to pursue. Don't assume that the previous business met zoning requirements or that your business will get away with not meeting the requirements because the previous business didn't meet the requirements. The act of applying for required licenses or other activities needed to open your business may trigger a visit from a zoning inspector. It is much easier and financially safer to find a location in the appropriate zone.

Local Laws Some business activities are strictly regulated or prohibited in a particular area. For example, restaurants have to meet many requirements that are designed to ensure the safety of the restaurant's customers. Adult bookstores or nightclubs may be prohibited in many areas of a city. Investigate local laws before you select a business site.

Security Employees and customers need to feel safe when they come to work or visit your establishment. Try to avoid high-crime areas and surroundings that are poorly lit. The building in which your business operates presents an image of your business. Make sure that the image you project shows your business in a positive light.

Community Growth Business sites located on the outskirts of a community are less expensive because they are less convenient for employees and customers. If you can accurately predict the direction in which a community will grow, you can obtain a location that will be good after the community grows to reach it. Until the community grows, such a location may inhibit the success and growth of your business. If you have the financial resources to operate your business until a community grows, this may be a good strategy. However, most new businesses cannot afford to wait for the community to grow to their location.

On the other hand, you must be cautious about selecting a location in an area with a declining population. A location that looks like a good deal now will not be as attractive when employees and customers move away.

Building When you select a business location, evaluate its physical characteristics. Examine the building as carefully as you would examine a potential home for your family. Ask a building inspector to evaluate the physical characteristics of the building. The inspector may identify problems you would not locate alone.

Identify the age of the building. Older buildings have higher maintenance costs and may need some items, such as the heating equipment and wiring, repaired or replaced. If you plan to open a business that requires a computer network in the building, older buildings probably won't have the wiring to support the technology you need. Check the roof, heating system, air conditioning, lighting, plumbing, and the quality of the construction. Newer buildings will probably be in better shape and require fewer repairs.

Identify the image the building projects. Examine the interior of the building. Verify that it can be adapted to meet your needs. If your business would benefit from window displays, ensure that it has windows that are well located for the purpose. If the building has a unique feature that would benefit your business, such as an unusual stained-glass window or an open loft, this building may be more attractive than others you visit.

Cost Each characteristic that makes a site more attractive also makes it more expensive. Before you shop for a location, determine the amount that you can spend and get the best site for that amount. If you choose the best site before you calculate the amount you can spend, you will waste time looking at sites that are too expensive or commit yourself to a site that you can't afford. A site that looks too good to be true may have hidden problems. Carefully examine every aspect of the location.

Selecting a Manufacturing Site

Most of the products sold today do not occur naturally. Sweaters, rubber tires, and necklaces do not grow on trees. Manufacturing produces these items. **Manufacturing** is the process of making a product by processing, assembling, or converting raw and semifinished materials.

Types of Manufacturing Choosing a site for a manufacturing business can be difficult because few sites are available for the activities involved in manufacturing products. Your needs, the type of manufacturing you perform, your equipment, your product, and your by-products determine the locations that will work for your business. There are several types of manufacturing—mass production, continuous processing, repetitive production, intermittent processing, and custom manufacturing.

Mass Production Using machines to produce identical products in large quantities using the same process is **mass production.** In the early 1900s, Henry Ford used the first assembly line to produce automobiles. The assembly line is now used to produce a variety of products, including computers, toys, and, of course, cars. An assembly line is made up of several stations. The raw material begins at the first station. As the product passes through the assembly line, employees or robots add components or adjust the existing components to assemble the product. By the time the product reaches the last station, it is fully assembled. An assembly line usually requires a large amount of space. It assumes that the product can move smoothly from one station to the next. It also requires machinery and employees skilled in using the equipment.

Most new businesses do not engage in mass production. Mass producing any product presumes that the product has proven itself and is popular enough to sell mass quantities. Most new businesses start a little smaller.

Continuous Processing Some manufacturers run day and night. Raw materials constantly pass through equipment that changes the form of the product to something more useful. This manufacturing method is known as **continuous processing.** Raw material may be transformed for weeks or months without ever shutting down the equipment. Paper mills, for example, run constantly, transforming pulp into paper. The process may be stopped only when the mill changes the type of paper it is manufacturing. Continuous processing may not require as much work from employees, but the manufacturing equipment could require a large amount of space. Employees test the finished product constantly, verifying that it meets requirements for consistency and quality.

Repetitive Production Companies that engage in **repetitive production** perform the same simple manufacturing activity over and over. The entire process can usually be completed in a few hours. Usually, repetitive production involves assembling premanufactured components to produce a finished product.

New companies are more likely to engage in repetitive production than continuous processing or mass production. The space requirements are less and harmful by-products are less likely to result, making it easier for new businesses to perform this type of manufacturing.

Intermittent Processing Many products are made in a single short production run that manufactures a limited quantity of different products. This manufacturing process is known as **intermittent processing.** Examples of companies that routinely perform intermittent processing include printers and bakers. Printers set up their printing equipment to produce a limited number of items such as brochures, résumés, or newsletters. Bakeries produce a limited number of cinnamon rolls, cookies, or loaves of bread.

Many new and small businesses are able to engage in intermittent processing that requires smaller and less expensive equipment. The entire manufacturing process may be completed by a single individual, limiting the need for a large amount of space and a large number of employees. The lower costs of this process make it an easier type of manufacturing for small businesses to perform. The product is normally purchased by individual consumers. This means that customer access is more important for manufacturers engaged in intermittent processing.

Custom Manufacturing A company or an individual may request a product designed specifically to meet a need that cannot be met by other standard products. The manufacturer may engage in **custom manufacturing,** the process of designing and building a unique product to meet the customer's needs. A custom product might not be something a customer can physically hold. It could be a software program, a component of a house, or a piece of jewelry. The process could require a single individual or 100 individuals. For example, a software company may produce software to run the equipment used by a paper mill or the machines used by another manufacturer.

A new or small company may perform this type of manufacturing. The requirements for space and equipment vary widely, depending on the nature of the finished product. The process could require an hour or a year. Customer access may not be required. This type of manufacturing often requires specialized skills and equipment.

Additional Selection Factors Manufacturing a product is the primary business of a manufacturer. However, a manufacturer performs many other business tasks that require space. The manufacturer must maintain the equipment used in the assembly line, purchase and receive raw materials and supplies, train employees, market the product, package the finished product, and ship the product to customers. Customers may be other businesses or individual consumers. All of these activities require space. They also require items such as office equipment, machinery, and maintenance equipment. All of these items require more space to store and use.

If you manufacture products sold directly to individual customers, as a bakery or printer does, your business performs manufacturing and retail activities in the same facility. Manufacturers who make and sell products from their sites should also use the selection factors identified for retail locations.

Supply and Cost of Raw Materials The presence of a nearby supplier is not only convenient, it may reduce the cost of the raw materials because transportation costs are lower. It also increases the convenience of the location because the time required to deliver the supplies is less if the supplier is near your location. For example, a manufacturer requires beads to make the final product. If the beads are produced across the street and can be delivered in a single business day, the manufacturer can wait to order the beads when the supply in the storage room is fairly low.

Access by Suppliers Suppliers should be able to make deliveries directly to your location. The more times a supplier has to repackage a load or transfer materials from one transportation mode to another, the higher the cost will be and the longer the delivery will require. For example, if you require a large quantity of aluminum from a supplier who is located a few miles away, you may be able to receive supplies delivered by trucks, trains, or river barges. It is more convenient for a supplier to use a single shipment method to transport supplies to your location. If materials have to be unloaded from a barge and transferred to trucks, the time and work will increase the cost and lengthen the delivery time.

Loading Dock Deliveries or shipments of large products or a large quantity of products should be made through a loading dock. The loading dock enables large trucks to back up directly to your storage area, making it easy to load and unload shipments.

Storage Space If you manufacture products that require large components or large quantities of smaller components, you will need to keep supplies on hand that will enable you to manufacture products for a predetermined length of time. A printer may receive shipments of paper that will enable the business to operate for several weeks without ordering additional quantities. It is necessary to store the supplies at the printer's site, requiring storage space for the paper quantities that will last several weeks.

Disposal of By-products Most manufacturing processes create **by-products,** items produced in addition to the main product. By-products could be harmless, such as steam or water. By-products can also be noxious, harmful to the environment or living beings. Regardless if the by-products are harmful or not, manufacturers must find acceptable ways of disposing of them. Even if the manufacturing process creates only water as a by-product, you must find an acceptable method of disposing of it. The location you select must provide a method of disposing of by-products or accessibility to an acceptable disposal method.

Selecting an Office Site

Many businesses that require office space rent space in a freestanding building. Generally, these are businesses that require office space and a professional atmosphere. The developer ensures that the building is maintained and rents space to tenants. When choosing a freestanding building, verify that other businesses in the building will not disapprove of your activities, and that their activities are acceptable to you and your customers. If customers are expected to visit your site, you should also use the selection factors identified for retail locations.

Additional Selection Factors A good office site is easier to find and acquire than a good manufacturing site. The way that you use office space makes the square footage easier to select because the way that you lay out the space is more flexible than a manufacturing site that has requirements for the placement of large machinery. If your entire workforce works at desks, which is common for businesses such as software development or financial services, the work space can be configured in a variety of ways to accommodate the available space. This means that your requirements for an office can also be flexible.

Workforce Many businesses that operate in an office hire employees with specific skill sets. For example, engineering firms and software development firms require employees with technical degrees in areas such as electrical engineering or software engineering. A business located near schools that offer these degrees will benefit from the ability to find nearby employees and interns with the education and experience needed to perform the job.

Parking Office space located in freestanding buildings may suffer from lack of adequate parking. For example, many downtown areas do not have access to a sufficient number of parking spaces for employees, visitors, and shoppers. Always identify the location where your employees and customers will park. Because of limited space, employees in downtown locations may have to pay for parking in attended garages or lots. Verify that the location is large enough, close enough to the office, and not too expensive.

Selecting a Retail Site

As a shopper, it seems like there are good retail sites all around you. As a retailer, you realize that good retail sites are not easy to find, particularly in an acceptable price range. Aspects of a location that are not important to other types of businesses are critical to the success of a retailer.

Theories of Retail Location Sociologists and economists have developed several theories to explain why shoppers choose one retail location rather than another, causing retailers to succeed in some locations and fail in others. Understanding these theories will help you choose the right location for your retail business.

Law of Retail Gravitation In 1929, William J. Reilly developed the **Law of Retail Gravitation.** This theory describes how large cities attract customers from smaller communities because they are more attractive to shoppers. The number of shoppers who choose to shop in a city is directly related to the population of the city and the distance the customer has to travel. Customers will travel farther to shop in a large city than they will to shop in a smaller community.

Converse's Revision Twenty years later, Paul Converse studied the Law of Retail Gravitation. He determined that there is a boundary between two cities at which customers will shop in either city. He identified this boundary as the **point of indifference** because shoppers at this location are indifferent, not caring which community they visit to shop.

Central Place Theory Walter Christaller also studied the economics of retail. He examined the items that shoppers purchase and determined that there is an explanation for the way that goods are distributed. He identified each community as a **central place,** a center of commerce consisting of several retail establishments. He evaluated the assortment of goods and services that are available in each community. The most basic communities have only the most basic assortment of products, usually gas stations and grocery stores. As communities grow, they have a wider variety of products. Consumers will travel farther to purchase specialized products found in the larger central place. For retailers, this means that basic goods should be sold near the consumer. Specialized goods can be sold farther away.

Christaller's Central Place Theory identifies the threshold of a retail establishment and the range of a product. **Threshold** defines the minimum demand for a product or service that must exist in an area to maintain a store's existence. The **range** of a product is the maximum distance a consumer will travel to buy it. If a retailer draws a circle that marks its products' range around the retail location, as shown in Figure 6.1, the circle identifies the outer boundary of the store's market area.

FIGURE 6.1   Central Place Theory

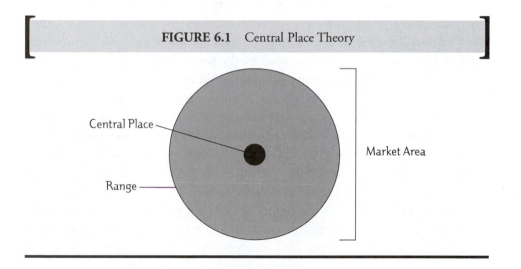

Together, the threshold and range provide important information that will help you select a retail location. If you sell specialty products, you have a better chance of success in a larger central place. You can predict the goods or services the community will need as it grows and be able to estimate the community size needed to support your store. The range determines your market area. The size of your market area, the local demographics, and the price of your products can help you estimate the number of potential customers and your projected sales.

Additional Selection Factors Unless you sell products only on the Internet, customers will visit your location. This makes location critical to retailers.

Customer Accessibility The more accessible your site is, the more likely customers will be to visit. A site near a major road or intersection makes it easier for customers to access your location. Public transportation, such as a bus or subway, also increases the accessibility of your site.

Traffic Patterns Being located on a major roadway with plenty of automobile traffic does not guarantee that your location is accessible. There may be barriers that prevent passing consumers from entering your location. Barriers could include traffic congestion during your peak business hours or the lack of traffic lights. Examine the traffic flow at various times of the day before evaluating this characteristic of a site.

Visibility A retail location should be visible from the street or point of entry. The second-best alternative is a sign identifying the business that is visible from the street. Gas stations often have tall signs that are visible from nearby highways. Within a shopping center, locations that are visible from the main walkways are more desirable and more expensive. Locations on the side, away from the main walkways, are not as visible and are therefore less desirable. A distinctive storefront that is recognizable by consumers can attract any passing customer.

Additional Customer Parking Although parking is needed by all businesses, it is critical to retailers. A customer who cannot find a parking space will not enter your store. If the parking area looks crowded, customers will assume that the store is also crowded and may decide to shop elsewhere. In many areas, the size and visibility of your parking area are regulated by the zoning ordinances that pertain to your site. There are also requirements for a specific number of parking spaces for disabled customers. These parking spaces are usually larger and closer to the entrance of your store. They provide accessibility for customers in wheelchairs. Although it is not required, because of a similar need for additional space, it has been suggested that retailers provide parking spaces for parents with children in strollers. It remains to be seen if this will become a trend of the future.

Competition The presence of nearby competition reduces the chance of success for a new retailer selling the same products. Compare your products to those sold by the competition. If your products match the demographics of the area better than those sold by the competition, you may still succeed. However, as a new retailer, it is better to establish your store in a geographic area that has not already been claimed by competitors.

Security Although safety is important to all businesses, a retail business requires an area where customers feel secure. An older area with a reputation for crime will not attract large numbers of customers. Shoppers prefer areas that are well lit and crowded. Dark, isolated retail sites will encourage shoppers to find alternative shopping areas.

Operating a Business in Your Home

In the past, it was not considered professional to operate a business in your home. Today, sole proprietors working in their own homes operate many businesses. Advances in technology have made it easier for individuals to work at home without being isolated from other businesses or workers. In fact, the advent of electronic mail and other communication methods has made location unimportant for many businesses. If you hire an architect, for example, unless you physically visit the office, you would not know if the architect worked in an office located in an industrial area or an office located in his or her home.

Additional Selection Factors Before you decide to open a business in your home, there are many factors you should consider. Some considerations include the potential impact on your personal and professional life.

Cost One of the main reasons for establishing a home-based business is cost. Operating from your home removes expenses that result from purchasing or renting business space elsewhere. If you work from home with minimal customer contacts, it also reduces wardrobe expenses. If the space that you use for business in your home is dedicated exclusively to your business, you may be able to deduct some of your home expenses that are related to your business on your tax return. Be aware, however, that claiming home office expenses is one of several "red flags" in the IRS auditing system and may invite an audit. Consult a tax expert for more information.

Convenience As a proprietor, a location could not be more convenient than one in your own home. However, for customers, your home is probably off the beaten path. If customers need to visit your office frequently, you may want to consider acquiring a more commercial site.

Facilities A business that requires large group meetings, many employees, or large equipment may require a commercial site. A frequent need for meetings with a large number of attendees may mean that your home is not the best location for your business. In the past, another factor was Internet access, which was usually much faster from an office that could be equipped with special lines dedicated to reaching the Internet. In the last several years, the speed and availability of Internet access for the home-based user has increased due to advances in technology.

Personal Considerations Privacy is an issue that you will have to consider. Customers, employees, and coworkers will be in your home. This may be easier for you if you are able to maintain your office in a separate room, preferably with a separate entrance. If your only workspace doubles as the dining room table, meetings may well infringe upon your privacy. Another issue involves your motivation. You may find it difficult to separate your personal and professional activities when they both occur in the same place. You could find yourself distracted by other household members or events that should remain outside of your working time and location.

Hypothetical Scenario

Michael made a list of the requirements for his business site. Each craftsperson will need a work area. Although many pieces of jewelry are made by following the same design, each is handmade without the use of any large machinery. Suppliers will deliver the raw materials, but the quantities shipped in and out of the building will not be large enough to require daily visits by suppliers. Parking needs will be minimal. He does not plan to sell to consumers, but he expects to show samples and give a tour of the work area to a few large jewelers who may be interested in purchasing his designs in the future. With this list in hand, Michael is ready to contact a Realtor.

Select a Site

Determining the square footage that your business needs is crucial to selecting a site for your business. If you acquire a site that is too small, your operation will be cramped and you may not have the space necessary to operate your business. If you acquire a site that is too large, you will be paying for space that you don't want and can't use.

Calculate the Size To determine the correct amount of space, make a list of your business activities and identify the amount of space that each activity requires. For example, if you plan to open a bakery, identify the space required for food preparation, equipment, storage of supplies, display shelves, a customer area, and an office to perform standard business tasks. The most basic office should have room for a desk, computer, and storage of records and other paperwork. Remember to include space to move around and access stored supplies and equipment. If your business requires a large number of employees, you can include space for break rooms, a cafeteria, and meeting rooms. If your business will be an office site, identify the amount of space required for each worker. Work areas in an office setting for each employee can vary from 6×7 feet to 8×8 feet or more, based on standard cubicle sizes.

Use Table 6.3 to calculate the square footage you need.

1. Identify the business tasks you perform and the space required for each task.
2. Add these numbers to identify the amount of space you currently need.
3. On the next line, identify the amount of extra space you will need if your business grows as projected in the next year.
4. Add this number to the subtotal to identify the size of your ideal location.

TABLE 6.3 Space Needed

Business Task	Equipment	Square Feet
	Subtotal	
	Room to Grow	
	Total Square Footage	

Site Visit The characteristics of specific sites will become confused after you have visited several locations. You may not remember which site has the best parking, the easiest access, or the technical college across the street. Use Table 6.4 to identify your requirements and evaluate sites you visit. Make a copy of the table for each site you visit.

1. List your specific requirements.
2. Check Yes or No to signify that the site has the required feature.
3. Rate each location on a scale of 1–10 to evaluate how well it meets your needs.
4. Write comments about particular features of a specific location.

TABLE 6.4 Site Evaluation Form

Requirement	Yes	No	Rating	Comment
Demographics for employees				
Demographics for customers				
Taxes				
Zoning regulations				
Local laws				
Security				
Size				
Community growth				
Cost				
Supply and cost of raw material				
Access by suppliers				
Disposal of by-products				
Workforce				
Parking				
Additional customer parking				
Customer accessibility				
Traffic patterns				
Visibility				
Competition				
Security				
Convenience				

Building Evaluation Most businesses are established in existing buildings. The cost of construction prohibits most entrepreneurs from designing and constructing a building specifically to meet business requirements. Therefore, you must take the time to evaluate an existing building carefully. Use Table 6.5 to identify your requirements and evaluate buildings you visit. Make a copy of the table for each site you visit.

1. List your specific requirements.
2. Check Yes or No to signify that the building has the required feature.
3. Rate each feature on a scale of 1–10 to evaluate how well it meets your needs.
4. Write comments about particular features of a specific location.

TABLE 6.5   Building Evaluation Form

Feature	Yes	No	Rating	Comment
Age				
Construction quality				
Construction materials				
Construction style				
Number of stories				
Color				
Number of entrances				
Number of windows				
Image projected				
Roof				
Heating system				
Air conditioning				
Lighting				
Plumbing				
Wiring				
Loading dock				
Storage space				
Stairs				
Elevators				
Cafeteria				
Break rooms				
Restrooms				
Customer reception area				
Employee offices				
Meeting rooms				
Accessibility for disabled employees or customers				

Hypothetical Scenario

Michael created a table to determine the amount of space he needs. He calculated that about 1,500 square feet will provide enough space for his business activities. He believes strongly that natural lighting is important and helps him create his unique designs. Therefore, windows are high on his list of special features.

Acquire a Business Site

If you plan to operate your business in your home, congratulations! You have already acquired your business site. Other businesses need to exert more effort to acquire a site. The difficult part of the process was finding the location. Acquiring the site is a matter of negotiation and price. There are three ways to acquire a business site—build, buy, or lease.

Building a Business Site

Although every business would like to operate in a business site constructed specifically for it, very few will ever do so. The cost of constructing a building is high and requires a large cash down payment. Most entrepreneurs have a variety of expenses when they establish a business that makes a sizable dent in any cash reserves they had before starting the process.

Financing, such as a bank loan, is available. However, a bank requires a good reason to give a construction loan to a new entrepreneur. It would probably take your business a long time to earn the amount spent on the down payment for a construction loan, much less pay the loan itself.

Another disadvantage of building a business is the time required for construction. Depending on the size, location, and complexity of the building, construction can take from several months to almost a year. For most entrepreneurs, constructing a business site is not a wise decision.

Buying a Business Site

Building and buying a business site have many of the same advantages and disadvantages. Buying a site also requires a large cash down payment. Many entrepreneurs can put their cash to better use than tying it up in a down payment. Again, financing is available. However, a bank will be very cautious about loaning such a large amount to a new business. On the plus side, you can modify the building in any way you want without requiring permission from an owner. On the minus side, you will be responsible for all repairs and maintenance.

Leasing a Business Site

The majority of entrepreneurs lease business space for the life of the business. A **commercial lease** is a contract between a property owner and a business that permits a business to use the owner's location for a specific time period in exchange for payment. Commercial leases vary. They do not have a standard rental fee, length of time, or terms. Most of the conditions within a commercial lease are negotiable.

The degree to which they are negotiable depends on factors such as the current economy and the desirability of the location.

Terms of a Lease **Always remember that a commercial lease is written to favor the owner, not the business leasing the site.** Protect yourself by examining every condition identified in your lease. Do not make a verbal agreement to lease a business site. A written lease is much easier to enforce. All verbal claims made about the property, including those made by the Realtor, should be placed in the lease agreement. The length of the written contract can be anywhere from a single page to 60 or 70 pages. Obviously, almost every event that could possibly occur can be described and accounted for in a 70-page contract. Although the terms of a commercial lease are negotiable and the details identified in a contract can vary, it should have a description that identifies the space to be leased, the amount of rent to be paid, the frequency with which the rent should be paid, the time period of the lease, the amount the owner is allowed to increase rent, the responsibility for the insurance and taxes, the responsibility for maintenance and repairs, the security deposit, the responsibility for improvements, regulations regarding signage, rules about subleasing, options to renew the lease, lease termination conditions, and dispute handling.

Description A lease should include a description of the business property. This includes the location of the property, the size of the commercial lot, the location within the building, and any common areas shared by the business leasing the site and other tenants. A description should also include the square footage of the building or portion of the building that is being leased with a description of how the square footage was calculated. This is necessary because some calculation methods include the thickness of interior walls while others do not. It is often beneficial to have the space measured again before you sign a lease agreement. If the space is smaller than defined, you could easily end up paying too much per square foot for the business site.

Rent Payment You should know how much rent you are expected to pay and where and how the payment will be made. For example, the property owner may collect the rent in person, you could drop the payment in the mail, or the funds could be transferred electronically into the owner's bank account.

Term of the Lease This section of the contract identifies when the lease begins and ends. The lease may provide an option to renew the lease under certain conditions. For new businesses, it is a good idea to ask for a short-term lease of two years or less with an option to renew. If your business fails, you will not be stuck with a long-term lease of 10 or 15 years. Generally, the rent will increase when the lease is renewed. Commonly, a fee is charged for the convenience of offering a renewal. However, it may be worth it to pay the fee if the location is good for your business. Do not agree to a lease that is longer than you are willing to stay in the building. Remember that your business may grow or fail in the future. If your business fails, you may have to pay a sizable penalty for breaking the lease.

Rent Increases An owner may try to build in an automatic annual rent increase. Negotiate to put a limit on the annual increase. Without a limit, rent increases can be very high. Remember that the value of this site could go down for a variety of reasons, including economic depression or changes in the neighborhood. If your agreement increases the rent every year, you may end up paying much more than the site is worth.

Assign Responsibilities Obviously, the more responsibilities that can be assigned to the owner, the better the lease will be for you. Responsibilities that can be assigned include insurance, property taxes, the cost of maintenance and utilities, repair fees, and improvements required before you can move into the building. If you need improvements to the building for your business, you may be able to negotiate the terms so the owner pays for the improvements. After all, the improvements will remain after your business has left the building, thereby providing the owner with long-term benefits.

Signage and Exterior Appearance Zoning regulations may stipulate the requirements for signage and the exterior appearance of the building. Your sign and any modifications to the building's exterior may be dictated by local regulations.

Subleasing The ability to sublease all or a portion of the business space is a benefit to you. The ability to sublease a portion of the space means that you can lease the space that is more than you need at this time in your business. You can sublease the portion that you don't need in order to pay part of the rent for the entire space. When your business needs the additional space, you can reclaim it from the tenant. The ability to sublease all of the business space will help you if your business closes. Rather than being stuck paying the lease after your business has failed, you can sublease the space to another tenant.

Termination Conditions Before signing a lease agreement, ensure that the termination conditions are clearly defined. The owner should not be able to evict you just because a better offer has been made. If you sign a month-to-month agreement, you have the option of leaving at the end of every month. However, the owner has the option of asking you to leave at the end of every month. If you have a month-to-month agreement, add the requirement that the owner must notify you at least three months before the eviction date.

Dispute Handling Although you hope it doesn't happen, you must make provisions for the process used to handle a dispute between you and the owner. Rather than going straight to court, you may prefer to meet with an arbitrator or a mediator. One of the best ways to prevent such disputes is to make sure that all of the terms and conditions are stated clearly in your written lease agreement. Do not rely on verbal arrangements. People can change their minds or an owner's representative may change jobs. Any terms contained in a written agreement can be enforced at a later date without assistance from an individual who has left the area or left the owner's employ.

Hypothetical Scenario

Michael found an ideal location. A display area can easily be created in the front of the building. A stained-glass window in the front door adds a creative touch for the building. The work area has plenty of natural light. He managed to hide his enthusiasm for the site and negotiated an excellent lease agreement. As he left the meeting with the lease agreement in his briefcase, Michael was already picturing the first time he would turn the key in the lock.

Technology Insights

Tracking Shipments

As your business operates, you will ship raw materials, finished products, and supplies to and from your business site. In the past, you or your suppliers placed items in a box, addressed it carefully, and hoped that it would reach its destination. The technological advances in the past decade have made it possible to track the shipment from your hands to the hands of the recipient. Each item shipped through a carrier, such as the U.S. Postal Service, United Parcel Service, or Federal Express, is identified by an electronic bar code. At each point where the item arrives, departs, or is transferred to another vehicle, the item's bar code is scanned and its location is saved into a database. You can access this information by telephone or Internet to discover where the package is at every point in the shipping process. When the package arrives safely into the addressee's hands, the package is scanned again and the identity of the individual receiving the package is recorded. If an addressee claims not to have received the package, the record can be examined and the package is usually located. Any item that must be delivered should be sent using a service that is able to track packages in this manner.

Think Critically Identify the shipping companies in your area that can track packages electronically.

CHAPTER REVIEW

Your business location can make or break your business. Spend as much time and effort as necessary to find a location that meets your needs and benefits your business. A poor location can doom a good business to failure. Location is also one of the highest expenses faced by an entrepreneur and it is difficult to change. A purchase or lease agreement requires contracts that may extend for several years. Research your potential location carefully.

Zoning ordinances regulate the use of private land within a community. Zoning laws identify agricultural, residential, commercial, industrial, and mixed-use areas. Categorize your business to identify the zone that it belongs in and find an appropriate location within that zone. This prevents you from being fined or penalized for zoning violations.

Each type of business has its own requirements. Manufacturers need space for large equipment. Retailers must provide convenient and easy access for consumers. Based on the Central Place Theory, retailers can identify the order in which goods and services will be needed by a community as it grows. This helps retailers identify the size of the community that can support a business and the demographics needed to support a specific store. The least expensive location to establish a business is your home. However, many businesses cannot be operated within a private home.

To select a specific site, determine the amount of space your business needs. Identify the tasks your business will perform and calculate the space needed for each task. The total will be the space you need for all of your business activities. When you visit a specific site, evaluate how well it meets your requirements and write comments that will help you evaluate and remember each location. Take a separate sheet to evaluate the building in which your business would operate. Again, evaluate how well it meets your requirements and write additional comments.

Most businesses lease their business space for the life of the business. The most important thing to remember about a commercial lease is that it was written to favor the owner. Examine every condition in the lease and negotiate to improve the terms if possible.

USE BUSINESS TERMS

Fill in the blanks with the appropriate term.

agricultural zone	Law of Retail Gravitation
anchor store	manufacturing
business district	mass production
business incubator	merchant association
buyer's agent	mixed-use zone
by-products	neighborhood business district
central business district	neighborhood center
central place	point of indifference
commercial lease	range
commercial zone	regional center
community center	repetitive production
continuous processing	residential zone
custom manufacturing	secondary business district
demographics	shopping center
freestanding location	super-regional center
industrial zone	threshold
intermittent processing	zoning ordinance

1. If you are looking for commercial property, it is a good idea to retain a(n) ___?___ to help you.
2. A business district is located in a(n) ___?___ zone.
3. ___?___ are primarily used by new businesses for the first two to three years.
4. ___?___ will help you identify the age and income of the local population.
5. An assembly line is often used in ___?___ to produce many identical products.
6. At the ___?___, shoppers do not prefer one nearby city over another.
7. Many terms in a(n) ___?___ are negotiable.

TEST YOUR READING

8. How is a commercial Realtor different from a residential Realtor?
9. What type of information can you gain from the local media that will help you select a location?
10. What is the purpose of zoning ordinances?
11. Where can you find information about the zoning ordinances for your community?
12. Why won't most small retailers establish a business in a freestanding location?
13. Why is the average income of the local population important to businesses that are not retailers?

14. How does information about the growth of the community help you select a good location?
15. What are the types of manufacturing?
16. How does the Central Place Theory help a retailer select a location?
17. What is the main reason for establishing a home-based business?
18. How do most businesses acquire a business site?
19. Why do some businesses sublease their business space?

THINK CRITICALLY ABOUT BUSINESS

20. Walk through a nearby shopping center. Describe the planning that went into selecting the mix of businesses in the center.
21. Examine the zoning ordinances for an area in your community. Identify one of the most unusual and one of the most practical regulations. Explain your choices.
22. Identify a business incubator close to your community. Call or write for information about the criteria for using the incubator to start your business.
23. Return to the business plan that you started in Chapter 5. Add information about the location to your business plan.

REAL-LIFE BUSINESS

Ghirardelli Chocolate Company, Inc.

The name may be difficult to spell or pronounce, but there is nothing difficult about eating Ghirardelli chocolate. Ghirardelli's products include confection, gifts, beverages, and baking items sold through specialty food stores. They also sell a variety of confection products in retail shops owned by the company. Ghirardelli has a reputation as one of the best chocolate manufacturers in the United States.

After prospecting for gold, Domingo Ghirardelli opened a general store near Sacramento. The store sold chocolate and other provisions to local miners. In 1852, Ghirardelli moved to San Francisco to begin the chocolate factory that eventually became a local legend and attracts many tourists today.

Manufacturing chocolate is a long process that starts with cocoa beans grown in tropical rain forests around the world. Cocoa beans grow in a pod. Each pod contains 20 to 50 cocoa beans. About 400 beans are needed to make one pound of chocolate. After the harvested beans are dried, they are shipped to chocolate manufacturers around the world.

The manufacturer cleans and roasts the cocoa beans, a process that can take 30 minutes to two hours. The inside of the cocoa bean is milled, transforming the cocoa butter into liquid chocolate. The liquid chocolate can be molded into unsweetened chocolate or pressed to produce cocoa butter and cocoa powder. Ingredients are combined in large mixers to create a paste with the consistency of dough. This is crushed into flakes and placed in a conching machine, a machine with large paddles that stirs the chocolate for a few hours or several days, depending on the requirements of the product. The chocolate is melted and cooled as it is placed into molds. The molded chocolate is cooled in another machine for 20 minutes to two hours. The finished product is packaged and shipped. The chocolate that you eat in minutes requires hours, even days to manufacture.

Think Critically

1. Where are the raw materials for chocolate located?
2. Why does the process of making chocolate take so long?
3. Categorize the type of manufacturing performed by Ghirardelli.
4. Describe the site requirements for a chocolate manufacturer.

protection. A state may choose to enforce standards that are more stringent than the federal regulations. At the state level, a state agency enforces laws related to pollution control, an important environmental issue. This includes the disposal of hazardous waste and prevention of accidental release of harmful materials. The state agency determines which requirements apply to your business and issues permits.

Seller's Permit In some states, a **seller's permit** is required for businesses that sell or lease tangible property. This permit applies to wholesalers and retailers.

Permit to Operate Businesses that have elevators or amusement rides must obtain a permit to operate the equipment. A safety inspection is normally conducted before the permit is issued.

Automobiles Businesses that sell vehicles and the individual sales representatives may be required to obtain a vehicle dealer license. This can be issued by the Department of Motor Vehicles. A separate registration may be required for businesses that repair vehicles.

Many businesses operate commercial vehicles. Although this includes taxis, buses, and limousines, the most common commercial vehicles are used for delivery of goods to warehouses, retailers, and consumers. Some locations require the business to obtain a special permit for each vehicle. Each driver must be licensed to operate a commercial vehicle.

Barbering and Cosmetology Licenses Businesses that perform personal services such as cutting and styling hair and performing manicures are required to obtain a license. Facilities that instruct cosmetologists and barbers must also be licensed.

Weights and Measures Device Registration Businesses that use scales, fuel pumps, and electronic scanning devices must obtain a license. When prices are determined by the amount purchased, it is important to measure the amount correctly. This license ensures that the devices have been properly calibrated and inspected.

Animal Husbandry Businesses that deal with animals such as cattle or sheep are also inspected. They must apply for registration for brands used to identify ownership and pass the physical inspections of the pens in which the animals are fed and maintained. A separate license is required for the disposal of solid waste produced by the animals. Another separate registration ensures that poultry is routinely tested for specific diseases.

Pesticide Businesses that use or dispense pesticides must obtain a state license. This ensures that pesticides are used safely around the general population and any items consumed by the public.

Construction Businesses that construct new buildings or alter existing buildings must obtain several different permits and licenses. These include separate certifications to work with asbestos, trenching, scaffolding, and carpentry. Some contractors must also obtain licenses and are required to display their license numbers on all vehicles, stationery, business cards, and advertisements.

Federal Requirements

Most business activities are regulated by the city, county, or state. Few businesses encounter federal regulations, with the exception of the Americans with Disabilities

UNIT 3

Prepare to Open for Business

CHAPTERS

Prepare Your Site

GOALS

- Acquire licenses to operate
- Create a layout for your manufacturing site
- Prepare the interior of your office site
- Design the interior of your retail site
- Set up your home office

Sophia Gabriel has many fond memories of baking bread, pies, and desserts with her mother on weekend mornings. Several years ago, Sophia married and moved away, establishing a home in Boston. However, the smell of fresh bakery products always brings back fond memories. When she decided to establish a business, she knew that the only choice was a bakery.

Acquire Licenses

The day you received your driver license symbolized the dawn of your adulthood and granted freedom. It also assigned responsibility. Each state requires drivers to pass a written test and demonstrate their driving proficiency. This ensures that drivers know the rules and apply them appropriately in the real world. Only responsible adults who prove their ability are given a license to operate a vehicle.

Some businesses also require a license to operate. This requirement could be based on the type of product or service the business sells, the number of employees working for the business, or the geographic location of the business establishment. To obtain a license, you may have to meet requirements such as minimum education, experience in the occupation, or passage of a certification exam. To operate your business legally, you must obtain all the permits and licenses needed.

Granting a license is a governmental task. To identify the licenses you need to obtain, contact your secretary of state, county agency, and city clerk. These offices

can provide a complete list of the licenses you need to operate your business in your chosen location. This section contains general information about licenses that are required to operate a business in most locations. The requirements for your business may be different.

Note: Several additional requirements are based on regulations concerning employees and employee safety. These topics will be discussed with human resources information in a later chapter.

Local Requirements

Local licenses or permits are issued by the county or community. There are a variety of permits and licenses required by county or community agencies. Some of the most widely held requirements are listed here. Your business may require additional licenses. Contact your city, town, or village clerk to obtain local licenses.

Alcoholic Beverages You must obtain a local license to pursue business activities such as serving alcoholic beverages. Some communities set a limit on the number of licenses they distribute to serve alcohol. If the community has already issued the predetermined number of licenses, you will not be able to acquire a license unless a business holding one of the licenses closes, its license is revoked, or it is allowed to sell or transfer its license to you.

Certificate of Occupancy Your building requires a **certificate of occupancy**, a legal document that certifies that the building has been inspected and meets the requirements for the business to operate on the premises. The requirements may differ for different types of businesses occupying the same space. Therefore, even if another business previously inhabited the same commercial space, the location may require a new certificate of occupancy. A certificate is issued only after the building has been inspected and met construction, plumbing, and electrical requirements. Businesses are often required to display the certificate where it can be viewed by employees and customers. A certificate can be revoked if a building inspection discovers violations of the building code.

Public Safety In some cities, the police department may issue a permit to businesses that impact public safety. Affected businesses include those selling adult products, peddlers, entertainment businesses, secondhand dealers, solicitors, pawnbrokers, taxis, etc. The requirements vary from city to city.

Health Permit Inspectors examine retail facilities where food and drink are handled, stored, served, or sold. This process is meant to ensure that food is properly handled, adequately cooked, and maintained in a sanitary environment. This protects consumers from food-borne illnesses.

State Requirements

There are a variety of permits and licenses required by state agencies. Some of the most widely held requirements are listed here. Your business may require additional licenses.

Environment Environmental regulations are often set at the federal level but enforced by state and local governments. In many communities, the city or county health department is responsible for enforcing laws related to environmental

Act, which affects most businesses. However, some businesses do need to obtain licenses and prove their compliance with federal regulations. Businesses involved in alcohol, meat, drugs, tobacco, firearms, and broadcast communications may require a federal license. Federal licensing is more likely in an industry that is highly regulated by the government.

Americans with Disabilities Act The **Americans with Disabilities Act (ADA)** impacts businesses of all sizes. The ADA guarantees equal opportunity for individuals with disabilities in public accommodations, employment, transportation, state and local government services, and telecommunications. It affects your business if you have 15 or more employees or provide products or services to the public.

Employers Under the provisions of the ADA, employment discrimination is prohibited against individuals with disabilities who are qualified for employment. A qualified individual with a disability is a person who meets the skill, experience, education, or other requirements of a position that is held or sought by the individual, and who can perform the essential functions of the position with or without reasonable accommodation. A **reasonable accommodation** is any modification to a job or the work environment that will enable a qualified applicant or employee with a disability to apply for or hold a position. Reasonable accommodations include making existing employee facilities accessible to and usable by an individual with a disability, modifying work schedules, and acquiring or modifying equipment. An employer is not required to make accommodations if they would impose an undue hardship on the operation of the business. *Undue hardship* is an action that would require significant difficulty or expense for the business. The difficulty level and expense are rated by the employer's size, income, and resources. Therefore, a large business would be required to make more accommodations than a small business because the smaller business makes less money and has fewer resources available. Tax credits (subtracted from your tax liability after you calculate your taxes) and tax deductions (subtracted from your total income before taxes to establish your taxable income) are available to assist businesses in complying with the ADA. Consult a legal or tax professional for more information.

Public Accommodations Even as a sole proprietor with no employees, you will be impacted by the ADA if you are a public accommodation. A **public accommodation** is a private business that provides goods or services to the public. This includes businesses such as restaurants, hotels, and retail stores. If you own, operate, lease, or lease to a business that serves the public, you will be responsible for meeting ADA requirements. You will be obligated to meet requirements for existing facilities and ensure that regulations are met when a facility is altered or constructed.

According to the ADA, if you own or operate a building that serves the public, you must remove any physical barriers that prevent accessibility as long as it is readily achievable to do so. The determination of *readily achievable* is based on the size, income, and resources of the business. Therefore, large businesses are expected to meet the requirements faster and more fully than smaller businesses. For example, a small business located in an older building may not have the finances to install an elevator that would provide access to a second floor or there may not be room to build a ramp that would provide access to the building from the sidewalk. However, businesses are expected to make changes to comply with the ADA as resources become available.

Architectural barriers are one of the first areas in which a business should make changes. Architectural barriers include stairs outside the entrance of the building, parking spaces that are too narrow, counters that are too high, and checkout lanes that are too narrow. Accessible parking spaces must be located as close to the building as possible on a flat area. An additional area should be provided next to the parking space that can be used by a vehicle equipped with a wheelchair lift. If the building has steps at the entrance, the business should provide an alternate entrance, build a ramp, or provide alternatives such as curbside service to customers with mobility impairments.

After a customer is inside the building, additional barriers should be removed. Each aisle should be a minimum of 36" wide and a 3×3 feet turning space is needed where turns are necessary. Merchandise or displays should not block or restrict movement in the aisle. If an individual in a wheelchair cannot reach a specific area in the business, staff must be available to provide assistance by reaching the merchandise or bringing it to the customer. Again, tax credits and deductions are available to comply with ADA requirements. For information about additional ADA requirements and more detailed information, consult your local library. For information about tax credits and deductions, consult a lawyer or tax professional.

Firearms Federal law requires that firearms dealers, manufacturers, and importers, as well as ammunition manufacturers and importers, obtain federal licenses to operate. A firearms dealer is any business that sells firearms at wholesale or retail, repairs firearms or certain components of firearms, or operates as a pawnbroker. To obtain a federal firearms dealer license, file an application with the Department of the Treasury, Bureau of Alcohol, Tobacco and Firearms or visit their web site at www.atf.treas.gov.

Television and Radio Stations The Federal Communications Commission (FCC) issues licenses to television and radio broadcasters. Regulations ensure that broadcasters serve the public interest, but the agency does not select the programming to be broadcast. It grants licenses to new stations based on the needs of the community and the engineering standards that prevent interference between stations. Only stations that broadcast over the air fall under the FCC. Cable stations are not included.

Changing Regulations

As a business owner and a citizen, business regulations are not only yours to follow, they are yours to establish. Stay informed. If regulations are unreasonable, your participation in government affairs that pertain to the business environment can have a positive impact on your industry. If industries require more regulations, your participation can have a positive impact on your community. Either way, knowing about regulations that affect your business is your responsibility. Read your local newspaper, magazines about your industry, and current news publications. Join local business associations. Take an active role in your local government. Vote on all issues that affect your business and your community.

Hypothetical Scenario

Sophia Gabriel found an ideal location for her bakery in a suburban area not far from her home. She plans to prepare and bake the products and sell them to commuters traveling to work in the city. The site also provides a unique alcove that is large enough to hold several small tables and chairs. In the future, Sophia thinks she will offer a comfortable setting for customers to spend a few minutes eating breakfast and chatting with friends. Before she makes any final plans, she decides to investigate the local regulations that affect her business and identify any licenses she has to obtain based on her business activities and location.

Prepare Your Manufacturing Site

When you prepare and cook a meal in your kitchen at home, you want all of the ingredients and kitchen tools where you can easily reach them. This is why you don't keep the refrigerator in the guest bedroom and the frying pan in the coat closet. When you prepare the layout for your manufacturing business, you must consider the same factors—convenience and efficiency.

Convenience and Efficiency

Some products are assembled in long assembly lines that may measure a mile in length. Individuals add components at several stations along the length of the assembly line. Other products are assembled in one location by a group of people who add small components and test the product as it is assembled.

A common theory used to manufacture products is known as **Just-In-Time** (JIT). In a JIT production environment, components arrive at a workstation when they are needed. This decreases the amount of time needed to manufacture an item because time is not wasted in moving, storing, and moving components repeatedly. It increases convenience and efficiency because parts are available when and where they are needed. It reduces the amount of storage space needed because components are used as they are produced and the product moves steadily through the assembly process. The JIT process also reduces the time that money is tied up in inventory.

Before you design the layout of your manufacturing site, you must ask a few questions about how the product is manufactured. Design considerations will include the delivery and storage of components, the order in which the components are assembled, the size of each assembly station, the time that the product spends at each station, and the method used to ship the finished product. The answers to these questions should determine the placement of each workstation.

Delivery and Storage of Components For the highest level of efficiency, components should be stored as close as possible to the place where they will be used. This is particularly true if the components are large or heavy. If the components are very heavy, such as a large engine, a manufacturer may install tracks on the ceiling to maneuver components into place. If components are smaller and production is steady, you can predict the number of components that will be needed at each workstation during a day or work shift. If the entire supply of available components cannot be stored near the station where they will be used, store the number of components that will be used during the specific time period near the workstation, reducing the number of deliveries that must be made.

Assembly Order Create a flowchart, as shown in Figure 7.1, which identifies the order in which the product is assembled. Use this flowchart to identify the order in which the product passes through each workstation. A station that performs a task should be located immediately after the station completing the previous task.

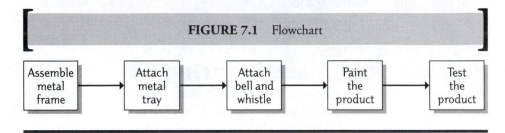

FIGURE 7.1 Flowchart

You can think of the assembly process as a group of tasks. The workstations needed for each group of tasks should be located close together. Draw a map of the assembly line. Number each workstation to identify its order in the assembly line. Use a ruler to draw a line between each station that shows the path the product will take through the assembly line as shown in Figure 7.2. If your assembly line is efficient, the line will not cross itself or pass through a workstation unnecessarily.

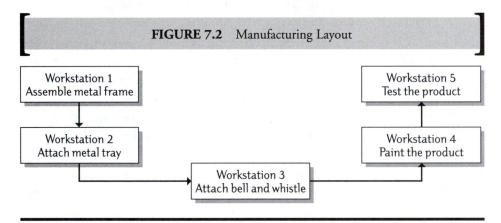

FIGURE 7.2 Manufacturing Layout

A common mistake made by manufacturers with more than one assembly line is grouping similar equipment together without considering the most efficient path through the assembly process. They get stuck on the logic that similar equipment should be placed together. In fact, the path of the product through the assembly line is more important than grouping similar machines or workers with similar tasks. To test the efficiency of your assembly line, calculate the time that the product will spend at each workstation and the time spent moving the product from one station to the next. If too much time is required to move components to the workstations, consider establishing smaller storage areas closer to the workstation needing the component.

Production scheduling identifies the steps in a manufacturing process, the time required to complete each step, and the sequence of the steps. Today, production scheduling is often done by sophisticated software. To calculate the most efficient sequence, schedule future production and monitor the progress during the manufacturing process.

Assembly Stations A workstation is designed to complete a specific task in the assembly process. Therefore, more than one worker may use each workstation. It should be equipped to handle the task as efficiently as possible. If several workers are required for the task, the workstation should enable the workers to act together as a team without getting in each other's way. Components should be available when they are needed. When the product is ready to move to the next workstation, all workers at this station should have completed their tasks.

Handling of Finished Products When assembly is complete, the finished product will be inspected and packaged. It should be ready to move to your warehouse or loading dock for any further packaging and shipping.

Single Workstations

A single employee or a small team of employees may assemble some products at a single workstation. In this situation, it is important that the components be stored as close as possible to the workstations. The design of each workstation must enable employees to work together without crossing into the space needed by another worker or another task at the same time. The locations of the workstations are affected by the location of other facilities in the building. For example, workstations are usually located near restrooms, drinking fountains, and coffee machines.

Additional Facilities

Even though the main business activity of a manufacturer is making a product, additional business activities are required. Purchasing, shipping, management, and administration are all tasks performed by most businesses, regardless of the main business activity. These functions require space and equipment to be performed correctly. Restrooms are an obvious necessity. Break rooms and a cafeteria are optional for many businesses. The proximity of these facilities to the manufacturing area should be dependent on the frequency with which the facilities are used. For example, a worker who has to walk through the entire building to get to the cafeteria once a day for lunch probably won't complain. A worker who has to walk through the entire building to get to a restroom several times a day will not be happy. Use the following sections to plan the layout of office or retail space in your building.

Hypothetical Scenario

Sophia's new bakery is a type of manufacturing site. The kitchen must be set up for her and another baker to work at the same time. Supplies will be delivered in the afternoon, during the bakery's slow time. For the products to be fresh, baking will begin several hours before the shop opens at 6:00 every weekday morning. To prepare the kitchen layout, Sophia spends hours poring through catalogs, visiting appliance vendors, and mapping out the baking tasks.

Prepare Your Office Site

The interior of your house reveals information about you, such as your personality, hobbies, and priorities. The furniture you select, the colors and decorations you choose, and the ways you use the space present an impression to your visitors. A bright, well-equipped kitchen suggests that you enjoy cooking. A large study dominated by the latest home computer and various high-technology devices implies that you employ the latest advances in entertainment and practical applications.

The interior of your business site also reveals information about your business, such as its work ethics and priorities. The physical arrangement of the office, the equipment, and appearance create an image of your business. Visiting customers and potential employees will judge your business by the impression you create. The amount of work performed by your employees and their willingness to help your business succeed will be affected by the environment in which they work.

Physical Layout

The floor plan of your business site should accommodate and encourage the efficient flow of work between departments and individuals. It should also present a favorable first impression to customers and enable employees to work at their best. Before you begin to plan the layout, consider the business tasks that must be accomplished, the amount of space needed to accomplish each task, and the interaction between departments in your business. This will help you decide how spaces should be allocated and used.

Customers Although it is common wisdom not to judge a book by its cover, the first impression you receive about a business or an individual is often a lasting one. The first impression can be the basis for decisions a potential customer or employee makes about your business. Naturally, you want the first impression your business gives to be positive.

The reception area is the location where customers and potential employees enter your business. It should be located just inside the front entrance so visitors don't wander around the building looking for assistance. The reception area should be located near departments that work with customers or visitors, such as the marketing and personnel departments. There should be access to nearby restrooms and meeting rooms, but employees should not use the area as a main route. Internal meetings that might involve confidential material or heated discussions should not occur near the reception area.

Departments Consider how departments in your business work together. Diagram the flow of material between departments. Departments that interact frequently should be closer to each other than departments that never interact.

Although it is important for each employee to have individual workspace, many resources and workspaces can be shared. For example, items such as photocopiers, scanners, and fax machines may be placed in areas accessed by all employees. It is also common for a department to share a single clerical resource or receptionist.

Members of a single department are usually placed together, but occasionally individual employees may sit together in task groups rather than departments. A

task group may be comprised of individuals from several departments who work together to complete a single task. A task group could include a project manager, several programmers, and a technical writer who are dedicated to creating a customized software package for a single customer. Because the members of this group work closely together, they may be seated together rather than with their separate departments. Assignment to a task group is usually not permanent. The task group is dissolved when the task is completed, so the employees in the task group remain members of their departments.

Employees As a general rule, each employee needs approximately 75 to 100 square feet of workspace. This includes open floor area, room for their equipment, desk, and an equal share of the public aisle outside of their workspace. Generally, each public aisle should be 4 feet wide. This enables employees to move freely and pass each other comfortably as they move from area to area.

Ergonomics The applied science of designing and arranging tools so that they can be used safely and efficiently is **ergonomics.** It includes such diverse activities as investigating the distance you should sit from your computer monitor and designing a comfortable handle for a toothbrush. Because you spend so much of your time working, ergonomics should be a decisive factor in setting up your workspace and the workspaces of your staff. Lawsuits from workplace injuries have been increasing in recent years. Workplace injuries can include severe injuries in a manufacturing environment or repetitive stress injuries from repeating the same motions time after time. The use of ergonomic equipment and principles will protect your employees from injury and your business from lawsuits.

Many modern office environments use cubicles. A **cubicle** is an area surrounded by panels containing surfaces for workspace and equipment and seating designed to be used by a worker or group of workers. Panels are structures, usually covered with fabric or glass, used to separate spaces, support shelves to hold equipment, or create office space. Cubicles are flexible. They can be set up and configured to create workspaces of different sizes and the panels can be easily taken down and moved to reconfigure the workstations in the office as the needs of the business change and grow.

Most office workers use a computer in the performance of their business responsibilities. Consider this when you design your office layout. Use ergonomics to make your staff more comfortable and more efficient. Proper equipment, seating, and lighting will help your employees perform at their best.

Hypothetical Scenario

Although office work is not the primary business activity of Sophia's bakery, it is necessary. Sophia plans to work alone in the office, staying in the office only long enough to do the required paperwork. Still, she spends some time examining and selecting her office furniture and equipment. She believes that doing paperwork is bad enough. She plans to be comfortable and well equipped to complete it as quickly as possible.

Prepare Your Retail Site

Plan the layout of your retail space very carefully. It will have a big impact on the success or failure of your retail business. Customers are more likely to buy items that they see. Therefore, the physical layout of the store should try to move the customer past as much merchandise as possible and the atmosphere should encourage customers to stay.

Physical Layout

The type of layout you choose should be based on the products you sell, the image you want to project, and the type of customer you want to target. Answer the following questions to help you design the appropriate layout:

- **What products do I sell?** Some products are more likely to be purchased if customers spend time browsing or moving slowly through the store, examining an item here or there. A bookstore or gift shop, for example, will make more sales if the layout encourages customers to take their time looking at the merchandise.

- **What image do I want to project?** A store laid out in straight aisles presents a very different image than a store that displays its merchandise in attractive groupings. Straight aisles present an image of efficiency and organization. In contrast, items displayed in groupings have more aesthetic appeal, attracting attention by design, color, and location.

- **Who are my customers?** Demographics such as age and gender will help you design your layout. Demonstration models that can be touched and moved intrigue children. Women are more likely to browse. Men often prefer to enter the store, go directly to the item they want to purchase, take it to the checkout counter, and leave immediately, preferably without coming to a complete stop.

- **When do my customers shop?** If your customers tend to come in on their lunch hour or on their way home from work, they will prefer a predictable, organized layout. Shoppers at this time of day have little time or patience. If you stop at the grocery store on your way home from work, you don't want to guess where the orange juice or milk might be in the store.

The physical layout of your business determines the path that customers will take through your store. Regardless of which layout you choose, the more products customers pass, the more products customers will buy. There are two basic layout designs. With only slight alterations, most retailers use the grid layout and the free flow layout.

Grid Layout Few people would include grocery shopping as one of their favorite recreational activities. Usually, when people go to the grocery store, they have to be there. The cupboards at home are bare or the basic necessities such as bread and milk are gone. They want to buy the items they need as quickly as possible. The task of the retailer in this situation is to create a path that will move customers past as much merchandise as possible. This is why dairy products, fruits and vegetables, and bread, the items purchased most often in a grocery store, are not located near each other between the door and the checkout lane. Customers would buy the few items they need and be done shopping in only a few minutes. Placing these items around the edge of the store ensures that customers will pass from one end of the store to the other. As they shop, they may remember additional items they need or impulsively toss items that look appealing into the cart. The physical layout of the store has added profit for the retailer and provided a more interesting meal for the shopper's future enjoyment.

Most grocery stores, discount stores, and pharmacies use the grid layout shown in Figure 7.3. In a grid layout, counters are placed at right angles to each other. The layout is fairly predictable. Most grocery stores, for example, follow the same pattern. Dairy, meat, bread, and fresh produce are found in the outer aisles. Products are displayed at the end of every aisle and signs encourage shoppers to enter aisles for additional products.

FIGURE 7.3   Grid Layout

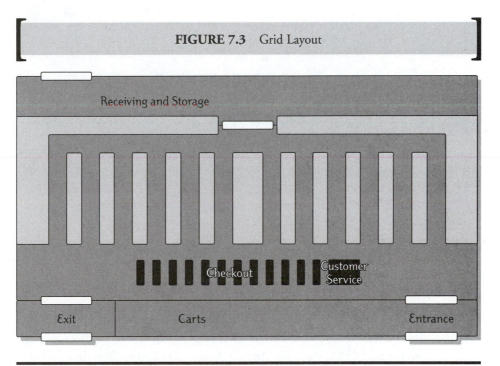

The grid layout has several advantages for retailers. Because the layout is standard, it is cheaper and easier to build. Customers are familiar with the layout, so requests for assistance are minimal. The arrangement is easy to maintain, clean, and restock. All products receive maximum exposure as customers travel up and down each aisle. On the other hand, the arrangement of aisles makes it difficult to create unique displays to attract customer attention. It limits browsing because customers tend to travel through the aisles at a similar pace. A customer who stops to compare products or examine new products creates a traffic jam when other customers try to stop in the same location or pass the browsing customer. Because most of the space is taken up by shelving and merchandise, the choices for décor are limited and one store looks much like another. In fact, once you're inside a grocery store, it is often difficult to tell which retailer you selected.

Free-Flow Layout If you prefer that your customers browse through your merchandise, the free-flow layout is better for you. Specialty stores, boutiques, and gift stores frequently use a free-flow layout. In this layout, merchandise is grouped on freestanding displays. The customer is encouraged to browse, following an unstructured and unpredictable path through the merchandise, pausing or changing direction to examine items that appeal to them. As you can see in Figure 7.4, merchandise displays can form irregular shapes such as semicircles or arches.

FIGURE 7.4　Free-Flow Layout

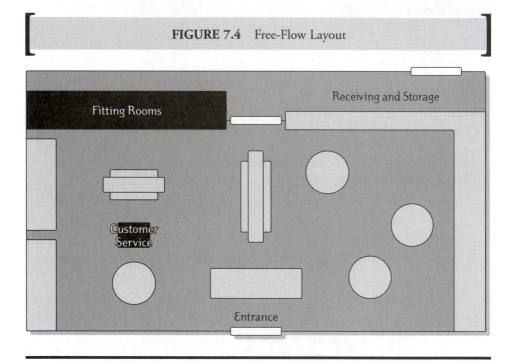

The free-flow layout has advantages for the retailer. The flexibility of the arrangements enables retailers to create unique displays to attract and hold customers' attention, resulting in increased sales. In fact, many consumers have admitted that they made a purchase based on the way a product was displayed. The store and the products are more visually appealing, enabling the retailer to attract foot traffic that would otherwise pass by the store. On the other hand, the display configuration requires more floor space, reducing the number of products that can be displayed. Because products are not well organized and displays are movable, customers could become confused or be unable to find the product they want. The cost of building and maintaining the displays is higher than the displays used in a grid layout.

Layout Variations Small businesses that have customers who move quickly through the business without passing any extensive product displays may want to use a standard layout. These businesses may have only an entrance, a counter, a checkout area, and an exit. A ticket agency or fast-food restaurant would be an excellent candidate for the standard layout.

The boutique layout groups merchandise based on the designer, manufacturer, or a common theme. For example, a department store may group clothing by the designer, creating an area that has only clothing designed by Liz Claiborne. An appliance store may group appliances by manufacturer such as Maytag. Rather than displaying all washing machines made by different manufacturers together, the appliance store will display all appliances made by Maytag together. This encourages customers to purchase all Maytag kitchen appliances to have matching appliances.

Atmosphere

Retailers create an atmosphere to attract customers they believe will purchase their products. The right atmosphere will draw customers into your store, make them comfortable while they're there, and encourage them to purchase your products. The atmosphere is important in creating a unique image for your store that distinguishes it from the other stores that sell similar products. The physical layout contributes to the atmosphere of your store, but other factors work with the physical layout to create the right environment for your customers. Fixtures, décor, and merchandise density help to create the atmosphere.

Fixtures are the physical items used to hold merchandise and create displays. Some fixtures are predictable. Grocery stores display the majority of their merchandise on shelves. Many retailers can project a unique image by using nontraditional fixtures. A retailer who sells bath towels could display the towels on the edge of a bathtub. A florist could use the same bathtub to display floral arrangements, creating a very unique presentation that will make a memorable impression.

Décor includes several aspects of a retailer's physical presentation. Colors and lighting can be used to make the same retail space appear to be very different. Colors create a mood that attracts your target customers. Bright primary colors present a different image than pastels or colors that are muted. Lighting can emphasize specific merchandise or create an image as customers enter the store. A grocery store is usually bright and well lit. A specialty store that sells candles will probably use more subtle lighting designed to imitate candlelight.

Merchandise density is the amount of merchandise displayed or shelved per 1,000 feet. A small high-quality store will display less merchandise per square foot than a similar store selling lower-quality merchandise. If merchandise is crowded on the racks or shelves, it seems that the retailer, and therefore the customer, places a lower value on the products. You will never walk into a jewelry store and see diamond rings crowded onto a shelf. Instead, the rings will be displayed in individual boxes inside a display counter.

Additional factors that affect the atmosphere in a store include sounds and scents. Many stores play background music. The type of music you choose to play should appeal to your target customers. If you choose music that appeals to a young audience, older shoppers may leave before they examine the merchandise. Small specialty shops may use scents to interest customers in their products. A candle shop may burn scented candles. A florist will usually have a light floral scent. Within a department store, the perfume and makeup department may have a light perfume scent, attracting customers and promoting the perfume they sell.

Hypothetical Scenario

Many of the characteristics of Sophia's bakery will appeal to customers. The red brick alcove with its long windows faces the east, allowing the morning sun to shine into the store. The smell of the baked goods will make anyone hungry. Sophia adds flavored gourmet coffee to the menu to further entice customers when they enter the store.

Prepare Your Home Office

There are many advantages to operating your business in your home. The commute is short and the coffee is always fresh. However, there is much more to setting up an office in your home than buying a coffee pot. To properly set up and equip a home office, you will need to start by clearly defining the area you have chosen. Ideally, your workspace will be located in a separate room. If this is not possible, you will need to separate the space by other means. Use your desk to identify your office space or set up screens that will visually separate the area.

Regardless of whether your office is located in your home or in an office building, you will need many of the same items. When you purchase your desk and equipment, choose ergonomic options that will make it easier and more comfortable for you to work. Purchase files and file cabinets to organize the materials your business will need. Select lighting that will enable you to work comfortably. Use task lighting or lamps to light your work area clearly.

Other items you may need include proper seating, additional phone lines, and communication devices such as a fax machine and modem. An additional phone line enables you to have a phone number for your business that is different from your home phone number. You may also need a phone line for Internet access or your fax machine.

If customers will visit your home office, your office should have furniture for them to use. If you want to serve refreshments, consider purchasing a small refrigerator and coffee maker for your office. This separates your professional and personal activities by ensuring that you do not use your private property or kitchen for your business guests.

Hypothetical Scenario

Sophia dislikes paperwork. Because her days at the bakery will start very early, she doesn't plan to linger after the shop is closed just to do paperwork. She decides to set up an office in her home where she can work in the late afternoon and evening. This space will not be visited by vendors or customers, so she decides to design the space to please herself. A large attractive desk, a comfortable easy chair, and a small stereo system provide the comforts of home and meet her office needs. Because she plans to complete paperwork at home and at the bakery, Sophia decided to purchase a laptop computer that she can use in either location.

Technology Insights

Personal Assistant

When you are setting up your new business site, you will talk to many suppliers, visit many stores, and set many appointments. Without a personal assistant, it may be difficult to track so much information. When you need help to maintain your schedule, you can turn to an electronic assistant. In 1998, Palm Computing introduced the first Pilot, a small electronic device that could replace your paper calendar, sticky notes, and address book. Although it had enough computing power to perform many of the scheduling activities you would normally track on a full-size computer, it was small enough to fit into a pocket and easy to use. As the devices grew in popularity, presidential candidates, corporate executives, and high school students purchased them to keep their busy social and professional lives on track and manageable. Today's generation of handheld computing devices is smaller, more powerful, and just as easy to use. The devices can communicate with your desktop computer, access the Internet, and respond to voice commands. In a competitive business world, this device can help you stay on top of your communications and activities.

Think Critically Identify the information you would track with a handheld device.

CHAPTER REVIEW

There are many tasks you must complete to prepare your business for the grand opening. Before your business can open, you must acquire any necessary permits and licenses and meet the requirements of any governmental regulations. Regulations may be based on the size of your business or the type of business activities it performs. For example, a restaurant will have to meet requirements that are different from those established for a clothing retailer. Requirements are set by local, state, and federal regulations. Contact the regulatory agencies in your geographic area to determine the regulations that apply to your business.

The type of business you operate determines the physical layout of your business and the specific business activities it performs. To prepare a layout for a manufacturing business, you must consider convenience and efficiency. The storage facilities and the steps in the manufacturing process determine the location of the workstations.

An office site has different priorities than a manufacturing site. The location of individual workstations should be determined by the flow of work between departments and individuals. Employees require the proper equipment and enough space to work efficiently and comfortably. When making decisions about workstations and equipment, incorporate ergonomic principles into your choices.

A retail site has many specific requirements. The type of products determines the physical layout, the image you want to project, your customers, and the way in which your customers shop. The purpose of the store's layout is to guide customers past the most merchandise possible. The most common physical layouts are the grid layout and the free-flow layout. The grid layout is rigid and predictable. The free-flow layout is unpredictable and encourages customer browsing. The physical layout, combined with fixtures, décor, merchandise density, color, sounds, and scents, creates an atmosphere designed to attract your target customers.

Although it seems simple to set up a home office, many of the decisions you make are similar to the choices you would make if you leased space in an office building. You must separate your office space from your personal space and purchase the equipment you need. Again, ergonomics should be an important consideration in your selections.

USE BUSINESS TERMS

Fill in the blanks with the appropriate term.

Americans with Disabilities Act (ADA)   merchandise density
certificate of occupancy   production scheduling
cubicle   public accommodation
ergonomics   reasonable accommodation
fixtures   seller's permit
Just-In-Time (JIT) manufacturing   task group

1. The ___?___ requires businesses that provide products or services to the public to provide accessibility to customers with mobility impairments.
2. Many employees in office sites work in a(n) ___?___ that holds their work-station and equipment.
3. ___?___ selections identify the most comfortable and efficient equipment a worker should use.
4. Unusual ___?___ can create an appealing atmosphere for a specialty retailer.
5. If a store's ___?___ is high, it implies that the retailer does not place much value on the merchandise.
6. A(n) ___?___ consists of members from several departments assigned to complete a single business activity.
7. A characteristic of ___?___ is the delivery of components when they are needed.

TEST YOUR READING

8. What is the basis for many of the licenses issued to businesses?
9. Whom should you contact to obtain local licenses?
10. What does a certificate of occupancy indicate?
11. How is a qualified individual defined by the Americans with Disabilities Act?
12. Provide an example of a reasonable accommodation for a disabled employee.
13. How is it determined that a business must make additional efforts to provide physical accessibility to customers?
14. How can you affect business regulations?
15. What are the main factors you must consider when preparing a layout for a manufacturing business?
16. What factors should you consider before determining the physical layout of an office site?
17. How can choosing ergonomic equipment protect your business?
18. What are the characteristics of a grid layout?
19. How can you define the physical space in your home office?

THINK CRITICALLY ABOUT BUSINESS

20. Select a local business. Identify the licenses this business had to obtain before it could open.
21. Select a nearby business establishment. Evaluate the site for any features that would make it difficult for an individual with a physical disability to visit the site.
22. Contact a nearby business site. Ask a company representative for a tour of the site. Determine the factors that influenced the physical layout of the site.
23. Visit a nearby retail establishment. Identify the layout and describe the factors that create the retailer's atmosphere. Describe why this atmosphere attracts customers.

REAL-LIFE BUSINESS

Buddy's Carpet & Flooring

For a business started in a barn, Buddy's Carpet & Flooring has become quite a success. In 1974, Leif Rozin established the Carpet Barn in an undeveloped area of Fairfield, Ohio. In the barn, Rozin used a trailer as the office and showroom. Eventually, Fairfield grew to encompass the barn holding the business.

At the time it was established, the Carpet Barn specialized in working with builders. As the business grew, Rozin purchased land in Fairfield and built a store that still operates today. In 1983, Buddy Kallick joined the business as a partner. This enabled the business to expand to selling carpet to retail customers. The business was renamed Buddy's Carpet Barn.

The business continued to grow and opened retail stores in other Ohio cities, including Cincinnati, Dayton, Columbus, Canton, Akron, and Cleveland. Eventually, it expanded into Florence, Kentucky, and Indianapolis, Indiana. Citizens in these cities became very familiar with the commercials for Buddy's Carpet, which was renamed as the company expanded into Cleveland, where another business used the word barn in its name. To distinguish the two companies, Buddy's Carpet dropped barn from its name.

In 2000, the business changed its name again by adding the word flooring. This change was the result of expanding their business into alternative flooring choices such as tile and laminates. Today, the business is the second-largest privately held specialty flooring company in America.

The original owners, Rozin and Kallick, sold the business to an investment group. Although the founders are no longer owners, they have remained consultants and Kallick continues to produce the commercials so familiar to consumers in the area.

Think Critically

1. How did the store acquire such a good location?
2. Why did the name of the business change several times?
3. Why has the company continued to produce similar commercials even though the ownership of the business has changed?
4. How did the company continue to expand?

CHAPTER  8

Select Suppliers

GOALS

- ◆   Develop a channel of distribution for your products
- ◆   Create a merchandise plan
- ◆   Set a merchandise budget
- ◆   Identify and choose your suppliers

Kevin Shen combined his artistic skills and technological expertise when he designed a web page for a classmate. He enjoyed the experience and received many compliments on the web page's appearance. Kevin decided to investigate the possibility of developing web pages as a business.

Develop a Channel of Distribution

Every business has suppliers. No matter what product or service you sell, you need to buy raw materials, tools, or business supplies to operate your business successfully. A landscaper buys lawn mowers, gardening tools, and plants. A restaurant buys ingredients, utensils, and restaurant furniture. A freelance accountant buys software, a computer, and office furniture. A retailer buys items to sell to customers. A delivery company buys trucks, gasoline, and uniforms. Choosing suppliers who will deliver quality products on a schedule that meets your needs time after time is critical to the success of your business.

Distribution Channels

Products do not magically appear on your doorstep or the doorsteps of your customers. The process of moving a product to the final consumer is **distribution.** The process varies from business to business and product to product. The distribution process for eggs is different from the distribution process for a book. Depending on the distance the product travels, the number of businesses needed to distribute the product, and the nature of the product itself, distribution can take minutes, days, or weeks.

Products can be shipped on planes, trains, ships, and delivery trucks. Some products can even be delivered electronically from the seller's computer directly to the buyer's computer. The path of the product from the producer to the consumer is the **channel of distribution.** A channel of distribution can be simple or complicated. A product may go directly from the manufacturer to the consumer or it may pass through several companies to reach the consumer. Businesses that facilitate the transfer of goods from the manufacturer to the consumer are known as middlemen. A **middleman** includes any business that helps to distribute the producer's goods to consumers. Middlemen include retailers, wholesalers, and agents. The complexity of a channel of distribution increases as more middlemen become involved.

Producer to Consumer   The simplest method of distribution is **direct distribution,** the sale of products directly from the manufacturer to the consumer as shown in Figure 8.1. In the past, many companies sent sales representatives from door to door in residential neighborhoods. When a consumer answered the door, the sales representative gave a standard presentation and demonstrated the product. Products sold this way included vacuum cleaners, encyclopedias, life insurance, and siding for houses. Services such as music lessons and lawn care were also sold directly to consumers.

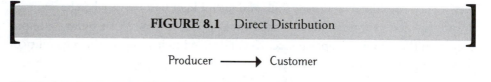

FIGURE 8.1   Direct Distribution

Producer ⟶ Customer

Over time, door-to-door selling has virtually disappeared, beginning its decline in popularity during World War II. Today, a few companies sell products such as storage containers and makeup directly to consumers through parties, friends, and work associates. Groups like the Girl Scouts regularly sell items from door to door.

That doesn't mean direct distribution no longer exists. In fact, it has become more common in the past few years, primarily due to the Internet. Many producers have established web sites where individual consumers can order products directly from the producer.

Direct distribution also occurs in other situations. A farmer who builds a roadside stand sells produce directly to passing consumers. Many manufacturers establish their own stores, usually attached to their factories, where products are sold directly to consumers. This provides an excellent opportunity for consumers to obtain products at greatly reduced prices. In fact, some people make plans to visit manufacturers' stores while they are traveling. Many manufacturers produce catalogs, which enable them to inform potential customers about their products and encourage consumers to buy the products directly from them.

Distribution through Retailers Many producers choose not to sell directly to consumers for a variety of reasons. Retailers can reach a much larger group of consumers than a single producer can reach. A producer would rather deal with a single retailer than the hundreds of consumers the retailer handles. For example, many consumers buy combs every year. If every person who bought a comb showed up at the gate of the factory to make a purchase, the manufacturer would be overwhelmed. Additionally, consumers who do not live near the factory would not travel to the site to make a purchase, so many potential sales would be lost. As you can see in Figure 8.2, it is much easier for a producer to sell thousands of combs to a limited number of retailers who can then sell the combs to thousands of consumers in grocery stores and convenience stores across the country.

FIGURE 8.2   Distribution through a Retailer

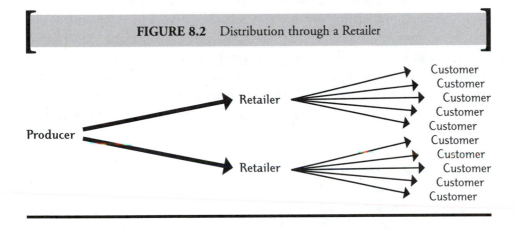

It is easy to see that producers and consumers benefit from this arrangement. Producers are able to sell much larger quantities and consumers are able to purchase products at locations that are more convenient. Retailers also benefit from their positions as middlemen. When retailers buy from producers, they are **buying direct.** The retailer is able to buy the latest products at low prices, without any additional cost from a middleman. Also, a producer may create advertising materials, such as signs or television commercials, that can be used by the retailer. However, many manufacturers will sell their products only in large quantities. For retailers to take advantage of buying direct, they have to purchase a large quantity of the product. This may not be reasonable or affordable for small retailers. For example, a large chain of convenience stores may be able to sell 1,000 combs in a few months. A small mom-and-pop grocery store might sell only five or six combs in a month. Purchasing 1,000 combs would not be a wise business decision for the small grocery store.

Distribution through Wholesalers You can already see the problem faced by small retailers who do not have the financial resources or physical space to purchase and store a large quantity of a single product. If you think again of the small mom-and-pop grocery store, you realize that they carry a fairly wide assortment of products. They sell items such as breakfast cereal, toilet paper, newspapers, and milk, as well as combs. Most have very little storage area behind the retail section of the store. How does the store manage to carry such a large variety of items?

Where there is a need, a business will usually be established to fill the need. In this case, a wholesaler fills the need. A **wholesaler** is a middleman that buys directly from a producer and sells to retailers or large commercial users. Usually, a wholesaler purchases large quantities of a product directly from the producer, gaining the price advantage of buying direct. The wholesaler stores the products in large warehouses. When it receives an order from a retailer, the wholesaler repackages the products in smaller quantities and ships them to the retailer. For example, a wholesaler may purchase a case of combs that contains 10 boxes of 100 combs. When a small retailer orders 100 combs from the wholesaler, the wholesaler opens the case and ships a single box containing 100 combs to the retailer.

Of course, the retailer pays for the wholesaler's services by paying the wholesaler more for each comb than the wholesaler paid. In this situation, it is the wholesaler that gains the financial advantage of buying direct from the producer. The retailer is the wholesaler's customer, paying more for the product than the wholesaler paid so that the wholesaler earns a profit. In turn, the retailer charges the final customer more than it paid the wholesaler so the retailer also earns a profit. Each middleman between the producer and the final customer earns a profit from its business transactions.

Adding a wholesaler into the distribution channel is beneficial to all the parties. The producer deals with fewer businesses, as shown in Figure 8.3. The wholesaler provides a valuable service by distributing smaller quantities of the product, thereby increasing the number of retailers that can sell the product. This increases potential sales for the producer. Smaller retailers can carry a wider assortment of products because they can purchase the items in smaller quantities.

FIGURE 8.3   Distribution through a Wholesaler

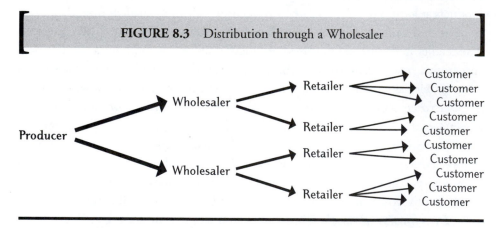

It is obvious that small retailers can benefit from working with a wholesaler. There are also advantages for medium and large retailers.

- Wholesalers are often able to deliver merchandise faster than a producer. Quantities stored in their warehouses can be shipped quickly when an order is received.

- Some wholesalers offer credit to retailers. This enables retailers to buy more merchandise than they could afford to purchase with their available cash.
- A single wholesaler often carries items made by several producers. This enables retailers to negotiate with one wholesaler rather than have to approach several producers.
- A retailer can place small orders at frequent intervals, reducing the need to store a large quantity of a single product.
- Some retailers can eliminate the need to store any products. For example, a furniture retailer could keep only samples at the retail establishment. When a customer buys a sofa, the retailer asks the wholesaler to ship the sofa directly to the customer.

Distribution through an Agent The producers, wholesalers, and retailers actually own the product at some point in the distribution process. A wholesaler purchases the products from the producer. A retailer purchases the goods from the producer or a wholesaler. The consumer purchases the goods from the retailer. An agent is considered to be a middleman in the distribution channel that never actually owns the product. An **agent** is an individual or business hired by the producer to find buyers for the product. The agent is usually paid a commission when the buyer is found and the sale occurs. This is much more common for the sale of imported goods rather than domestic products. A producer might hire an agent to represent it in a country in which it does not have a local office and may not be familiar with the regulations, culture, or business environment in the country. Although the agent represents the producer, the agent does not own the merchandise. Therefore, when negotiating with potential buyers, the agent may not have the authority to change the price of the product.

Your Place in the Distribution Channel

As a business, your company has a role in distributing products or services. The activities you perform, the items you purchase, and the businesses and individuals who are your customers determine your place in the distribution channel.

Many businesses provide the products and services that make physical distribution possible. They drive trucks, sort and deliver packages, and manufacture boxes and envelopes. Without businesses such as these, physical distribution could not occur.

Hypothetical Scenario

Kevin Shen discovered that many small businesses are entering the business arena by creating web pages that market their products directly to their potential customers. Kevin decides to follow the same tactics. He designs a web page that describes the services he can provide and examples of his work. He incorporates several design elements that demonstrate his abilities and provide a link to the web page he created for his friend. Kevin hopes that this direct approach will attract potential customers.

Create a Merchandise Plan

Success can happen accidentally, like winning the lottery because the winning numbers match some arrangement of your birth date, your anniversary, and your high school locker combination. For most businesses though, success is the result of planning.

Purpose of a Merchandise Plan

Your business plan describes your business, your objectives, and your business activities. It describes the products you buy and sell in a general way. If you are a retailer or a wholesaler, the business plan does not provide enough details to manage your merchandise. You need a merchandise plan. A **merchandise plan** describes the specific items you acquire to sell in each department at each retail establishment. For example, your business plan may state that your retail business sells women's clothing. Your merchandise plan specifies the number of sweaters, skirts, and other items you plan to buy and sell. It identifies characteristics such as the brand, size, and color of each product.

The information in your merchandise plan helps you create a merchandise budget. The plan tells you what you need to purchase. The budget tells you how much it will cost. Making a plan helps you control your spending by purchasing the right quantities.

Collecting Information for the Merchandise Plan

In a small business, the owner writes the merchandise plan and prepares the budget. In a larger retail business, each division may have a merchandise manager who prepares the plan for a division. The merchandise manager is knowledgeable about the products in the division and uses the knowledge, sales information, and estimates of future sales to prepare a merchandise plan.

In large businesses, more individuals are involved in the planning process. The individual who prepares the plan uses input from several sources that are closer to the merchandise and the customers who purchase the merchandise. Each division may have one or more **buyers,** individuals who negotiate with suppliers to purchase the needed merchandise. The only job of a buyer is selecting and buying merchandise.

If a retailer has several establishments, each store manager may report merchandise information, including current sales, to a district manager who works at the corporate headquarters. The district manager is responsible for merchandise at all of the stores within a specific geographic area. For example, a store manager in Cleveland reports the store's merchandise information to the district manager. The district manager collects the merchandise information from stores in Cleveland, Columbus, Dayton, and Cincinnati. The merchandise plan, which is used by the buyers to purchase the necessary merchandise, is prepared at the company's headquarters after the merchandise information from all the stores is combined and evaluated.

Preparing the Merchandise Plan

To develop a merchandise plan that is thorough and effective, the merchandise needs of every department in every store must be met. The planner prepares the merchandise plan for four levels of retail, listed below from the most general to the most specific.

- **Business**—As a retail business, profitability is the basic goal of each establishment. The divisions and departments must work together to increase the profit earned by the business.

- **Divisions within the Business**—A **division** is an operating unit of a business. In a retail environment, a division might be based on a geographic area, such as the northern region, or a broad product classification, such as clothing and home furnishings. In a nonretail business, a division may focus on the tasks associated with a particular product, including manufacturing, marketing, and service.

- **Departments within the Divisions**—In a retail business, a **department** is a section of a store that handles a particular type of merchandise. A department store, for example, has departments that specialize in children's clothing, women's clothing, and men's clothing. In a nonretail business, a department is usually focused on a single business activity such as accounting, marketing, or customer service.

- **Merchandise Classifications within Departments**—**Stockkeeping units** (SKUs) are merchandise classifications based on the characteristics of the merchandise such as type, material, color, price, size, or brand.

A merchandise plan must consider the needs of the consumers and the capabilities of the business to purchase the merchandise and perform the necessary business tasks. Merchandise planning can be performed from the top down or from the bottom up.

Top-Down Planning Merchandise planning that starts at the most general level is top-down planning. The planner sets the initial goals for merchandise, sales, and expenses for the entire business. The goals for the business are divided among the divisions, departments, and merchandise classifications.

Planners who use this method are looking at the big picture first. After setting the goals for the business, the merchandise, sales, and expenses are distributed to the smaller business units. The objectives do not have to be distributed evenly. In fact, they usually aren't distributed evenly to all business areas.

Bottom-Up Planning Merchandise planning that starts at the most specific level is bottom-up planning. The planner sets the initial goals for merchandise, sales, and expenses for the departments, divisions, and store in the specified sequence. When these goals are added, the sum is the goal for the business.

In bottom-up planning, information is collected at the lowest level. Information about sales and stock level are collected for each merchandise classification first. Next, information about departments and divisions is gathered and passed up to the planner. The information is totaled and the sum becomes the total for the entire store. This approach is usually more accurate than top-down planning because the information is gathered from store personnel who are most familiar with the merchandise and the customers they serve.

Blend In reality, most retailers use a blend of the two methods. Setting an overall goal for the store first provides a sense of direction for the business. Collecting information from the people who deal most closely with the merchandise and the customers provides a realistic picture of how the merchandise is selected by consumers and sold by store personnel. Thus, the most accurate information is provided from different management levels. This realistic approach gives a business a much better chance of success than relying on a single method. More information leads to a better plan.

Writing Objectives for the Merchandise Plan

The order in which merchandise objectives are written and the way they are determined depends on the type of stock planning method the planner uses. Top-down and bottom-up planning may produce different results, leading to differences in objectives.

Objectives are written for each division, department, and merchandise classification. For example, the clothing division may have an objective to increase sales by 12 percent. In top-down planning, the division's objective determines the objectives for the departments in the division. Based on the size of each department and its previous contributions to the division's income, the men's clothing department must increase sales 15 percent, the women's clothing department must increase sales 6 percent, and the children's clothing department must increase sales by 2 percent. Department objectives are related to the objectives for merchandise classifications.

Regardless of how an objective is determined, a written objective should be easy to understand and written clearly for the unit assigned to complete the objective. It must include the criteria to measure success, the measurement method, and the time period to achieve the objective.

A merchandise plan is usually written for a six-month time period. The first six months includes February through July or spring and summer. The second six months includes August through January or fall and winter. However, it takes time to purchase and receive merchandise, particularly imported merchandise. Therefore, the merchandise plan for spring and summer is actually prepared and finalized the previous August and the merchandise plan for fall and winter is prepared and finalized the previous February. For example, the merchandise plan prepared in August 2005 will identify the merchandise that will be stocked and sold in February through July 2006.

Planners often make errors when planning this far in advance. Planning errors include ordering too much, ordering too few, and ordering the wrong products. These errors can have a tremendous impact on the retailer's profits. Although the merchandise plan is developed to meet the needs of the business, those needs are created and driven by the needs of consumers.

Calculating the Amount of Merchandise to Purchase

The merchandise plan calculates the amount of merchandise you should have in inventory at the beginning of each month. If you could simply order the same amount of every item you sell, it wouldn't be necessary to plan your sales and purchases.

However, different products sell at different rates. For example, a hardware store sells more hammers than lawnmowers. If the retailer purchased 20 hammers and lawnmowers every month, the hammers would be sold but unsold lawnmowers would soon take up every inch of the available retail space and parking lot. Buying too much merchandise ties up your funds and requires storage space. Buying too little merchandise results in lost sales. If you order too few lawnmowers and find yourself without lawnmowers in stock, the consumer who wants to buy one will turn to another retailer. Purchasing the right quantity is a critical decision. To calculate the correct quantity to purchase, you need several pieces of data, including the average stock figure, stock turn rate, sales, ending inventory levels, and beginning inventory levels.

Note: You can use the retail price (amount the customer will pay), cost price (amount you paid), or number of units to calculate the value of the inventory, average stock, and stock turn rate. However, you must be consistent in the type of data you use in all of the following calculations.

Step 1—Average Stock The first value is the **average stock figure,** which is the average amount of merchandise you have in inventory during the year. Retailers count their inventory 13 times during the year—on the first of every month and at the end of the year. To calculate the average stock figure, add the stock in inventory on the first of every month to the stock in inventory at the end of the year. Divide the sum by 13. The result will be the average value of the stock in your inventory. At any specific time during the month, your inventory is worth more or less than this amount.

Average Stock Calculation
(First-of-Month Inventory + End-of-Year Inventory) ÷ 13 = Average Stock

Step 2—Stock Turn Rate The average value of your stock is used to determine the **stock turn rate,** the number of times the average stock is sold during the year. The stock turn rate identifies the rate at which you sell your inventory, which fluctuates during the year. The stock turn rate is a hypothetical number because you never sell your entire inventory at one time unless your shelves are completely empty several times a year, which should never happen with proper merchandise planning.

Some items sell faster than others and some products are sold only during certain times of the year. The stock turn rate is useful in merchandise planning because it uses the average stock value in the calculation. Use the same type of value (retail price, cost price, or number of units) to calculate your stock turn rate. Use the following calculation that matches the type of value used in the average stock calculation.

Stock Turn Rate Calculation
Based on retail price:
    Annual Net Sales ÷ Average Stock = Stock Turn Rate

Based on cost:
    Annual Cost of Stock Sold ÷ Average Stock = Stock Turn Rate

Based on quantity:
    Annual Number of Units Sold ÷ Average Stock = Stock Turn Rate

Use the following example. You know your average stock figure and your net sales. If your average stock figure is $3,000 and the value of your net sales last year was $12,000, your stock turn rate is four.

Annual Net Sales ÷ Average Stock = Stock Turn Rate
$12,000 ÷ $3,000 = 4

How do you know if this is a good stock turn rate? Investigate the average stock turn rate in your industry and use the knowledge to set goals for your business. If this is your first year of operation, use your projected sales information and target stock turn rate to calculate the stock you should have in inventory.

Step 3—Ending Inventory Time Period To determine the amount of merchandise you need to purchase, you need to identify the number of items you plan to sell and the number of items you want in inventory at the end of the month. The ending inventory is based on your stock turn rate. The higher your stock turn rate, the less merchandise you need in inventory at the end of each month. To calculate the ending inventory you need, divide 12 months by the turn rate. This identifies the number of months that the merchandise in inventory should be able to fill sales.

Ending Inventory Time Period Calculation

12 ÷ Stock Turn Rate = Ending Inventory Time Period

Use the following example. If your turn rate is six, you should keep enough inventory in stock at the end of each month to satisfy two months of sales (12 months ÷ 6 stock turn rate = 2 months).

Step 4—Ending Inventory Novice retailers often have trouble deciding how much merchandise they should have in stock. To determine the amount of merchandise you should have in inventory at the end of each month, simply multiply your projected monthly sales by the ending inventory time period.

Ending Inventory Calculation

Sales × Ending Inventory Time Period = Ending Inventory

Use the following example. If your projected sales value for each month is $4,000 and you need to maintain two months of inventory, your ending inventory should be $8,000 ($4,000 × 2 months = $8,000 ending inventory).

Step 5—Open to Buy The final step in constructing a merchandise plan is calculating the amount of merchandise to purchase each month. Like the previous calculations, you can use retail price, cost price, or quantity, but use the same type of data throughout all of the calculations. There are four variables in the open-to-buy calculation:

- Sales is the amount you sold during the month.
- Ending inventory is the merchandise you want to have available at the end of the month, which is usually more or less than one month of merchandise sales.

- Beginning inventory is the amount of inventory you started with at the beginning of the month.
- Purchases is the amount of inventory to buy.

The values can vary from month to month. For example, if you expect to sell $7,000, but sell $7,500 instead, you can easily adjust the sales value number and recalculate the values. The result clearly shows that you need to increase the amount you purchase this month. Next month, the situation may be different.

Open-to-Buy Calculation

Sales + Ending Inventory − Beginning Inventory = Purchases

Use the following example. If you sell $4,000 in merchandise, require $8,000 in ending inventory, and have $6,000 in your beginning inventory, you will need to purchase $6,000 in merchandise ($4,000 + $8,000 − $6,000 = $6,000).

Purchases should be planned for your entire list of merchandise. Once the basic numbers have been established, calculating the amount to purchase is a single-step process performed before you place any orders.

Stock Plan

Retailers develop a list of merchandise that should be in stock at all times known as a **basic stock list.** It identifies products that customers expect to see when they enter the store. This list will vary from retailer to retailer. A customer expects a hardware store to have hammers, nails in a variety of sizes, and several types of screwdrivers. (Refer to the CD for an example of a stock list.)

A **model stock plan** lists any merchandise sold by the retailer that is not on the basic stock list. For example, hardware stores often have books that contain plans for building decks or making household repairs. Customers don't always think of a hardware store as a place to purchase books, but they obviously fit into the hardware store's product assortment.

Additional Resources

Planning for Non-Retail Businesses

Every business buys some items such as supplies and equipment. If your business does not sell merchandise, you do not need a merchandise plan. However, you do have to determine the number of products you expect to sell, components you need to purchase, time required, and other factors that affect the number of items you can produce, purchase, and sell. For example, if you work alone, you must be careful not to commit yourself to more work than you can perform in the number of available hours. If you have several employees in a consulting firm, you must keep track of their available hours and work requirements as well as your own. Manufacturers require components. Producers require raw materials. Each type of business must keep track of the items it needs, the items it can produce, and the items it can sell.

Note: Software packages are available to help you plan your merchandise purchases. However, the software only serves as a guide. Merchandise planning is your responsibility.

Hypothetical Scenario

Kevin is not a retailer. He sells a service, the service of designing web sites. Although he doesn't buy merchandise, Kevin does have to plan. He has decided that he wants to spend 30 hours a week designing web sites and pages, five hours a week in marketing activities, and five hours a week in administration. When he published his site, he received 20 responses in the first week. He will have to use his planning schedule to determine which jobs to accept.

Set a Merchandise Budget

Use the merchandise plan to create the merchandise budget, a guide for merchandise activities such as purchasing and sales during the six months covered by the merchandise plan. Like a budget that you prepare to guide your personal finances, a merchandise budget is built on estimates of income and expenses. An accountant can help you prepare a realistic merchandise budget by calculating the amount you can afford to spend. A basic budget always includes profit, sales, inventory, purchases, and expenses. A more detailed budget may include more categories and details.

Profit

The primary goal for a retailer—and most other businesses—is profit. Calculate profit by subtracting expenses from income (Income – Expenses = Profit). To earn a profit, your income must be higher than your expenses. You can increase your profit in two ways:

- Earn more income.
- Spend less money.

Businesses spend a great deal of time and money creating ways to earn more money and reduce expenses. One of the best methods is often overlooked: Create a reasonable budget and follow it.

To create a budget you can follow, estimate a realistic amount of profit your business can earn. Base the estimate on (1) your profit in the last few years, (2) any changes that might occur in your sales and expenses, (3) changes in key personnel, (4) changes in your competition, and (5) current economic conditions. If this is your first year of operation, your profit estimate should be based on (1) averages for businesses of the same size in the same industry, (2) information about your competition, (3) information about your products, (4) information about the surrounding community, and (5) current economic conditions.

Sales

Generally, sales are estimated on a monthly basis. The factors that affect profit will also have an impact on sales. To estimate potential sales, consider (1) your sales in the last few years, (2) the profit you have already estimated, (3) any changes in expenses, (4) changes in key personnel, (5) changes in your competition, and (6) current economic conditions. If this is your first year of operation, your sales estimate should be based on (1) averages for businesses of the same size in the same industry,

(2) information about your competition, (3) information about your products, (4) information about the surrounding community, and (5) current economic conditions.

Inventory

At any time during your business operations, you have a great deal of money invested in the merchandise in your inventory. Following your merchandise plan reduces your financial risk and increases your available cash by freeing funds that could be tied up unnecessarily in more merchandise than you need.

Purchases

To sell merchandise, you need to purchase merchandise. Your merchandise plan identifies the cost and quantity of the products or services you plan to buy and sell. Be prepared to modify your purchases based on actual sales and changes in the factors that affected your merchandise plan at the time it was created. The ability to react quickly to changes in the business environment is an important asset for small businesses.

Expenses

A business has many expenses, such as office supplies, rent, and electricity bills that are not related to the purchase of merchandise and do not belong in the merchandise budget. Expenses related to merchandise should be carefully planned and controlled. Items such as unnecessary trips and unplanned purchases should be reconsidered and evaluated by their contribution to your profit. If the expenses are not beneficial, they should be rejected or avoided.

Hypothetical Scenario

Although Kevin does not sell merchandise, he does have expenses associated strictly with the service he sells. Expenses include the services of a professional photographer when necessary and occasional trips to client sites to gather information for the web sites he builds.

Identify and Choose Your Suppliers

Every business supplies something to someone. You must identify the companies that supply the products you need. A variety of sources are available. Trade journals, business-to-business telephone books, trade shows, Internet searches, and referrals from other businesses are only a few examples of resources you can use to identify potential suppliers. The more difficult task is choosing the right supplier.

As a consumer, you have favorite places to shop. Your choices are based on criteria such as location, price, service, product selection, and experience with the business. As a business owner, you select suppliers for your merchandise and supplies. Your criteria are the same as any other consumer. You consider the supplier's location, product type, product characteristics, the frequency and size of your orders, price, service, and experience with the supplier.

Location

Many suppliers deliver their products to your business location. The variety of available transportation methods and the convenience of overnight delivery have made location less of a consideration. Location does impact delivery fees, which affects the price of the product. Generally, location is not important if the supplier is reliable and your purchases are well planned. Therefore, the location of the supplier may not be a factor in your selection process.

On the other hand, many businesses prefer to purchase from a local company. They believe that it is easier to work with a local company and develop a professional relationship that will benefit both businesses.

Product Type

A large variety of products are purchased by businesses. Product type can be identified by the way it is used by the business. Products may be used directly by the business, used to manufacture or produce the items the business sells, or sold to other consumers.

The business and its employees use some products as they conduct business. In other words, these products are not sold to another layer of consumers. They are purchased and consumed by the business. Examples include computers, office furniture, cash register receipt tape, and cleaning supplies. Many of these items are not critical to the operation of the business and are purchased in small quantities. After every employee has a desk, you probably won't purchase more desks. Most of these items are sold by a large number of suppliers.

Businesses purchase items that are used as components in the products they manufacture and sell to consumers. A computer manufacturer purchases hard drives, keyboards, memory chips, and DVD drives that it uses to assemble computers sold to final consumers. A restaurant purchases eggs, milk, and sugar to produce menu items sold to consumers. Without the necessary components, production grinds to a halt.

Businesses also purchase merchandise that is sold to consumers. This merchandise is often purchased in large quantities and repackaged or divided for sale to other consumers. For example, retailers purchase boxes of pens and pencils that they separate and sell to consumers. If merchandise is not in stock, it can't be sold.

Product Characteristics

Businesses purchase a wide array of products. Some products are very specialized, limiting the number of available suppliers. For example, prescription drugs are patented for many years. Until the patent expires, the drug can be manufactured only by the owner of the patent, limiting the choice of suppliers for drugstores and doctors. An airline that wants to purchase new passenger airplanes may have only a handful of suppliers that can manufacture large aircraft. In this situation, your choices are limited. You will have to purchase from one of the few available suppliers.

Order Frequency and Size

If you prefer to purchase small quantities or can afford to purchase only small quantities, you probably won't be able to buy directly from the producer. Based on the quantity you order, you may be able to purchase products from a wholesaler. Often, businesses operate just to supply you and other businesses in your industry. For example, a restaurant supplier sells dinnerware, flatware, napkins, and table linen. A hotel supplier sells towels, bed linen, and soap. Suppliers that primarily serve your industry are more likely to carry the products you use in the quantities you need.

Price

The cheapest supplier isn't always the best choice. As a final consumer, do you want to know that the cheapest suppliers the automobile manufacturer could find made the seatbelt and airbag in your car? The most expensive supplier isn't always the best choice either. If you want a watch that tells the time accurately, you don't need jewels around the face of the watch and a gold wristband. Like any consumer, you need to find suppliers who fit your needs and budget. Verify that the supplier provides what you need at a reasonable price. Don't pay for frills and services you don't need.

Service

A good supplier does more than provide assistance when everything is going right; it also provides assistance when something is wrong. Before you select a supplier, ask about the services it provides. Ask how your orders are processed and how the supplier handles errors after an order is delivered. A supplier that does not have procedures for correcting errors or providing assistance to its clients will not be able to take quick, efficient action when it is needed.

Referral

A supplier, like any business, maintains a list of customers. Ask the supplier to give you a list of customers who will provide a referral. A **referral** is a testimony of the supplier's good business practices. Contact several businesses on the list. Ask questions about the supplier and its products. Ask the business to describe what happened when an error was made or it needed service. Ask the business to identify other customers. Contact these customers, who may not be on the list the supplier provided. Ask the same questions. This provides a true picture of the supplier's quality and business practices.

Restrictions for Suppliers and Retailers

Retailers and suppliers are part of the distribution channel that provides goods to the final consumer. This relationship is affected by legal restrictions. These restrictions are designed to ensure **fair competition,** which is competition based on price, quality, and service. As a retailer, you must be aware of any restrictions imposed by the manufacturer, supplier, or government regulations.

Territorial Restrictions A supplier can place **territorial restrictions,** which limit the geographic area in which the retailer can resell its merchandise. Territorial restrictions are legal when the agreement is between the supplier and the retailer, businesses with a vertical relationship in the distribution channel as shown in Figure 8.4. If the agreement is between suppliers—businesses with a horizontal relationship in the distribution channel—territorial restrictions are illegal because they violate the practice of fair competition. Horizontal territorial restrictions violate the customer's right to choose because only one brand is sold within the geographic area. The lack of competition creates an environment in which prices can increase to a much higher level than they could if competition exists in the geographic area.

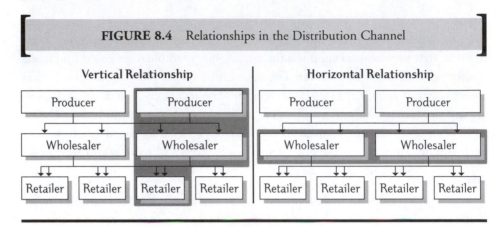

FIGURE 8.4   Relationships in the Distribution Channel

Tying Arrangement   Suppliers often carry many products. Some are strong products that sell better than others do. A supplier with a strong product that forces a retailer to buy a weak product before allowing the retailer to buy the strong product establishes a **tying arrangement.** This is illegal because the retailer is forced to buy the weak product.

Exclusive Dealing   A one-way exclusive dealing arrangement is legal. A two-way exclusive dealing arrangement is illegal. When the supplier gives the retailer the exclusive right to sell a product in a specific area, but the retailer does not do anything for the supplier, a **one-way exclusive dealing** arrangement is created. In a **two-way exclusive dealing** arrangement, the retailer offers to do something for the supplier, such as not selling competing brands, in exchange for the exclusive right to sell a product in a specific area. Two-way exclusive dealing arrangements are illegal because they violate the principle of fair competition. The arrangement can take sales away from small manufacturers and retailers.

Hypothetical Scenario

Kevin realizes that he has a constant need for professional photographs. He decides to identify photographers in several locations who can provide quality photographs. To identify potential photographers, he consults the Internet. He carefully examines samples of their work and asks for referrals. He identifies a pool of five photographers whom he can call when he needs specific photographs for the web sites he develops.

Technology Insights

Bar Codes

Every piece of merchandise in a store has a tag. The tag usually contains at least two pieces of information: the retail price and a bar code. When the cashier scans the bar code, what type of information is being scanned into the system? Contrary to what you may think, a bar code does not contain a lot of detailed information about the product. The bars of varied widths represent numbers and letters. When a scanner scans the bar code, it translates the bars into numbers and letters. The most common formats for bar codes are Code 39 and Code 128. In Code 39, each character requires 5 black bars and 4 white bars. Code 128 is more flexible. Each character requires 3 bars and 3 spaces. The remaining text on the label probably provides more information than the bar code can represent.

Think Critically Identify the information you would want on your product's tag.

CHAPTER REVIEW

Every business is a member of a channel of distribution because it is involved in distributing goods or services to consumers. Distribution can be simple if the product goes directly from the producer to the consumer. More complicated channels can include retailers, wholesalers, and agents.

A merchandise plan describes the specific items you acquire to sell in each department at each retail establishment. Merchandise managers perform the planning. Buyers purchase the merchandise. Planning identifies the quantities of each product to keep in inventory, determining the quantity to purchase each month. Use your merchandise plan to create your merchandise budget.

A merchandise budget is a guide for your merchandise activities during the six months covered by the merchandise plan. A basic budget always includes profit, sales, inventory, purchases, and expenses. The primary goal of your merchandise budget is profit. Use the budget to help you increase your income and reduce your expenses.

The suppliers you select have a significant impact on your success, so it is important to choose wisely. When you select a supplier, consider the supplier's location, product type, product characteristics, the frequency and size of your orders, price, service, and experience with the supplier. Referrals from other businesses that have dealt with the same supplier are valuable.

USE BUSINESS TERMS

Fill in the blanks with the appropriate term.

agent	merchandise plan
average stock figure	middleman
basic stock list	model stock plan
buyer	one-way exclusive dealing
buying direct	referral
channel of distribution	stock turn rate
department	stockkeeping unit
direct distribution	territorial restrictions
distribution	two-way exclusive dealing
division	tying arrangement
fair competition	wholesaler

1. The wholesaler and retailer are members of the ___?___ that brings products from the manufacturer to the consumer.
2. A(n) ___?___ is the only channel member that doesn't own the merchandise.
3. Actions that restrict ___?___ are illegal because consumers should have the right to choose between products.

4. The merchandise budget is based on the ___?___.
5. A supplier can place ___?___ on retailers but not on other suppliers.
6. The ___?___ is a hypothetical number because you never sell your entire inventory at one time.
7. Each ___?___ is classified by merchandise characteristics such as type, material, color, price, size, or brand.

TEST YOUR READING

8. How has the Internet affected distribution channels?
9. Why does a manufacturer sell its products through retailers?
10. What advantages does a retailer receive by purchasing merchandise from a wholesaler?
11. Why do middlemen add cost to a product?
12. How is your place in the distribution channel identified?
13. What is the relationship between the merchandise plan and the merchandise budget?
14. What are the four levels of retail addressed by the merchandise plan?
15. Why is bottom-up planning more accurate than top-down planning?
16. Identify the information you need to calculate the correct quantity of merchandise to purchase.
17. What is the difference between a basic stock list and a model stock plan?
18. Why do nonretailers need to plan?
19. Why shouldn't you always buy products from the cheapest supplier?

THINK CRITICALLY ABOUT BUSINESS

20. Create a basic stock list for a local retailer.
21. Visit a local retailer. Examine the SKUs for several products. Identify the product characteristics that are the basis for the classifications.
22. Select a nonretail business. Identify the product planning it should perform.
23. Select a local business. Identify 10 suppliers the business could use. Evaluate two of the suppliers.

REAL-LIFE BUSINESS

Chinook Bookshop, Inc.

Chinook has been an independent bookstore in Colorado Springs, Colorado, since Dick and Judy Noyes established it in 1959. The Noyes continue to operate the bookstore today.

The couple selected a location that fronted on a park and had a significant amount of pedestrian traffic. The couple then visited and evaluated the stores that would be their competition when Chinook opened. They decided that there was room for Chinook in the local book market.

The couple determined that they would need $25,000 to establish the business. Dick Noyes did his homework. Before asking his family for financial assistance, he prepared a 32-page prospectus that explained why Chinook would be unique and successful. The prospectus included a budget for the first year. The first year of inventory was projected to cost $15,000 and additional expenses were predicted to be $13,000. Together, the couple drew a monthly salary of $380.

They projected sales of $40,000 for the first year. When the first year of operation was over, they were pleased to report sales of $65,000 to the family investors. Every year, sales grew 20 to 25 percent. By 2001, the store had 30 employees and annual sales were well over $2,000,000.

Several unique ideas drew customers to the store. The store windows featured creative displays accompanied by puns. The couple made a special effort to interest people who didn't usually read for fun. They carried special-interest books about offbeat topics to attract these customers. Their success in encouraging readers and attracting customers is obvious.

Think Critically

1. How did Dick and Judy Noyes acquire the funds to open the store?
2. What did the initial inventory cost?
3. How well does Chinook perform today?
4. How does the store attract new customers?

CHAPTER 9

Set Prices

GOALS

- ◆ Add value to a product or service
- ◆ Describe the role of cost in setting prices
- ◆ Establish prices that cover expenses and earn a profit
- ◆ Avoid deceptive pricing techniques

Oki Reynolds decided to open a business that would be more fun than her current job as a shift supervisor in a warehouse. She noticed that three hotels were building new facilities only a few miles from several acres owned by her cousin. After some research, Oki decided to open a miniature golf course, targeting the families she expected to use the new hotels.

Add Value

It has been said that the best things in life are free. However, you want to *sell* your product or service. For consumers to part with their hard-earned cash, they have to believe that your product has value. **Value** is the worth, utility, or importance of an item.

Individuals often place a different value on the same item. This simple statement tells you why value is important and why consumers make specific decisions. For example, some people buy luxury cars while others buy motorcycles. Some shoppers prefer plastic bags while others prefer paper bags to carry their groceries. First, you must identify the type of value your product provides. In later chapters, you will identify the customers who are likely to purchase your products and select methods of reaching them.

Every item has some value. However, the value of every item isn't **marketable**— able to be offered for sale and wanted by consumers. The value of an item is often tied to the item's **utility** or usefulness. For example, a huge oak tree isolated in the deep woods has limited value to the majority of consumers speeding to and from work every day who never see the tree. If the same tree is located in your yard, it has a much higher value. In the summer, it provides shade for backyard picnics. In the fall, it provides autumn color. For children, it provides a location for a tire swing or support for a tree house. If you choose to sell your house, mature trees in the yard increase the value of your property on the real estate market. Thus, the tree increases the marketability and value of the property.

Making Products

Many businesses sell physical goods. Most of these businesses can be classified as extractors, manufacturers, or retailers. The process of making goods begins with the raw materials and ends with the finished products purchased by the consumer as shown in Figure 9.1.

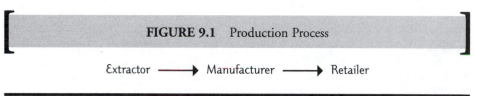

FIGURE 9.1 Production Process

Extractor ⟶ Manufacturer ⟶ Retailer

Extractors Look around you. The chairs, books, and lamps you see didn't grow in a field or on a tree. The majority of products you purchase have been manufactured from **raw materials,** matter that can be converted by manufacturing or processing into new and useful products. Raw materials include varied materials such as wood, water, rocks, coconuts, and wheat.

Extractors are businesses that remove raw materials from the land, water, or air. Farmers, ranchers, and miners are extractors. They raise crops, herd cattle, and dig minerals out of the ground, taking advantage of the natural resources.

Manufacturers Producers transform raw materials into products that consumers can use. They transform trees into chairs, grain into cereals, and coal into electricity. All of these transformations create products that are marketable—items that can be sold by owners and purchased by consumers.

Manufacturing creates useful items from raw materials. The changes increase the value so the manufactured product is worth more than the raw material. The dining room set is worth more than the wood. An in-ground swimming pool is worth more than the water and concrete used to make the pool.

Retailers It is possible to "live off the land," extracting items you need from the environment to produce food, shelter, and clothing for you and your family. However, most Americans can't imagine life without grocery stores, gas stations, and pastry shops.

Retailers also add value to the products they sell. They may repackage or install the product, educate the consumer, and service the product after it is purchased. All of these activities add value to the product.

Value Added to a Product

Products advance through several stages before they are purchased. At each stage, value is added to the product in form, place, time, or possession.

Form The production process changes the raw materials into a product that can be sold and used. The new form is more marketable and has more value than the raw materials that were used to make the product. The computer has more value than the monitor, the keyboard, and the electronic components. The new shirt has more value than the cotton used to make it. Extractors, manufacturers, and retailers add form value. Extractors acquire the raw materials. Manufacturers make the products, and retailers may repackage the products for sale.

Place The value of place is added when products are moved to a location where they can be processed or sold. Extractors, manufacturers, and retailers add value in place. Extractors harvest the raw materials, often from locations that are difficult to reach. They ship the raw materials to manufacturers. Manufacturers assemble components or transform the raw materials to make their products. The finished products are shipped to retailers. Retailers collect merchandise from a variety of locations, making them available in a single location to consumers. Consumers can acquire the products they want without traveling around the world to find them.

Time Value is added in time if products are available when customers want to buy them. For example, snow tires and boots are sold in the autumn or early winter. Gardening tools are purchased in the spring. If the products are not available when they are desired, the products will lose value. Retailers provide value in time. They arrange to provide products at the time they will be purchased, even though manufacturers produce the products all year.

Possession When the ownership of the product is transferred to the consumer, value is added in possession. Retailers add possession value when they sell products to consumers. After ownership is transferred, the consumer can use or consume the items.

Value Added to a Service

When a consumer purchases a service, a physical object may not be produced or transferred to the consumer. Therefore, value is not added in form or possession. A consumer who purchases a service is generally buying time and expertise. Value is added to the service in place and time.

Place Value is added in place when the service is provided where it is needed. For example, a landscaper provides the purchased service in your yard. A lawyer provides services in the courtroom. A service offered or performed in an inappropriate location will not be marketable.

Time Value is added in time if the service is performed when it is needed. A bald man is not likely to pay for a haircut. A lawyer won't be hired if the consumer doesn't need legal advice.

Value Adds Cost

At each stage in the development and delivery of a product or service, value and cost are added. Each stage requires time, materials, or skill provided by the extractors, manufacturers, retailers, and service businesses. Time, materials, and skills cost money, paid by the product or service providers. These costs are eventually added to the price paid by the consumer.

Hypothetical Scenario

Oki Reynolds expected that the miniature golf business would provide value to the families visiting the area, but she didn't know how to turn the value of her service into a price. She determined that her service provided value in the form of place and time. The location provides a nearby source of family entertainment for visitors and local residents. The only other miniature golf facility is located an hour away. Oki plans to keep the facility open during daylight hours and add special night hours during the busy summer months.

Cost Affects Price

Buyers have a critical role in managing the cost of the merchandise purchased by retailers and the items needed by service businesses to provide the services they sell. A buyer wants to obtain high-quality goods at a reasonable price. This is the same goal that every consumer has on every trip to the grocery store or visit to the dentist. People want to "get what they pay for," which usually means they want more than they can afford. They want larger diamonds, more horsepower, and better service than the model in the right price range provides. The buyer must be aware of the product's features and the needs of the final consumer at all times.

Buyers Estimate Cost and Price

Many factors affect the **retail price,** the amount a customer pays for an item. However, the cost of the product has the most impact on the price. An experienced buyer studies a specific type of product, including how it is made, the materials in the product, and the cost of making the item. The buyer uses this knowledge to determine the probable cost of manufacturing the product and a reasonable retail price. The buyer's methods of determining acceptable cost include estimating a reasonable retail price, building up prices, and memorizing prices.

Estimate Retail Prices Knowledgeable buyers who are familiar with a particular type of product can estimate the amount a consumer is willing to pay for the product. Based on the retail price and the amount the retailer wants to earn on each sale, the buyer can calculate the maximum cost the buyer can pay for the product.

Cost Based on Retail Price Calculation

Retail Price – Desired Profit = Maximum Cost

Based on the maximum cost, directives from the retailer, and knowledge of the retailer's customers, the buyer makes a purchase decision about the merchandise. This means that a buyer rejects merchandise that is not identified by the merchandise plan or doesn't meet the requirements of the customers, even if it could generate the desired profit.

Build Up Prices Only knowledgeable buyers can use this method of evaluating the cost of a particular product. The buyer must have a thorough understanding of the product's components and the production process. To calculate a reasonable cost, the buyer "builds up" the price by adding (1) the cost of the material, (2) the labor needed to make the product, (3) the cost of packaging and transporting the product, and (4) a reasonable profit for the retailer.

Build Up Price Calculation

Material + Labor + Packaging and Transporting + Profit = Reasonable Cost

The buyer compares the result of the calculation to the price requested by the supplier. If the supplier requests a higher price, the product has some value undetected by the buyer or the supplier has overpriced the product. If the supplier can't explain why the price is higher, the buyer should not purchase the product. If the supplier can't justify the higher cost to the buyer, the retailer will not be able to justify the higher price to the final consumer.

Be cautious if the price requested by the supplier is less than the reasonable cost calculated by the buyer. The product may be inferior. The materials, components, or skill used to make the product is less than expected or the product is not selling well. Consumers will not pay for a product that is lower in quality, less popular, or less functional than indicated by the purchase price.

Memorize Prices Buyers who are less knowledgeable about the details of the merchandise and how it is manufactured may choose to memorize prices for the items they intend to buy. The buyer simply compares the price requested by the supplier to the memorized price. The disadvantage to this method becomes obvious when the buyer encounters a new product or an improved process. Without understanding how the product is manufactured, the buyer can't price the new product or modification.

Buyer Discounts

When a consumer purchases products from a retailer, the consumer hopes to get a good deal by purchasing products on sale, using coupons, or taking advantage of rebates. Buyers also hope to get good deals when they buy merchandise for retailers.

Although buyers can't use coupons, they have other options for obtaining good deals from suppliers.

A supplier sets a price, known as the **list price,** for each product it sells. However, retail buyers rarely pay the full list price. Buyers usually receive **discounts,** amounts subtracted from the list price. Each discount is written as a percentage of the list price, such as "list less 20," meaning "list price minus the 20 percent discount." For example, the amount a buyer pays for "list less 20" of a garment listed as $125 is calculated by $125 - (125 \times .20)$, which is $100.

Discount Calculation

List Price - Discount = Buyer's Cost

Although every supplier doesn't offer all of the possible discounts, discounts are so common that many buyers will not purchase merchandise unless they receive a discount. Discounts help both the supplier and the buyer. The buyer gets a better price and the supplier sells more merchandise. A supplier may offer one or several of the most common discount options—quantity, promotional, seasonal, cash, and trade.

Quantity Discount Suppliers encourage buyers to purchase large quantities of merchandise at the same time by offering a quantity discount. A **quantity discount** is the dollar amount based on the quantity of merchandise purchased that is subtracted from the list price. Because the discount is based on an objective fact—the number of items purchased—the discount is applied equally to every buyer. For example, if a 10 percent discount is offered for purchasing 1,000 combs, every buyer who purchases 1,000 combs receives a 10 percent discount. The supplier often has a table, such as Table 9.1, that identifies the standard break points and the associated discount. **Break points** identify the quantity at which the discount changes. In Table 9.1, the break points are 1,000, 2,500, 5,000, 7,500, and 10,000.

TABLE 9.1 Quantity Discount

Product	Product Code	Quantity	% Discount
Green pocket comb	745982	1,000	10
		2,500	15
		5,000	20
		7,500	25
		10,000	30

Promotional Discount A supplier offers a **promotional discount** to retailers that perform an advertising or promotional service for the supplier. National suppliers typically offer this type of discount to local retailers. Local businesses are charged lower rates to encourage the companies to use local media. Therefore, local retailers are often charged lower rates for advertising by local media. A promotional discount enables the national suppliers to take advantage of local advertising opportunities.

The promotional discount can be given as a lower price for the merchandise or free additional merchandise. If a supplier offers this discount to any buyer, it must be offered to all buyers.

Seasonal Discount A supplier gives a **seasonal discount** to retailers that take delivery of products during the off-season. The discount is offered because the retailers assume some risk by taking delivery of the merchandise when consumers won't be interested in buying the products for several months. The retailer's risk is present in several forms:

- The retailer ties up cash in inventory, lowering the amount of cash available for other purchases, bills, or business emergencies.
- The additional merchandise increases cost by requiring additional storage space.
- Between the time of the delivery and the time the merchandise can be sold, fashions may change or new technology may become available. This reduces the value of the merchandise and the chance of making a profit by selling the goods to consumers.

Suppliers, on the other hand, reduce their risk when retailers purchase seasonal products early. Suppliers experience several advantages:

- The supplier receives cash for merchandise that would have sat in storage for several months. This cash can be spent on activities that generate additional income and improve the products.
- The sale decreases cost by requiring less storage space.
- After the merchandise is sold, the supplier faces less risk caused by changes in fashions or the development of new technology.

Cash Discount Like many consumers, retailers often don't pay bills until the last minute. Suppliers offer a **cash discount** for paying bills before they are due. This is an advantage to the supplier because payment is received earlier than necessary. Plus, it encourages retailers to avoid paying bills late. The discount also provides an advantage for the retailer by lowering the cost.

A cash discount is typically written as "6/10, net 30." This means that the retailer is given a 6 percent discount if payment is received in 10 days. If payment isn't received in that time period, the net amount is due in 30 days.

Trade Discount When a buyer performs wholesale or retail services for the supplier, the supplier provides a **trade discount.** The amount of the discount is determined by the service the buyer performs. The trade discount is calculated differently than the standard discount. It is usually written as a chain, such as "list less 40-20-10." Only the first discount is deducted from the list price. Each following discount is deducted from the amount reduced by the previous discounts in the chain.

Trade Discount Calculation
List Price $-$ (List Price $\times$ Discount 1) $=$ A
A $-$ (A $\times$ Discount 2) $=$ B
B $-$ (B $\times$ Discount 3) $=$ Buyer's Cost

Hypothetical Scenario

Oki purchases several items regularly. When she made a list of items, it was longer than she anticipated. Frequent purchases include refreshments, refreshment cups and trays, scorecards, prizes, and souvenirs. Infrequent purchases include replacement balls and clubs. She identified several businesses that specialize in miniature golf supplies. Oki discussed cost and available discounts with several representatives before selecting the supplier that provided the most value.

Establish Prices

The price you set for your products determines the profit you earn for each sale. Therefore, price decisions are critical to the success of your business.

Price Factors

Prices are not set in a vacuum. Every business owner's situation is different. For example, a month ago you purchased 200 concrete garden gargoyles for $50 each, set the samples out for display, and prepared to write the retail price on each price tag. How do you determine the right price? Several factors need to be considered.

Expenses Operating a business costs money. Expenses include all the money spent to operate the business, sell the product, and manage the business. Examples include money spent on utility bills, postage, and equipment. An expense can be defined as money leaving your business.

Expenses are paid by the total of all your sales. Each individual sale is important because it contributes to the big picture. However, you can make a pricing mistake on one item, such as the garden gargoyles, as long as the big picture is in focus—your customers are satisfied and your business earns a profit.

Cost The money you pay to manufacture or acquire a single unit of the product you sell or the amount you spend to provide service to one customer is classified as a cost. It is another way that money leaves your business.

To earn a profit on each *individual* item, considering only the cost of the product (not business expenses), the price for the item must be higher than the amount you paid for it. You paid $50 for each garden gargoyle. To earn more than you paid for each gargoyle, the price must be at least $50.01. Of course, one penny isn't much of a profit, certainly not enough to justify going through the bother and expense of operating a business.

Profit Profit is the money that remains after expenses and costs are subtracted from sales. The prices you set must cover expenses and costs. If prices are too low, your business loses money. If prices are too high, customers may not buy your products.

Consider the amount of profit you want to earn. One penny of profit on every garden gargoyle you sell is not enough. Identify the number of sales you make in a specific time period, such as a year, a month, a week, or a day. Based on the amount of profit you want to earn in that time period and the number of sales you expect to make, you can determine the average profit you must earn for each sale.

Average Profit Calculation

Desired Profit ÷ Number of Sales = Average Profit Per Sale

For example, if you want to earn $4,000 in one month by selling all of the 200 garden gargoyles, you can perform the average profit calculation. You learn that each gargoyle sale should earn $20 profit to reach your profit goal ($4,000 ÷ 200 = $20).

From the average profit per sale and the cost of the merchandise, you can determine a price for the product. In the case of the garden gargoyles, simply add the cost of each gargoyle ($50) to the average profit per sale ($20). The price for each garden gargoyle is $70. Use this price as a guideline. Other factors, such as demand for the product, may increase or decrease this price later.

Price Calculation

Cost + Average Profit Per Sale = Price

Image The type of business you operate affects profit expectations and prices. An upscale landscaper who provides landscape designs can charge a higher price for services than a landscaper who only provides and plants trees and shrubs.

Examine the image you want to present for your business. Ask yourself if a $70 garden gargoyle fits your business image. If your customers would set the value of the product within the same price range, your price is acceptable.

Demand The consumer's desire to buy your product affects the price. Popular products can be priced a little higher. Sometimes a product can be priced differently because of minor variations that make one item more popular than another. A green bicycle may be priced higher because the green bicycle is more popular than the standard beige bicycle.

Your customers influence your pricing decisions. If your customers want low-cost products, they won't buy expensive products or products that don't offer enough value for the price. Refer to the Supply and Demand charts in Chapter 1. At higher prices, fewer gargoyles will be sold. Examine the product and evaluate its value. Talk to customers. See how many are sold in the first week for $70. If demand is high and the gargoyles are sold in a few weeks, you probably want to acquire more and may consider increasing the price.

Competition If you charge $50 for a product that sells for $40 next door, most customers will happily buy the item next door. You must keep track of your competition and the prices they charge. Examine advertisements for similar products and visit competitors' stores or web sites. Compare your product and your price to available alternatives.

If you are the only business selling the garden gargoyles in your area, you may be able to charge a higher price. If the plant nursery on the next block sells the gargoyles for $60, you will lose some sales if you set the price at $70. In today's technological age, you also have to consider competitors who operate only on the Internet. Items such as books and sweaters are frequently purchased from Internet retailers. However, there are advantages to having a "brick-and-mortar" retail establishment. Customers may be reluctant to order a 40-pound concrete object from a company doing business on the Internet when it means they have to pay for shipping it.

Price Policies

Every business has an image it wants to project. For example, a children's clothing store might want to seem fun. A shoe store could present an image of providing good value. Businesses present their images in many ways, such as advertising, service, and décor. Price policies are another tool for presenting an image.

Price-Line Policy Some businesses establish **price lines,** in which all products are categorized by cost and quality, then assigned one of several standard prices. Usually, a business establishes three price lines—low, medium, and high. Items in the low price line are lower in price and quality. Items in the middle price line are better and cost a little more. They may include more services. The highest price line is reserved for the best quality of products the business sells. It may include extras such as delivery, installation, and a guarantee.

Price lines are informative for the customer. Without too much comparison, they can easily determine which products fill their basic needs and which products provide additional features they want. For example, an appliance manufacturer could make several types of dishwashers, but use price lines to set the prices at $250, $300, and $450. The difference between each price line does not have to be the same. The cost, quality, and characteristics between the lines determine the differences in prices.

If your business uses price lines, the garden gargoyles would probably fit into the middle category. Smaller, less-complicated concrete figures of rabbits and frogs could be sold for $45. Deer, gnomes, and garden wall plaques could also be priced at $70. More complex statuary, such as birdbaths, could be priced at $100.

Price Endings When you shop, you probably haven't consciously noticed that all of the prices in a single store either end with even cents ($15.50) or odd cents ($15.53). Businesses that assign prices with odd endings are presenting the idea that the consumer is buying a good value because they don't charge a penny more than necessary. Businesses that assign prices with even endings present an image of high-quality products. Most professionals and service businesses use even endings. For example, when your lawyer sends a bill, each hour is priced $120, not $117.43. It would seem unprofessional for the lawyer to include 43 cents in the bill.

Markups

The difference between the cost-of-goods sold and the retail price is the **markup.**
It is the amount you add to the cost of the product before you sell it. Markup is
expressed as a percentage of the retail price, such as "a 40 percent markup." To calculate the markup, divide the markup amount by the retail price.

Markup Percentage Calculation

Markup Amount ÷ Retail Price = Markup Percentage

Businesses track two kinds of markup—initial markup and maintained
markup. The **initial markup** is the difference between a product's cost and initial
retail selling price. If the product doesn't sell well, remember that prices are not set
in stone. The price can be reduced. The difference between the product's cost and
the price paid when the item is sold is the **maintained markup.**

A business can decide to apply the same initial markup to all or most of the
products it sells. However, some manufacturers dictate retail prices for their products. This prevents other businesses from modifying the price.

Markdowns

A price reduction is known as a **markdown.** Markdowns become necessary for a
variety of reasons, but the basic cause is a desire to sell products that are not selling
well at the current price.

- **Buying errors**—Purchasing items that don't sell well because they are unpop-
ular, unfashionable, or technologically outdated are common buying errors.
Buying too many items also leads to eventual markdowns.
- **Pricing errors**—Setting initial prices that are too high results in markdowns
to sell the products. A sweater that can't be sold at $80 may be quickly sold
for $50 or $60.
- **Returned items**—Items that have been purchased and returned may be sold
again at a reduced price. This is very common for video games.
- **Poor inventory control**—Older merchandise may accumulate in a neglected
storage area. Older merchandise can often be sold at a reduced price, even
when newer merchandise is available. Last year's athletic shoe styles can be
marked down and sold right next to this year's newest styles.
- **Promotions**—Special dates and seasonal changes are often occasions marked
by sales. Seasonal items are usually marked down when the season changes.
Many holidays, including Presidents' Day and Thanksgiving, are usually marked
by sales at several retail businesses. Although you won't see too many sales
launched by your dentist or advertising firm, manufacturers and service businesses can hold promotions. A landscaper, for example, may reduce the price
of landscape designing during the fall or winter months.

Hypothetical Scenario

It was time to set prices. Oki carefully recorded her estimates for expenses, cost, profit, image, demand, and competition. She hopes to earn $30,000 in the first year of operation. She projected the number of sales and ongoing expenses. Using the average profit calculation and price calculation, she set the prices for golfing, refreshments, souvenirs, and other products she will sell.

Pricing Regulations

In an environment of fair competition, price is one of the major criteria consumers use to select retailers, service providers, and manufacturers. This leads businesses to compete by setting lower prices and holding sales designed to attract even the most reluctant consumer.

Because fair competition is an essential part of the American economic environment, regulations have developed to provide economic protection for businesses and consumers. Set reasonable prices by considering expenses, cost of the product, profit, image, demand, and competition. Occasionally, businesses get carried away by the competition element and are tempted to use questionable pricing methods. Understand the regulations governing pricing to avoid stepping over the line.

Deceptive Pricing

A misleading price intended to lure customers into your business is **deceptive pricing.** Laws against deceptive pricing protect consumers and honest retailers. There are many varieties of deceptive pricing, but the most common are false price comparisons and free offers that aren't really free.

♦ If you advertise a *reduced* price, you must be sure that the new price is lower than a previous price offered for several days. Purchasing a product from a supplier and selling it for a reduced price when it was never sold for a higher price is deceptive.

♦ If you compare your price to a competitor, you must be sure that the competitor's product is *exactly* the same. Additionally, your competition must have sold a significant number of the product at the higher price.

♦ A product sold with an accompanying free item must not be priced higher than its regular price.

♦ A product sold with an accompanying free item must still provide all free products or services that were previously provided.

The Federal Trade Commission (FTC) has jurisdiction over deceptive pricing. Consumers can sue a business that uses deceptive pricing. Consumers have pursued several cases in court and been awarded significant financial judgments that cover the deceptive price and provide additional financial reward.

Below-Cost Pricing

In many states, businesses are required to apply a minimum percentage markup to the cost of any product. The product can't be sold for less than this amount, which is equal to cost plus the minimum percentage markup. This requirement prevents **below-cost pricing,** which a business may be tempted to use to attract customers by offering lower prices on one or more items. Obviously, a business could not operate for long if they sold every product below cost. Therefore, below-cost pricing is a method of luring in customers while hoping that they will purchase other products that do earn a profit.

Below-cost pricing is difficult to prove. Competitors rather than customers usually file complaints. In states that require a minimum percentage markup, it is a good idea to keep records of your products' costs and the markups you apply.

Predatory Pricing

A business that charges different prices in different locations to eliminate competition is practicing **predatory pricing.** The key element in identifying predatory pricing is the intention to eliminate the competition. Predatory pricing is difficult to prove. A retailer may have many reasons to charge different prices in different geographic areas. For example, transportation costs and expenses vary from one site to another.

Hypothetical Scenario

Oki decided to run a few specials to attract new customers shortly after opening her business. In Oki's situation, the most common pricing regulations that affect her business refer to deceptive pricing. She planned to run several promotions. The first offers a 50 percent discount for new customers. The second allows one customer to golf free if two other golfers pay full price. Are these promotions examples of deceptive pricing?

Technology Insights

Data Backup

As you operate your business, you collect and create valuable information, which is usually stored on your computer. It stores your business plan, a list of suppliers with phone numbers and addresses, financial data, and a few attempts at creating marketing fliers. What would happen if you lost this information? Recreating these documents would take a great deal of time and effort. Some documents could never be reproduced. Back up your critical business information so it doesn't disappear if your hard drive crashes or lightning strikes the building. Several backup methods are available. Options include the hard drive of a networked computer, a tape drive, a writable CD, and a Zip® drive. Several businesses sell storage space on a server you reach through the Internet. Regardless of how you choose to back up your data, follow three rules:

◆ **Make a backup at regular intervals.** Decide how much information you can afford to lose to determine the frequency of your backups.

◆ **Keep several backups in storage.** If you decide to back up your data weekly, keep a month of backups. Problems often take a while to become apparent. For example, a corrupted file from your accounting software won't be noticed until you open the program to enter new data.

◆ **Keep the previous backup off-site.** Leave a copy at your mom's house, your best friend's house, or your Uncle Rick's house. This protects your data even further.

Think Critically Identify the information you need to backup, the backup method, and your off-site storage location.

CHAPTER REVIEW

To reach a consumer, products go through a production process. As products are made, they pass through an extractor, manufacturer, and retailer. At each stage, value is added. Value, the worth of an item, is added to the product in form, place, time, or possession. Because each stage requires time, materials, or skill, cost is also added. When the product is purchased, these costs are built into the price paid by the consumer.

Buyers use three methods of determining if a product's cost is reasonable. They can estimate a reasonable retail price, build up prices, or memorize prices. A buyer who is familiar with a specific industry is able to evaluate products and product prices more accurately than buyers who are less familiar with the products. Buyers rarely pay the product's list price. They receive common discounts based on purchased quantity, promotional activities, seasonal purchases, early cash payment, and trade activities performed by the buyer.

The situation for pricing each product is different. Critical factors include expenses, cost, profit, image, demand, and competition. Price policies such as price lines and price endings simplify pricing decisions. Markups assigned to products can be raised or lowered later.

Fair competition is a basic principle of the American economy. Government regulations protect consumers and businesses from unethical pricing techniques such as deceptive pricing, below-cost pricing, and predatory pricing.

USE BUSINESS TERMS

Fill in the blanks with the appropriate term.

below-cost pricing	markup
break point	predatory pricing
cash discount	price line
deceptive pricing	promotional discount
discounts	quantity discount
extractor	raw material
initial markup	retail price
list price	seasonal discount
maintained markup	trade discount
markdown	utility
marketable	value

1. A farmer and a miner are examples of ___?___.
2. ___?___ is under the jurisdiction of the Federal Trade Commission.
3. ___?___, which use one of several standard prices, categorize products by cost and quality.
4. Retailers that take delivery of products during the off-season receive a(n) ___?___.
5. Retail buyers rarely pay the full ___?___.
6. Individuals often place a different ___?___ on the same item.
7. A business can decide to apply the same ___?___ to all or most of the products it sells.

TEST YOUR READING

8. How is value related to marketability?
9. How is value added to a product?
10. Why should a buyer be knowledgeable about a particular industry?
11. Why do suppliers offer a promotional discount?
12. What is different about the method used to calculate a trade discount?
13. How does a cost differ from an expense?
14. How are products assigned to a price line?
15. What is the difference between the initial markup and the maintained markup?
16. List the reasons merchandise prices are marked down.
17. Describe the most common methods of deceptive pricing.
18. Why do many states require a minimum percentage markup?
19. Why is predatory pricing difficult to prove?

THINK CRITICALLY ABOUT BUSINESS

20. Select five local businesses. Guess which type of price endings each business uses. Call or visit each business to check your accuracy.

21. Visit a local retailer. Examine merchandise that has been placed on sale. Determine the reason the price has been marked down.

22. Investigate the laws in your state. Is a minimum percentage markup required? If it is required, how much is the minimum markup?

23. Select an item sold by several local businesses. Call or visit to get pricing information about the product. Identify the highest, lowest, and average price.

REAL-LIFE BUSINESS

Dell Computer Corporation

Michael Dell, born in 1965, revolutionized the computer industry when he was only 19 years old. Dell used $1,000 to establish Dell Computer Corporation in 1986. The company was the first personal computer company to sell custom computers directly to consumers.

The idea for Dell Computer Corporation came when Dell was building a computer system for himself. He realized that traditional stores sold a computer for $3,000, even though the components cost only $700. The operators of the traditional stores knew little about computers and were not able to provide assistance to customers, although they did add cost to the product. Dell knew that he could build and sell high-quality computer systems and back the product up with the product support consumers needed.

Dell opened the first international subsidiary in the United Kingdom in 1987. The company now has sales offices in several countries and currently has over 34,000 employees. The company's sales have grown to $31.8 billion. The value of Dell's stock has risen nearly 50,000 percent in the last 10 years. Obviously, Dell's business model is a success.

Think Critically

1. How did Michael Dell get his business idea?
2. Why did Dell want to avoid selling his computers through retailers?
3. What type of value does Dell add to his product?
4. What was the markup percentage for computers sold in traditional stores at the time Dell was established?

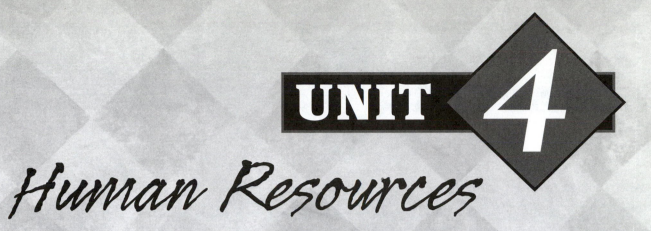

UNIT 4

Human Resources

CHAPTERS

CHAPTER 10

Hire Employees

GOALS

- ◆ Decide to hire employees
- ◆ Write and place a job advertisement
- ◆ Interview applicants
- ◆ Hire a candidate

Frank Lin grabbed three more berry-scented green Lin Candles and stuffed them in the box. He would have preferred to be at the baseball game instead of helping his wife pack shipments. A year ago, Janice made a few candles and sold them at a local craft show. The candles were very popular. One thing led to another and Janice opened a web site to sell the candles three months ago. Since then, the number of orders seemed to grow every day. Lin Candles was succeeding, but Frank and Janice had little free time to enjoy the success.

Decide to Hire Employees

Many small businesses operate for decades without ever hiring a single employee. A musician who teaches students to play the piano, an architect who designs private residences, and a surveyor who determines the boundaries of a plot of land operate independently as small businesses without assistance from employees. Other businesses, such as restaurants, clothing stores, and delivery services, could not operate without employees.

It is up to you to determine if your business could operate more effectively, creating happier customers and earning more profit, with or without employees. Several questions can help you decide if employees are necessary.

- **Will an employee improve the quality of the product or service you provide?** Providing a high-quality product or service includes the physical quality of the product and the timeliness of the product's delivery. If you have too much work, the quality of your product can slip because you don't have enough time to dedicate to each product. If you have more orders than you can fill, the time required for product delivery—between the order date and the delivery date—may be too long, resulting in lost customers and sales.

- **Will an employee increase the number of products you make or customers you serve?** If your schedule is full, turning down additional orders or customers is the only solution to keeping your existing customers happy. To make your business grow, you need to hire employees. In this situation, the real question may be, "Do I want my business to grow?" The answer to this question depends on your personal goals. You can decide that you do not want your business to grow any larger than the work you can finish yourself.

- **Will an employee increase the profit earned by the business?** If you have turned down orders because you didn't have the time or skill to perform the work, you can probably increase your profit by hiring an employee who enables you to accept more orders or add new products or services. Can the business afford to hire an employee? If the employee increases your business, will the additional profit pay the employee's salary? Financially, it makes sense to hire an employee if the worker earns enough to pay the additional salary and creates profit for the business.

- **Will an employee provide specialized skills the business needs?** If the primary activity of your business requires skills that you don't have, an employee is required. After the business has operated for a while, you could decide to expand by offering new services that require additional skills. For example, a craft store that decides to offer framing as an additional service needs to hire a skilled framer. Many companies add employees when the amount of specialized work justifies the expense. For example, most small businesses pay for legal work when it is needed. Large corporations keep a lawyer on staff to handle legal issues.

- **Will an employee perform tasks that you can't or prefer not to perform?** Many tasks don't require special skills. They could require strength, late hours, or precision work that you prefer not to perform. Hiring an employee can reduce the amount of "grunt work" you perform, leaving you free to concentrate on the tasks you enjoy.

- **Will an employee improve the quality of your life?** Starting and operating a small business requires a lot of time and energy. To keep up with your business, you could be working long hours, losing contact with your friends and family, and getting little sleep. Some entrepreneurs decide to hire an individual to operate the business or share the responsibilities.

Your responses to these questions, recorded in Table 10.1, determine if you need to hire an employee. They reveal your motivation and help you make a final decision.

TABLE 10.1   Hiring an Employee

Motivation	Yes	No
Will an employee improve the quality of the product or service the company provides?		
Will an employee increase the number of products the company makes or customers it serves?		
Will an employee increase the profit earned by the business?		
Will an employee provide specialized skills the business needs?		
Will an employee perform tasks that I can't or prefer not to perform?		
Will an employee improve the quality of my life?		

Write a Job Description

You decided to hire an employee. Now you have to determine how the employee can help your business succeed. Write a **job description,** a written list of the employee's responsibilities that defines your expectations of the employee's performance as shown in Figure 10.1. A complete job description should include several elements: job title, responsibilities, supervisor, job classification, location, qualifications, salary range, hours, and career path.

FIGURE 10.1   Sample Job Description

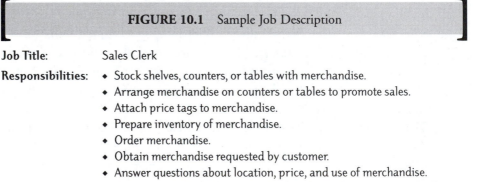

Job Title: Sales Clerk

Responsibilities:
- Stock shelves, counters, or tables with merchandise.
- Arrange merchandise on counters or tables to promote sales.
- Attach price tags to merchandise.
- Prepare inventory of merchandise.
- Order merchandise.
- Obtain merchandise requested by customer.
- Answer questions about location, price, and use of merchandise.
- Total price and tax of merchandise purchased by customer on cash register.
- Accept payment and make change.
- Wrap or bag merchandise for customers.
- Clean shelves, counters, or tables.
- Remove and record amount of cash in register at end of shift.
- Keep a record of each sale.

Supervisor: Shift Supervisor

FIGURE 10.1   Sample Job Description (continued)

Job Classification:	Part-time
Location:	Retail store in Redwood Mall or Rosewood Town Center
Qualifications:	No prior experience required.
Salary Range:	$6.50 per hour
Hours:	May be required to work evenings or weekends.
Career Path:	Sales Clerk, Shift Supervisor, Store Manager

Job Title The name assigned to a worker's position in a company is the worker's **job title.** The title usually describes the employee's major responsibilities and position in the company's hierarchy. For example, the title of an individual who writes computer software for a company is a programmer. The individual who greets customers when they enter the building is the receptionist. The individual who manages the customer service department is the customer service manager.

Most companies define the responsibilities of each job title. If two individuals have the same job title, they are expected to perform the same work at the same level of proficiency. Creating a standard description for each job title protects the business if an employee becomes dissatisfied with the job responsibilities and protects the employee if the business tries to make unreasonable changes in assigned tasks.

The government provides some standard job titles and descriptions, but the list is far from exhaustive. New jobs and job titles are created often. Government agencies that collect and publish occupational data use the Standard Occupational Classification System (SOC). The Census Bureau publishes data about detailed occupations that can be accessed at www.census.gov. Every two years, the Department of Labor publishes the *Occupational Outlook Handbook, Career Guide to Industries,* and *Occupational Projections and Training Data.*

Use the government classifications as a guideline for your business. Start with a standard title that has responsibilities similar to the position in your company. Edit the specific responsibilities to match your needs.

A job title is more important to some workers than others. It signifies the importance of the work they perform. Keep this in mind as you develop the job titles for your business.

Responsibilities The tasks that an employee is expected to perform or supervise are the employee's **job responsibilities.** This is the key section of a job description. It identifies exactly what the employee is expected to do during work hours. The description should be at least one paragraph in length. A bulleted list that identifies each task is an ideal form of presentation.

More detail is needed in the description of lower-level positions, as shown in Table 10.2. For example, the job description of a sales clerk is very detailed, including individual tasks such as answering customer questions, stocking shelves, and ringing up sales on the cash register. In contrast, the job description of a marketing manager is more general, such as developing marketing strategies. This general task includes more specific items such as trade show presentations and designing marketing brochures, tasks that are not specifically listed.

TABLE 10.2   Job Responsibilities

Sales Clerk	Marketing Manager
◆ Answer questions from customers	◆ Develop marketing strategies
◆ Stock shelves	◆ Communicate with customers
◆ Complete sales transactions on the cash register	◆ Supervise sales force

It's a good idea to include a generic phrase, such as the phrases in Figure 10.2, in every job description. It states that an employee may have to perform additional duties outside the normal activities listed in the job description. This is particularly important for a small business. Employees should know that they may be asked to assist each other in completing tasks that are not related to their primary responsibilities.

FIGURE 10.2   Generic Phrases

◆ Assume additional responsibilities as requested.
◆ Perform additional tasks as needed.

Supervisor A detailed description identifies the employee's **supervisor,** the job title of the individual who manages the employee. Generally, the supervisor assigns tasks and evaluates the employee's performance. Employees are usually required to contact the supervisor if they are late, ill, or unable to perform their tasks for any reason.

Supervisors are often expected to resolve conflicts between workers or tasks. They also create schedules, assign deadlines, and track the status of specific tasks, ensuring that tasks and projects are completed in a timely manner.

Job Classification Several terms are used to classify different types of employment. The various classifications have a variety of implications in the financial and legal arenas. Federal and state laws regulate job classifications and their effect on employees. The **Fair Labor Standards Act (FLSA)** is a federal law that sets standards for many employment situations. The FLSA does not affect all businesses. In fact, many small businesses are not affected. To be covered, a business must meet the following criteria:

♦   Business is engaged in interstate commerce.
♦   Business has an annual gross volume of sales made or business done of at least $500,000.
♦   Business operates a hospital, provides medical or nursing care for residents, or operates schools and preschools.
♦   Business is a government agency.

When federal and state laws don't agree about how workers should be treated, the laws that are most beneficial to the *employees* are applied. Regulations vary from state to state. Consult the laws in your state. Classifications include exempt, nonexempt, part-time, full-time, temporary, and permanent.

Exempt/Nonexempt The line that separates exempt and nonexempt employees is not always clear. This classification method is based on a variety of factors, such as the type of work performed, the number of hours worked, the number of employees supervised, and the salary earned. Of these factors, the type of work performed is the most important. An **exempt** employee performs work that is intellectual rather than manual labor, exercising discretion and independent judgment. Exempt employees are paid at least $1,150 per month for most jobs or $900 for other jobs that meet the criteria of exempt employment. Generally, exempt workers are not paid an additional amount for **overtime,** hours worked above the standard schedule. Their salary is not reduced, also known as **docked,** for reporting to work late or missing standard work hours.

Nonexempt employees perform manual or intellectual labor that does not require the individual to exercise discretion or independent judgment. Nonexempt employees are paid at least the minimum salary for each hour they work. They are paid at least one and one-half times their regular pay rate for overtime work, but they are also docked for missing work hours.

Part-time/Full-time Each employer determines the definitions of part-time and full-time employment. The Bureau of Labor Statistics (BLS) states that a standard workweek consists of 35–44 hours. Using this as a guideline, **part-time** employees work less than 35 hours per week. **Full-time** employees work 35 hours or more per week.

Temporary/Permanent Many businesses hire workers to provide assistance during busy times. For example, retailers hire additional sales personnel before Christmas. Farmers hire additional workers to harvest crops. Temporary workers are hired for short periods of time for many reasons.

♦   Temporary workers assist when the workload is particularly heavy for a short period of time.
♦   Temporary workers fill in for permanent employees who are absent for some time. The permanent employee could be on vacation; taking maternity leave;

or taking a temporary leave of absence for illness, military service, or educational requirements.

◆   Temporary workers fill a need until the employer determines that the position is a permanent requirement.

Location Define the location or geographic area where the employee performs the required tasks. If the employee will be assembling dollhouses in your garage, your garage is the location. If the employee delivers packages to several businesses in town, the location is the area where the packages are delivered.

Many jobs involve frequent travel to different locations to meet with customers or attend seminars. If the position involves travel, the percentage of time the employee will spend out of town should be defined.

In today's age of technology, many workers never have to leave their homes. Workers can **telecommute**—work at home by using an electronic linkup with the employer. This is more common for high-tech workers who perform their tasks on a computer and turn in the result via an Internet connection. Programmers and writers are common telecommuters. Local telecommuters come into the office for meetings when necessary, but work at home most of the time.

Qualifications A standard that must be met to be considered for a specific position is a **qualification.** Qualifications identify the requirements an applicant must meet to be considered for a specific position. They limit the applicants who can apply for a position, preventing you from wasting time evaluating applications from individuals who are not able to do the job.

Salary Range One of the most important considerations to an applicant is the amount of money paid for performing a job. Generally, exempt employees are paid a **salary,** a fixed amount every week or two weeks, regardless of minor variations in the number of hours worked each week. Although many nonexempt employees are paid a salary, the majority are paid **wages,** which is payment based on the number of hours worked or pieces produced.

A **salary range** is the minimum and maximum amount an employee can be paid for performing a job. The salary range is defined for each position. An employee with little experience in the job is paid a salary or wage close to the minimum amount. A more experienced employee is paid a higher salary, closer to the maximum amount.

Hours The time that a job is performed and the number of hours worked in a specified time period are part of the job description. This is important if the employee is expected to work hours that are long or unusual. For example, if an employee is expected to work on weekends or until a business closes in the evening, it should be stated clearly in the job description.

Career Path Individuals who become managers and chief executive officers usually held several previous jobs. Positions that provide related experience and increasing responsibility form a **career path,** such as the example in Figure 10.3. Many employees who want to advance their careers look for positions to help them reach their goals. Defining the position's place in the career path helps employees decide if the position is a step in the right direction for their career.

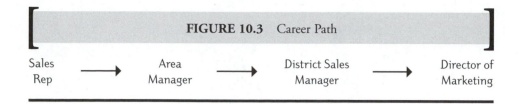

FIGURE 10.3 Career Path

| Sales Rep | → | Area Manager | → | District Sales Manager | → | Director of Marketing |

Employee Characteristics

When hiring an employee, you should consider more than the individual's experience. Personality and work behavior can be critical to an employee's success.

Personality Many jobs require more than experience and education. Characteristics such as dependability, detail-orientation, or creativity are necessary for specific positions. For example, a sales clerk who opens the store each morning must be dependable and punctual. A marketing assistant should be creative.

Hiring Relatives Financial reasons or family politics cause many small business owners to rely on relatives to complete some business tasks. If you have to depend on relatives when you would prefer to hire outside assistance, try to match appropriate tasks to the interests and skills of the family member. You may discover talents you didn't expect in your family. After all, your family may not have identified you as an entrepreneur, either.

Hypothetical Scenario

Frank and Janice Lin calculated that Lin Candles was currently earning $2,500 a month, but it had the potential to earn much more. Only the week before, a local gift shop owner approached Janice about selling Lin Candles in her store. If Janice and Frank accepted the order, their business income would immediately double. However, Janice would not be able to complete the needed work with only the limited hours that Frank was able to help. Frank and Janice decided to hire some part-time help, someone who could package the candles while Janice concentrated on designing and manufacturing new scents and candles.

Write and Place a Job Advertisement

The purpose of publishing information about an available position is to attract the right person for the job. The advertisement has to interest the individual enough to apply for the position. Therefore, the advertisement has to say the right thing in the right location to reach the right person.

What to Say

Start with the job description. It contains all the information you need to write a job advertisement. A variety of approaches can be used to write a job advertisement. The style can be objective, intriguing, or humorous. Regardless of the approach you use, the ad should contain several pieces of necessary information. Additional information is optional. The advertisement in Figure 10.4 can be placed in a newspaper to advertise the sales clerk position described in Figure 10.1.

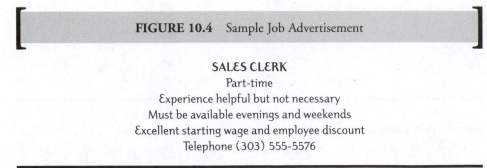

FIGURE 10.4   Sample Job Advertisement

SALES CLERK
Part-time
Experience helpful but not necessary
Must be available evenings and weekends
Excellent starting wage and employee discount
Telephone (303) 555-5576

As you write the advertisement, remember that your purpose is to find and hire the right individual, not to receive an application from every unemployed person in the city. Include information that limits the number of applicants to those individuals who are qualified to fill your needs.

Necessary Information
*   **Job title**—The title enables the applicant and the business to identify the advertised position.
*   **Responsibilities**—A brief description of the tasks to be performed helps the reader decide to apply for the position.
*   **Contact information**—The advertisement must contain a method of contacting your business to apply for the job. However, you do not have to provide your name, the name of the business, your phone number, or your address. If you want to remain anonymous, rent a post office box and provide only the box number and address in the ad. This protects you and your business from being flooded with phone calls, letters, or personal appearances from hopeful applicants.

Optional Information
*   **Responsibilities**—Additional details limit the number of applicants.
*   **Supervisor**—Use the title of the supervisor, not the supervisor's name. This gives an applicant an understanding of the position's place in the business hierarchy.
*   **Job classification**—This information filters applicants. For example, individuals looking for full-time permanent employment won't apply for a part-time temporary position.
*   **Location**—If the position requires a large percentage of time traveling, many potential applicants will lose interest.
*   **Qualifications**—List your requirements. For example, if the position requires fluent Spanish, desktop publishing skills, or a pilot's license, placing this information in the advertisement limits the number of applicants.
*   **Salary range**—Salary information limits applications. When you hire an individual, this prevents any questions or negotiation about the salary.

◆ **Hours**—Readers assume a regular 8 to 5 workday. Deviations from a normal schedule limit applicants.

Where to Say It

The right location depends on whom you are trying to reach. Teenagers who want work in your restaurant probably don't read *The Wall Street Journal.* Accountants won't walk in your door asking for a job. Select the location that is most likely to reach the applicant you are seeking.

Local Newspapers An excellent location that reaches a variety of readers is your local newspaper. Many job seekers read the classified ads in the Sunday paper, prepared to circle your ad with a red pen while they drink their morning coffee.

The ads are usually grouped by the type of position advertised. Categories usually include Professional, Part-time, Sales, and Management. Be sure that your advertisement is placed in the right category in the Help Wanted section.

Trade Journals If you are seeking applicants with knowledge in a particular field, a trade journal reaches a target segment of the population that is knowledgeable, or at least interested, in the field. Trade journals specialize in a specific industry such as steel, paper, or programming. Most trade journals contain advertisements in the last few pages. Because trade journals are directed to a group of people with shared interests, they usually are not limited to a specific geographic region. Therefore, most positions advertised in trade journals are seeking high-level employees, usually well-paid professionals who are willing to relocate to find employment.

Schools Part-time workers and new graduates can be reached at local high schools, technical schools, and colleges. Instructors, counselors, and campus employment offices are happy to work with employers to place their students and graduates in appropriate positions. Prepare your job advertisement, contact the school, and wait to hear from hopeful applicants.

Employment Agencies State and private employment agencies are excellent sources of applicants. Nonprofessional workers can often be reached by government agencies. The employer does not pay a fee for the employment services provided by the state.

Private agencies are more useful in identifying applicants for professional and management positions. Private agencies filter applicants and conduct the first round of interviews. By the time a potential employee reaches your door through a private agency, he or she has advanced to the short list of qualified applicants. Of course, a fee is charged for the service the agency provides. The employer always pays a fee. If an individual is hired, the new employee may have to pay a fee to the agency as well. It is usually calculated as a percentage of the salary earned by the employee. The employer can choose to pay both fees so the new employee doesn't pay any fee. Before working with any private agency, be sure that you understand the services provided and the fees to be paid.

Internet Many companies place advertisements on web sites that specialize in providing space to businesses and job seekers. Individuals post information about their experience, qualifications, and the type of position they want. Employers post information about the company and available positions. The site presents information about the job seekers whose qualifications match the employer's requirements.

The fees charged by some large sites can be steep. For example, one site charges employers a $2,500 fee to post 1–5 job openings. If you choose to post openings on the Internet, be cautious about the site you select. Understand the fees and services.

Additional Sources of Applicants

Sometimes you are given the opportunity to hire an excellent employee without conducting an extensive search that can be expensive. The right employee may come to you.

Walk-Ins Hopeful job seekers visit many businesses, such as restaurants and retailers, every day. **Walk-ins,** people who walk into your business to ask for a job, are most likely to apply for low-level nonprofessional positions. Many are seeking part-time temporary jobs for the summer months or Christmas holidays. Be sure to consider these applicants when you want to fill an appropriate position. Walk-ins have already demonstrated interest in your business and personal initiative, two important characteristics of successful employees.

Referrals "Who you know" is important in finding a good job and finding a good employee. Use your connections. Talk to people you trust. If you already have an employee who is performing well, he or she may be able to recommend someone else who would also perform well. Referrals happen all the time. When people talk, they exchange information. If you are alert, you will often receive information about someone who could be the person you need.

Temporary Employees Don't miss the opportunities right under your nose. If a position is really necessary, someone may already be doing the work. If you hired a temporary employee who has been filling the position, consider offering the individual a permanent job if you are happy with the current results. You've already done the training and the temporary employee is performing the work well. Take advantage of the situation.

Hypothetical Scenario

Janice and Frank prepared an advertisement to place in the newspaper of a local college. They both worked while they were in college, so they decided to create a position for a local student. The advertisement stated: "Part-time. Flexible daytime work hours. Packing and shipping products for small local company. $10 per hour. Call for more information." Seven students responded to the ad and requested additional information and an interview.

Interview Applicants

At this point, you are ready to review the responses you received from your advertisement. The type of responses you receive depends on the level and complexity of the position and the contact method you specified. Buyers, administrative assistants, or managers may submit résumés through the mail, e-mail, or fax machine. A **résumé** is a document that summarizes an individual's qualifications, education, and experience.

Review the information you receive from the job candidates. Highlight or note any information that makes one applicant stand out over another. Compare the qualifications of the candidates and the description of the job to be performed. Select the candidates who are the best match. Contact them by telephone and schedule interviews.

Preparing to Interview Applicants

An **interview** is a meeting at which information is obtained from a person. Although the applicant is there to answer your questions, you are also being interviewed. The applicant wants to determine if you are a good employer. It is an opportunity for you to get to know each other, determine if the applicant can perform the job, and evaluate how the employee will "fit in" with your work style, the business, your customers, and other employees or professionals involved in the business.

Illegal Questions An interview is not an opportunity to discover information you could not ask on the application. Similar topics are forbidden because they could cause discrimination in hiring practices. Avoid the following topics:

- Religion
- Color
- Race
- National origin
- Marital status
- Sexual orientation
- Childcare arrangements
- Family plans
- Disability

You can't ask questions designed to solicit information about these topics. Illegal questions include the following examples:

- Are you married?
- Who cares for your children when you work?
- What is your political party?
- Do you have any illnesses?
- What church do you attend?

Although you can't ask questions about these topics, applicants will often bring up the topic. If the applicant starts the topic, he or she may provide information that you cannot request.

Types of Interviews The Department of Labor identifies three interview styles—patterned, nondirective, and group. Use the format that makes you the most comfortable.

A **patterned interview** is very structured. You have identified areas you want to investigate and prepared a list of questions. All interviewees are asked the same questions.

A flexible format is characteristic of the **nondirective interview.** This interview style is conversational. Questions asked vary from one interview to another because they are not written in advance and the interviewer responds to the conversation.

A **group interview** is usually more intimidating for applicants. A panel of several managers from the company takes turns asking questions. A group interview is probably the most stressful format for the applicant.

Prepared Questions The most common approach is a mix of the patterned and nondirective interview styles that includes some standard questions. Make a list of questions to ask or topics to investigate with all the applicants. Be sure to ask all of these questions in every interview. You don't want to complete an interview without knowing if the candidate has the skills to perform the necessary tasks.

Use the job description to write the list of prepared questions. Your questions should enable you to determine the extent of each applicant's knowledge and skills. Ask how to perform specific tasks. Review the necessary qualifications and ask how the candidate meets each requirement. These standard questions provide a yardstick to measure each candidate's abilities.

Additional Questions Interviews can be as interesting and challenging as you want them to be. The questions you ask set the tone for the interaction between you and the applicant. Some interesting interview questions make the experience more challenging for the applicant and reveal additional information about the applicant's experience and personal characteristics. Consider asking some of the following questions:

- What can you do for us that someone else can't do?
- What qualities do you find important in a coworker?
- How will this job fit into your career plans?
- What were your biggest responsibilities in previous jobs?
- How much supervision have you typically received in previous jobs?
- What kind of people do you find it most difficult to work with? Why?
- In your previous jobs, what kind of pressures did you encounter?
- What do you think are the most important characteristics and abilities a person must possess to become a successful in this career field? How do you rate yourself in these areas?
- What was your most difficult decision in the last six months? What made it difficult?

Conducting an Interview

Just hearing the word "interview" is enough to cause many people to break into a cold sweat. Relax. You're on the other side of the table now. You're interviewing them!

Job Application When candidates arrive, ask them to fill out an application. An application, like a résumé, summarizes an individual's qualifications, education, and experience. The application contains the same standard questions in standard locations. You don't have to search for answers to a specific question that interests you. The information requested is the same for every candidate, making it easier to objectively compare candidates.

You do not need to create an application. Standard applications that meet federal regulations are available at office supply stores such as Staples and Office Depot. Federal regulations concerning employment applications are designed to prevent discrimination on the basis of gender, nationality, race, age, appearance, religion, or disability. Therefore, applications avoid the following questions:

◆ Original or unmarried name
◆ Place of birth of the applicant or the applicant's family
◆ Age or date of birth
◆ Salutations such as Mr. or Mrs.
◆ Marital status or number of children
◆ Race or color, including color of skin, hair, or eyes
◆ Height or weight
◆ Photograph of the applicant
◆ Religion
◆ Disability
◆ Citizenship
◆ Arrests that did not result in convictions

Skills Test Before interviewing, you can ask each applicant to take a skills test related to the tasks in the job description. For example, ask a chef to prepare a dish, an administrative assistant to complete a typing test, or a programmer to write a program. Scores or test results provide accurate information about the applicant's skills and help you compare similar applicants. Some applicants could be disqualified almost immediately.

You can require that the applicant take a test that evaluates the skills needed to succeed in the job. You can also require a practical demonstration of their skills, such as cooking. The test you require does not have to be complicated or require hours for the applicant to complete. Use the job description to identify skills that can be tested. Write a simple test that requires an applicant to use the basic skills needed for the job.

Interview the Applicants Prior to each interview, review the information you have about the applicant, the job description, and the list of questions you want to ask. If a skills test was given, evaluate the result. This prepares you to conduct the interview.

Meet the individuals in a business location where you won't be interrupted. For example, meet in your office or an available meeting room. If this isn't possible, consider meeting in a nearby restaurant with a quiet atmosphere. Don't try to serve customers and interview applicants at the same time. Hiring someone is a serious decision that deserves your full attention.

Greet applicants with a firm handshake. Open the interview by discussing a topic that makes you comfortable—an overview of your business. When the applicants are more relaxed, you can spring the tough questions.

Give the applicants enough time to answer questions. Notice how long a response requires and how applicants choose and phrase their responses.

Provide time for the applicants to ask questions. They need enough information to decide about accepting a position with your business. The questions the applicants ask reveal information about them, too. Are they concerned about the work schedule, promotions, the amount of travel involved, or the company's financial performance?

During the interview, be sure to ask any standard questions that apply to every applicant. Ask for permission to contact any references provided. Ask applicants if you can contact their current employer. Request explanations if they don't want you to speak to references or employers.

You can take brief notes if necessary, but it adds extra tension to a situation that is already stressful for the applicants. When the interview is complete, tell each applicant when a decision will be made and when you will make contact. Shake hands again and escort the applicant to the exit.

Evaluate Each Applicant   The evaluation process began when the applicant responded to your advertisement. As you continue to interact with the applicant, your image of the person becomes clearer. The interview brings the information together to form an opinion that provides the basis for selecting the right person who can help your business succeed.

When you select employees, you are looking for three things—individuals who *can* do the job, who *will* do the job, and who *fit* in with other personnel and the business situation. The proper qualifications provided by education and training prove that an individual *can* do the job. Experience in performing a similar job indicates that an individual *will* do the job. The individual's behavior in the interview helps you determine if he or she will *fit* smoothly into your business without creating problems.

Look for several characteristics or signs during the interview. Applicants should be knowledgeable, enthusiastic, prepared, honest, and professional. They should have knowledge and experience with your product or in your industry. An enthusiastic applicant is excited about the opportunity to work in your business. A prepared applicant researched your business as much as possible. An honest applicant evaluates his or her skills objectively and answers questions truthfully. A professional is able to present himself or herself in a businesslike manner.

Immediately after each interview, while the experience is fresh in your mind, complete the evaluation form in Figure 10.5. If you have two or more interviews scheduled back-to-back, take the time to evaluate the first applicant before meeting with the second applicant. You may not believe it now, but the applicants will blur in your memory after the interview.

FIGURE 10.5   Applicant Evaluation Form

Applicant Evaluation Form

Applicant: _____

Position: _____

Date: _____

5—Excellent   4—Good   3—Average   2—Below Average   1—Unsatisfactory

Application:

Area	Rating	Comments
Application—Complete and readable	1 2 3 4 5	
Qualifications—Has required education and experience	1 2 3 4 5	

Skills Test:

Score—Performance and accuracy	1 2 3 4 5	
Timely—Reasonable length of time	1 2 3 4 5	

Interview:

Knowledge—Product and industry	1 2 3 4 5	
Enthusiasm—Interested in working for your business	1 2 3 4 5	
Prepared—Researched business	1 2 3 4 5	
Honest—Evaluates skills accurately and answers truthfully	1 2 3 4 5	
Presentation—Promptness, appearance, self-confidence, energy level	1 2 3 4 5	
Communication skills—Verbal and nonverbal; articulate, effective, good listening skills	1 2 3 4 5	
Teamwork—Able to work with others	1 2 3 4 5	
Problem solving—Can identify issues, solve problems, and evaluate potential consequences of actions	1 2 3 4 5	
Personality and behavior—Connection with applicant, fit with business and personnel	1 2 3 4 5	
Reference—Contact references	1 2 3 4 5	
Sum of ratings		

Additional Notes:

_____
_____
_____
_____
_____

Are applicant's skills a match for position?   Yes   No

Should applicant be considered for the position?   Yes   No

Hypothetical Scenario

Janice and Frank asked the college for an available room to conduct interviews. The college placement office was happy to provide assistance. They took product samples and a laptop computer with them to the interviews. When they met with the applicants, they asked each student to fill out an application and displayed the best-selling candle products. Because the students would need to create address labels and keep computer records of the sales and shipments, each applicant was asked to demonstrate computer skills by accessing the business web site and creating labels.

Hire a Candidate

Selecting and hiring the right candidate for a position in your business is very rewarding. It creates a relationship between the business and the employee that could last a very long time.

Make an Offer

Any employment offer should be made in writing. This prevents any confusion for you and the candidate. The **employment letter** should include the following elements, as shown in Figure 10.6.

- **Job title**—Confirms the job to be performed.
- **Job description**—Briefly describes the tasks to be performed and confirms the responsibilities and actions expected of the employee.
- **Start date**—Identifies the employee's first day of work for the business.
- **Probation**—Describes the length of time and details of any **probation,** the trial period when an employee is subject to testing and evaluation to determine fitness for the position.
- **Starting salary**—Confirms the amount the employee will be paid for performing the job.
- **Employee handbook**—Identifies any benefits or perks the employee receives, vacation time, and termination procedures.
- **Disclaimer**—States that the employment offer from the company is made in writing. No oral commitments have been made. This protects the business from false claims by an applicant who could have claimed that a higher salary or better position was offered verbally.
- **Deadline for acceptance**—If the candidate has not accepted the job by a specific date, the offer can be withdrawn. This enables you to offer it to someone else.
- **Your name and signature**—Confirms that you are the individual authorized to make a job offer.

FIGURE 10.6   Employment Letter

\<Company's Name – Company's Address – Company's City, State, Zip Code\>

\<Date\>

\<Candidate's Name\>
\<Candidate's Address\>
\<Candidate's City, State, Zip Code\>

Dear \<Candidate's Name\>:

I am pleased to offer you a \<full-time\> position with \<Company's Name\> as \<Job Title\> beginning \<Start Date\>. Your starting salary is $\<Dollar Amount\> per \<Hour/Week/Month/Year\>.

As a(n) \<Job Title\>, you are responsible for the following activities.
\<Job Description\>

An employee handbook is enclosed. It describes employee benefits, vacation, and termination procedures. The employee handbook and this employment letter form the entire commitment offered to you. No oral commitment has been made. The company and any representatives of the company are not authorized to make oral commitments regarding employment.

To accept this position, please sign the bottom of this letter as indicated and return it to me by \<Date\>. Contact me at \<Phone Number\> if you have any questions. I look forward to hearing from you.

Welcome to the team,

\<Your Signature\>

\<Your name\>
\<Your title\>

Enclosure

I accept your employment offer. I have received a copy of the current employee handbook. I acknowledge that no oral commitments have been made. The employee handbook and this letter form the entire employment offer.

Employee's Signature: _____

Date: _____

Contingencies

An employment offer can be made with **contingencies,** meaning that the offer depends on something else occurring first. The employment offer does not occur if the contingency doesn't occur. The contingency must be identified in the employment letter. Alter the text in the first paragraph of the letter as shown in Figure 10.7.

FIGURE 10.7   Contingency in Employment Letter

I am pleased to offer you a full-time position with ‹Company's Name› as ‹Job Title› beginning ‹Start Date›. Your starting salary is $‹Dollar Amount› per ‹Hour/Week/Month/Year›. This employment offer is contingent upon ‹Description of Contingency›.

Common contingencies include a medical examination, a drug test, and background checks. **Check the laws in your state. Some options may not be permitted in your state or permission from the applicant may be required before you can pursue any testing or background checks.**

Medical Examination   An employment offer can be contingent on the results of a medical examination. However, the business must require all new employees in the same job category to have a medical exam. If a disability is found, the business can't reject the potential employee unless the disability prevents the applicant from performing the job. A medical examination can't be required before making the job offer. The Americans with Disabilities Act is a federal act that regulates this.

Drug Test   Federal and state laws regulating drug testing are complex. State laws vary. Generally, you can require that an applicant pass a drug test after making the employment offer if you tell applicants that the test is part of the required screening process, test all applicants for the same type of job after an employment offer is made, and use a state-certified laboratory to administer the tests.

Background Check   Federal and state laws regulate a variety of background checks. State laws frequently differ. The most common information to examine during a background check includes driving records, criminal convictions, and credit history.

Driving Record   If the list of responsibilities includes driving a company vehicle, you can check the applicant's driving record. Contact the Department of Motor Vehicles (DMV) in your state. You may be required to pay a small fee of $2 to $10 and complete a form. The DMV can provide information about the applicant's traffic violations, driving-related offenses, and data on the license. You may need to provide the applicant's full name, date of birth, address, and license number.

Criminal Convictions   Many jobs deal with sensitive information or people who require protection. Some states prohibit convicted criminals from working in specific career areas, such as nursing homes and day care centers, or having access to weapons, drugs, and master keys. Conviction records are public information, available to anyone who wants to search the records. Most states do not permit you to research arrests that didn't result in convictions.

Credit History If the responsibilities of the position include dealing with valuable items or large sums of money, a credit check is reasonable for potential employees. Again, obtaining this information is a regulated activity. Many states require you to inform the applicant in writing and receive written permission from the applicant. After permission is received, you can contact a credit agency. For a fee of $25 to $50, the agency will provide a credit report. A credit report contains information about the applicant's address, Social Security number, bankruptcies, tax liens, judgments, child support obligations, loans, and the name of any other employer who has requested a credit check on the applicant.

Reject Candidates

You will reject many more applicants than you hire. When you interviewed applicants, you told them when the hiring decision would be made. Don't keep them in suspense. Send rejection letters immediately after the successful candidate has accepted your offer. The rejection letter in Figure 10.8 provides an example that can be sent to applicants who were interviewed but not selected. The standard rejection letter identifies your company, the position that has been filled, your name, your title, and your signature.

FIGURE 10.8   Rejection Letter

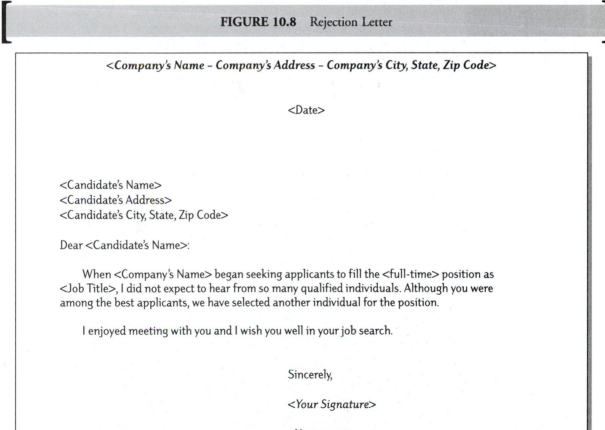

Hypothetical Scenario

Frank and Janice decided that four of the applicants had the skills they needed. However, one student stood out from the others. As an art major, her computer database skills were not as advanced as one of the other students, but she seemed alert enough to learn quickly. The most convincing feature was her enthusiasm for the growth of the business. She volunteered her art skills in designing more creative labels for the candles. Janice felt that the girl was smart and likable. She believed that the girl could perform the job well and contribute a little extra to the business if they took advantage of her skills. After discussing the candidates, Frank and Janice made their selection and offered her the job.

Technology Insights

Telecommuting Employees

Home-based telecommuting is gaining in popularity. It has advantages for employers and employees. Employers do not need to provide on-site workspace. They gain increased job performance, decreased absenteeism, decreased employee turnover, and reduced office expenses. Employees gain flexibility in arranging their work schedules and reduce the time and expense consumed by traveling to and from work. Telecommuting has some equipment requirements. Telecommuters need a computer, preferably a laptop, and a modem to connect directly to your network or the Internet. This enables the employee to transfer files to and from your computer or Internet site. You can also lease a high-speed telephone line to reduce the time needed to transfer files. Hiring telecommuting employees benefits you and the employee.

Think Critically Identify the equipment you would need to purchase for a telecommuting employee.

CHAPTER REVIEW

It is often difficult to determine when your business would benefit from hiring an additional employee. The reasons to hire more workers vary. Some companies add employees to help the business grow while others add employees to make the business experience more enjoyable for themselves and their families. After deciding to hire an employee, you must write a job description entailing the tasks the employee will perform and the qualifications they need.

After identifying the responsibilities of the new employee, you can determine how to attract qualified candidates. Use the job description to write an advertisement. Place the ad in a location where the perfect candidate will encounter it and respond. Options include your local newspaper, a trade journal, a web site, and an employment agency.

After the ad is placed, sift through the responses. Select the most qualified individuals for interviews. Most interviewers use a combination of prepared questions and conversational interaction to gather information to select one candidate and eliminate others. If it is appropriate, a skills test can help you select the most qualified candidate. Evaluate each candidate immediately after he or she is interviewed. Be sure to avoid illegal questions during the interviews.

After making a decision, extend an offer in an employment letter. The letter should contain the basic information about the job, including the title, responsibilities, and salary. When your candidate accepts, inform the other applicants by sending rejection letters.

USE BUSINESS TERMS

Fill in the blanks with the appropriate term.

career path   nonexempt
contingency   overtime
docked   part-time
employment letter   patterned interview
exempt   probation
Fair Labor Standards Act (FLSA)   qualification
full-time   résumé
group interview   salary
interview   salary range
job description   supervisor
job responsibilities   telecommute
job title   wages
nondirective interview   walk-in

1. Nonexempt employees are usually paid ___?___ .
2. An employment offer does not occur if the ___?___ doesn't occur.
3. New employees may have a period of ___?___ when they are subjected to testing and evaluation to determine fitness for the position.
4. A(n) ___?___ interview is very flexible.
5. Buyers, administrative assistants, or managers may submit ___?___ through the mail, e-mail, or fax machine.
6. Employees who advance to higher positions are following a(n) ___?___ .
7. ___?___ limit the applicants who can apply for a position, preventing you from wasting time evaluating applications from individuals who are not able to do the job.

TEST YOUR READING

8. What elements should be included in a job description?
9. Why is a job title significant to workers?
10. What qualifies a business to be covered by the Fair Labor Standards Act?
11. Why is a job position considered to be exempt?
12. How many hours does a full-time employee work?
13. What services does a private employment agency provide?
14. What determines the number of applicants who will respond to your advertisement?
15. Why does an employer ask a job seeker to complete an application?
16. Why should an employer avoid asking some questions during an interview?
17. Identify the elements in an employment letter.

18.   Why would an employer check an applicant's driving record?

19.   How do you inform an applicant that he or she was selected?

THINK CRITICALLY ABOUT BUSINESS

20.   What is the current minimum wage? Calculate the annual salary of a worker who works full time for minimum wage. Describe the standard of living for this individual.

21.   Describe the career path you have followed or expect to follow.

22.   Write a job description for your current job or the job of someone you know.

23.   Where would you advertise to find a pediatrician to join your medical practice?

REAL-LIFE BUSINESS

Task Masters

Julie Morgenstern started her business with a $100 loan from a friend. She spent $25 on an ad and $75 on business cards and stationery. When she established Task Masters in 1989, it was based on the idea that many people have tasks they don't want to do or don't have time to complete. The first advertisement included a list of tasks that Task Masters could perform, such as errands, cleaning rooms, managing a move, and planning parties. Her first client asked her to perform a difficult task that most people don't want to tackle—organizing and submitting years of health insurance claims.

Additional advertising attracted about five clients every month. She shopped for groceries, renewed passports, created scrapbooks, and organized work and living spaces. She quickly reached the point where she could not perform all the requested tasks herself. She chose to hire assistance to expand her business.

Creative marketing ideas, such as "the messiest office in New York City contest" received national attention. She was a guest on *Good Morning America, Oprah,* and *The Today Show.*

Today, Task Masters specializes in helping individuals and businesses get organized. It provides workshops and seminars about organizational skills. The company has expanded to Boston, Los Angeles, Minneapolis, New Jersey, and New York City.

Think Critically

1.   What idea was the basis for Task Masters?

2.   What type of tasks does the business perform?

3.   How did marketing help Morgenstern?

4.   Look at Task Masters' web site at www.juliemorgenstern.com/task_masters.html. What else has Morgenstern done to expand her business?

CHAPTER 11

Human Resources Activities

GOALS

- Write an employee handbook
- Provide benefits
- Train and evaluate employees
- Terminate and recommend employees

When Rebecca Carter started her business two years ago, she had no idea it would be so successful. Her experience in art restoration made her notice the graffiti that appeared on buildings, park benches, and bus stops. After a few months of research and hard work, she established Carter's Clean Slate, a business that specialized in removing graffiti and restoring building exteriors and statues.

Write an Employee Handbook

Many owners of small businesses often wonder if it is necessary to write down formal rules and procedures you want employees to follow. Lawsuits against employers are common. Sometimes the complaint is legitimate. Other times it isn't. However, it takes only one lawsuit to financially ruin your small business. An **employee handbook,** a written document containing your personnel policies, is the first line of protection for your business.

Note: Laws regarding employees and company policies vary from state to state. Consult the regulations in your state and obtain legal advice before finalizing your employee handbook.

Purpose of the Employee Handbook

An employee handbook does more than offer some protection from lawsuits. An employee handbook performs several functions:

- **Describes the purpose and goals of the business**—A brief statement describes the purpose of the business and the principles that guide the operation of the business.
- **Provides guidelines for employees' behavior**—A handbook defines the rules regarding employee activities. This can include the use of company property, smoking policy, and attendance requirements.
- **Provides guidelines for employer's behavior**—The handbook also looks at behavior from the other side by defining the rules regarding the employer's activities. This can include topics such as sexual harassment, hiring practices, and employee evaluation procedures.
- **Ensures that all employees are treated equally**—Recording the guidelines your business follows ensures that your reaction is the same each time you encounter the same situation. For example, if two employees arrive an hour late, both receive the same disciplinary action. One won't be fired while the other employee is merely warned.
- **Describes employee benefits**—Identifying and explaining the benefits employees receive guarantees that employees are informed. Topics include vacation, medical insurance, and retirement plans.

Basic Requirements

When you hire your first employee, you should be able to place an employee handbook in the employee's hands. Many small businesses start with only a basic handbook. As the company grows, they add more policies and information. However, several topics should be covered in the most basic employee handbook. These items include an acknowledgment form, mission statement, nondiscrimination policy, safety rules and guidelines, use of company property, work hours, absence, pay periods, performance evaluation procedures, vacation days, and holidays.

Acknowledgment Form It is your responsibility to provide each employee with an employee handbook. It is the employee's responsibility to become familiar with the handbook. The **acknowledgment form** is a written statement the employee signs to declare that he or she has received the employee handbook. File the acknowledgment form in a secure place. This statement proves that you provided the handbook, fulfilling your responsibility. The employee can't claim he or she "didn't know." The form shows that the employee was provided with the information.

Verify that the employee has read the handbook and has no questions about its content. Schedule an appointment within the first week or two of the employee's hire date. Review the policies and procedures documented in the handbook. Be sure to answer any questions the employee may have. Keep a list of questions asked or information that wasn't clear. This helps you update the handbook in the future.

Many companies send an employee handbook with the employment letter. The new employee must sign and return the letter, as shown in Figure 11.1, to accept the position and acknowledge receipt of the employee handbook.

FIGURE 11.1   Acknowledgment Form in Employment Letter

I accept your employment offer. I have received a copy of the current employee handbook. I acknowledge that no oral commitments have been made. The employee handbook and this letter form the entire employment offer.

Employee's Signature: _____

Date: _____

If you don't include the acknowledgment form in the employment letter, it should be on the first page of the handbook. After the employee signs the form, remove the form and file it as you would file the signed employment letter. The acknowledgment form in an employee handbook, as shown in Figure 11.2, should contain several statements.

- The employee acknowledges that he or she has received and read the handbook.
- New information and policies can be implemented at any time.
- The handbook is not an employment agreement and does not guarantee employment.
- It confirms the employee's status as an **"at will"** employee. Either the employee or employer can terminate the employment relationship between an "at will" employee and employer at any time.
- It states that no agreements made by any company representative conflict with the statements in the acknowledgment form.
- The employee's signature and date ensure that the employee has received and read the acknowledgment form and handbook.

FIGURE 11.2   Acknowledgment Form in Employment Handbook

Acknowledgment Form

I acknowledge that I have received and read a copy of the <Company Name> employee handbook.

I agree that:

- New information and policies can be implemented at any time.
- The employee handbook is not an employment agreement and does not guarantee employment.
- I am an "at will" employee. My employment may be terminated by <Company Name> or me at any time for any reason or no reason.
- No statements, agreements, or promises made by any representative of <Company Name> conflict with the statements in this acknowledgment form.

Employee's Signature: _____

Date: _____

Mission Statement When you wrote your company's business plan, you created a mission statement for your business. The mission statement is a brief description of your company's purpose that sets expectations for your customers and employees. Although it is limited to one or two sentences, the mission statement contains: (1) the product or service your company provides, (2) a description of the company's customers, (3) the geographic area you service, (4) your company's unique business idea, (5) your methods of doing business, and (6) your vision for the future of the company. The example in Figure 11.3 contains the mission statement for a small candy manufacturer.

FIGURE 11.3   Mission Statement for Kingston Candy Maker

Mission Statement

To design and manufacture unique nonfat candy treats for customers requiring alternatives to chocolate and provide fast, friendly service to stores and Internet customers.

This area can be expanded later to include additional information such as the importance of the employees in the success of the business and a short history of the business. For the basic employee handbook, the mission statement provides important information about your business.

Nondiscrimination Policy When you interviewed and hired an employee, you acted as an equal opportunity employer. You did not consider employee characteristics such as race, religion, gender, age, or disability.

Your responsibility as an equal opportunity employer does not end when the employee is hired. Just as physical characteristics could not be used to discriminate against potential employees, they cannot be considered after an employee has been hired. For example, you cannot award or deny promotions based on criteria such as religion or gender, criteria that are not related to the employee's ability. Businesses that do not follow equal opportunity guidelines will eventually encounter an employee who protests unfair practices. Therefore, it is a good idea to state your nondiscrimination policy, such as the example given in Figure 11.4, at the beginning of the employee handbook, and follow it faithfully.

FIGURE 11.4   Nondiscrimination Policy

Nondiscrimination Policy

<Company Name> is an Equal Opportunity Employer, providing equal opportunities to applicants and employees without considering race, religion, color, gender, national origin, age, disability, or sexual orientation. All employees should take advantage of any opportunities for promotion that occur. Every employee is expected to create a work environment in which all employees are treated fairly and feel respected.

Safety Rules and Guidelines The type of business you operate and the activities the employees are expected to perform determine the rules and guidelines you should document as well as the length of this section in the employee handbook. A receptionist who answers the phone in an office faces less danger on an average day than a worker at a construction site or steel mill.

It is your responsibility to provide appropriate safety equipment. Periodic training and evacuation drills ensure that employees know how to respond when an emergency occurs. If you or any of your employees has a mobility impairment that prevents the use of stairs, consult the local fire department for assistance in developing an evacuation plan if the standard plan is not sufficient.

The **Occupational Safety and Health Administration (OSHA)** was established to prevent work-related injuries, illnesses, and deaths. It was created on December 29, 1970, when President Richard M. Nixon signed the Occupational Safety and Health Act. OSHA inspects workplaces and charges fines of up to $70,000 for safety violations. In 2000, OSHA conducted 36,350 inspections; states conducted an additional 54,510 inspections. Most inspections were conducted at construction and manufacturing sites.

Employers are required to display posters about health and safety issues. Check the OSHA guidelines to determine which posters your business is required to display. Posters, such as the example in Figure 11.5, can be downloaded from www.osha.gov and enlarged to meet legal specifications. OSHA provides free workplace consultation to small businesses that want on-site assistance establishing safety and health programs as well as identifying and correcting workplace hazards.

FIGURE 11.5   OSHA Poster

A notice, such as the example in Figure 11.6, could be placed at the beginning of the safety section. Safety rules and guidelines specific to your business should follow, or the notice can refer to a separate safety handbook.

FIGURE 11.6   Safety Notice

Safety Notice

<Company Name> provides a safe work environment that complies with the Occupational Safety and Health Act of 1970. You are expected to actively maintain this environment. Follow all posted safety rules and safety instructions provided by your supervisor. Use safety equipment when it is required.

<Company Name> provides all necessary safety equipment. Learn its location and maintain and use the equipment correctly. Report any defects or malfunctions immediately. Any employee who deliberately violates a safety rule or creates a hazard will be disciplined and may be terminated.

Use of Company Property   Your business has a variety of equipment that is used by your employees. To protect your business income, value, and reputation, it is often necessary to place limitations on employee usage. For example, a sales clerk who spends hours chatting on the phone ties up your business phone and neglects customers who need assistance. This behavior loses sales and hurts your reputation. A programmer who surfs the Internet during work hours is not performing necessary business tasks. A delivery driver who runs personal errands while driving the company vehicle risks the company's property unnecessarily.

A problem in many companies is **software piracy,** violating a software copyright by unauthorized copying and distribution of the software program. This includes employees who install a second copy of a game already installed on their home computers, or take your business software home to install on a personal computer. When you purchase a software program, you are buying a **user license,** permission to use the program. You can purchase a single-user license for a single user or a multiuser license that enables several individuals to use the application. Watchdog companies investigate reports of software piracy. If a software company discovers that you are violating your license agreement, you can face legal consequences such as fines or lawsuits. If employees use your computers, be sure to include usage rules in the employee handbook as shown in Figure 11.7.

FIGURE 11.7   Company Property

Company Property

<Company Name> provides any equipment needed to perform your job. Company equipment can be used only to perform assigned tasks for the company. Company equipment is not intended for personal use. Do not remove company property from the premises without written authorization from your supervisor.

FIGURE 11.7   Company Property (continued)

Computer equipment is not available for personal use. Do not install any software that is not licensed to the company. Do not install, copy, or remove any software without a written authorization form signed by your supervisor.

<Company Name> telephone lines are restricted to business use only. Personal phone calls should be limited to emergency situations. Do not place any long-distance business calls without permission from your supervisor.

Work Hours   A business can't operate efficiently without employees performing the necessary tasks. This means they must be at work performing their jobs during the expected work hours. Policies for exempt and nonexempt employees are usually described separately. Overtime occurs when a nonexempt employee works more than 40 hours in a workweek. Be sure to describe when overtime is authorized and how the nonexempt employee is compensated as shown in Figure 11.8. Check the regulations in your state regarding overtime and compensation.

FIGURE 11.8   Work Hours

Work Hours

At <Company Name>, all full-time employees are expected to work 40 hours during a normal workweek. Exempt employees may work additional hours if needed and are not eligible for overtime pay.

Overtime for Nonexempt Employees
Although a 40-hour workweek is standard, nonexempt employees are not guaranteed 40 hours of work every week. Nonexempt employees will be paid only for the hours they work. Occasionally, a supervisor may request that you work overtime. Nonexempt employees will be paid time and one-half pay for time worked exceeding 40 hours in any given workweek. Wages paid for overtime hours are paid in the pay period following the overtime.

Time Cards
Each nonexempt employee must sign in when reporting for work and sign out when taking breaks or leaving work. Do not sign in or out for another employee. Any absences must be marked on the time card. Time cards are submitted to your supervisor for approval by noon every other Friday.

Absence and Tardiness   Even though the need for employees to show up for work seems self-evident, it is still a good idea to document this requirement and identify the consequences of an employee's absences. An employee can have many valid reasons for absence. Illness, jury duty, and scheduled vacation are legitimate reasons. Many more creative reasons for absence are used in businesses across the United States every day. If employees are not disciplined for unapproved absences, this can easily become a problem for your business.

Another problem that plagues many businesses is employee tardiness. Nonexempt employees can easily be docked for tardiness if they are paid only for the hours they work. Excessive tardiness should result in disciplinary action for exempt and nonexempt employees alike. The employee handbook is the right place to describe the consequences of unapproved absences and excessive tardiness as shown in Figure 11.9.

FIGURE 11.9   Absence and Tardiness

Absence and Tardiness

Attendance is an important component of your job performance. Except for sick time, all absences must be requested and approved in advance. Excessive absences will result in disciplinary action, which could include termination.

You are expected to be at your workstation when your work hours are scheduled to begin. Any nonexempt employee who is more than five minutes late will be docked 15 minutes of pay. This occurs every 15 minutes. For example, if you are 5-15 minutes late, you will be docked for 15 minutes of pay. If you are 16-30 minutes late, you will be docked 30 minutes of pay.

Pay Periods New employees are interested in when and how they will be paid. Document the schedule for distributing paychecks. If special options such as **direct deposit,** which automatically deposits your paycheck into your savings or checking account, are available, they should be described in the employee handbook as shown in Figure 11.10.

Deductions are dollar amounts taken from an employee's pay every pay period. Federal and state regulations require you to deduct federal social security and income taxes. Additional amounts may be deducted for various reasons such as insurance coverage.

FIGURE 11.10   Pay Periods

Pay Periods

Employees are paid every two weeks.

Direct Deposit
Direct deposit is available. If you choose direct deposit, your paycheck is automatically deposited into your savings or checking account. This convenient service makes your money immediately available without visiting the bank. You will continue to receive a pay stub that provides information about the amount you were paid and any amounts deducted from your pay such as taxes and insurance.

Deductions
To comply with legal requirements, <Company Name> deducts federal social security and income taxes from your pay every pay period. The amount deducted is identified on every pay stub. Keep your pay stubs for your financial records.

Performance Evaluation Procedures Every employee should receive periodic performance reviews. A **performance review** is a process that enables an employee and supervisor to discuss and evaluate the employee's job performance. These reviews are usually conducted at specific time intervals. For example, employees are usually reviewed three to six months after they are hired. Reviews then occur annually, based on the employee's hire date. Annual performance reviews are usually associated with an increase in salary.

The employee handbook does not describe the process involved in conducting the performance review. It should contain a general description of the purpose, timing, and evaluation criteria, as shown in Figure 11.11.

FIGURE 11.11 Performance Evaluations

Performance Evaluations

A performance review is conducted six months after your hire date. After the first performance review, employees are reviewed annually.

Purpose
A performance review provides an opportunity for you and your supervisor to discuss and evaluate your performance since the last review occurred. Your performance is measured against the criteria for your position. If you perform well, you may be given an increase in salary based on merit.

Criteria
The tasks identified in your job description form the basic criteria to measure your job performance. If you are promoted or change positions within the company, you will be given a new job description.

Additional criteria can include, but are not limited to, items such as the manner in which your job is performed, attitude, and attendance. For example, your work should be completed on time, the quality of your work must be acceptable, your attitude toward customers and coworkers should be positive and friendly, and you should report to work when scheduled.

Vacation and Holidays In the United States, an employer is not required to give employees vacation or pay the employee during a vacation. If you give employees vacation time, it is only because it is generally expected.

If you give employees paid vacation, your employee handbook should describe your vacation policy as shown in Figure 11.12. This includes the employees eligible for vacation, the rate at which vacation is given, when vacation can be taken, and what happens to vacation when an employee leaves the business.

FIGURE 11.12 Vacation Policy

Vacation

After six months of employment, all full-time employees are given one paid day of vacation for each month of employment, up to a maximum of 10 working days in one year. Part-time employees who work less than 20 hours a week are not given paid vacation time.

> **FIGURE 11.12** Vacation Policy (continued)

Vacation should be taken in the year it is earned. No more than five days of vacation can be carried to the following year.

Vacation must be requested in writing and approved by your supervisor at least one month in advance. Vacation can be taken only in whole or half days.

Employees who notify their supervisors that they intend to resign at least two weeks before their last day of employment at <Company Name> will receive payment for accrued vacation. Any vacation taken before it was earned will be deducted from the final paycheck.

Holidays are usually taken on the date specified by the employer. The employee handbook describes your holiday policy, as shown in Figure 11.13. Every year, publish a memo notifying employees of the specific holiday schedule for that year.

> **FIGURE 11.13** Holiday Policy

Holidays

<Company Name> recognizes seven holidays: New Year's Day, Easter, Memorial Day, Independence Day, Labor Day, Thanksgiving, and Christmas. When a holiday occurs on a weekend, <Company Name> will observe the holiday on the Friday before or the Monday after the actual date. Full-time employees will receive full pay for the observed holiday. Part-time employees are paid for the hours they would normally work on the designated date.

Advanced Employee Handbooks

As your company grows, you may decide to provide additional benefits or guidelines for your employees. Situations that occur often inspire additions to the handbook. For example, an employee may require an extended leave to recuperate from an accident or request flexible hours to care for a long-term illness in the family. These situations can create company policy so all employees are treated equally.

When you make additions or changes, be sure to distribute an update to your existing employees. All of your employees must be informed of any new or modified policies or rules.

Hypothetical Scenario

Initially, Rebecca Carter hired students to provide part-time help at Carter's Clean Slate. Last month, Rebecca landed a contract with the city. She estimated that she needed to hire seven additional employees in the next month. Before she went too far in the hiring process, she decided to write an employee manual that could be given to each employee with an offer letter. She included all the topics on the list of basic items and added policies regarding smoking and drug use, two topics that are important to her.

Provide Benefits

Offering a good salary and pleasant working conditions aren't enough to attract and keep high-quality employees with developed skills. Employees compare compensation packages offered by different employers. **Compensation** is direct and indirect payments made to an employee. Direct payments are made in the form of wages, commissions, and bonuses. Indirect payments are made in the form of insurance, vacation time, and retirement plans.

Employees are looking for a complete compensation package. The complete package includes the highest salary possible, ideal working conditions with the most modern and effective tools, and a rewarding benefits package. **Benefits** are rewards the employee receives, in addition to a salary, for performing a job.

There is a vast array of benefits that you can provide for your employees. Minor benefits, sometimes called **perks,** can include items or services such as a reserved parking place, free coffee and snacks, and a larger cubicle with a window. Major benefits, which are usually more expensive to provide, can include on-site day care for employees' children, use of a company car, tuition assistance, and a cafeteria.

Selecting Benefits to Provide

Hiring and training new employees is expensive. You lose productivity from the individual who trains the new employee and the difference in productivity between the new employee and the former worker. You also lose the knowledge and skill that took time for the former employee to gain. Therefore, it is better for your business to retain good employees as long as possible.

Several criteria should be considered when you select benefits to offer your employees. State and federal requirements, characteristics of your employees, and the amount of money you want to spend are the three main considerations.

Legal Requirements Some benefits are mandated by law, which varies from state to state. Generally, legal requirements are based on the number of employees. Small businesses usually have fewer requirements than large businesses. In most states, legal requirements do not become a factor until you have at least three employees. This was intentionally designed to help small businesses succeed. Large businesses have more resources; therefore, they are expected to provide benefits that small businesses can't afford.

Employee Characteristics Examine the characteristics of your employees. This information helps you determine the benefits that will give you "the most bang for the buck." Match the benefits to the needs and priorities of the majority of your employees. For example, young employees who hope to complete a college degree are attracted by a tuition reimbursement plan. Older workers show interest in a retirement plan. Married employees with families prefer an insurance package that cares for spouses and children while single employees consider insurance for themselves only.

Use Table 11.1 to describe your employees. In the last column, identify benefits that would be appropriate for your employees.

General Characteristics	Your Employees	Appropriate Benefit
Average age		
Marital status		
Family size		
Interests		
Activities		
School		
Goals		

TABLE 11.1   Employee Characteristics

Cost of Benefits Review the potential benefits you identified in Table 11.1. Try to think of some alternatives that reward your employees without costing a lot of money. Be creative. Benefits can include free pizza for lunch once a month, an employee discount on your products, and a season pass to the local amusement park or zoo.

Common Benefits

Many companies offer similar benefits that employees rely on and expect. Workers' compensation, health insurance, disability insurance, and life insurance are several of the most common benefits. Insurance companies can provide these benefits. Contact an insurance agency for a price quote. Some insurance companies specialize in selling insurance benefits to employers or offer special packages to small businesses.

Workers' Compensation In most states, employers with three or more employees are required to buy **workers' compensation insurance,** which pays medical and disability benefits according to a state-approved formula when a worker is injured. It provides replacement income, medical expenses, and some rehabilitation if necessary.

Health Insurance Medical care is expensive. An illness or injury that requires a visit to a doctor's office or emergency room or a stay in the hospital can be a significant expense. Employee **health insurance** is purchased to provide financial assistance in paying medical expenses.

Health plans vary in the type of coverage they provide. Some plans pay a larger percentage of the employees' medical expenses than others. Some plans limit the physicians available for selection. Before you select a provider, create a chart that compares the services each package covers. Even if you have a small number of employees, group health plans usually cost less than buying individual health insurance policies with similar coverage. As an extra bonus, your business may receive a tax advantage for providing health insurance for your employees. As an employer, your contribution may be tax deductible. Consult your accountant and the laws in your state.

Disability Insurance The American Council of Life Insurers has determined that a 35-year-old individual is six times more likely to become disabled than die before reaching the retirement age of 65. Becoming disabled can end your ability to earn enough money to support yourself or your family. However, the value of disability insurance is often underrated. **Disability insurance** provides income replacement by paying 60 to 80 percent of the employee's normal salary when he or she can't work because of an illness or accident. Short-term disability payments are usually paid to an employee for a maximum of 26 weeks. Long-term disability benefits are paid after short-term disability payments are terminated. These payments continue until the disability ends or the recipient reaches normal retirement age.

Life Insurance Older employees and employees with families are attracted by **life insurance,** which pays one or more specified individuals when the insured employee dies. It is intended to provide financial security to the family members who rely on the employee's income.

Hypothetical Scenario

Carter's Clean Slate isn't earning enough money yet to provide more than basic benefits that are required by state law. However, Rebecca has gathered a wide range of perks to attract workers. So far, perks include a pass to the local amusement park and water park, free access to the state parks, and a discount at a local building supply store. She expects to be able to offer more common benefits in the next year.

Train and Evaluate Employees

Several activities are involved in monitoring an employee's job performance. A new employee must be trained in performing the necessary job tasks. After several months, evaluate the employee's performance. If the employee is performing well, you are on your way to a satisfying professional relationship that could last many years.

Training

After hiring a new employee, you will both experience one of the most frustrating periods in your employer–employee relationship—training. As an employer, you want the new employee to be productive and successful immediately, without any additional training or orientation required. Unfortunately, that isn't possible. The "sink or swim" approach to training a new employee just doesn't work. Skipping necessary training steps or shortening needed training time often backfires. The usual result is inadequate performance and low-quality work.

Imagine the following scenario. You're away on vacation. Suddenly, you double over with extreme abdominal pain. You're rushed to the emergency room where a doctor with the talent to make you feel better greets you. He shrugs his shoulders, and tells you, "Sorry, I haven't been taught to use the equipment yet."

Your employees may not be faced with a life or death situation. Remember, however, that they are responsible for items that are important to you, including your customers, your reputation, and your profits.

Introducing the New Employee Especially in a small group, the introduction of a new employee is an important event for the business, the new employee, and the existing staff. Depending on the mix of skills and knowledge your new employee brings, your business may be reaching a turning point. A single individual can have an enormous impact on a small business.

The new employee is entering a new situation on someone else's turf. Reinforce the new employee's place in the group. Describe the contribution the employee is expected to make. Identify any hierarchy if necessary. For example, introduce the new employee by saying, "This is Lee Smith. At his previous company, Lee increased the sales in his territory 20 percent and supervised five sales reps. When we begin selling our products next month, his responsibilities here will include establishing sales territories, hiring additional salespeople, and meeting with potential clients."

The existing staff may feel threatened by the addition of another employee. Be sure to reinforce your current employees by identifying the most important tasks they perform and a unique skill or benefit they contribute to the company's success. Introduce a current employee by saying, "This is Kristen Seldon. She keeps our computers and network running in tip-top shape. You'll work together to create the perfect web site for our business by the end of the year."

What to Teach You don't need to put too much thought into *what* to teach your new employee. When you decided to hire a new employee, you created a job description. The job description contains a list of responsibilities and tasks. To train the employee, you need to teach him or her:

◆   an overview of your business, and
◆   everything needed to perform the tasks in the job description.

Small companies don't hire a large number of employees at one time, so they usually don't have a formal training program. New employees are expected to hit the ground running but often aren't given enough information to determine the speed and direction they should run. This results in a lot of wasted time and effort spent searching for information and making false starts in the wrong direction.

A better approach organizes the information your new employee needs. In small companies, one-on-one training is common. Ask your current employees to teach specific sections that are most familiar to them. Knowing the tasks the new employee will perform, your current staff can probably determine the information the new employee needs from each area. Even if you are training your first employee, this organized approach enables you to identify the information you need to teach your new worker.

In Table 11.2, the new employee's responsibilities are listed on the left. In the second column, identify the topics needed to perform the task. You'll notice that each task has room for several topics because the employee may need several pieces of information to perform a single task. In the final column, identify the current staff member who can teach each topic. The overview and first job responsibility are completed as examples.

Note: To go to the next planning level, ask each staff member to estimate the time each topic requires. Use the information to create a training schedule.

TABLE 11.2 Employee Training Plan

Responsibilities	Topics	Staff Member
Company overview	Company history	Owner
	Products and customers	Owner
	Company goals	Owner
Order merchandise	Identify restock level	J. Maines
	Complete order form	K. Lind
	Contact supplier and place order	K. Lind

How to Teach Choosing a training method is more of a challenge than deciding what to teach. The best training method is determined by the information or skill to be taught and the method by which the student learns best.

Skill Physical activities are often best taught by showing the learner how it is done and asking him or her to practice the action. Practice can improve many physical business skills, including poise and confidence when giving a sales presentation, assembling equipment, and using specialized tools.

Learning Style Individuals learn in different ways. When you want to learn something new, do you ask someone to show you how to do it, tell you how to do it, or let you try it? Your response classifies you as a visual learner, auditory learner, or kinesthetic learner.

- **Visual learners**—Learn best by seeing how something is done. They convert words into pictures and visual images. Slides, graphics, and charts are important print elements for visual learners. Visual learners easily learn by reading instructions.
- **Auditory learners**—Learn by hearing and processing information. Listening to a lecture is more useful than reading the same information. Auditory learners easily learn by hearing instructions.
- **Kinesthetic learners**—Learn by interacting and processing the information. Performing the task is more valuable than seeing or hearing about it.

The best trainers use a variety of approaches to teach and reinforce skills. For example, to teach sales skills, instructors can provide a written script of a sales transaction to read, ask the trainee to read the script out loud, and ask the trainee to act out the sales transaction with another person.

Trainers If you and your staff have the necessary knowledge, time, and materials, it makes sense to teach the new employee yourselves. New employees learn your business and your business methods. However, you lose the productivity of your current staff while they prepare materials and perform the training.

If you or your staff lack the needed skills or time, you can seek assistance from outside your company. Depending on the topics, you can purchase training from companies that specialize in training employees in your industry, local vocational schools, or seminars presented on the topic.

A third option is known as **train the trainer.** One employee is trained by an outside resource, then teaches the information to others in the company. This is a cost-effective option when several employees need the new skills but you want to send only one employee to an outside source for training.

Feedback When training is complete, ask the new employee for feedback. Ask again when the employee has been performing the tasks for a month or more. After doing the job, he or she can evaluate the information, point out anything that was missing, and identify the areas that were fully covered. The response can help you improve the training for your next employee.

Conduct a Performance Review

You thought report cards were a thing of the past when you finished school. Report cards still exist in the professional world in the form of performance reviews. A performance review enables a supervisor to evaluate the employee's job performance, much like the teacher evaluates the student and assigns a grade.

Note: Standard performance review forms are available from office supply stores such as Office Depot.

Purpose of a Performance Review Employee performance affects the business and the employee. Therefore, the business has the right and responsibility to evaluate the employee's performance. The process of giving a performance review is designed to accomplish several purposes that affect the business and the employee:

- Employees receive formal feedback about their performance on a regular basis.
- The supervisor sets objectives for employee performance. Achieving these objectives help the business become successful.
- The review process is the same for every employee, creating a fair and objective evaluation of every employee's performance.
- Documenting information about the employee's performance protects the business if it becomes necessary to terminate the worker's employment or a legal dispute occurs between the employee and the business.
- Effective employees are rewarded, usually by a salary increase based on merit, which is determined by the performance review.

Preparing to Conduct a Performance Review The employee handbook set the guidelines for the timing of employee performance reviews. Remind the employee in writing that the performance review is approaching about a month before the review is due to occur. This enables the employee to prepare and provides reassurance that you know the review is approaching.

Collect materials during the year. After the first performance review, which usually occurs six months after the employee is hired, reviews are given annually. Unfortunately, this means that tasks accomplished near the beginning of the review period or even several months ago tend to be forgotten. The accent is placed on the question, "What have you done for me lately?" This is not fair to the employee and misrepresents his or her value to the business. Collect materials or make notes during the entire review period. When an event occurs in which the employee makes a significant contribution or forms an obstacle, provide instant feedback to the employee and make a note that reminds you of the event when it is time for a performance review. Creating a record of the employee's performance, including achievements and setbacks, presents a more balanced picture of the employee's actions and value.

Review the employee's job description. Review the list of tasks that the employee is expected to perform. This helps you recognize when the employee exceeds expectations or fails to meet basic requirements.

Review the business objectives for the current review period. Check the notes you made about the employee during the year against the objectives for the business. Identify the employee's actions that aided or impeded the business in meeting its objectives.

Review the business objectives for the next review period. Knowing the business objectives for the next year helps you set employee performance objectives for the next period. Each employee's objectives should help the business accomplish its objectives. If an employee has no role in the success of the business, the position is not necessary and should be eliminated.

Fill out the employee's performance review form. Complete the performance review form one to two weeks before the scheduled review meeting. This enables you to make additions or changes before the meeting.

Select a location for the meeting. Meet the employee in a business location where you won't be interrupted, such as your office or an available meeting room. If this isn't possible, consider meeting in a nearby restaurant with a quiet atmosphere.

Conducting the Review You spent time preparing for the review. Use the checklist in Figure 11.14 to bring the necessary materials and information to the meeting.

FIGURE 11.14 Materials Needed for a Performance Review

Check	Material
❒	Completed performance review form
❒	Employee's job description
❒	Business objectives for the current review period
❒	Business objectives for the next review period
❒	Materials to take notes

A performance review can be stressful. Remember the following tips when you meet with the employee.

- **The feedback and evaluation you provide during the performance review should never be *new* information.** Regardless if the news is good or bad, the employee should already know what to expect because you provided feedback during the year. Never give positive feedback throughout the review period then slam the employee's performance during the review. The review should only confirm the praise and corrections the employee received during the year.
- **Be honest.** Avoiding justified criticism denies the employee the chance to improve and hurts the business by allowing poor performance to continue.
- **Remind the employee that this is a dialogue.** Be an active listener by encouraging the employee to respond and provide additional information and new ideas.

◆   **Don't be confrontational.** When an employee's performance is poor, the meeting can become tense. Stay calm. Don't make accusations such as, "You're always late."

Step 1: Arrive on time for the meeting and provide a comfortable atmosphere. Schedule at least an hour for the meeting. Prevent any unnecessary interruptions. Encourage the employee to discuss any information that pertains to the review.

Step 2: Review the employee's job description. Ask the employee if this description is accurate. If the employee is performing additional tasks or some task descriptions are inaccurate, note any changes on the form.

Step 3: Evaluate the employee's performance of each task in the job description. Identify specific occasions that led to your opinion about the employee's performance of each task. Rate the employee's performance of each task from one (unsatisfactory) to five (exceeds performance expectations). Ask the employee to respond to the individual ratings.

Step 4: Evaluate the employee's general attitude and behavior. This step includes general behavior such as tardiness, teamwork, and impact on other employees. Rate the employee's general attitude and behavior by assigning a number from one to five.

Step 5: Review the business objectives for the current review period. Ask the employee to identify how his or her actions aided or impeded the business in meeting its objectives. Rate the employee's effectiveness in promoting the success of the business.

Step 6: Review the business objectives for the next review period. Ask the employee how he or she can help the business accomplish its objectives. This enables the employee to see his or her position in the bigger picture of the business as a whole.

Step 7: Write performance objectives for the coming year. Be sure the objectives are reasonable, measurable, and achievable in the next review period. Longer-term goals can be used to identify a direction. Objectives that require more than one year to achieve can be broken down into parts that can be accomplished and evaluated in a year.

Step 8: Write an action plan for the employee. An action plan describes activities or training that help the employee perform better or gain additional skills to increase his or her value to the company. Be sure the action plan is reasonable. The funds needed to attend seminars or take additional training classes may not be available. Perhaps a subscription to an industry journal or membership dues in a professional organization are more affordable options that can still provide benefits to the employee and the business.

Step 9: You and the employee sign the performance review. Your signature confirms that you met with the employee and reviewed the information together. The employee's signature also confirms that you reviewed the information together. It does not imply that the employee agrees with everything in the review, only that the information in it was discussed.

Hypothetical Scenario

Carter's Clean Slate hired five employees and purchased several pieces of equipment. Rebecca understood the large tools because she used smaller versions of the same type of equipment when cleaning and restoring some interior walls in a class project. On the first day, Rebecca and her new employees attended the training session conducted by the equipment manufacturer. Future training will be conducted by Rebecca or her current staff.

Terminate Employees and Provide Recommendations

Regardless of how well the employee performs, most employment situations eventually end. Employee departures can be classified as voluntary terminations and involuntary terminations.

Employees choose to leave a job, known as **voluntary termination** or **resignation,** for a wide variety of reasons. They move, find better jobs that advance their careers, return to school, or decide to start a new business. Customarily, an employee is expected to tell you at least two weeks before his or her last day of employment with your company. This gives you time to begin searching for a new employee. If you're lucky, you can hire a replacement before the current employee leaves. This enables the employee to train the replacement.

Involuntary termination occurs when the decision to end employment is made by the employer. Regardless of the reason, terminating an employee is never easy. It is also covered by regulations that vary from state to state. Consult the laws in your state before taking any action.

Terminating Employment

Sometimes the best decision you can make for your business is choosing to terminate an employee. When an employee is not contributing to the success of the business, it is time to consider terminating the worker's employment. An employer may terminate employment for three reasons—layoff, cause, and poor performance.

Layoff A temporary interruption of the employment relationship because work is not available is a **layoff.** In this situation, the termination of employment is the result of a necessary reduction in the company's workforce.

The Department of Labor states that over 3.3 million people are laid off from their jobs each year. Layoffs are common during times of poor economic conditions but they also occur when individual companies have financial difficulties. In some cases, you may be required to provide a 60-day warning to your employees. This enables them to seek other employment. Consult the laws in your state.

Terminate Employment for Cause **Termination for cause** occurs when an employee's behavior seriously violates company policy or creates significant jeopardy for the company or its employees. When terminating for cause, be sure to thoroughly document the employee's behavior.

Many reasons can be given to terminate for cause including physical violence, theft, drunkenness, or illegal drug use at your business during work hours. These reasons should be documented in the employee handbook.

Terminate Employment for Poor Performance Termination for poor performance does not happen on the spur of the moment. Before an employee can be terminated for poor performance, you must create a paper trail proving that the employee has been informed that his or her performance is not acceptable and the employee had the opportunity for improvement. The process requires several steps. Terminations are often the subject of lawsuits, making it important to follow every step required in your state. Consult legal counsel to avoid any unnecessary risk of a lawsuit.

Step 1: Issue a verbal warning. When consistently poor performance is noticed, issue a verbal warning. Inform the worker that job performance is not acceptable. Document the verbal warning in writing and place it in the employee's file. The document should describe the performance issue and the verbal warning given to the employee. Many disciplinary actions end here because no further action is necessary.

Step 2: Issue a written warning. The next step in the disciplinary procedure is a written warning. The written warning should describe the performance issue and the verbal warning that was given previously. It should also state that the employee's job is *in jeopardy.* Review the written warning with the employee and ask the employee to sign the warning. If the employee refuses to sign, note the refusal on the document. You may want to have your lawyer or a witness present.

Step 3: Terminate the worker's employment. Because you followed the progressive steps of issuing verbal and written warnings, the employee shouldn't be surprised by the termination. Give the employee a written termination notice. If the worker is terminated because of absence, send the notice via certified mail. Tell the employee that the decision is *final.* Describe any benefits that may apply such as insurance. Request the return of all company property including keys, equipment, and manuals. You may want to consider changing security codes before the end of the business day. Document the termination meeting and place the information in the employee's personnel file.

Inform any employees who are affected. In a small business, everyone is affected to some extent. Reassign any tasks as needed. Be careful about your comments when referring to the employee. The terminated employee may sue for slander if you make derogatory remarks about the worker.

Recommending an Employee

When you hired employees, you contacted previous employers for references. When one of your employees moves on to another job, you may be asked to provide a reference. If the employee was a superstar, you can provide a glowing reference. Sometimes an employee had potential but didn't quite fit into your business. You can still provide positive information. However, what do you say when a potential employer calls about an employee you terminated for cause or poor performance?

Inform the caller that you can only confirm the individual's job title, responsibilities, and employment dates. For employers, refusing to comment on anything else about the employee is almost a statement or warning flag and avoids any potential accusation of slander from your previous employee.

Hypothetical Scenario

Carter's Clean Slate initially hired five employees. Although Rebecca thought she selected good employees, one of them doesn't seem to be working out. He shows up late, leaves early, and takes long lunch breaks. Rebecca has already given a verbal warning. Currently, she is drafting a memo that provides the written warning that his job is in jeopardy. If he does not improve to an acceptable level by the end of the month, Rebecca will be forced to terminate his employment.

Technology Insights

Software Piracy

The Software and Information Industry Association (SIIA) is a trade association composed of leading companies in the software and information industry. In this role, the association has formed the SPA AntiPiracy division, devoted to educating users and enforcing antipiracy regulations. Software is protected by copyright. Therefore, when you make unauthorized copies, you are infringing on the maker's copyright, also known as stealing. Worldwide, the revenue lost in business applications in 1999 was $12.2 billion. As an employer, if you instruct your employees to install pirated software, you are responsible for copyright infringement under the U.S. Copyright Act. A software pirate can be fined $150,000 in civil penalties for each work infringed. A pirate can also be fined up to $250,000 and receive a jail term of five years.

Think Critically What are the maximum penalties for software piracy?

CHAPTER REVIEW

An employee handbook performs several important functions. Its primary purpose is providing guidelines for the employer and employee. The basic handbook contains an acknowledgment form, mission statement, nondiscrimination policy, safety rules and guidelines, guidelines for the use of company property, work hours, absence, pay periods, performance evaluation procedures, vacation days, and holidays. As the company grows, add new policies and information. Distribute the revised handbook to all of your employees.

Good employees are attracted and retained by a good compensation package, which includes the worker's salary and benefits. Some benefits such as insurance are considered to be standard in many benefit packages. Inexpensive unique perks can attract employees with specific characteristics.

Your existing staff, outside firms, or schools can conduct training. Each new employee should receive all the training necessary to perform the tasks identified in the employee's job description. Incomplete training creates incompetent employees. After training is completed, feedback can help you improve future training programs. Performance reviews provide a formal structure for evaluating employee performance on a regular basis.

Employees who resign are voluntarily leaving your business. Involuntary termination occurs when the decision to end employment is made by the employer. Employers terminate employment for three reasons—layoff, cause, and poor performance. Termination for cause or poor performance is based on the employee's actions. Layoffs are caused by financial or business reasons. Employee terminations can result in lawsuits. It is important to follow established procedures to reduce this risk.

USE BUSINESS TERMS

Fill in the blanks with the appropriate term.

acknowledgment form	life insurance
"at will"	Occupational Safety and Health Administration
auditory learner	(OSHA)
benefits	performance review
compensation	perks
deduction	resignation
direct deposit	software piracy
disability insurance	termination for cause
employee handbook	train the trainer
health insurance	user license
involuntary termination	visual learner
kinesthetic learner	voluntary termination
layoff	workers' compensation insurance

1. _____?_____ are rewards the employee receives, in addition to a salary, for performing a job.
2. The employment relationship between a(n) _____?_____ employee and employer can be terminated by the employee or employer at any time.
3. The _____?_____ was established to prevent work-related injuries, illnesses, and deaths.
4. _____?_____ pays medical and disability benefits according to a state-approved formula when a worker is injured.
5. Performing the task is more valuable to a(n) _____?_____ than seeing or hearing about it.
6. A voluntary termination is also known as a(n) _____?_____.
7. Physical violence and drunkenness are valid reasons for _____?_____.

TEST YOUR READING

8. What is the purpose of an employee handbook?
9. List the components of the basic employee handbook.
10. What is the purpose of the Occupational Safety and Health Administration?
11. How many employees can a small business have before investigating state regulations?
12. How do you identify training needed by a new employee?
13. Who can train a new employee?
14. Describe three different learning styles.
15. What is the purpose of a performance review?
16. Identify the role of the company's objectives in an employee's performance review.

17. When should an employee inform you that he or she is resigning?
18. Which reason for employment termination is not caused by the employee's actions?
19. Describe the steps you should follow to terminate a worker's employment for poor performance.

THINK CRITICALLY ABOUT BUSINESS

20. Describe an attractive compensation package.
21. Describe how you would train someone to use a new software application.
22. Evaluate your own performance as an employee or student.
23. Investigate methods of evacuating disabled workers from a building with several floors. On September 11, 2001, several disabled workers perished in the terrorist attack at the World Trade Center in New York City while they were waiting in the stairwell for firefighters to come to their rescue. A plan and equipment such as evacuation chairs might have saved some of them.

REAL-LIFE BUSINESS

Always Home Incorporated

In April 1998, Mary Ewing and Veanne Stewart established a business that is truly unique. As Realtors, they discovered that many senior adults were facing the need to downsize their homes or relocate to another area. The need to move was often the result of an illness, an accident, or the death of a spouse. The transition is emotionally and physically difficult for the older individuals. Family members are often unavailable to provide assistance because they live far away or don't have the necessary time.

Almost Home provides a variety of services that smooth the transition between homes. These services include preparing and selling the current home, sorting and organizing possessions, locating and preparing a new home, and providing physical assistance in packing and moving possessions.

After operating the business alone, Mary and Veanne decided to sell franchises in several states. They realize that the population is aging. The children of today's senior adults are accustomed to paying others to perform services they don't want to perform or don't have the time to perform themselves. These adult children often convince their aging parents to use the services of Always Home.

Think Critically

1. How did the founders get the business idea?
2. Why is the market growing?
3. When are the services of a business such as Always Home needed?
4. Evaluate the growth potential of the business.

CHAPTER  12

Human Resources Responsibilities

GOALS

- ◆ Fulfill responsibilities to employees
- ◆ Pay employees
- ◆ Maintain employee records
- ◆ Deal with conflict in the work environment

One rainy summer afternoon, Eric Okano realized that his children, ages 8 and 10, were bored. He watched them flip through dozens of television channels and reject a stack of library books they'd read earlier in the week. He decided to start a game that would be both fun and educational. He placed six objects on a covered tray. Each child earned points by listing the objects after they were displayed briefly and then covered again. Then Eric asked them to identify a silly use for each object. From there, Eric asked them to describe a location where the silly use would be performed. Eric named it "The Chain Game," a game that entertained and developed imagination and logical thinking. The idea that led to White Hats Software was born.

Fulfill Responsibilities to Employees

Every relationship comes with responsibilities and expectations. When you hire an employee, you create a professional relationship between you and the employee. The employment relationship creates expectations on both sides. You expect your employees to come to work, complete their assigned tasks, and help your business meet its objectives. Employees also have expectations. They expect the company to provide a safe work environment and fair treatment, which it promises to do in its employee handbook.

Safety

Every work environment carries its own set of dangers. Some dangers are more obvious than others. Falling materials can injure construction workers. Farm equipment or lifting heavy items can injure farmers. Even environments that seem safe can hide dangers. A common complaint of office workers who spend a lot of time using a computer keyboard is the repetitive strain injury known as **carpal tunnel syndrome**—weakness and tingling in the hand caused by pressure on the medial nerve in the wrist. The Bureau of Labor Statistics, the principal fact-finding agency for the federal government in labor economics and statistics, provided the data found in Table 12.1 regarding work-related injuries, illnesses, and fatalities that occurred in private industry in 2000:

TABLE 12.1   Work-Related Incidents in Private Industry in 2000

Nonfatal Injuries and Illnesses in Private Industry	
Total recordable cases	5,650,100
Cases involving days away from work	1,664,000

Fatal Injuries in Private Industry	
Total recorded cases (preliminary)	5,344
Highway incidents (preliminary)	1,205
Falls to a lower level (preliminary)	640
Homicides (preliminary)	599

Ergonomics   As an employer, you are responsible for providing a safe work environment. Some actions you can take to improve safety are common sense or common practice without regulations to dictate specific safety requirements. For example, many employers provided ergonomic computer equipment when it became available. **Ergonomics** is an applied science that designs and arranges equipment and workspace so people and equipment interact efficiently and safely. Computer equipment such as monitors and keyboards have been improved because of ergonomic studies. For example, the best distance and angle of the monitor to the user has been identified to reduce discomfort and eye strain. Ergonomics now affects everything from industrial equipment to consumer products such as toothbrushes and bicycles.

Emergency Equipment and Procedures   Regardless of how safe the environment or how carefully employees behave, accidents and emergencies occur. When they happen, employees must have the correct equipment and procedures to deal with the result. When customers are on your property, you may have some responsibility for their well-being.

Injury   A small business doesn't have enough employees or income to justify hiring medical personnel. However, a first-aid kit should be kept on hand for minor injuries such as cuts or scrapes. A doctor should treat any injury that requires more attention. If a severe injury occurs that demands immediate medical attention, do not hesitate to dial 9-1-1 for assistance.

Medical Emergency Awareness of any pre-existing medical conditions affecting your employees helps others to recognize medical emergencies when they occur. For example, conditions such as diabetes or epilepsy have specific symptoms that signal the need for immediate medical attention. Recognizing the signs and knowing the correct assistance to provide can prevent medical complications. Training one or all of your employees in first aid can be beneficial to employees and customers. Post a list of trained employees so others know whom to contact if a medical emergency appears. Contact your local American Red Cross for information about available first-aid training in your area.

Act of Nature It is impossible to plan for every possible type of emergency that can occur. However, a plan can make the difference between recovering from a natural disaster and closing your business forever. An **act of nature,** also known as an act of God, is an unpredictable interruption of the normal environment caused by a natural event such as an earthquake, flood, or severe storm.

For a business, response plans should include protecting your employees and customers, minimizing the damage, and recovering as quickly as possible. Physically, this means training your employees to go to the safest location. Clearly mark doors that lead outside your building. Store electronic data in more than one geographic location. A recovery plan helps your business reassemble the necessary components, returning to operation quickly and efficiently.

Environmental Hazard Chemicals and other man-made products create hazards for employees, customers, and others near the business location. The hazard may create an immediate emergency or a long-term environmental catastrophe by poisoning nearby streams or causing air pollution. Employers must be aware of potential emergencies created by products used during business operations. For example, strong chemicals are used in many manufacturing processes. Be sure that your employees are properly trained and equipped to handle the product and any foreseeable consequences of its use.

OSHA Regulations The purpose of the Occupational Safety and Health Administration (OSHA) is the prevention of work-related injuries, illnesses, and fatalities. Obviously, prevention is your goal as well. Guidelines established by OSHA affect businesses in a wide variety of industries, probably more industries than you can name. As a business owner, you must investigate and follow the guidelines that affect your business.

Most workplace accidents can be prevented. With some thought and planning, the cause of most accidents can be removed before the accident occurs. Health hazards are different. An accident isn't necessary to cause injury. **Health hazards,** which occur during routine job performance, can cause injury, illness, or death. The effect of a health hazard may be delayed. For years, X-ray technicians were exposed to low levels of radiation without realizing their health was placed in jeopardy.

When businesses and individuals realized the health risk that resulted from long-term exposure, some of them provided lead aprons or moved the switches controlling the equipment to a separate room to protect the technicians. Even your dental hygienist triggers dental X-rays from outside the room. Every business wants to protect its employees from accidents and health hazards.

OSHA State Plan Partners Many states operate their own OSHA-approved programs. These programs provide assistance that is closer to home for many businesses. States must provide protection that is as effective as the federal program or better. Therefore, state programs may be stricter than the federal guidelines. Every business should follow the state guidelines that apply to their business activities.

Four-Point Workplace Programs Compliance with the guidelines established by OSHA's Four-Point Workplace Program is voluntary. However, the program forms a solid base for meeting required safety and health regulations:

- **Management commitment and employee involvement**—Your commitment to employee safety convinces employees and managers to promote safety and health concerns. Involvement by managers and employees encourages enthusiastic compliance.

- **Work site analysis**—Examine the physical characteristics of the work environment you provide to identify the source of potential accidents and health hazards.

- **Hazard protection and control**—After identifying potential accidents, eliminate or control hazards to protect your employees.

- **Training for employees, supervisors, and managers**—Training enables employees to perform their jobs correctly. Employees incorrectly performing specific activities or incorrectly using materials and equipment cause many accidents.

Records Maintain records that document your preventative actions. These records prove that you reviewed your workplace environment and identify the actions you took to prevent accidents and protect your employees.

OSHA requires some paperwork that must be submitted regularly. Employers must report every injury that requires medical treatment that is more serious than first aid. At the end of each year, you must submit a summary of the injuries that occurred during the year. All work-related injuries and illnesses must be recorded on forms provided by OSHA. Contact your state OSHA office to obtain the correct forms.

Inspection Complaints An individual who reports unsafe or hazardous working conditions to OSHA is a **whistle-blower.** Every complaint is evaluated based on the individual who filed it and the complaint itself. Complaints by active employees carry more weight than complaints by past employees or visitors. Complaints about serious hazards that can cause a fatality carry more weight than hazards that can't cause immediate injuries.

Complaints are categorized as an inspection complaint or an investigation complaint. An **inspection complaint** is a complaint about a hazard that causes an OSHA representative to visit the business site. A complaint must satisfy one of the following criteria to trigger an inspection:

- The written complaint is signed by a current employee or employee representative and describes a specific illegal hazard.
- The complaint alleges that the hazard has caused physical harm and the hazard still exists.
- The complaint describes an imminent danger, a condition that could cause death or serious physical harm before it is eliminated by normal business procedures.
- The complaint identifies a business engaged in an industry or using equipment targeted by OSHA.
- The complaint was treated as an investigation complaint but the employer did not provide a satisfactory response.
- The complaint identifies a business that OSHA has cited in the last three years.

Investigation Complaints Every complaint does not trigger an on-site inspection by OSHA personnel. Complaints that don't meet the conditions needed to trigger an inspection are categorized as **investigation complaints.**

Investigation complaints made by individuals, usually by telephone, are handled as quickly as possible. When an investigation complaint is received, the following procedure produces fast results:

- An OSHA compliance staff member calls the employer to discuss the issue.
- The OSHA representative faxes a letter describing the complaint to the employer.
- The employer must respond within five days by denying that the hazard exists, stating that the hazard has been eliminated, or stating that the process of eliminating the hazard has been started.
- OSHA contacts the individual filing the complaint to inform the person of the employer's response. If the complainant does not agree with the employer's response, OSHA decides if the complaint warrants an inspection.

Fair Treatment

Your employee handbook states that you are committed to being an equal opportunity employer. Equal opportunity doesn't end when the employee is hired. It is a business philosophy that rewards employees for good performance without considering factors such as age, gender, race, nationality, country of origin, or disability.

Equal Opportunity The American dream of liberty and justice for all assumes the promise of equal opportunity for all citizens. Every child born in America can dream of being president—of a major corporation or of the entire country. Your position as an entrepreneur proves that you benefited from the principle of fair treatment and took advantage of the opportunities available to you. As an employer, you offer your employees the same fair treatment.

Equal opportunity for employees in the **private sector** and workers not employed by a local, state, or federal government office or agency is guaranteed by several federal laws and enforced by the U.S. Equal Employment Opportunity Commission (EEOC). Additional laws affect businesses and employees who work with or for government agencies. Private businesses must meet the following federal laws. Your state may have additional requirements:

◆   The Equal Pay Act of 1963 (EPA) protects men and women who perform substantially equal work in the same establishment from gender-based wage discrimination.

◆   The Civil Rights Act of 1964 (Title VII) prohibits employment discrimination based on race, color, religion, gender, or national origin.

◆   The Age Discrimination in Employment Act of 1967 (ADEA) protects individuals who are 40 years of age or older.

◆   The Americans with Disabilities Act of 1990 (ADA) prohibits employment discrimination against qualified individuals with disabilities.

◆   The Civil Rights Act of 1991 provides monetary damages in cases of intentional employment discrimination.

After hiring, these laws protect employees from discriminatory practices that could occur during normal business operations. Many states have additional laws designed to protect equal opportunity. The federal laws listed previously address the following activities:

◆   Termination, transfer, training, promotion, layoff, or recall
◆   Compensation, assignment, or classification of employees
◆   Use of company facilities
◆   Harassment or personnel decisions based on race, color, religion, gender, national origin, disability, or age
◆   Personnel decisions based on characteristics of the employee's family

Statistics Discrimination is not always easy to identify and can be difficult to prove. Examining the characteristics of a company's upper management can indicate the presence of discrimination in employee decisions. For example, the ratio of female and minority managers in upper management should be similar to the ratio in lower management and the general workforce. If the ratio is not similar, employees may complain about a **glass ceiling,** an intangible barrier within a company hierarchy that prevents women and minorities from obtaining upper-level positions. Catalyst, a nonprofit research and advisory organization, states that government statistics show that 52 percent of America's workers are women, yet they hold only 12.4 percent of all board seats in top corporations, as shown in Figure 12.1.

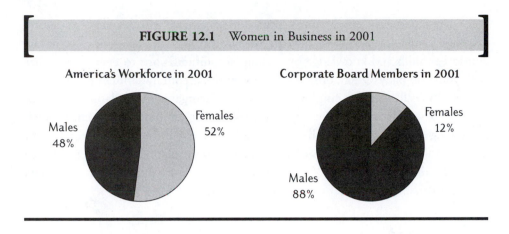

FIGURE 12.1   Women in Business in 2001

America's Workforce in 2001

Males
48%

Females
52%

Corporate Board Members in 2001

Females
12%

Males
88%

In the long run, a business that practices discrimination is hurting itself. A business that passes over skilled employees to select employees who fit a specific image is misusing its most important asset—its employees. Eventually, poor management decisions such as discrimination affect the employer's profits. To maximize your profits, select the best individual for every position.

Americans with Disabilities Act As a business that provides goods or services to the public, the Americans with Disabilities Act requires you to provide accessibility to your customers if providing accessibility is reasonably possible. (See Set Up Your Site in Chapter 7.) However, as an employer, you need to provide equipment and accommodations to enable all of your employees to be productive, including your disabled employees.

According to the Department of Labor, businesses with fewer than 15 employees are not covered by the ADA. A small business with more than 15 employees but few financial resources is often protected by claiming **undue hardship** based on the difficulty or expense of providing accommodations for a disabled employee.

The primary employment market is 18 to 64 years of age. Therefore, this age range is used to measure employment rates. The National Organization on Disability presents data about many aspects of life with a disability, including employment. Statistics, as shown in Figure 12.2, indicate that disabled citizens are unemployed in much higher percentages than those without disabilities.

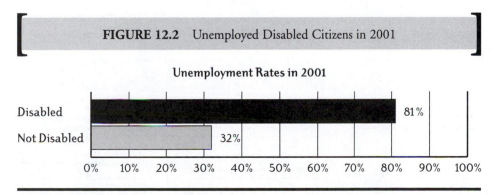

FIGURE 12.2   Unemployed Disabled Citizens in 2001

Unemployment Rates in 2001

Disabled   81%

Not Disabled   32%

0%   10%   20%   30%   40%   50%   60%   70%   80%   90%   100%

Terminating the employment of a valued employee who becomes physically disabled is not necessary, and may prove harmful to your company. Retain the employee's skills and knowledge by making accommodations to keep him or her with your company. Often, only small, inexpensive accommodations are needed to keep a physically disabled employee productive. Reorganizing available workspace can permit wheelchair access to a specific area. Minor equipment adjustments such as moving a lever or altering the grip on a handle make the worker's equipment more usable. Your best source of information about helpful adjustments is the physically disabled employee. Ask the employee to describe the accommodations needed to enable him or her to continue to work.

Hypothetical Scenario

Eric Okano's Chain Game became a popular computer game. He established a web site where subscribers could download new chains every week, maintaining the children's interest. Several other software ideas were lurking, but Eric didn't have the time to develop them. He hired a group of 10 programmers with a background in education. Several years ago, his lead programmer was diagnosed with a muscular degeneration disease. As her disability increased over time, Eric provided accommodations such as computer equipment and adjustments to the building that helped her continue to work.

Pay Employees

Employees expect a safe working environment, fair treatment, and payment. Some consider paying employees as simply writing checks every two weeks. Of course, it's not that simple. Paying your employees is more than a simple business arrangement between you and your employees. Additional forms and payments are required to meet government regulations, pay taxes, pay social security, and withhold funds for other reasons. The process of preparing and calculating your **payroll,** the list of employees entitled to pay and the amount each employee is paid, can be complicated.

Payroll Process Overview

Each step in the flowchart shown in Figure 12.3 requires dozens of forms, actions, and interactions with individuals, businesses, government agencies, and financial institutions. The flowchart is a simplified version of the payroll process.

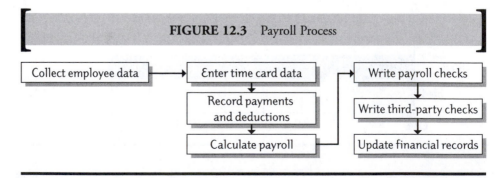

FIGURE 12.3   Payroll Process

1. **Collect information for new employees or update information for existing employees.** Employee information includes data such as name, address, social security number, marital status, hourly pay rate or standard salary, and authorized deductions.

2. **Enter time card data for the pay period.** Enter the number of hours worked, vacation taken, and sick time taken.

3. **Record automatic, recurring, and special payments or deductions.** Record common and unique instances of payments and deductions for exempt and for nonexempt employees. Deductions are dollar amounts routinely taken from the employee's pay such as federal social security and income tax.

4. **Calculate payroll.** Calculate the **gross pay,** total amount paid to an employee before deductions are applied, for each employee and employee payroll taxes. Apply the deductions scheduled for the current payroll to compute the **net pay** for each employee.

5. **Write payroll checks.** When you are satisfied that your payroll is correct, create your payroll checks or transfer funds electronically to the employee's bank account, directly depositing the salary payment. Even if the funds are directly deposited, the employee should still receive a check stub that identifies the amounts paid and deducted.

6. **Write third-party checks.** Checks to a **third party** are written to a business, individual, or government agency other than your business or the employee. They are used to transfer funds that have been withheld from an employee's pay. This can include garnishments, dependent care, and 401(k) savings.

   - **Garnishments** are amounts deducted from an employee's salary to pay a debt to a creditor. The funds are usually sent or transferred directly to the creditor, ensuring that the creditor is paid before the employee can spend his or her income.
   - Dependent care usually means child support. However, alimony or other court-ordered support can be included.
   - Retirement plans, such as a **401(k),** are popular benefits. The 401(k) diverts funds from the employee's salary, enabling the employee to save for retirement and reduce his or her current taxable income.

7. **Update financial records.** Update the year-to-date information with data from the current payroll. This includes your financial statements, payroll tax liability data, 401(k) report, and bank statements.

Outsource Payroll Processing

The complexity of the payroll process and the serious consequences of errors make it a critical business function, one that you may not have the ability to perform alone. Payroll is usually processed every two weeks or every month. Additional tasks are required when tax payments are made and at the end of the year. Depending on the number of employees you have, payroll probably doesn't require a full-time employee. However, the detailed knowledge and specific procedures do require the attention of a specialist.

Advantages of Outsourcing Payroll Processing You don't have to hire specialists with experience in payroll and human resource activities. You can buy the level of expertise and time you need by **outsourcing** the entire process, paying an outside company to perform a specific business activity. Outsourcing the payroll process provides several advantages. It enables you to:

- Concentrate on your core business activities.
- Lower business expenses by eliminating the need to invest in personnel, technology, and training for a specialized function that isn't part of your core business activity.
- Increase security by maintaining personnel and payroll information at the provider's site.
- Eliminate the need to perform complex accounting tasks that require time and specialized training.
- Forego the requirement to perform research to constantly keep up with changes in tax and compensation regulations.

Selecting a Payroll Processing Provider Many businesses provide human resource activities, including payroll processing, for employers. After you decide to outsource payroll activities, use Table 12.2 to help you select the right provider.

TABLE 12.2 Selection Criteria for Payroll Processing Provider

Criteria	Yes	No
Does the provider service businesses of your size? Providers may specialize in servicing small or large employers, based primarily on the number of employees you have.		
Does the provider perform related human resource activities that you want? If you decide to outsource additional human resource activities, it's easier to purchase all the services from the same provider.		
Does the provider have a reputation for providing accurate financial data on time? Check references. If your employees' paychecks are wrong or late, it will quickly become a serious problem for your business. Errors in tax statements can result in penalties such as fines and interest payments.		
Do the provider's services match your needs? List your needs. Be sure that the provider fills all of your needs, such as electronic fund transfers, direct depositing, and suitable payments.		
Is the provider available when you need assistance? The provider should be available to answer questions regarding any step in the process, such as paycheck amounts or possible errors.		
Is the contact method acceptable? You may prefer a local provider who can speak with you in person. If face-to-face service isn't necessary, many providers are available on the Internet.		
Is the cost of the service reasonable? Compare prices among several providers.		
Note any additional criteria that affect your decision.		

Many providers offer similar services. Compare the information for several providers. Select the provider that is the best fit for your business and your business methods.

Hypothetical Scenario

Eric was an excellent programmer and developed his business ideas with a flair that attracted and held customers. However, he wasn't an accountant. He decided to admit his weakness and hire a small business to manage the payroll functions. A thorough search found a business on the Internet that filled every need, leaving Eric free to concentrate on business activities he enjoyed much more.

Maintain Employee Records

In grade school, you worried that some minor misdeed would be entered on your "permanent record." You imagined a stone tablet with a column for good behavior next to a column for bad behavior. When you became an adult, your employee file became your permanent record. Now, you enter a new role. As an employer, you maintain the **employee files,** which contain all documents related to the employee's activities related to your business.

Organization of the Employee Files

Information about your business and your employees is valuable. Organizing the files you maintain makes it easier to find critical data when it is needed. Many human resource experts divide employee files into three sections, shown in Figure 12.4, which can be maintained in three separate folders if necessary—compensation, events, and medical information. Within each section, store items in reverse chronological order, placing the most recent item on the top and the oldest items on the bottom. This keeps the most recent information at your fingertips.

FIGURE 12.4   Organization of Employee Files

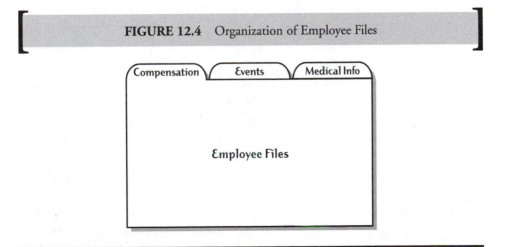

Compensation   When an employee is hired, his or her job description, salary, and benefits are recorded and the employee completes tax liability forms.

The employee's compensation should be recorded when the employee is hired and when a change occurs. After employment, this usually happens when the employee receives a promotion or merit increase. In less common situations, a change in compensation can occur when an employee changes departments, switches to part-time employment, or returns to the company after leaving for a period of time.

If the employee is required to submit a time card, the time card can be kept in this folder. If the employee's attendance is unsatisfactory, time cards can be valuable evidence. The compensation and time card information can also be used to answer IRS questions regarding employee income, unemployment, or tax liability for the employee or employer.

Events Start this folder when the employee accepts your job offer. Include the employee's application, résumé, and references. Significant events include promotions, performance reviews, and disciplinary actions. A signed **confidentiality agreement** protects the company by guaranteeing that inventions, methods, and company information will not be revealed to individuals or businesses outside your company. The employee usually signs all documents.

Medical Information Everyone considers his or her medical information to be confidential. A high level of security is necessary to protect the employee's privacy. Medical information may be provided to an employer because absences are required for treatment or recovery. A change in an employee's duties or special equipment may be necessary because of an illness or injury.

Security and Storage Requirements

Much of the information contained in your employee files is private. Like you, your employees do not want to broadcast personal information such as their income, performance evaluations, or medical needs. In fact, employees may sue your business if sensitive medical information is revealed. In many states, regulations identify the security measures that must be used to protect the information.

Locked file cabinets and locked offices can protect paper documents. Personal computers and servers often have files that should be protected from unauthorized personnel. For example, managers may write performance appraisals on a computer in their offices. Protecting the printed document does not provide security if the files are available on unsecured computers. Use security software to protect your electronic files by limiting access to the electronic storage in your business.

Employee Access In many states, laws guarantee employees access to their personnel files. Regardless of whether it is required in your state, it is good policy to allow employees to access their own employee files at any time.

The employee signs most documents, including performance reviews. Therefore, they should be familiar with all the information in their files. Viewing and copying the documents should be permitted. Refusing to permit access implies that you are keeping information from the employee, a policy that could cause problems between management and employees.

Employee Files for Previous Employees State and federal regulations specify the number of years that you must store employee files while an individual remains an employee and after an employee leaves your business. Consult legal advice before setting this policy. Employee records can be used in lawsuits against employers. The minimum length of storage time should not be less than the time limit in your state that an individual has to sue a previous employer for employment issues such as discrimination and harassment.

Checklist of Items in the Employee File

The following items are kept in employee files. Your business may keep additional information. Create a list similar to the example in Figure 12.5. Attach it to the main folder for each employee. Next to each item, record the date the item was most recently updated. For example, a new job description should be inserted when the employee is promoted.

FIGURE 12.5 Contents of Employee Files

Date	Item
	Application
	Résumé
	References
	Acknowledgment receipt for employee handbook
	Confidentiality agreement
	Tax liability
	Benefits
	Job description
	Salary
	Time cards
	Performance reviews
	Disciplinary action
	Medical information
	Emergency contact information

Hypothetical Scenario

Eric required every new employee of White Hats Software to sign a confidentiality agreement, which he carefully stored in the employee files. When he learned that a competitor was trying to recruit one of his programmers, he invited her into his office. He learned that the job offer was one he couldn't defeat with a counteroffer. He wished her the best of luck and reminded her of the confidentiality statement she had signed several years ago. Although White Hats was losing her skills, it wasn't losing any business methods or program secrets.

Deal with Conflict in the Work Environment

It seems like stories about violence in school and work situations are frequently in the news. Violence is one of the top three causes of workplace fatalities for all workers. The Bureau of Labor Statistics states that violence in the workplace was responsible for 16 percent of all work-related fatal injuries in 2000.

Workplace Violence

A major cause of fatalities among taxi drivers, police officers, and sales representatives is workplace violence. The three most common causes of workplace fatalities are traffic accidents, homicides, and falls. However, the picture is not as bleak as it looks. Most violent fatalities in work situations are the result of robberies, not assaults by employees or previous employees. The Bureau of Labor Statistics, as shown in Figure 12.6, identifies the hardest-hit industries, based on fatality rates, as mining, agriculture, construction, and transportation. **Fatality rates** are calculated by dividing the number of fatalities by the number of individuals in the field. If you consider only the number of fatalities, the most dangerous industries are construction, transportation, and service businesses, which include law enforcement and firefighting.

FIGURE 12.6   Work-Related Fatality Rates by Industry

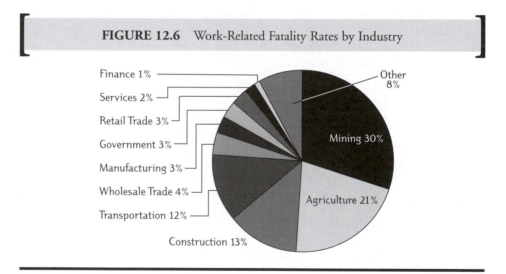

When Conflict Occurs

Although conflict doesn't always result in violence and fatalities, it can certainly make your work environment uncomfortable. It is impossible for two individuals to agree all the time. In the personal arena, friends, spouses, and family members disagree from time to time. The same is true in the business arena—coworkers, managers, and other individuals in business relationships occasionally disagree. To succeed, you must unite differing viewpoints to reach a common goal.

Conflict occurs when disagreements are *uncontrolled.* Shouting matches in the company boardroom, deliberate attempts to undermine or sabotage another's work, and unauthorized employee activities can result from uncontrolled disagreements.

Controlled disagreement combines the opposing energy from two or more individuals. This forms **synergy,** interaction that creates a total effect greater than the sum of the individual parts. Synergism results in creative approaches to problems and new solutions.

Conflict between Employees Disagreement between employees can be caused by many different reasons or no reason at all. Disagreements can result from a misunderstanding, an error, or a different viewpoint. Simple dislike based on differing personalities can cause disagreements about almost every topic. You can do several things to prevent conflict between employees:

- **Create an environment of openness and trust.** As the group's leader, your behavior establishes the ground rules for everyone else.
- **Emphasize the value of each employee and his or her viewpoint.** Encourage employees to make suggestions. Innovations, practical improvements, and money-saving methods can come from any quarter.
- **Give praise publicly.** Everyone likes a pat on the back.
- **Give criticism privately.** Don't criticize an employee in front of his or her peers. Adding public humiliation to a criticism isn't necessary.
- **Treat all employees fairly.** Fair and equal treatment for all employees establishes trust and reinforces the value you set on each employee.
- **Establish boundaries between employees' responsibilities.** Refer to their job descriptions to define the boundaries.
- **Avoid filling the role of a parent between two employees who are acting out.** You are a supervisor, not a parent. Use your standard disciplinary procedures.
- **Don't get involved in a personal conflict between employees.** If their behavior is not acceptable, follow your standard disciplinary actions.

Conflict between employees creates a tense work environment. This is particularly true in a small business. Other employees may get involved or refuse to work with the problem employees. It may be necessary to take your disciplinary actions to the final conclusion and terminate one of the difficult employees. If you don't take action, you could lose other employees who are more valuable because they can work with others.

Conflict between Managers The role of a manager is leadership. Conflict between managers can easily snowball to include the employees reporting to the managers. Before you realize it, you have armed camps rather than departments in your company. Take action before the conflict between your managers reaches this point.

Like you, the managers in your business must have the good of the company as one of their highest priorities. Managers should be aware of the big picture, the direction the company is moving, and your goals for the business. Their actions should be directed to the success of the business. You can encourage this attitude in several ways:

- **Set business goals together.** Solicit input from your managers. They will work harder to achieve goals they helped set.
- **Keep managers informed of the company's progress.** Hold regular meetings to keep the managers informed and committed to the company's success.

- **Explain each manager's role in achieving success for the business.** Understanding their roles encourages them to work together to accomplish business goals.

Managers may create conflict even if they have the company's success as a goal because they don't agree on *how* the company can achieve the goal. As long as the disagreement is controlled, managers try to find ways to make their ideas more likely to succeed. When the disagreement becomes uncontrolled, the managers are reduced to shouting in meetings. Employees who overhear the disagreement start to take sides. The disagreement becomes conflict, holding the company back rather than moving it toward success.

Before it becomes conflict, intervene to make a decision or encourage the managers to make a decision. As the business owner, making final decisions or leading the way to a final decision is your role. The longer conflict continues, the more harmful it becomes. Allowing conflict to continue doesn't benefit the company or the managers. If the conflict can't be resolved, don't be afraid to terminate a manager before the situation damages your company.

Conflict between Employees and Managers Because the manager has an obvious position of authority over the employees in his or her group, open conflict between employees and managers is less likely to occur. When it does happen, it should be addressed and resolved immediately. An unhappy employee who blames the managers or the company for unfair treatment can quickly spread discontent and create morale problems.

To support the manager's authority, encourage the manager to handle the conflict alone. That doesn't mean you shouldn't confer with the manager before he or she takes action. To the average employee, managers represent the company, establishing and affecting the company's reputation. Be sure that the manager's actions accurately reflect the image you want to present.

Defusing Individual Confrontations

Every individual has a different viewpoint based on factors such as experience, values, economic status, and personality. The difference in viewpoints causes individuals to seek different goals and different approaches to achieving a goal.

- **Gather adequate information before a conflict starts.** The more information you gather about an issue, the more you are able to evaluate the situation and offer realistic solutions. You might realize that you don't disagree with the other individual's viewpoint at all.
- **Don't make it a personal battle.** Keep your feelings and opinions about the other person out of the issue. Do not encourage personal disputes. The disagreement is about an issue, not a person.
- **Pick your battles.** Most items aren't worth an argument. If you limit your disagreements to important topics, others are more willing to listen.
- **Stay on the topic.** Deal with a single issue. Don't bring up old disagreements, personal subjects, or events not related to the current topic.

- **Listen to the other person.** While the other person is speaking, listen rather than plan your response. In fact, your next statement won't be a response to the other individual's comments if you weren't listening well.

- **Process and reflect before you respond.** Don't repeat the same words the other person just said. Use words that show the speaker how you processed and interpreted the statement. This gives the speaker the opportunity to correct any misunderstanding before it creates more problems than you had initially.

- **Look for value in the individual's viewpoint.** If you can find value in his or her position, the individual is more likely to find value in your viewpoint.

- **Be creative.** One side isn't 100 percent right while the other side is 100 percent wrong. The best solution is usually a mix of both positions or an alternative that hasn't been created yet.

- **Win and lose gracefully.** This disagreement probably won't be the last. Your response to the end of this disagreement sets the stage for the next one. If you win gracefully, the other party may be more willing to lose next time, knowing he or she won't be ridiculed or embarrassed. If you lose gracefully, you provide an example for appropriate behavior and keep personal issues out of the arena.

Solving Conflict

Disagreements don't have to create conflict. A business thrives when its owners, managers, and employees unite their different viewpoints to achieve a common goal—a successful business.

Reduce Causes of Conflict In today's business world, few employees start their careers in one business and stay with the company until they retire. Many people spend only two or three years working for a company before moving to another company, often for a better job title and a higher income. Long-term success of *your* business is not one of *their* goals. In a few years, they plan to be somewhere else, regardless of whether your business still exists.

Conflict within a company is often caused by personal ambition. Individuals may want personal success more than they want the business to succeed. This causes employees to emphasize short-term strategies and ignore the long-term effect. When consequences of shortsighted actions arrive, they are already gone. "Winning" disagreements or conflicts that create short-term gains are only items to list on their résumés to advance their personal careers.

As the owner, you have to create an atmosphere that emphasizes the common goal of success for the business. Reducing the emphasis on personal success reduces conflict and increases the likelihood of success for your business.

Set Goals for the Business Although managers should be involved in goal setting, the ultimate responsibility belongs to the owner. If the goals suggested by the managers conflict with the goals you want for the business, you win. After all, you opened a business so you could make the big decisions. Success or failure is your responsibility.

If more than one owner is involved in setting goals, any disagreement should be handled before it becomes a conflict. If conflict between owners can't be resolved, refer to the procedure for conflict settlement established when the business was formed. Your partnership agreement or other legal document created when your business was established should specify how a deadlock is resolved.

Role of Human Resources Like every other element of your business, human resources is focused on helping your business achieve its goals. However, it doesn't perform your core business activity. Human resources makes it possible for employees to do their jobs. It reduces conflict and increases morale by selecting and training employees to perform their tasks correctly and efficiently.

Part of training employees and improving efficiency is molding them into a united group with a common goal. This can be done by expensive methods such as seminars and outside trainers. Shaping the group into a single unit can also be done less expensively:

- **Participate in sports leagues with other small companies.** Playing as a team teaches employees to work together and cheer each other's small successes.
- **Hold a company picnic.** The social activity creates an opportunity for employees' families to meet. Family friendships create networks among the employees.
- **Order pizza when a group completes a project.** Celebrating success as a group encourages the group to create more success.
- **Give tickets to a local sporting event that your employees can attend as a group.** Reward the group for working together successfully.

Hypothetical Scenario

Eric's company, White Hats Software, thrived. Company dinners and excursions were common. The group became close, working and socializing together. When necessary, employees worked additional hours to complete projects or fix problems. They knew their time and skills were appreciated by Eric and their coworkers.

Technology Insights

Speech Recognition Software

The ultimate ergonomic tool for text input is speech recognition software. It doesn't take up space on your desk or get in the way when you're reaching for the telephone. It won't tire out your fingers or injure your wrists. Current technology enables the computer to process the sound of your speech and interpret those sounds into text, which it places in a document. In addition to dictating text, you can issue commands to the software such as selecting text and changing its appearance. Some packages enable you to control the operating system, performing tasks such as copying and moving files. Before you purchase a speech recognition software package, make a list of how you plan to use the software. If you plan to use it only to dictate text into a document, Microsoft Word and other word processing programs have built-in speech recognition features. If you plan to manage your operating system as well, your choices are more limited.

Think Critically What can speech recognition packages do for you or your business?

CHAPTER REVIEW

An employer has responsibilities to the employees, including a safe work environment and fair treatment. Providing an ergonomic workstation benefits the employer by creating employees who are more productive and content. You can also protect your employees by providing emergency equipment and safety procedures. OSHA has the responsibility of preventing work-related injuries, illness, and fatalities. OSHA investigates every complaint it receives about work sites that are not safe. If necessary, OSHA inspects the site. If dangerous situations are found, OSHA has the right to issue fines. Equal opportunity employers continue nondiscrimination policies after the employee is hired. Legislation has been passed and enforced to guarantee equal opportunity to all employees.

The payroll process is complicated and critical to the success of your business. Employees who aren't paid won't work. Because taxes are involved, there's a chance the government will be looking over your shoulder to make sure everything is done correctly. For small businesses, it is usually a smart decision to outsource the entire process. When you select a provider to perform your payroll process, investigate several options to find a provider that meets your criteria.

Employee files document every significant event in a worker's time with your company. Topics are organized into compensation, events, and medical information. The nature of the information demands privacy and the files should be stored under lock and key.

Workplace conflict doesn't usually result in violence but it can make the difference between enjoying your work and preferring to stay home. Controlled disagreements help workers find unique solutions to problems. Uncontrolled disagreement results in conflict, which is a problem that quickly causes additional problems that are even more serious. The best defense against conflict is establishing an environment that treats every employee with respect, acknowledging the value of every individual.

USE BUSINESS TERMS

Fill in the blanks with the appropriate term.

401(k)   inspection complaint
act of nature   investigation complaint
carpal tunnel syndrome   net pay
confidentiality agreement   outsourcing
employee file   payroll
ergonomics   private sector
fatality rates   synergy
garnishment   third party
glass ceiling   undue hardship
gross pay   whistle-blower
health hazard

1. Businesses should have an emergency plan to protect employees when a tornado or other ___?___ occurs.
2. An employee who reports high levels of radiation at a work site is a(n) ___?___ .
3. A highly qualified woman who can't get promoted to upper management despite her qualifications has encountered the ___?___ .
4. ___?___ is a complicated process that is often outsourced by small businesses.
5. Documents signed by an employee, such as a performance review, should be kept in the ___?___ .
6. An employer may be required to set up ___?___ to pay an employee's creditors.
7. A(n) ___?___ protects your inventions and business methods when an employee leaves your company to work for another business.

TEST YOUR READING

8. How does a business benefit from using ergonomics?
9. Identify the items that should be included in an emergency response plan.
10. What triggers an OSHA inspection?
11. What business activities are regulated by equal opportunity legislation?
12. How does the ADA affect small business employers?
13. Describe the steps in the payroll process.
14. Why would a small business outsource the payroll process?
15. How is information organized in employee files?
16. Why should employee files be kept in a secure location?
17. When is new information placed in an employee file?
18. Based on fatality rates, identify the most dangerous industries.
19. How do you avoid conflict in the workplace?

THINK CRITICALLY ABOUT BUSINESS

20. Describe the elements of a disaster recovery plan for your business or the business where you are currently employed.
21. Describe how OSHA regulations impact your business.
22. Select a large business. Examine the ratio of female and male board members. Explain why you believe the company has or doesn't have a glass ceiling.
23. Investigate and compare three businesses that provide payroll processing services.

REAL-LIFE BUSINESS

Cracker Barrel Old Country Store

In the late 1960s, Dan Evins was a young man working for his family's gasoline business. America's system of interstate highways was still developing. Fast-food restaurants were springing up all over the country. Dan saw the need for restaurants that serviced travelers, but he didn't like the idea of fast food. He believed that travelers would appreciate a respite from the road, a place to relax and eat nourishing food before continuing on their way. In 1969, Dan Evins and Tommy Lowe opened the first Cracker Barrel Old Country Store in Lebanon, Tennessee.

The Cracker Barrel concept included more than a nourishing menu. Dan wanted an environment that was welcoming and homey, an atmosphere that encouraged customers to relax and take their time. The original Cracker Barrel sites provided the atmosphere of a country store, a place to relax as well as a variety of merchandise that met the needs of small town residents. A large fireplace warmed the restaurant area. The merchandise assortment included food, dishes, toys, candy in large jars, and gasoline to help travelers meet all their needs before hitting the road again. Cracker Barrel no longer sells gasoline, but the merchandise assortment and atmosphere remains the same.

By the end of 2001, there were 443 Cracker Barrel Old Country Stores in the country and more locations are planned. Every location is owned and operated by the company. No franchises have been sold. The company still operates under the leadership of Dan Evins, the original cofounder. Dan states that the mission of every location is pleasing its customers.

Think Critically

1. What characterizes each Cracker Barrel location?
2. How is Cracker Barrel different from its competitors?
3. What is the mission of each location?
4. How would franchising change the business?

UNIT 5

Financial Services

CHAPTERS

CHAPTER 13

Banking Services

GOALS

- ◆ Choose a type of financial institution
- ◆ Open accounts and select financial services
- ◆ Select credit and loan services
- ◆ Apply for a loan

Norma Ramos quickly finished cleaning the small cabin, one of five cabins located on her property five miles from the state park. Norma's cabins remained full all year every year, but she wished for extra cash so she could build a few more. Limited to only five cabins, Norma constantly turned down requests for reservations. She was sure that several more cabins would increase her profit, helping her save money for her daughter's college education.

Financial Institutions

Operating a business requires financial activities that affect a large number of individuals and businesses. Your customers, suppliers, and employees are only the most obvious groups affected. The success or failure of your business affects individuals you may never encounter. Your financial decisions also affect many businesses that don't seem related in any way. Keep that in mind when you make your financial choices.

Types of Financial Institutions

You probably pass several financial institutions on your drive to work. With the time and temperature display and a little standard landscaping, they all seem to be the same. However, differences between financial institutions can help you determine which one is the best match for your needs. Financial institutions can be categorized as commercial banks, thrifts, or credit unions. The differences are based on the services they provide, their areas of specialization, the regulations they must obey, and the way their activities are monitored and supervised by government agencies.

Commercial Banks Financial institutions that provide the widest variety of services are **commercial banks.** They can place your deposits in a variety of accounts and loan money to individuals and businesses. Stockholders own commercial banks, which are traded on the stock market. As a result, banks are driven to earn a profit for their stockholders, just like any other publicly traded business.

State or federal governments charter commercial banks. The **charter** is also known as articles of incorporation. Banks can file their articles of incorporation at the state or federal level. The selected level determines the business activities they can pursue.

Supervisory Structure Created by Congress in 1913, the **Federal Reserve System,** the central bank of the United States, is responsible for maintaining a healthy banking system and a healthy economy. It is comprised of 12 regional Reserve Banks supervised by the Board of Governors in Washington, D.C. The Board of Governors consists of seven members, who are appointed by the president of the United States. Each Reserve Bank is located in a different geographic area, known as its **district,** which is made up of several states. Each Federal Reserve Bank supervises and regulates the state-chartered banks in its district.

Regulations Congress gave the Board of Governors the responsibility to implement the regulations affecting the Federal Reserve System. The Code of Federal Regulations contains laws that affect banks in the Federal Reserve System. The regulations affect activities, such as the amount of cash a bank must keep in reserve, changes to the basic discount rate, and membership requirements for state-chartered banks.

The Federal Deposit Insurance Corporation (FDIC) insures deposited funds. Each individual depositor is insured for a maximum of $100,000 deposited in the same bank. Any amount over $100,000 is not insured, even if it is deposited in more than one account in the same bank.

Thrifts Savings and loan associations and savings banks were originally known as **thrifts** because the only services they provided were savings accounts and home mortgages. Today's thrifts provide a much wider array of financial services. However, thrifts still maintain a high percentage of their loans in real estate.

The federal Office of Thrift Supervision (OTS) or a state regulator charters thrifts. To keep its charter, a thrift must provide a specific percentage of loans to purchase, build, or remodel homes, and maintain its membership in the Federal Home Loan Bank System.

Shareholders can own thrifts. Depositors and borrowers, known as **mutual ownership,** can also own their thrift institutions.

Supervisory Structure In the 1980s, many savings and loan associations were closed as a result of financial instability. The OTS supervises the remaining thrifts. Like banks, thrifts can be chartered at the state or federal level.

Regulations The OTS is also the primary regulator of all federal and state-chartered thrift institutions that are members of the Savings Association Insurance Fund (SAIF), which provides deposit insurance for thrifts. Authorized by Congress in 1989, SAIF is administered by the FDIC. Individual depositors are insured for a maximum of $100,000. If an individual deposits more than $100,000, even if it is deposited in more than one account, the additional amount is not insured.

Credit Union A group of individuals with a common bond can form a credit union, pooling their money to form a financial base for the credit union. The individuals who form the credit union become the owners. Only individuals who share the same common bond can take advantage of the credit union's services. The common bond can be sharing an employer, a club, or a community. Credit unions are nonprofit organizations. They encourage members to make sound financial decisions and offer services to members at lower rates than the average bank or thrift institution.

Supervisory Structure Credit unions can be chartered at the state or federal level. All federal credit unions and state credit unions that are federally insured report to the National Credit Union Administration (NCUA), a federal agency. The president of the United States appoints the three-member board.

Regulations Like most financial institutions, individual depositors are insured for a maximum of $100,000. The National Credit Union Share Insurance Fund provides insurance. This fund is administered by the NCUA.

Choose a Type of Financial Institution

Although you may not think about it, financial institutions are businesses too. They compete for your patronage just as you compete to attract and keep your customers. Choosing the right financial institution is similar to selecting any other professional to work with your business, such as a lawyer or accountant. Make a list of the criteria that are important to your business and evaluate the available alternatives.

- **Keep your business and personal accounts separate.** Business funds should always be kept separate from your personal funds. Although you can accomplish this by opening a separate business account, the separation will be easier to track and maintain if your business account is opened at a different financial institution.

- **Identify the products and services the financial institution offers.** Use the following sections in this chapter to determine the services you need. Rate each potential financial institution based on the range of services each institution provides. It's easier to track your financial activities and creates a better relationship with the institution if you fill all of your business needs at one place.

- **If you plan to request a business loan, identify the criteria the institution uses to qualify its loan recipients.** Even if you don't *plan* to need a loan at this point, check out the institution's requirements. Your plans could change if an opportunity presents itself or economic conditions cause a temporary dip in business income.

- **Verify that the institution provides services to small businesses.** Some types of financial institutions are more likely to work with small businesses than others. For example, commercial banks are more likely than credit unions to provide a loan to a small business.

- **Identify the minimum balance needed to open an account.** If you can't keep that amount in the account, you may have to pay additional fees.

- **Identify the fees associated with the products or services you need.** Fees can be based on the type of financial institutions you evaluate. For example, the U.S. Public Interest Research Group stated in 2001 that fees at large commercial banks are higher than fees in other institutions. The group identified small, locally owned banks as service providers that offer lower rates.

- **Ask your accountant, lawyer, and other small businesses for recommendations.** Your accountant and lawyer have probably dealt with several small businesses and their financial institutions. Other small businesses are usually happy to express satisfaction or frustration with their choices.

- **Consult your local Chamber of Commerce and Small Business Administration office.** They are aware of financial institutions that are active in the small business community.

- **Introduce yourself to the institution's manager and loan officer.** You don't need to be best friends with these individuals, but you should be able to work comfortably with them in mutual respect.

Hypothetical Scenario

Norma Ramos decided that she would apply for a loan to build five more cabins, doubling the capacity of her business in one big growth spurt. As a first step, she investigated the financial institutions in the nearby town. The most helpful information came from Bill, a friend who owned a restaurant in town. Six months ago, he received a loan from the commercial bank for new kitchen equipment. Bill claimed that the loan officer was very helpful.

Select Financial Services

In the past, banks offered items such as toasters, clock radios, and luggage to new customers opening an account. Shrewd business owners don't select a financial institution to get a toaster. They evaluate the individual accounts each institution offers, the complete array of services offered by each institution, the fees charged by the institution, the reputation of the institution, and its personnel.

Accounts

The characteristics of the available accounts in your area vary among financial institutions. Investigate the characteristics of several different types of accounts and several accounts of the same type at different institutions.

If possible, select accounts that earn **interest,** an amount paid to use someone else's money, that is usually expressed as an annual percentage of the amount used.

When you deposit money in an account, the financial institution uses those funds to earn money by loaning it to other customers or investing it. In exchange, the institution pays interest, automatically depositing the interest into your account. It is a simple way for your money to make more money.

Commercial Checking Accounts When you deal with a financial institution, you are usually putting money into your account or taking money out of your account. A commercial checking account enables you to easily perform both activities. Many institutions calculate the service fee for a checking account based on the account balance, the interest earned (if it is an interest-earning account), and the amount of account activity. If the balance of the checking account is high enough and the account earns interest, the amount of interest earned may be higher than the service fee, eliminating the need to pay a fee.

Each institution usually offers several types of checking accounts. Differences in the account's characteristics determine which one is right for your business.

- **Minimum opening deposit**—This amount is required to open a checking account. A common figure is $100.
- **Statement**—A **statement,** a document identifying the account transactions, is usually issued every month for checking accounts.
- **Automated Teller Machine**—Most checking accounts provide unlimited access to the account through an **Automated Teller Machine (ATM),** a machine designed to perform many of the services a human teller provides. ATMs, patented in 1973, accept deposits and enable you to withdraw cash and check your account balance. The ATM is linked electronically to your account to provide up-to-date account information.
- **Check images**—Some accounts provide a copy of the front and back of every check written from the account. This is useful in identifying mistakes or locating checks you forgot to record at the time they were written.
- **Transaction activity**—Limits may be placed on the number of account transactions performed in a month, including deposits and checks paid.
- **Monthly maintenance fee**—This fee is charged for keeping the account open and performing any services for the account such as tracking the balance and performing account transactions. The fee may not be charged if a minimum balance is maintained.
- **Per item fee**—The account is charged for every account transaction processed.
- **Stop payment**—Issuing a **stop payment** instructs the financial institution to refuse payment when a specific draft or check you wrote earlier is presented.
- **Wire transfers**—A **wire transfer** is an order, transmitted electronically, that instructs an institution to pay a specific amount to an individual or business.
- **Minimum daily balance**—The **minimum daily balance** is the lowest amount in an account during a specified time period, usually a month. If the balance in your account drops below this amount at any time, you may be charged an additional fee.

◆   **Interest rate**—This value identifies the rate at which the money in your account earns interest. When you are the one earning interest, a higher rate is better than a lower rate.

Savings Account If you want to store and accumulate funds, an interest-earning savings account is an option. However, it isn't a good choice if you need frequent access to your money or the convenience of writing checks. Some savings accounts may require a waiting period before the funds can be withdrawn. Many savings accounts limit the number of withdrawals and require a minimum daily balance to avoid a fee. An account statement may only be issued quarterly.

Consider opening a savings account if you are saving funds for a specific business purchase or a rainy day fund for emergencies. Because interest rates paid for savings accounts are usually very low, savings accounts should be used only for short-term savings needs.

Money Market Account You may decide that you want to keep some money set aside for purchases or emergencies but you want to earn more than a savings account can provide. A **money market account** is a savings vehicle that earns a higher interest rate than a savings account. However, a money market account is usually more restrictive than a savings account. For example, the minimum opening deposit is often much higher. Money market accounts may require an initial deposit of $2,500, $10,000, or $25,000. Some money market accounts charge fees. Others limit the number of withdrawals.

The interest paid on a money market account depends on the current financial environment and the amount of your opening deposit. A lower rate of interest is usually paid if the balance drops below the initial deposited amount.

Certificate of Deposit Another savings option is a certificate of deposit (CD). A depositor is given a **certificate of deposit** that identifies the amount deposited and contains the institution's promise to return the amount deposited plus a defined interest amount on a specific date. In most cases, a CD pays a higher rate of interest than a savings or money market account.

The interest rate paid for a CD is based on the amount deposited and the length of time the money is retained by the institution, also known as the **term** of the CD. A CD with a longer term pays a higher interest rate. If you withdraw all or part of the deposited funds before the term expires on the day the CD **matures,** a penalty is charged. If the penalty is more than the interest earned at the time, you lose some of your original deposit. Select a CD only if you are certain you won't need the original amount until the CD matures. Terms can vary from several months to several years. If you select a CD, choose an appropriate term that pays the highest rate of interest possible without tying up your funds too long.

Retirement Accounts Many financial institutions provide tax-deferred investment plans with FDIC insurance. Several types of investment plans are approved by the IRS and follow government regulations regarding the amount that can be contributed annually and when funds can be withdrawn. The most common account types include the Individual Retirement Account, Simplified Employee Pension, and Keogh.

- **Individual Retirement Account (IRA)**—Any individual, and the individual's nonworking spouse, who received taxable compensation during the year can contribute to an IRA. The funds are intended to be withdrawn after age 59½, when the individual retires.
- **Simplified Employee Pension (SEP)**—This retirement investment plan was designed specifically for small business owners and self-employed individuals.
- **Keogh**—This qualified retirement plan is designed for self-employed individuals.

Sweep Account Managing your cash flow does not need to take a great deal of time. A **sweep account** enables you to identify the amount of cash you want to retain in a specific account, usually a checking account. At the end of each day, the financial institution transfers any funds that are over the specified amount into a different account, usually an account that earns a higher interest rate, such as a money market account. This enables you to earn additional interest as soon as possible on funds that do not need to be used for day-to-day expenses.

Services

Financial institutions offer a variety of services. Each service is designed to earn income for the institution. Therefore, the services must appeal to a broad range of businesses by simplifying a common task, increasing the company's income, or decreasing the company's expenses. You don't need every service. For example, some services are more attractive to large companies. Evaluate the benefit and cost of each service to your company to avoid paying for services you don't need.

Direct Deposit Many employers choose to deposit employee paychecks directly into the employees' accounts. This service is much easier when the business account and the employees' accounts are located at the same financial institution. Therefore, many financial institutions offer a direct deposit package. Employees who choose to bank with the same institution receive additional benefits with their accounts such as lower minimum balances and better mortgage rates. The process of documenting and transferring the funds directly into the employees' accounts often runs smoother, even when a third-party business prepares your payroll. When the direct deposits occur, troubleshooting is easier if the money is transferred between accounts within the same institution.

Lock Box Payment Processing A post office box opened in your company's name is a **lock box.** A financial institution that provides lock box payment processing collects customer payments mailed to your lock box at least once a day. The envelopes are opened and the payments are deposited into your account. Check images and deposit information can be sent electronically to you or your accountant. This has obvious benefits for a small business. You save time when the institution picks up and processes the payments for you. Also, payments are deposited immediately. They do not sit around at the post office or on someone's desk until they can be processed and deposited.

Internet Access You can do a million things online. You can shop, play games, and send an e-mail to Great-aunt Ethel. Many financial institutions now provide full access to your accounts over the Internet. Using a secure Internet connection, you can view the current balance in your accounts, transfer funds from one account to another, and stop payments on checks you wrote earlier. You may be able to download the information into a database or accounting software application used by you or your accountant.

Night Depository Box If your business hours are different than your financial institution, closing after the institution is already closed, a **night depository box** enables you to deposit cash or checks after the institution has closed for the day. Deposits made after hours are usually credited to your account on the next business day. This simple service enables you to physically deposit funds without rushing to get to the bank before it closes or starting your day at the bank before you open your business the next day.

Tax Payments Paying taxes isn't fun. However, it doesn't have to be a stressful task that you perform at the last minute so you can keep your funds working for you until taxes must be paid. Some institutions enable you to make your federal and state tax payments by calling the institution and transferring the funds to the IRS. You can do this one business day before the tax is due. Although this may not seem like an important service, depending on the amount of taxes you pay, this service can earn additional interest and guarantees that the payment will not be late or lost before it can be delivered.

E-commerce Many small businesses operate on the Internet. Customers select merchandise and provide credit card information to make a purchase. After the credit card transaction is authorized, your institution processes the transaction and deposits the funds into your account. This process occurs without any work on your part. When you view your current account information, the sales made on your web site have already been deposited.

Merchant Credit Card Consumers are using their credit cards more than ever. Large or expensive purchases are commonly paid by credit card. If you enable your customers to use a credit card, you won't lose sales to other companies that permit credit card purchases. A financial institution that provides **merchant credit card service** accepts credit card payments and deposits the funds into your account. Usually, payment is deposited within 48 hours of the time the purchase was made. Many institutions can also provide the equipment used to accept credit card information. More information about granting customer credit is available in Chapter 14.

Evaluate the Options

Use the form in Figure 13.1 to evaluate the available alternatives. Identify the accounts and services you need. Call or visit the institutions to gather the information. Prepare a form for each institution so you can compare the options.

FIGURE 13.1   Evaluate Accounts and Services

Institution: _____

Account Type: Checking

Account Feature	Provided	Fee	Comment
Opening deposit			
Statement frequency			
ATM			
Check images			
Transaction activity			
Maintenance fee			
Per item fee			
Stop payment			
Wire transfer			
Minimum daily balance			
Interest rate			

Account Type: Savings

Opening deposit			
Statement frequency			
ATM			
Check images			
Transaction activity			
Maintenance fee			
Per item fee			
Stop payment			
Wire transfer			
Minimum daily balance			
Interest rate			

Account Type: Money Market

Opening deposit			
Statement frequency			
Transaction activity			
Maintenance fee			
Minimum daily balance			
Interest rate			

Account Type: Certificate of Deposit

Opening deposit			
Term			
Interest rate			

FIGURE 13.1   Evaluate Accounts and Services (continued)

Institution: _____

Account Type: Retirement

Service	Provided	Fee	Comment
IRA			
SEP			
Keogh			

Account Type: Sweep

Services

Direct deposit			
Lock box			
Internet access			
Night depository box			
Tax payments			
E-commerce			
Merchant credit card			

Hypothetical Scenario

Norma followed Bill's advice and spoke to the loan officer at the commercial bank. He seemed interested in her ideas, hoping to make the area more prosperous by attracting tourists. Norma's business would bring additional visitors to the area who wouldn't come without a place to stay.

Select Credit and Loan Services

Businesses of all types, even successful ones, may need loans. You may need a loan to expand your business, buy equipment, remodel your existing location, or buy a new site. The amount you need could be large or small. You may need the money for a few months or a few years. You might prefer to repay the loan in small payments over a long period of time or pay the entire amount a few years from now. Regardless of what you need, a financial institution can probably provide the funds and conditions that meet your needs.

Loan Terms

Borrowing money after your business is operating is similar to finding capital to start your business. It requires a promissory note, such as the example in Figure 13.2, that states the details of the loan and the conditions for the loan's repayment. The promissory note identifies the amount of the loan, the interest rate, the payment terms, and the borrower's possessions that can be sold or claimed by the lender, if necessary, to repay the loan.

FIGURE 13.2   Simple Promissory Note

Promissory Note

Amount: _____   Date: _____

Promise to Pay:
For value received, the undersigned hereby jointly and severally promise to pay <Financial Institution> $<Borrowed Amount> and interest at the annual rate of <Interest Rate>%.

Terms of Loan:
<Your Business> will pay <Number of Payments> of $<Payment Amount> on the <Day of the Month> beginning <Date> until the principal and interest have been paid in full. All payments are applied to the interest first. The remaining amount is applied to the principal. <Your Business> may make additional payments that will be applied to the principal, paying all or part of the principal, without penalty.

Security:
Until the principal and interest are paid in full, this promissory note is secured by <Your Company's Property>.

Default:
If <Financial Institution> prevails in a lawsuit to collect the unpaid amount, <Your Company> will pay the <Financial Institution's> court costs and legal fees.

<Your Signature>
<Your Title>
<Your Business>
<Your Business Structure>

Promise to Pay   A promissory note is a business document that gets right down to business. It quickly identifies the lender or financial institution, the borrowed amount or **principal,** and the annual interest rate you pay to borrow the funds. Interest rates are usually higher for a commercial loan than a personal loan.

Terms of a Loan   The promissory note defines how and when the principal and interest will be repaid. The sample promissory note in Figure 13.2 describes an installment loan. However, a variety of terms are available to meet your needs.

◆   **Installment loan**—The borrower makes **amortized payments,** paying the same amount each month for a specified number of months. When the payments are complete, the loan has been fully amortized. Each payment is applied to interest first. The remaining amount is applied to the principal.

- **Interest-only payments and a single balloon payment**—Usually for a short-term loan, the borrower makes regular payments of interest for a specified period of time. The final payment, the **balloon payment,** is a much larger amount consisting of interest and principal, paying off the loan.

- **Installment payments and a single balloon payment**—The borrower makes a predetermined number of installment payments consisting of interest and principal. After the final installment payment, the remainder of the loan is paid in a single large balloon payment.

- **Single payment**—A single large payment pays both the principal and the interest at a specified time.

Be sure that the terms of the promissory note state that a penalty won't be charged if you are able to pay the full amount of the loan before the final payment is due. Paying a debt early enables you to release yourself from a serious financial burden as quickly as possible. It also reduces the total amount you pay because interest stops accruing when the loan is paid. For example, if you repay an installment loan two years early, you repay the entire principal, but you do not pay the final two years of interest.

Security When you borrow money from a financial institution, it is usually a secured loan. If you are unable to repay the loan, the lender has the right to take the property you offered as security or collateral. The lender can sell the property and keep the proceeds.

Default If you are unable to repay the loan, the lender may pursue the matter in court. If the lender wins, you are required to pay the specified amount and any amount the lender incurs in suing you.

Signature Signing the promissory note binds you to the terms of the agreement. The business structure indicates your ability to bind the business to the terms of the promissory note as well.

Loan Types

Financial institutions offer several specific types of business loans. Some are designed to attract small businesses. Investigate all options carefully. The right loan can help your business succeed or advance to the next level of success. The wrong loan can hang over your business like a dark cloud for the entire length of the loan.

Financial Institutions According to the Small Business Administration, 55 percent of the small businesses that sought financing in 1998 acquired traditional commercial loans. In 1999, small businesses received over $172 billion in loans. Your business could benefit from one of the following common commercial loans. The financial institutions in your area may offer different loan products.

- **Commercial operating line of credit**—Some successful businesses have long-term projects and don't receive full payment until the project is complete. They still need funds for day-to-day expenses. An **operating line of credit** provides a specific amount that is available to the business over a specific time period. A short-term line of credit may be available for several months. A long-term line of credit may be available for several years. The institution may permit you to renew the loan when the term expires. Interest rates vary among institutions.

- **Commercial mortgage**—Apply for a **commercial mortgage** to buy a building, refinance an existing mortgage, or expand your operations. Mortgages are usually large amounts and long-term loans.
- **Term loan**—If you need funds for property improvements, expansion, or changes that provide long-term benefits, apply for a **term loan.** The lengths of time and interest rates vary among institutions.

Small Business Administration (SBA) If a financial institution rejects your loan application, you still have options. The SBA works with lenders to provide loans through financial institutions by guaranteeing the repayment of a major portion of the loan. The loan officer who rejected your application for a standard commercial loan can often help you apply successfully for an SBA loan. To determine eligibility for a loan, the SBA examines four factors—the type of business, size of the business, intended use of the funds, and any special circumstances.

- **Type of business**—The business must be operated for profit in the United States. The owner must invest in the business and seek standard commercial financing first.
- **Size of business**—Your business must qualify as a small business.
- **Use of funds**—The funds can be used for most legitimate business purposes.
- **Special circumstances**—Specific business activities and situations are not eligible.

The most common available SBA loan programs include the 7(a) Loan Guaranty Program, SBALowDoc program, SBAExpress, and SBA Export Express. Check with your financial institution, contact your local SBA office, or visit www.sba.gov for more information.

Evaluate the Options

Use the form in Figure 13.3 to evaluate the available alternatives. Identify the terms for each possibility. You don't have to apply for a loan to gather the information. Call or visit the institutions and speak to the loan officer who would handle your application. Prepare a form for each institution so you can compare the options. When you are ready to meet with the loan officer, you can calculate payments.

FIGURE 13.3   Evaluate Available Loan Options

Institution: _____

Loan Product: _____

Characteristic	Data
Length of time	
Payment schedule	
Interest rate	
Security required	
Penalty for early payment	
Default	
Comments	

Loan Product: _____

Length of time	
Payment schedule	
Interest rate	
Security required	
Penalty for early payment	
Default	
Comments	

Loan Product: _____

Length of time	
Payment schedule	
Interest rate	
Security required	
Penalty for early payment	
Default	
Comments	

Loan Product: _____

Length of time	
Payment schedule	
Interest rate	
Security required	
Penalty for early payment	
Default	
Comments	

Hypothetical Scenario

> Although Norma believed she preferred to deal with the commercial bank, she decided to talk to the two savings and loan institutions in town as well. She had a personal savings account and checking account at one of the savings and loans, but no one there seemed interested in talking to her about a business loan. Norma decided to apply for a loan at the commercial bank.

Apply for a Loan

Don't rely on a financial institution to tell you how much you can borrow. You may not need to borrow the maximum amount the financial institution offers. Determine the maximum amount you want to borrow by calculating the amount you can comfortably afford to pay when each payment is due. If you choose a loan with a balloon payment, be sure that you save funds to pay the balloon payment when the loan matures. Consult with your accountant to calculate the amount you need and the payment schedule you can afford. Repay your loan as quickly as it is financially advantageous to do so.

Loan officers see dozens of loan applications every week. Every application can't be approved. Your application needs to stand out from the others, convincing the loan officer that your loan request is more deserving than the other applications stacked on the desk.

Lender's Criteria

Financial institutions operate to earn money. An institution that gives money away will not be in business long. When evaluating a loan application, the lender's main criterion is your ability to repay the loan in full and on time. To receive a loan, you must convince the loan officer that you are able to repay the loan within the specified time period. Lenders look at several characteristics to determine your ability to repay the loan.

- ◆ **Management experience**—Your experience is very important. Ideally, you have experience in the industry and in management. If you don't have experience in both, the next best situation is successful experience in management. Finally, experience in the industry demonstrates that you have some knowledge of how your business should operate.
- ◆ **Personal investment**—You become a better credit risk if you invest your time and money into establishing and operating your business. If you have a personal stake in your business, the lender assumes that you will work harder to ensure its success.
- ◆ **Credit history**—When you need to obtain credit, it is better to have a history of borrowing and repaying funds rather than a history that does not include loans. Ideally, you have borrowed and repaid a loan that is similar in size. Even a personal credit card that does not show any penalties for late payments helps to prove that you are capable of repaying a debt.

- **Character**—References should provide evidence of your honesty, integrity, and business acumen. Suppliers, major customers, and previous employers can testify to your character as a business professional.
- **Security**—The property you offer as collateral for the loan must have a value high enough to secure the loan. If the lender takes possession of the property, it should be able to recoup its losses if you are unable to repay the loan.
- **Cash flow**—Your business must generate enough income to pay each loan payment, continue to pay expenses, and generate a profit for the business. If the business can't do this, the loan gradually sinks the business, lowering the lender's chance of receiving repayment for the loan.

Select a Financial Institution

Review the information you collected about the financial institutions, the accounts and services they offer, and the type of loans they have available. This information helps you select several financial institutions that can potentially meet your business needs.

An additional piece of data might give you the edge in selecting a financial institution that provides loans. Every year, the SBA evaluates financial institutions that provide loans. These institutions are rated for their "friendliness" toward small businesses. Friendliness is interpreted as "significant lending activity" of loans to small businesses, indicating a willingness to provide loans to small businesses. This information is available from the SBA. You can visit your local SBA office or the SBA web site at www.sba.gov and enter the search criterion "friendly" in the search field. Select the report for the most recent year and select your state. Financial institutions evaluated by the SBA are listed in order, based on their friendliness to small businesses. Selecting a financial institution with a high rating or avoiding a bank with a low rating helps you select a financial institution which will make the best use of your time when you apply for a loan.

Prepare a Loan Proposal

You already collected much of the information you need for a loan proposal when you wrote or updated your business plan. A loan proposal is similar to a business plan. It contains much of the same information regarding your business, your management, and your plans for the future. A loan proposal contains several additional pieces of information—the amount of money you need to borrow, the way the funds will be used, when the loan will be repaid, how the loan will be repaid, and what will happen if your plans don't work.

The loan proposal contains the following elements. Information that can be drawn from the business plan is identified with an asterisk (*). Each bulleted item identifies a major heading in the loan proposal.

- **Business Summary**—Describe your business. Include your mission statement* and a description of the product or service you sell.* Identify the amount of money you need, the way the funds will be used, and how the loan will be repaid. Be brief. This is a summary. Provide more details later in the document.

- **Management Profiles**—The lender wants to know that your key personnel are experienced.* If any managers have previous experience with business loans, this additional information can make a loan more likely.

- **Business Description**—Identify the company's legal structure* (sole proprietorship, partnership, etc.) and the organizational structure* with a basic organizational chart.* Include the age of your business and the number of employees. Describe your product,* your location,* and your product market.* Identify your competition* and advertising strategy.* Describe the inventory levels you need to maintain.

- **Projections**—Identify your strategic and tactical objectives.* Describe the opportunities for growth represented by the objectives.

- **Financial Statements**—Add a cash flow statement,* income statement,* and balance sheet* for the last three years. Work with your accountant to prepare two sets of projections—one projection assumes you receive the loan and one projection assumes you don't receive the loan. Include copies of your personal tax returns for the last three years.

- **Purpose of the Loan**—Describe exactly how the funds will be used.

- **Amount of the Loan**—Restate the amount of the loan. Include supporting information such as the cost of the equipment, inventory, or other items to be purchased.

- **Repayment Plan**—Describe how the assets you purchase will generate the additional income needed to repay the loan. Generally, a lender expects you to be able to pay interest as you pay any other expense. The principal is paid from your profit. Your repayment plan must demonstrate that your cash flow and assets enable you to repay the debt. Identify the value of the property that serves as your security if you are not able to repay the loan.

Apply for a Loan

When you go to the financial institution to meet with the loan officer, present a professional image. Review your documents so you are prepared and knowledgeable. Be sure to bring all the documents listed in Figure 13.4.

FIGURE 13.4 Checklist for a Loan Application

- ❏ Loan proposal
- ❏ Business plan
- ❏ Owners' résumés
- ❏ Owners' personal credit histories
- ❏ Owners' character references
- ❏ Information about security
- ❏ Business bank account information
- ❏ Personal financial data
- ❏ Cash flow statements for the last three years
- ❏ Income statements for the last three years
- ❏ Balance sheets for the last three years
- ❏ Information about the items to be purchased with the funds

Hypothetical Scenario

Norma prepared her loan proposal with some help from the accountant who prepared her tax returns and financial statements. She carefully collected the materials she needed for the meeting and reviewed the financial information. Although she couldn't prepare the statements without assistance, she wanted to sound knowledgeable if any questions were asked. She placed the materials in her portfolio and prepared to leave for the meeting.

Technology Insights

Electronic Fund Transfer

You can be rich without having a single dollar in your wallet, tucked under your mattress, or buried in your backyard. You can buy ice cream or a diamond ring without physically handling a single dime. An electronic fund transfer, the process of moving money from one place to another or from one owner to another, is a benefit of modern technology. Computers are used in so many aspects of business that tracking business funds is a natural development. Adding, subtracting, and moving money from one bank account to another is a task that requires numerous calculations, which a computer can perform before you can sharpen your pencil. Businesses that operate in locations across the ocean from each other can transfer funds around the world with a few keystrokes. Transferring funds electronically has several advantages. Funds are transferred immediately. Money transferred electronically can't be lost or stolen like checks or cash can. The process is much easier and more convenient, particularly when long distances are involved.

Think Critically Describe several business situations in which electronic fund transfers are used.

CHAPTER REVIEW

Every community has a variety of financial institutions. They can be distinguished by the services they provide, their areas of specialization, government regulations, and government supervision. Commercial banks, thrifts, and credit unions compete for your patronage, just as other businesses compete for customers and market share.

Accounts and services offered by each financial institution vary slightly. Investigate several alternatives before selecting a financial institution for your business. The best way to make your money work for you is to keep the lowest amount necessary on hand. The remainder should be placed where it can earn interest as quickly as possible.

A variety of loan products are available to meet your business needs. The terms of a loan are defined in the promissory note. Signing the note indicates that you agree to the terms and promise to repay the loan. If you can't repay the loan, the lender can claim the property you identified as security. If you can't qualify for a standard business loan, the SBA may be able to help you by guaranteeing a major part of the loan.

Lenders evaluate you as a credit risk. They want to know that you have the resources to repay the loan. With this in mind, they examine you and your business. When you prepare to apply for a loan, you must write a loan proposal, which contains much of the information from your business plan with information about the loan you are requesting and the way the funds will be used.

USE BUSINESS TERMS

Fill in the blanks with the appropriate term.

amortized payments

Automated Teller Machine (ATM)

balloon payment

certificate of deposit (CD)

charter

commercial bank

commercial mortgage

district

Federal Reserve System

interest

lock box

matures

merchant credit card service

minimum daily balance

money market account

mutual ownership

night depository box

operating line of credit

principal

statement

stop payment

sweep account

term

term loan

thrift

wire transfer

1. A(n) ___?___, the final payment, is a much larger amount than the previous payments.
2. A financial institution that provides ___?___ accepts credit card payments and deposits the funds into your account.
3. A penalty is charged if you withdraw all of the initial deposit before the CD ___?___.
4. A(n) ___?___ instructs an institution to pay a specific amount to an individual or business.
5. A borrower pays interest on the loan's ___?___.
6. If your business closes after your financial institution, you can deposit each day's earnings in the ___?___ at the end of each day.
7. Open a(n) ___?___ where customer payments can be mailed.

TEST YOUR READING

8. Where are the 25 Federal Reserve Banks located?
9. What is the purpose of the FDIC?
10. What criteria should you use to select a financial institution for your business?
11. Why is it beneficial to receive images of the checks written from your business account?
12. Which common savings vehicle usually earns the most interest?
13. What are the most common types of retirement plans for small businesses?
14. What type of business would find lock box processing to be a beneficial service?
15. What information is in a promissory note?
16. Identify several different payment terms.
17. What happens if you are not able to repay a loan?

18. How does a lender determine your eligibility for an SBA loan?

19. What characteristics do lenders examine to determine your ability to repay a loan?

THINK CRITICALLY ABOUT BUSINESS

20. How does the FDIC stabilize today's business environment?

21. Use an amortization table (available on the Internet) to calculate the monthly payment for a $90,000 loan with an annual interest rate of 8 percent that will be paid off in five years.

22. Use the Small Business Association's web site to identify several financial institutions in your community that are interested in lending money to small businesses.

23. Contact the financial institution where you currently bank. Evaluate the accounts and services it offers. Is this a good choice for a small business?

REAL-LIFE BUSINESS

Pretty Bird International, Inc.

A successful product can be manufactured for pets rather than people. Pretty Bird is a leader in exotic pet nutrition. Founded by Michael Massie, Pretty Bird introduced its first products to the market in 1990. Pretty Bird researched animal nutrition and new technology to formulate nutritious food for pet birds and other exotic pets.

Initially, Pretty Bird identified prominent breeders as its target market. As the food products became popular with breeders, individual pet owners began to purchase the food. Pretty Bird's reputation and customer base grew quickly.

Research and technology led to new products. Research identified the nutritional needs of individual bird species, leading Pretty Bird to develop nutritional formulas for specific species. To make the pellets seem more interesting and attractive to the birds, Pretty Bird introduced pellets in a variety of colors and shapes.

Pretty Bird continues its research, developing new products and improving existing ones. It currently manufactures several different products for birds. It has opened a new division, Pretty Pets, and expanded into nutritional food for other exotic pets such as iguanas, bearded dragons, and hedgehogs.

Think Critically

1. Describe the information Michael Massie would provide in a loan application.

2. How did Pretty Bird's decision to target prominent breeders rather than individual pet owners impact the amount of money needed for advertising?

3. Identify several possibilities for the Pretty Pet division of Pretty Bird.

4. How do you think Pretty Bird should continue its growth in the future?

CHAPTER  14

Granting Credit

GOALS

- Describe how consumers use credit
- Accept credit cards
- Provide security and protect your business from credit card fraud
- Follow credit regulations

Al Lamas owns Little Bitty Books, a small children's bookstore in Arizona. His store has become the leading children's bookstore in town. However, Al has bigger dreams. He wants to become the leading children's bookstore in the state and eventually the leading children's bookstore in the country. Al believes that the earnings generated by large releases, such as the series about Harry Potter, prove that the market for children's books can be very profitable.

How Consumers Use Credit

If you are like millions of other Americans, when you dine at an expensive restaurant, go on a shopping spree, or make reservations for a vacation, your first option to pay is with a credit card. Credit cards are an established way to pay for goods and services large and small. Businesses that don't accept credit cards lose sales.

"Just put it on my tab" is a common statement from movies about the Old West. Customers purchased food and other necessities from the town's general store and paid for the items after harvesting and selling their crops. Although most consumers' incomes are no longer tied to the harvest, buying on credit is standard for many Americans.

Credit Usage
Credit is the exchange of goods or services for the promise of payment. Consumers buy products on credit all the time. Cost, location, and convenience are the most

common reasons for credit usage. An expensive home theater equipment package and a special deal available only on the Internet are only two examples of situations that frequently result in credit usage.

Credit is a loan. To buy a house, consumers get a mortgage loan. To buy a car, consumers get an installment loan. To buy products from merchants, consumers frequently use a credit card. A **credit card** is a plastic card used by a consumer to make purchases by borrowing money from the financial institution that issued the card. The card charges funds to a specific account registered to the individual, group, or business obtaining credit from the financial institution.

The credit card company is a business built to provide a service. Credit card companies pay the business for the product then collect payment from the customer. For this service, credit card companies collect interest from the customer for the loan. Many credit card companies also charge fees to the merchant and the customer.

According to the American Express Company, the average consumer has six credit cards, which include retail cards from particular stores, gasoline cards from specific gas stations, and **charge cards,** which don't charge interest but require full payment each month. CardWeb.com, a leading publisher of information about credit, calculated in November 2001 that the average American household that had at least one credit card had $8,523 in credit card debt, not including home mortgages, car payments, or other debts.

This trend toward frequent credit usage is causing an increase in bankrupt-cies. When individuals spend more money than they earn, they eventually run out of money and declare **bankruptcy,** a legal condition that enables the court to use the individual's assets to repay the creditors and lenders. As shown in Figure 14.1, the incidence of bankruptcy doubled in the 1990s.

FIGURE 14.1   Bankruptcies in the 1990s

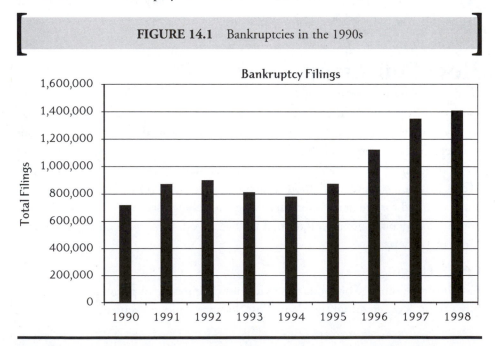

Credit Card Characteristics

Probably every American consumer (and even some of their pets!) has received at least one credit card offer in the mail. Although many of the offers sound similar, credit cards have characteristics that set them apart from each other.

Financial institutions known as **issuing banks**—not the credit card companies themselves—issue most credit cards. Differences among credit cards reflect differences among issuing banks. When consumers and businesses select a credit card, they should examine the disclosure statement carefully. The **disclosure statement** identifies valuable information about the card and the rules regarding its usage, including how the interest is calculated and any fees or penalties that can be applied.

Credit Limit Each account has a **credit limit,** a maximum amount that can be charged by the cardholder when making purchases. To increase the credit limit, a cardholder can request an increase after having the card for six months. Some credit card companies occasionally raise the credit limit without a specific request from the cardholder.

Interest Rate The amount of interest a credit card company advertises is the APR, the annual percentage rate. The **APR** identifies the amount of interest charged for any unpaid credit card balance. Many credit cards offer a special introductory rate for new customers. This rate is usually much lower than the regular APR. The introductory rate expires after one to six months and the regular APR becomes effective.

The APR can be fixed or variable. A variable rate is tied to an economic index that fluctuates as the economy trends up or down. For example, the prime rate, an economic indicator, is also used to determine the interest rate for other loans such as mortgage and installment loans.

The interest rate can also change if the cardholder is late making a payment. A **penalty APR** is used for all future payments. The penalty APR is usually much higher than the regular APR.

Grace Period Consumers who pay their accounts in full every month benefit from a credit card with a **grace period.** A credit card with a grace period doesn't charge interest if the balance is zero at the beginning of the billing period and the new balance is paid before the due date. A credit card that doesn't offer a grace period charges interest from the date of the transaction or the date the transaction is posted to your account. If the card has a balance carried over from the previous month, a grace period is not granted for the existing balance and usually isn't granted for any new transactions.

Fees Credit card companies charge a variety of fees. Every card is slightly different so consumers should investigate carefully before selecting a card.

- **Annual fee**—Many credit card companies charge an annual fee. This fee can range from $25 to several hundred dollars.
- **Transaction fee**—Most companies do not charge additional fees for a standard purchase transaction. However, they may charge for additional services such as a cash advance or trying to pay the card's balance with a check supported by insufficient funds in your checking account.

- **Late fee**—Submitting a late payment can have severe consequences. The cardholder is charged a fee for making a late payment. Additional interest is charged because the balance isn't paid and the penalty APR is used for all future transactions.
- **Over-the-limit fee**—If a consumer charges more than the allowed amount for the credit account, an additional fee may be charged.

Balance Calculation Three different calculations can be used to determine the balance on a credit card. The balance is important because it is used to determine the amount of interest a cardholder pays each month. Each calculation has a different result, which can be more or less advantageous to the cardholder. The disclosure statement for the credit card describes the calculation used. If a cardholder doesn't carry a balance forward each month and the card has a grace period, the method used to calculate interest is not as important to the cardholder.

- **Average daily balance method**—The balance of each day during the billing period is added together. The total is divided by the number of days in the billing period to calculate the average daily balance. This is the most common method.
- **Previous balance method**—The unpaid balance at the end of the last billing period is used to calculate interest.
- **Adjusted balance method**—Any payments made by the cardholder are subtracted from the previous balance. The result is used to calculate the interest.

Balance Transfer Credit card companies encourage new cardholders to transfer debt from another credit card. This enables the cardholder to close the account with the credit card that has a zero balance. However, the cardholder is only transferring the debt from one credit card to another. This makes sense only if the new credit card has a lower APR.

Hypothetical Scenario

Al Lamas's Little Bitty Books has been in operation for one year. His retail and storage space is limited, so the selection he is able to offer is also limited. Regardless of the limitations, sales increased steadily in the past year. His cash flow has become more even and reliable. However, sales have reached a plateau. Therefore, Al has decided that it is time to investigate the process of accepting credit cards to increase sales.

Accept Credit Cards

Not all businesses accept credit cards. In fact, many businesses accept only cash. However, the majority of businesses that sell directly to consumers accept credit cards.

Business Types

Some businesses can operate on a cash-only basis. For example, most coin-operated laundromats and self-service car wash businesses don't accept credit cards. However, businesses may be limiting their income by not offering alternative payment methods.

Internet and Catalog Many catalog companies also provide a web site to place orders. Although companies that sell products through catalogs have existed longer than businesses that operate only on the Internet, they have many similarities. An Internet or catalog business is not usually located where the consumer can physically access the merchandise. Therefore, Internet and catalog businesses ask consumers to purchase items they can't touch and visually examine.

Accepting credit cards is required for businesses that sell products on the Internet or through a catalog. Sending cash or checks through the mail is time-consuming and requires more effort by the customer. Additionally, checks require more time to receive and process, increasing the length of time the customer must wait to receive the product.

Placing an order with a credit card is as simple as reading the credit card account number over the phone or typing the number into an entry field. The easier and faster you can make the order process, the more likely a customer is to make a purchase. According to American Express, their cardholders who purchase items from catalogs spend an average of $387 with catalog companies each month.

Retail Bricks-and-mortar retailers usually accept many forms of payment. Retailers don't want to see a potential purchase walk out the door because they weren't able to handle the payment method offered.

B2B Business-to-business (**B2B**) companies sell goods and services to other businesses. A business often prefers to pay by credit card, or it asks the provider to submit an invoice. For the provider, payment is more timely when the customer uses a credit card rather than an invoice.

Advantages of Accepting Credit Cards

Convenience is an obvious advantage for customers with credit cards. Businesses gain other advantages from accepting credit cards, including:

- **Flexibility**—A customer who doesn't carry enough cash to purchase your product probably carries a credit card. Alternative payment methods increase the possibility of a purchase.
- **Speed**—Credit card payments can be deposited in your account in two to three days. Checks take additional time to process.
- **Safety**—The risk of nonpayment is low. Payment isn't dependent on the amount in the customer's checking account.
- **Accuracy**—Mistakes in billing and making change are more common when handling cash than during a credit card transaction.
- **Additional business customers**—Many businesspeople who travel or purchase items for their businesses prefer a credit card receipt they can submit to their accounting department. To business customers, this alternative is better than using their own cash and waiting to be reimbursed by their employers.
- **Image**—Businesses that accept credit cards, compared with cash-only businesses, present a more professional image. A cash-only business seems more like a garage sale than an established business that has operated for a respectable length of time and will continue to operate in the future.

Requirements to Accept Credit Card Payments

A credit card transaction is more complicated than a cash transaction. Money doesn't move directly from the customer's wallet to yours. It requires a middleman. To accept credit card payments, you need a merchant account at a financial institution, point-of-sale equipment, a transaction clearinghouse, and a gateway to the clearinghouse.

Merchant Account When you selected the financial institution for your business, you investigated the services and fees for several institutions. (See Chapter 13.) If you planned to accept credit card payments, a merchant account was on your list of necessary financial services. A financial institution that provides merchant credit card service accepts credit card payments and deposits the funds into your account.

Some financial institutions offer a complete package that includes or recommends a transaction clearinghouse, a gateway to the clearinghouse, and equipment and software if necessary. If you don't want the package offered by your financial institution, you can shop around for a different financial institution or component providers.

You are charged a transaction fee based on the average number of credit card transactions you have within a specific time period and the method you use to collect the credit card number. The fee is usually lower for bricks-and-mortar retailers who handle the card and collect the number by passing it through equipment that reads the magnetic strip. Fees are higher for Internet merchants who rely on the cardholder to enter the credit card number accurately and honestly. The financial institution can charge a flat fee or a minimum fee regardless of the number of credit card transactions you have.

Point-of-Sale Equipment A bricks-and-mortar retailer can collect the credit card number in several different ways. Select a method that meets your needs and budget. To purchase equipment or software, contact your transaction clearinghouse, gateway, or a vendor that sells supplies to retailers. If you don't want to purchase the equipment, you may be able to lease it from your financial institution or transaction clearinghouse. Whether you purchase or lease the equipment or software, ensure that it is compatible with the other components in your credit card package.

♦ **Manual transactions**—This old-fashioned transaction method requires a manual imprinter and sales slips. The sales slip and credit card are laid in a small mechanical device and a heavy piece is dragged over them, making an imprint of the card on the sales slip. The cardholder is present and signs the receipt. The advantage of this method is its mechanical nature. Since it doesn't require electricity, it can be useful at trade shows or fairs, but it is too labor intensive and time-consuming to use for a large number of transactions.

♦ **Hand-keyed transactions**—Retailers who don't handle the card use hand-keyed transactions. Internet and catalog businesses commonly use this method. Transactions can be entered through a special electronic terminal or software on your personal computer.

- **Swiped transactions**—The most common type of credit card transaction today is performed with an electronic terminal or a track reader. The retailer **swipes** the card, passing it through a piece of equipment that reads the information on the magnetic strip. The cardholder is present and signs the receipt.

Transaction Clearinghouse An important step occurs in every transaction between swiping the credit card and handing the merchandise to your customer—authorization. If your equipment can transmit information electronically and is connected to a phone line, the credit card information is transmitted to the clearinghouse. If your equipment doesn't have an electronic connection to the clearinghouse, you can call the clearinghouse and dictate the credit card data. The **transaction clearinghouse** verifies the credit card information and validates the customer's credit line. You receive an **authorization code,** which ensures that the credit card has passed the criteria to make the purchase. After receiving the authorization code, you can complete the sales transaction and give or ship the merchandise to the customer.

Internet and catalog businesses are slightly different. Rather than transmitting the credit card information as the transaction occurs, small Internet and catalog businesses collect the information and transmit it in a batch at regular intervals, usually once a day. The business then ships merchandise only if the credit card involved in the transaction has been given an authorization code by the clearinghouse. Other sales transactions are rejected. This process helps prevent sending merchandise without receiving payment.

Gateway For Internet businesses, real-time access to your transaction clearinghouse is provided by a **gateway** consisting of hardware and software. A gateway also provides electronic protection for the sensitive customer information transmitted during a credit card transaction. The data is encrypted and protected from other computers and Internet users. The transaction clearinghouse or financial institution usually selects the gateway.

Complete a Credit Card Transaction

Regardless of whether the sales transaction is completed in person or over the Internet, several steps are necessary. Usually, payment is deposited within 48 hours of the time the purchase was made.

Steps in the Sales Transaction During a sales transaction, the most visible and familiar steps occur between the time the customer presents the credit card and the time the customer receives the merchandise. If a credit card transaction is rejected, it occurs during this part of the transaction, before you give or ship the merchandise to the customer.

Steps in a Swiped Transaction
- **The cardholder presents a credit card.**
- **Physically examine the card.** Look for damage or alterations. Verify that the card is signed and hasn't expired.
- **Swipe the card.** This records the card's information and transmits it to your transaction clearinghouse.

◆ **Receive the authorization code.** If you don't receive an authorization code, terminate the sales transaction.

◆ **The customer signs the receipt.**

◆ **Give the merchandise and a copy of the receipt to the customer.**

Steps in a Manual Transaction

◆ **The cardholder presents a credit card.**

◆ **Physically examine the card. Look for damage or alterations.** Verify that the card is signed and hasn't expired.

◆ **Take an imprint of the card.** This records the card's information.

◆ **Call the transaction clearinghouse.** Provide the credit card and purchase information.

◆ **Receive the authorization code.** If you don't receive an authorization code, terminate the sales transaction.

◆ **The customer signs the receipt.**

◆ **Give the merchandise and a copy of the receipt to the customer.**

Steps in a Hand-Keyed Transaction

◆ **The cardholder provides the credit card information.** This data includes the credit card number, billing address, and expiration date. The card isn't presented to the merchant.

◆ **Enter the credit card information.** Depending on your setup, this could be performed when the cardholder enters the data at your web site or you enter information given when the cardholder calls to place an order.

◆ **Transmit the information to your transaction clearinghouse.** Depending on your setup, this could be performed automatically when the order is placed. The information could also be transmitted in a batch at the end of the day. This delay is usually acceptable to today's educated cardholders who expect a slight delay until credit card authorization is given.

◆ **Receive the authorization code.** If you don't receive an authorization code, terminate the sales transaction.

◆ **Give the merchandise and a receipt to the customer.**

Steps After the Sales Transaction When the sales transaction is complete, the customer has the merchandise, but you don't have the money. The steps that occur after the sales transaction, which are invisible to the cardholder, transfer the cash into your merchant account.

◆ **Submit the receipts to your financial institution.** Depending on your setup, swiped transactions and nonswiped transactions from a web site may be submitted automatically. At the end of every business day, **settle accounts** by submitting any receipts that aren't submitted automatically. Settle accounts regularly. Some credit card companies limit the length of time they will pay a receipt.

◆ **Your financial institution submits a request for payment to the transaction clearinghouse.** The financial institution and transaction clearinghouse charge a fee for their services.

- **The transaction clearinghouse submits a request for payment to the credit card's issuing bank.**
- **The issuing bank subtracts the purchase from the cardholder's line of credit, bills the cardholder, and transfers the funds back up the line where they are eventually deposited in the merchant account.**

The funds are transferred electronically. Therefore, payment usually arrives in your account in two to three days. Receipts that are manually taken to your financial institution may require additional time to transfer from paper to electronic form.

Discount Rate

A discount is usually a good thing. However, when you are discussing credit card transactions, the **discount rate** is the amount of money you *pay* to process and deposit credit card transactions. The discount rate is calculated by adding the transaction charge, interchange rate, and transmission cost as shown in Figure 14.2. If the credit card is not swiped, an additional fee is charged for the transaction.

FIGURE 14.2 Discount Rate Calculation

$$\text{Transaction Charge} + \text{Interchange Rate} + \text{Transmission Cost} + \text{Nonswipe Charge} = \text{Discount Rate}$$

Although some fees are expressed as a flat rate per transaction, others are calculated as a percentage of the credit card sale. The total discount rate varies because the financial institution, credit card company, and transaction clearinghouse charge different fees but it is usually less than 6 percent of the credit card sale.

- **Transaction charge**—This fee is paid to the financial institution for accepting and processing the payment.
- **Interchange rate**—This fee is paid to the transaction clearinghouse for the service of allowing you to accept the cardholder's credit card.
- **Transmission cost**—This fee is paid to transmit the transaction information through the gateway to the transaction clearinghouse.
- **Nonswipe charge**—This charge is applied only when the card is not swiped during the transaction. Therefore, Internet and catalog businesses can expect to pay this fee on all of their transactions.

Hypothetical Scenario

Al met with his banker to discuss the steps necessary to accept credit cards. He established a merchant account with the financial institution and authorized the bank to set up an arrangement with the transaction clearinghouse and gateway. He purchased the equipment necessary to swipe cards and a manual imprinter to use as backup during the occasional power outages caused by construction in the area.

Security and Credit Card Fraud

Credit card information is critical to the finances of businesses and consumers. As a business, it is your responsibility to protect your customers' information as well as your business. Your business must implement procedures to prevent the theft of the credit card information it possesses and protect your business from **fraud,** which is deceit intended to gain something of value. Individuals using credit cards that are stolen or not legitimate are committing credit card fraud.

Security

Many of the precautions you must take to protect your customers' credit card information are the same as the measures required to protect your employees' information. Some are common sense. Others require specialized software or assistance from a third party to execute.

Common Sense Security Guidelines The most basic forms of credit card security are simple for your business to enforce. They require common sense rather than specific skills or technology.

- **Limit physical access to credit card information.** Store the information in a secure location that can be locked. Any papers, such as receipts or correspondence containing credit card information, should be kept in a locked file cabinet. Never leave this information where it is readily available.
- **Establish a security policy and document the policy in the employee handbook.** This ensures that your employees are aware of the security policy and they are responsible for following it.
- **Security includes confidentiality.** Discourage employees from discussing customer or order information.
- **Return credit card receipts to customers.** Don't let customers leave a receipt behind or dispose of it improperly. Thieves can recover receipts to gather credit card and customer information.
- **Don't send credit card information in e-mail messages.** Others can intercept it.

Electronic Security Guidelines Many businesses store credit card information electronically. However, consumers are more aware of the fact that Internet and catalog businesses have their credit information. This doesn't mean that these businesses have more responsibility to protect their customers' information. All businesses have the same responsibilities, but cardholders who purchase products over the Internet or by telephone are more likely to investigate how the business protects their data. For example, as a consumer, you don't worry about using your credit card at an expensive restaurant, even though the card leaves your sight for several minutes. However, you always check for the padlock icon on a web page that indicates a secure web page before you provide any personal or financial information.

A third-party business that specializes in setting up computer networks and web sites can provide the expertise needed to establish security for your electronic data. The business should be familiar with encrypting data, network security, and establishing a **firewall**—software that prevents unauthorized access to your data by outside users.

Credit Card Fraud

Most cardholders are only responsible for the first $50 fraudulently charged on their cards. Unfortunately, businesses have no limit for the loss they assume when they are the victims of credit card fraud. Opportunity for fraud is easy to find for a credit card criminal. Several web sites list stolen cards. Other sites can automatically generate realistic credit card numbers that have never been issued to a legitimate cardholder. Because many instances of credit card fraud involve items valued at less than $500, police are reluctant to become involved.

Contrary to what you may think, the authorization code doesn't guarantee that a transaction isn't fraudulent. The theft of the card could be unreported or unknown by the cardholder, enabling an unauthorized user to make the purchase. Warning signs can indicate a problem with the transaction.

Warning Signs A small business doesn't have the resources to recover from a number of fraudulent sales transactions or a single large fraudulent transaction. Shipping your merchandise without receiving payment can quickly close a new business. You might as well leave your merchandise at the curb and invite passing pedestrians to take it home. Watch for the following warning signs that might indicate credit card fraud:

- **Orders that are larger than normal could indicate that a thief is planning to get away with as much as possible at one time.**
- **Overnight delivery adds significant expense.** Thieves don't mind the additional expense if they don't plan to pay the bill.
- **A shipping address that differs from the billing address could indicate a gift or a theft.**
- **An e-mail address at a site that provides free e-mail service can be temporary.** A free e-mail address can be easily obtained and discarded.
- **The signature on the receipt doesn't match the signature on the card.** The user is probably not the cardholder.
- **The card looks like it was altered.** The name, number, or signature may have been changed.
- **A single shipping address is used for several credit cards.**
- **Several orders are placed within a short period of time.**

Precautions Protect your business by looking for the warning signs and following some simple precautions. Some of these precautions would not be acceptable to customers of a large business. For example, Amazon.com can't reject every order placed by a customer who specifies a different shipping address. However, they operate on a much larger scale. If they process a few fraudulent transactions in a week, they can absorb the loss. If you process four transactions in a week and one of them is fraudulent, you just lost 25 percent of your income from that revenue center for the week. The following precautions can reduce your financial losses caused by fraud and help your business survive to become large enough to follow only the precautions used by other large businesses.

♦   **Ship merchandise only to the billing address for the credit card.**
♦   **Don't accept orders from customers who give you an e-mail address from a site that provides free e-mail addresses.**
♦   **Call the customer to verify the order.** A quick phone call can protect your business from fraud and alert the cardholder to a potential problem.
♦   **Return all receipts to the customer.** Don't throw receipts away where thieves can retrieve them.
♦   **Don't accept cards if they are unsigned or the signature on the card doesn't match the signature on the receipt.**
♦   **Don't accept cards that appear to be altered.**

Chargebacks

A common result of a fraudulent transaction is a **chargeback,** which occurs when a cardholder claims that a purchase was unauthorized or the product was unsatisfactory. The issuing bank removes the charge from the customer's card and does not deposit anything in your merchant account. For cardholders, the most liability they face is $50.

A business that follows established procedures and performs swiped transactions may not be held responsible for unauthorized charges. Unfortunately, businesses that perform nonswipe transactions, such as Internet and catalog businesses, are usually left holding the bag after losing the merchandise and any chance of receiving payment for the merchandise. This difference in treatment leaves Internet and catalog businesses dangerously vulnerable to fraud.

Businesses face penalties for chargebacks. Most businesses are charged a fee for each chargeback. Businesses that have frequent chargebacks are penalized further. They could lose their merchant account. Their discount rate, the fees businesses pay to process credit card transactions, could be increased. The best protection you have against chargebacks is correct procedures, a generous return policy, and documentation.

Procedures Follow all of the required steps for every sales transaction. In swiped transactions, be sure to compare the signature on the receipt to the signature on the card. For nonswiped transactions, collect all the needed information. Conduct verification procedures, such as calling the cardholder to validate the order.

Return Policy A customer can start the chargeback process if the merchandise is damaged or unsatisfactory. A generous return policy encourages the dissatisfied customer to deal directly with you rather than involve the credit card's issuing bank.

Documentation Keep detailed records of your sales. If you ship products, use shipping methods that enable you to verify that the products were delivered. This prevents customer complaints that the merchandise wasn't delivered, another valid reason for a chargeback.

![icon] **Hypothetical Scenario**

After several months, Al evaluated the results of his decision to accept credit cards at Little Bitty Books. Initial expenses were high. He hired a business to set up procedures and equipment necessary to protect the customer credit information collected with each credit transaction. Although the initial cost was high, the results were better than he had hoped for. In the past three months, the store's profit increased 35 percent.

Follow Credit Regulations

Many consumer activities are protected by federal and state regulations. It shouldn't be a surprise that consumers' credit usage is also covered by regulations. The laws governing the use of credit cards are designed to protect the consumer. Consumers who feel safe using credit cards make more purchases than consumers who are afraid to pull the plastic cards out of their wallets. Making consumers feel safe supports the American economy.

Federal and state regulations protect consumers by limiting their responsibility when a credit card is stolen or lost, guaranteeing full disclosure of credit terms, and dictating procedures to follow when a dispute arises. These regulations are important to you because they provide guidelines for your actions and help you predict the consumers' and issuing banks' actions and the potential results of those actions.

Federal Regulations

Laws enacted at the federal level affect consumer issues in every state. Federal regulations regarding credit cards are enforced the same way in every city and state in America. Federal statutes include the Consumer Credit Protection Act, the Truth in Lending Act, the Fair Credit Reporting Act, the Fair Credit Billing Act, the Equal Credit Opportunity Act, and the Fair Debt Collection Act.

Consumer Credit Protection Act Passed in 1968, the Consumer Credit Protection Act was one of the first laws passed to regulate credit and give some protection to the individual consumer. It required lenders to explain the cost of a loan in standard terms that are defined and used consistently, enabling consumers to compare credit offers.

Truth in Lending Act Enacted in 1969 and amended repeatedly, the Truth in Lending Act, known as Regulation Z, requires lenders to disclose information about credit transactions, regulates credit advertisements, and limits a cardholder's liability to $50 for unauthorized credit usage. The primary purpose is consumer education.

Fair Credit Reporting Act Credit reports contain a history of each consumer's credit activities, including any loan, loan payment history, credit card balance, and personal information, such as the consumer's address and employment history. Enacted in 1971 and amended several times, the Fair Credit Reporting Act gives consumers the right to view their credit reports and make corrections if the reports contain errors. If the credit bureau that created the report is unable or unwilling to make a requested change, the consumer has the right to add a statement that is attached to future copies of the report. Lenders use the credit report to assess an applicant as a credit risk.

Fair Credit Billing Act Enacted in 1975, the Fair Credit Billing Act applies to **open-ended credit** transactions, credit that can be used repeatedly until the consumer reaches a credit limit. Bank credit cards and store credit cards are examples of open-ended credit. The law is designed to protect consumers, but it also protects businesses by documenting the procedure a business and its customers must follow to resolve billing disputes.

Passed to protect consumers from unfair billing practices, the Fair Credit Billing Act guarantees consumers the right to correct billing errors, withhold payment for defective products, prompt credit for payments, and protection of their credit rating while disputes are settled. If consumers find billing errors, they must notify the creditor in writing within 60 days. Billing errors covered by the Fair Credit Billing Act include a variety of situations:

- The consumer did not authorize the charges.
- The consumer was charged for the wrong merchandise.
- The price of the merchandise was incorrect.
- The charges were billed for the wrong date.
- The consumer didn't accept the product.
- The merchandise wasn't delivered.
- The bill was incorrect because of accounting errors.
- Credit was not given for returned items.
- Disputed charges are included on the bill.
- The bill was mailed to an incorrect address.
- Products purchased with a credit card were poor quality or damaged and the consumer tried to resolve the issue with the business where the product was purchased.

Equal Credit Opportunity Act Passed in 1974, the Equal Credit Opportunity Act was designed to ensure that all people are given an equal right to borrow money. Credit can't be denied because of race, color, religion, national origin, gender, marital status, age, and receipt of public assistance income. Applicants can only be rejected on the basis of criteria related to credit risk. In other words, a minority single female applicant can't be rejected for being a minority, female, or unmarried. She can be rejected if her income is too low to repay the loan or she already owes a large amount of money, increasing the lender's risk of not receiving full repayment of the loan.

If a loan application is denied, the consumer has the right to know why the application was rejected. If the consumer isn't satisfied with the explanation, he or she can file a complaint with the regulating agency for the financial institution.

Fair Debt Collection Act Enacted in 1978 and amended in 1986, the Fair Debt Collection Act limits the actions a third-party collection agency can take to collect funds for outstanding debt. For example, contact can only be made from

8:00 A.M. to 9:00 P.M. and contact can't include threats or obscene language. Although this law doesn't apply to a small business collecting its own debts, it is a good idea to follow the same guidelines.

State Regulations

Individual states often have additional laws regarding credit reporting, disclosure, and transactions. If federal and state regulations can be applied to a specific situation, the laws that are the most beneficial to consumers are used. Investigate and follow the credit regulations in your state.

Hypothetical Scenario

Al wasn't happy. Even though profits increased by 35 percent, he faced problems he never had when the business accepted only cash. Little Bitty Books had two chargebacks in the last three months. That wasn't a high percentage, but it was irritating. After some thought, he decided to change his delivery methods and alter the store's return policy. Al hoped these changes would allow him to experience fewer chargebacks in the future.

Technology Insights

Firewall

The term *firewall* is based on the concept of a "fire wall," a term coined in the 1700s. A fire wall was originally intended to identify a physical wall built to contain a fire, preventing it from spreading. Today, a firewall is used to describe the hardware and software used to prevent unauthorized access from an outside user to the computer's data or other computers on a network. Businesses and individuals that access the Internet should protect their computers with a firewall. Generally, a business places security software—a firewall—on a separate computer that is connected to the Internet. Other computers connect to the selected computer to access the Internet, preventing any direct access to the computers used by its employees. A firewall examines packets of information coming in from outside users and going out from internal users. Unauthorized data packets are blocked, prevented from entering or leaving the firewall. Although a firewall protects your data from some threats, it doesn't protect your network or your data from viruses, employees who give your data away, or employees who place sensitive data on a laptop and then connect directly to the Internet after they leave the office.

Think Critically How does a firewall work?

CHAPTER REVIEW

Consumers use credit frequently and heavily. They use credit for expensive items, for purchases from businesses that aren't local, and for convenience. In fact, some consumers use their credit cards a little too much. Many consumers have at least one credit card and carry a balance of over $8,000. To select a credit card, examine the disclosure statement and evaluate the card's characteristics, such as its credit limit, interest rate, grace period, fees, the method used to calculate the card's balance, and its guidelines for a balance transfer.

Most businesses that sell to consumers accept credit cards. Businesses prefer to offer a variety of payment methods, increasing the opportunity to make a sale. To accept credit card payments, a business needs a merchant account at a financial institution, point-of-sale equipment, a transaction clearinghouse, and a gateway to the clearinghouse. Businesses may be able to fill all of the requirements through their usual financial institution. Businesses can carry out a sales transaction by swiping the card, making an imprint of the card, or hand-keying the card's data. The information is passed to the issuing bank for the credit card and payment is deposited in the merchant account for the business. The value of the discount rate for each transaction is deducted before the payment is deposited.

Credit card companies haven't released statistics for credit card fraud but it is quite common. Protecting information about your customers can help limit fraud by reducing the theft of credit card data. Chargebacks can be the result of fraud. You can prevent some chargebacks by following correct procedures, establishing a generous return policy, and documenting any special customer interactions and shipping data. The paper copies of your sales transactions and the electronic data should be protected. Securing the documentation can easily be done without requiring any special skill. Establishing electronic data security requires technical skills possessed by an individual or business with the necessary expertise to encrypt the data and create a firewall.

Several federal and state regulations protect consumers who are using credit cards. Businesses don't receive the same type of governmental protection as consumers. However, following the credit guidelines that are intended to assist consumers also benefits the businesses involved. The regulations define the responsibilities of the business by detailing the actions businesses perform when customer credit activities occur.

USE BUSINESS TERMS

Fill in the blanks with the appropriate term.

APR	discount rate
authorization code	firewall
B2B	fraud
bankruptcy	gateway
charge card	grace period
chargeback	issuing bank
credit	open-ended credit
credit card	penalty APR
credit limit	settle accounts
credit report	swipe
disclosure statement	transaction clearinghouse

1. Examine the ___?___ carefully before you select a credit card for your personal use.
2. You should ___?___ at the end of every business day so you receive payment as quickly as possible.
3. Most businesses are charged a fee for each ___?___ and could face further penalties if it happens often.
4. Businesses have no limit for the loss they assume when they are the victims of credit card ___?___ .
5. If the card has a balance carried over from the previous month, a(n) ___?___ usually isn't granted for any new transactions.
6. A business should establish a(n) ___?___ to protect its electronic data from outside users.
7. Many credit cards offer a special introductory rate that is usually much lower than the regular ___?___ .

TEST YOUR READING

8. What is the difference between a credit card and a charge card?
9. How does a consumer increase the credit limit for a credit card?
10. List the characteristics you would use to evaluate a credit card offer.
11. Describe the balance calculation methods used to determine the interest the cardholder is charged each month.
12. How does accepting credit cards affect a business's image?
13. What is the role of a merchant account in accepting credit cards?
14. Give an example of a business that uses each type of credit card transaction.
15. How long does it take to process a credit card transaction?
16. How do you protect your customers' credit card information?
17. How much liability do Internet businesses bear when credit card fraud occurs?
18. How can a business protect itself from chargebacks?
19. How does the Fair Credit Billing Act protect consumers?

THINK CRITICALLY ABOUT BUSINESS

20. Find a credit card calculator on the Internet. Calculate the length of time and total interest paid if you use a credit card that charges 15 percent interest to purchase a product for $1,200 and make only the minimum payment each month.
21. If a credit card has a variable rate, the rate is tied to an economic indicator such as the prime rate. Define the prime rate and explain why it is used to determine a credit card's rate.
22. Laws may be passed that regulate how credit cards solicit students. Describe the guidelines you feel are necessary.
23. Select a credit card. Describe the information in the card's disclosure statement. Explain why you would or would not recommend this card to a friend.

REAL-LIFE BUSINESS

Ocean Spray Cranberries, Inc.

Farmers, dependent on the weather and the demand for their products, often face financial difficulties. In the 1800s, a business concept known as the cooperative movement started in Denmark. The purpose of the cooperative movement was purely financial. Farmers wanted to increase their profits by working together to provide urban communities with produce and other products. By working together, farmers found new markets for their products and increased their profits.

The actions of a cooperative are decided democratically. Each member votes on business activities that affect the group. The movement is successful in Denmark and has become a stable part of its economy. Currently, more than 90 percent of milk and pork production in Denmark is carried out by cooperatives.

In 1930, three American cranberry farmers formed an agricultural cooperative to increase the size of the cranberry market. Marcus L. Urann developed a cranberry sauce that could be canned and sold, the same type of cranberry sauce that was probably served at the most recent Thanksgiving or Christmas dinner you attended. Ocean Spray also developed an innovative product that greatly expanded the demand for cranberry products—cranberry juice drinks. Innovations continued over time as Ocean Spray sought to increase their product offerings and market size. In 1963, Ocean Spray introduced the first cranberry juice blend, a mix of cranberry and apple juice. Several new mixes consisting of cranberries and other fruit juices were introduced to an eager reception. In 1976, grapefruit growers joined the Ocean Spray cooperative. The product list expanded to include dried fruit. The success of the agricultural cooperative is undeniable, currently consisting of more than 900 cranberry and grapefruit growers who sell their products in 50 countries.

Think Critically

1. Why is it difficult for many farmers to earn a profit?
2. What is an agricultural cooperative?
3. What was Ocean Spray's strategy?
4. Why has Ocean Spray been successful?

CHAPTER 15

Insurance and Taxes

GOALS

- ◆ Describe your product responsibilities
- ◆ Identify the necessary bonds
- ◆ Purchase insurance
- ◆ Pay taxes

Emi Waters attended college, pursuing a Bachelor of Fine Arts. During the summer, she worked for a building contractor painting houses. The work was low stress and Emi found the painting process to be soothing. As she gained experience, the building contractor began placing her in charge of the painting crew.

Product Responsibilities

A small appliance starts a house fire. A herbicide intended to kill weeds destroys an entire garden. A diner patron gets food poisoning. A safety seat fails and a child is killed. If your business makes or sells a product that causes damage or injury, you may be liable for damages.

Product Liability

Damage and injury caused by product defects are common enough that a specialized area of law, known as **product liability,** has developed. Legally, **liability** assigns responsibility for the damage or injury. If the business is responsible, it is held accountable and is usually required to compensate the product's buyers and users.

Liability To assign liability for damage or injuries, you usually have to prove that the individual was **negligent**—did not take proper care or exhibited careless behavior. This isn't difficult to prove in individual situations. For example, if a driver runs a red light and causes an accident, negligence is obvious. The driver's careless behavior caused the accident.

Strict Liability It is much more difficult to prove that a business is negligent. Often, there isn't a single event such as a car running a red light and causing an accident that demonstrates negligence. Therefore, the evidence required to prove liability is different. To be compensated by the manufacturer or seller, a consumer needs to prove **strict liability,** which assigns liability without requiring any evidence of negligence. Strict liability must meet several requirements.

- **The product has a defect that causes unreasonable danger to the user.** Even if the manufacturer is not careless, a defect can be built into the product when it is made, packaged, or handled for shipping.
- **The seller frequently sells the same product.** The seller is familiar with the product. This protects sellers who sell the product in temporary situations, such as a garage sale or flea market.
- **The user has not substantially changed the product.** The user hasn't introduced the defect into the product by making changes that affect the product's performance.
- **The user is not aware of the defect.** If the user knows about the defect but continues to use the product, the manufacturer has a valid defense against strict liability.
- **The length of time after the consumer's purchase that strict liability can be used to prove liability is limited.** The time period varies among states, but it is usually six to 12 years.

Manufacturer When you hear about a product liability case, the manufacturer is usually cited. Product defects that cause injury can be categorized as design defects, manufacturing defects, and warning defects.

- **Design defect**—The product operates as it was designed to operate, but the design creates dangers for the user. The injury occurred because the product was poorly designed.
- **Manufacturing defect**—The product is made from parts that are defective or the product isn't assembled correctly.
- **Warning defect**—The user isn't informed that the product is dangerous or the documentation doesn't provide warnings.

A manufacturer can be found responsible for a variety of defects. Examples include an automobile with seatbelts installed incorrectly, foreign objects in canned or bottled food products, and incorrect or missing usage instructions. A candle containing flowers that could flare and start an uncontrolled fire is the manufacturer's responsibility.

When a product is defective, the manufacturer can issue a **recall,** a public call for the return of a defective or contaminated product. Recalls are frequently announced on newscasts. Magazines such as *Consumer Reports* evaluate products and announce recalls. Specialized web sites also publicize recalled products.

Seller Sellers who are familiar with the product type share responsibility. However, the product type doesn't have to be the seller's main product. For example, fast-food restaurants may be held responsible if a toy packaged in a child's meal proves to be a choking hazard for toddlers.

The Consumer Product Safety Act of 1972 requires sellers to monitor the safety of merchandise. If a product is unsafe for consumer usage, a seller may participate in a manufacturer's recall. This enables consumers to return the defective product at the same location where it was purchased rather than ship it to the manufacturer.

Service Provider Businesses that provide a service also face product liability issues. Businesses that enable consumers to participate in high-risk or physical activities, such as skydiving, sports facilities, and flight instruction facilities, are more at risk for liability claims than other businesses. Other business examples include providers of software, temporary office assistants, and equipment rental.

Frequency If your product causes damage or injury, you have lost a customer. A single dissatisfied customer is the least of the potential consequences for your business. Many product liability cases end in a lawsuit when the damaged party seeks compensation. However, most product liability cases never make it to trial. Three-fourths of product liability lawsuits are settled out of court, which means that the injured party and the business reach an agreement without judgment by a judge or jury. The agreement could include financial compensation, a nondisclosure agreement, and actions by the company to change the product and repair the damage if possible.

When small financial amounts are involved, a dispute can be resolved in **small claims court.** Depending on the state in which your business operates, the maximum amount that can be awarded in small claims court is between $3,000 and $7,500. The high cost of legal representation and the limited financial risk means that most lawsuits in small claims court are handled without lawyers. To prevail in court, assemble your supporting evidence and be prepared with as much detail as possible.

If a product is defective, every customer who bought the product can sue the business. The customers can become members of a **class action** lawsuit, a case in which a large number of people were injured by the same product. A small business is much more likely to be involved in a dispute resolved in small claims court than in a class action lawsuit.

Results The concept of product liability is beneficial to businesses and consumers alike. It requires that businesses communicate with their customers regarding safety and liability issues related to their products. The potential results of product defects and product liability include damages, legal action, and product improvements.

Potential Damages Defective products can cause minor or major damages. Injuries and death are unacceptable consequences of some defects. Other defects cause environmental damage and property damage.

- **Injury**—Severe physical injuries can be caused by defective products, even if the products are operated correctly. A car with a defective gas tank can explode when struck by another vehicle. Children's pajamas that are incorrectly labeled as "flame-retardant" do not slow flames. Injuries can also be more subtle but just as damaging. For example, side effects from medications can cause physical and mental injuries or disabilities.

- **Death**—**Wrongful death,** which is caused by the fault of another, can also be caused by defective products. Injuries from which an individual doesn't recover result in long-term disability or death.

- **Environmental damage**—Damage to the environment doesn't have to be as obvious as a large oil spill near a nature preserve. Engine exhaust, aerosol products, and leakage from dead batteries have contributed to environmental damage. Many products and their manufacturers must meet strict standards regarding by-products of the item or its manufacturing process.

- **Property damage**—A defective product can easily damage physical property. Defective software can damage valuable electronic data and physical property, such as a computer or other equipment.

Legal Action A lawsuit produces economic results. If a lawsuit goes to trial and compensation is awarded to the consumer, the financial toll on a business can be extreme. Your business can be required to pay economic damages, noneconomic damages, and punitive damages.

Economic damages include any losses that can be measured by a dollar amount. They can include replacement or repair of damaged property, medical care, lost income, and the cost of hiring others to complete tasks the injured individual can no longer perform.

Noneconomic damages include any loss that can't be measured by a dollar amount. Nevertheless, an economic value is assigned because it is the only compensation that can be offered. Noneconomic damages include the claims commonly seen on television legal dramas—pain, suffering, and mental anguish. The true effect of a physical disability, mental disability, or disfigurement resulting from an injury is difficult to quantify.

Punitive damages are not common. In 1990, after conducting a four-year study, the American Bar Foundation announced that punitive damages are awarded in less than 5 percent of civil jury verdicts. Punitive damages are awarded to punish the business and encourage other businesses to use more caution. To award punitive damages, the business must be proven to manufacture and distribute the product even though it *knows* that the product is dangerous.

Product Improvements The most important and enduring result of product liability is product improvement. Holding manufacturers, sellers, and service providers accountable to consumers guarantees that products will improve, defects will be removed, safety will be increased, and product labeling will become more accurate and useful.

Precautions A manufacturer often provides a warranty with its products, ensuring that the product or parts will be repaired or replaced if they are defective. A retailer can also provide a warranty. The retailer's warranty can extend the length of the manufacturer's warranty or cover specific parts of the product. Parts that may wear out faster than the rest of the product may not be covered by the warranty. For example, an automobile is expected to last much longer than its tires. When the tires wear out, they are simply replaced.

A recall is also a precaution. A manufacturer issues a recall, hoping to protect consumers by preventing them from using the defective product and protect itself from liability claims.

The Consumer Product Safety Act requires manufacturers, importers, distributors, and retailers to report products that present a risk to consumers. The reported product may fail to comply with consumer safety guidelines, have a defect that creates a substantial hazard, or create an unreasonable risk of serious injury or death. If a product can cause injury or death, it should be reported to the Consumer Product Safety Commission within 24 hours. A product must be reported within 10 days if it meets one of the following requirements:

- The product is involved in three or more settlements or judgments within two years.
- The settlements or judgments involve serious injury or death.
- A specific model of the product causes the injury or death.

Consumers and the media must use caution when reporting potential product defects. A false spoken statement that injures the reputation of a business, known as **slander,** or a false written statement that injures the reputation of a business, known as **libel,** can enable the business to file a lawsuit against the source of the statement.

Hypothetical Scenario

Generally, builders were happy with the work performed by the contractor and Emi Waters's work crew. Their work was high in quality and completed on schedule every time. The contractor began expanding into commercial work, painting business locations. When a restaurant owner asked Emi if she knew of someone who could paint murals on the restaurant walls, Emi referred the restaurant owner to her supervisor.

Purchase Bonds

Many businesses provide services that require entry into customers' homes, offices, or locations guarded by security measures such as banks and museums. Others require the operation of equipment owned by the customer or access to confidential information. A bond creates security for your customer.

A **bond** is a written agreement purchased from a surety company that guarantees an individual will complete a specific task. If the task isn't completed, the surety company pays the customer the amount specified by the bond. When you bond your employees, you are assuring the customer that the work will be done. The following steps enable you to purchase a bond. Figure 15.1 demonstrates how the bonding process works. If you don't have a specific customer or job opportunity, you can establish a **bond line.** The bond line enables you to purchase a number of individual bonds up to the limit of your bond line.

- Identify a **surety company** that provides the type of bond you want.
- Identify yourself as the principal, the individual purchasing the bond.
- Identify the **obligee,** the customer who the surety company will pay if the service isn't completed.
- Identify the amount to be paid.
- Purchase the bond.
- If you don't perform the service, the obligee files a claim with the surety company.
- The surety company pays the obligee.
- You must reimburse the surety company for its loss and associated expenses.

FIGURE 15.1 Bonding Process

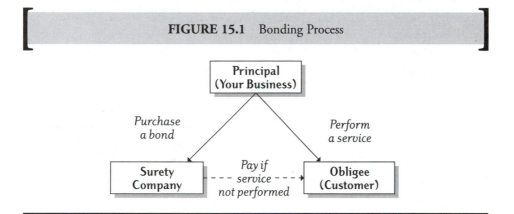

Types of Bonds

A bond basically provides a guarantee that a specific action or event will occur. This type of guarantee is useful in many situations. In fact, many different types of bonds are available to fit a variety of situations, from a court appearance to a contractor's bid for a new project. Several types of bonds are commonly used, but only three are frequently used by small businesses.

- **License bond**—A business buys a **license bond** to guarantee that it will comply with state and local codes. In many cases, the federal, state, or local government requires a business to purchase a license bond.
- **Permit bond**—A licensed business buys a **permit bond** to guarantee that it will comply with local codes that apply to a specific situation. The local government may require its purchase.
- **Contract bond**—A contracting business buys a **contract bond** to guarantee that it will fill the terms of the contract, usually a construction project. The terms include the construction plans and building specifications.

Businesses That Use Bonds You can gain an advantage over other businesses in your industry by bonding your business activities and employees. Consumers searching for a particular type of service prefer to hire companies such as yours that provide a guarantee that the service will be performed. Whether a bond is purchased to fill government requirements or meet customer preferences, bonds are important for a variety of businesses. Several business types are identified in Table 15.1.

TABLE 15.1	Businesses That Use or Require Bonds	
Auctioneer	Financial lender	Process server
Check casher	Fuel tax	Produce dealer
Collection agency	Health club	Registration service
Commercial photocopier	Insurance adjuster	Security service
Contractor	Insurance broker	Talent agency
Convalescent facility	Janitorial service	Tax preparation
Cosmetology school	Livestock dealer	Telemarketing
Dance studio	Notary public	Traffic violation school
Detective agency	Nursing home	Vehicle dealer
Driving instruction	Parking	Waste transport
Dry cleaners	Pawnbroker	Wildlife guide
Employment agency	Pest control	
Farm laborer	Postal contract station	

Specific Bonds Your requirements or need for a specific bond varies by the type of business you operate and its location. Your state and local government dictate some requirements. A business in San Diego may face different bond requirements if it operated in Atlanta or Los Angeles. However, some bonds are more common than others.

Contractor's Bonds A contractor follows a procedure when bidding for a project. First, the contractor submits a bid for the project. If the bid is accepted, the contractor purchases a performance bond and a payment bond. Depending on the type of building, the contractor may purchase a bond to build a specific item, such as a subdivision, roof, or swimming pool.

- **Bid bond**—When a contractor submits a bid for a project, the project manager usually requires a bid bond. The bid bond ensures that the contractor has submitted a bid in good faith and the numbers are accurate to the best of the contractor's ability.
- **Performance bond**—The performance bond protects the obligee from losing money if the contractor can't fulfill the terms of the contract. Most public sector projects require a performance bond.
- **Payment bond**—The payment bond guarantees that the contractor will pay the subcontractors necessary to complete the work and purchase the needed materials.
- **Subdivision bond**—If the project involves a housing development, a subdivision bond guarantees that the contractor will comply with the local building codes and regulations.

License and Permit Bonds Required by federal, state, or local government, a specific bond may be necessary before the license or permit is granted. Examples include a notary public, tax preparation business, and an insurance broker.

Fidelity Bond If your business has employees that have access to your clients' property, a fidelity bond, also known as an employee dishonesty bond, protects you and your customers. Janitorial services, security services, and health clubs may purchase a fidelity bond.

Applying for a Bond

The purpose of a bond is to ensure the obligee that your business has the resources to perform the desired service. Therefore, the surety company must evaluate your resources and business activities. The process of applying for a bond is similar to applying for a loan. The surety company needs to be confident that your business can repay them if they are required to pay an obligee. This makes the application process similar to applying for a loan. Most surety companies require the following information:

- **Financial statements**—Surety companies prefer to see three years of financial statements for your business that have been prepared or reviewed by a certified public accountant.
- **Current schedule**—Comparing your resources to your current commitments helps the surety company evaluate your ability to complete the project.
- **Company history**—Comparing the size of the projects your business has completed to the current project helps the surety company evaluate your ability to complete the project. For example, if this project is much larger than any previous projects, the surety company may ask for additional information to ensure that your business can perform the task.
- **Personal history**—Your professional experience supports the evaluation that you are capable of managing the tasks required to fill the contract.
- **Financial references**—The surety company is seeking confirmation that your business has previously borrowed and repaid amounts similar to the value of the current bond.
- **Application**—The surety company may ask for additional information on the bond application.

Hypothetical Scenario

The conversation between Emi and her supervisor took a turn that surprised Emi. The supervisor recalled several of Emi's paintings he viewed in a student art show. Painting a mural, he reasoned, was simply using a larger canvas. Although Emi knew there was more of a difference than the size of the canvas, she was intrigued by the idea. After some negotiation with the customer and obtaining a bond, the supervisor committed Emi to her first mural project.

Purchase Insurance

Everyone wants to feel safe. They protect themselves, their loved ones, and their property. As a business owner, you also want to protect your business, your business property, and your employees. One way to provide this protection is **insurance,** a contract that protects the policyholder from financial loss caused by a specific danger. Insurance can't prevent a fire or an injury, but it can protect you from the financial consequences of the loss.

Insurance Principles

There are circumstances in which your business might need several types of insurance. For example, a customer might slip on a wet spot on the floor, upsetting the large saltwater aquarium in your office, which causes a short in the wiring and sets the office on fire. You are left with damage to your property, an angry customer, and several dead fish. Insurance can help you replace the aquarium, repair the damage to the office, and provide assistance when the customer files a lawsuit.

Basic Insurance Concepts Many insurance companies sell insurance for businesses. A quick look at the business pages in your telephone book illustrates the point. Your task is selecting the insurance coverage you need, consulting with one or more insurance agents, and purchasing the insurance appropriate for your business.

Insurance companies are not all the same. Similar insurance coverage is often packaged differently. One company may sell a type of insurance separately while another company includes it as a component of a policy and won't sell it separately. Before you purchase, examine the policy or policies carefully. **Avoid paying for the same coverage twice.**

Some insurance companies provide packages for small businesses. Just because the package is designed for a small business doesn't mean it's a good fit for *your* small business. Assembling the perfect package for your business is like assembling a jigsaw puzzle. When all the pieces are in place, the picture is complete, without any missing pieces. When your insurance coverage is right, your business is adequately protected without leaving vulnerable areas that could jeopardize it. When you examine a policy, take note of the following information.

- **Deductible**—You can agree to pay a **deductible,** a specific amount per claim or accident that is applied toward the insured loss. For example, if your deductible is $1,000, you pay $1,000 before the insurance company pays anything. A higher deductible reduces the cost of the policy because it reduces the insurance company's risk.

- **Endorsement**—Also known as a rider, an **endorsement** is an attachment to a policy that adds a benefit or feature to the policy. Check the endorsements on a policy against any separate policies you purchase. If it is an endorsement on one policy, the additional policy might not be needed.

- **Exclusion**—A policy may contain an **exclusion,** a provision that identifies dangers, property, or locations that aren't covered by the policy. For example, property damage caused by earthquakes may be excluded in some parts of the country.

- **Replacement cost**—Insist that the policy cover the replacement cost for damaged property. If replacement cost is not specified, the insurance company only pays for the damaged property, not the **replacement cost,** the price you have to pay to replace it. For example, a top-of-the-line computer you bought two years ago may be worth less than $2,000. A new computer that is currently the top-of-the-line may cost $4,000.

Types of Insurance Available Selecting the right insurance coverage for your business can be complicated. Many different types of coverage are available. Some insurance contracts should be purchased by most businesses. Other insurance contracts are appropriate only for specific types of businesses. The most basic coverage usually includes property insurance, general liability insurance, and commercial automobile insurance. To ensure that your business is fully insured, consult a qualified insurance broker.

Note: Your business has some additional insurance requirements if you employ workers. Most states require workers' compensation insurance, unemployment insurance, and state disability insurance. Consult with a qualified insurance broker who is familiar with your state requirements and has experience in employee insurance.

Property Insurance Three broad categories of business property can be protected by property insurance. It protects the building in which your business operates, your business personal property, and personal property owned by another individual or business. Insurance that covers your building protects the structure and the permanent fixtures in the building, such as installed machinery, flooring, and heating equipment. Business personal property includes items used for the business that are in the building or within a specified distance, but aren't considered to be part of the building. Business personal property can include furniture, computers, and fixtures. Personal property owned by others is property that your business doesn't own but it is in your control or custody. It can include furniture, equipment, or other items in or near the building. Endorsements that can be added to the property insurance policy include:

- **Cargo coverage**—This component protects your business property, such as inventory, while it is in transit or storage.
- **Tool and equipment coverage**—This component protects your business tools while they are in your business vehicle or at an off-site work location. Any business that transports its tools to a work site should consider this coverage.
- **Umbrella excess liability coverage**—This component provides protection for the value of property that exceeds the limit of the basic coverage.

General Liability Insurance Unexpected events can have good or bad results and consequences. Insurance provides protection from some of the financial losses caused by accidents. General liability insurance protects your business from claims for bodily injury or property damage.

- **Advertising liability coverage**—This component protects your business from claims filed as a result of the advertising activities your business has performed.

- **Bodily injury liability coverage**—This component protects your business from claims that your business caused a physical injury to another individual while performing business operations.
- **Personal injury liability coverage**—This component protects your business from claims that your business caused a nonphysical injury to another individual while performing business operations. This includes claims of slander, libel, false arrest, eviction, and invasion of privacy.
- **Property damage liability coverage**—This component protects your business from claims that your business caused physical injury to someone else's property while performing business operations.

Commercial Automobile Insurance If your business uses or relies on vehicles, insuring the vehicles can prevent an expensive loss. Commercial automobile insurance protects your business from financial loss when its vehicles are damaged or destroyed. It also limits your exposure when your business vehicle is involved in an accident. Commercial automobile insurance should cover several situations:

- **Collision coverage**—This component helps you pay for repairs to correct damage to your business vehicle caused by a collision.
- **Comprehensive coverage**—This component helps you pay for repairs to correct damage to your business vehicle caused by fire, theft, and glass breakage.
- **Liability coverage**—This component provides some financial protection if an accident involving your business vehicle results in a lawsuit.
- **Rental reimbursement coverage**—This component provides financial assistance to temporarily replace your business vehicle if it has been damaged in an incident covered by your commercial automobile insurance. The time period is limited by the length of time the vehicle is unavailable because it is receiving repairs.

Product Liability Insurance If your business manufactures or sells products that could cause injury to others, product liability insurance provides some protection. The insurance provides assistance when a consumer makes a claim against your company.

Business Interruption Insurance If your business is unable to operate for any reason identified by your insurance coverage, such as fire or storm damage, your business is protected from financial loss. The length of time for the coverage may vary among insurance companies. The coverage may not begin to pay benefits until 48 hours after the incident.

Crime Coverage Insurance Theft is frequently a problem for small businesses. Crime coverage insurance protects your business from financial loss caused by theft or vandalism by employees and others.

Key Person Insurance A **key person** is one who is critical to the operation of the business. You are a key person in a business you operate. If you have partners, they are also key people. Key person insurance provides financial assistance to your business when it experiences loss caused by the death or long-term disability of the specified key person. The financial assistance continues until the key person is replaced or returns.

Buy-Sell Insurance Partnerships usually rely on all of the partners to succeed. If a partner dies or faces long-term disability, the remaining partners may wish to purchase the shares in question. This insurance provides the remaining partners with the funds necessary to buy the shares. Review the value of your business regularly. If the value increases significantly, the original value of the buy-sell insurance may not be adequate.

Errors and Omissions Insurance Service businesses should consider errors and omissions insurance. It provides protection when a customer is injured because you made a mistake or didn't complete all or part of a task. For example, a house sitter who forgets to feed the fish could face a claim from the angry homeowners when the expensive saltwater fish are found floating rather than swimming. Medical malpractice insurance also falls into this category.

Home-Based Business When you operate a business in your home, you perform business activities that aren't normal for most homeowners. You store inventory, manufacture products, operate equipment, and accept a large quantity of packages. Your business equipment and activities aren't covered by the standard homeowner's policy. In fact, operating a business in your home could make your homeowner's policy void.

Examine your homeowner's policy carefully. You may be able to upgrade your policy to include some business activities and equipment. If you have frequent deliveries or your customers visit your site, be sure to carry liability insurance that protects your business if a visitor is injured at your site.

If you operate from your home, you lose your place of business as well as your home if the site is temporarily or permanently damaged. The insurance you purchase should provide a method that enables you to continue to work.

Purchase Insurance Policies

Insurance is a critical part of keeping your business in operation during difficult times. The decisions you make now, while the situation is calm and you have the time to investigate your options, drastically affect the outcome if a catastrophe occurs in the future. The following steps help you make decisions about the insurance coverage you need.

Step 1—Identify the Items and Individuals to Protect

Make a checklist of the property and individuals you want to protect with insurance. The items that have a high financial value, that would take time and money to replace, should be listed. If you insure a building, be sure to list the equipment and items that are part of the building, such as installed machinery.

Know the value of your business property. Identify the value of each item to be insured as shown in Figure 15.2. If part of the building is new, such as the roof, note the date the item was purchased or replaced. If you have trouble determining the value of the building, consult one or more insurance brokers. Consultations are free. Ask several insurance brokers to evaluate the property's worth.

FIGURE 15.2 Items to be Insured

Building Feature/ Equipment/Key Personnel	Date Purchased or Replaced	Value Replacement Cost	Coverage	Insurance Cost

Step 2—Select Insurance Companies to Provide Quotes

Even without selecting a specific coverage, you can choose the insurance companies you want to investigate. Your insurance broker and insurance company provide security for your business. You must be able to trust them.

The A.M. Best company rates the ability of insurance companies to meet their obligations to their customers. The rating is based on each company's financial strength. For large insurance companies, Best's Ratings range from A++ to F, shown in Table 15.2. For small insurance companies, the ratings range from 9 to 1.

TABLE 15.2 A.M. Best Ratings

	Rating	Interpretation	Description
Secure	A++ and A+	Superior	Strong ability to meet obligations to policyholders
	A and A–	Excellent	Strong ability to meet obligations to policyholders
	B++ and B+	Good	Good ability to meet obligations to policyholders
Vulnerable	B and B–	Fair	Able to meet obligations to policyholders, but vulnerable to underwriting and economic changes
	C++ and C+	Marginal	Able to meet obligations to policyholders, but vulnerable to underwriting and economic changes
	C and C–	Weak	Able to meet obligations to policyholders, but very vulnerable to underwriting and economic changes
	D	Poor	May not be able to meet obligations to policyholders and extremely vulnerable to underwriting and economic changes
	E	Under regulatory supervision	Significant supervision by regulatory supervision prevents the company from conducting normal business
	F	In liquidation	Company is being liquidated so it can't conduct normal business
	S	Rating suspended	Sudden events prevent Best's evaluation

A.M. Best ratings can be found in the reference section of your local library or ordered from the company. When you select an insurance company, verify its rating. Select a company with a secure rating.

Step 3—Identify the Coverage
The insurance broker reviews your property and your list. The broker may suggest additions or subtractions to your list. When the list is satisfactory, the broker identifies the type of insurance coverage and the cost of the coverage for each item on the list. Verify that items are not covered by two types of insurance. Insert the name of the coverage and cost in the list in Figure 15.2.

Step 4—Purchase Policies
When you are satisfied with the insurance coverage you have selected, purchase the insurance policies. Your choices should consider the items you need to protect, the coverage available for the items, and the rating of the insurance company.

Hypothetical Scenario

Eventually, Emi gained a reputation for her skill in painting unique murals. Emi opened her own business and sold her services directly to the client rather than a contractor. After purchasing some expensive equipment and materials, Emi decided it was time to purchase insurance to protect her financial investment in her business.

Pay Taxes

An accountant should prepare the income tax forms for your business. Even if you enter all of your financial records into a software package during the year that can produce a tax return at the end of the year, an accountant should still review your records and your tax forms. This can provide several advantages:

- **An accountant is an expert.** Although you excel at performing your main business function and operating your business, accounting is probably outside your area of expertise. Take advantage of an accountant's knowledge and skill.

- **An accountant is less likely to make errors.** You can be penalized for errors. Every year, the IRS issues millions of penalties.

- **An accountant can provide assistance if your business is audited by the IRS.** If the IRS suspects errors in your tax return, it can conduct an **audit,** a formal examination of your financial records.

- **An accountant can often lower your taxes.** Accountants may identify expenses that can be deducted from your business income or apply beneficial tax regulations that are not familiar to you.

- **An accountant can provide business advice throughout the year.** The accountant that helped you establish your business and bookkeeping system is familiar with your business and can offer meaningful advice.

- **An accountant saves time.** Your accountant is familiar with current tax regulations. This information takes time to gather and comprehend.

Information for Your Accountant

Although your accountant prepares the income tax forms, you need to provide the basic information about your company's income, expenses, and business activities. The following tips can help you prepare the information your accountant needs. Use the checklist in Figure 15.3 to gather the information.

- **Don't wait until the last minute.** Most accountants are busy during tax season.
- **Organize your invoices and receipts.** More organization means less time for the accountant. If you are paying by the hour, organization lowers the cost of hiring the accountant.
- **File your documents in a logical order.** Invoices, receipts, bank records, customer information, and data about your suppliers should be organized by date, number, or alphabetic order.
- **Provide data about the value of your current assets.** A copy of the receipt with the purchase date helps accountants calculate the current value of the items.
- **Provide a list of individuals and businesses that owe your business money.** Include the amount each debtor owes and the length of time the amount has been owed. Some debts may not be collected.
- **Provide a list of individuals and businesses you owe.** Include the amount you owe to each creditor and the date it is due.

◆ **If you operate a home-based business, provide information about your house and your business usage.** Include the size of your home, the size of your workspace, the rent or mortgage payment, property taxes, insurance payments, repair expenses, and utility expenses.

◆ **If you have employees, provide information about your employees and their compensation.** Include the employees' names, social security numbers, benefits, and salaries.

FIGURE 15.3   Information for Accountant

Collected	Information	Collected	Information
❐	Invoices		**Home-based business (continued)**
❐	Receipts	❐	Rent or mortgage payment
❐	Bank records	❐	Property tax
❐	Customer information	❐	Insurance payments
❐	Vendor information	❐	Repair expenses
❐	Receipts for assets	❐	Utility expenses
❐	Debtors and amounts		**Employees**
❐	Creditors and amounts	❐	Names
	Home-based business	❐	Social security numbers
❐	Size of home	❐	Benefits
❐	Size of workspace	❐	Salaries

Business Taxes

Having a basic understanding of tax issues related to your business is a good idea. Your accountant requires some basic information about your business and you should be able to understand the concepts used to create your tax return.

Employer Identification Number   The IRS assigns an **Employer Identification Number (EIN)** to identify businesses that must file tax returns. The number contains nine digits (00-0000000) and a letter (A) or a plan number (000). You must get an EIN if you form a corporation or partnership, pay wages to an employee, have a retirement system such as a Keogh plan, or pay an excise tax.

When you have employees, you are required to withhold some amounts from their salaries or wages. You must withhold social security taxes, Medicare taxes, and federal income tax. In some states, you are also required to withhold state income tax and contribute to a state disability fund. Additionally, you must pay federal unemployment taxes (FUTA) for the first $7,000 of each employee's wages.

You are also required to match some amounts withheld from the employee. You must match the social security and Medicare taxes paid by your employees.

Excise Tax   Your business may be required to pay an excise tax if it is involved in specific activities. An **excise tax** is required by the state or federal government for the manufacture and sale of nonessential products such as alcohol. Excise taxes are often paid in the communication, environmental, air transportation, fuel, and manufacturing industries.

Deductions An amount you subtract from the total income on which you are taxed is a **deduction.** Deductions include items such as charitable contributions, operating a business from your home, and some expenses.

Home Office Deduction If you operate a business from your home, you may be eligible for a tax deduction. To qualify, the area must be used regularly and exclusively. It must also be the principal location for your business. Tax ramifications of selecting this option are considerable.

Major Purchases A business makes major purchases throughout the year. When taxes are prepared, you can deduct the entire cost of the item or depreciate the cost. If you **depreciate** an item, you deduct the cost in proportional amounts over several years.

Employees or Independent Contractors When people perform work for your business, they can be classified as employees or independent contractors. The difference between the classifications is significant, as shown in Table 15.3.

TABLE 15.3   Employees or Contractors

Employees	Independent Contractors
Employer withholds income taxes from payment	Responsible for paying all income taxes
Employer withholds social security and Medicare taxes	Responsible for social security and Medicare taxes
Eligible for benefits	Not eligible for benefits
Employer has the right to direct and control the worker	May work for several businesses
Receives salary or wages regularly	Responsible for profit or loss

For independent contractors, your business must file a 1099 with the IRS and send a copy to the contractor. The 1099 informs the IRS that you paid a specific amount to the contractor. The contractor is responsible for paying taxes for the earned amount.

Hypothetical Scenario

As her business grew, Emi discovered new markets for her skills. Homeowners building large, expensive homes requested murals for their ceilings, sunrooms, and kitchens. After experimenting by painting a large mural on tile for a hearth room wall, Emi decided to hire contractors who could paint simple designs coordinated with the room's mural. As tax season approached, she contacted her accountant to help her determine the financial arrangements with the contractors.

Technology Insights

File Taxes Electronically

According to the Internal Revenue Service, more than 40 million Americans filed income tax returns electronically in 2001. The IRS is encouraging electronic filing, known as e-file. The IRS identified several advantages of filing electronically.

- **Refunds are sent faster.** E-file refunds are usually issued and mailed within three weeks. Returns not filed electronically may take six to eight weeks.
- **Tax returns are more accurate.** Computers can check information much faster and more accurately than manual processing.
- **Electronic confirmation is sent when the IRS receives the return.** The filer knows that the tax forms have been received.
- **Consumers who owe money can transfer the funds electronically.** Consumers can pay with a credit card or transfer funds from an account in a financial institution directly to the IRS. In 2001, more than 280,000 used a credit card and more than 350,000 taxpayers paid their taxes using electronic fund withdrawals.

Think Critically How does the IRS benefit from electronic returns?

CHAPTER REVIEW

A company doesn't plan to hurt consumers, damage property, or destroy the environment when it opens for business. Unfortunately, it happens from time to time. A child chokes on a small toy. A nonabrasive cleaner scratches the kitchen counter. Cities issue smog alerts caused by exhaust and by-products. The manufacturer and the seller of a product share the responsibility or liability for the consequences of consumer usage of their products. The product manufacturer and seller can face a lawsuit and may be required to pay for damages if they are found to be responsible.

A bond guarantees that a specific task will be completed. It reassures the customer because the surety company that issues the bond has evaluated the provider's resources and determined that the company can perform the task. If the work isn't completed, the customer is paid a specified amount. Contractors are usually bonded. To purchase a bond, you must provide enough information to enable the surety company to evaluate your ability to complete a specific job.

Insurance protects the policyholder from financial loss caused by a specific danger. Most businesses purchase property, general liability, and commercial automobile insurance. Property insurance protects you from financial loss when damage occurs to the building in which your business operates, to your business personal property, and to personal property owned by another individual or business. General liability insurance protects your business from claims for bodily injury or property damage. Commercial automobile insurance protects your business from financial loss when its vehicles are damaged or destroyed and limits your exposure when your business vehicle is involved in an accident.

Ask an accountant to prepare the income tax forms for your business. An accountant's expertise can reduce the time required, increase accuracy, and may reduce the amount of taxes you pay. To help the accountant, collect the necessary information before meeting to prepare the tax forms. If you operate a home-based business, provide the accountant with information about your home and its business usage.

USE BUSINESS TERMS

Fill in the blanks with the appropriate term.

audit

bond

bond line

class action

contract bond

deductible

deduction

depreciate

economic damages

Employer Identification Number (EIN)

endorsement

excise tax

exclusion

insurance

key person

liability

libel

license bond

negligent

noneconomic damages

obligee

permit bond

product liability

punitive damages

recall

replacement cost

slander

small claims court

strict liability

surety company

wrongful death

1. A computer you bought two years ago may be worth $2,000, but its ___?___ is $4,000.

2. A higher ___?___ reduces the cost of your insurance policy.

3. A licensed business buys a(n) ___?___ to guarantee that it will comply with local codes that apply to a specific situation.

4. ___?___ are awarded to punish the business and encourage other businesses to use more caution.

5. ___?___ insurance provides financial assistance to your business when it experiences loss caused by the death or long-term disability of the specified person.

6. The cost of some expenses can be deducted or ___?___ when you prepare your company's tax return.

7. ___?___ protects the policyholder from financial loss caused by a specific danger.

TEST YOUR READING

8. What is the difference between liability and strict liability?
9. Why does a retailer have product liability?
10. Describe the damages a business may be required to pay if it loses a lawsuit.
11. Describe how a bond works.
12. What types of bonds are used by small businesses?
13. Explain the bonds a contractor purchases.
14. Identify the information required by a surety company.
15. Why does a business purchase insurance?
16. How could your business end up paying for the same insurance coverage twice?
17. Identify three local companies that could use tool and equipment coverage.
18. How can an accountant lower your taxes?
19. Why does a business need an EIN?

THINK CRITICALLY ABOUT BUSINESS

20. Identify a product that has been recalled recently and explain why it was recalled.
21. Contact a surety company. Investigate the fees for different types of bonds.
22. Identify the insurance coverage needed by your business or a local business.
23. Contact several accountants who prepare taxes for small businesses. Compare their rates and services.

REAL-LIFE BUSINESS

Starbucks Corporation

Success, social responsibility, and happy employees—Starbucks seems to have it all. Starbucks buys and prepares coffee products for consumers who enjoy coffee. Starbucks sells coffee through company-operated retail stores, supermarkets, and Starbucks.com. Starbucks plans to be the most recognized and respected brand in the world. It is already on its way. In 1971, the first Starbucks opened in Seattle. Several years later, a new director of retail operations and marketing, Howard Schultz, started the company on a new path to success. Starbucks' reputation increased when it began to sell coffee to fine restaurants in 1982.

In 1983, Howard Schultz traveled to Milan, Italy. The espresso bars he found there led him to encourage Starbucks to try the idea of a coffee bar in the United States. Since then, growth has been rapid with the company expanding into foreign markets in 1995. Starbucks didn't limit its growth to coffee bars. It developed additional distribution methods through agreements with companies such as Barnes & Noble; United Airlines; Dreyer's Grand Ice Cream, Inc.; Kraft Foods, Inc.; and Pepsi-Cola Company.

In its success, Starbucks hasn't forgotten the consumers and suppliers who have made it a success. In 1997, it established the Starbucks Foundation to assist literacy programs operating in communities where Starbucks coffeehouses are located. In 1999, Starbucks partnered with Conservation International to encourage coffee-growing methods that won't harm the environment. Starbucks continued the effort in 2001 by releasing the Coffee Sourcing Guidelines developed with a division of Conservation International. Also in 2001, Starbucks offered $1 million to support coffee farmers and established the Starbucks Cares Fund to assist the victims of the September 11, 2001, attack on the World Trade Center.

Employees also benefit from Starbucks' success. In 1991, Starbucks offered a stock option program that included part-time employees. In 1992, Starbucks became a publicly traded company on the NASDAQ Market. In 1998, 1999, and 2000, Starbucks appeared on *Fortune* magazine's list of "The 100 Best Companies to Work For."

Think Critically

1. Why are Starbucks' employees happy?
2. What was the source of the idea of opening coffeehouses?
3. How does Starbucks exhibit social responsibility?
4. How have Starbucks' associations with other companies affected Starbucks?

CHAPTER  16

Financial Statements

GOALS

- Select an accountant
- Describe the importance of accurate financial records
- Explain financial statements
- Manage the cash flow for your business

TJ Goto worked as a meteorologist at a large investment firm for 10 years. He provided up-to-the-minute weather forecasting for brokers who trade commodities and for other industries affected by the weather, such as the transportation industry and importers. Last year, TJ began setting up his own company, Goto Weather Updates. He plans to provide weather information, via e-mail and a web site, to individual investors interested in the same markets.

Select an Accountant

The role an accountant plays in a small business is critical to your success. Your accountant can be a valuable part of your business strategy. You may picture an accountant sitting in an office endlessly adding and subtracting long columns of numbers. Although accountants do add and subtract, they perform many other tasks as well. They assist management in strategic planning, monitor a company's financial health, and advise when critical financial decisions are necessary.

Requirements

Most accountants have a bachelor's degree in accounting. Many accountants obtain a master's degree in accounting or a master's degree in business administration with a specialization in accounting. Some universities enable accounting students in a concentrated program to earn a bachelor's and a master's degree in five years.

A state regulatory agency, known as a Board of Accountancy, issues practice licenses to qualified accountants to permit them to operate in that state. Therefore, requirements applicants must meet to become a **Certified Public Accountant** (CPA) differ from state to state. All states require that applicants earn a degree in accounting or take a specific number of college-level classes in accounting and pass the Uniform CPA Examination, a test graded by the American Institute of Certified Public Accountants (AICPA), a professional organization representing the accounting profession. Some states also require experience in public accounting, a recommendation from a CPA who supervised the applicant's work, and an ethics examination.

An accountant can't be a Certified Public Accountant (CPA) until meeting the state's requirements where he or she plans to operate. A CPA is entitled to use the CPA logo if the individual is a CPA and holds a membership in the AICPA or a state society where the accountant operates.

Accountants in America follow rules established by the Financial Accounting Standards Board (FASB), which is sponsored by the U.S. **Securities and Exchange Commission** (SEC). The SEC protects investors by educating consumers and regulating the disclosure of information by public companies.

A CPA in most states must take continuing education classes in the accounting field to renew the CPA certificate, ensuring that a practicing CPA remains current with changes in the field and advances in related technology.

Select Your Accountant

You turn to an accountant because the individual has skills your business needs. Choosing the right accountant requires some time and effort.

Tasks Performed by Public Accountants Small businesses often use the services of a consultant to perform accounting tasks. Before you hire an employee, identify the tasks the employee performs. When you hire a consultant whose expertise is outside your experience, such as an accountant, you can research the tasks the consultant will perform. This knowledge enables you to make a better decision when you select an accountant. You should know what you can expect for the money that you pay.

Accountants can perform a variety of tasks. Identify the role you want your accountant to play in your business. After meeting with candidates, you may be able to add to the list of tasks an accountant can perform to assist your business. The following list of basic accounting tasks provides a starting point for a complete list customized for your business.

- **Sort and file financial documents.** Financial records must be stored for several years. The length of time specific records must be kept is determined by state and federal regulations.
- **Pay vendors.** Write checks or transfer funds to vendors for items purchased.
- **Prepare invoices.** Accurate and timely invoices increase the percentage of invoices that are paid quickly and without argument.

- **Process payroll.** Calculate and process salaries, wages, and withholdings for employees. Maintain payroll reports.
- **Record financial transactions.** Accurate financial records help managers make decisions.
- **Compile and prepare financial reports.** Standard financial statements track profit, cash, and inventory.
- **Create a budget.** Estimated expenses and revenue can be used to determine a **budget** that identifies the amount of money available for a specific purpose.
- **Prepare tax forms.** An accountant can save you time and increase the accuracy of your tax returns.
- **Ensure compliance with state and federal regulations.** Financial information must be documented for several government agencies. These requirements increase if the company sells shares to the public.
- **Use accounting software to perform financial tasks.** Experience and comfort with current technology ensure that reports can be prepared quickly and accurately.

Make a Decision Choosing the accountant who is right for your business is similar to selecting a good employee. You need to evaluate the accountant's abilities and experience, and the fit between the individual and your business needs.

- **Write a job description.** A description enables you to limit the applicants who are appropriate for the position. For an accounting position, the job description should include a job title, responsibilities, supervisor, job classification, location, qualifications, salary range, and hours.
- **Write and place a job advertisement or look through the business section in your phone book.** Alternate methods include asking other small business owners or professionals for a recommendation. Your banker or lawyer may be familiar with an accountant who could meet your needs.
- **Select candidates to interview.** Limit the interviews to applicants who match your criteria.
- **Interview candidates.** Determine that the applicant's experience and expertise make the individual a good fit. The consultant must be familiar with your type of business and fit in with the current personnel.
- **Select a candidate.** Establish a professional relationship with the accounting consultant who meets your needs.

Hypothetical Scenario

TJ Goto worked closely with his lawyer and insurance agent. When the business was ready to start setting up financial matters, he turned to his lawyer and agent for recommendations. TJ knew that he needed to maintain accurate records and make reasonable forecasts. He met with two candidates and selected the first individual because she seemed to be more aggressive in pursuing her goals, a characteristic that TJ believed fit his own management style. TJ knew that he would need to rely on her analysis as he moved forward with his business plans.

Maintain Financial Records

At some point, you have probably picked up merchandise in a store and moved toward the checkout counter, discovering in front of the cashier that you didn't have the money in your pocket or purse to pay for the item. After apologizing profusely, you left the store in embarrassment. As a business owner, you can't afford to make financial errors. You can't order merchandise you can't afford, hire employees you can't pay, or sell merchandise you don't have.

Information Gathered from Financial Records

Your day-to-day business operations create an enormous number of documents. Bills, receipts, and shipping records are only a small number of the paper and electronic documents created every week. The documents enable you to create an accurate picture of your company's status and its progress.

Record the Information When your accounting system is established, an accountant creates accounts in your accounting software. An **account** is a collection of related financial information based on your business operations. Some accounts are common to many businesses while others are specific to your business. For example, many businesses maintain a petty cash account, but only your business has an account for each of your vendors and customers.

When a financial transaction occurs, it is recorded in your **journal,** a record of all the financial transactions that occur each day. Each transaction entry contains the date the transaction occurred, a short description of the transaction, the amount of money involved in the transaction, and the accounts involved in the transaction. The data is posted to the individual accounts, which are stored together in the **ledger,** a collection of accounts.

Use the Information Accurate financial records answer questions that help you make the right decisions for your business. For example, if you are working 60 hours a week but don't seem to be earning a profit, financial records can tell you where your money is going and how your time can be more profitable. Analyzing the financial records can help your business succeed by answering the following questions.

- **How is your income generated?** You may establish a business intended to generate income by selling a product, but discover that servicing the product instead generates the majority of your income. Realigning your efforts to emphasize your service capabilities could take advantage of consumers' need for product service and increase your income.

- **How much income are you currently generating?** Knowing the amount of income you are currently generating and the trend in your income can help you project your future income, enabling you to create a budget.

- **Are any of your products or services draining funds from your business?** If a product isn't profitable, it could be time to drop it from your assortment.

- **How much cash is currently available?** If a business opportunity becomes available, will you have the cash to take advantage of it?

- **How much money do you currently owe and when are the payments due?** To plan ahead, you must know how much you owe and when the funds must be available to make the payment. It may mean that you have to postpone a purchase to ensure you meet your debt obligations.

♦ **How does your profit compare to other businesses in the same industry?** If your business isn't making a profit when your competition is profitable, it's time to make some changes.

Financial Record Retention Requirements

Each financial transaction is supported by physical documents. Legally, you are required to store the physical documents for a specific length of time. Figure 16.1 identifies the basic financial records and the length of time they should be stored. Check the current regulations for a complete list of records and the record retention requirements.

FIGURE 16.1   Financial Record Retention

Record	Description
Three Years	
Bank reconciliations	**Bank reconciliations** verify the match between the bank statement and your company's records.
Petty cash vouchers	**Vouchers** document the transaction when money is disbursed from the petty cash fund. **Petty cash** is a small supply of cash, usually around $100, used to pay small expenses.
Inventory records	**Inventory records** identify the merchandise in storage at a specific time.
Internal audit reports	**Internal audit reports** evaluate a company's operations and performance.
Expired insurance policies	**Insurance policies** protect a business from financial loss caused by a specified risk. Most policies are worthless after the coverage period is over.
Bank deposit slips	**Deposit slips** document the transfer of money into the specified bank account.
Seven Years	
Accounts payable ledger	The **accounts payable ledger** contains data about money your business owes to others.
Accounts receivable ledger	The **accounts receivable ledger** contains data about money owed to your business for goods or merchandise sold.
Business vehicle log	The **business vehicle log** contains information about the value and usage of the vehicles owned by the business.
Bank statements	**Bank statements**, usually issued every month, document any activity within the specified account such as deposits, withdrawals, interest earned, and fees paid.
Bills of lading	**Bills of lading** are contracts between a business or individual and a cargo carrier to transport goods to a specific destination.
Commission records	**Commission records** identify any commissions paid. A **commission**, which is paid to the employee responsible for the sale, is a flat amount or percentage of the amount received from the proceeds of a sale.
Contracts	**Contracts** legally bind two or more parties to a specific course of action. After expiration, the contracts are worthless, but must be kept for historical reference.

FIGURE 16.1   Financial Record Retention (continued)

Leases	**Leases** are contracts that enable one party to use property belonging to a second party in exchange for a specified payment. After expiration, leases are worthless, but must be kept for historical reference.
Employment tax report	The **employment tax report** documents taxes withheld during the specified time period.
Expense reports	**Expense reports** record the products or services purchased as an expense, a loss expended to acquire a benefit.
General journal	The **general journal** records all the financial transactions not recorded in a specialized journal.
Inventory records	**Inventory records** identify all the assets owned by the business, including the quantity of goods and materials in stock.
Invoices sent	**Invoices** you send to customers identify the goods you sold to the customer. The invoice, usually sent with the products, specifies the quantity and cost of the items, and the deadline for paying the bill.
Invoices received	**Invoices** you receive are bills issued by a supplier for goods or services you purchased. The invoices, usually sent with the products, specify the quantity and cost of the items, and the deadline for paying the bill.
Payroll records	**Payroll records** identify amounts paid to employees and withheld from paychecks.
Purchase orders	**Purchase orders** are legally binding offers sent to a supplier to buy products or services on specific terms and conditions. They specify the quantity, price, size, etc. of the items.
Sales tax returns	**Sales tax returns** document the sales taxes collected and paid to the state or local government.
Permanent	
Audit reports by public accountants	**Audit reports** result from an examination of a company's accounting and financial records.
Canceled checks for government payments and critical purchases	**Canceled checks** are paper checks that have cleared the bank. They serve as proof that payment has been made.
Deeds	**Deeds** are legal documents that transfer ownership of real estate.
Mortgage agreements	**Mortgage agreements** are legally binding contracts in which the borrower agrees to give the creditor the deed to the property offered as collateral if the borrower is not able to repay the loan.
Depreciation schedule	A **depreciation schedule** identifies all the assets that are depreciated, listing the date the item was acquired, the cost, depreciation, and current value.
Year-end financial statements	Retain a copy of the financial statements created at the end of each business year.
General ledger	The **general ledger** contains accounts in which all transactions are classified.
Property appraisals by outside appraisers	**Appraisals** are estimates of the value of your property, including real estate, equipment, and other business assets. Appraisals performed by an appraiser who is not associated with your business are more objective.
Tax returns	**Tax returns** report your tax liability to federal, state, and local governments.
Insurance records	An **insurance policy** is a contract that protects the policyholder from financial loss caused by a specific danger.

Hypothetical Scenario

TJ listened and observed as Liz Bettle, his new accountant, set up his accounting software and printed labels for the boxes of new file folders she purchased for his business. As they applied the labels and set up the file cabinets, Liz instructed him in record retention. They decided that after the accounting system was set up, Liz would come in for several hours every week. Initially, they planned to keep a very close eye on the financial situation as the business grew.

Explain Financial Statements

Many people would say that they don't have enough money. Yet many of these same people would be hard pressed to say exactly how much money they have or how much money they owe. For example, you might have money in your wallet or purse, on your dresser, in the ashtray of your car, in your coat pocket, in the bottom of your gym bag, in a checking account and savings account, and invested in the stock market. At the same time, you might have a student loan, a car payment, rent, utilities, a balance on your credit card, and a small library fine for overdue books. You have a part-time job and a partial scholarship. Are you saving money or falling further into debt? The increasing number of bankruptcies shows that many people are falling deeper into debt.

Many consumers lack awareness of the big picture. They don't know where their money comes from or where it goes. A business that doesn't know where its money is earned or spent will probably find that all of its money is spent very quickly. A wise business owner carefully examines and understands the income statement and balance sheet, two critical financial statements.

Income statement

Also known as the **profit and loss statement,** the **income statement** summarizes your earnings and expenses over a specified period of time. An income statement is usually prepared for a month, three months (a quarter), or a year.

Purpose of an Income Statement Business owners track income and expenses, as reported in the income statement, to evaluate business performance during the time period. You can also identify unusual expenses, an increase in manufacturing or merchandise costs, and trends in sales for a specific product. Using this information, you can make a variety of business decisions to increase your profit. For example, if you discover that the cost of manufacturing a product has increased dramatically this quarter, you can search for less expensive suppliers to lower production costs in the next quarter.

Your income statement is also useful for individuals and businesses outside your company. Financial institutions examine your income statement when they evaluate your business before providing a loan. Investors use the income statement to evaluate the potential return if they choose to invest in the business. Vendors use it to evaluate your business as a credit risk if they ship products before receiving payment. Potential employees, particularly those in management, examine an income statement to evaluate the stability of the business as an employer.

Content of an Income Statement The format of an income statement may vary among companies. An income statement can be much more complex than the simple example in Figure 16.2 and some labels will vary. However, the following information is usually present.

Net Sales

- **Sales**—The sales data represents the total income earned by the business.
- **Sales Returns and Allowances**—This category identifies the value of products returned after they were purchased and sales discounts. If this amount seems high, it might indicate a problem in product quality or sales methods.
- **Net Sales**—The difference between Sales and Sales Returns and Allowances *(Sales − Sales Returns and Allowances = Net Sales).*

Cost of Goods Sold

- **Beginning Inventory**—The value of the products in inventory at the start of a specified time period is the beginning inventory.
- **Cost of Goods Purchased**—The amount you paid to make or buy your products during the specified time period identifies the cost of goods purchased.
- **Ending Inventory**—The value of the products in inventory at the end of a specified time period is the ending inventory.
- **Cost of Goods Sold**—This is the total cost of the merchandise actually sold during a specified period *(Beginning Inventory + Cost of Goods Purchased − Ending Inventory = Cost of Goods Sold).*
- **Gross Profit**—Also known as gross income, the gross profit identifies the profit before operating expenses and income tax is subtracted *(Net Sales − Cost of Goods Sold = Gross Profit).*

Expenses

- **Operating Expenses**—The day-to-day expenses incurred in running your business include administration and sales, but not the expenses involved in manufacturing or acquiring your products.
- **Net Income Before Taxes**—This figure identifies the income earned from ongoing operations before taxes are deducted *(Gross Profit − Operating Expenses = Net Income Before Taxes).*

Taxes

- **Taxes**—Taxes paid to the federal, state, and local governments are totaled.

Net Income

- **Net Income**—The final amount is the business income earned after income taxes are deducted *(Net Income Before Taxes − Taxes = Net Income).*

FIGURE 16.2   Income Statement

Net Sales			
Sales			$25,450
Less: Sales Returns and Allowances			500
Net Sales			24,950
Cost of Goods Sold			
Beginning Inventory	$12,000		
Cost of Goods Purchased	7,000	19,000	
Less: Ending Inventory	5,550		
Cost of Goods Sold			13,450
Gross Profit			11,500
Expenses			
Operating Expenses			4,200
Net Income Before Taxes			7,300
Taxes			2,044
Net Income			$ 5,256

Balance Sheet

A snapshot of your business, including its assets, liabilities, and capital, is the **balance sheet.** It describes the current condition of your business. Like a snapshot, it shows only the current moment, not the events that preceded it or the changes that could follow.

Purpose of a Balance Sheet A business owner can examine the balance sheet to evaluate the company's current capabilities. The company's **assets,** items that have economic value, can be used to improve or expand the business. The amount owed by the business identifies its financial responsibilities. Lenders, including financial institutions and vendors, use this information to determine the risk of granting a business loan. Potential employees are reassured when the balance sheet indicates stability and the resources for future growth. Investors evaluate the amount of debt and the value of the company's assets.

Content of a Balance Sheet Information in the balance sheet, shown in Figure 16.3, includes assets, liabilities, and net worth. Assets can be categorized as current assets and fixed assets. **Current assets** include cash and items that could be converted to cash in less than a year. **Fixed assets** include all other assets that won't be converted to cash in less than a year. **Liabilities,** debts owed by the company, are usually listed by the order in which they are paid. Those to be paid in less than a year are presented first. Long-term liabilities follow. **Capital,** also known as **net worth** or **owner's equity,** is the portion of the company's assets owned by the business's owners. It is calculated by subtracting the company's liabilities from its assets.

Current Assets

♦   **Cash**—Currency, checks, and funds available in bank accounts are classified as cash.

♦ **Accounts Receivable**—Classified as current assets, **accounts receivable** are funds owed to the company by your customers.

Fixed Assets

♦ **Land**—Classified as a fixed asset, land never depreciates.
♦ **Buildings**—Classified as a fixed asset, buildings depreciate.
♦ **Equipment, Machinery, and Vehicles**—Classified as fixed assets, these items are often expensive but they depreciate over time.

Total Assets

♦ **Total Assets**—This is the total amount of current and fixed assets *(Current Assets + Fixed Assets = Total Assets)*.

Liabilities

♦ **Accounts Payable**—**Accounts payable** is comprised of short-term debts owed by your business.
♦ **Mortgage**—Debt owed for real estate that extends beyond a year is a long-term liability.

Total Liabilities

♦ **Total Liabilities**—This is the total amount of liabilities owed by the business *(Short-term Liabilities + Long-term Liabilities = Total Liabilities)*.

Owner's Equity

♦ **Capital**—This is the difference between total assets and total liabilities and represents the business owner's share of the assets of the business *(Total Assets − Total Liabilities = Capital)*.

Liabilities and Capital

♦ **Liabilities and Capital**—This value should be the same as the total assets *(Total Liabilities + Capital = Total Assets)*.

FIGURE 16.3 Balance Sheet

Assets	Totals	Liabilities and Net Worth	Totals
Current Assets		Liabilities	
Cash	$ 1,200	Accounts Payable	$ 650
Accounts Receivable	289	Mortgage	18,000
Total Current Assets	1,489	Total Liabilities	18,650
Fixed Assets		Capital	9,339
Land	7,500		
Buildings	15,000	**Liabilities and Capital**	**$ 27,989**
Equipment	3,000		
Vehicles	1,000		
Total Fixed Assets	26,500		
Total Assets	$ 27,989		

Hypothetical Scenario

TJ watched carefully as Liz, his accountant, created the first income statement. Although they expected the numbers to be good, they were delighted with the first month of financial data. The number of customers was growing faster than TJ's most optimistic projections.

Cash Flow

Every day your business operates, it earns and spends money. Profit results when the amount of money coming into your business is larger than the amount leaving your business. **Cash flow** is measured by the difference between the cash receipts and cash payments during a specific time period. Positive cash flow indicates that a profit was earned during the time period but doesn't guarantee an overall profit. Negative cash flow indicates a loss for the time period.

Analyzing Your Cash Flow

Cash constantly flows in and out of your business. As shown in Figure 16.4, money comes into your business in the form of sales and leaves your business to pay short-term and long-term liabilities.

FIGURE 16.4   Cash Flow

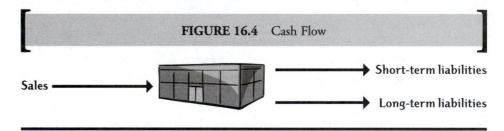

Sales ⟶ □ ⟶ Short-term liabilities

⟶ Long-term liabilities

Problems can occur when a payment is due if a sale hasn't been made recently and the business doesn't have the cash to cover the payment. This occurs more frequently for small businesses that have a low sales volume or make infrequent sales. Even if the company shows a profit for the year, it could encounter dry spells during the year, times when the outflow during the month or the last several months is much higher than the cash inflow.

Managing Your Cash Flow

The game of Monopoly® teaches some important facts about cash flow management. Every time a player passes Go, she collects $200. When another player lands on her property, she receives rental income. She occasionally receives cash or pays fees when she draws Community Chest and Chance cards. When she lands on another player's property, she pays rent. The cash inflows and outflows are identified in Figure 16.5.

FIGURE 16.5   Cash Inflows and Outflows of Monopoly®

Cash Inflows	Cash Outflows
Pass Go	Purchase property
Sell property or buildings	Purchase houses and hotels
Earn rental income	Pay rent
Receive awards from Chance and Community Chest	Pay fees to Chance and Community Chest

---

As you know from playing the game, the order in which events occur often determine the winner. Landing on a high-rent property just before you collect $200 for passing Go can take all your resources, forcing you to declare bankruptcy when you are only $80 short. One more turn would have enabled you to pass Go and stay in the game.

In the real world of business, the time period in which the business suffers from a lack of cash is known as a **cash flow gap.** In the real world, you don't lose the game. You go out of business. Several commonsense business practices can help you prevent or reduce cash flow gaps that put your business at risk.

Plan Ahead Use a calendar, as shown in Figure 16.6, to project your cash flow for the next six months. This enables you to take precautions to avoid cash flow gaps, such as scheduling additional work or moving anticipated purchases.

1. **Identify the dates you expect to receive payment from sales or services.** Write down the amount you expect to receive on these dates.
2. **Identify the dates when payments must be made to your creditors.** Write down the amount you expect to pay on these dates.
3. **Calculate your available funds throughout the time period.**
4. **Identify any projected cash flow gaps.**

FIGURE 16.6   Cash Flow Planning Calendar

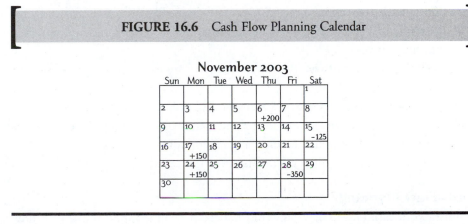

November 2003

Sun	Mon	Tue	Wed	Thu	Fri	Sat
						1
2	3	4	5	6 +200	7	8
9	10	11	12	13	14	15 -125
16	17 +150	18	19	20	21	22
23	24 +150	25	26	27	28 -350	29
30						

Decrease the Time between Cash Inflows Bringing cash into your business more frequently decreases the risk of cash flow gaps. This assumes that the business is profitable in the long run. The problem causing the cash flow gaps is the timing of the cash inflows and outflows.

- **Fill orders quickly.** Perform the task or ship the product as quickly as possible. You will receive payment faster and have more time to complete additional items or services to be sold.
- **Send invoices immediately.** If your business sends invoices to request payment, send invoices as quickly as possible. Customers won't pay until they are billed. Every day that you postpone invoicing postpones the day you receive payment.
- **Offer a discount for immediate cash payment or early payment of invoiced items.** A discount encourages customers to pay promptly.
- **Contact customers who are late making payments.** Call customers who are late paying your invoice. Remind the customer of the due date and politely request payment.
- **Request partial payment before the product or service is complete.** Long-term projects that take several weeks or more to complete can require partial payment when the work is 25, 50, 75, and 100 percent complete. If the product must be manufactured, request partial payment when you accept the order.

Increase the Time between Cash Outflows Having less frequent cash outflows decreases the risk of cash flow gaps. Again, this assumes that the business is profitable in the long run. The problem causing the cash flow gaps is the timing of the cash inflows and outflows.

- **Establish credit accounts with your vendors.** A credit account delays payment until the invoice is due.
- **Don't make payments early.** Keep your cash as long as possible without making the payment late.
- **Don't make payments late.** Vendors and financial institutions can add a fee if payments are late. If you are consistently late, a vendor may refuse to sell products to you.
- **Reduce your inventory.** Buying more inventory than necessary ties up your available cash.
- **Increase your cash reserves.** When you have cash you don't need immediately, keep it in an accessible location for emergency use. A savings account keeps your cash available while earning a small amount of interest. This cash can be used to make required payments when the cash inflow is slow.

Cash Flow Planning

Monitor your cash flow closely. Signs of financial problems appear in the cash flow statement long before the end of the year. The **cash flow statement** summarizes the cash flow over the specified period of time. A cash budget, shown in Figure 16.7, is an excellent planning tool. Headings across the top of the statement usually identify the months. Labels on the left identify the specific inflow or outflow data.

FIGURE 16.7   Cash Budget

	Jan	Feb	March	April	May	June
Inflows						
Sales	450	515	310	290	250	600
Investments	0	0	0	0	0	0
Total In	450	515	310	290	250	600
Outflows						
Lease	250	250	250	250	250	250
Shipping	15	17	12	12	10	20
Supplies	75	20	30	30	25	22
Utilities	110	100	90	95	97	120
Total Out	450	387	382	387	382	412
Total Cash Flow	0	128	-72	-97	-132	188

Hypothetical Scenario

The growth of TJ's business created problems. The number of hits on his web site was far larger than the service provider expected. To accommodate the amount of traffic the site was generating, TJ needed to purchase a much higher service level. Although TJ didn't have a lot of cash available, the change had to be made immediately. If customers could not access the site when they needed the service, TJ would lose customers quickly. TJ negotiated with the service provider. Based on the obvious potential of TJ as a customer, the service provider agreed to upgrade TJ's service immediately. TJ agreed to pay for the service as soon as possible and pay an additional 25 percent fee for the first three months of service. The additional fee compensated the service provider for providing the additional service immediately and the risk incurred by delaying payment.

Technology Insights

Accountants Use Technology

Colleges are expanding the curriculum for future accountants. The use of software to perform accounting tasks is so common that most colleges are requiring some classes in information systems as well as accounting. Information systems include the use of personal computers, networks, and software applications. Programming classes are also gaining in popularity and may be required in some accounting programs. This requirement is very practical because accountants in the corporate world are frequently involved in the design and development of customized software packages. Many large corporations maintain an information systems department to develop software used specifically by their businesses or industry. Accountants are frequently involved in this effort because the results can be channeled directly into the accounting department's projections and final numbers.

Think Critically   Why can programming classes benefit an accountant?

CHAPTER REVIEW

An accountant can be a valuable part of your business strategy. A Certified Public Accountant has completed four to five years of college to earn a bachelor's or master's degree and passed the Uniform CPA Examination. To select an accountant for your business, identify the tasks the accountant will perform, interview accountants that might fit your needs, and select the best candidate.

The financial information gathered from your documents tells the story of your company's successes and failures. It provides details that help you make management decisions about your product, your business methods, and the direction that can enable your company to grow successfully. Government regulations and common sense require you to store most of your financial records for a specific length of time. If storage space is not a problem, keep your records as long as possible.

The income statement and balance sheet provide critical information that can help your business grow. Business decisions made by an informed owner can avoid pitfalls and increase revenue. The income statement can alert you to potential problems, such as increased costs or decreased sales, before they destroy your business. The balance sheet describes the current condition of your business. Potential lenders use this information to evaluate the risk of granting a business loan.

Cash is a valuable element in your business. If you don't have cash when it's needed to pay vendors, bankers, and employees, you could be forced to close your business. Managing your cash flow means identifying any potential cash flow gaps and taking measures to avoid them. This includes decreasing the time between cash inflows and increasing the time between cash outflows.

USE BUSINESS TERMS

Fill in the blanks with the appropriate term.

account
accounts payable
accounts payable ledger
accounts receivable
accounts receivable ledger
appraisal
asset
audit reports
balance sheet
bank statements
bill of lading
budget
business vehicle log
canceled check
capital
cash flow
cash flow gap
cash flow statement
Certified Public Accountant (CPA)
commission
contract
current assets
deed
deposit slips
depreciation schedule
employment tax report

expense reports
fixed assets
general journal
general ledger
income statement
insurance policies
inventory records
invoices
journal
lease
ledger
liabilities
mortgage agreement
net worth
owner's equity
payroll records
petty cash
profit and loss statement
purchase order
reconciliation
sales tax returns
Securities and Exchange Commission
    (SEC)
tax returns
voucher

1. The profit and loss statement is also known as the ___?___.
2. An accountant can't be a(n) ___?___ until meeting the state's requirements where he or she plans to operate.
3. When your accounting system is established, an accountant creates a(n) ___?___ for each vendor.
4. The ___?___ contains data about money owed to your business for goods or merchandise sold.
5. The ___?___ is a snapshot of your business, including its assets, liabilities, and capital.
6. A(n) ___?___ can force your business to declare bankruptcy.
7. Signs of financial problems appear in the ___?___ long before the end of the year.

TEST YOUR READING

8.   Describe the experience of an accountant who would fit your business needs.

9.   Describe the tasks an accountant performs.

10.   Identify the benefits of working with an accountant.

11.   How do accurate financial records benefit your business?

12.   Identify the bank records that must be retained.

13.   Explain the difference between an income statement and a balance sheet.

14.   Describe the information in an income statement.

15.   Why does a business prepare an income statement?

16.   How can you identify a problem with the quality of a company's product?

17.   Why is a balance sheet described as a snapshot?

18.   Identify the values in a balance sheet that should match.

19.   Why is cash flow important?

THINK CRITICALLY ABOUT BUSINESS

20.   Use your local phone book. Identify at least two accountants who might meet the needs of a small business. Ask each one to describe the services they provide for local businesses.

21.   Why are you required to keep financial records for a specific length of time?

22.   Many large, publicly traded businesses publish financial information, including income statements and balance sheets, on the Internet. Select a company. Examine its published financial information. Describe what you have learned about the company. Evaluate the business as an investment.

23.   Prepare a letter to your customers that explains changes you are making to improve your cash flow. Make the changes sound beneficial to them rather than to your business.

REAL-LIFE BUSINESS

BIC Corporation

Every day, accountants and millions of other consumers add numbers, write notes, and sign their names with BIC pens. BIC is up to the challenge of providing BIC pens for every consumer who needs or wants to use a pen. To meet the need, BIC manufactures almost three million ballpoint pens each day.

Marcel Bich established his business in a factory outside Paris in 1945. In 1949, he introduced the BIC ballpoint pen. The company grew rapidly and expanded to the U.S. market in 1958, purchasing a pen company in Connecticut. The first BIC pens in America sold for 29 cents. In 1963, BIC established its corporate headquarters in Milford, Connecticut. BIC Corporation continued to grow and became a publicly traded company in 1971.

Not satisfied with limiting itself to pens, BIC introduced its lighter in 1973. In 1976, BIC entered a completely different market, offering a shaver that was much less expensive than any competitor's products. Again, BIC entered a new market, one in an entirely different field. BIC established a subsidiary known as BIC Sport, marketing the sailboards that have become the most popular sailboards in the world. Throughout the 1990s, BIC continued to develop and introduce products within its existing fields of expertise. When Marcel Bich passed away in 1994, BIC Corporation was a world-leading corporation. Today, BIC manufactures 2.5 million shavers and one million lighters every day. It has approximately 3,000 employees in the United States as well as factories and offices in several other countries.

Think Critically

1. Use the Internet. Identify the most recent stock price for BIC.
2. Describe the recent trend in BIC's stock price.
3. Visit BIC's web site at www.bicworldusa.com. View the most recent financial statements. Evaluate the current financial status of the company.
4. Evaluate BIC as an investment.

Marketing

CHAPTERS

CHAPTER  17

Marketing Functions

GOALS

- ◆ Explain how consumers make decisions
- ◆ Identify your market segment
- ◆ Select a positioning strategy
- ◆ Create an image
- ◆ Develop your marketing mix

Nikita Gibson is the lead singer and manager for the Scarlet Lighters, a country music band that recently played at a few small fairs and nightspots in Texas. Their original music has proven to be popular in the small places they have played. Nikita hopes that a few marketing strategies can help the group break into the big leagues.

Consumers Make Decisions

Many consumers believe that marketing and advertising are the same thing. They aren't. Advertising is only part of the marketing function. **Marketing** is the process of promoting, selling, and distributing your product or service. Marketing activities include research, direct marketing, sales promotion and event sponsorship, advertising, and public relations. The first step in successful marketing is understanding the consumers' motivations and decision-making processes.

Consumers' Characteristics

An old joke starts with the question, "Why did the chicken cross the road?" The chicken's only motivation was "to get to the other side." In other words, the chicken didn't have a complicated reason to cross the road. Consumers, on the other hand, must be motivated to take an action such as entering your store, buying your product, or purchasing your service. Before you can motivate a consumer, you have to understand the consumer's characteristics that can be used to create motivation. Consumer characteristics include culture, social class, community, gender, age group, family, and individuality (Figure 17.1).

FIGURE 17.1   Consumer Characteristics

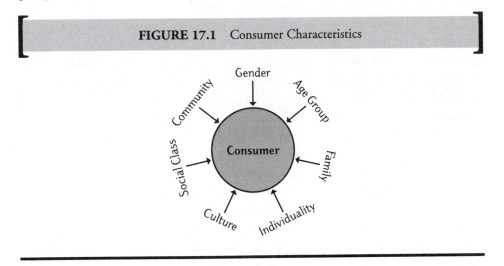

Culture Individuals from the same culture share many significant characteristics. **Culture** is an integrated pattern of behavior, knowledge, and beliefs that are acquired from a group and passed on to future generations. Culture can be determined by large groups of people based on a single factor, such as nationality, ethnic heritage, race, or religion.

Culture is more than having a single factor in common. Citizenship is one factor among many in defining American culture. Culture influences a wide variety of behavior and characteristics such as personal appearance, leisure activities, values, and rituals performed by groups or individuals.

Appearance Fashion is an obvious example of the influence of culture. For example, turbans are common in the Middle East and southern Asia. Beards are more common in some cultures than others. Specific clothing, such as hats, shawls, or dresses, often indicate members of a specific cultural group. Amish people wear "plain" clothing. Conservative Jewish men may wear a yarmulke—a skullcap—when they go to synagogue.

Leisure Activities Culture also affects the activities people pursue during their free time. Some activities, such as reading and conversing, are leisure activities all over the world. Organized sports, such as baseball, which has been called "the great American pastime," are played regionally. Curling, a little-known sport born in Scotland in the early sixteenth century, was introduced to the world when it became an Olympic sport in 1998. Some sports have spread to other cultures. Baseball is now popular in Japan. However, it will probably take a few more decades before curling is played by leagues of teenagers in Tucson, Arizona.

Values Culture strongly influences what people value and how they behave. Cleanliness, patriotism, and honesty are learned as part of your culture. For example, you learn to value and exercise good personal hygiene. You bathe, comb your hair, and brush your teeth before you present yourself to others. Other members of your cultural group have learned the same behaviors and react to you in a negative fashion if you are not well groomed.

Rituals Members of a culture also share rituals. A **ritual** is a formalized act or series of acts that is performed frequently. The rituals reinforce the values of your culture. For example, the Thanksgiving and Fourth of July holidays are full of rituals that reinforce the American values of freedom and individuality. Daily rituals also reflect your cultural values. An activity as simple as brushing your teeth is a daily ritual that reflects the value your culture places on cleanliness.

Social Class A subset of your culture is your social class. A social class is a group sharing the same economic or social status. In America, social classes are not well defined and individuals can move from one class to another. Class membership is based on many factors, but the most typical are income, education, and occupation. A higher social class implies higher income, more education, and a more prestigious occupation. Most moves to a new social class are caused by a change in one of the three most important factors. Many marketers believe that studying social class is one of the best methods of identifying potential customers.

Community You can be a member of only one culture or social class at a time. However, you can belong to several communities at the same time. A **community** is a group of people with a common characteristic or interest living within a larger society. Communities can be based on where you live, age, or interests.

Members of a community do not have to live near each other geographically. A community can be made up of individuals connected only by a common interest such as collecting baseball cards or restoring classic cars. Today, communities based on mutual interest can live in different cities, states, and even countries. They can communicate through media such as magazines, web sites, and newsletters delivered electronically or through the mail.

Gender A characteristic that would seem to be an obvious factor in purchasing decisions is gender. This can be deceiving. The person who uses the product may not make the purchase and may not even care about the available choices. For example, a wife or mother may make most of the purchases for the members of her household.

Men and women often buy similar items for the same reasons. Tools, furniture, and household appliances are purchased by both genders.

Age Group Across all other groupings, age creates some common characteristics and needs. At each developmental stage, specific items are required. Infants need cribs and diapers. School children need clothing and school supplies. Teenagers need transportation. Young adults get married, buy houses, and start the cycle over again.

Family The family unit is a group of consumers. It is difficult to explain or even anticipate the roles played by individual family members in making purchasing decisions. Although young children don't make decisions about the items to buy, they are the reason for many purchases. Parents often overlap in decision-making responsibilities.

You can tell a lot about the needs and purchasing habits of a family when you know the age of the youngest child in the family. This identifies the type of products the family buys, the money they need to save, and even the vacations the family might plan.

When children leave home and begin to shop for themselves, they often buy the same products and brands their parents bought. Following their parents' purchasing patterns provides some security for the newly independent person. In this way, brand loyalty can be passed from one generation to the next. People tend to buy a certain brand of detergent, pudding, or batteries because they remember those brands from their parents' home.

Individuality Regardless of any group membership or outside factors, every consumer is an individual with unique characteristics and experience. Products that appeal to one consumer won't appeal to another, even one with a similar background and interests. It makes the world a little more interesting, but adds both challenge and opportunity for product manufacturers and other businesses. The challenge is created because a business can't create a product that all people will like all of the time. The opportunity is created because there is a market for a variety of products. New companies produce products that appeal to enough people to make them successful.

The Process of Making a Decision

Figure 17.2 outlines four steps consumers follow when they make purchasing decisions: (1) Recognize a need. (2) Search for information and compare alternatives. (3) Buy the product. (4) Use and evaluate the product. Businesses use marketing to influence consumers at each step.

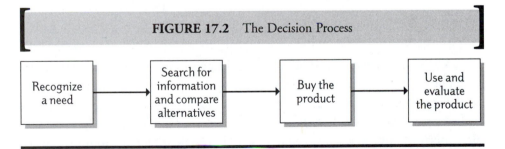

FIGURE 17.2   The Decision Process

The amount of time consumers spend going through this process depends on the complexity of the decision. Buying a pack of gum can be a quick impulsive decision that happens in less than a minute while standing in the checkout lane. Buying a house can take days, weeks, or longer.

Recognize a Need Before making any purchasing decision, consumers must satisfy the basic needs for food, clothes, and shelter. Marketing activities, particularly advertising, can also create needs. How many times have you headed into the kitchen for a snack after watching a food commercial on television? Often, an advertisement for a product can inspire you to think, "That would be great! I *need* that." Five minutes before the advertisement, you would never have thought of *wanting* the product, much less *needing* it. Marketing can influence consumers' desires for products from dog toys to automobiles.

Search for Information and Compare Alternatives Recognizing a need sets the decision-making process in motion. Next, consumers look for a way to satisfy their needs. The search begins for the items they need—a frozen pizza, diamond earrings, or a picture to hang on that bare wall.

Before consumers search for information, they recall anything they already know about the products they need. They may have used the product before or seen it used by family or friends. Sometimes recall is enough. Simple consumer decisions, such as choosing spearmint or cinnamon chewing gum, can be made quickly without additional research.

If the product is complex and the consumer doesn't have any personal experience or knowledge about the product, he or she needs to spend more time searching for information. This could include looking up product reviews on the Internet or in consumer publications, asking people who own the product, and examining or trying the product.

Marketing is a critical part of this step. Consumers remember or notice items related to the products that could satisfy their needs. For example, if they recognize a need to purchase a new vehicle, they probably notice advertisements for tires, auto supplies, and sports utility vehicles (SUVs) with four-wheel drive. News stories about automobile safety catch their attention. They might also notice automobiles used by the characters in television shows they watch.

Buy the Product At this point, the consumer has decided that he or she needs something, researched, compared the alternatives, and made a choice. He or she steps up to the counter and pays for the product. Theoretically, the business has succeeded and shouldn't show any more interest in the consumer who has already made a purchase.

Use and Evaluate the Product After the consumers' money has moved into your pocket, why would you continue to pursue them? No matter what the product is, if they bought it once, they will probably buy a similar product again. This includes small items, like hot chocolate, and large items, like cars or houses. Also, after they own a product, their opinion could become important to someone else searching for information about purchasing the product.

This makes the time after the consumer's purchase very important to your business. You want the consumer to feel good about his or her decision and satisfied with the product. Reinforcement after the purchase can include contact via the telephone or mail. After a major purchase, your sales or service representatives can contact the consumers by telephone to offer assistance or answer questions. A survey can ask consumers to rate the quality of the product and level of satisfaction with the company. Information gathered through these contacts can improve your sales and service in the future.

Your business can offer customers a small fee or discount on their service rates if they refer any new customers. You can also offer a discount on maintenance if the customer brings the product in for service. This increases the possibility that they might make additional purchases from your business. For the same reason, you can send tips about using the current model and information about upgrades or new models as they are produced.

Hypothetical Scenario

Nikita Gibson and the other Scarlet Lighters met to discuss the band's future. Nikita suggested that some marketing activities could do a lot to increase the band's popularity in the local arena, hopefully generating some interest in the local media and reaching more listeners.

Identify Your Market Segment

Businesses need to determine who is likely to purchase their products. After the buyers are identified, the business can direct its marketing efforts toward the specified group, known as its target segment. A **target segment** is a subgroup of a market that is chosen to be the focus of the marketing and advertising campaign.

Define a Market Segment

A business divides the entire market into smaller submarkets in the process of market segmentation. These smaller subgroups are market segments. A **market segment** is a group of people that have common characteristics and similar needs and wants. They buy the same products for many of the same reasons.

Businesses define market segments to target their marketing efforts. To segment a market, the market must meet these criteria:

- **The market must be large enough to divide.** If a product appeals to only 500 people, there is no point in segmenting the market.
- **The market must be accessible to marketing efforts.** If your business can't reach the group, there is no point in creating marketing materials that group members won't be able to view.
- **Each market segment must have distinct characteristics.** The differences between group members form the basis that can be used to create the segments.

Businesses use five common methods to identify and create market segments: usage, demographics, geographics, psychographics, and benefits. Regardless of the differences among them, each segment must have two characteristics.

- **The members of the segment must have common characteristics that cause them to respond to a marketing program in a similar way.** A single marketing method must work the same way for each member of the group.

- **The same form of mass media must reach all the members of the segment. Mass media** is a form of communication designed to reach a large number of people. Examples of mass media include magazines, newspapers, television, and radio.

Usage The consumer's usage level and commitment to the product are common methods of segmenting markets. For some products and services, heavy users are responsible for the majority of sales. Therefore, businesses often select heavy users as the primary target segment. However, heavy users may not need encouragement to buy the product. By concentrating on the heavy users, the business loses the opportunity to encourage other segments to buy the product. Table 17.1 compares the consumer's usage and commitment to the cost and effect of a marketing approach targeting the specified group.

TABLE 17.1   Consumer Usage, Commitment, and Impact

Usage	Commitment	Impact
Nonuser	None	Most difficult to persuade
Switcher	None	Difficult to keep
New consumer	Medium	Low short-term return
Brand-loyal consumer	High	Difficult to convert
Heavy user	High	May not need persuasion

Based on this information, businesses can predict the cost and effect of their marketing efforts. These conclusions reflect consumer behavior when money and effort are engaged in marketing to the following target segments.

- **Nonuser**—A **nonuser** is a consumer who has never used your product or service. They are the most difficult group of consumers to persuade because they see no need for your product.
- **Switcher**—A **switcher** is a consumer who switches from brand to brand. They buy your product if you have a sale, offer coupons, or provide some incentive, like the toy in a box of cereal. Because they don't pay full price, your profit per sale is reduced. Odds are high that they will easily switch to another product when your marketing efforts end.
- **New consumer**—A new consumer is a young adult establishing his or her own home. They inherit some brand loyalties from their parents, exhibited by purchasing many of the same products and brands their parents purchased. These products have a higher comfort level because they feel like "home" for the new consumer.
- **Brand-loyal consumer**—Every business hopes to have a core of **brand-loyal consumers.** These customers always purchase the same brand. Even if prices go up or the product becomes difficult to find, these consumers remain loyal.

◆ **Heavy user**—A **heavy user** purchases large amounts of the same product. Marketing efforts might be wasted. They purchase substantial amounts of your product whether or not you select them as a target market.

Demographics The statistical characteristics of human populations are **demographics.** Demographics include information such as age, race, gender, income, marital status, education, and occupation.

Demographics are commonly used with one of the other market segmentation methods to identify target segments. For example, as shown in Figure 17.3, new consumers can share certain demographics of age (18–25), marital status, etc. This helps a business target the group more specifically. The tighter the definition of the target segment, the better chance the business has to connect successfully to the consumer.

FIGURE 17.3 Demographics and Usage Identify Target Segment

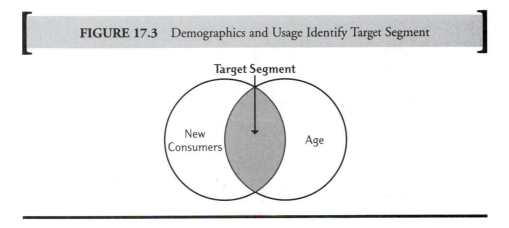

Businesses use demographics to select the media to reach a target segment. Characteristics such as age, income, occupation, and gender often identify a common exposure to the mass media. For example, teenagers and young adults who like the same television shows often listen to the same radio stations.

Geographic Market segmentation based on the consumers' geographic location is also common. Consumers that live near each other share a variety of characteristics. For example, culture, values, and recreational activities are affected by the consumers' geographic location. Consumers who live in Colorado are more likely to ski than to surf. Even the foods that are available and preferred by consumers are affected by geographic location. In the United States, for example, spicy Cajun food is a favorite in Louisiana and clam chowder is popular on the northeast coast.

Combining demographics with geographic market segmentation provides a strong method of identifying a specific target market. The combination can provide a common contact method for advertisers and identify which local media are best suited for the target segment. Local media, sorted by demographic appeal, are more easily identified for the target segment.

Psychographics Businesses created the **psychographics** category to describe a market segmentation method that concentrates on the consumer's activities, interests, and opinions. Businesses connect to the consumers by reflecting their lifestyle, creating marketing messages that seem valid to the target market.

Insight into the consumers' motivation enables you to understand the reasons for their behavior and apply that understanding to any number of products. For example, some consumers are constantly looking for ways to save time. They might eat fast food, buy frozen meals, use drive-through banking services, and choose a store based on its convenient location. Focusing on the timesaving features of your product attracts this target market.

Benefits Businesses using benefit segmentation create segments based on the benefits that different customers want from the same category. For example, consumers want different benefits from purchasing a house. People with children want a large house. Elderly consumers want a smaller, more comfortable home with easy accessibility. Each group of consumers is drawn to a different type of home.

Select a Target

After the market segments have been established, you can select one or more of the market segments to become the target segments. Before choosing a target market, take a long look at its advantages and disadvantages. Choosing the wrong target can have disastrous results. You can spend a large amount of money on marketing without increasing your sales.

Regardless of how the market is segmented, each segment has a different level of appeal to a business. It may seem that two segments could produce similar sales in response to a marketing campaign. Use several criteria to select the best target segments.

- **Examine the current size of the market.** Is the current target market for the product too big or too small? If it's too big, your business won't be able to meet the demand. If the market is too small, it might not be worth the time and money required to reach the market segment.

- **Evaluate the expected growth of the market segment.** If the current market is the right size, will it continue to grow? Can your business keep up with the market's growth? Can you influence the growth of the market segment through your marketing efforts?

- **Calculate the cost of reaching the segment.** How much will it cost to reach the market segment through your marketing efforts? Is the profit worth the cost? If the cost is high and the predicted return is low, it may not be worth the time and effort. Another segment may fit your needs better.

- **Evaluate the compatibility of the market segment with your objectives and resources.** Do the market segment's characteristics fit into your plans for your future? Do the values of the segment fit into your corporate image? Do you have the resources available to make, ship, and sell the product? Will it be necessary to increase your manufacturing capabilities or personnel?

Hypothetical Scenario

The Scarlet Lighters band consists of all women. They determined that their target segment consists of young single women in their own age group, 20 to 30 years of age. With the target segment in mind, the group began discussing methods of reaching their potential audience.

Select a Positioning Strategy

You know that your product is unusual, different from other products on the market. To persuade a consumer to purchase your product, you must demonstrate that your product meets his or her needs better than other products on the market.

Positioning is the process of making your product different from other products in the consumer's mind. The real differences between the paint you manufacture and the paint manufactured by another company next to yours on the store's shelf are probably minor. A consumer might choose the second type of paint only because of the difference he or she remembers from a television commercial shown several times in the past week. As the consumer buys the competitor's paint, you realize that your competitor's positioning strategy was successful.

Elements of a Positioning Strategy

Positioning strategies provide consumers with reasons to purchase specific products. An effective positioning strategy must have the elements of substance, consistency, and a simple distinctive theme.

Substance For a positioning strategy to remain effective over time, it must be backed by substance. Statements about the product or service must be true and backed up by facts.

If your restaurant claims to have fast, friendly service, you must back the claim with service that is indeed fast and friendly. If you don't, your campaign will fail. When consumers find slow and unfriendly service at the restaurant, they won't return for another visit.

The target market for your paint is young adults who are new homeowners and have young children. You determine that they want bright colors and washable paint that is fashionable and protects their new home from a child's adventures with crayons, toys, and muddy dogs. To sell your product successfully to this target market, your paint must be available in a wide variety of bright colors and be able to withstand repeated washings without peeling off the wall when it is wiped with a wet cloth.

Consistency The advertising message must be consistent internally and over time. Internally, everything must work together to reinforce the message. Consistency over time requires that you send the same simple message day after day.

To manufacture bright, washable paint, you must use the right ingredients and procedures. Purchase bright dyes and manufacture the paint with durable ingredients that make the paint washable.

Theme Even though individual marketing activities are different, the basic message must be the same. This message becomes the theme of your positioning strategy. A complicated message won't be understood or remembered by the audience.

Positioning Themes

Your business and your marketing activities need a focus. A **positioning theme** is a central motivating idea that creates a focus for marketing activities and helps your business make internal decisions that create substance for your customers. It should be short, to the point, and easy to remember. Select a single idea as the focus. If more than one idea is selected, the message may become confusing or lack focus.

Positioning themes can be physical or perceptual. **Physical positioning strategies** emphasize the objective physical characteristics of the product. A car can go from 0 to 60 miles per hour in a few seconds, for example, or the airbags deploy when the car collides with something at 25 miles per hour. **Perceptual positioning strategies** emphasize emotional or subjective opinions about the product. A specific type of car is exciting, safe, or adds to the owner's status. You can choose from several basic themes and emphasize physical or perceptual characteristics within each theme. The three basic positioning themes are based on the product's benefits, the user, and the competition.

Benefit Positioning Every product or service has features and benefits. A characteristic that is part of a product or service is a **feature.** A **benefit** is the advantage the consumer gets from that feature. Features are valuable, but it is the benefit that will sell the product. Table 17.2 demonstrates the relationship between features and benefits.

TABLE 17.2 Features and Benefits	
Feature	**Benefit**
100 percent cotton flannel sheets	Keeps you warm on a cold winter night
12 locations in the city	Convenient location near your home or office
Available in seven colors	Match the appliances in your kitchen

Select a single benefit that is important to the consumer. **Benefit positioning** interests consumers searching for that feature. If consumers are looking for a car that is reliable, marketing messages that emphasize low maintenance interest them. If they want a car that is safe, marketing messages that emphasize the car's safety record or safety features attract their interest.

User Positioning Rather than focusing on any aspect of the product, **user positioning** focuses on the user. This is common when the target segment has been chosen by using demographic and psychographic criteria that reveal a complete picture of the target's lifestyle. The marketing messages show how the product fits into that lifestyle. For example, an advertisement for pudding shows a family enjoying dessert together. Marketing messages for jewelry demonstrate occasions for giving jewelry, such as wedding anniversaries or Valentine's Day.

Competitive Positioning To make a product stand out in a crowded product market, use competitive positioning. **Competitive positioning** emphasizes the differences between your product and similar products on the shelf. Your product tastes better, works more effectively, or costs less than your competitors' products. Smaller companies use this method to carve out part of the larger market for their products.

Repositioning Despite your best efforts, your positioning strategies may not work. The market changes constantly. The competitor may have changed its operations or the popularity of specific styles may have changed.

When it is necessary to start over, **repositioning** is always a special challenge. For example, in the past decade, cruise lines have tried to change their image. Cruises used to be purchased by elderly consumers. To attract younger consumers, several cruise lines began to emphasize the adventure of traveling and provide more activities for young adult passengers.

Hypothetical Scenario

Identifying the target segment enabled Nikita and the other Scarlet Lighters to identify the positioning strategy they believed would be most effective. User positioning enabled the women to suggest marketing activities that would reach their target audience. The similarities between the band members and the audience led to several good ideas.

Create an Image

Consumers frequently make decisions based on a "feeling" about a company and its products. That feeling or impression is often based on very little evidence. The consumer gains a positive impression from the company's friendly staff, well-organized display area, and favorable news stories. You can create and reinforce consumers' opinions by creating an image for your business and reinforcing that image with your marketing mix.

When you named your business, you took the first step in creating a public image. Since then, you made many decisions that affected the impression you give to consumers about your company and your products.

Logo

An image used to represent your company is a **logo.** Your logo can be a picture, text, or a combination of the two. When consumers see the image, you want them to think of your business. Without thinking about it, you can probably identify a large number of businesses by viewing the logo:

- NIKE, Inc.
- McDonald's Corporation
- Hallmark Cards, Inc.
- National Broadcasting Company

The color and design of your logo also contribute to your company's image. For example, bright primary colors suggest excitement and high intensity.

Companies that manufacture children's products, amusement parks, and a comedy club could easily choose bright colors for their logos. Darker colors can create a more professional, sophisticated image. Financial institutions, legal firms, and expensive restaurants often use darker colors.

Business Documents

Stationery, invoices, and business cards are among the business documents used by many businesses. These documents should conform to your company's image. The colors and design should reflect the impression you wish to give. Any document available to consumers should use the same colors and design elements to present a consistent image.

Signage

Inside and outside, the signs displayed in your business must stay within the image you are presenting. If you want an upper-class look, don't use poster board and a marker. Pay a few dollars extra for appropriate signs.

Signs Provided by the Manufacturer Aids to retailing that are displayed in the store to attract attention to a product or service are known as **point-of-purchase (P-O-P) advertising.** P-O-P advertising includes signs, banners, flags, and special merchandise displays. These items are meant to draw consumers to the product and encourage them to make a purchase. P-O-P advertising might be sleek and sophisticated, colorful and brash, informational or amusing. It could have moving parts, lights, sounds, or video. The product manufacturer, rather than the retailer, provides many P-O-P advertising displays. They are usually created by advertising agencies skilled in attracting and persuading customers.

Signs Provided by the Retailer The retailer develops some displays and store signs. These can include signs that direct shoppers to different areas of the store, identify different departments, and highlight groupings of associated products. The combination of P-O-P advertising is unique to your store. It contributes to the atmosphere in your store, which encourages potential customers to stay or makes them leave within seconds or minutes. For example, elderly consumers quickly leave a store that targets young teen consumers.

Personnel

Your employees, particularly your sales and service representatives who have contact with your customers, also affect the customers' impressions of your business. The way that your personnel dress and interact with your customers creates an impression of the service and products your business sells. Personnel who are similar to the type of customer you want to attract draw in similar shoppers. A dress code or clothing similar to the customer or coordinated with the product reinforces the atmosphere. For example, employees in a sporting goods store dress casually, while employees in a men's store that sells suits often wear suits.

Personnel density describes the number of store employees per 1,000 square feet of retail space. Fewer employees are found in discount stores or stores where the customer does not expect much assistance. However, if the personnel density is too high, customers feel that the employees are interfering with the shopping process and may leave without making a purchase.

Product Inspection Policy

A customer's ability to visually inspect, touch, try on, taste, or otherwise experience your products is an essential part of the selling process. This is true for expensive items as well as low-cost products. Inspecting the product gives the consumer an impression of the product's quality. You wouldn't buy a new car without kicking the tires, touching the upholstery, and driving it around the block. On the other end of the spectrum, grocery stores often have a "sample" day to encourage shoppers to try new products such as pizza treats or ice cream cones.

Atmosphere

Any location your customers see must follow the guidelines you set for the image of your business. Retail businesses have always been aware of the importance of the appearance and mood generated for customers. Other types of businesses sometimes ignore the physical appearance of their location. This can be a costly mistake. A restaurant, for example, relies heavily on its atmosphere to attract customers. No one wants to eat in a dark, dirty restaurant. **Atmospherics** is the design and use of your business space to create an atmosphere or mood in the environment.

Retail Businesses The design and use of the retail space creates an atmosphere in the store. This is particularly important when the products are consumed at the site, such as a restaurant, or when there are many stores that sell similar merchandise, such as women's clothing stores. **Merchandise density** is the amount of merchandise displayed or shelved per 1,000 feet. A retail store with high merchandise density does not project a high-quality image. Merchandise stacked too high or too closely does not make the products seem exclusive. Generally, a small high-quality store displays less merchandise per square foot than another store that sells merchandise that is lower in quality.

The physical items, known as **fixtures,** used to hold merchandise and create displays also contribute to the store's atmosphere. These items should be consistent with the store's image. Retailers can create a unique look by exploring nontraditional fixtures that support the store's image and make the displays more attractive or memorable.

Sounds are part of the retailer's tools for creating an environment that encourages shoppers. Music is most frequently used. However, sounds can include wind chimes or gurgling water in a florist shop or garden store, televisions or stereos in an electronics store, or a broadcast of a sports event in a sporting goods store. The sound or music you select and its volume must be appropriate for the retail environment. It has been established that music with a slower beat can increase sales. Music with a faster beat increases the speed of shoppers' movements but not their purchases.

Odors can also be used to create a positive retail atmosphere. The right type of odor encourages customers to buy the product. Scented candles in a gift shop are consistent with the store's merchandise and create a positive environment. The scent should be noticeable when the customer enters the store or the product area. If the store is located in a mall, the scent may extend into the main walkway outside the store. The scent, pushed out by airflow if necessary, entices customers to enter the store.

Finally, visual factors present the overall picture. Colors create moods and focus the customer's attention on merchandise. Lighting creates an effect as well, enhancing colors and focusing attention.

Nonretail Businesses If a customer visits your place of business, even if you don't consider yourself to be a retailer, atmospherics are important. Rather than fixtures, your business may have equipment or office furniture. The quality and arrangement of your business environment creates an impression with the visiting customer.

Home-Based Businesses Atmospherics are important for home-based businesses as well. Try to separate your business area completely from your living area, preferably using a separate entrance and washroom. If that isn't possible, treat the areas exposed to the customer as public areas. Customers make judgments on all that they see. Verify that your toddler's tricycle isn't blocking the driveway. Keep the public areas clean, particularly the washroom and kitchen. Ensure that the customer has access to a phone he or she can use privately, preferably in your office. Otherwise, the customer may ask to use the phone in your bedroom, discovering all the items you cleared from the public rooms.

Web Site and Catalog

Many businesses are never physically visited by a consumer. They perform services at the customer's location or sell their products through web sites or catalogs. In this situation, the web site or catalog represents your business. The colors, design, and content must present the desired image of your business.

Services

Delivery, installation, gift wrapping, and return policy are a few examples of the services you can provide for your customers. The quantity and quality of the services you provide affect consumers' impressions of your business. Businesses that provide high-quality products usually provide more services than businesses that provide low-quality products. Of course, prices are usually higher as well.

Hypothetical Scenario

Nikita and the other Scarlet Lighters chose user positioning. They made a list of adjectives that described themselves and their lifestyle. They included the activities they enjoyed and the places they went regularly, seeking items that matched their target segment.

Develop Your Marketing Mix

Businesses use an integrated approach to marketing communication. In other words, although advertising is the most visible marketing element, it doesn't stand alone. Instead, it is part of the **marketing mix.** The marketing mix includes all marketing activities, such as advertising, sales promotions, sponsorships, and public relations. Every component of the marketing mix works together to support your positioning strategy and image for your business and products.

Advertising

Consumers often confuse marketing and advertising, assuming them to be two terms for the same thing. Marketing and advertising are related, but they aren't the same. Marketing is the process of promoting, selling, and distributing your product or service. As shown in Figure 17.4, advertising is only one of several activities involved in marketing your business and your products.

FIGURE 17.4   Marketing Mix

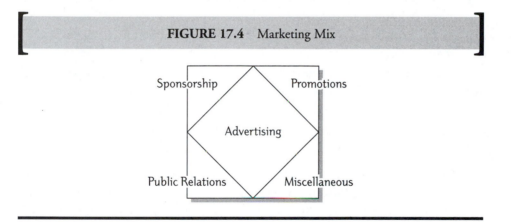

Advertising is the most well-known marketing component, appearing during most television shows and on many pages of your favorite magazine. However, advertising is a complex topic. See Chapter 18 for more detailed information about the advertising process.

Sponsorship

Businesses can choose to sponsor international, national, or local events as well as individuals or teams who participate in public events. **Event sponsorship** occurs when a business helps to fund an event in exchange for displaying a brand name, logo, or advertising message at the event, in any literature about the event, or any broadcasts of the event. Events can be large, such as the international Olympic Games, or small, such as a local craft show held in the park each summer.

Businesses can also sponsor individuals or teams in some events. In NASCAR racing, for example, businesses often sponsor a single racing team. This means that the business helps pay the team's expenses in exchange for displaying the company's logo or product name on the team's car and uniforms. For the entire race, viewers in the stands and the television audience watch the car and the company's logo drive around the track time after time.

Smaller businesses often sponsor local events or teams. A local bank or restaurant can sponsor a children's soccer league by purchasing uniforms for the teams in exchange for displaying a business logo on the uniforms.

Sponsorship can benefit the business, the event or team, and the community. Businesses gain prestige, improve their public image, and receive marketing opportunities. Events or teams benefit by receiving funds that enable them to hold the event or participate in the event. Communities benefit by gaining visitors for the event and increasing the satisfaction of its citizens.

Sales Promotions

If you have ever entered a contest or sweepstakes sponsored by a company, you have responded to a sales promotion. **Sales promotion** is the use of incentives to increase the brand value for consumers or distributors. Promotions are aimed at consumers or distributors.

Promotions for Consumers Sales promotion is meant to cause an immediate purchase rather than a long-term change in consumer behavior. Sales promotions encourage consumers to buy new products, return for additional purchases, buy larger amounts at one time, or try a new brand. Techniques such as coupons, contests, and rebates encourage consumers to buy specific products.

- **Coupons**—A **coupon** provides a reduction in price for a buyer. Coupons might cause a consumer to change brand loyalties or buy your product again. Sunday newspapers usually have dozens of coupons. Others can be printed on your product packaging, fliers, or included in coupon booklets sold by nonprofit organizations.

- **Premiums**—Items that are free or cost less with the purchase of another item are **premiums.** Cold cereals use this tactic, adding small toys to each box, to encourage purchases.

- **Contests**—When consumers use a skill to compete for a prize, they participate in a **contest.** Contests can be expensive to administer because each entry must be judged. Simple contests, such as a children's coloring contest, require less time and effort to manage and judge.

- **Sweepstakes**—When winners are determined by chance, consumers have entered a **sweepstakes.** These require no judging. Simply collect entries, draw a winning entry, and award the prize. Many restaurants hoping to attract the employees of nearby businesses hold a sweepstakes drawing every week, awarding a free lunch. They hope to encourage the winners and their coworkers to return.

- **Sampling**—Businesses often give away samples of their products, a practice known as **sampling.** Food products and perfume can easily be given as samples. The samples are intended to persuade consumers to buy the products.

- **Rebates**—A manufacturer can return a portion of the purchase price, known as a **rebate,** to the consumer. The retailer, where the consumer bought the item, is not involved in the rebate procedure.
- **Frequency**—Regular buyers are rewarded with special deals or offers. Retailers issue a card that can be punched or stamped.

Promotions for Distributors Businesses also offer promotions to distributors. Promotions can interest distributors in a product and create enthusiasm about selling the product. They persuade distributors to sell new products, place larger orders, and assist with promotions for consumers. Running a promotion for distributors at the same time as a consumer promotion may ensure the distributors' cooperation.

- **P-O-P displays**—Retailers want displays that sell the product. Provide unique displays that attract attention to your products.
- **Incentives**—Rewards for reaching specific sales goals are very effective. Incentives can include discounts or additional products.
- **Cooperative advertising**—Free product advertising provides space for the retailer to insert its name. For example, the manufacturer provides many automobile commercials. The local dealership inserts its name and location at the end of the commercial.

Public Relations

A company handles news about itself by controlling the release of company information as much as possible. **Public relations** is the business function that works with the media. Because public relations includes the company's public image, it is also a marketing function.

Objectives Improving and maintaining the company's public image is an important part of public relations. This includes telling the media about good deeds performed by the company or the company's employees. For example, the company could donate computers to a local school or help a community struck by a natural disaster. Employees might donate time to an adult literacy project or spend weekends helping to build housing for low-income families.

Product announcements made by the public relations department can also be newsworthy. The medical field, in particular, often makes product announcements. Sometimes thousands of people can be affected by a single medical breakthrough or a new medication. Obviously, every product announcement won't be on the evening news. While a new toy for dogs may make millions of dogs happy, it doesn't have the same impact on the audience viewing the news as advances in cancer treatment.

Preventing negative events from damaging the company's image is also a public relations function. A worker injured on the job can lead to negative information or rumors of poor safety practices. An employee involved in an auto accident while driving a company vehicle can open the door to all kinds of negative stories in the media.

Publicity A major responsibility of public relations is publicity. **Publicity** is information about a company's activities that is covered by the news media without payment. Press releases are a valuable tool in controlling what the media says about your company.

Miscellaneous A variety of additional methods of marketing are available. In fact, you can create marketing activities that no one has thought of before. Be creative. Distribute balloons, printed with your business name and address, at the technical college down the street. Donate a sample of your customized desserts to a lottery sponsored by a local group for a good cause. Before you act, ensure that the idea fits your image and positioning strategy. The possibilities may surprise you.

Hypothetical Scenario

The Scarlet Lighters came up with some unique marketing activities that fit their business, product, and target market. Nikita had additional copies made of their CD and the Scarlet Lighters designed and printed several dozen T-shirts. They distributed the CDs and T-shirts to beauty shops throughout the city. At each beauty shop, they provided two tickets to the places they performed. At each location, the tickets would be awarded to the winners of a weekly sweepstakes. After several months, they realized their strategy was working. Attendance was increasing. Beauty shops requested additional T-shirts. Finally, a local radio station contacted Nikita to request an interview.

Technology Insights

Branded Customer Loyalty Swipe Cards

Businesses have often tracked customer loyalty by tracking purchases. In the low-technology method, businesses assigned a number to a customer and tracked the dollar value of their purchases. They awarded points when the purchases were totaled later. The customer could redeem the points during a future visit. The high-tech version adds speed, convenience, and data tracking. Each customer is issued a swipe card. When a purchase is made, the card is swiped. Your business instantly records the purchases and adds points for the purchases to the customer's account. The customer receives points for the purchase, enabling him or her to redeem the points immediately. The customer receives an instant award for making a purchase and you are able to track every purchase the individual makes using the card. The tracking information assists you when making critical management decisions and enables you to customize correspondence and offers for each customer, encouraging return visits and additional purchases.

Think Critically Describe the important differences between the low-technology and high-technology customer loyalty cards.

CHAPTER REVIEW

Consumers make purchasing decisions every day. Marketing is a combination of art and science that persuades consumers to purchase your products. It is the process of promoting, selling, and distributing your product or service. To market your products successfully, you should understand the consumers' motivations and decision-making process. Consumers are influenced by their culture, social class, community, family, gender, and age. These characteristics affect the results of the decision-making process by influencing their priorities and values. The decision-making process consists of several steps: (1) Recognize a need. (2) Search for information and compare alternatives. (3) Buy the product. (4) Use and evaluate the product.

Consumers can be grouped by criteria such as location, gender, and common interests. After consumers are categorized, businesses can determine which groups are more likely to purchase their products and direct their marketing efforts at a specific target market.

A positioning strategy persuades consumers that your product is different from other products on the market. An effective positioning strategy has the elements of substance, consistency, and a simple distinctive theme. The three basic positioning themes are based on the product's benefits, the user, and the competition. If a positioning strategy doesn't work, you can design another strategy.

Consumers make decisions based on impressions they have about your business and your product. You can create an image to influence the impression consumers receive about your business. Use your company's logo, business documents, signage, personnel, product inspection policy, atmosphere, web site or catalog, and customer services to create the image.

Support the image you create with the elements of your marketing mix, which includes all the marketing activities you conduct. Your mix includes advertising, sales promotions for consumers and distributors, sponsorships, and public relations. Advertising is the most familiar aspect of marketing, but it must be supported by the other elements of your marketing mix to be successful.

USE BUSINESS TERMS

Fill in the blanks with the appropriate term.

atmospherics	nonuser
benefit	perceptual positioning strategy
benefit positioning	personnel density
brand-loyal consumers	physical positioning strategy
community	point-of-purchase (P-O-P) advertising
competitive positioning	positioning
contest	positioning theme
coupon	premium
culture	psychographics
demographics	public relations
event sponsorship	publicity
feature	rebate
fixture	repositioning
heavy user	ritual
logo	sales promotion
market segment	sampling
marketing	sweepstakes
marketing mix	switcher
mass media	target segment
merchandise density	user positioning

1. The first step in successful ___?___ is understanding the consumers' motivations and decision-making process.

2. Your ___?___ can be a picture, text, or a combination of the two that makes consumers think of your business.

3. ___?___ is a form of communication designed to reach a large number of people.

4. Every business hopes to have a core of ___?___.

5. ___?___ is the process of making your product different from other products in the consumer's mind.

6. If the ___?___ is too high, customers will feel that the employees are interfering with the shopping process and may leave without making a purchase.

7. ___?___ is meant to cause an immediate purchase rather than a long-term change in consumer behavior.

TEST YOUR READING

8. Identify several cultural values in the United States.
9. Describe the decision-making process.
10. How do marketing activities affect individuals?
11. Why does a business contact customers after a sale has been made?
12. Identify the criteria a market must meet before it can be segmented.
13. Identify two characteristics every market segment must have.
14. How does a business select the best target market?
15. Describe the three elements of a positioning strategy.
16. Why would repositioning be needed?
17. What type of signs do manufacturers supply to their distributors?
18. How does a business create an atmosphere for its customers?
19. Describe the components of the marketing mix.

THINK CRITICALLY ABOUT BUSINESS

20. Describe how your culture, social class, community, family, gender, and age affect your purchasing decisions.
21. Identify the characteristics of a specific market segment.
22. Select an advertisement. Identify the positioning strategy. Explain why this strategy was selected.
23. Describe the image you want for your business. Identify the steps needed to create that image.

REAL-LIFE BUSINESS

Eddie Bauer, Inc.

Eddie Bauer established the first Eddie Bauer's Sport Shop in Seattle, Washington, in 1920. Through integrity, innovation, and business acumen, the business grew to its current size—more than 600 stores, several web sites, and multiple catalogs.

Eddie Bauer, Inc., established an unconditional guarantee and dedicated itself to earning its customers' high esteem. It still follows its high principles of commitment to its customers and the environment today by supporting local volunteer projects and environmental projects, such as planting trees in wildlife areas devastated by natural disasters.

Innovation is demonstrated through many of the company's initial products and expansion moves. In 1934, Eddie Bauer patented a shuttlecock, popularizing badminton. Only two years later, Eddie Bauer patented the first goose-down insulated jackets. In 1942, the company was commissioned to produce more than 50,000 flight parkas for the U.S. Army Air Corps. In the mid 1900s, Eddie Bauer outfitted several exploratory expeditions to Antarctica and other locations.

Eddie Bauer retired in 1968, selling the business to his partner, William Niemi. In the same year, the business expanded to San Francisco, California. General Mills purchased the company in 1971 and growth skyrocketed. The product line changed to include casual apparel for consumers. Growth has continued as the store expanded into home furnishings and other products, but the company has retained its focus on integrity and innovation.

Think Critically

1. How did Eddie Bauer's creativity affect his company?
2. How does the company reflect Eddie Bauer's priorities?
3. How has the company changed since Eddie Bauer retired?
4. Use the Internet to evaluate Eddie Bauer, Inc. as an investment.

CHAPTER 18

Advertising

GOALS

- ♦ Describe the role of advertising
- ♦ Set your advertising objectives and budget
- ♦ Select an advertising agency
- ♦ Select media and prepare an advertisement

Dan Nazami disliked shopping for gifts. When he was forced to shop, he could never find what he wanted. He always ended up buying a gift certificate at the recipient's favorite store, restaurant, or entertainment provider. At Christmas, he had to visit several shopping centers, restaurants, and other local businesses. The following summer, he negotiated with several local businesses. They provided gift certificates that he sold from central locations in each shopping center and a web site. Nazami Gift Certificates was in business.

Role of Advertising in Business

Every time you watch television, read the newspaper, listen to the radio, or browse your favorite magazine, you encounter advertisements. Advertising is beneficial to many businesses, making it worthwhile to spend so much time, effort, and money on the process.

Purpose of Advertising

An **advertisement** is a paid public announcement, usually emphasizing desirable qualities, to persuade consumers to buy an item or service. By definition, an advertisement must meet three criteria:

- ♦ The advertiser must pay for the message.
- ♦ The message must be delivered to the audience by mass media.
- ♦ The message must try to persuade the audience to perform some action or adopt some belief.

Advertising is the most visible component of your marketing strategy. For most consumers, the advertisements you create and distribute may be the only information they learn about your business. Businesses that advertise hope to persuade consumers to purchase their products. As part of the marketing process, advertising has five responsibilities:

- Support the marketing positioning strategy
- Make the product unique
- Target a market segment
- Contribute to revenue and profit
- Enhance customer satisfaction

Support Positioning Strategy Your positioning strategy provides consumers with reasons to purchase specific products. Your advertisements must fit into your positioning strategy and the message must be supported by substance. You can't advertise "overnight delivery" if you ship your product via second-day air.

Advertisements also reinforce the marketing theme and provide consistency. To provide consistency, the basic message, or theme of your positioning strategy must be present in every advertisement you create. Many businesses provide this reinforcement through a single sentence or phrase that is present in every advertisement. The phrase becomes attached to the company's image in the consumer's mind.

Imagine that your business manufactures paint. In the store, your paint is placed next to paint manufactured by other companies. Some of those paints cost less than your product. Your positioning strategy emphasizes that your paint is fashionable and protects the consumer's home.

Make the Product Unique If your product isn't unique, consumers have no reason to select your product rather than one of the dozen similar products offered by your competitors. Emphasize or create unique characteristics for your product that enable your target market to select your product for its differences. Even if the products are very similar, you must give the consumer a reason to think that your product is different. Advertising can create the difference in how consumers perceive your product.

When your paint is displayed next to other paints, a consumer might not be able to determine the differences between the products. In this situation, consumers frequently recall the advertisements they have recently viewed. They remember that your paint is fashionable. When they examine the available colors, they discover that your bright colors are more appealing, and thus worth the extra cost.

Target a Market Segment Targeting the type of consumer most likely to purchase your product is an important part of advertising. One of the key elements of many advertisements is using actors who look like the target consumer. If the consumer identifies with the people in the advertisement, he or she remembers the ad and sees himself or herself buying and using the product or service. This trend is obvious when you watch commercials for specific products. Brawny young men drive pickup trucks. Attractive young women happily clean their houses.

In your paint advertisement, a happy young couple chases after a charming toddler armed with a crayon, drawing a line on the wall as he runs down the hall. The young pregnant couple standing in the store with their active toddler identifies with the parents in the commercial. They select your paint without seriously considering your competition.

Contribute to Revenue and Profit   You operate your business to earn money. Therefore, all of your business decisions should result in profitable actions. Advertising is no exception. Businesses spend money on advertising because they expect the advertising to pay off in increased sales. If you spend money to persuade consumers to buy your products, your business should earn more money than you spent for the advertisements. If your income doesn't increase, your advertising isn't working successfully.

When you create and distribute advertising, you invest time and money in the process. The finished product is designed to persuade consumers to purchase your products or services. The revenue generated by the advertisement should compensate you for your time and expenses. Good advertising generates revenue and profits throughout the lifetime of the product.

Enhance Customer Satisfaction   Before consumers purchase your product, advertising creates good feelings about it. Advertising creates interest and persuades them to make the purchase. After the purchase, the same advertisement reinforces the buyer's decision. He or she continues to identify with the happy customer in the advertisement. However, this works only if the product satisfies the customer's needs. Viewing an advertisement won't appease a dissatisfied customer. The advertisement increases the customer's satisfaction level only if the customer is already happy with the product. Good advertising enhances customer satisfaction with a good product before and after the sale.

The young couple that purchased your paint is satisfied with their decision. Just a few days after repainting their toddler's room, the youngster discovered the magic part of magic markers. Fortunately, the marker easily washed off the painted walls. Every time the couple sees the advertisement, they recall the incident and their satisfaction with the paint increases. When friends ask, they happily recommend your paint.

Role of Advertising in the Economy

Advertising is a huge industry, making it an important force in today's economy. In 1997, advertisers in the United States spent nearly $188 billion. Worldwide, an estimated $450 billion was spent on advertising. It encourages consumers to spend money and increases your business revenue. Advertising supports businesses that produce advertisements and supports mass media. It increases competition and affects prices. Advertising also educates consumers.

Business Cycles   The economy goes through times of prosperity and recession. Your business operates regardless of the current state of the economy. In times of economic depression, consumers are reluctant to spend money. Advertising reminds consumers of the items they want, encouraging them to spend money on the products and services. An increase in demand requires an increase in supply. With many other economic factors, an increase in demand helps a depressed economy to recover.

During a downturn in the economy, many small businesses reduce spending on advertising, thinking it is an expense they should reduce or eliminate to survive poor economic conditions. Other businesses increase spending on advertising to fight a recession, hoping to "buy" their way out of the downturn. When the economy recovers, companies that maintained a steady level of advertising during the downturn perform better than companies that cut advertising during the recession.

Another theory suggests that advertisements persuade consumers that they need or want the advertised products. As soon as the consumer has the money, he or she makes the purchase. The desired effect of the advertisement is delayed until consumers can afford the products during better economic conditions, but the ads are still effectively increasing your business revenue.

Mass Media Money spent on advertising gives consumers low-cost or free access to a variety of information and entertainment providers. Television and radio broadcasts would not be free without income from advertising. The price of your local newspapers and national magazines would be much higher than their current costs. Specialized programs or magazines with a limited audience might not survive without advertising support.

Competition Advertising stimulates competition among companies, motivating businesses to develop new products and better production methods that reduce the time and cost of making the products. Advertising also helps companies break into new markets, creating competition across geographic and industry boundaries.

Advertising has detrimental effects as well. New businesses that can't afford to advertise at the same level as their competitors may not have a chance to succeed because they can't attract enough attention from consumers. To compete successfully without spending the same amount of money requires creative marketing approaches.

Prices Advertising is an expense that increases the cost of doing business. This cost is passed to the customers in the form of higher prices. In 2001, the effect of advertising on pricing in the pharmaceutical industry was frequently debated. According to a report on ABC News, Americans spent $208 billion on prescription medication in 2001. The cost of prescription drugs in the United States is much higher than for the same medications in Canada. Advertising has been named as one of the leading causes of the higher prices. In early 2002, government representatives began discussing potential regulations to limit advertising by the pharmaceutical industry to make medications more affordable for those who need them.

Potentially, advertising should be able to reduce the price of some items because advertising increases the demand for specific items. To keep up with the demand, a company has to make more of the items at the same time, lowering the cost of production for each item. If the company passes this on to its customers, each item is cheaper.

Educate Consumers Advertising teaches consumers about the purpose, features, benefits, and value of your product. Advertisements equip consumers with the information needed to make wise purchasing decisions. Educated consumers improve their lives in several ways:

♦ **Educated consumers buy better products.** Educated consumers know about technological advances, upgrades, and new products. The young couple that purchased your paint learned about washable paint from your advertisements. Without your ads, the couple wouldn't look for that particular feature.

♦ **Educated consumers pay lower prices.** Advertising enables consumers to compare prices among several providers. It also increases demand, causing producers to increase the supply. Increasing production lowers the cost per individual unit. The savings in cost can either be retained as profit or passed on to the customer as a lower price.

♦ **Educated consumers spend less time shopping.** Advertising reduces **search time,** the amount of time the consumer spends to find products or services he or she wants.

Hypothetical Scenario

Dan Nazami waited patiently for consumers to discover Nazami Gift Certificates. While he waited, he paid operating expenses, including rent, utilities, and the salary for an assistant. His financial resources were beginning to feel the pinch. Dan noticed that the retailer next to him, who opened her business only a week earlier, had a steady stream of customers. Finally, he opened a conversation with his business neighbor. Callie was happy to help. Increased foot traffic would help her business as well. She gave Dan the name of the advertising agency she used.

Set Your Objectives and Budget

Any activity that has a strong effect on the success of your business must be carefully planned, including advertising. Before spending any money on advertising, determine what you hope to accomplish and the amount you can spend to accomplish it.

Set Your Objectives

You advertise for a reason. Before you can make decisions about advertising strategies or approaches, identify the goal of your advertising. Most businesses have similar objectives. Your objectives must be clearly stated before they can be reached. Each objective should include a value that can be measured, the method used to measure the results, and a reasonable time period in which the objective should be achieved.

Measure the Result The objective must include a value that can be measured before and after the advertisement has been created and distributed. For example, an objective might be to increase recognition of your washable paint from 20 percent to 25 percent. Product recognition must be 25 percent after advertising to be considered successful.

Measurement Methods Your objective must identify how the result is measured. For example, recognition of your washable paint can be measured by conducting a survey. Be sure to measure the specified criterion, such as product recognition. It's nice if sales increase, but if it wasn't the objective, it isn't fair to measure sales to determine success.

Time Period The objective must specify the time period in which the result should be accomplished. Usually, the time period ends when the advertising campaign ends in a few days or weeks. For example, recognition of your washable paint must increase 5 percent by December 31. Your three-week campaign was not successful if brand recognition increases 5 percent, but it requires five years to do so.

General Objectives

Almost every business has the same general objectives. Regardless of the product or service your business sells, you can probably agree that these general objectives are desirable for your business as well:

◆   Increase consumer awareness of your company, product, or service.

◆   Persuade consumers to try your product or service and return to buy it again.

Specific Objectives

The general objectives aren't specific enough to plan an advertising strategy. They can't help you select a target segment and choose a positioning strategy for an advertising campaign. More detailed objectives that fit your needs are required. Although your complete objective includes a measurement method and a time period, you can incorporate the following common goals in your objectives.

◆   **Increase consumer awareness of your products.** Consumers are more likely to purchase a brand that they recognize than an unknown brand. **Top-of-the-mind awareness** identifies the leading brands in a specific product category by asking a consumer to name brands in that category. This is an easy test to conduct. Simply ask consumers to name products of a specific type, such as tires, paper towels, or real estate companies.

◆   **Change consumers' attitudes about your business or products.** Negative attitudes toward your business or products affect sales. Advertisements that provide additional information or use humor might create a better image for your company or product. You must decide if you want to address the reason for the negative attitude in your advertising campaign. Both approaches have advantages and disadvantages. For example, addressing the reason could make it sound like a legitimate concern. On the other hand, addressing the issue could emphasize the fact that the problem was recognized and fixed, demonstrating your dedication to the consumer and the quality of your product. The nature and severity of the issue determine your actions.

◆   **Promote replacement of outdated products with new products using superior technology.** You want to encourage current customers to buy a newer model in the same product line. This type of advertising encourages brand loyalty in expensive or high-tech products such as cars or computers. In some products, such as computers, technological advancements occur so rapidly that consumers are constantly encouraged to upgrade or replace their computers.

- **Persuade the consumer to try a sample of the product.** Providing a sample of your product is a way of getting your foot in the door. When the consumer tries a sample, the product must meet or exceed the advertised benefits. If the consumer is pleased with the sample, a purchase or repeated purchases may follow.

- **Persuade consumers that they intend to buy the type of product you produce.** Although this tactic increases the size of the market, it doesn't guarantee that you will get a larger share of the market. However, making the market larger means that you and your competitors will make more sales. In the example illustrated in Figure 18.1, 500 consumers intended to buy your product or a similar product before the advertising campaign. Your share of the market—40 percent—was 200 consumers. The advertising campaign persuaded 300 additional consumers to buy your product or a similar product. Your market share remains the same at 40 percent, but the number of consumers who purchase from you increases to 320.

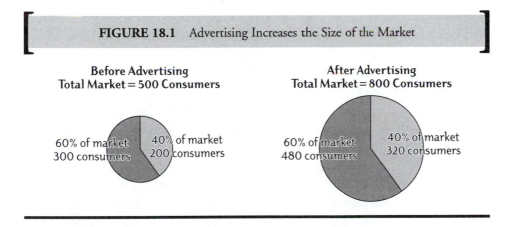

FIGURE 18.1   Advertising Increases the Size of the Market

Before Advertising
Total Market = 500 Consumers

After Advertising
Total Market = 800 Consumers

60% of market
300 consumers

40% of market
200 consumers

60% of market
480 consumers

40% of market
320 consumers

- **Convert consumers that used the product once or occasionally into regular users.** After consumers have used your product, this tactic encourages the sample recipients or occasional users, who use your product infrequently or when their preferred brand isn't available, to become regular users. This is more likely to occur if the consumers are not loyal to a different brand. Brand loyalties are difficult to change.

- **Persuade consumers to switch from a competitor's product.** A consumer who isn't loyal to a specific brand is more likely to change to your product. Persuading a consumer who is loyal to another brand to switch to your product is one of the most difficult advertising tasks. On the other hand, if the customer is loyal to your brand, it works in your favor. It is difficult for a competitor to "steal" a customer who is loyal to your brand.

◆ **Increase sales.** Every advertising campaign is designed to increase sales. A campaign that increases sales directly encourages consumers to purchase specific products. A campaign that increases sales indirectly improves the consumers' attitude toward the company or increases the size of the market.

Set Your Budget

Before you can make many decisions about the advertising you want to create, determine the amount of money you can spend to design and distribute the advertisements. In 1999, American companies spent about $200 billion on advertising annually. Globally, advertisers spent $450 billion. Those figures grow about 7 to 8 percent every year.

Some methods of setting your budget are more effective than others. After you determine your budget, compare the cost to the standard amount for your industry and previous budgets for your company. Finally, set a time frame, evaluate the budget, and make any necessary changes.

Affordable Method Small inexperienced businesses frequently use the **affordable method,** spending the amount the business believes it can afford to spend. This method doesn't consider the products sold, the economic conditions, revenue, or any other factor affecting the business. If the business owner believes the business can't afford to advertise, he or she will discontinue any current advertising. The business doesn't know if it is spending too much or too little. Only after years of experience can a business estimate the correct spending level. This is not considered a preferred method of setting an advertising budget.

Historical Method Another less-than-ideal method of setting an advertising budget is the **historical method.** Compounding the mistakes made using the affordable method, the amount for the current budget is based on the amount the business spent the previous year. To calculate the current budget, multiply last year's budget by the rate of inflation. However, since the amount the business spent the previous year was determined by what it could afford, the current year's budget may be even less reasonable. This method is flawed because it doesn't consider any changes to the business since last year, such as new competition or growth. Plus, a new business can't use this method because it is based on historical data.

Historical Method

Last Year's Budget × Rate of Inflation = Current Budget

Percentage of Sales Method Large companies commonly use the **percentage of sales method.** The amount for the current budget is a percentage of last year's sales or a percentage of the sales the business expects to make this year. Companies spend different amounts for advertising based on the industry, product, and market conditions.

- Across all industries, the amount spent on advertising ranges from 1 percent of sales in the auto and retail industry to 15 percent of sales in the personal care and luxury items business. In 1997, General Motors spent $3 billion on advertising, about 3 percent of its sales. The percentage you select depends on the standards for your industry.
- Spend a higher percentage on new products. It costs more to build a consumer's awareness of a new product. Companies should spend at least 10 to 12 percent of the expected sales of the new product. Companies might decide to spend a much higher percentage, as much as 35 percent, if they are comfortable with the expected sales.
- When market conditions are poor, don't eliminate advertising completely. When conditions improve, consumers make purchases they postponed when the economy was poor.

Results from the percentage of sales method are often disappointing because it is primarily based on expected sales. If sales are declining, spending on advertising also decreases. This could be bad if the business would benefit from an increase in advertising. Also, this method could lead to overspending because the funds have been budgeted for advertising without considering the amount of advertising needed.

Percentage of Sales Method

Last Year's Sales $\times$ Percentage $=$ Current Budget

or This Year's Expected Sales $\times$ Percentage $=$ Current Budget

Share of Voice Method The amount spent by your competition is the basis for the **share of voice method.** The idea is to spend more than your competition so consumers become more aware of your product than your competitor's product. A larger share of voice increases your company's or product's top-of-the-mind awareness. Consumers are more likely to purchase your product because your advertising has made your product more familiar. However, this method has several disadvantages because it relies heavily on your competitor's budget decisions.

- **Competitors' spending information might be impossible to obtain.** Competitors won't publish their advertising data. Small businesses such as yours are even less likely to distribute confidential financial information.
- **Your competitors might not set a reasonable budget.** Your competitor could be using the affordable or historical method. This means your budget could be completely wrong for your business.
- **Your competitor could spend large amounts of money on advertising.** If you try to keep up with a competitor who has more funds than your business, you may spend much more than you can afford.
- **The same amount of money doesn't automatically create a campaign of the same quality.** Your design and distribution selections create a different advertising campaign than your competition. The quality and quantity of ads differ from your competitor's.

Share of Voice Method

Competitor's Advertising Budget +

Percentage of Competitor's Advertising Budget = Current Budget

Objective and Task Method When you make advertising decisions, you set specific goals you want to attain. The **objective and task method** is the only tactic that recognizes and uses the relationship between what you want to accomplish and the amount you want to spend. Because this method uses your objectives, it is important that your objectives are specific and clear. The budget must enable you to achieve your goals.

Obtaining each level of your objectives requires a different spending level. For example, increasing brand awareness requires one level of spending. Persuading consumers to sample your product takes more effort, requiring a higher spending level. After you select specific objectives, determine costs for each individual task. Costs are based on the level of the objectives and the tasks that form the components of each objective you want to accomplish. Several common tasks required to meet your objectives can be identified and assigned a cost.

- **Reach**—The percentage of the target audience that is exposed to an advertisement in the specified time period is the **reach.** If 20 percent of the advertiser's target segment reads the same weekly magazine, the magazine has a reach of 20 percent.

- **Frequency**—The number of times the audience is exposed to an advertisement in a specified time period is the **frequency.** Analysts can't agree on the number of times a consumer needs to be exposed to an advertisement to make it effective. One exposure probably isn't enough to affect the consumer's behavior. However, fewer exposures are necessary for a simple message.

- **Message weight**—The number of times, including duplication, that the audience is exposed to the advertising message by a specific media vehicle is the **message weight.** In other words, if you see the ad twice while you are watching the same television show, it counts as two separate exposures.

- **Production**—The cost involved in designing, creating, and producing the advertisement can be significant.

- **Media**—Purchasing media time includes selecting the time and placement of the advertisement. For broadcast ads, media selection includes the media provider and specific air times. For print ads, media selection includes the media provider, printing expenses, and specific print times and location in the document.

- **Ancillary costs**—Related costs not included in any other category are **ancillary costs.** This can include shipping expenses, equipment rental, and catering while a commercial is filmed.

- **Promotional costs**—Expenses resulting from coordination of the marketing effort are promotional costs.

Objective and Task Method
Cost of Objective 1 + Cost of Objective 2 + Cost of Objective 3 . . . = Current Budget

Hypothetical Scenario

Dan immediately protested that Nazami Gift Certificates didn't have any extra money for advertising. Callie confessed that she initially thought the same thing. She asked him how long Nazami Gift Certificates could survive when it was losing money every day. Then she asked him what his sales projections were when he established the business. Somehow, he had to move from losing money to earning money.

Select an Advertising Agency

Not all businesses hire an advertising agency. Many think the service is too expensive. Before you decide not to work with an agency, examine your advertising needs and abilities. Contact several agencies in your area. Some agencies are also small businesses. They often specialize in working with other small businesses like yours. Investigate the services and the fees your local agencies charge before you decide to develop advertising alone. Like accounting and legal tasks, marketing is a specialized area that can be complicated, requiring specific skills and expertise. Hiring an advertising agency has several advantages:

- **Your business is not familiar with the field of advertising.** It needs to concentrate its time and expertise on its core business product or service. If your business manufactures paint, concentrate the efforts of your business on making paint.
- **Agencies can maintain a larger, more diversified pool of advertising specialists than your business could employ.** Any specialists you maintain as full-time employees contribute to your core business functions.
- **It is more cost-effective to pay a consultant to do a specific task when it's needed than to maintain a staff of specialists you would need only occasionally.** You can't afford to keep employees on staff when their specialized skills are needed only for a few weeks during the year.

The Advertising Process

Your business starts the process, shown in Figure 18.2, by deciding to advertise. You can either hire an advertising agency or design your own advertising. The agency or your advertising department designs the advertisements. These groups can choose to do everything themselves or use an external facilitator to perform tasks such as advertising research and physical production of the advertising components. After the advertisement is produced, it is placed in the media and distributed to consumers.

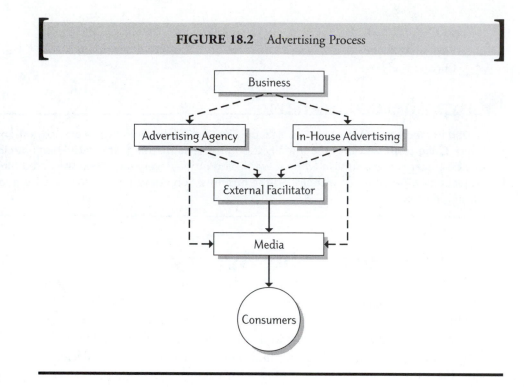

FIGURE 18.2   Advertising Process

Business   Some business sectors use advertising to create a different mix and a unique approach. Manufacturers of consumer goods and services advertise the most. For example, Procter & Gamble and General Foods, which provide products such as laundry detergent and food, advertise heavily. Service providers include hospitals, beauty shops, restaurants, and organizations such as your local symphony and museum.

The U.S. government is also an advertiser. It spent more than $620 million on advertising in 1997. When the U.S. Mint made the first gold $1 coin, it launched an extensive advertising campaign that included national broadcast, print, radio, and Internet advertising featuring George Washington as spokesman for the Golden Dollar. The government also advertises frequently for military recruits.

Advertising Agency   An **advertising agency** is a company made up of professionals who specialize in providing many different services, from creating advertisements to measuring the effectiveness of the advertising before and after it is distributed. Some specialize in a specific part of the advertising process, such as buying media time, creating graphics, or designing interactive media like CDs or web sites.

External Facilitators   Even advertising agencies occasionally need specialized personnel with skills that they don't maintain as regular employees. **External facilitators** perform specialized services related to advertising for small businesses and advertising agencies. These services include a variety of tasks such as providing sets, equipment, and work crews for commercials or photography sessions. Others provide research to assist in planning future advertising or evaluating advertising that has already been released. Regardless of the type of extra service needed, an external facilitator can probably fill the need.

Types of Agencies

When you look for an advertising agency, you quickly notice that the available agencies have some important differences. Some specialize in specific steps in the advertising process, specific business industries, or specific types of advertising. The five types of agencies are in-house agencies, creative boutiques, media-buying services, interactive agencies, and full-service agencies.

In-House Agency An advertising department operating inside a company whose main business isn't advertising is an **in-house agency.** Advertising produced within your business has some advantages:

- **The personnel designing the advertising are familiar with your business, your product, and your industry.** The ideas they generate can use this valuable knowledge and experience.

- **Personnel in an internal department are under your management.** You have direct control over the direction and schedule of the project.

Operating an in-house agency has drawbacks as well. Your employees may be limited in the approaches they consider because they lack objectivity for your products. Under your direct control, the number of ideas presented may be limited. Depth and variety of skill and experience are difficult to maintain in an in-house agency. A small business doesn't have the financial resources to keep advertising talent on the payroll when their skills are not always needed and they do not help to produce the company's main product.

Creative Boutique Ideas, and the people who create them, are available at a **creative boutique,** which specializes in developing creative concepts, writing creative text, and providing artistic services. Hired by advertising agencies or small businesses such as yours, this type of agency adds more creativity to the advertising message or adds excitement to a single advertisement. The group that hired the creative boutique performs the other tasks of preparing and placing the advertisements or distributes the tasks to other specialized agencies.

Media-Buying Service When you purchase a large quantity of an item, you receive a discount based on the quantity you purchase. A **media-buying service** makes a profit by purchasing large quantities of time directly from the media provider at a discounted rate and selling portions of the time to other businesses at a higher rate. This is a specialized service purchased by other agencies.

Interactive Agency Some media are interactive; they respond to a person's input. These media include the Internet, CD-ROMs, and interactive television. **Interactive agencies** specialize in helping clients prepare advertising for new interactive media. These services require specific expertise that isn't common yet in many full-service agencies. Interactive agencies can maintain web sites and build databases. This special service is purchased by other agencies.

Full-Service Agency A full-service agency offers the most complete service. It provides a wide range of services designed to meet a client's complete advertising needs, from the beginning of a project to the end. In a typical full-service agency, client services include account management, marketing planning and management, creative design, production, media planning, and media buying.

Individuals in the Full-Service Agency

When you work with a full-service advertising agency, you work with individuals who are employees of the agency. The individuals play a specific role in the creation and production of advertising for your business. The services provided by the agency can be divided into six categories—account services, marketing services, creative services, production services, media services, and administrative services. Each category is responsible for specific tasks associated with your project.

Account Services You work closely with the **account services** personnel. Services include identifying the benefits of your product, the possible consumers to target with advertising, and the best positioning against competing products. With this information, the group develops a complete advertising plan. Services sometimes include research if more information is needed about any of the components of the advertising plan. Account services consists of two principal positions.

- **Account managers**—Often known as account executives or account supervisors, the primary duty of an **account manager** is keeping the agency teams working on your account on schedule and within the budget. They also work with your business and creative services to create effective advertisements using the correct cultural and consumer values.
- **Analysts**—Research to identify the consumer's behavior and values is conducted by **analysts.** This information provides insight that helps create successful advertising.

Marketing Services Advertising is part of an overall marketing function. **Marketing services** include research, sales promotion and event sponsorship, direct marketing, and public relations. The agency locates previous studies related to your product's market or objectives. It might recommend events you can sponsor, such as community events, bridal shows, or golf tournaments.

- **Event marketing specialists**—Many events are held every day. **Event marketing specialists** identify the events your business could support. They consider elements such as your product, the target segment, the reputation and size of the event, and its location.
- **Researchers**—Data is collected by **researchers.** They study areas such as advertising results and target audiences.

Creative Services The heart of advertising is creativity. **Creative services** develop the advertising message. They use words and images to deliver that message to consumers. The creative group usually includes a creative director, art director, illustrators, and copywriters.

- **Creative director**—The **creative director** manages the group and ensures that the art and text come together to create the desired results on schedule.
- **Art director**—The **art director** manages the art production for the group, ensuring the quality of the graphics for each project.
- **Illustrators**—The **illustrators** draw or create the graphics for each project. Today, graphics are frequently created with specialized software. An illustrator "draws" with a computer as well as a pencil.
- **Copywriters**—The **copywriters** write the text (also called copy) that works with the images. Well-written advertising copy creates images and emotions that persuade the audience to purchase the product.

Production Services A good idea relies on a good production crew to make it concrete. **Production services** produce polished advertising messages. The production crew brings the images and words to life for radio and television commercials.

- **Producers**—The crew includes **producers.** Print and television advertisements require producers to create the desired effect.
- **Production assistants**—Assistants carry out the production tasks.

Media Services A large portion of your money is spent on media time or space. It also determines the consumers reached by the message. These two factors make **media services** very important.

- **Media planners**—Planning creates more effective advertising. **Media planners** help you select the most effective media option.
- **Media buyer**—A **media buyer** purchases large quantities of time at a discounted rate and sells a portion of the time to your business at a higher rate.
- **Media researcher**—A **media researcher** investigates media options and provides recommendations.

Administrative Services Advertising agencies are just like any other business in some ways. They have accounting, personnel, and billing departments, as well as a sales department that sells the agency's services to clients like you. Traffic management falls under administrative services.

- **Traffic managers**—Traffic management coordinates the action between creative services and media services. A **traffic manager** ensures that ads are ready for the media placement deadline.
- **Administrative personnel**—A variety of personnel provide administrative support.

Hypothetical Scenario

Dan made an appointment with the full-service advertising agency Callie recommended. After meeting with an account manager, reviewing samples of the agency's work, and calling two other businesses that worked with the agency, he agreed to meet again with the account manager to discuss advertising strategies.

Select Media and Prepare Your Advertisement

You've seen them on television, heard them on the radio, or cut them out to hang on your wall or refrigerator—an advertisement that stays in your memory. Sometimes it's a little tune that runs through your mind all day. It could be a catchy phrase that your friends adopt and repeat at every opportunity or the picture of your dream car you taped to your locker in high school. Now you want to create an advertisement that has the same effect. It requires the right combination of media and advertising elements.

Select Media

The choice of media class is based on your objectives and strategy. Media planners can choose to use a single medium, concentrating the media budget in that medium alone, or more than one media class, such as television and magazines. Advertisers primarily use print, radio, and television.

Newspapers   The advertising medium accessible to the most businesses is the newspaper media class. National newspapers, such as the *Wall Street Journal,* reach a national audience. Local newspapers target a more precise geographic area, making them invaluable to local retailers. Some newspapers target specific audiences. For example, the *Wall Street Journal* targets the business segment. As the media class for your advertisements, newspapers have advantages and disadvantages, as shown in Table 18.1.

TABLE 18.1   Newspapers

Advantages	Disadvantages
Reach over 50 percent of American homes	Black-and-white printing in body of newspaper
Produced and delivered every day	Discarded daily
Reputation of credibility	Limited creativity
Cost is lower than most media	Place ads more frequently because lifespan is short

Display advertisements are located in the body area. Limited to black and white, they are usually set apart from the text by a border or white space. Inserts are printed on separate pages, often using color and high-resolution graphics, and folded into the newspaper. Sunday editions usually contain the most inserts. Small businesses as well as individuals can place classified ads.

Magazines   Many magazines are published in the United States. They target individual consumers through sports, interests, or hobbies. Others target businesses based on the reader's profession or industry. Magazines, as shown in Table 18.2, have advantages and disadvantages for advertisers.

TABLE 18.2 Magazines	
Advantages	**Disadvantages**
Ability to target a specific audience	Costs more than newspaper advertisements
Creative flexibility using color, size, and some samples such as perfume	Requires a lead time of two or more months
Longer life than a newspaper or broadcast	Published on a monthly or weekly basis; most offer only limited frequency

Advertisements in magazines can be full-page, half-page, two-column, one-column, or half-column. Special effects draw attention. For example, ads can have a **bleed** page, which occurs when the background runs to the edge of the page, eliminating the white space border. A **gatefold** page folds out of the magazine to hold an extra-wide advertisement.

Radio Radio stations transmit continuously, distributing your advertising message day and night. Radio advertising is fast and easy to produce, making it as timely as newspaper advertising. Radio programming can be local or national. Your local station can be an affiliate of a national network, carrying only network programs. It could carry syndicated programs or all the programming could be locally produced. Consumers don't pay to listen to radio programming. Therefore, advertising is a major source of income for radio broadcasters. Radio, as shown in Table 18.3, has advantages and disadvantages for advertisers.

TABLE 18.3 Radio	
Advantages	**Disadvantages**
Low cost	Audio-only environment is a creative challenge
Reaches consumers everywhere	Listeners don't always pay attention, considering the radio to be background noise

Options include local spot advertising, network advertising, and national spot advertising in syndicated programs. The audience can be thousands or millions of listeners. Select the stations and programming that reach your target segment.

Television The best advertising medium may be television. It offers sight and sound to distribute your advertising message, stimulating a consumer to act. Television, as shown in Table 18.4, has advantages and disadvantages for advertisers.

TABLE 18.4 Television	
Advantages	**Disadvantages**
Reaches a very specific target segment	Low credibility
Able to repeat the message frequently	Commercials are so brief that they require repetition to affect a consumer
Creative freedom to use a variety of effects	Consumers frequently change the channel to avoid commercials
Almost every home in America has a television set	Commercials are expensive to make and airtime is expensive to buy

Options include local, syndicated, cable, and network television. Local programming includes news and programs of interest to the community. Syndicated shows can be original or older network shows that are rebroadcast. Cable and network television transmit a variety of programs.

Select the Advertising Message

Whether you are playing a game or planning your next career move, strategy is important. Advertising also requires strategy. Consider your objectives and design a strategy to reach your goals. Your strategy is based on your product or the targeted consumer.

Strategies Based on the Product Consumers' perceptions of your product affect your sales. Many purchase decisions don't require much consideration or product research. Decisions are based on familiarity with a product or brand. This familiarity is often the result of advertising.

Brand Name The consumer loyalty hierarchy in Figure 18.3 identifies the path consumers follow as they move from recalling the name of the branded product to loyalty to a specific brand. Your advertising goal is moving the consumer's preference higher in the hierarchy.

FIGURE 18.3   Consumer Loyalty Hierarchy

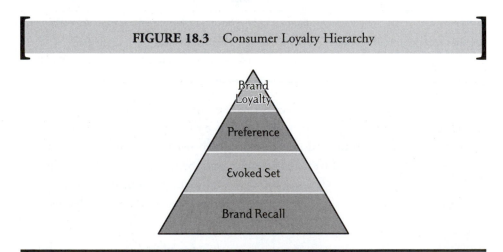

You want your brand to be the first brand consumers remember when they think of that particular type of product. If it isn't first, you want it to be among the first few brands they remember. The **evoked set** is a short list of brand names consumers think of when a product or service is mentioned. It is only a short series of jumps on the consumer loyalty hierarchy from brand name recall to brand loyalty, your ultimate goal. Three common methods of increasing a consumer's brand awareness are repetition, slogans, and jingles.

- **Repetition**—One of the easiest methods of getting consumers to remember a brand name is repetition. The more they hear the brand name, the more likely they are to remember it. Repetition includes the frequency of encountering the advertisement and the frequency of the brand name in the advertisement.

- **Slogan**—A catchphrase meant to help the consumer remember a brand name is a **slogan.** A slogan is memorable because of characteristics such as simplicity, rhyme, or rhythm.

- **Jingle**—A **jingle** has the same characteristics and purpose as a slogan, but it is set to music.

Brand Preference You want consumers to like your brand, making it more likely that they will eventually prefer your brand. If consumers dislike your brand, it will never become their preferred brand, even if it is in their evoked set. Like and dislike are feelings about a product that can be affected by advertisements. Happy and humorous advertisements are common.

- **Feel good**—Advertisements that make consumers feel good anticipate that they will transfer that good feeling to the product. Consumers prefer to do business with companies that make them feel good, companies that they like. This method doesn't always work. Consumers can like an advertisement without liking your product or your company.

- **Humor**—Humor can be risky in an advertisement. The humor has to tie directly to the product or consumers will remember the joke, but not the brand name or product. Like a knock-knock joke, humorous messages wear out quickly. After you've heard the joke a few times, it can wear thin and move from being humorous to irritating.

Key Attribute Linking the brand name to a single characteristic encourages consumers to remember the brand name and the attribute. Usually, trying to link a brand name to several attributes isn't very successful. A short and simple advertising message is more likely to be remembered.

Advertisements that emphasize only a single key attribute use the **Unique Selling Proposition (USP) philosophy.** The brand name helps you remember the attribute and the attribute helps you remember the brand name.

Social Context All objects have some meaning or value in society. The social setting in which your product is used in an advertisement lends some value to the product based on the social context. Slice-of-life and light fantasy ads use social context to demonstrate the value of your product.

- ◆ **Slice-of-life**—These advertisements recreate a moment when the product is used. The social setting around the product gives it meaning. For example, an older wealthy couple dancing on the deck of a cruise ship could suggest that the cruise is a reward for living prudently. A child recuperating from an injury demonstrates the value of insurance.
- ◆ **Light fantasy**—These advertisements encourage consumers to picture themselves "living the good life" as wealthy, athletic, or lucky. Your brand becomes associated with the desired characteristic portrayed in the advertisement.

Brand Image Impressions are sometimes just as important as reality. An image is a mental concept held by a group of people. People, objects, ideas, and brands all have images. Your advertisements can create and modify the image consumers have of your brand name. The brand's image is the characteristic that most consumers associate with your brand. Brand image is very important to your company's long-term success.

Advertisements that create an image for a brand name are usually placed in visual media such as television, print, or the Internet. Image advertisements don't give information about the product or the brand. They rely on the picture rather than the words to create the image.

Strategies Based on the Consumer   When you try to persuade your friend to take some action, such as going out to dinner, you don't read the menu to him. You tell him it will be fun or the activity celebrates a special occasion. You appeal to his emotions rather than his reason. Advertising messages based on the consumer also appeal to emotions rather than reason. The messages make emotional appeals or ask the consumer to make or change some type of action or behavior.

Fear   Scare tactics wouldn't seem to be a smart sales strategy. However, fear can be a powerful motivator. It motivates consumers to take action, such as buying or using the advertised product to protect them from danger.

This type of advertisement informs consumers of the risks associated with *not* using the brand. Products such as security systems, smoke detectors, and insurance are good candidates for this strategy. The products protect consumers from the dangers depicted in the advertisement. This strategy isn't always successful. Consumers may focus on the fear rather than the product that protects them. They may develop a negative attitude toward the business for telling them about the danger.

Anxiety   Not as powerful as fear, anxiety is concern about something rather than fear of it. Consumers often buy a product to protect them during an anxious situation.

Like the fear strategy, this type of advertisement informs consumers of the risks associated with *not* using the brand. Advertisements using the anxiety strategy point out this alleged danger and present a product that avoids or prevents the danger. Personal products such as mouthwash and shampoo are good candidates for this strategy. These products protect consumers from bad breath and dandruff during stressful social situations such as an interview or a date.

Transform Experience Every experience includes emotions and events. Your first date included both the butterflies in your stomach as well as the movie you saw. A consumer's experience can be transformed to enhance the experience. If the transformational strategy is effective, the emotions and memories suggested in the advertisement are triggered every time the advertisement is viewed or your product is bought or used. For example, every time the consumer drinks a specific brand of flavored coffee, she might remember lingering over coffee, chatting with friends, or a few minutes of relaxation at the end of a hectic day. The emotions and memories are linked to buying and drinking the coffee brand, enhancing the experience and reinforcing the consumer's purchasing behavior.

Direct Response The direct response strategy encourages consumers to act immediately. It communicates a sense of urgency to buying the product. The expected response is personal contact initiated by the consumer. The direct response also provides immediate feedback for the advertiser by counting the number of responses received.

The direct response strategy often includes a price-based reward for contacting the business immediately. Mail-order companies often send coupons to customers for orders placed within a certain time period. Television commercials offer discounts or additional merchandise for the next 20 callers. Internet advertisements promise special benefits to consumers who click on the advertisement to view the advertiser's web site.

Persuasion Motivating a consumer to buy a product is an advertiser's ultimate goal. The goal of the persuasive strategy is to convince consumers that a specific brand is better. Persuasion requires more work because it is more difficult to persuade consumers than to frighten them. The message is more complicated in a persuasive advertisement. Most persuasive strategies require some thought by the consumer to understand the message. To persuade, your ads can provide logic, create a sense of urgency, compare your product to another available product, provide a recommendation by an individual who has used the product, or demonstrate the product in use. The last print option is an **advertorial,** which is a special advertising section designed to look like an editorial in a publication. Finally, an **infomercial** is a televised advertisement presented as a documentary. It can last anywhere from five to 60 minutes, but most are 30 minutes long.

Prepare a Print Advertisement

It is easy for a consumer to turn the pages of a newspaper or magazine without looking at the advertisements. A print advertisement has no sound and no movement. You have only visual and textual elements to capture the reader's attention and deliver your advertising message.

Design the Print Advertisement The art and the text must work together. Generally, the text contains the message. The visual element supports and helps to deliver the message. When referring to advertising, **art** is everything in the advertisement that isn't copy, including the illustration and design.

The picture in the advertisement is the illustration. It can be any format, including a drawing, painting, photograph, or a computer-generated graphic. Many artistic elements can be manipulated. As the ad is designed, keep the principles of order and design in mind.

Order identifies the sequence in which any viewer notices the elements in a print ad. Your eyes move from left to right when you read. Therefore, your eyes naturally follow the same pattern when you look at any other object or advertisement. The sequence in which elements are noticed determines which items serve as the visual focus in the ad. Your gaze moves:

- left to right
- top to bottom
- large objects to small objects
- light to dark, and
- color to no color

White space, the part of your advertisement that has nothing in it, is just as important as anything in the advertisement. Too little white space makes an advertisement look cluttered and the product look cheap. White space used correctly can draw attention to the most important element and create a dramatic statement.

Create the Layout for the Print Advertisement The **layout** is a drawing that shows where each element in the advertisement is placed. Several stages are needed to create the final layout, which can be taken to a professional printer or submitted to your selected print media vehicle:

1. A **thumbnail** is one of the first few drafts of an advertisement. It shows a general idea of where the items will be placed in the final advertisement. It is one-fourth the size of the proposed advertisement.
2. A **rough layout** is more accurate than a thumbnail. It is usually created on the computer so the size of the text can be determined and placed accurately. It is the size of the proposed advertisement.
3. A **comprehensive layout** is a polished copy. All the elements are scanned into the computer so everything can be placed accurately. It is printed on a high-quality color printer.
4. A **mechanical** is the final version. Fine changes are made if necessary and you give final approval. The computer file is ready for production.

Prepare a Television Advertisement

Lights! Camera! Action! A television commercial requires a great deal of work before you bring out the cameras and start filming.

Plan the Format Think of several television commercials and programs you have watched recently. Television is a flexible medium. Cartoon dogs make sandwiches and talk. Aliens come down to Earth and humans walk on alien worlds. If someone can imagine it, you can see it happen on television. A variety of formats are commonly used for commercials. Don't limit your creativity to the following examples if something better occurs to you.

- **Demonstration**—The television medium is ideal to demonstrate the benefits of your product. Take advantage of this if it fits your message. Images taken before and after your product is used demonstrate its value.

- **Problem and Solution**—A product is the solution to a difficult situation. For example, an educational service helps a child who is a poor student perform better academically. The slice-of-life method works well with this format.

- **Music and Song**—Many advertisements use music, but in this format the music is the message. The music provides the mood while the images show the brand. Too much text can interfere with the message.

- **Spokesperson**—This format relies heavily on the text. The visuals merely support the copy. Select your spokesperson carefully. He or she represents your company and your product. If you use a celebrity, consider the celebrity's reputation.

- **Dialogue**—This format relies heavily on the text. The slice-of-life method works well with this format. For example, two friends discuss the convenience of a new store.

- **Vignette**—This is a series of commercials that feature the same product and characters. Each commercial is similar to a chapter in a book, moving the story forward. For example, the attraction between the main characters increases or a group of friends travel to different locations. The use of the product is featured during every episode.

- **Narrative**—The mood of these advertisements is personal and emotional. The text, supported by the visuals, tells a story. For example, a man describes how he lost weight or a business owner tells how an insurance company helped him after storm damage closed his business.

Plan the Content Television commercials require planning. For a commercial, the plan is a storyboard. The **storyboard** is a series of sketches that show the sequential visual scenes and the matching text for the commercial. The storyboard keeps track of the action and paces the action and text, ensuring a smooth flow of events in the commercial. It matches each movement with the music or spoken text. The characters perform specified actions while making specific statements. The storyboard maps the entire commercial.

Creating a storyboard is simple. Use graph paper or a graphic software application, and complete the following steps:

1. Draw a series of boxes, known as **frames,** that are three inches by three inches.
2. Sketch a scene in each frame. Use enough detail that it depicts where the elements and actors are when the copy is heard.
3. Write the words to any dialogue or voice-over below each frame. This matches the text to each significant action in the commercial.

The complete storyboard depicts the key actions and text in the commercial. The storyboard looks like a comic book version of the commercial.

Prepare to Produce the Commercial Before production of a television commercial can start, approval is necessary to make the financial commitment needed to film the ad. Time that you spend preparing before production keeps events running smoothly later, when delays cost you severe penalties in time and money. Complete the following steps before production:

1. **Approve the storyboard and script.** The written version of the storyboard is the script. The script is used to set the location, select actors and actresses, and set the budget. It also determines the schedule for making the commercial.

2. **Approve the budget.** A general agreement about the budget was made earlier in the planning process. At this step, the producer estimates cost based on items such as location, actors, and staffing. You must approve this more specific budget.

3. **Evaluate potential suppliers.** Hiring a director is one of the most critical decisions for your project. The director makes many decisions that create the final look of your commercial. Other needs include editors and musicians. Select suppliers that meet your requirements.

4. **Review bids from suppliers.** A production house is a business that provides workers to the film industry. Technicians such as sound specialists and camera operators provide necessary skills. Use the bid process to select providers with reasonable charges.

5. **Create a schedule.** Create a reasonable schedule for completing the commercial. Additional charges and expenses occur when you run over your scheduled dates.

6. **Select the location, set, and cast.** Your cast is critical. They should resemble your target segment. The actors have to match the product, the target segment, and the scene in the advertisement.

Produce the Commercial Now you are ready to say, "Lights! Camera! Action!" The production phase is the most exciting part of the process. The director and the technicians work hard to set up the correct lighting, a critical factor that could take all day. The director walks the actors and camera operators through the movements they will make during the commercial to prevent expensive mistakes later. Every day, the director views the film shot that day. If mistakes or inconsistencies are found, scenes may need to be filmed again. If you slip behind schedule, cost is added.

Finish the Commercial Postproduction requires specific skills. Film editors piece together the best shots and combine different camera angles to create the type of high-quality appearance usually shown on television. Sound, including music, dialogue, and voice-overs, are added. Editing is complete when the commercial is ready to broadcast.

Hypothetical Scenario

Dan and the advertising agency agreed that the right medium to advertise Nazami Gift Certificates was radio. Dan's customers would be similar to Dan—busy individuals who didn't want to spend time visiting different shopping centers, restaurants, and other businesses only to purchase gift certificates. Writing the ad copy and purchasing the media time took just a few days. Dan was delighted the first time he heard the ad on his way to work. Within a few days, business began to increase.

Technology Insights

Challenges of Advertising through Interactive Media

A successful advertisement through traditional media such as print and television reaches passive consumers. Although it forms an emotional connection to the viewer, the viewer only watches and listens. Interactive media, such as the Internet, enable the consumer to respond. Traditional advertisements, designed for passive viewers, aren't successful when directed at the Internet audience. A web surfer won't sit still to load a 90-second commercial, much less watch the advertisement. A linear passive story won't connect with the audience using interactive media. The new interactive media demand new methods of advertising. These methods must take advantage of the consumer's ability to respond. As interactive media become more familiar, advertisers will learn new techniques to use them effectively.

Think Critically Evaluate the capabilities of an Internet advertisement you viewed recently. How could it be improved to take advantage of available technology?

CHAPTER REVIEW

Advertising is a key component of your marketing strategy. Its responsibilities include supporting the marketing positioning strategy, making your product unique, targeting a market segment, contributing to revenue and profit, and enhancing customer satisfaction. Advertising also plays a role in the American economy by affecting businesses and consumers. It encourages consumers to spend money and increases your business revenue. During periods of economic depression, advertising strives to increase the demand for products, helping the economy recover.

Advertising requires careful planning and budgeting. Advertising objectives include a value that can be measured, the method used to measure the results, and a reasonable time period in which the objective should be achieved. Your objectives must be specific enough to plan your positioning strategy. Businesses use several methods to set an advertising budget. Some methods, such as the affordable method, historical method, and share of voice method, are poor methods of setting your budget. The most effective methods are percentage of sales and the objective and task methods. In the percentage of sales method, the amount for the current budget is a percentage of last year's sales or a percentage of the sales you expect to make this year. The objective and task method is the only tactic that recognizes and uses the relationship between what you want to accomplish and the amount you want to spend.

Although some small businesses decide not to hire an advertising agency, advertising is a specialized area that requires specific skills and expertise. Some agencies specialize in specific steps in the advertising process, specific business industries, or specific types of advertising. The five types of agencies are in-house agencies, creative boutiques, media-buying services, interactive agencies, and full-service agencies. You can hire an agency to complete all or some of your advertising tasks.

The choice of media class is based on your objectives and strategy. Advertisers primarily use print, radio, and television. The advertising medium accessible to the most businesses is the newspaper media class. Many magazines target individual consumers through sports, interests, or hobbies. Others target businesses based on the reader's profession or industry. Radio advertising is timely and affordable, but television is currently considered to be the best advertising medium. Advertising strategies are based on the product or the consumer. Product-based strategies are designed to gain brand recognition and loyalty. Consumer-based strategies are designed to persuade consumers.

USE BUSINESS TERMS

Fill in the blanks with the appropriate term.

account manager	jingle
account services	layout
advertisement	marketing services
advertising agency	mechanical
advertorial	media buyer
affordable method	media-buying service
analyst	media planner
ancillary cost	media researcher
art	media services
art director	message weight
bleed	objective and task method
comprehensive layout	percentage of sales method
copywriter	producers
creative boutique	production services
creative director	reach
creative services	researcher
event marketing specialist	rough layout
evoked set	search time
external facilitators	share of voice method
frames	slogan
frequency	storyboard
gatefold	thumbnail
historical method	top-of-the-mind awareness
illustrator	traffic manager
in-house agency	Unique Selling Proposition (USP) philosophy
infomercial	white space
interactive agency	

1. Consumers spend less time shopping because advertising reduces ___?___ .
2. Large companies commonly use the ___?___ of setting an advertising budget.
3. ___?___ write the text that works with the images in an advertisement.
4. The ___?___ ensures that ads are ready for the media placement deadline.
5. The part of your printed advertisement that has nothing in it is ___?___ .
6. A(n) ___?___ is memorable because of characteristics such as simplicity, rhyme, or rhythm.
7. The ___?___ is the final version of a print advertisement.

TEST YOUR READING

8. Identify the role of advertising as part of the marketing function.
9. How does advertising generate revenue?
10. How does advertising affect the economy?
11. Identify two general advertising objectives.
12. Describe three methods of setting an advertising budget.
13. Why is it advantageous for many businesses to hire an advertising agency?
14. Describe the advertising process.
15. Identify the role of each type of advertising agency.
16. Identify the advantages and disadvantages of print in advertising.
17. Why is radio a challenging medium for advertising?
18. Explain the meaning of the consumer loyalty hierarchy.
19. Describe the steps to create a print advertisement.

THINK CRITICALLY ABOUT BUSINESS

20. Given the current economic conditions, what spending level do you think businesses are using for advertising? Describe the effect on businesses.
21. Use the local phone book. Identify an agency of each type.
22. Identify the advertising media that reach your target segment.
23. Create a storyboard for an advertisement.

REAL-LIFE BUSINESS

Enterprise Rent-A-Car

The slogan of Enterprise Rent-A-Car is well known from its nationally broadcast commercials. "Pick Enterprise. We'll pick you up." Today, Enterprise Rent-A-Car is the largest car rental company in North America. It has more than half a million vehicles in its rental and leasing fleet. More than 50,000 employees work at over 4,800 locations in the United States, Canada, Germany, the United Kingdom, and Ireland.

The idea of renting or leasing vehicles wasn't common when Enterprise Rent-A-Car was founded in 1957. Enterprise was the result of an idea and commitment by Jack Taylor. He believed that consumers would understand the benefits of leasing, rather than buying, an automobile. Enterprise started as Executive Leasing, located in the basement of a Cadillac car dealership in St. Louis. A car body shop next door created challenging background noises for business phone conversations.

In 1969, the company changed its name to Enterprise. The name was chosen to honor the aircraft carrier Jack Taylor served on in World War II. The company continued to grow, opening locations across the country. The wrapped car was introduced in the Enterprise commercials early in the 1990s, becoming a symbol for Enterprise marketing efforts. In 1993, the business began operating 24 hours a day. Focus on customer service and convenience has enabled Enterprise to continue its record of success.

Think Critically

1. Where did Enterprise Rent-A-Car begin?
2. Where does Enterprise Rent-A-Car operate today?
3. Why was the company's success initially in doubt?
4. How has the company's advertising affected the business?

UNIT 7

Business Communication

CHAPTERS

CHAPTER 19

Verbal Communication

GOALS

- ◆ Give an effective presentation
- ◆ Participate in a one-on-one discussion
- ◆ Conduct an organized and effective meeting
- ◆ Negotiate successfully

Gloria Gramble taught English and communication skills to high school and college students for several years. Her students regularly won debate competitions, often advancing to the highest competition levels. To help the debate team raise funds to travel to a competition, she gave a presentation about the impact of effective communication skills to a group of parents. One of the parents approached her after the meeting. He asked her how much she would charge to conduct a seminar teaching communication skills to a group of his employees. Gloria Gramble established Gramble Communication Skills a few weeks later.

Give an Effective Presentation

If sweaty palms, a dry mouth, and shaking knees describe your reactions when asked to give a presentation, you may be comforted to know that public speaking is a common fear for many people, even individuals who do it frequently. Your first public speaking experience probably occurred in grade school as an oral book report or group project. Although you have gained experience making presentations since grade school, you may still feel uncomfortable in front of a group.

Business owners have many opportunities for public speaking. A presentation can interest potential investors, inform your employees, and attract media interest in your company or your product. The potential rewards make it beneficial to learn how to give a good presentation. To become a better speaker, learn the techniques used by many effective public speakers, develop your own variations, and practice until your presentation achieves the desired results.

Before the Presentation

Preparation begins long before you step into the spotlight. Initially, preparation and practice sessions require a lot of time. If you use the presentation more than once, the preparation time for each repeated performance is greatly reduced. Preparation can be grouped by tasks for the setting, the content, and the audience.

Prepare the Setting Atmosphere is an important element for any presentation. The setting must enable you to present your information in the best possible fashion and enable your audience to enjoy and understand the presentation. The setting includes the characteristics of the location and room where the presentation occurs. Consider every possible detail. In this area, preparation translates into fewer problems during the presentation.

Select the Location If the presentation is given to your employees and funds are limited, your choice of locations might be limited to your building where only standing room is available if all your employees attend. Consider giving the presentation twice, breaking your employees into two groups so they can comfortably attend. Depending on the reason for the presentation, consider some locations that are creative and affordable. For example, employee awards can be distributed during a short ceremony as part of your company picnic at the local park.

If the presentation is given to potential customers or possible investors, or more formal situations are planned, your choices are limited to more impressive options. Hotels or reception halls are possibilities. Additional factors must also be considered.

- **Available facilities—Facilities** are items built, installed, or provided at a particular location for a specific purpose. Facilities include meeting rooms, convenient parking, and catering.

- **Accessibility**—If attendees drive to the location, it should be easily accessible from highways and main roads at a distance that can be driven in a reasonable time. If attendees fly into town, the location should be near the airport. Accessibility doesn't stop at the door. Verify that all facilities can be reached and used by attendees with physical disabilities. These include handicap parking, elevators, and accessible dining facilities.

- **Audiovisual equipment**—Many locations provide audiovisual equipment such as video projectors, televisions, overhead projectors, and computers. This is convenient if you travel to another city to give a presentation. If the site is local, it's a good idea to use your own equipment.

Set Up the Room Unless your presentation is part of an event that lasts several days, the audience members spend the majority of their time in the setting that you control. Modify the setting to provide an environment that enhances your presentation. Place the audience as close to you as possible. This makes it easier for you to form a connection with audience members through proximity and eye contact.

Prepare the room as early as possible, preferably the night before your presentation. Verify that everything works and check the seating arrangements. If the facility is providing food or equipment, verify that they are aware of their commitments and test all the equipment. If you need to replace something, make sure the representative from the facility follows through on your request and gets what you need.

- **Seating arrangement**—The audience should be able to see you and each other. Reactions, such as laughter, and interest are easily passed from one individual to another when they can see other faces in the audience and make eye contact. Sitting in a semicircle, as shown in Figure 19.1, is ideal for a seated audience that doesn't need a writing surface. Other arrangements include a U-shape made from tables, a hollow square, and an arrangement of circular tables. These enable the audience to see you and communicate with each other.
- **Line of sight**—The speaker and any audiovisual materials must be clearly visible from every seat. Verify that pillars don't obstruct anyone's view.
- **Sound**—Verify that the audience can easily hear you. If you need to use a microphone, verify that it works long before the audience arrives so you have time to replace it if necessary.
- **Lighting**—The entire room should be well lit. If you need to darken the room for a slideshow or overhead transparencies, remember that the speaker should still be visible. Light from a podium or a small spotlight enables the speaker to see and be seen by the audience. Natural light is beneficial, but sunlight often interferes by causing glare. Adjust window coverings as needed.
- **Temperature**—Control the temperature in the room. If it's too warm, the audience may have to fight off drowsiness. If it's too cold, shivering audience members will be distracted by their discomfort.

FIGURE 19.1   Seating Options

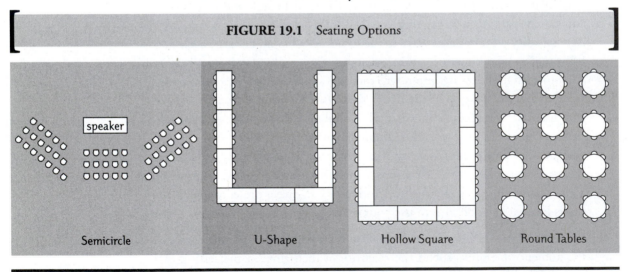

Semicircle   U-Shape   Hollow Square   Round Tables

Prepare the Content   A good speaker equipped with good content can deliver a good presentation. However, an audience may miss important content if a poor speaker delivers it. Research and creativity are the basis for good content.

Research Nothing can replace a thorough knowledge of your topic. Use many sources to gather information. Appropriate sources depend on the topic of your presentation. For example, if your topic is the growth of your business, you should be prepared with financial data about your company, the outlook for your industry, and the economic outlook for business in general. Appropriate sources include your accountant, industry-specific and business-oriented magazines, professional associations, and current news. If your topic is changes in landscaping trends, you'll use different sources. Gardening magazines, surveys of homeowners, and landscape designers can provide accurate, up-to-date information about current trends in that industry.

Gather all the information you can find, and learn to apply the specialized methods and techniques associated with the field. Someone in the audience will discover any gaps in your knowledge or errors in your presentation, particularly if your presentation includes a question and answer period. If you can't respond quickly and accurately, your credibility as a speaker will drop dramatically. Be sure that you have the resources to find the information during a break or recommend a source the questioner can pursue independently.

Audiovisual Materials Part of preparing the content of your presentation is planning and preparing your audiovisual material. Audiovisual materials add flair to your presentation that keeps the audience interested. As technology improves and becomes more portable, your options continue to grow. Audiovisual equipment can be purchased, carried with you, or rented on-site. Many facilities provide or rent audiovisual equipment to speakers when the facilities are rented for a conference or presentation. A variety of media are available.

- **Prop**—Be creative. **Props,** physical items used to illustrate or emphasize a particular point, can be any object associated with your topic including pencils, signs, dogs, and flowers.

- **Flip chart**—The low-technology option for audiovisual equipment is a flip chart. The **flip chart** is a large pad of paper displayed on an easel. Use it to outline your presentation as you speak or record suggestions, feedback, or answers from the audience. Be sure to write large enough and use a dark marker so that the audience can read the text. Involve audience members by asking a volunteer to write on the flip chart and requesting input or feedback from the audience to fill each sheet. Participation stimulates the interest of the audience. Tear off sheets as they are filled and tape them to the wall, creating a physical reminder for the rest of the presentation.

- **Overhead projector**—The ability to create or alter the materials by writing on the transparencies enables you to adjust your materials on the fly for your audience. You can preprint a basic overhead and manually add to it with a marker during the presentation.

- **Computer**—Presentations can be created on a personal computer and displayed on a large screen for an audience. If appropriate, a personal computer can be used by every audience member to complete a tutorial or hands-on exercises.

- **Videoconferencing**—The entire audience doesn't have to be in the room with you. With **videoconferencing** capabilities, audience members can be located anywhere in the world. Your presentation can be broadcast live or recorded and transmitted over the Internet to separate locations at the same time.
- **Teleprompter**—You've seen a teleprompter used by television news anchors and presidential candidates. A **teleprompter** unrolls a magnified electronic script in front of the speaker. Only formal presentations where each word is critical require this type of equipment.

Prepare for Your Audience Every group that you address is different in some way. The group's experience, position in the company, and familiarity with your topic are frequent differences. The depth of the information you want to provide, props, and audiovisual materials differ among groups.

Your personal appearance is an important element in your presentation. The audience makes instantaneous judgments about you, your knowledge of their background, and your presentation when you step into view. Your image shouldn't detract from your presentation.

- **Clothing**—Dress appropriately to fit into the environment and present a professional, knowledgeable image for the industry. For example, if your presentation includes a tour of an area using heavy equipment, wear steel-toed boots and keep your hard hat available. If your presentation includes a demonstration of making a stained-glass window, use the needed safety equipment. Don't wear new clothing or new shoes. Halfway into a presentation scheduled to last all morning isn't the time to discover that your new shoes are too tight.
- **Research**—Meet with your contact to discuss the group for the presentation. Be able to recognize the highest ranked attendees. Refer to your personal experience in their industry. This creates a connection to the audience.
- **Purpose**—Identify the reason for the participants' attendance. This helps you understand the audience's attitude coming into the presentation. If they are being forced to switch to your company's customized software, they have a negative attitude before they start your training session.
- **Objectives**—Identify your objectives for the presentation. If this is a sales presentation, you want to persuade the audience to purchase your product. If this is a training seminar, you want to teach the participants as much as possible, thereby reducing the support your business must provide later.
- **Audiovisual materials**—Adjust the materials to fit the needs of the audience. For example, an audience with less experience in the field needs more basic content and audiovisual materials than an audience with more experience.

During the Presentation

After all the preparation, it's finally time to begin the presentation. The audience has arrived and they are chatting softly, waiting for you to start.

The key to a good presentation is good delivery. You have to form a connection with the audience. A connection makes it much easier for the audience to pay attention and absorb the information. Without a connection, the audience hears only, "Blah, blah, blah, blah, blah." Specific techniques can help you connect to the audience and keep their interest during the presentation. Scheduling and delivery affect the success of your presentation.

Scheduling   The purpose of scheduling is to increase the comfort of your audience. A comfortable audience is more likely to enjoy and learn from your presentation.

- **Time of day**—The best time to learn is affected by a number of factors, including the time of day, most recent meal, and environment. Unfortunately, you can't adjust to every individual's needs. During the average workday, 8 A.M. to 5 P.M., many people are most productive during the middle of the morning, 9 A.M. to 11 A.M., and mid-afternoon, 2 P.M. to 4 P.M. If possible, cover the most complicated material during the time when your audience is most likely to absorb the information. Plan to start a little slower if your presentation begins at 8 A.M. or right after lunch.

- **Breaks**—Scheduled breaks should occur every 1.5 to 2 hours. If breaks are scheduled farther apart, individuals begin taking breaks on their own, causing minor disruptions as they leave their seats and exit the room. Scheduled breaks ensure that the majority of the audience remains seated until the break. Schedule 10 to 15 minutes for each break, enabling audience members to refill their drinks and make phone calls.

- **Ground rules**—Establish the ground rules for your presentation early. For example, if you prefer that audience members save questions for a specific time, mention this before a question is asked.

- **Question and answer**—If your presentation includes a segment when the audience asks questions, schedule it near the end of your session. However, don't end with the Q&A segment. Create a more powerful closing that leaves the audience with the impression you prefer.

Delivery   Use a variety of techniques to enhance your presentation. With a little practice, most of these can become part of your personal style, requiring no special effort during your future presentations. Videotape yourself during a practice session or presentation. You'll notice many characteristics, good and bad, of your delivery techniques.

- **Humor**—Use humor cautiously. You don't want to be offensive in any way. Humor that relies on criticism isn't appropriate during a presentation.

- **Eye contact**—Frequent eye contact with audience members forms a connection with the audience and presents an honest, trustworthy image. Avoiding eye contact appears suspicious, giving the impression that you aren't an authority on your topic or aren't revealing the truth.

- **Tone of voice**—A droning monotone can quickly put your audience to sleep. Vary your tone of voice as you do when holding a normal conversation.

- **Pace**—Speed up, slow down, and pause to create emphasis and maintain interest. Vary your pace as you do when holding a normal conversation.
- **Gestures**—Physical gestures can be used to emphasize or demonstrate, calling attention to specific points. Don't rock, make repetitive gestures, or constantly move your feet. Be aware of any irritating speaking or moving habits and try to avoid them.
- **Reactions**—Watch your audience. Nods signify agreement and indicate that they are involved in your presentation. Frowns indicate confusion or disagreement. Addressing audience concerns can overcome their objections before they are voiced.

After the Presentation

Your actions after the presentation depend on the purpose and objectives of the presentation. If you want further contact from audience members, encourage the contact and provide access.

- Discuss the results with the person who scheduled your presentation to determine if the presentation met the objectives.
- Distribute feedback forms to the audience. Suggestions might improve your future presentations.
- If you want audience members to get in touch with you, place contact information on all handouts. To encourage participants to keep handouts, include additional materials, resources, or other valuable reference materials.

Hypothetical Scenario

Gloria Gramble gave her first presentation to a group of sales representatives three months after she established Gramble Communication Skills. The fact that so many adults hadn't learned effective communication skills in school made a large pool of potential customers. Gloria discovered that individuals at every level of the business world are interested in improving their communication skills, hoping that these critical skills can improve or expand their career options.

Participate in a One-on-One Discussion

It doesn't require a presentation to accomplish most business objectives. Many require only a discussion. Personal communication is an essential component of many businesses. Doctors and counselors obviously need good communication skills. Doctors determine the tests and treatment a patient needs by physical examination and conversation with the patient. Counselors help troubled individuals through open discussions.

Other businesses also require communication skills. An architect must understand the client's needs to design a home or office. To select appropriate plants, a landscape designer has to know how much labor the client wants to perform regularly. Hairstylists keep up a steady stream of conversation with their clients. Conversations can create networks.

Networking

Individuals are connected in many ways, such as common interests, professional associations, and community. The connections between individuals form networks, as shown in Figure 19.2. **Networking** is the exchange of information and services among individuals and businesses. It's an effective way to make connections that can help your business on the way to success.

FIGURE 19.2   Networking

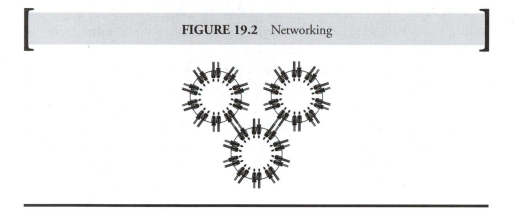

Conversations with your current customers often result in gaining new clients. However, current customers aren't the only sources of information and opportunity. Make connections through nearby small business owners, community associations, clubs, consultants, professional associations, and former classmates. Every conversation you have can lead to new connections. These connections could lead to additional customers, less expensive suppliers, or additional information that benefits your business.

Networking can help you find a **mentor,** an individual with more experience or knowledge in a specific area who provides advice or guidance. Structured mentoring programs are usually available through a college or university. Another resource is SCORE (Service Corps of Retired Executives). SCORE is a nonprofit resource partner with the U.S. Small Business Association. Working and retired executives and business owners volunteer through SCORE to educate entrepreneurs. Volunteers donate more than one million hours every year through SCORE. SCORE is located on the Internet at www.score.org.

Conversation

Success as a business owner requires much more than knowing how to manufacture your product or provide a service. Interaction with customers, suppliers, employees, investors, and other business owners can affect the success of your business just as much as does the quality of your product or current economic conditions. Good conversation skills can help your business succeed.

Be sure that you have real conversations. If you talk but don't listen to a response, you aren't having a conversation. A **conversation** is a verbal exchange of information or ideas. The key to a conversation is the *exchange*. During a conversation, you speak and listen. Before a conversation can take place, an introduction must occur.

Introduction Many people feel awkward in social situations. Fear of rejection may keep you from approaching someone to introduce yourself. Conquering this fear can improve your networking skills and increase the number of beneficial connections you form and maintain.

When you are introduced to someone, shake hands and repeat the other person's name. Don't address someone by first name until requested by the individual. Gender is no longer a consideration when initiating a handshake, but you should always stand for an introduction.

Introducing two people you know helps others form connections. Always use full names when performing an introduction. Include their job titles and company if you know the individuals professionally. When performing a social introduction, the sequence is based on age or gender. In business situations, always present the lower-ranked individual to the person of higher rank. Gender is not a consideration. Identify the higher-ranked individual first and present the lower-ranked person as shown in Figure 19.3.

FIGURE 19.3   Introduction

Ned Thornton, this is Melissa Andrews, our new accountant.

Discussion Conversation follows an introduction or greeting. Remember that conversation is an exchange. However, people will think you are a better conversationalist if you listen a little more than you talk.

- Focus on the other person. Use positive body language by facing the other person and leaning slightly forward. Maintain eye contact.
- Your response shouldn't put the focus on you. Rather than telling about a similar situation you experienced, paraphrase the speaker's comments. **Paraphrasing** expresses the same information in different words, verifying that you have correctly understood and interpreted the speaker's thoughts. This process helps the speaker clarify or correct your interpretation and prevents misunderstandings or confusion. The speaker also has the opportunity to reveal additional details that support his or her statements.
- Use humor with caution. Offensive humor is never appropriate. If you offend someone, the negative information is just as likely to be passed around your network as complimentary information.

Closing If you just met the individual, always close the conversation by commenting that it was nice to meet the new person. Restate the individual's name and your name as shown in Figure 19.4. Many people forget names heard only during the introduction. This reminder helps your new connection remember your name, preventing future awkwardness.

FIGURE 19.4   Closing

It was nice to meet you Mr. Thornton. Feel free to contact me at Company A.
Just ask for Melissa Andrews in the accounting department.

After meeting someone, enter any important information into a personal database. If it's a new contact, enter the individual's name, title, company, and any other information you want to remember. Review this data before you meet with the person again.

Hypothetical Scenario

After some investigation, Gloria discovered that many sources provide counseling for couples that need to communicate, but few sources teach businesspeople to communicate with individuals. She began creating marketing materials for a seminar about one-on-one discussions. Much of the communication performed by businesspeople occurs between individuals rather than groups. The response she received from companies requesting the seminar was overwhelming.

Conduct a Meeting

The more meetings you attend, the faster you learn that some go well and others do not. You want the meetings you conduct to go smoothly. The participants should feel that their time was well spent rather than wasted. A good meeting must be well planned and efficiently conducted, and the participants must follow through with any necessary activities.

Before the Meeting

In many ways, preparing for a meeting is similar to preparing for a presentation. However, you control only the outline of topics and events for a meeting. You aren't the only speaker. The content discussed during a meeting is the result of the knowledge, experience, and activities of the participants. Before the meeting occurs, you must perform several tasks. The readiness of the participants is based on the amount of preparation work you and the other participants perform. Meetings can be called for three reasons—status, project, and problem.

Status meetings are held regularly, enabling participants to inform others of the progress or status of their current responsibilities. The topics and information discussed are usually general, involving participants from several groups. A specific issue isn't discussed in any great detail or depth. A business owner can hold a status meeting every quarter to inform employees of the company's performance and projections.

Project meetings are also held regularly. All participants are involved in the project. Advances and obstacles are discussed in depth. Participants may be given assignments to complete.

Problem meetings are held when a serious obstacle blocks progress on a project or a critical problem faces the company. Time is critical and tension is high. The participants include anyone who can provide additional information or contribute to the solution. Preparation time before the meeting may be limited, but you should perform as much preparation as possible.

Identify the Topic   Every meeting has a purpose and one or more focus topics. If you can't identify a purpose and topics for a meeting, the meeting isn't necessary. Your business has more time to conduct its business and earn profit if managers and workers aren't tied up in meetings that waste time without gaining any benefit.

Limit the number of major topics to be discussed. More than one or two serious issues is too much for most meetings. Additional topics result in a lack of focus and progress because the tasks seem overwhelming when faced at the same time. Individually, each topic may require easily identifiable steps to succeed.

The topics determine the participants who should attend the meeting. If you try to cover too many topics, the number of participants grows to an inefficient throng of attendees whose only interest is the 5–10 minutes when their project is discussed. The rest of the one-hour meeting is wasted time for them. Avoid this by identifying the focus of the meeting.

Make a list of topics for the meeting as shown in Figure 19.5. Verify that the topics are related.

FIGURE 19.5   Original List

- Customer A complained that our help desk was unable to solve her problem.
- Several customers complained that they waited on hold for 20 minutes before reaching a customer service representative.
- Two experienced customer service representatives left the company last month.
- Customer service calls have increased in the last six months.

If your list is too long, organize the list into one or two focus topics that can be addressed successfully during the meeting. You may discover that one or more of the topics are actually characteristics or symptoms belonging to the same topic. The organized list in Figure 19.6 establishes the focus for your meeting.

FIGURE 19.6   Organized List

Customers are dissatisfied with our service.

- Customer A complained that our help desk was unable to solve her problem.
- Several customers complained that they waited on hold for 20 minutes before reaching a customer service representative.
- Two experienced customer service representatives left the company last month.
- Customer service calls have increased in the last six months.

Identify the Participants If you have identified the focus topics for the meeting, creating a list of participants is simple. The individuals you invite vary, based on the organization chart and assigned responsibilities. After reviewing the list in Figure 19.6, it appears that the focus is on your company's customer service. The initial meeting should include the group leaders and manager in your customer service department.

Schedule the Participants and Location Most meetings require one or two key participants to accomplish your goals. For example, you identified the manager and the group leaders as participants in the meeting about customer satisfaction. However, the solution requires the presence of the manager and a majority of the group leaders. If one of the group leaders isn't available, the meeting can still proceed. If the manager and half of the group can't attend, you should schedule a different time.

Identify one or more potential meeting times and check with the required participants. Check schedules early in the process to ensure the availability of the participants who can make progress on the issue.

If your location has only one meeting room, keep a sign-up sheet next to the room. Individuals can use the sheet to reserve the room. If you have more than one meeting room, keep a notebook with your receptionist or a secretary. The notebook should contain sign-up sheets for all the meeting rooms. This enables an individual to select a free room without going to each room to check the schedule for the room. Meetings that occur regularly can easily be scheduled in advance. The same meeting room can be reserved for each meeting.

Each reservation identifies the individual making the reservation, the meeting to be held, the date, the time the meeting starts, and the time the meeting is expected to end. This information helps others schedule meetings before or after your reservation.

Create an Agenda An **agenda** identifies the topics to be covered during the meeting. It establishes priority and provides focus for discussions. You can identify the topic leader and the estimated time required for each item on the agenda. This keeps the discussion moving, preventing the group from getting sidetracked.

The agenda alerts the participants to the topics, enabling them to research any needed data or bring related information to the meeting. A topic leader should have input regarding the length and timing of the presentation.

The sample agenda in Figure 19.7 identifies the objective, topics, scheduled date and time, and participants. Based on the agenda, participants know what to expect, any needed preparation, and the amount of time the meeting requires.

FIGURE 19.7   Agenda

Agenda

Objective
Determine and repair the cause of customer dissatisfaction.

Time
May __, 9:00 A.M.–11:30 A.M.

Location
Meeting Room B

Participants
Chuck Youngho, Lily Evans, Bill Warsek, Jill Raymond, Seth Wilson

Agenda

Time	Leader	Topic
9:00–9:20	Lily Evans	Customer Support Statistics—Identify the number of support calls and time required to assist a customer.
9:20–10:00	Bill Warsek	Customer Support Procedures—Describe how customer requests are currently handled.
10:00–11:00	Brainstorm	Identify areas of potential improvement and suggest changes to current methods.
11:00–11:30	Wrap-Up	Summarize suggestions and make any necessary research assignments. Schedule a follow-up meeting.

Based on the agenda, participants know that two presentations are planned. They can begin thinking of ways to improve current customer service procedures. The process of improving customer service probably won't be completed in a single meeting. In the last item, participants close the meeting by identifying their suggestions and assigning areas of research before the next scheduled meeting.

Distribute the Agenda   If possible, distribute the agenda two to three days before the meeting, giving the participants time to prepare. Distribute the agenda via e-mail or send a hard copy to each participant. Call or e-mail the attendees to remind them of the meeting on the day before it occurs.

During the Meeting

Your goal is organized and effective meetings. Writing a good agenda is the first step in holding an organized meeting. The key is following the agenda. Several guidelines can make your meetings more effective.

Guidelines Effective meetings don't happen accidentally. You have prepared and invited the right people to participate. The events and discussions that happen during the meeting and the way they are handled determine the meeting's effectiveness.

- **Schedule**—Always start a meeting on time. The participants have better things to do than wait for a meeting to begin. Waiting irritates the participants who arrive on time, which means that the group will already be quarrelsome before the meeting starts, a bad emotional environment for any meeting. If participants know that your meetings always start on time, they will make an effort to arrive on time.

- **Behavior**—Encourage participants to behave professionally. Attendees often feel strongly about an issue and disagreements within a business are common. Discussion, not a shouting match, is the key to resolving a disagreement and moving forward.

- **Research**—If an issue requires additional research, assign a group or individual to gather the needed information. Set a completion date and identify how the information will be distributed to those who need it.

- **Subgroup**—If a topic warrants further discussion, set up a subgroup that can meet separately. This practice prevents a single aspect of the larger topic from holding up progress for the entire group.

Prepare Minutes Three days or three months after a meeting, one of the participants may need to know what happened in a meeting. Individuals who were invited but weren't able to attend also need to know what occurred. **Minutes** meet this need by providing a brief summary of the meeting. During every meeting, one participant must be assigned to take the minutes.

Minutes are meant to summarize the meeting. Every comment doesn't need to be recorded. The easiest and most efficient way to take minutes is to start with the agenda, which already has information about the meeting and the scheduled topics.

Minutes should contain the meeting's objective, time, participants who attended, and participants who did not attend. It also summarizes the presentations and discussions, as well as identifies any assignments made or subgroups formed. If scheduled, the date of the follow-up meeting is recorded. The sample minutes in Figure 19.8 summarize the meeting about customer dissatisfaction.

FIGURE 19.8 Minutes

Minutes

Objective
Determine and repair the cause of customer dissatisfaction.

Time
May __, 9:00 A.M.–11:30 A.M.

Attendees
Chuck Youngho, Lily Evans, Bill Warsek, Jill Raymond

Absent
Seth Wilson

Topics
Lily Evans presented information about customer support statistics. Customer service calls have increased 20 percent in the last six months. Two experienced customer service representatives left the company last month. Both claimed to be "frustrated" with their work. Replacements haven't been hired and the remaining representatives are overscheduled.

Bill Warsek described the procedures followed by customer support. Currently, any available representative picks up calls. If technical information is needed, the call is placed in a queue for a technical support representative.

Activities
Brainstorming
- Call handling was identified as an area of potential improvement. A separate phone number can be provided for technical support, eliminating a level of call handling.
- Corporate customers can be assigned to a specific representative or group of representatives. This ensures that the representative is familiar with the customer and can provide more knowledgeable assistance.
- Provide additional training for customer service representatives.

Assignments
Bill Warsek will investigate the cost of establishing a phone number for tech support.
Lily Evans will investigate training suggestions from current representatives.

Next Meeting
May __, 9:00 A.M.–11:30 A.M.

After the Meeting

An effective meeting doesn't end when the participants leave. Meetings don't create progress unless they result in actions. Any assignments must be completed and decisions must be carried out.

The individual in charge of the meeting approves the minutes before they are distributed. Give the approved minutes to all attendees who were invited to the meeting, not just the ones who were absent. The minutes remind attendees of the suggestions and decisions made. Often, the minutes can clear up any confusion attendees felt during the meeting by clearly stating the events and decisions.

Hypothetical Scenario

Ineffective meetings are common in many businesses. Transforming these meetings can greatly increase a company's productivity. After receiving many requests for seminars teaching effective meeting skills, Gloria began to prepare the materials for a seminar.

Negotiate Successfully

Conducting business is the process of exchanging one item for another. Typically, you exchange your product or service for money. However the exchange isn't always so simple. When an exchange is suggested, an opportunity for negotiation is created.

Negotiation Skills

Negotiating is the process of dealing with another party to reach an agreement. Negotiating involves discussion and compromise. Both sides usually make concessions during a negotiation.

In some business exchanges, negotiation is not expected. For example, you don't negotiate the price of lettuce with the cashier when you go to a grocery store or the price of a hamburger at a fast-food restaurant. On the other hand, consumers expect to negotiate when they purchase more expensive items such as a house or a car.

Business owners making an exchange frequently negotiate because many prices aren't set as firmly as the price of lettuce in the grocery store. Conditions, such as the quantity ordered or the frequency of an order, can be altered to receive a different price. In other words, the price is negotiable. A business owner negotiates with suppliers, lenders, employees, and some customers, particularly if the customer is a business.

Skillful negotiation can resolve current conflicts and avoid future disputes. When a negotiation is successful, both parties should be satisfied with the agreement. Neither party should feel that it paid too much or received too little. This mutual satisfaction is known as a win-win situation because both parties benefit from the agreement. Successful negotiators have several specific skills, shown in Figure 19.9. Many of these skills can be learned and improved through experience.

- **Research**—Investigate the current availability and value of the items involved in the negotiation. This identifies the acceptable value of the items.
- **Listen**—Watch the other party's body language. Listen when the other party speaks. This enables you to analyze the party's reaction to your offer and evaluate the offers made by the other party.
- **Insight**—Researching before negotiations and listening closely during the negotiation can help you understand the other party's need. If you know what the other party really needs, you can adjust your offer to meet the need. This may mean that your offer has more value to the other party than it does

to you. For example, you have available storage space. Your supplier has more merchandise than she can store. You offer to purchase a large quantity for a lower price. You gain by paying a lower price and the supplier gains by freeing storage space and receiving a profit for the merchandise, even if the profit is a little less than originally planned.

- **Fairness**—Your offer must be fair. If you offer low value for a high-value gain, the other party will be insulted and may refuse to negotiate any further.
- **Presentation**—The method you use to present the potential exchange depends on the other party and the items involved. Make your presentation more impressive when the other party is powerful in the business world and the items have great value. For example, if you want to construct a building, but require agreement from local businesses and landowners, you may construct a model of the building to demonstrate the appearance of the finished building.
- **Flexibility**—Be prepared to offer unusual items or combinations to obtain the desired item. The other party is looking for some value you can offer. Rather than money, your business neighbor could ask you to photocopy fliers in exchange for placing your ad in his newsletter.
- **Behavior**—At all times, your behavior must remain professional. Negotiation occurs between adults. Emotional statements or offensive remarks are not acceptable.

FIGURE 19.9   Negotiation Skills

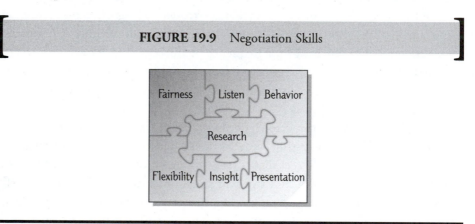

Negotiation Guidelines

Skill can result in successful negotiations. However, consider other factors and guidelines when you begin to negotiate:

- The parties you negotiate with are often individuals or businesses involved in long-term relationships with your business. Sometimes, it is better to give a little extra to keep the relationship solid. For example, when you deal with a supplier all the time, it doesn't pay to negotiate harshly in a specific instance. The goodwill of your suppliers is a long-term benefit that can be vital if you ask for special considerations in the future. The short-term gain in a single exchange isn't worth the loss of the supplier's goodwill.

- A successful negotiation isn't complete until the exchange occurs. If one of the parties avoids delivery, the negotiation wasn't successful.
- All of your business activities affect your reputation. Other businesses and customers can discover information about your behavior. Be sure that your behavior doesn't reflect poorly on your business.
- Compromise is part of negotiating. You might not get everything you want.

Contrary to popular sentiment, everything doesn't have a price. You may encounter an individual or business that simply refuses to negotiate. Don't waste your time and energy trying to force the reluctant party to negotiate. If you fail to receive a positive response after you've informed the party that you are interested, drop it and move on to other opportunities.

Hypothetical Scenario

Gloria's business was definitely growing. The latest seminar she added to her repertoire focused on negotiation skills. Businesses that held previous seminars quickly called to schedule the latest addition. After the seminar, businesses were happy to provide testimonials praising the effect the seminars were having within the company and how they were improving the company's relationships with customers and suppliers. Customers were more satisfied and conflict between employees dropped significantly, increasing everyone's productivity and job satisfaction.

Technology Insights

Electronic Meetings

Every day, business meetings take place all over the world. Attendees no longer have to be in the same place to attend a business meeting. Participants can be anywhere in the world. If you are out of town to meet with a client, you can also attend a meeting taking place in your office, hundreds of miles away.

Requirements include a personal computer at each end, a camera to provide images, and specialized software. Additional software features can include an electronic whiteboard, a tool that enables participants to sketch or record ideas that are visible to all participants.

The technology has some disadvantages. The participants notice a delay or lack of synchronicity between the video and audio, which can be distracting. The delay makes it more difficult for participants to take turns speaking. This causes interruptions and less assertive people may remain silent during the meeting. The camera can't focus on each individual who is speaking, so a remote attendee may not know who is making a comment or suggestion. The remote viewer also misses the body language of the speakers, which is often just as important as the spoken words.

Think Critically Describe how electronic meetings can affect the business world.

CHAPTER REVIEW

Fear of public speaking is common. Many individuals have conquered their fear to become excellent speakers. The setting for a presentation should enable your audience to enjoy and understand the presentation. This means it should be comfortable and provide all the needed facilities. The content must be understandable and interesting to the audience. If you give the presentation more than once, you may need to modify the content to reach the audience. An animated speaker who uses props and audiovisual materials delivers a more effective presentation than a speaker who simply reads the content to the audience.

Customers, friends, suppliers, and business associates are members of your personal network. They can introduce you to others who may become connections who can help you professionally. Good conversation skills help you interact successfully with your customers and connections.

Many companies hold meetings that turn out to be a waste of time. You can increase the effectiveness of your meetings through planning, creating an agenda before the meeting, and following the agenda during the meeting. After a meeting, write minutes that summarize the meeting. Distribute the minutes to all participants. Be sure that any follow-up activities are completed.

Negotiating is considered a life skill. It is used in many situations every day. Individuals negotiate with friends, parents, and spouses regularly. Negotiation also occurs in the business world to resolve current conflicts and avoid future disputes. Successful negotiators use their communication skills to present solutions and persuade the other party.

USE BUSINESS TERMS

Fill in the blanks with the appropriate term.

agenda   negotiate
conversation   networking
facilities   paraphrasing
flip chart   prop
mentor   teleprompter
minutes   videoconference

1. Effective speakers often use ___?___ to emphasize a particular point.
2. Meeting participants can record suggestions on a(n) ___?___ to stimulate the interest of the audience.
3. ___?___ is an effective way to make connections that can help your business succeed.
4. During a(n) ___?___, you speak and listen.

5. ___?___ helps the speaker clarify or correct your interpretation of his or her comments and prevents misunderstandings or confusion.

6. The ___?___ for a meeting can be based on its agenda.

7. Concessions are usually made by both sides when they ___?___.

TEST YOUR READING

8. Identify several reasons for a business owner to give a presentation.

9. Describe how a speaker prepares to give a presentation.

10. Why is a U-shape a good seating arrangement for a presentation?

11. Why do speakers use audiovisual materials?

12. How frequently should an audience take breaks during a presentation?

13. Why is networking important?

14. What is a mentor?

15. How can you remember someone's name after an introduction?

16. Why are meetings held?

17. Why are the minutes useful after a meeting?

18. What is the purpose of negotiating?

19. Identify the skills used by a good negotiator.

THINK CRITICALLY ABOUT BUSINESS

20. Identify a good presentation you attended. Explain why the presentation and the speaker were memorable.

21. Identify five individuals in your network of connections. How can you make additional connections?

22. Describe the characteristics of a friend you enjoy talking to regularly. Why is he or she a good conversationalist?

23. Write an agenda for a meeting to identify ways to rally support for or against a current political issue.

REAL-LIFE BUSINESS
Pixar Animation Studios

Children and adults alike view Pixar's animated films with delight. Unusual creatures, animals, or toys with very human stories attract large audiences to the theater. Steve Jobs established Pixar in 1986 when he purchased the computer graphics division from Lucasfilm, Ltd. The 44 employees transformed from a division to an entire company with the purchase.

As the company began developing animation tools and techniques, it also began winning awards. In 1987, Pixar won the Golden Gate Award for computer-generated imagery and Pixar began making animated short films. In 1989, Pixar made its first commercial for a business client, Tropicana.

The production of commercials generated income. In 1991, Pixar and Walt Disney agreed to create and distribute feature-length animated films. Computer-generated animation was finally ready for the public.

Pixar enjoyed a big year in 1995, the year it went public, selling shares of the business on the stock market. *Toy Story,* the first animated film to be fully computer-generated, was released during the Thanksgiving weekend. The film was a huge success. In 1998, A *Bug's Life* was released. Again, the public flocked to the theaters. Only a year later, *Toy Story 2* was released. It earned more than the original film. In 2001, *Monsters, Inc.* was another success and Pixar grew to 600 employees. *Finding Nemo* is scheduled for release in 2003.

Think Critically

1. Where did Pixar find its original employees?
2. What is Pixar's main product?
3. Why is the product unique?
4. What else has Steve Jobs done?

CHAPTER 20

Written Communication

GOALS

- ♦ Describe the characteristics of effective written communication
- ♦ Write business correspondence
- ♦ Prepare a press release
- ♦ Create a proposal

Marc Haefner waited anxiously in the doctor's office. He picked up and discarded several magazines. Who could settle down to read a magazine article, especially knowing that there may not be time to read a complete article? He glanced at another waiting patient when she pulled a newsletter from a local craft group out of her purse to read. When the nurse called her name, she placed the newsletter back in her purse before following the nurse to an exam room. A quick glance around the waiting room confirmed Marc's suspicion. No newsletters were displayed in the room. It was then that Marc conceived the idea of producing newsletters for doctors' offices.

Effective Written Communication

Long after you leave a meeting or hang up the phone, your words live on for your clients, employees, and suppliers—if they are written down. When you aren't able to speak in person, a letter, memo, or e-mail conveys your thoughts and represents you to the recipient. Like verbal communication, your written words can affect the success of your business.

You don't have to write like a best-selling author to produce effective business documents and correspondence. Your documents should be concise, well organized, and easy to understand. Several guidelines can help you write more effective business documents.

Guidelines

Every day, businesses produce millions of documents. Piled on desktops, tacked on cubicle walls, displayed on company bulletin boards, stored in file cabinets for years, or dropped immediately into the recycling bin, these documents have destinations. A document's destination is determined by its timeliness and importance.

Documents that aren't important to your main business functions may be saved for a few days or recycled immediately. For example, after attending the company picnic, employees throw away the directions and the signup sheet.

Documents that provide critical information are saved for a longer period of time. Documents such as correspondence with customers, status reports, and project schedules are usually stored together as project materials. These documents are stored with active projects until the project is complete. After completion, the documents may be moved to a location that is less accessible but the files can still be recovered for future reference.

Regardless if your words are read and recycled or used as a template for future documents, each document creates an impression of your character, priorities, and experience. To exhibit your best business skills, your documents must be well organized, clear, and accurate.

Organization Documents that follow a logical pattern are easier to understand than free-flowing text. When a document is organized in a **logical** manner, the sequence of facts or arrangement of elements is predictable. Predictability helps the reader understand the document because he or she expects what is coming next. You can provide predictability by structuring the information and following a common format.

Structure Based on its structure, you recognize a knock-knock joke immediately. In fact, you start smiling when you hear the first two words, "Knock knock." Since you recognize the structure, you can immediately respond, "Who's there?" The content of the joke varies, but the structure is always the same. The **structure** of a document defines the sequence in which the content appears.

Reporters around the world use the five Ws and H—who, what, where, when, why, and how, to structure a news story. Every document should answer these questions, whether you are setting up a meeting or requesting additional funding from your banker or investors:

- **Who**—Identify the individuals or businesses associated with the event.
- **What**—Identify the event or topic of the document or a specific section of the document.
- **Where**—Identify the location of the event selected in the first question.
- **When**—Identify the time and date for the event.
- **Why**—Identify the reason the event occurred.
- **How**—Identify the manner in which the event occurred.

To create an organized document, organize your thoughts. The following process identifies the information you want to communicate, groups similar information, and determines the sequence in which the information should appear in the document.

1. **List**—Make a list of the information to be included in the document as shown in Figure 20.1.

FIGURE 20.1   List of Information

50 participants

Individual meetings

Learn new methods.

Five meetings required.

Price is $60 per hour.

Initial consultation is two hours.

Follow-up meetings are one hour each.

Measure existing performance before you start.

Analyze before the first meeting.

Follow-up visits every two weeks.

Provide new measurement criteria.

Measure changes over time.

---

2. **Group**—Organize the list by grouping information that is closely related as shown in Figure 20.2. Grouping similar information creates paragraphs, a group of sentences focused on a single point.

FIGURE 20.2   Organized List of Information

50 participants
Individual meetings
Five meetings required.

Price is $60 per hour.
Initial consultation is two hours.
Follow-up meetings are one hour each.

Follow-up visits every two weeks.
Measure changes over time.

Measure existing performance before you start.
Analyze before the first meeting.
Learn new methods.
Provide new measurement criteria.

---

3. **Sequence**—Move each group of information so the document follows a logical sequence. Figure 20.3 shows the rearranged order. The sequence in this example is based on the order in which the meetings occur, followed by the price of the package. Use one of several common methods to determine a logical sequence.

- **General to specific**—Information that applies to all of the elements is given before information that applies to only a portion of the elements. For example, all local restaurants are crowded on the weekend, but only a few require reservations.
- **Specific to general**—Information that applies to a single situation is given before information that applies to a large number of elements. For example, Tom and Celia are getting a divorce. Fifty percent of marriages end in divorce.
- **Major importance to minor importance**—Provide critical information before the supporting details. News reports follow this sequence because readers usually read only the first paragraph or two of each story. If the most critical information is provided first, readers can skip the rest of the article without missing the critical data.
- **Easy to difficult**—Simple methods or tasks form a platform for elements that are more complicated or require more skill or effort. Documents designed to teach a skill follow this sequence, building new skills from existing abilities.
- **Cause and effect**—The first element results in the second element. For example, the absence of a traffic light caused the car accident.
- **Chronological order**—Elements are presented in order of occurrence. For example, start the tune slowly and gradually increase the tempo.
- **Alphabetical order**—Use the alphabet to arrange the elements. Lists of names are often presented in alphabetical order.
- **Numerical**—Base the sequence of elements on rank or current order, such as a contestant's post position in a race or a student's class standing.
- **Size**—The sequence is based on quantity, such as the number of participants or the number of products in stock.

FIGURE 20.3   Organized List of Information in Sequence

Information	Sequenced By
50 participants Individual meetings Five meetings required.	general
Measure existing performance before you start. Analyze before the first meeting. Learn new methods. Provide new measurement criteria.	chronological
Follow-up visits every two weeks. Measure changes over time.	chronological
Price is $60 per hour. Initial consultation is two hours. Follow-up meetings are one hour each.	specific

4. **Headings**—Longer documents use headings to identify groups of information. A **heading,** short for headline, is a title or subtitle that identifies the topic of the information. Figure 20.4 demonstrates the headings that could be used for a document containing several pages.

FIGURE 20.4   Sequenced List with Headings

Introduction
50 participants
Individual meetings
Five meetings required.

Procedures
Measure existing performance before you start.
Analyze before the first meeting.
Learn new methods.
Provide new measurement criteria.
Follow-up visits every two weeks.
Measure changes over time.

Pricing
Price is $60 per hour.
Initial consultation is two hours.
Follow-up meetings are one hour each.

Format The appearance of the document, known as its **format,** also helps a reader understand its content. Format applies to all business documents. Letters, e-mails, reports, and other common document types have formats recognized by most readers. For example, a business letter contains information, such as your address, the date, and the name of the addressee, in specific locations. You can use variations of these formats to create a customized look for your business. Several elements, shown in Figure 20.5 can be altered.

♦ **Stationery**—The paper on which your documents are printed is **stationery.** Many businesses purchase paper that is thicker, tinted, and preprinted with specific information. **Letterhead,** commonly used for letters, is a sheet of stationery that is preprinted or engraved, usually with the logo, name, and address of your business. Matching envelopes are often purchased with the letterhead stationery.

♦ **Margins**—The area outside the main printing on a sheet of paper is the **margin.** Alter the width of the margin to change a document's appearance. Some stationery has preprinted text or graphics in the margin.

♦ **Font**—A set of type that has a specific appearance is a **font.** Often, headings are printed in a different font than the main body of the text.

- ◆ **Color**—The appearance of a document that uses only black print on white paper doesn't attract attention. A document that uses color can create interest before a single word is read. Opportunities for color include graphics, headings, and art in the margins.
- ◆ **Headers**—The text that appears in the margin at the top of the page in a long document is the **header.** A header contains information you want repeated at the top of every page or every other page of a document. A header contains information such as the name of the document, the page number, or your company's name.
- ◆ **Footers**—The text that appears in the margin at the bottom of the page in a long document is the **footer.** A footer contains information you want repeated at the bottom of every page or every other page of a document. A footer contains information such as the name of the document, the page number, or your company's name.

FIGURE 20.5   Format Elements

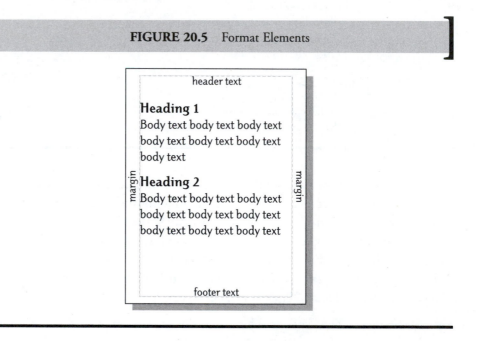

Clarity You don't get paid for each word, so making a document longer than necessary wastes time for you and the reader and can create confusion rather than clarity. Most people don't read business documents for fun. They want the necessary data to be supplied as quickly and simply as possible. If you bury the information in too many unnecessary words, the reader may give up before finding it.

Graphics add interest to your document by breaking up the text. They also add clarity by illustrating the important facts in the document. For many people, graphics are much easier to remember because of the visual impact. Compare your response to the following sentence to the impact of the chart in Figure 20.6. In the first quarter, sales for each month were $820, $900, and $1,200, consecutively.

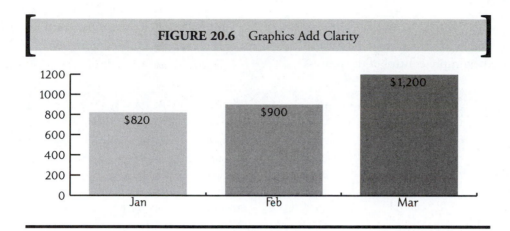

FIGURE 20.6   Graphics Add Clarity

Accuracy Mistakes lower the value of your document. Spelling or typographical errors imply that your work is sloppy and careless. Factual errors display a lack of knowledge. Errors such as misquoting a price or misspelling the customer's name can kill a project before it starts.

Before any document leaves your desk or your business, be sure it is reviewed for accuracy. Use the spell checker that is featured in your word processing software. Most spell checkers alert the user when they encounter misspelled words or grammatical errors. If another person isn't available to examine it, take a break for an hour before you reread the document for errors. The break clears the document from your immediate thoughts and increases the chance that you will find any errors. Many projects have been lost because of errors that could have been caught and fixed before releasing the document.

Wording

Your documents represent you when you aren't available. Just as you dress up to meet with a client, your document must be at its best. Good business documents look and sound professional. They follow the rules of grammar and they don't use slang or offensive terms. The author creates a document's image by selecting specific words.

Adjectives Words that describe nouns, such as *profitable* business and *large* office, are adjectives. Increase the impact of your document by using adjectives with a positive business image. The list of adjectives in Figure 20.7 can improve your business documents.

FIGURE 20.7   Adjectives

accurate	complete	direct	fundamental	original	qualified	tangible
advanced	comprehensive	distinctive	generic	permanent	quick	temporary
affordable	concise	economical	independent	popular	reliable	unique
attractive	consistent	effective	informative	powerful	skilled	unlimited
common	convenient	efficient	innovative	practical	specific	useful
compact	creative	experienced	necessary	precise	successful	valuable
competitive	dependable	fresh	new	professional	superior	

Verbs Actions are expressed by verbs. Some verbs, including those listed in Figure 20.8, are more powerful than others in the business environment because they imply control of the process.

FIGURE 20.8   Verbs

accommodate	assist	complete	design	estimate	gain	maintain
act	attain	conduct	develop	evaluate	generate	manage
adapt	balance	consolidate	diagnose	examine	identify	perform
administer	build	coordinate	direct	expand	implement	prepare
allocate	calculate	control	educate	expedite	increase	resolve
analyze	clarify	create	enable	extract	initiate	support
assemble	communicate	define	ensure	forecast	launch	track
assess	compile	demonstrate	establish	formulate	lead	verify

Hypothetical Scenario

No one knew more about effective written communication than Marc Haefner. Fifteen years of writing marketing materials honed Marc's skills to a fine edge. After some research, he prepared three separate newsletters, each directed at a different medical specialty. Each newsletter contained some shared material and some specialized articles highlighting developments or treatments in each medical area.

Write Business Correspondence

Business is often conducted through meetings and verbal exchanges. However, written correspondence in the form of letters, e-mail, and memos are used to confirm details, make official offers, and form agreements. To correspond with clients, employees, and other professionals, use the following writing techniques that make your documents more effective.

Business Letters

Even though much business correspondence is carried out electronically, traditional letters printed on stationery are still the preferred contact method for many situations. For example, most companies send an offer letter to extend a job offer. The ability to sign the document provides a legal advantage over electronic communication.

Guidelines Business letters should be as brief as possible, usually fitting on a single sheet of paper. If the information you want to send requires more than one page, create a separate sheet that can be sent as an attachment.

Many writers overuse the pronoun "I" in their correspondence. Use "you" more often.

Common fonts, such as Times Roman and Arial, present a professional image. Avoid fonts that are less common. The font size should be between 10 and 13 points.

This is large enough to read easily and small enough to fit a reasonable amount of text on a page.

Address your letter to a specific person in the company. If you don't know the right person to address, call the company and ask. Verify the individual's job title and the correct spelling for his or her name.

Format The most common formats are the full block style and modified block style, shown in Figure 20.9. The text in a letter using the **full block style** is always left justified. Some text in a letter using the **modified block style** starts in the middle of a line.

FIGURE 20.9   Common Formats for Letters

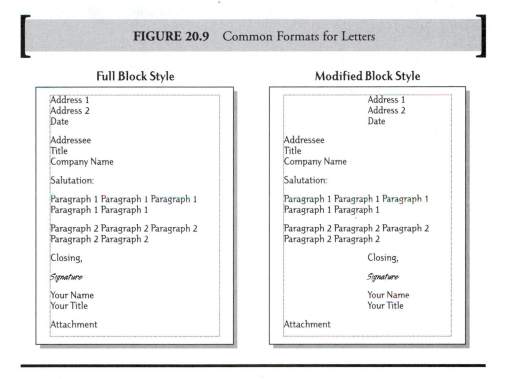

The full block style is considered more formal than the modified block style. Indenting your address and the closing is similar to the format of a friendly letter, creating the impression that this format is more casual. Regardless of which format you select, the elements in the letter are the same.

- **Your address**—Your mailing address appears first in the document. If your stationery has your address preprinted, don't repeat your address here. Optionally, you can include your e-mail address on a separate line after your regular mailing address.
- **Date**—Older typing books dictate that the date should appear on line 12. If you are using letterhead stationery, you may need to adjust the spacing so the date is a reasonable distance from the preprinted text or graphics.
- **Addressee**—Insert four blank lines. Type the full name of the person receiving the letter. For example, type "Jane Doe" or "John Smith."

- **Addressee's title**—Verify the addressee's job title by making a quick phone call or checking previous correspondence you received from the individual.
- **Company name**—Use the full name of the company, including any punctuation.
- **Recipient's address**—Enter the addressee's full mailing address.
- **Salutation**—Insert a blank line. The word or phrase that appears before the body of the letter is the salutation. The easiest salutation is "Dear Jill Smith:" which avoids the issue of selecting Mrs. or Ms. If you prefer to use Mr. or Ms., verify the recipient's gender. Names such as Chris, Kelley, and Jamie can be used by either gender. The colon (:) after the salutation is appropriate for business correspondence.
- **Body**—Insert a blank line after the salutation and between each paragraph of the body. The blank line may not be necessary if your software automatically adds extra space before each paragraph. Generally, the first paragraph contains an introduction or describes the reason for this contact. The middle paragraphs contain the details and supporting information. The last paragraph provides a summary and tells the recipient how to contact you.
- **Closing**—The concluding word or phrase indicates that the body of the message is complete. "Sincerely" is a common closing for business correspondence.
- **Your name**—Insert four blank lines to allow space for you to sign your name after printing the letter. Type your name the same way you sign it. For example, don't sign "Shelley" and type "Michelle."
- **Your title**—Type your job title under your name.
- **Attachment**—Insert two blank lines. The word "Attachment" alerts the recipient that an attachment is part of the mailing. If an attachment isn't included in this mailing, leave the line blank.

E-mail

The use of electronic mail is becoming more popular. However, many people send e-mails to business associates that sound like they are chatting with a friend. Even though e-mail is a more casual form of communication, when you use it to write business correspondence, follow the more formal guidelines used in business letters.

Guidelines Business e-mails should be as brief as possible, usually fitting on a single screen. If you send attachments, contact the recipient to verify that he or she has the software to open the document.

Use software that screens your incoming messages and attachments for computer viruses. A **virus** is a program hidden in a message or attachment that performs an undesirable act such as destroying your computer files or sending messages to every e-mail address in the address book of your e-mail program.

Many writers overuse the pronoun "I" in their correspondence. Use "you" more often.

Common fonts, such as Times Roman and Arial, present a professional image. Avoid fonts that are less common. The font size should be between 10 and 13 points.

This is large enough to read easily and small enough to fit a reasonable amount of text on a screen.

Call the company to verify the addressee's job title and the correct spelling for his or her name. Mistakes irritate recipients before they read your message.

Format Some of the format decisions are dictated by the features and limitations of the e-mail program you use. For example, some of the most basic applications don't enable you to select the font used in your messages. More advanced e-mail applications enable you to design "stationery" that is used as a background for the e-mail messages you send. The stationery can include color, a logo, and graphics, as well as the name, address, and phone number for your company.

When an e-mail is received, it is displayed in a list with other e-mails that have arrived. The list identifies the sender, the topic, and a time stamp that states the day and time the e-mail arrived. Figure 20.10 illustrates an e-mail that has been prepared to send and the same e-mail after it is received.

FIGURE 20.10 E-mail Format

E-mail to Send | E-mail Received by Customer

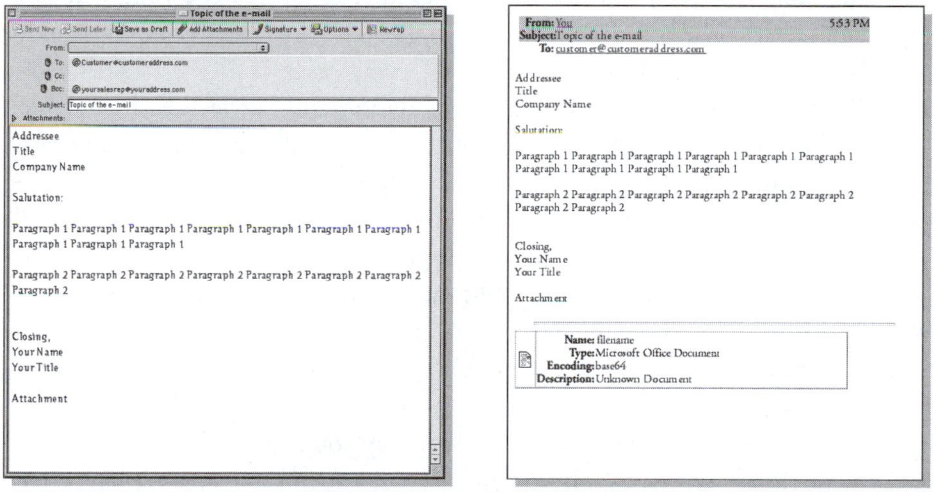

Many elements used in a business letter are also present in business e-mail. The ability to attach an electronic file has advantages over sending a paper copy of the same document. The recipient can modify and return the attached file.

- **To**—Enter the addressee's e-mail address.
- **cc**—Enter the e-mail address of any additional individual who should receive a copy of this e-mail. Recipients listed in this field usually aren't expected to take any action because of the message. They are simply informed about the subject. The recipient identified in the "To:" field will know these people received a copy of the message.

- **bcc**—Enter the e-mail address of any additional individuals who should receive a copy of this e-mail. The recipient identified in the "To:" field will *not* know these people received a copy of the message.
- **Subject**—Identify the topic of the e-mail.
- **Attach**—Identify the document to be sent to the recipient with the message. If an attachment isn't included with this e-mail, leave the line blank. In the e-mail received by the customer, the paper clip icon indicates the presence of an attachment.
- **Addressee**—Type the full name of the person receiving the e-mail. For example, type "Jane Doe" or "John Smith."
- **Addressee's title**—Verify the addressee's job title by making a quick phone call or checking previous correspondence you received from the individual.
- **Company name**—Use the full name of the company, including any punctuation.
- **Recipient's address**—Enter the addressee's full mailing address.
- **Salutation**—Insert a blank line. The word or phrase that appears before the body of the letter is the salutation. The easiest salutation is "Dear Jill Smith:" which avoids the issue of selecting Mrs. or Ms. If you prefer to use Mr. or Ms., verify the recipient's gender. Names such as Chris, Kelley, and Jamie can be used by either gender. The colon (:) after the salutation is appropriate for business correspondence.
- **Body**—Insert a blank line after the salutation and between each paragraph of the body. The blank line may not be necessary if your software automatically adds extra space before each paragraph. Generally, the first paragraph contains an introduction or describes the reason for this contact. The middle paragraphs contain the details and supporting information. The last paragraph provides a summary and tells the recipient how to contact you.
- **Closing**—The concluding word or phrase indicates that the body of the message is complete. "Sincerely" is a common closing for business correspondence.
- **Your name**—Type your name the same way you sign it.
- **Your title**—Type your job title under your name.
- **Signature**—Some e-mail programs enable you to create and store a **signature,** which can contain graphics or text. The signature can be automatically added to every message you send. Therefore, you can place data such as your contact information in the signature to save the time and effort required to enter the information every time.

Memo

A brief document written for interoffice communication is a **memorandum,** commonly called a memo. Use memos to announce meetings, promotions, or new employees. Memo topics could include a new procedure for processing orders, details about the company Christmas party, or new parking information while the lot is repaved. A memo doesn't leave your company.

Guidelines A memo is more casual than a formal document sent to a customer. However, the content should still be organized, clear, and accurate.

Common fonts, such as Times Roman and Arial, present a professional image. Avoid fonts that are less common. The font size should be between 10 and 13 points. This is large enough to read easily and small enough to fit a reasonable amount of text on a page.

Anyone in a company can send a memo, regardless of the rank of the sender or the receivers. You can send a memo to an individual, a list of individuals, a group, a department, or the entire company.

Format The casual approach to a memo is reflected in the format, which is less formal than business correspondence sent to customers. For example, memos are usually printed on plain white paper rather than the company's stationery.

The company's name may not appear anywhere in the document. As shown in Figure 20.11, the title of the sender and receiver are rarely in the document unless the company is very large.

FIGURE 20.11   Memo Format

Memorandum

To:	Recipients
From:	Your Name
Subject:	Topic of Memo
Date:	Today's Date
cc:	Additional Recipients

Paragraph 1 Paragraph 1 Paragraph 1 Paragraph 1 Paragraph 1 Paragraph 1 Paragraph 1 Paragraph 1 Paragraph 1 Paragraph 1 Paragraph 1 Paragraph 1 Paragraph 1

Several elements in a business letter aren't included in a memo. The address, title, and company name of the sender and recipients aren't included. A formal salutation and closing are also omitted.

- **To**—Enter the names of the recipients.
- **From**—Enter your name.
- **Subject**—Identify the topic of the memo.
- **Date**—Identify the day the memo was sent.
- **cc**—Enter the names of any additional individuals who should receive a copy of this memo. Individuals listed in this field aren't usually expected to take

any action because of the message. They are simply informed about the subject. The recipient identified in the "To:" field will know these people received a copy of the message.

- **Body**—Insert a blank line between each paragraph of the body. The blank line may not be necessary if your software automatically adds extra space before each paragraph.

Hypothetical Scenario

Marc distributed sample copies of his newsletters to dozens of medical offices in the city. He included a cover letter that described the newsletter service he offered. Details in the cover letter included the frequency of new editions, the number of copies to be printed, and the price for the newsletter service.

Prepare a Press Release

When you look through the business section of your local newspaper, you often see stories about local businesses. Sometimes, the business is small and the story contains information about a special display or the opening of a second location. Reporters don't go from business to business asking every owner if he or she has done anything that could be newsworthy. Since the reporter won't come to you, you must go to the reporter.

Role of a Press Release

Marketing is the process of promoting, selling, and distributing your product or service. As described in Chapter 17, public relations is a marketing activity, a component of the marketing mix. Publicity, information about a company's activities that is covered by the news media without payment, is an inexpensive method of bringing your business into the public eye. Press releases help you affect or control information about your company distributed to the public via the news media. In Figure 20.12, you can see the relationship between press releases, a single method of creating publicity, and marketing.

FIGURE 20.12   Relationship between Press Releases and Marketing

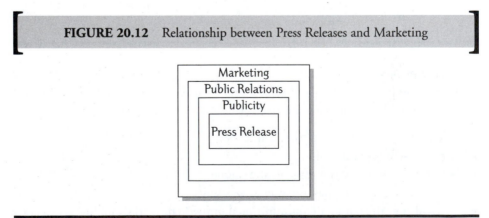

A **press release** is a statement prepared for distribution to the media. It is one of the most important tools you can use to communicate with your investors, customers, and consumers through the media. By preparing a press release, you are neatly packaging the information you want distributed. Presenting a press release that is well written, thorough, and timely increases the chance that the press release will be published. A press release can be used to accomplish several objectives.

- **Announce a significant event that occurs for your company.** Significant events include winning an award, sponsoring an event, opening a new office, hiring or promoting new corporate officers, or introducing a new product.
- **Interest the media in writing about your product or company.** Although you may be tempted to call the media when an event occurs, a press release is the method of contact preferred by the media.
- **Create awareness of your company or your product.** Depending on the level of media coverage generated by your press release, thousands or millions of people could be exposed to your company or your product.

The level of press coverage generated by a press release is based partly on the potential impact on the audience. For example, if you own one sandwich shop that employs 15 part-time workers and you open a second sandwich shop on the other side of town, your press release might generate some local coverage because it is a local event. It affects the potential employees and consumers near the new location. If it is a new neighborhood and you own the first restaurant in the area, it generates more interest than it would in a well-developed area with several restaurants. If you own a major American software company that employs thousands of workers and you open another office in a different state or a different country, your press release might generate national or international news.

A press release is intended to provide information for journalists. Regardless if the media ever use the press release, it can be an effective marketing tool. You can distribute a press release at a trade show or speaking engagement, mail it to associations related to your industry, or include it in a direct mailing package.

Guidelines

Several guidelines can help you prepare a press release to be used by the media. A submitted press release that appears to follow a standard format and structure will receive more attention from the media.

- **Verify the facts.** Never give information to the media that hasn't been checked. If they find mistakes when they verify the information independently, you will lose credibility.
- **Use a journalistic style.** Avoid long, flowery phrases that aren't appropriate for a news story. Don't include personal opinions. Use the third person. For example, describe "the company," not "my company." Refer to yourself by name, not "I" or "me."
- **Write in a simple and straightforward manner.** Use brief sentences.

- **Use letterhead stationery.** The letterhead stationery makes the press release appear more legitimate and professional.
- **Place the important information first.** Use the five Ws and H—who, what, where, when, why, and how. The headline, lead paragraph, and body contain the information that you want to distribute. Keep the most important information near the top so readers won't miss any critical details if they stop at the halfway point. Limit the press release to two pages.
- **The headline must attract the reader's attention.** Keep it short, never more than a sentence in length.
- **The lead paragraph is critical.** Readers will either stop here or read most of the press release. Set the tone for the article. Keep the pace lively. Don't get bogged down in specifics in your first paragraph.
- **The body of the press release contains the details.** Use quotes and bulleted lists wherever possible. This will break up any long blocks of text and highlight critical information. Quotes also enable you to insert opinions into the article. Although you can't say it's a good product, you can quote someone else saying it's a good product.

Format

Every press release should follow the same structure and format shown in Figure 20.13, making it easy for the media to find the important facts in the document. Reporters receiving your press release don't want to search for the information on the page.

FIGURE 20.13   Press Release Format

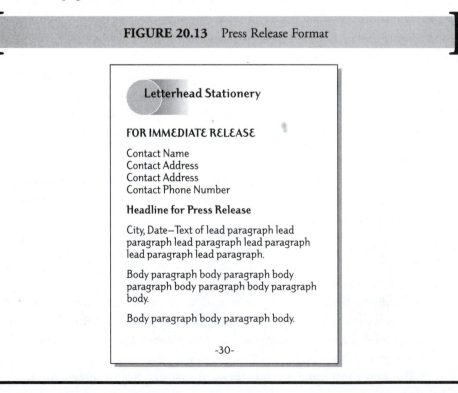

Every press release received by the media isn't published. However, the correct format automatically improves the chance that the newspaper, magazine, or industry publication will print your press release.

- **For immediate release**—Type the words "FOR IMMEDIATE RELEASE" in all capital letters directly under the letterhead. Make the text bold and use a font size that is a bit larger than the remaining text.
- **Contact information**—Leave one or two blank lines after the release statement. Enter the name, title, telephone number, and fax number of the person in your company who can be contacted for more information. Include a home phone number. Journalists may need to make contact in the evening if a deadline is approaching.
- **Headline**—Leave one or two blank lines after the contact information. Type the headline. Make it bold.
- **Dateline**—Enter the city where the press release originated and the date the press release was mailed. Begin your first paragraph on the same line.
- **Lead paragraph**—Start on the same line as the date.
- **Body**—Type the main text of the press release. Double-space the text or leave a blank line between paragraphs. At the bottom of each page, except the last page, type "-more-" centered alone on the last line.
- **Conclusion**—Restate the important information in the press release. At the end of the article, type "###" or "-30-" centered on a line by itself to indicate the end of the article.

Hypothetical Scenario

When Marc was ready to expand his business, he prepared a press release describing his service, tying it to developments in several medical areas. He sent the press release to several medical journals, hoping to reach doctors who would purchase his newsletter service.

Create an RFP or a Proposal

All businesses, large and small, encounter the need for services or materials they can't provide for themselves. To fill this need, they can purchase the products from a supplier that is located nearby or recommended by another business owner. However, some businesses prefer to select a supplier based on cost, services provided, or the supplier's experience. One method of discovering this information about several potential suppliers is requesting proposals to fill your requirements.

As a small business, you may find yourself on either side of the fence. You may find your business requesting proposals from several vendors or responding to a proposal request, competing against businesses much like yours. This means you may be preparing a request for a proposal one day and responding to a request from another business several months later.

Write a Request for a Proposal

A business prepares a **Request for a Proposal (RFP)** to select a supplier. An RFP describes a task or project to be completed. It sets guidelines to complete the project and criteria to evaluate the work performed. Qualified businesses submit a proposal to complete the project. Essentially, a **proposal** is a bid, a document created to respond to an RFP by describing how the supplier can fill the listed requirements.

Determine the Requirements for a Project You may need a project completed, but you don't know enough about the process of creating the product to write a thorough RFP. For example, your business needs customized software to run heavy machinery that makes paper from wood pulp. To gather the information you need, meet with several vendors that write customized software. Vendors can make suggestions that are helpful in stating the parameters and the criteria for the project. You can also perform research by reading trade journals.

Prepare the RFP Generally, an RFP has a detailed description of the task, the location where the task is to be completed, the methods used to complete the task, the deadline, and the criteria for successful completion. Every RFP doesn't follow the same structure. However, every effective RFP contains many of the following elements.

- **Deadline for proposal**—An RFP is usually distributed eight to ten weeks before the deadline for the proposal. The **closing date** is the date and time of the deadline for the submission of a proposal. Proposals received after the deadline won't be considered.

- **High bid**—You can choose to identify the upper limit for a supplier's bid by stating a limit such as, "Vendor bids may not exceed $75,000." This can eliminate unreasonable bids or high-priced vendors.

- **Additional costs**—If travel is required, identify any limits on travel methods and the rate at which travel is reimbursed.

- **Work site**—Identify where the work is to be performed. Building contractors work at the building site, not your home office. Writers and programmers might work from their own homes.

- **Content of the proposal**—Specify the information every submitted proposal must contain. For example, you can require a price quote, résumés for the project managers, and technical specifications for the machinery or components used. Specify the format in which the information must be submitted. It is easier to compare data, such as a quote, submitted using the same format. You can also provide a sample table of contents for the proposal, identifying exactly what the proposal should contain and the sequence in which the information should be placed.

- **Delivery method for proposal**—Proposals can be submitted electronically as an attachment to an e-mail message, sent through the postal service, or delivered by a courier. When a project doesn't require the worker's physical presence, companies that aren't local submit proposals.

- **Decision date**—The RFP must specify the date on which the supplier will be selected and the method used to inform the applicants of the decision. Applicants may be planning their manpower and supply needs around the prospect of winning the project.

- **Selection criteria**—Identify the criteria used to select the provider: (1) You can assign points to each project specification and select the supplier with the most points. (2) You can select the supplier that gives the lowest bid. (3) You can use an alternate selection system, but be prepared to prove that the system was fair to all bidders.

- **Contact**—Identify the individual and the contact method for applicants who have questions about the RFP or the project requirements.

- **Ownership**—The RFP must clearly state that the ownership of the deliverable product is transferred to your business. It is not retained by the supplier. If the deliverable is a document, this is known as work made for hire. The supplier performs the work, but the document's copyright belongs to your business.

- **Project description**—"You get what you ask for" is a good principle to remember when you describe the task to be performed by the bidder. Provide a comprehensive description of the work you expect to be completed. Document every detail. If the deliverable is a report, specify the page count, format, application to create the report, number of copies, paper, and binding method. More details result in a deliverable that meets your expectations. Don't leave it to the supplier to determine the characteristics of the deliverable. You could end up with a 200-page report as you required, but the document uses wide margins, double-spaced text, and a large font. In other words, the supplier could use the same techniques you used in high school to meet a page requirement for an assigned report.

- **Demonstration**—If appropriate, ask the vendor to provide a demonstration or sample of previous projects. A vendor that designs web sites should be able to provide several web site addresses you can examine.

- **Contributions**—Identify the role your business plays in completing the project. This includes the time, materials, and expertise contributed by members of your business. If you have to review the project at several points in the production process or provide specific materials, it must be noted in the RFP.

- **Schedule**—Set reasonable deadlines for the finished product and any critical interim stages.

- **Applicants**—Specify the qualifications of the supplier and the individuals performing the work. If you want a framer with at least three years of experience, make it a requirement. This prevents the supplier from substituting workers who are unqualified or inexperienced.

- **Experience**—Applicants should describe previous experience that applies to the current project in responsibility, scope, and price range.

- **References**—Ask applicants to identify several previous employers who are able to describe the applicant's work.

◆ **Payment**—Identify when payment will be made. For long projects, you may decide to pay when the project reaches a milestone or a certain percentage of completion. For example, you could make a partial payment when the project is started, when the product is ready for quality testing, and when the project is complete. Each payment implies satisfaction with the progress of the project up to that point.

Select Vendors to Receive an RFP An RFP is a substantial document to prepare, representing dozens of hours of work. You want to select the best vendors to respond to the RFP and perform the task. First, you have to select the vendors to receive an RFP. Several methods are available.

Internet Publish the RFP on the Internet. Many government offices publish RFP documents on web sites established and operated for the purpose of distributing requests. Vendors that typically bid on these projects are familiar with the sites and check them regularly for new RFP postings. This enables the government to provide equal opportunity to all vendors. The diversity of vendor responses received by the government office increases the chance that a qualified, cost-effective vendor will respond to the RFP. On the other hand, it increases the number of proposals that have to be reviewed. Many of these proposals will be from businesses that are not qualified to complete the project.

Industry Journal Publish general information about your needs in an industry journal or related publication. Be sure to include enough information. Invite responses to a general description of the project. Review the responses and select the most qualified vendors. Send an RFP to each of these prequalified applicants.

Research Select the vendors you learned about during your research. Based on the information you already gathered, these vendors may be able to fill your requirements.

Write a Proposal

You can become involved in submitting a proposal in several ways. You can actively search for an RFP on the Internet, respond to a general advertisement placed by a business searching for a vendor, or be selected by reputation or referral to receive an RFP. You could deal with a satisfied customer time after time.

The decision to prepare and submit a proposal has a deep impact on your business. Writing a proposal requires time, research, and expertise. The time spent preparing a proposal is time that can't be spent performing the core business activity that earns money for your business. In fact, unless your proposal is accepted, your business will not earn any money for the time and effort required to prepare the proposal. Therefore, the commitment to prepare a proposal is significant to your business.

Guidelines Your proposal is a response to an RFP. The RFP describes exactly what the business requires. Your proposal must describe how your business meets every requirement identified in the RFP. Therefore, make a checklist as you read the RFP. Check off each item as it is incorporated into your proposal.

Some businesses include a sample table of contents for the submitted proposals. This tells you exactly what the proposal should contain and the sequence in which the information should be placed.

Bind, label, and deliver the proposal in the manner specified by the RFP. Include a cover letter with your proposal. This gives you the opportunity to directly address the contact individual for the project. Take advantage of this opportunity by summarizing the key points of your proposal, stating why your business is the best applicant. Emphasize the quality of the work your business performs. Finally, cross your fingers and hope that the abilities of your business match the requirements in the RFP and your business is selected.

Format Proposals should be as brief as possible. However, be sure to respond to every requirement in the RFP. Most proposals are 20 to 100 pages in length. If the RFP included a sample table of contents for the proposal, follow the structure closely.

Use headings and provide a table of contents for the proposal. This makes it easier for the company to find specific information. It also demonstrates that you are efficient, organized, and have the ability to follow instructions, which is proven by your ability to follow a sample table of contents.

Common fonts, such as Times Roman and Arial, present a professional image. Avoid fonts that are less common. The font size should be between 10 and 13 points. This is large enough to read easily and small enough to fit a reasonable amount of text on a page. Headings should be bold so they stand out from the text. Often, headings are printed in Arial and the body text is printed in Times Roman.

To submit a bound proposal, be sure to adjust the margins of your document. The left side, where the binding is applied, requires more white space than the right side. This enables readers to view all the text rather than having some text missing because the binding covers it or the document doesn't open wide enough to view the text on the inside margin.

Address the cover letter to the contact person identified in the RFP. Use the full block style or modified block style for the letter. Select the format that is most similar to the format of your proposal.

Hypothetical Scenario

Marc's newsletter business expanded rapidly. His printing costs were also growing rapidly. From his experience in marketing, Marc was familiar with several printers who could regularly produce large quantities of newsletters. Marc spent time preparing an RFP and distributed it to four printers he worked with in the past. The proposals he received in response were well prepared and reflected a capability to print the newsletters. The deciding factor was a service offered by only one printer. A strategic alliance between the printer and another small business enabled him to offer the additional service of shipping the newsletters directly to the medical offices, eliminating a potential distribution problem.

Technology Insights

Document Templates

Every major word processing application comes with several document templates. A template contains the basic structure and format settings for a type of document. The template contains sample text and headings that can be replaced by text specific to your document. To replace the sample text, simply click on the sample text and type the replacement text that you want in the document.

Templates contain styles, formatting characteristics applied to the elements in a document. Styles enable you to change the appearance of text, tables, and lists. Styles can affect the alignment, tabs, spacing, and borders of a paragraph. Styles also affect the appearance of individual characters by changing the font, size, color, bold, and italic characteristics.

The variety of templates that accompany most word processing applications provides a template for almost any occasion or purpose. For example, templates for letters, e-mail messages, reports, faxes, mailing labels, brochures, and newsletters are already on your computer. Use the template as it appears or modify it slightly to customize the template for your needs.

Think Critically Describe the templates that accompany your word processing software.

CHAPTER REVIEW

Effective written communication is essential for a small business to succeed. The documents your business produces must be well organized, clear, and accurate. To prepare organized documents, organize your thoughts by making a list and placing the items in a logical sequence. If possible, add graphics to illustrate the critical information. Always verify the information in your documents before releasing them.

Correspondence should be brief, clear, and organized. Follow standard formats for letters, e-mail messages, and memos.

Press releases are a form of publicity, a responsibility of the marketing function. Press releases help you affect or control the company information you distribute to the public via the news media. Your press release must interest and inform readers from the headline to the last period. Follow the standard format to increase the chance of publishing the press release. Even if a press release isn't published, it can still be distributed to potential customers or investors.

As a small business, you may request a proposal from specialized vendors or prepare a proposal hoping to acquire a project offered by another business. The keys to preparing an effective Request for a Proposal (RFP) are organization and writing an accurate description of the project to be completed. To write a successful proposal, describe how your business meets every requirement identified in the RFP.

USE BUSINESS TERMS

Fill in the blanks with the appropriate term.

closing date	memorandum
font	modified block style
footer	press release
format	proposal
full block style	Request for a Proposal (RFP)
header	signature
heading	stationery
letterhead	structure
logical	virus
margin	

1. A proposal must be submitted by the _____?_____.
2. A business prepares a(n) _____?_____ to select a supplier.
3. The _____?_____ can be automatically added to every message you send.
4. Use a(n) _____?_____ to announce meetings, promotions, or new employees.
5. The text in a letter using the _____?_____ is always left justified.
6. The _____?_____ contains information you want repeated at the top of every page or every other page of a document.
7. A(n) _____?_____ is intended to provide information for journalists.

TEST YOUR READING

8. Explain how the five Ws and H can improve your business documents.

9. Identify the criteria that can be used to determine the sequence of information in a business document.

10. Explain the difference between the structure and the format of a document.

11. Which fonts are more common in business documents?

12. Describe the difference between the full block style and the modified block style used in business correspondence.

13. When do you use the abbreviation *bcc?*

14. What type of document is appropriate to notify your employees of a meeting?

15. How does a press release fit into your company's business functions?

16. Why do you use letterhead paper to submit a press release?

17. Describe the elements in a press release.

18. Identify the components of an RFP.

19. How do you select vendors to submit a proposal for a project you want completed?

THINK CRITICALLY ABOUT BUSINESS

20. Use the five Ws and H to describe a current project.

21. Write a business letter to Dave McCairn using the information in Figures 20.1 to 20.4.

22. Write a press release about a recent event at your business or school.

23. Search the Internet or industry publications for an RFP that your business could respond to by submitting a proposal for consideration. Make a checklist of the requirements identified in the RFP as you read.

REAL-LIFE BUSINESS

Gannett Co., Inc.

When you think of written communication, you think of newspapers, one of the earliest methods of distributing news to a large number of people. One of the largest news and information companies in the world is Gannett Co., Inc. In 2002, the company had approximately 51,500 employees. The company has more than 265 million shares of common stock, which are held by approximately 13,700 shareholders. Its operating revenue in 2001 was $6.3 billion. More than 7.2 million individuals read its newspapers every day.

Obviously, the company wasn't always a giant that earned billions of dollars and operated on several continents. In 1906, Frank Gannett purchased an interest in the *Elmira Gazette* in New York. He established the Gannett company in 1923. At the time, Gannett Co., Inc. consisted of six newspapers in New York.

The newspaper industry proved to be profitable. Gannett expanded rapidly. It also made a point of staying on the edge of technological developments in the news and communication fields. Gannett utilized teletypesetters, shortwave radio sets, color printing presses, and the Internet before other news media companies were equipped with the devices or technological advances.

Gannett also emphasized a commitment to quality. A quality award, known as the Best of Gannett, rewards news personnel for excellence in reporting and public service.

Through all of these activities, Gannett continued to grow. It purchased radio and television stations, an outdoor advertising plant, and a research firm.

Gannett realized the importance of information and opinions from all sources. Minorities and women were encouraged to apply because they were offered opportunities to work and advance in their chosen career field. Individuals advanced to the highest positions, regardless of race or gender.

Think Critically

1. Where was Gannett Co., Inc. established?
2. How has Gannett diversified?
3. What is the Best of Gannett?
4. What directions do you think Gannett should investigate for future expansion?

CHAPTER 21

Communication Challenges

GOALS

- ◆ Resolve conflict
- ◆ Close a sale
- ◆ Improve your management style
- ◆ Practice business etiquette

Chelie Pennant earned a master's degree in business 12 years ago. She worked for several years, and then chose to stay home to raise her three boys. When all three were attending school all day, she started looking for work. Economic conditions were poor and many of her friends who were business professionals had been laid off when offices were closed or personnel reductions were required. It wasn't a good time to look for a full-time position. Many businesses were hiring temporary workers, workers possessing the same skills as Chelie and her friends. Chelie opened her new business, Pennant Temporaries, a few months later.

Resolve Conflict

Good communication is critical to creating and operating a successful business. Communication between individuals is more than an effective presentation or a perfectly worded memo. In the workplace, communication occurs from the second you pull into the parking lot to the instant you pull out of the lot at the end of the day. It occurs in offices, hallways, break rooms, restrooms, and loading docks. It's verbal, nonverbal, and written. It's every exchange between every member of your business throughout the day.

Communication Process

Communication is the exchange of information between individuals through symbols, signs, or behaviors.

Most people believe that they are effective communicators. The most common accusations when a communication problem occurs are, "You aren't listening!" and "You don't understand!" It's easy to blame misunderstandings and problems on the other person.

The communication process, illustrated in Figure 21.1, explains where communication problems occur. At every stage, noise interferes with the accurate transfer of the message. **Noise** is anything that distorts or slows the message transfer. Noise includes uncomfortable surroundings, tight deadlines, and competition with other messages.

FIGURE 21.1   Communication Process

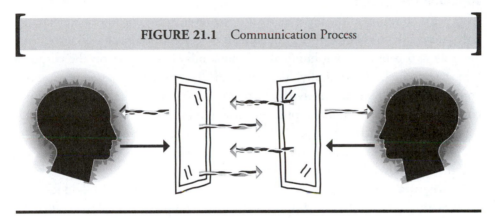

Step 1—Sender Creates Message   The **sender** is the originator of the message. In the sender's mind, the thought is crystal clear and well defined. Unfortunately, this is the last time in the communication process that the idea is pure, uncorrupted by the steps in the process.

Step 2—Sender Encodes Message   To express the idea and communicate it to someone else, the sender must encode the message. To **encode** it, the sender converts the message into words, symbols, sounds, images, numbers, gestures, and movements. Encoding the message passes the thoughts through a screen or filter established by the sender's unique characteristics, such as age, gender, education, and experience. For example, a young child can have a complicated thought about an elephant at the zoo, but be unable to express it because his or her vocabulary isn't fully developed. In a similar way, an individual who has experienced a devastating loss finds it difficult to express the resulting emotions.

Step 3—Transmit the Message   The idea has been encoded by passing it through the sender's unique filter. The encoded message must be transmitted to another individual. Transmission requires a **channel,** such as your voice, gestures, or a written medium. The message is further corrupted by the limitations of the channel or translation from one channel to another. For example, facial expressions that transmit grief or excitement lose much of their impact when they are described in words.

Step 4—Decode the Message After the message is transmitted, it must be decoded when it arrives at the other end. To **decode** the message, it is filtered through the receiver's unique characteristics, which differ from the sender's characteristics. The receiver's age, gender, or nationality may alter the interpretation of the message.

Step 5—Understand the Message The message is again converted into an idea by the **receiver,** the person decoding the message. However, after the communication process, the thought held by the receiver's mind may bear little resemblance to the idea that was originally created in the sender's mind.

Reasons for Conflict

Conflict is common in the business world. However, small businesses are particularly vulnerable to conflict. If two individuals in a large corporation disagree, they are only two people among hundreds or thousands. The impact on the corporation is minimal. If two individuals in a small company disagree, the entire company could become involved. A situation that would be minor in other circumstances becomes a major problem that could disrupt the entire business.

Goals Conflict can begin when leaders do not have the same goals. Employees pull in different directions when they disagree on the desired results and the methods used to reach the goals.

Organization Every business needs a leader, a group or individual who chooses the direction for the business. In many companies, employees work in teams without clearly defined leaders. When team members work together, contributing their skill and knowledge without conflict, much can be accomplished. However, conflict can arise when team members disagree about the team's goals, methods, or individual tasks. When this happens, the team becomes a canoe with only one oar, spinning rather than making progress.

Communication A single individual who lacks self-control and anger management skills can instigate misunderstandings or escalate existing misunderstandings into conflict. Training in communication can help some individuals channel their emotions and behavior more productively.

Conflict Resolution

Conflict isn't necessarily bad. Disagreements are beneficial when different viewpoints and solutions are presented which can help the business succeed. Regardless of the issue, conflict must be resolved before a business can take advantage of the benefits:

- **Use the company's resources more efficiently.** Conflict requires time and wastes money. These resources could be used on the company's core business activities.
- **Increase work quality.** Conflict causes stress, which decreases productivity and increases errors.

- **Gain loyalty to the company.** During a conflict, employees may be loyal to one leader rather than the business. Employees who have the best interests of the business at heart are upset by conflict between company leaders.
- **Decrease complaints by customers.** If your business works closely with customers, the customers may become aware of the conflict. This can make them nervous about working with your business and encourage them to switch to one of your competitors.
- **Increase morale.** When conflict divides a business, employee morale drops.
- **Decrease turnover.** Conflict causes employees to search for new jobs, arrive late, leave early, and take more sick days than happy employees.

If your business experiences internal conflict, it must be resolved. Problems caused by differences in goals, organizational needs, and miscommunication can be solved.

Goals Individuals within a business have unique ambitions. For example, some employees want to be promoted while others want to work on a specific project or learn additional skills. However, everyone in the company must share the goals for the business. Conflict occurs when the activities of the business are not directed toward the company's goals. Periodically, review your business plan and evaluate your current business status and activities. If your activities will not help your business reach the goals expressed in your business plan, make changes to your activities or your goals to resolve the conflict.

Organization The structure of a business is usually based on its business functions. When a company changes its business activities, modifies its business methods, or struggles financially, management often restructures the business. **Restructuring,** also known as reorganizing, assigns new responsibilities to existing employees. Individuals or entire departments may report to a new manager. Sometimes, restructuring enables a business to add new products, lower expenses, or resolve conflict caused by the previous structure.

Communication Every individual communicates in a unique way. However, these communication methods can be grouped into four basic communication styles. You can build rapport, a feeling of harmony or friendship, by sharing common topics, such as interests or values, or by sharing a common communication style.

Communication styles are defined by the way individuals express themselves. Each style definition includes speech patterns, gestures, facial expressions, and the content that influences the individual the most:

- **Analytical communicators** are driven by the content of the message. They are more influenced by what is said rather than how it is said. In conversation, they may seem impersonal and cold. Influence these individuals by providing facts, numbers, and charts.
- **Direct communicators** are driven by the content of the message. They are more influenced by what is said rather than how it is said. In conversation, they may seem assertive, blunt, or dominating. Influence these individuals by providing facts, numbers, and charts.

- **Expressive communicators** are driven by the context of the message. They are more influenced by how it is said rather than what is said. In conversation, they may seem disorganized or scattered. Influence these individuals by using action and emotion.
- **Supportive communicators** are driven by the context of the message. They are more influenced by how it is said rather than what is said. In conversation, they may seem warm and approachable. Influence these individuals by using emotion.

Hypothetical Scenario

When she established Pennant Temporaries, Chelie Pennant worked alone. She sought temporary assignments that matched the skill sets of her unemployed friends, family, and neighbors. Occasionally, she completed a temporary assignment herself. As her business grew, her brother joined the company, matching workers to temporary assignments. Conflict occurred frequently when his selections were not the ones Chelie would have chosen. To resolve this conflict, Chelie and Joe set aside an afternoon to create a set of guidelines that they agreed to follow when accepting assignments and selecting workers.

Close a Sale

You've probably known one. You might even be related to one—the kind of person who could sell ice to Eskimos, sand in the desert, or swampland in Florida. A few people on your staff with sales talent can make the difference between profit and loss.

Characteristics of Good Salespeople

To *have* good salespeople, you must *hire* good salespeople. You can teach salespeople about your product and you can train them to use specific sales tools and techniques. However, most successful salespeople share personal characteristics that can't be taught:

- **Financially motivated**—Sales commissions are powerful motivators for sales representatives. For each sale, representatives earn a percentage of the sales price, which can differ among industries. A trade association can tell you the normal commission amount in your field.
- **Self-confident**—More sales attempts are rejected than accepted. A sales representative must have the self-confidence to believe the rejection isn't personal.
- **Persistent**—Sales representatives must be willing to keep trying, even when the majority of their contacts don't result in a sale.
- **Good communication skills**—Sales representatives must communicate well. Listening to customers is often more critical than speaking to them.

Personal Selling

In many situations, buying and selling are impersonal actions. The vendor is interested in selling a large quantity of the company's products and is focused on earning a profit rather than satisfying individual customers. Customers select and purchase items without any assistance from a sales representative. They may not even see a sales representative during the transaction.

In contrast, personal selling focuses on people rather than products. **Personal selling** is direct communication between a sales representative and a consumer when the intention of the communication is a purchase. Direct communication usually occurs face-to-face, but it can also involve telephone conversations and business correspondence. In the current business atmosphere, large businesses use personal selling in limited situations:

- **Expensive**—Items such as automobiles and houses that have a high value use personal selling.
- **Custom**—Items designed or manufactured for a single customer use personal selling.
- **Technical**—Complex items may require explanations delivered by a trained sales representative.

As a small business, you can use personal selling to give you an advantage over larger businesses offering the same products or services. In an environment that emphasizes profit more than customer satisfaction, your focus on the customer can be a welcome change to many consumers. Table 21.1 describes the advantages and disadvantages of personal selling.

TABLE 21.1   Personal Selling

Advantages	Disadvantages
Message can be customized for each consumer	Requires a large time commitment
Creates a satisfied customer	Additional expenses caused by time and effort
Develops a relationship between the sales representative and the customer	Depends on the sales representative's skill in making a sale
Targets the consumers most likely to make a purchase	Time and cost limit the number of customers who can be targeted

Process of Personal Selling

The process of personal selling can take hours, days, or even months. The length of time required depends on some factors that are concrete and others that are more difficult to quantify, such as the value of the product, the "fit" of the product offered, and the weather that day. For example, selling a pair of diamond earrings can be done in a few hours. Selling a house may take months of looking for a buyer who can afford the house, a family that "fits" the house and neighborhood, and a crisp fall day when the autumn colors lend the house a secure, comfortable feeling. When all the elements come together, the house is sold.

The time required to complete each step in the process in Figure 21.2 varies as well. The same step in the process may require more or less time for different customers.

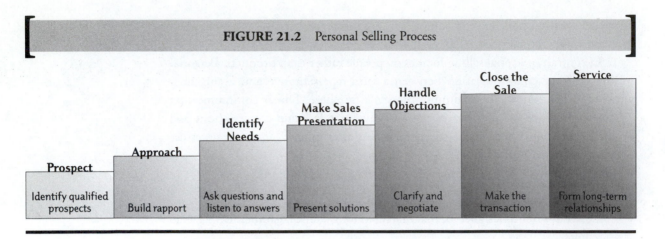

FIGURE 21.2   Personal Selling Process

Step 1—Prospect Customers don't grow on trees. You have to find them somewhere. Identifying potential customers is known as **prospecting.** The use of this term in business is based on the idea of searching for gold or other valuable substances in a likely location. In business, you search for prospects, a limited number of individuals who could become customers, who are hidden in a large number of disinterested consumers. Prospecting is performed in many ways:

◆ **Referrals**—Ask satisfied customers to suggest others who may be interested in your product or service. If your customer is reluctant to give you a friend's name, give him or her a business card or brochure. Customers may want to tell friends, but don't want you to contact the friends directly. Your business card or brochure encourages your customers to tell others about your business while protecting their friends from unwanted sales calls.

◆ **Existing customers**—When you introduce a new product or plan ways of increasing your business income, don't forget your existing customers. They may be interested in trying a related product or increasing the frequency of their purchases. For example, a personal fitness trainer could introduce a new package that includes three visits a week instead of two.

◆ **Related businesses**—Exchange information with another small business that is in a related field but doesn't compete with you. For example, if you open a business that grooms dogs, exchange customer information with a veterinarian or pet supply retailer.

◆ **Advertisements**—When you place advertisements, you can expect that some individuals will respond by calling, visiting your location, or contacting you as requested in the ad.

◆ **Observation**—As you go about your business, you may notice people who could benefit from your product or service. For example, when you walk at the park, you might encounter another walker who chats about her daughter's upcoming wedding. This is a good opportunity to talk about your photography business.

◆ **Trade shows/seminars**—Individuals at a trade show or seminar have already declared an interest in your type of product by attending.

◆ **Cold calls**—Perhaps the most difficult method of prospecting, **cold calling** is calling a list of new contacts to ask if they are interested in purchasing your product. Quantity is the theory behind cold calling. If you call enough people, you'll find a few who are interested in your product.

All of your prospects will not be qualified. Don't waste your time pursuing a sale that won't happen with an unqualified prospect. To be qualified, a prospect must meet several criteria: (1) The prospect must be able to benefit from the product. You won't buy a sailboat if you don't want to go sailing. (2) The prospect must be able to pay for the product. You can't sell a yacht to someone who can afford only a canoe. (3) The prospect must have the authority to make a purchasing decision. A 12-year-old may want his family to own a sports car, but he doesn't have the authority to spend the money. (4) The prospect must be accessible, able to purchase and receive the product. You probably won't find someone to buy your llamas in the heart of New York City. (5) The sale must provide a reasonable profit. A prospect who only wants to pay the cost price doesn't earn a profit for you.

Step 2—Approach In this step, greet the individual and establish rapport to increase the chance of obtaining a sale. If you are observant, you may notice some clues that can help you establish rapport with a qualified prospect. Family photos on a desk, a team logo on a shirt, and a degree framed and hung on the wall can provide clues to the qualified prospect's interests. The conversation doesn't have to be lengthy. Make a comment about the team's current standings or mention that your daughter is about the same age. Listen to the prospect's response and move on to the next step. If you "chat" too long, you create the impression that you are ineffective or too inquisitive about the individual's personal or business affairs.

In a retail situation, this step is accelerated. The prospect is in the store to browse or buy an item. He or she may approach the sales representative to ask for assistance. If a sales representative notices that a prospect is examining a product, the representative can offer assistance. In this situation, the approach might be a simple question. "I noticed that you are looking at the paint. Can I help you?"

Step 3—Identify Needs The key to identifying needs is listening to the prospect's questions and statements. The information you gather at this stage helps you make a successful presentation for the right products. A few probing questions can identify the prospect's needs and concerns:

◆ **Goal**—What do you want to accomplish?
◆ **Experience**—Have you used a similar product?
◆ **Method**—How do you want to accomplish it?
◆ **Characteristics**—What features do you want?
◆ **Price**—What price range are you considering?

If you sell only one product, the answers to these questions determine if your product is a good fit for this prospect. If you sell several products, the prospect's answers determine which, if any, of your products fit the prospect's needs. If your products don't fit the prospect's needs, recommend a product that does. The individual will remember your honesty when he or she needs products in the future.

Step 4—Make Sales Presentation If your product fits the prospect's needs, present it as the solution for the prospect. The sales presentation can be simple or detailed. The product you sell determines the type of sales presentation that is appropriate. For example, if you own a hardware store, the sales presentation may be as simple as leading the customer to the saws and pointing out the saw that performs the task the customer specified. If your business writes custom software priced at $500,000 or more, your sales presentation may include a proposal, a slide show, and meetings with your satisfied customers.

During the sales presentation, take advantage of the information you gathered in the previous step. Respond to each of the consumer's needs:

- **Goal**—Confirm or demonstrate that the product can help the consumer accomplish the objective.
- **Experience**—Verify that the product matches the consumer's experience level.
- **Method**—Describe or demonstrate how the product works.
- **Characteristics**—Describe the benefits of using the product, not its features.
- **Price**—Verify that the product is in the consumer's price range or explain why the price is higher than the consumer expected. Few consumers ask for an explanation if the cost is lower than expected unless the difference is dramatic.

Be honest during the sales presentation. If you sell a product that doesn't fit the consumer's needs, you will have a dissatisfied customer and a damaged reputation that could easily impact your future earnings. This is particularly true when you sell to a limited market. For example, if your target market is dentists in your city, a bad experience with one dentist may reduce the number of dentists who will meet with you, much less buy your product.

Step 5—Handle Objections A consumer who isn't ready to purchase will voice objections. Listen closely before you respond. Sometimes the consumer makes an objection, but the objection isn't the real roadblock to the purchase. A consumer might object that the price is too high. As you review the consumer's needs, you discover that he or she doesn't really need all the options on the selected product. The basic model, which is also less expensive, meets the consumer's needs. Objections help you further define the consumer's needs and provide the opportunity to reinforce the benefits of the product.

Step 6—Close the Sale The most difficult part of the sales process for many sales representatives is closing the sale. They can talk to the consumer and present the product comfortably, but when it comes to asking the customer to make the purchase, sales representatives are often more reluctant than the customer. Their fear of rejection makes sales representatives hesitant to ask the customer to commit to a purchase.

Knowing when to close a sale is the key to success. Pay attention to the customer's body language as well as his or her words. For example, nodding implies agreement with your statements.

Review the product's benefits and match the benefits to the customer's needs. Listen and watch for clues in body language. When the customer is ready, ask for commitment. A variety of questions can be used to close the sale.

- **Do you need anything else?** This question is similar to the standard, "Do you want fries with that?" It assumes the customer is already committed to the purchase.
- **Can I take this to the counter for you?** This indirect question doesn't ask if the customer is buying the product, but an affirmative answer commits to the purchase.
- **Can we set up a schedule?** More complicated business products require a schedule for installation and training.

Successful representatives often ask for referrals when they close a sale. The customer is confident and expects a positive result. The customer provides contact information for additional prospects.

Step 7—Service Contact the customer after the product has been installed. This helps you form long-term relationships with your customers. It pays off in referrals now and additional purchases in the future.

Hypothetical Scenario

Chelie was delighted to discover that her brother seemed to be a natural salesman. He associated comfortably with their existing business customers. Chelie and Joe agreed to split the work by assigning Joe to deal with the businesses. Chelie worked with the temporary workers, adding more workers to their "stable" of workers and selecting workers to fill each position. Joe maintained weekly contact with their steady business clients.

Improve Your Management Style

If you have been an employee for any length of time, you have had at least one manager. Whether your experience with the manager was positive or negative, you learned something about managing. You may have vowed never to use the same techniques to manage your employees or made a mental note to remember a technique that worked well. However, the odds are good that you forgot every management technique you planned to use on the day you opened your business.

Entrepreneurial Management Style

From the instant your business idea struck, it has been your baby. You dreamed about it, planned for it, tried different names for it, and imagined it growing and expanding. When the doors opened for the first time, you watched anxiously and worried about the cost of every rubber band and paper clip. As your business began to attract customers and make sales, you rejoiced in triumph.

Standard Entrepreneur If you resemble the typical entrepreneur who works alone, you share several work habits. You do everything yourself, taking care of every detail. You work long hours, which limits your activities outside your business.

Small problems can become large issues if critical meetings or deadlines are neglected. You may feel stressed, harried, and exhausted. Finally, your business requires more work than you can perform alone. It's time to hire employees to help your business grow.

Hands-On Technique After hiring employees, entrepreneurs tend to be **hands-on managers,** leaders who take an active personal involvement in every business activity. In fact, entrepreneurs who hire employees tend to be very much like entrepreneurs without employees. They do everything themselves, taking care of every detail. They work long hours, which limits their activities outside their business. Small problems can become large issues if critical meetings or deadlines are neglected. They may feel stressed, harried, and exhausted.

An entrepreneur who hires employees, and then retains a chokehold on every business detail is losing the most important benefits of having employees. For example, you lose the ideas that could be generated by employees who are not tightly controlled by the manager. You lose the free time that would be available if employees took over some of the workload. You also haven't reduced your stress level. In fact, you have only added more reasons for concern because you now worry about the employees.

Improvements in Management Techniques

For better or worse, a manager sets the tone for the employees who report to him or her. If you currently have the characteristics of a hands-on manager, you can make improvements in your techniques. These improvements can increase productivity, create a happier work environment, and help your business grow.

Planning In the past, you performed all the planning for your business. You researched, investigated options, selected a path, and moved forward. If you succeeded or failed, the responsibility and the consequences were yours.

Employees can bring a fresh perspective to problems you have examined time after time from a single point of view. Seek opinions from the employees you hired. Ideas and plans generated by the group incorporate knowledge and experience that are outside your personal scope. Your business planning adds new dimensions, contributing to the success of your plans and improved results.

Use your business plan. It contains strategic and tactical objectives that determine the direction your business is moving. Used practically, a business plan determines the projects that need to be completed and establishes the priority for each task. Expand the strategic and tactical objectives into detailed action plans. Share this information with your employees. If an employee is assigned more than one project, you or the employee must be able to prioritize the tasks so that critical assignments are completed on schedule.

Supporting Planning is a good start to any project. However, you could plan hundreds of projects that are never completed. Support is required to enable employees to successfully complete a project. Success requires reasonable schedules, appropriate training, and the needed resources:

- **Schedule**—Don't set deadlines in a vacuum. Ask the individuals who are responsible for completing a task to estimate the time required. Employees will be motivated to meet deadlines they set for their assignments.

- **Training**—If an employee is assigned a task, be sure that the employee has the needed skills. It may be more efficient to select an employee who already has the skills rather than train an inexperienced worker.

- **Resources**—Managers must supply funds, equipment, time, and additional manpower to complete any project.

Training "If you want something done right, do it yourself" is a mantra common to managers who believe in doing every task to ensure it is done correctly. This type of manager may be limiting the number of products or services your business offers because of his or her need to personally complete every task. Instead, train an employee to correctly perform the task. Training others enables you to spend your time more profitably rather than performing each minor task.

Delegating Hands-on managers are unable to delegate tasks. Even when a hands-on manager **delegates** a task by assigning the responsibility to someone else, the manager seems unable to let go of the task. The manager constantly requests updates and makes suggestions. The employee can quickly become frustrated with the situation.

Delegate some tasks without dumping all of your unpleasant chores. Some tasks are more fun than others. However, if you keep the fun tasks for yourself and ask others to do all the difficult and tedious jobs, employees will resent it.

Responsibility Managers can make a serious error when they delegate a task if they assign responsibility for the task without granting the authority to complete it. An individual who has **responsibility** for a task is expected to complete it and answers to another individual for the task. An individual who has the responsibility to finish a task often requires **authority,** the ability to influence or control individuals or objects to obtain resources needed to finish the task. If the employee doesn't have the authority to acquire needed items and you don't supply the resources, you can't expect the employee to complete the task.

Rewarding Employees who perform well should be rewarded. The reward must be relative to the size of the task completed. For example, an "Atta-boy" pat on the back is appropriate for completing a minor task, such as organizing an employee meeting. Tasks that require more time and effort deserve better rewards, such as recognition in front of other employees, additional financial compensation, or a promotion.

Everyone needs to feel appreciated. In addition to extra rewards for extraordinary accomplishments, employees should feel appreciated for the work they perform every day. "Thank you" shouldn't be a rare phrase in your company. Good employees who feel appreciated respond by working harder and choosing to stay longer with your business.

Technology Most businesses use several types of technology in their daily operations. The technology used to pursue their primary business function is usually different than the technology used to record and track business operations. For example, a cruise line incorporates new technology every time it builds a new cruise ship. Improvements may include advances in building techniques, materials, and design. The cruise line's business activities are probably tracked through another technology, specialized software.

Technology is improving at an incredible pace. Trying to keep up with all of the advances in your specific area of expertise may be a full-time job by itself. Additional technology is used to track your business operations, such as computers, software, and cell phones. Each piece of technology in these areas becomes rapidly outdated.

In many companies, an individual is assigned the responsibility of maintaining computers and software for all employees. This is cost-efficient because it requires less time and money for a single individual to remain up-to-date and become skilled at computer maintenance than it does to educate every employee in redundant skills.

Hypothetical Scenario

As Pennant Temporaries grew, Chelie and Joe added perks and training for their best workers. Workers interested in learning new skills were encouraged to identify businesses that would pay for these skills. Chelie and Joe discovered that this new prospecting method identified several potential customers.

Practice Business Etiquette

You might think that knowing which fork to use at a formal dinner isn't important to the success of your business. When you invite a client to dinner at an expensive restaurant or attend a business event sponsored by an industry leader, this knowledge can make you feel more confident. **Etiquette,** correct conduct in social situations, can help you succeed.

Business Situations Require Etiquette

Customer contact occurs in many different situations. Your behavior determines the ease or difficulty you encounter in your professional relationships. Knowing what to say or do at the right time makes it easier for you and your associates to discuss and conduct business.

Telephone Skills Almost any business relationship eventually includes a phone call. Telephone skills enable you to conduct business and avoid misunderstandings.

Answer the Phone A friendly greeting starts a conversation on the right foot. If you answer calls from outside the office, state the name of your business and your name. If your calls are passed through a secretary or assistant, state your name as shown in Figure 21.3.

FIGURE 21.3   Answer the Phone

Good morning. Pennant Temporaries. This is Chelie Pennant.

or

Good morning. This is Chelie Pennant. How may I help you?

Place a Call   Again, a friendly greeting starts the conversation on a positive note. If a secretary or assistant answers the phone, a courteous greeting will get you much farther than an abrupt demand. In fact, they are the gatekeepers for their supervisors. A pleasant professional approach will ensure that the gate may be opened a little faster and a little wider for you. As shown in Figure 21.4, be sure to let the secretary know if you are returning a call. This assures the assistant that his or her supervisor will welcome the call.

FIGURE 21.4   Place a Call

Good morning. I'm returning a call from Jason Hunter about a temporary receptionist. This is Chelie Pennant.

or

Good morning. This is Chelie Pennant. I'm returning your call about a temporary receptionist.

Leave a Message   Answering machines and voice mail are a fact of life. When you have to leave a message, include the elements in Figure 21.5:

- **Your name**—Identify yourself clearly. State your first name, last name, name of your business, and your business title. Provide this information at the beginning and end of every message.
- **Your phone number**—Speak clearly and a little slower than usual to enable the recipient to write down the number if necessary. Include the area code if the recipient must dial it to reach you or if the number is toll-free. Provide this information at the beginning and end of every message.
- **Reason**—Summarize your reason for calling in a single sentence. Don't ramble for five minutes. Long messages create confusion if the recipient even bothers to listen to the entire message. A brief sentence gives the recipient time to acquire any needed information before returning your call.
- **Time**—State the date and time. Most phone message equipment adds a time stamp to the message, but state the time to be sure, especially if time is critical.
- **Reply**—Identify when and how the recipient should reply.

FIGURE 21.5   Leave a Message

Good morning. This is Chelie Pennant, your account representative from Pennant Temporaries. My number is 555-0238. I need the requirements for the temporary worker you requested. It's 10:00 A.M., Tuesday, May __. I will be here until 5:30 P.M. or you can call me tomorrow morning. Again, this is Chelie Pennant, your account representative from Pennant Temporaries. My number is 555-0238. Thank you.

Record an Outgoing Message The outgoing message on your business phone is not the place to exercise your sense of humor. Your message should confirm that the caller has reached your office. If you are out of town and someone else in the office can help the caller, provide the individual's name, title, and phone number. As shown in Figure 21.6, state when you will return calls if you are out of town.

FIGURE 21.6   Outgoing Message

Hello. This is Chelie Pennant of Pennant Temporaries. I will not be in the office until September 14, but I will return calls every afternoon between 4:00 and 5:00. Please leave a brief message that includes your name, telephone number, and the reason for your call. If you need assistance before this afternoon, please call Joe Pennant at 555-0239. Again, that's Joe Pennant at 555-0239 if you need assistance before this afternoon. Thank you.

Attire Proper dress is determined by the industry and the situation. A landscaper can wear shorts and light boots to work at a customer's site, but the same attire isn't appropriate for an accountant or a retailer. If your industry doesn't require specialized clothing, you make the best impression by dressing conservatively and professionally, like an administrator who works in a business office. If you work in an office in your home without customer contact, you are freer to choose any attire you want.

Dining Out When you dine with a business associate, you are developing and strengthening your business relationship. If you usually dine alone in front of the television or at a table populated by several children who still use their fingers to get most food from the plate to their mouths, a business dinner may seem daunting. However, like most rules of etiquette, the guidelines are designed to make you and others feel comfortable. If you want to review all the rules of fine dining, consult an etiquette handbook. A few simple tips can keep you from making basic errors:

- When formal place settings are used, use the silverware on the outside first. Use the next piece of silverware on the next course.
- You can begin to eat when half of the diners at your table have been served.
- Place each used piece of silverware flat on your plate. If the food is served in a bowl, place the used silverware on the plate under the bowl. This keeps your used silverware from staining the tablecloth.

- Reach only for items directly in front of you.
- When you pass serving dishes, pass to the right unless dishes are already being passed to the left.
- If you are dining at someone's home, don't salt or pepper an item before tasting it.
- Avoid smoking.

Cell Phones   A new method of interrupting a productive meeting or dinner with a customer is the cell phone. Turn off your cell phone before entering a meeting. This demonstrates respect for the other participants or attendees.

If you don't want to miss a call, inform the individual or group that you are expecting a critical call and ask for permission to take the call. When it comes, excuse yourself and move to a private location. Keep the call as brief as possible and turn off your phone to prevent additional calls.

Calls are often dropped in an elevator. Close your conversation before entering an elevator.

Cultural Differences

The most important thing to remember when dealing with individuals from other cultures is respect. It is unlikely that you can learn everything about another culture; however, others will respond favorably if you make an effort to learn the most basic elements of etiquette for their culture. Learn how to formally greet a customer from a different culture. Your effort will be appreciated. A few additional guidelines can be helpful in establishing and developing your business relationship:

- Address individuals by a title and his or her last name. Just as you would address an American as Mr. Smith, use the title appropriate to his or her culture.
- Learn a few words or phrases used in his or her language.
- Pay attention to the time zone where the business is located. You don't want to call when it is midnight in the customer's time zone.
- Respect the individual's daily and annual work schedule. Everyone needs a lunch break. Be aware that other countries celebrate different holidays.

Hypothetical Scenario

Chelie frequently met with temporary workers during lunch. This enabled her to talk with workers who were out on assignment and were unable to come to the Pennant office during work hours. Chelie and Joe shared the task of representing Pennant Temporaries at business events such as job fairs and chamber of commerce dinners. This socializing frequently resulted in new prospects for their services.

Technology Insights

Customer Relationship Management

Although successful selling usually takes place between people, computers have become involved in the sales process. Customer relationship management (CRM) software enables you to manage your relationship with your customers. It tracks sales leads, from first contact to closing the sale. After the sale is made, CRM software tracks customer service information. Store sales and service information in a single database to enable your workforce to manage the customer throughout the life cycle of the business relationship. It saves time and avoids duplication of effort. Communication among your employees is streamlined and effective. Representatives in the field can access the information through an Internet connection. Sales and service representatives communicate effectively, increasing their productivity and customer satisfaction.

Think Critically Identify customer information that is valuable to both sales and service representatives.

CHAPTER REVIEW

Communication is a critical business skill that can make the difference between success and failure. Miscommunication is caused by noise and differences in the way the sender and receiver view the world around them. It is impossible for a receiver to receive and understand any message exactly as the sender conceived it. Differences in goals, business organization, and communication can cause conflict. Resolve differences by reviewing your company's goals that are documented in the business plan, restructuring to meet business needs, and building rapport through meeting the needs of an individual's communication style.

To build a good sales force, hire people with sales skills. Sales representatives are financially motivated, self-confident, persistent, and have good communication skills. Personal selling focuses on people and the relationship between the business and its customers. It can be used by small businesses to compete effectively with much larger businesses. The personal selling process occurs in several steps—prospect, approach, identify the customer's needs, make the sales presentation, handle objections, close the sale, and service the customer after the sale. Communication skills help the successful salesperson close a sale, which is considered by many to be the most difficult step in the process.

Entrepreneurs who micromanage employees and projects reduce their efficiency and increase employee frustration. You can make significant improvements in your management style by improving your skills in planning, supporting your employees, training, delegating, assigning responsibilities, rewarding employee achievements, and keeping up with technological advances.

Knowledge of business etiquette can help you succeed by removing roadblocks in communication. Etiquette establishes guidelines for business activities such as telephone communication, dining, and cell phone usage. When communicating with individuals from other cultures, respect and an effort to make accommodations for differences has a positive impact on your business encounters.

USE BUSINESS TERMS

Fill in the blanks with the appropriate term.

authority	hands-on manager
channel	noise
cold call	personal selling
communication	prospecting
decode	receiver
delegate	responsibility
encode	restructuring
etiquette	sender

1. ___?___ can make you feel more confident in business situations.
2. An employee requires ___?___ to obtain resources needed to complete a project.
3. ___?___ some tasks without dumping all of your unpleasant chores.
4. Use a phone book to contact prospects when you make ___?___.
5. ___?___ focuses on people rather than products.
6. ___?___ transfers employees to other departments and assigns new responsibilities.
7. Transmitting a message requires a(n) ___?___.

TEST YOUR READING

8. Make a flowchart that describes the communication process.
9. How is a message encoded?
10. Identify five communication channels.
11. What causes conflict?
12. Describe the characteristics of a good salesperson.
13. Why don't large businesses use personal selling?
14. How is a prospect qualified?
15. Describe the sales presentation portion of the personal selling process.
16. How do you know when to close a sale?
17. Describe three ways to improve your management style.
18. Explain the difference between responsibility and authority.
19. Describe business attire in a specific industry.

THINK CRITICALLY ABOUT BUSINESS

20. Identify seven factors that affect how you encode or decode a message.
21. Identify your communication style and explain how you fit the style.
22. Interview a Realtor. Ask him or her to describe the sales process and his or her closing technique.
23. Describe three methods of identifying qualified prospects for your business.

REAL-LIFE BUSINESS

Wild Birds Unlimited

Most people didn't think it was possible to earn a living selling bird seed. However, Jim Carpenter didn't listen to most people. He believes that the foundation for his business career was built from problem-solving skills and an interest in exploring new concepts.

When Jim Carpenter earned a master's degree in ecological plant physiology, jobs in his selected field were hard to find. He chose to manage a lawn and garden center for a year and a half before he opened the first Wild Birds Unlimited in 1981. He leased store space for $400 per month. He discovered that many consumers were interested in attracting and feeding wild birds. Not only consumers were interested. Many individuals wanted to work for the business or become franchisees.

The first franchise store opened in 1983. Wild Birds Unlimited consisted of eight stores in 1986 and offered mail-order service. By 1992, Wild Birds Unlimited had opened 50 new stores. Although growth was rapid, Jim Carpenter continued to carefully select employees and franchise operators. He hasn't abandoned his true interest in birds and the environment. Wild Birds Unlimited supports several environmental groups.

Start-up costs for a Wild Birds Unlimited franchise range from $80,000 to $140,000. The exact cost is determined by factors such as the store's location, size, rent, etc. Every franchise pays an ongoing royalty fee.

The market for Wild Birds Unlimited consists of 52 million consumers who feed birds and watch wildlife in their backyards. Annually, they spend about $4.7 billion on birdseed, bird feeders, birdbaths, nesting boxes, binoculars, and spotting scopes.

Think Critically

1. Would salespeople at Wild Birds Unlimited use personal selling techniques?
2. Describe how you would approach a customer and close a sale.
3. Identify the tasks a manager at Wild Birds Unlimited can delegate.
4. Write an outgoing telephone message to be used when the store is not open.

UNIT 8

The Growth and Expansion of Your Business

CHAPTERS

CHAPTER 22

Growing Your Business

GOALS

- ◆ Finance the growth of your business
- ◆ Avoid deceptive advertising
- ◆ Protect your business from theft

Berto Salas owns a single go-cart racetrack just outside the city limits. Salas Speedway has performed well in the past year. It's located near a major tourist attraction, so its busiest time is the "tourist" season. However, Berto knows that the racetrack is frequently empty. He needs to think of ways to help his business grow.

Finance the Growth of Your Business

You've done well. Your business has survived and thrived. Now you are searching for financing to help your business grow.

Business Life Cycle

Like a living being, a business goes through a life cycle, illustrated in Figure 22.1. The five stages are start-up, growth, maturity, decline, and death. At each stage, your business has different characteristics and needs:

FIGURE 22.1 Business Life Cycle

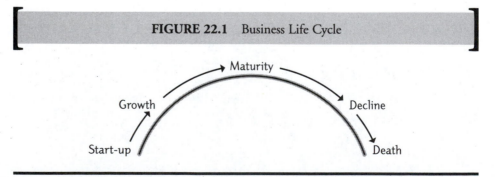

- ◆ **Start-up**—In many ways, the start-up period is the most difficult stage in the life cycle of a business. You don't know if it will succeed or fail. In fact, it may hover on the brink of failure more than once. The business requires a great deal of time, effort, and financial injections to establish and keep going. The cost of starting a business is high and sales are low. Advertising informs the public that the business exists, and it educates them about the company's products and services. An entrepreneur is needed to establish the business in the start-up phase.

- ◆ **Growth**—During the growth phase, the business turns the corner; it earns a steady profit and develops a reliable customer base. To keep growing, the business needs to attract more consumers who will buy its products. The increase in sales means that the business must also increase its productivity to meet the demand, which reduces the cost of making or acquiring each individual unit. The business's prices may be higher because it lacks competition. Advertising persuades consumers to purchase its products and services. Helping the business grow requires new ideas and risk-taking entrepreneurial skills. However, increasing productivity is an administrative skill involving planning and organizing groups of people and materials.

- ◆ **Maturity**—In the maturity phase, the profit and number of customers reach their peak. While the number of competitors is increasing, they haven't yet challenged the business's grip on the market. Consumers are aware of the business and its products. Advertising continues to persuade consumers to purchase its products and services. Naturally, a business should try to stay in the maturity phase for as long as possible. Many large corporations have remained in the maturity phase for decades. Good administration can keep the business at maximum performance for many years.

- ◆ **Decline**—Eventually, customers begin to purchase products and services from the competition, businesses that are more convenient, less expensive, or more innovative. The declining business means decreasing profits, even if the economy and other businesses in the industry are stable or increasing. The creative skills of an entrepreneur may enable a business to recover or delay the death of the business, but the decline is always fatal.

- ◆ **Death**—Closing a business that has a long history of success is a difficult decision. However, the chronic decline indicates that the business is nearing its end. Close the business before it drains all the company's remaining resources.

Many entrepreneurs enjoy the challenge of the start-up and growth periods, but lose interest when the business becomes established. They may sell a business once it matures and move on to start another business.

Ways to Grow

A business can grow and expand in four ways—market penetration, market development, merchandise expansion, and diversification. The first two options, illustrated in Figure 22.2, encourage growth and require the least risk. The second two options, which are discussed in Chapter 23, encourage expansion and require the most risk.

> **FIGURE 22.2**   Methods of Growth and Expansion
>
> | Less Risk | More Risk |
> |---|---|
> | Encourage growth through | Encourage expansion through |
> | ◆ Market Penetration | ◆ Merchandise Expansion |
> | ◆ Market Development | ◆ Diversification |

Market Penetration   You identified your target segment during the start-up phase of your business. A target segment is a subgroup of a market chosen to be the focus of the marketing and advertising campaign. You select a group because the individuals in the group share common characteristics and have similar needs and wants. For example, if your business manufactures sealer for wood decks, your target market could be new homeowners between the ages of 25 and 35 who have purchased a home with a wood deck for the first time.

Market penetration is a strategy that increases the sale of your existing products to your current market without altering the products. The risk is the amount you spend on marketing and any changes in your company's image or the image of your products. Within your target segment, individuals use your products or services, use a competitor's products or services, or don't use any products or services provided by you or your competition. Each group requires a different marketing approach:

◆   **Your customers**—You design the market penetration strategy to target your existing customers and increase the frequency of their purchases and usage. For example, your ads could emphasize that deck sealer should be applied annually to provide the best protection. Sales and coupons issued in the late summer or late winter can encourage your customers to purchase deck sealer in the spring to prepare the deck for summertime use, or in the fall to protect the deck from winter weather.

◆   **Competitor's customers**—Your competitor's customers already know the value of using deck sealer. Your strategy should convince them that your product is better in some key ways. It could be longer lasting, easier to use, or less expensive.

◆   **Nonusers**—Some individuals in your target segment have wood decks, but have never bothered to use a deck sealer. Your strategy should convince this group that sealing a deck would preserve the wood, maintaining the beauty and durability of the deck.

Market Development   To help your business grow, you may increase sales through **market development,** a strategy that sells your existing products to a new market. The new market might be interested in your product for a different reason or can be reached through a different method. Like market penetration, the risk is the amount you spend on marketing and any changes in your company's image or the image of your products. For example, your original target market was new home-owners between the ages of 25 and 35 who have purchased a home with a wood deck for the first time. A new market could be older homeowners or builders who construct homes for others. Reach these consumers by advertising in different magazines or selling through different retailers.

Finance the Growth

You may be surprised to learn that you have many of the same options for financing the growth of your business as you had for financing the start-up of your business. Again, the most common sources of capital for new businesses include personal savings, friends and family, and financial institutions. New sources to pay for growth expenses include partners and the profit earned by operating your business.

Personal Savings You may have depleted your personal savings by paying start-up expenses for your business. Funding the additional expenses to help your business grow enables you to retain ownership and control of your business and its business activities.

Friends and Family You may have already repaid any funds you borrowed from your friends or family. If the situation ended profitably and amicably, they may be interested in investing additional funds. Don't accept a loan without a promissory note. Although you are borrowing funds from individuals who have a personal relationship with you, the loan should be offered and accepted for business reasons.

Financial Institutions Banks and credit unions are still the most popular sources of business loans. The successful operation of your business helps you convince the loan officer that your business will continue to grow. You must be well prepared with plans, facts, and numbers. The loan officer needs to know how much money you need, how you plan to use the money, and how the proposed expansion of your business will cause it to succeed. Update your business plan and prepare a new presentation.

Partners Regardless of your company's current stage, you can always bring in another partner, as long as you follow the terms of the partnership agreement. The new partner can bring new cash into the business, enabling you to move forward with your plans for growth.

Profit In the growth phase, your business is gaining customers and earning a profit. You can use the profit to pay for additional growth.

Hypothetical Scenario

Berto Salas has some ideas that will help Salas Speedway grow. He noticed that most of his customers were children and college students on vacation. However, local college students rarely came to the racetrack. Berto decided to start an advertising campaign directed at the students at the local college.

Avoid Deceptive Promotions

In your role as a consumer and business owner, you will encounter dishonest methods of increasing profit. Your actions are based on your personal ethics and your knowledge of the laws regulating promotions in an environment of fair competition. Competitors that suffer because of dishonest methods used by another company may pursue the matter in court.

Businesses promote their products and services through marketing activities, such as advertising and event sponsorship. Advertising is an opportunity for businesses to make statements about their products, services, and competitors. It is also an opportunity to make misleading statements, either deliberately or accidentally. Because advertising is a public statement, deception is easy to identify and prove.

The **Federal Trade Commission (FTC),** www.ftc.gov, was created in 1914 to stop unfair methods of competition. In 1916, the FTC determined that false advertising was an unfair method of competition. Advertising became a primary interest of the agency.

Deceitful Diversion of Patronage

A competitor that publishes or verbalizes false statements about another business to try to divert patrons from the business is engaging in **deceitful diversion of patronage.** The injured business can contact the FTC or pursue the issue in court by charging the competitor with libel or slander for making untrue statements that hurt the company's reputation.

However, businesses do not often pursue cases of deceitful diversion in court. It may be simple to prove that the statement is false, but it is difficult to prove that the business lost sales or customers as a result of the false statement. However, injured businesses do win cases often enough that other businesses have learned to be more cautious about the statements they, their advertising, and their employees make about the competition.

A second form of deceitful diversion of patronage is known as **palming off.** A retailer buys merchandise from one manufacturer, but places the label of a more popular manufacturer on the products. This is not only deceitful but it also infringes on trademarks owned by both manufacturers. Paying more than the product is worth injures the consumer. The better manufacturer is injured because its reputation may be damaged when the relabeled product breaks, works less efficiently, or otherwise demonstrates its lesser quality.

Bait and Switch

Businesses may lure customers by using the **bait and switch** tactic, which is advertising an attractive low price, and then trying to persuade the customer that the low-priced model is a poor buy because of its quality. These businesses hope consumers will buy the better, more expensive model. They bait the customers with the low-priced model, and then switch to the more expensive model. If the business runs out of the advertised item, it should issue a rain check or sell an item of comparable value to the customer rather than attempting to persuade him or her to purchase a more expensive item.

Substantiation and Retraction

A business may be asked to **substantiate**—provide proof—that its advertising claims about a product's quality, safety, or performance are true. If the advertising statements cannot be proven, the FTC can require that the business issue a public retraction. The **retraction** publicly withdraws the false statements, admitting that they were not true.

Hypothetical Scenario

Berto distributed some fliers at the local college. The fliers contained a sketch of a go-cart, a map of the route from the college to Silas Speedway, and the line "15 minutes free!" Berto meant that every customer who purchased 15 minutes would receive an additional 15 minutes at no extra charge. Unfortunately, Berto's first customers responding to the flier were law students who were more than happy to point out the deceptive nature of the ad in the flier. Berto ended up watching unhappily as a large group of students raced for 15 minutes without making a purchase or spending a single dime.

Prevent Theft

Increasing profit and decreasing expenses by reducing theft can help your business grow. Businesses lose property and merchandise every day. It doesn't fall off the back of the truck or disappear in a dark corner. Small items leave the premises hidden in customers' pockets or employees' lunch bags.

It may be called **shrinkage,** loss, or shoplifting. Whatever you call it, it is a serious problem for retailers and other businesses. Every year, businesses lose billions of dollars in stolen merchandise and property. Businesses can take a variety of actions to prevent loss.

Store Layout

Retailers primarily design the store layout to increase sales by encouraging customers to pass as much merchandise as possible. Including features to reduce shoplifting could increase your profit. Increasing visibility is an important factor in reducing shoplifting. Most shoplifting occurs where customers or merchandise are not easily seen, such as in fitting rooms, behind tall displays, or in crowded aisles. Reduce shoplifting by using display fixtures that employees can see over, keeping all areas of the store well lit, and placing employee stations near fitting rooms and exits.

Check Fraud

Every year, U.S. consumers write more than 68 billion checks. Each day, U.S. consumers write more than 1.2 million bad checks. Ernst & Young, a major accounting firm, reports that annual losses from check fraud total more than $10 billion.

The *American Banker,* a journal for the banking industry, projects that loss caused by check fraud will increase 2.5 percent every year.

Regardless of the chance of check fraud, most businesses cannot afford to refuse to accept checks. Checks are used as payment in approximately one-third of all retail transactions. A company that does not accept checks will lose business. To help limit check fraud, establish standard procedures for accepting and handling checks:

- ◆ Require specific forms of identification.
- ◆ Verify that the photo and description on the identification match the customer in front of you.
- ◆ Make sure the customer's name, address, and phone number are on the check.
- ◆ Make sure the name and address on the check match those on the identification.
- ◆ Set a dollar limit.

Employee Theft

Although shoplifting by customers can be a serious problem, theft by a retailer's employees accounts for more losses every year than shoplifting. In 2000, employee theft accounted for more than 22 percent of the merchandise loss experienced by retailers; the average retailer lost $1,023 for each dishonest employee. As a retailer or business owner, you can take several steps to decrease the chance of theft by your employees:

- ◆ Use video surveillance in the store, particularly at the checkout counter. This practice is not widely accepted outside a retail situation.
- ◆ Perform thorough background checks before hiring any employee.
- ◆ Limit access to the building's key.
- ◆ Pay higher wages to attract and keep better employees.

False Refunds

Returned merchandise is an opportunity for both consumer and employee theft. Consumers may request a cash refund when trying to return merchandise stolen from your store or purchased with a bad check. Avoid these types of false refunds by requiring an original receipt and waiting until the check has successfully cleared the bank.

Employees left alone or unsupervised may invent false refunds to explain cash missing from the register. Prevent this type of false refund by requiring that customers returning merchandise provide contact information and a signature. Occasionally, go through these forms and contact random customers to verify the merchandise return.

Hypothetical Scenario

Berto wasn't sure what to do. His nephew worked alone at Silas Speedway three evenings every week. On those three evenings, the speedway seemed to do less business than usual. Berto suspected that business wasn't actually slower on those days. He was afraid that his nephew was keeping some of the proceeds for himself. Berto felt silly playing private detective, but he spent Wednesday evening parked across the street from Silas Speedway, counting the customers he saw at the speedway during his nephew's shift. The next day, he compared his tally to the receipts reported by his nephew. After a few quick calculations, Berto determined that his nephew wasn't reporting all of the customers. Although it would be unpleasant, Berto decided to fire his nephew.

Technology Insights

Detect Counterfeit Currency

Counterfeit currency was probably created one day after real currency was created. During the American Civil War, American currency didn't have a standard appearance. Instead, 1,600 state banks designed and printed currency. The differences among the authentic bills made it difficult to identify counterfeit currency.

It wasn't until 1862 that a standard national currency was created. However, counterfeiting continued. The United States Secret Service was established in 1865 to curtail counterfeiting. Although counterfeiting was successfully suppressed, it is increasing again.

You can protect your business from loss due to counterfeit currency in two ways. Learn how to recognize authentic currency and purchase a machine or pen that identifies counterfeit bills. A pen is the easiest and most economical method. The pen contains a chemical that leaves no mark on authentic currency, but leaves a dark mark on counterfeit bills. Keep a pen near every cash register.

Think Critically Describe how to protect your business from loss caused by counterfeit currency.

CHAPTER REVIEW

Every business has a life cycle that consists of five stages—start-up, growth, maturity, decline, and death. The entrepreneur's skills are needed during the start-up and growth stages to establish the business and apply creativity to the product or service offered. During the maturity and decline stages, an entrepreneur may be able to use creativity to reinvigorate a business. A business can grow through market penetration, market development, merchandise expansion, and diversification. Market penetration and market development incur less risk because they involve changes to your marketing approach rather than your product or service.

In a desire to increase profit, a business owner may accidentally or intentionally use promotion tactics that don't belong in an environment of fair competition. Dishonest promotion tactics include deceitful diversion of patronage and bait and switch. The Federal Trade Commission is a government agency that monitors and regulates advertising to ensure fair competition.

Theft is a serious problem for many businesses. It reduces profit by increasing expenses. You can reduce theft in several ways. Retailers can increase visibility. Businesses can set strict guidelines for hiring employees, accepting checks, and giving refunds.

USE BUSINESS TERMS

Fill in the blanks with the appropriate term.

bait and switch
deceitful diversion of patronage
Federal Trade Commission (FTC)
market development
market penetration

palming off
retraction
shrinkage
substantiate

1. The ___?___ strategy directed at your existing customers is designed to increase the frequency of their purchases and usage.
2. The ___?___ tactic lures customers into a store by advertising a low price, but encourages the purchase of a more expensive product.
3. The ___?___ determined that false advertising was an unfair method of competition.
4. If the advertising statements cannot be proven, the Federal Trade Commission can require that the business issue a public ___?___.
5. Store layout can discourage loss due to ___?___.
6. ___?___ is deceitful and infringes on trademarks owned by the manufacturers of the more popular and the relabeled products.
7. A business may be asked to ___?___ its accurate advertising claims.

TEST YOUR READING

8. Describe the business life cycle.
9. Describe the difference between market penetration and market development.
10. How do you decide to close your business?
11. How can you increase market penetration of your existing customers?
12. How can you finance growth?
13. Describe the criteria for identifying a deceptive advertisement.
14. Which government agency regulates advertising?
15. What can a business do if it is a victim of deceitful diversion of patronage?
16. How can a store layout discourage shoplifting?
17. Why is check fraud a problem?
18. How much do retailers lose to employee theft?
19. How can a retailer protect the business from false refunds?

THINK CRITICALLY ABOUT BUSINESS

20. Select a local business. Identify its life cycle stage. Explain how you identified its current stage.
21. How would you finance the growth of your business? Explain your answer.
22. Describe a situation that demonstrated dishonest promotion tactics.
23. Visit a local store. Evaluate its visible shoplifting prevention methods.

REAL-LIFE BUSINESS

John Paul Mitchell Systems

In 1980, John Paul DeJoria and Paul Mitchell borrowed $750 to establish a business that makes products for hairstylists. The company began marketing its hair care products using the brand name Paul Mitchell. Funds were so tight during the first year that they couldn't afford to use colored ink on their product packaging. The black-and-white packaging became a distinctive product identifier.

Many of the expenses incurred during the first year were the result of their unique approach. They conducted product demonstrations and guaranteed that any products not purchased by customers could be returned for a full refund. The guarantee ensured that the company grew quickly. The company's annual retail sales now exceed $600 million. Approximately 90,000 U.S. hair salons and 15,000 hair salons in 45 countries sell their products.

Think Critically

1. How much money did DeJoria and Mitchell borrow to start the company?
2. What is their product?
3. How was their approach unique?
4. How much does the company earn now?

CHAPTER 23

Expanding Your Business

GOALS

- ◆ Expand your business
- ◆ Develop additional distribution methods
- ◆ Describe the evolution of a company's web site

Emma Jensen operated Funny Bunny Party Poppers, a party entertainment business, for a year. Most customers requested clowns or magicians for children's birthday parties. The business grew steadily through word-of-mouth and referrals from party suppliers and catering companies.

Expand Your Business

A company's growth must be managed and directed. Successful growth is the result of the right blend of conservative action, risk-taking behavior, and a chain of good decisions. Businesses can grow with limited risk by using marketing strategies that increase their market penetration and develop their markets. Businesses that are ready for more risk, because of factors such as profit or current size, can expand. Expansion occurs through merchandise expansion and diversification. When your business grows sufficiently, you can choose to sell shares of your business through the stock market.

Merchandise Expansion

Merchandise expansion is risky because the expense involved in this growth method can be high. If your actions are not successful, financial recovery may be difficult or impossible. As shown in Figure 23.1, merchandise expansion has different requirements for each business type—retailers, manufacturers, and service businesses. Retailers need the basic requirements, while manufacturers and service providers have a few additional needs based on the business type.

FIGURE 23.1   Requirements for Merchandise Expansion

Manufacturers
Equipment
Raw Materials
Expertise
+ Basic Requirements

Service Providers
Equipment
Expertise
+ Basic Requirements

Retailers

Basic Requirements
Customer Wants and Needs
Customer Expectations
Available Space
Financial Limitations

Retailers Many retailers choose to grow by opening additional retail establishments that sell the same merchandise. However, merchandise expansion enables retailers to grow in other ways. Your current merchandise mix was selected to meet the wants and needs of your customers, fill customer expectations, fit into the space available to display or keep merchandise, and stay within the financial limitations of your business. Use the same criteria to identify additional lines of merchandise.

Customer Wants and Needs Your merchandise mix attracts a specific type of customer searching for a particular type of item that they want or need. When you consider adding new products, reexamine the wants and needs of your customers. Determine the wants that your current merchandise doesn't fill. For example, if your merchandise mix currently consists of gourmet cooking equipment and utensils, your customers may also need cookbooks, ingredients, and major appliances.

Customer Expectations Based on the image of your business and past experience in your store, your customers expect you to carry specific merchandise. If you add a new line of merchandise, customers would not be surprised to see cookbooks when they enter the store. In fact, they will probably buy the cookbooks that feature recipes using the cooking equipment they just purchased. However, if you add a refrigerator case and try to sell milk and eggs, which are ingredients in many recipes, customers will not purchase them. The ingredients are inappropriate merchandise selections because customers don't expect your store to carry fresh ingredients that they can easily purchase at a grocery store. The ingredients will spoil before they can be sold, resulting in a financial loss for your business.

Available Space When you select additional merchandise, you must consider the amount of space available to display and store merchandise. Small items, such as cookbooks, are much easier to add to your merchandise than large items, such as stainless steel grills or ovens.

Financial Limitations You can purchase only the merchandise you can afford. Even if you determine that your customers would purchase more expensive items, you must be able to pay for the merchandise first. Although you may be able to use credit to purchase merchandise, be cautious in your use of credit. You could end up owing money for merchandise you can't sell, draining your company's financial resources.

Manufacturers The concerns of a retailer considering merchandise expansion are common for manufacturers as well. Manufacturers must examine how additional product lines will meet the wants and needs of their customers, fill customer expectations, fit into the space available to display or keep products and materials, and stay within the financial limitations of their business. Additionally, manufacturers must consider equipment, raw materials, and expertise.

Equipment If your business manufactures products, it may own expensive equipment required in the manufacturing process. When you decide to add products, you must have manufacturing time available on your existing equipment or purchase additional equipment. Examine both alternatives to select the most cost-efficient option.

Raw Materials The materials needed to produce your new products must be available and affordable. To be considered available, the raw materials must exist in sufficient quantities and be accessible through methods such as pickup or delivery.

Expertise Many manufacturing processes require knowledge and skill. **Knowledge** is the possession of information. A graduate of a training class knows how to perform a certain action. For a manufacturer, the necessary knowledge includes use of the equipment as well as the preparation and mix of raw materials. **Skill** is the ability to use your knowledge effectively, often as a result of experience. An individual with knowledge and skill is an **expert.** If you add new products and new equipment, you may need to hire additional employees who can use the equipment.

Service Business The concerns of a retailer considering merchandise expansion are common for a service business as well. Service business owners must examine how additional services can meet the wants and needs of their customers, fill customer expectations, fit into the space available to display or keep equipment, and stay within the financial limitations of their businesses. Additionally, a service business must consider equipment and expertise.

Equipment A service business sells an individual's time and abilities. Depending on the service you sell, the equipment to perform the service could belong to your business or to your customers. For example, landscapers use their own equipment when they plant shrubbery or mow the lawn. However, a temporary service that provides programmers expects the customer to supply the equipment used by the programmer at the customer's site. Therefore, the type of service you provide determines the need to purchase additional equipment if you provide additional services.

Expertise A service business sells the expertise of its employees. For a service business to expand, it must acquire additional employees with expertise in the new areas it has selected for expansion.

Diversification

Expansion can also be accomplished through **diversification,** starting or acquiring businesses that are outside a company's products and markets. Most large businesses have a wide variety of business activities, as displayed in Table 23.1.

TABLE 23.1 Diversification	
Company	Business Activities
The Procter & Gamble Company	Markets more than 250 brands, including products such as dog food, coffee, and pharmaceuticals
AOL Time Warner, Inc.	Brands include products such as music, cable systems, publishing, and interactive services
The Walt Disney Company	Operates businesses such as the ABC Television Network and Walt Disney World Resort, sells apparel, and publishes books

A business can grow through diversification by merging with or acquiring another company. **Mergers** usually occur when two companies that are similar in size join forces. **Acquisitions** occur when a larger, wealthier company buys a smaller company and its assets. Depending on the size and value of the companies involved, a merger or acquisition may require approval by the Federal Trade Commission (FTC). The FTC is involved because mergers and acquisitions by large businesses may jeopardize fair competition. Fair competition means consumers are free to choose different businesses to serve their needs. If one company drives others out of business and merges with or acquires any other major competition, consumers will have fewer choices. Therefore, mergers and acquisitions are not always approved. If the two companies are in the same business and operate in the same market, approval could be withheld to prevent unfair competition.

Enter the Stock Market

At some point in its growth, a company may decide to take a larger risk by "going public." In order to go public, shares of its company must be offered and sold to the general public after meeting all registration requirements of the Securities and Exchange Commission (SEC). When a company registers with the SEC to sell stock to the public for the first time, it is called an **Initial Public Offering (IPO).** Company stock is sold on a stock exchange, such as the New York Stock Exchange or the American Stock Exchange.

Advantages to becoming a publicly traded company include increasing the value of the company, providing easier access to capital, and increasing public recognition of your brand name. There are also disadvantages. The company no longer belongs only to its owners. Therefore, they do not have the authority to make decisions alone. Shareholders must be consulted or considered in every decision that affects the value of the company. Any financial gain is not the owner's alone. It must be divided among all the company shareholders.

Investors and shareholders risk their personal funds when they choose to invest in a company. Their financial success becomes tied to the success of the company. The amount of money they have to pay for new homes, a college education for their children, and retirement depends on their investment decisions. To protect investors, the SEC requires every publicly traded company to reveal information about its operations and financial condition. The company is required to file periodic reports with the SEC that describe the company's business, property, and financial condition. The company's annual report provides additional information about the company's activities and strategies.

Hypothetical Scenario

Emma Jensen's business, Funny Bunny Party Poppers, has been supplying party entertainment for a year. To continue growing, Emma decides to add party planning. Her experience and connections should help her organize and schedule the necessary elements for any party. The risk level is low because it doesn't require any major purchases. She informed her network of business connections of the new services.

Develop Additional Distribution Methods

When you established your business, you selected your role in a channel of distribution, the path of a product from the producer to the consumer. Your role is based on the activities you perform, the items you purchase, and the businesses and individuals who are your customers. When you consider alternative methods of selling your products, services, or merchandise, take advantage of your current distribution methods and the information you have already gathered. Match an appropriate distribution method to your type of business and product.

Retailer

By definition, a retailer sells goods directly to the final customer. Your methods of enabling a customer to purchase your products are already established. However, you can usually increase sales by providing additional methods of customer contact.

In the past, individuals who sold products to the public had to open a retail establishment because the only payment method was the exchange of goods or currency. The transaction required the presence of the seller and the buyer to physically transfer the payment to the retailer and transfer the product to the buyer.

The physical presence of the buyer and seller is no longer necessary to complete a business transaction. Credit cards enable a buyer to pay for merchandise without physically handing the payment to the retailer. The electronic transfer of funds frees the retailer to sell products without a physical location for customers to visit.

Retail Establishment Many small retailers operate from a single retail establishment selling a specialized collection of merchandise. Initially, growth occurs by moving to a larger physical location or opening additional locations. Retail establishments have advantages and disadvantages, as shown in Table 23.2.

TABLE 23.2 Retail Establishments

Advantages	Disadvantages
Enables customers to see and handle the merchandise	Limited range for attracting customers
Space to store available merchandise is often on the same premises	Limited capacity for holding a large number of customers at the same time
Limited hours of operation enable the owner and employees to keep a predictable schedule	Expense of maintaining a building can be high

Alternative growth methods include establishing phone orders and creating a site that enables customers to place orders on the Internet. To lure your existing customers into placing orders via the phone or Internet, inform customers that the new option is available. Distribute fliers to customers entering the store. Create and send a catalog or direct mail package to reinforce the availability of the new order placement services.

Telephone Retailers can establish themselves as businesses that accept orders placed only through phone calls. Customers are informed about these products via direct mail packages, catalogs, and e-mail messages. Telephone vendors have advantages and disadvantages, as shown in Table 23.3.

TABLE 23.3 Telephone Retailers

Advantages	Disadvantages
Unlimited range for attracting customers	Customers cannot see and handle the merchandise
No expense of maintaining a building for customer visits	Customer relationships are difficult to establish and maintain
Products can be stored and shipped from any location	Additional employees are needed to staff the phone beyond the standard 9 to 5 hours

Alternative growth methods include opening a retail establishment and creating a web site that enables customers to place orders. A retail establishment located near the majority of your customers or easily accessible from a major city can attract customers who are either from the area or passing through the area. For a company that sells through catalogs, a retail establishment also functions as a catalog showroom, enabling customers to examine an article before buying it. If you grow by establishing a web site, inform your current customers. Place the address of your web site on every page of your catalog. Include the web address in any direct mail package you send. Inform callers of the new web site when they make a purchase.

Web Site   Today's technology enables retailers to establish and operate a business through the Internet without physically meeting a single customer. Customers find the web site by searching, random surfing, or responding to an advertisement on another web site. Internet retailers have similar advantages and disadvantages as telephone retailers, as shown in Table 23.4.

TABLE 23.4   Internet Retailers

Advantages	Disadvantages
Unlimited range for attracting customers	Customers cannot handle the merchandise
No expense of maintaining a building for customer visits	Customer relationships are more difficult to establish and maintain
Products can be stored and shipped from any location	Orders can be placed at any time of the day or night

Alternative growth methods include obtaining a retail establishment and phone lines that enable customers to place orders. A retail establishment located near the majority of your customers or easily accessible from a major city can attract customers who are either from the area or passing through the area. For a company that sells through the Internet, a retail establishment also functions as a product showroom, enabling customers to examine an article before buying it. If you grow by establishing phone lines, inform your current customers. Place the phone number on every page of your web site.

Manufacturer

Many manufacturers sell their products to consumers through retailers or to businesses that use their products. Manufacturers can choose to eliminate the retailer by selling directly to the final consumers. Eliminating a middleman can increase the profit from each sale, decrease the price paid by the final customer, and reduce the time between manufacturing and delivery. On the other hand, it may require additional staff to complete the new retail tasks.

When a manufacturer sells directly to consumers, it has the same alternative growth options as a retail business. Limited only by the requirements of the product, a manufacturer can choose to open a physical location where products are sold to consumers at a lower price than a retailer would charge. Additional staff and facilities may be needed to respond to individual customers and prepare the smaller shipments sent to individual consumers rather than retailers.

Service Business

Most services are performed in person, requiring the physical presence of the worker. The product you sell—the time and skill of your employees—isn't easily sold through a retail establishment. For example, it would be difficult to store accountants and architects on a shelf waiting for a customer to select one. For the same reason, it's difficult to sell services through the telephone or Internet. Services that don't require the worker's presence, such as designing web sites or programming, can be sold through telephone or Internet distribution methods.

Hypothetical Scenario

The majority of Emma's business is the result of referrals from party supply stores and satisfied customers. To provide basic information about her services, Emma developed a web site for the business and a brochure to be mailed to prospective customers.

Establish a Web Site

Many small businesses use the Internet to reach customers through a company web site, advertise on other web sites, and send and receive e-mail messages. However, some businesses refuse to hop on the bandwagon. These reluctant businesses cite a variety of reasons:

- **Lack of time**—The business owner doesn't have the time needed to investigate the advantages and disadvantages of establishing a web site or learn the skills needed to create the site.
- **Lack of resources**—The business doesn't have the financial resources to purchase the skill or equipment needed to create or maintain a web site.
- **Audience**—Many small business owners target local consumers, so they believe the Internet is not an appropriate tool for their businesses.

These arguments against creating a web site for your small business aren't valid. Software packages enable you to build a basic web site in minutes without requiring any design skills. A professional web designer can create a "look" for your web site that is more customized and more complex, but the basic site doesn't require a high spending level.

Web sites that sell storage space and web services to small businesses such as yours charge a specific amount to set up the site and a monthly fee based on the amount of data transferred. For example, a site may charge you a one-time setup fee of $25 and a monthly fee of $50. Additional fees may be charged for each product, sales transaction, or the amount of revenue earned. Prices are based on the options you select, so setup and maintenance fees vary among vendors.

Consumers are increasingly turning to the Internet for information. They are just as likely to search for information about your small business located a mile away as they are to seek information about a large business operating in a different state.

Internet Terminology

Before hiring a consultant to create a web site for your business or taking on this task yourself, do some homework. Familiarity with some of the terms in Table 23.5 enables you to make management decisions about your web site.

TABLE 23.5   Internet Terminology

Term	Definition
Banner	An advertisement placed on a web page that opens the advertiser's web site when a user clicks it.
Button	An icon that causes an action, such as calculating a total or displaying another web page, when the user clicks it.
Click trail	Identifies where visitors clicked as they moved through your web site.
Counter	Tracks the number of hits for a web site.
Domain name	A unique name that identifies a web site.
E-commerce	Doing business online. Requires specialized software, a secure web site, and a method of processing payments.
Hit	Electronic request to view a specific web page.
Home page	The entry page for a web site.
Hyperlink or link	Electronic connection between one specific location in a document to another location in the same document or a different document.
Internet Service Provider (ISP)	An organization that provides access to the Internet via a dial-up connection, cable connection, satellite connection, etc.
Navigation	Moving among pages on a single web site or between web sites.
Secure Socket Layer (SSL)	Data encryption method to protect data, such as online payment information, transferred between an Internet host and the browser.
Shopping cart	Software program incorporated into a web site to collect and record purchasing information.
Uniform Resource Locator (URL)	Identifies the address for a specific web page.
Unique visitor	A single individual visiting your web site.
Web hosting	A company that provides electronic storage space for individuals and businesses.

Advantages of Maintaining a Web Site The most basic web site can achieve several goals. It can:

◆ **Increase consumer awareness of your company and its products or services.** A web site displays the name of your company and its products or services 24 hours a day every day.

◆ **Reach a market outside your local area.** Consumers can view your web site from anywhere in the world.

◆ **Quickly distribute time-sensitive information.** Sales, announcements, and instructions can be placed on the Internet within minutes.

- **Increase income.** A web site encourages consumers to purchase your products. Consumers who purchase items in your bricks-and-mortar store or online obtain information and make comparisons to other products online.

- **Reduce the cost of customer support.** Provide answers to common questions and solutions to common problems, reducing the need to provide phone support to repeatedly answer the same questions.

Web Site Development Web sites can be categorized by the level of interaction that occurs between the customer and the business. The complexity of the site determines the level as basic, interactive, or online store.

Basic Web Site Even the most basic web site provides some information for consumers searching for your company or your products. A basic web site, such as the example in Figure 23.2, should contain basic information about your company, your product, and contact information. Remember that consumers visiting the site may be comparing your products to a competitor's products. The site usually contains only a single web page without any links to other pages or e-mail applications:

- **Company Name and Logo**—Identify the name of your company. Include the logo so consumers associate your logo with your company.

- **Product**—Identify and describe your product. You can choose to include a picture of the product, its function, directions for use, price, delivery method, etc.

- **Contact Information**—Provide the contact information you want customers to use, such as a phone number, fax number, mailing address, or e-mail address.

FIGURE 23.2   Basic Web Site

Interactive Web Site Add links to other pages, interactive forms, and a link to an e-mail application that enables the consumer to send an e-mail message to your business. If product options are available, the consumer could select specific options to build a complete product, which the site can use to calculate a price. An interactive web site, such as the example in Figure 23.3, should contain more than the basic information about your company, your product, and contact information.

FIGURE 23.3   Interactive Web Site

Online Store A web site that enables consumers to purchase your products on the Internet is an **online store.** An online store, such as the example in Figure 23.4, should use security measures and interactive forms that enable customers to select, price, and pay for the selected products.

FIGURE 23.4   Online Store

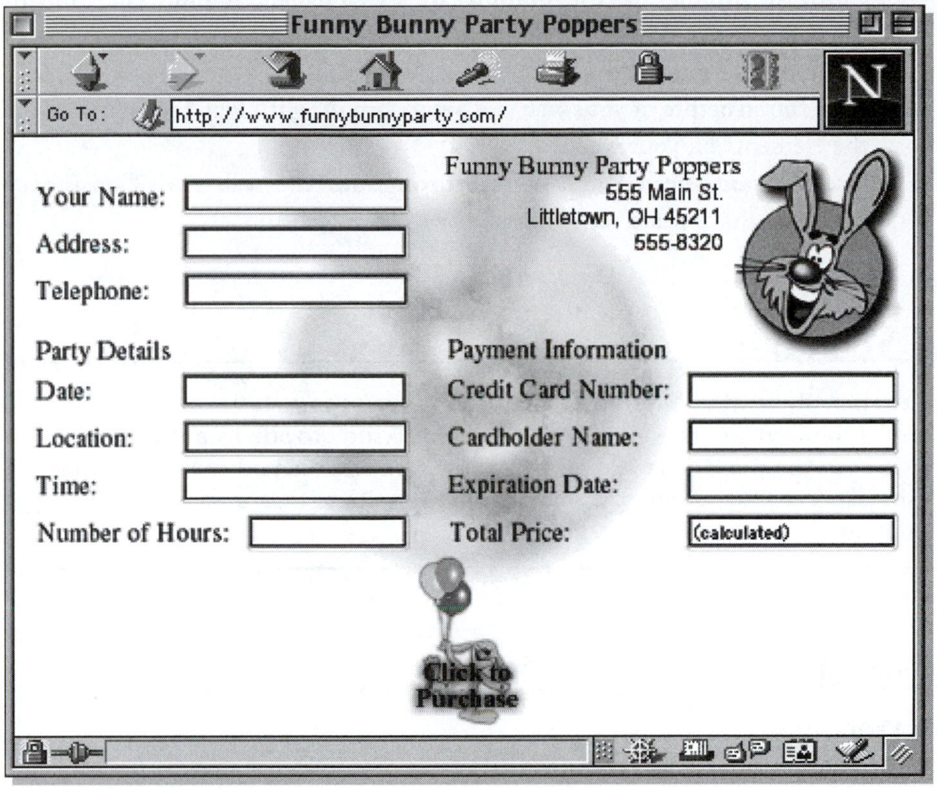

Funny Bunny Party Poppers

Go To: http://www.funnybunnyparty.com/

Your Name:

Address:

Telephone:

Funny Bunny Party Poppers
555 Main St.
Littletown, OH 45211
555-8320

Party Details

Date:

Location:

Time:

Number of Hours:

Payment Information

Credit Card Number:

Cardholder Name:

Expiration Date:

Total Price: (calculated)

Click to Purchase

Design Tips and Guidelines   Your web site represents your business. Be sure that the image it presents is the image you want for your business. Use the following guidelines to build your web site:

- **Use a design that is attractive to your target segment.**   Use graphics, fonts, and text that help you connect with the targeted consumers.
- **Avoid using long blocks of text.**   Text displayed on a computer screen is difficult to read.

- **Limit the moving items on a web page.** If the page is too busy, the important information is difficult to find.
- **Limit the number of large graphics on a web page.** Graphics take time for the consumer to download. If a page takes too long to download, consumers will move on to a different site.
- **Map the structure of your web site before building it.** Plan the links between the elements on your web site.
- **Use the same design and colors throughout the web site.** Consistency improves the appearance and usability of your web site.

Hypothetical Scenario

Emma's first web site contained the most basic information. She added the web site address to her brochure and business card. When the business hosting the web site provided statistics for the number of unique visitors to the site, Emma was surprised. The web site seemed to have a larger number of visitors than she expected. She decided to improve the web site to create an alternative method of generating business.

Technology Insights

Graphic Formats for Web Sites

Effective web pages contain graphics such as photographs, sketches, or cartoons. Each graphic is saved as a separate file on the server, where it is linked to the web page. When a consumer opens the web page, the elements on the page are downloaded to the user's computer. The format of most graphics used on a web page is JPEG (Joint Photographic Experts Group) or GIF (Graphics Interchange Format) because these formats can be displayed by most browsers. JPEG graphics are used to store photographs, pictures with many colors (more than 256), or very detailed graphics. GIF graphics are used when the image contains a transparent area that enables viewers to see text or other items under the graphic. GIF graphics are also used when the graphic contains text or no more than 256 colors.

Think Critically Why would you use a JPEG image rather than a GIF image?

CHAPTER REVIEW

Growth is a critical phase in the life cycle of any business. Expansion is a method of growing that requires some risk. To expand, a business can select additional merchandise to sell, diversify, or offer shares of the business for public purchase through the stock market. To be successful, a business evaluating merchandise expansion must consider the wants and needs of its existing customers, the expectations of its customers, the amount of space available to display and store the merchandise, and its financial ability to purchase the merchandise. Manufacturers must also consider the equipment that must be purchased, the cost and availability of the needed raw materials, and the expertise required to produce the new products. To expand, service providers must consider the basic requirements, any equipment that must be purchased, and the expertise they must acquire by hiring new employees or training existing employees. Selling shares of your business through a stock market is the most risky method of expansion.

When you established your business, you selected a distribution method. An additional distribution method can help you succeed by reaching new and existing customers. Consider the type of business you operate and the product you sell when you evaluate additional distribution methods. For example, products that consumers like to taste or touch are easier to sell through a retail establishment. However, a food product that is already popular can be sold through the Internet if it can be delivered successfully. Telephone orders can support an established business or succeed as the primary distribution method. Internet sales can succeed as a primary sales method and support businesses that primarily sell through other avenues.

E-commerce is gaining in popularity every day. Many businesses are developing web sites to support their products and make additional sales. The most basic business web site provides information about the business and its products. An interactive web site provides additional information, contains hyperlinks, and provides a method of contacting the business. The most advanced web site, the online store, enables consumers to purchase a product through the Internet.

USE BUSINESS TERMS

Fill in the blanks with the appropriate term.

acquisition	Initial Public Offering (IPO)
banner	Internet Service Provider (ISP)
button	knowledge
click trail	merger
counter	navigation
diversification	online store
domain name	Secure Socket Layer (SSL)
e-commerce	shopping cart
expert	skill
hit	Uniform Resource Locator (URL)
home page	unique visitor
hyperlink or link	web hosting

1. A business operating a(n) ___?___ that enables customers to make purchases on the Internet should use security measures.
2. A business must meet SEC requirements before its ___?___.
3. A business can diversify by ___?___ a smaller company that manufactures different products.
4. Consumers shopping in an online store place items in a(n) ___?___ before they are purchased.
5. The web address for a business site is a(n) ___?___.
6. A business wants its name to appear in its ___?___.
7. Consumers can click a(n) ___?___ on another web site to open your web site.

TEST YOUR READING

8. Identify the basic requirements a retailer must consider before growing through merchandise expansion.
9. Why is growth through merchandise expansion risky?
10. Identify the factors a manufacturer must consider before growing through merchandise expansion.
11. Identify the factors a service business must consider before growing through merchandise expansion.
12. What is the difference between a merger and an acquisition?
13. How has technology changed the retail industry?
14. Identify the advantages of a retail establishment as a distribution method.
15. How does a consumer learn about a product that can be purchased only through a phone call?
16. How does a web site help a bricks-and-mortar retailer grow?

17. Why is it difficult to sell some services over the Internet?
18. Describe the evolution of a business's web site.
19. Describe the characteristics of a well-designed web site.

THINK CRITICALLY ABOUT BUSINESS

20. Identify a local business that could grow through merchandise expansion. Write a proposal, addressed to the business owner, that describes how it should use merchandise expansion to grow.
21. Use the business section of your newspaper or the Internet to identify a recent merger or acquisition that has occurred. Explain why the companies chose this method to expand.
22. Select a business traded in the stock market. Identify the information you should know before investing in the company.
23. Visit an online store. Evaluate the web site.

REAL-LIFE BUSINESS
The Scotts Company

The Scotts Company is the world's leading supplier of lawn and garden care products. Orlando McLean Scott established the company in 1868 when he bought a hardware store that also sold seed. His original company was named O.M. Scott & Sons. The first service the business performed used a seed-cleaning machine to remove weeds and inert matter from farm seed.

After 1900, the company evolved into a mail-order seed business. An advertisement in a farm journal resulted in the sale of grass seed to one of the country's first golf courses. Today, golf courses around the world use Scotts grass seed.

The company grew through merchandise expansion. In 1928, Scotts invented and sold lawn fertilizer. Scotts also invested money in research, resulting in inventions such as the lawn seed spreader and Kentucky bluegrass. The company expanded in 1972 by opening a hotline that provides lawn care advice.

Scotts also grew through diversification. It acquired several companies, including Hyponex, which produced soil products. Mergers included Stern's Miracle-Gro Products, which added new products to its merchandise lines. Another agreement enabled Scotts to enter the pesticide industry. Scotts has grown successfully for several decades.

Think Critically

1. What does the Scotts Company sell?
2. How was the company started?
3. How did the company grow through merchandise expansion?
4. How did the company grow through diversification?

GLOSSARY

401(k)   Diverts funds from the employee's salary, enabling the employee to save for retirement and reduce his or her current taxable income.

A

At will   Either the employee or employer can terminate the employment relationship between an "at will" employee and employer at any time.

Account   A collection of related financial information.

Account manager   Advertising executive who keeps the ad agency team working on a particular account on schedule and within the budget; also works with businesses and creative services to create effective advertisements using the correct cultural and consumer values.

Account services   Group within ad agency that identifies the benefits of a product, the possible consumers to target with advertising, and the best positioning against competing products. With this information, the group develops a complete advertising plan.

Accounts payable   Short-term debt owed by a business.

Accounts payable ledger   Data about money a business owes to others

Accounts receivable   Funds owed to a company by its customers.

Accounts receivable ledger   Contains data about money owed to a business for goods or services sold.

Acknowledgement form   Written statement the employee signs to declare he or she has received the employee handbook.

Acquisition   When a larger, wealthier company buys a smaller company and its assets.

Act of nature   An unpredictable interruption of the normal environment caused by a natural event such as an earthquake, flood, or severe storm.

Advertisement   A paid public announcement, usually emphasizing desirable qualities, to persuade consumers to buy an item or service.

Advertising agency   A company that specializes in providing many different services, from creating advertisements to measuring the effectiveness of the advertising before and after it is distributed.

Advertorial   A special advertising section, which is designed to look like an editorial in a publication.

Affordable method   Approach to advertising by a business that spends only what it thinks it can afford and does not consider the products sold, the economic conditions, revenue, or any other factor affecting the business.

Agenda   Identifies the topics to be covered during a meeting and establishes priority and provides focus for discussions.

Agent   An individual or business hired by the producer to find buyers for the product.

Agricultural zone   Land on which farming or ranching activities take place.

Americans with Disabilities Act (ADA)   Guarantees equal opportunity for individuals with disabilities in public accommodations, employment, transportation, state and local government services, and telecommunications.

Amortized payments   Paying the same amount each month for a specified number of months.

Analyst   A person who researches to identify consumers' behavior and values

Anchor store   A major store that attracts customers to a shopping center.

Ancillary cost   Advertising expenses including shipping expenses, equipment rental, and catering while a commercial is filmed.

Angel investor   Wealthy or experienced businessperson who provides venture capital to emerging companies in exchange for the opportunity to become involved in a business.

Appraisal   An estimate of the value of property, including real estate, equipment, and other business assets.

APR (Annual Percentage Rate)   Identifies the amount of interest charged for any unpaid credit card balance.

Arbitrator   A neutral third party who meets with the two parties to resolve a dispute without going to court.

Art   In advertising, art is everything in the advertisement that isn't copy, including the illustration and design.

Art director   Manages art production for an advertising group, ensuring the quality of the graphics for each project.

Articles of incorporation   Documents filed with the state to establish a corporation.

Asset   Item of economic value.

Atmospherics   The design and use of space to create an atmosphere or mood in the business environment.

Audit   A formal examination of a company's financial records.

Audit reports   Result from an examination of a company's accounting and financial records.

Auditory learner   One who learns by hearing and processing information.

Authority   The ability to influence or control individuals or objects to obtain resources needed to finish the task.

Authorization code   Ensures that a credit card has passed the criteria to make a purchase.

Automated Teller Machine   A machine designed to perform many of the services a human bank teller provides.

Average stock figure   The average amount of merchandise a business has in inventory during the year.

B

B2B (Business-to-business)   Companies that sell goods and services to other businesses.

Bait and switch   Advertising an attractive low price, and then trying to persuade the customer that the low-priced model is a poor buy because of its quality.

Balance sheet   A snapshot of a business, including its assets, liabilities, and capital.

Balloon payment   Large, final payment that pays off a loan.

Bank reconciliation   Verifies the match between a bank statement and a company's records.

Bankruptcy   Legal condition that enables the court to use an individual's assets to repay his or her creditors and lenders.

Bank statements   Document any activity within a specified account such as deposits, withdrawals, interest earned, and fees paid.

Banner   An advertisement placed on a web page that opens the advertiser's web site when a user clicks it.

Basic stock list   List of products customers expect to see when they enter a store.

Below-cost pricing   Pricing an item below its minimum cost plus a markup to attract customers.

Benchmark rating   Standard expectations of company performance, based on business activities.

Benefit   The advantage the consumer gets from a feature of a product or service.

Benefit positioning   Strategically positioning benefits to interest consumers searching for that benefit.

Benefits   Rewards an employee receives, in addition to a salary, for performing a job.

Bill of lading   Contract between a business or individual and a cargo carrier to transport goods to a specific destination.

Binding arbitration   Arbitration wherein the arbitrator can impose a decision on the opposing parties.

Bleed   When the background in a graphic file runs to the edge of the page, eliminating the white space border.

Bond   Written agreement purchased from a surety company that guarantees an individual will complete a specific task.

Bond line   Limit of bonds an individual is allowed to purchase.

Brand-loyal consumer   A customer who always purchases the same brand.

Breadth   The number of merchandise lines carried by a business.

Break point   The quantity at which a supplier's discount changes.

Budget   Estimate of expenses and revenue that identifies the amount of money available for a specific purpose.

Business broker   A person who introduces qualified buyers to an owner planning to sell a business.

Business cycle   A time period identified by a specific level of economic activity.

Business district   An unplanned grouping of businesses in a single location.

Business incubator   An organization that offers inexpensive space, dispenses business advice, and shares equipment and office expenses to assist new businesses.

Business plan   A document that describes a company's purpose, objectives, and methods for achieving the objectives.

Business vehicle log   A document containing information about the value and usage of vehicles owned by the business.

Button   An icon that causes an action, such as calculating a total or displaying another web page, when the user clicks it.

Buyer   Individuals who negotiate with suppliers to purchase the needed merchandise.

Buyer's agent   A Realtor who represents the buyer, not the seller.

Buying direct   The practice of a retailer buying directly from the producer.

Buy-sell agreement   A document that defines who can buy a partner's interest in a business, the situation that activates the buy-sell agreement, and the price to be paid for the partner's interest.

Bylaws   Statements that define the internal regulations and procedures a corporation follows.

By-products   Items produced in addition to the main product.

C

Canceled check   A paper check that has cleared the bank.

Capital   The portion of the company's assets owned by the business's owners.

Career path   Positions that provide related experience and increasing responsibility.

Carpal tunnel syndrome   Weakness and tingling in the hand caused by pressure on the medial nerve in the wrist.

Cash discount   Discount offered by suppliers to encourage and reward the paying of invoices before they are due.

Cash flow   The movement of cash in and out of a business.

Cash flow gap   The time period in which a business suffers from a lack of cash.

Cash flow projection   A forecast of the funds a business expects to receive and pay out during a specific time period.

Cash flow statement   A summary of cash flow over a specified period of time.

Central business district   An unplanned shopping area created around a community's public transportation system.

Central place   A center of commerce consisting of several retail establishments.

Certificate of deposit   A certificate given to a depositor that identifies the amount deposited and which contains the institution's promise to return the amount deposited plus a defined interest amount on a specific date. In most cases, a CD pays a higher rate of interest than a savings or money market account.

Certificate of occupancy   A legal document that certifies that a building has been inspected and meets the requirements for the business to operate on the premises.

Certified Public Accountant   An accountant who has met the requirements of state law and has been granted a license to practice accounting.

Channel   Medium of communication, including voice, gestures, or writing.

Channel of distribution   Path a product travels from a producer to a consumer.

Charge card   A type of credit card that doesn't charge interest but requires full payment each month.

Chargeback   Credit card transaction wherein a cardholder claims that a purchase was unauthorized or the product was unsatisfactory. The issuing bank removes the charge from the customer's card and doesn't deposit anything in the business's merchant account.

Charter   Documents, also known as Articles of Incorporation, a commercial bank files with the state which determine its level of business activity.

Class action   A lawsuit in which large numbers of people were injured by the same product.

Click trail   Identifies where visitors clicked as they moved through a web site.

Closing date   The date and time of the deadline for the submission of a proposal.

Cold call   Type of prospecting for clients in which a salesperson calls a list of new contacts to ask if they are interested in purchasing the company's product.

Command economy   The government owns most of the nation's resources and commands businesses to produce specific items or perform specific jobs.

Commercial banks   Financial institutions that provide the widest variety of services.

Commercial lease   A contract between a property owner and a business that permits a business to use the owner's location for a specific time period in exchange for payment.

Commercial mortgage   Loans made to businesses as opposed to individuals.

Commercial zone   A zone that may include areas that provide retail sales, services, professional offices, and other commercial activities for a neighborhood or community.

Commission   Flat amount or percentage of an amount paid to an employee responsible for a sale.

Commission record   A document that identifies any commissions paid.

Communication   The exchange of information between individuals through symbols, signs, or behaviors.

Community   A group of people with a common characteristic or interest living within a larger society.

Community center   Type of shopping center that meets the basic needs of a neighborhood and provides a few additional products such as clothing and appliances.

Compensation   Direct and indirect payments made to an employee.

Competitive positioning   Marketing strategy that emphasizes the differences among similar products.

Comprehensive layout   A type of advertising layout that is polished, with all the elements placed accurately.

Conception date   The date the idea for an invention is conceived.

Confidentiality agreement   Protects a company by guaranteeing that inventions, methods, and company information will not be revealed to individuals or businesses outside the company.

Consumer   Individual who uses goods.

Contest   Using skill to compete for a prize.

Contingency   An offer that depends on something else occurring first.

Continuous processing   Type of processing where raw materials constantly pass through equipment that changes the form of the product to something more useful.

Contract   Agreement that legally binds two or more parties to a specific course of action.

Contract bond   Bond a contracting business buys to guarantee that it will fill the terms of the contract.

Contraction   A period of general economic decline.

Convenience goods   Merchandise purchased frequently by consumers.

Conversation   A verbal exchange of information or ideas.

Copyright   Grants an author the exclusive right to copy, modify, publish, perform, display, and sell creative work.

Copywriter   A member of the advertising team who writes the text (also called copy) that works with the images.

Corporation   A business structure, created and regulated by state law, that functions as an independent legal entity.

Cost of goods sold   The amount a business pays to manufacture or acquire a single unit of the items it sells.

Counter   Tracks the number of hits for a web site.

Coupon   Provides a reduction in price for a buyer.

Creative boutique   An advertising firm that specializes in developing creative concepts, writing creative text, and providing artistic services.

Creative director   A person in an ad agency who manages work groups and ensures that the art and text come together to create the desired results on schedule.

Creative services   A group of personnel in an advertising agency responsible for developing the advertising message and delivering the message to consumers using words and images.

Credit   The exchange of goods or services for the promise of payment.

Credit card   Plastic card used by consumers to make purchases by borrowing money from the financial institution that issued the card.

Credit limit   Maximum amount that can be charged by the credit cardholder when making purchases.

Credit report   History of each consumer's credit activities, including any loan, loan payment history, credit card balance, and personal information such as the consumer's address and employment history.

Cubicle   An area surrounded by panels containing surfaces for workspace and equipment and seating designed to be used by a worker or group of workers.

Culture   An integrated pattern of behavior, knowledge, and beliefs that is acquired from a group and passed to future generations.

Current asset   Cash or items that can be converted to cash in less than a year.

Custom manufacturing   Process of designing and building a unique product to meet the customer's needs.

D

Deceitful diversion of patronage   The practice of publishing or verbalizing false statements about another business to try to divert patrons from the business.

Deceptive pricing   Misleading prices intended to lure customers into a business.

Decode   The part of the communication process where a sender's message is filtered through a receiver's unique characteristics, which differ from the sender's characteristics.

Deductible   A specific amount per claim or accident that is applied toward an insured loss.

Deduction   Dollar amounts taken from an employee's pay every pay period. Federal and state regulations require you to deduct federal social security and income tax.

Deed   A legal document that transfers ownership of real estate.

Delegate   To assign responsibility for a task to someone else.

Demographics   The statistical characteristics of human populations.

Department   The section of a store that handles a particular type of merchandise.

Deposit slips   Records that document the transfer of money into a specified bank account.

Depreciate   To deduct the cost of items in proportional amounts over several years.

Depreciation schedule   Identifies all the assets that are depreciated, listing the date the item was acquired, the cost, depreciation, and current value.

Depression   A recession that is major in scale and duration.

Depth   The number of items in various colors, sizes, styles, and price ranges offered within a merchandise line.

Design engineer   Converts concepts and information into detailed plans and specifications that are used to manufacture a product.

Design patent   A patent based on the look of a product; appropriate if an invention is new, original, and ornamental design for a manufactured item.

Direct deposit   Paycheck is automatically deposited into a savings or checking account.

Direct Distribution   The sale of products directly from the manufacturer to the consumer.

Directors   Elected members of the board of a corporation who make major decisions affecting the corporation, such as deciding to purchase a location and hiring or appointing officers, particularly the chief executive officer.

Disability insurance   Insurance that provides income replacement by paying 60 to 80 percent of an employee's normal salary when he or she can't work because of an illness or accident.

Disclosure statement   Identifies valuable information about a credit card and the rules regarding its usage, including how the interest is calculated and any fees or penalties that can be applied.

Discount rate   The amount of money a business pays to process and deposit credit card transactions.

Discounts   Amounts subtracted from the list price of a good or service.

Distribution   Process of moving a product to the final consumer.

District   Geographic division, made up of several states, which comprise the Federal Reserve System.

Diversification   Expanding a company through starting or acquiring businesses that are outside a company's existing products and markets.

Dividend   A portion of a corporation's profit paid to shareholders.

Division   An operating unit of a business.

Dock   A reduction of pay for missing work.

Doing business as (DBA)   A business situation in which a business operates under a name that is different from the real name of the owner.

Domain name   A unique name that identifies a web site.

Ɛ

E-commerce   Doing business online; requires specialized software, a secure web site, and a method of processing payments.

Economic damages   Any losses that can be measured by a dollar amount.

Economic system   The way a nation uses resources to produce goods and services.

Economist   A specialist who studies the economy.

Employee file   Contains all documents related to an employee's activities related to a business.

Employee handbook   Provides guidelines for an employer and employee.

Employer Identification Number (EIN)   The number the IRS assigns to identify businesses that must file tax returns.

Employment letter   A written offer of employment.

Employment tax report   A report that documents taxes withheld during the specified time period.

Encode   Part of the communication process in which the sender converts a message into words, symbols, sounds, images, numbers, gestures, and movements.

Endorsement   An attachment to an insurance policy that adds a benefit or feature to the policy.

Entrepreneur   An individual who owns, manages, and assumes the financial risk of a business enterprise.

Equilibrium price   The price at which the quantity supplied exactly equals the quantity demanded of a product.

Ergonomics   The science of designing and arranging equipment, workspace, and seating for safe and efficient use.

Establishment   A single location where a business operates.

Etiquette   Correct conduct in social situations.

Event marketing specialist   A person who identifies the events a business could support. He or she considers elements such as the product, the target segment, the reputation and size of the event, and its location.

Event sponsorship   A business helps to fund an event in exchange for displaying a brand name, logo, or advertising message at the event, in any literature about the event, or during any broadcasts of the event.

Evoked set   A short list of brand names consumers think of when a product or service is mentioned.

Excise tax   A tax required by state or federal government for the manufacture and sale of nonessential products such as alcohol.

Exclusion   A provision that identifies dangers, property, or locations that aren't covered by an insurance policy.

Executive summary   A summary of the information contained in the rest of a business plan.

Exempt   A classification of employee who performs work that is intellectual rather than manual labor, exercising discretion and independent judgment.

Expansion   A period of general economic improvement.

Expense report   A report that documents products or services purchased as an expense, a loss expended to acquire a benefit.

Expert   An individual with knowledge and skill.

Extended warranty   A warranty that lasts longer than the warranty offered by a product's manufacturer.

External facilitators   People who perform specialized services related to advertising for small businesses and advertising agencies, including providing sets, equipment, and work crews for commercials or photography sessions.

Extractor   Businesses that remove raw materials from the land, water, or air.

F

Facilities   Items built, installed, or provided at a particular location for a specific purpose.

Fair competition   Competition based on price, quality, and service.

Fair Labor Standards Act (FLSA)   A federal law that sets standards for many employment situations.

Fashion goods   Merchandise that follow changes in style and thus change constantly.

Fatality rates   A percentage calculated by dividing the number of workplace fatalities by the number of individuals in the field.

Feature   A characteristic that is part of a product or service.

Federal Reserve System   The central bank of the United States; responsible for maintaining a healthy banking system and a healthy economy.

Federal Trade Commission   The federal agency responsible to stop unfair methods of competition.

Firewall   Software that prevents unauthorized access to data by outside users.

Fixed assets   Assets that can't be converted to cash in less than a year.

Fixtures   The physical items used to hold merchandise and create displays.

Font   A set of type that has a specific appearance.

Food and Drug Administration   The agency under the U.S. Department of Health and Human Services that regulates a variety of products, including food, drugs, medical devices such as pacemakers and hearing aids, biologics such as vaccines, animal feed and drugs, cosmetics, and radiation-emitting products.

Footer   Text that appears in the margin at the bottom of the page or every other page of a document.

Format   The appearance of a document.

Frames   Three-by-three–inch boxes used in storyboarding.

Franchise   A commercial relationship in which a franchisee is permitted to use the licensed trademark and marketing plan of the trademark owner, the franchiser, in exchange for an initial fee and possible ongoing royalty payments.

Franchise agreement   The contract between a franchisee and franchiser.

Franchise broker   An individual who sells or arranges for the sale of a franchise.

Franchise disclosure statement   A Federal Trade Commission-required document that contains information about the franchiser and franchisee; it is intended to protect potential franchisees from taking unreasonable financial risks.

Fraud   Deceit intended to gain something of value.

Free market economy   Resources are privately owned and each business determines the products or services it will produce and sell.

Freestanding location   A retail site not connected to other buildings or part of a shopping center.

Frequency   The number of times an audience is exposed to an advertisement in a specified time period.

Full block style   Style of formatting for letters that uses left-justified text.

Full-time   Status of employees who work 35 hours or more per week.

G

Garnishment   An amount deducted from an employee's salary to pay a debt to a creditor.

Gatefold   Page in a magazine that folds out to hold an extra-wide advertisement.

Gateway   Hardware and software that provides real-time access to credit card transactions.

General journal   A record of all financial transactions not recorded in a specialized journal.

General ledger   Contains accounts in which all transactions are classified.

General partners   Partners equally involved in operating a business, indicated by participation in business decisions and unlimited liability for company debts.

General partnership   One form of business structure. *See also* General partners.

Glass ceiling   An intangible barrier within a company hierarchy that prevents women and minorities from obtaining upper-level positions.

Grace period   No interest is charged on a credit card balance if the balance is zero at the beginning of the billing period and the new balance is paid before the due date.

Gross pay   Total amount paid to an employee before deductions are applied.

Group interview   A type of employment interview in which a panel of several managers from a company takes turns asking questions to a prospective employee.

H

Hands-on manager   A manager who becomes actively and personally involved in every business activity.

Header   Text, usually repeated, that appears in the margin at the top of a page or every other page.

Heading   Short for headline, is a title or subtitle that identifies the topic of the information.

Health hazard   Occur during routine job performance; can cause injury, illness, or death.

Health insurance   Provides financial assistance for medical expenses.

Heavy user   Consumer who purchases large amounts of the same product.

Historical method   Basing a company's current advertising budget solely on what the company spent the previous year.

Hit   Electronic request to view a specific web page.

Home page   The entry page for a web site.

Hyperlink   Electronic connection between one specific location in a document to another location in the same document or a different document.

I

Illustrator   A person in an ad agency responsible for drawing or creating the graphics for each project.

Income statement   Summarizes a business's earnings and expenses over a specified period of time.

Incorporator   The person appointed to sign the articles of incorporation.

Individuality   The distinctive characteristics that make each individual unique; affects each consumer's purchasing decisions.

Industrial zone   A geographical location occupied by manufacturers of various products.

Industry   Companies that perform similar business activities that are distinct from those performed by other businesses.

In-house agency   An advertising department operating inside a company whose main business isn't advertising.

Infomercial   A televised advertisement presented as a documentary.

Initial markup   The difference between a product's cost and initial retail selling price.

Initial public offering (IPO)   When a company registers with the SEC to sell stock to the public for the first time.

Inspection complaint   Complaint about a hazard that causes an OSHA representative to visit the business site.

Insurance   A contract that protects a policyholder from financial loss caused by a specific danger.

Intellectual property   Products created by the mind, rather than made by hand.

Interactive agency   An ad agency that specializes in helping clients prepare advertising for new, interactive media.

Interest   An amount paid to use someone else's money, usually expressed as an annual percentage of the amount used.

Intermittent processing   Products made in a single short production run that manufactures a limited quantity of different products.

Internal accountant   An accountant on company staff.

Internal audit reports   Reports that evaluate a company's operations and performance.

Internet service provider (ISP)   An organization that provides access to the Internet via a dial-up connection, cable connection, satellite connection, etc.

Interview   A meeting at which information is obtained from a person.

Inventory   Merchandise in storage at a specific time.

Inventory records   Record of merchandise in storage at a specific time.

Investigation complaint   Complaint to OSHA that does not meet the conditions needed to trigger an inspection.

Invoices   Documents that specify the quantity and cost of items purchased, and the deadline for paying the bill.

Involuntary termination   The decision to end employment is made by the employer.

Issuing bank   A financial institution that issues credit cards.

J

Jingle   A company slogan set to music.

Job description   A description of the tasks to be performed; confirms the responsibilities and actions expected of an employee.

Job responsibilities   Tasks that an employee is expected to perform or supervise.

Job title   Name assigned to a worker's position in a company.

Journal   Record of all financial transactions that occur each business day.

Just-In-Time (JIT) manufacturing   Production environment in which components arrive at a workstation when they are needed.

K

Key person   Identification for insurance purposes of someone in a business who is critical to the operation of the business.

Kinesthetic learner   A person who learns by interacting and processing information.

Knowledge   The possession of information.

L

Law of demand   Consumers will buy more of a product at a lower price than at a higher price.

Law of Retail Gravitation   Theory that describes how large cities attract customers from smaller communities because the larger cities are more attractive to shoppers.

Law of supply   Producers are willing to sell more of a product at a higher price than at a lower price.

Layoff   Termination of employment is the result of a necessary reduction in a company's workforce.

Layout   A drawing that shows where each element in an advertisement is placed.

Lead time   The amount of time between ordering and receiving an item.

Leading economic indicators   Statistics that reliably move up or down before the general economy follows.

Lease   A contract that enables one party to use property belonging to a second party in exchange for a specified payment.

Ledger   A collection of accounts.

Letterhead   A sheet of stationery that is preprinted or engraved, usually with the logo, name, and address of a business.

Liability   Assigns responsibility for damage or injury.

Libel   False written statement that injures the reputation of a business.

License bond   Bond a company purchases that guarantees it will comply with state and local codes.

Life insurance   Pays one or more specified individuals when an insured employee dies.

Limited liability company (LLC)   A business structure that features pass-through taxation and limited personal liability.

Limited partners   Partners in a corporation who have only limited personal liability for a company's debts and no voice in company decisions.

Limited partnership   One form of business structure. One or more of the partners is a limited partner and one or more of the partners must be a general partner. *See also* General partners, limited partners.

Limited personal liability   A partner's financial risk is limited to the amount invested in the business.

List price   A supplier's published price for each product it sells.

Lock box   A post office box opened in a company's name; used to collect customer payments.

Logical   Organization of material in a document wherein the sequence of facts or arrangement of elements is predictable.

Logo   An image used to represent a company.

M

Maintained markup   The difference between a product's cost and the price paid when the item is sold.

Make or buy strategy   A decision based on a host of factors of why it is better to either manufacture or purchase components, or vice versa.

Manufacturing   The process of making a product by processing, assembling, or converting raw and semi-finished materials.

Margin   The area outside the main printing area on a sheet of paper.

Markdown   A price reduction.

Market development   A strategy that sells existing products to a new market.

Market penetration   A strategy that increases the sale of existing products to a current market without altering the products.

Market research   The systematic collection of information about customers, competition, and the business environment.

Market segment   A group of people with common characteristics and similar needs and wants.

Marketable   Products able to be offered for sale and wanted by consumers.

Marketing   A combination of art and science that persuades consumers to purchase a company's products.

Marketing mix   The mix of all marketing activities, such as advertising, sales promotions, sponsorships, and public relations.

Marketing services   Services an ad agency provides, including research, sales promotion and event sponsorship, direct marketing, and public relations.

Markup   The difference between the cost of goods sold and the retail price.

Mass media   Forms of communication designed to reach large numbers of people.

Mass production   Using machines to produce identical products in large quantities using the same process.

Maturity date   The date at which a certificate of deposit completes its term.

Mechanical   Final version of an advertising layout.

Media buyer   A person who purchases large quantities of media time at a discounted rate and sells portions of the time to other businesses at a higher rate.

Media planner   Specialists who help businesses select the most effective media options.

Media researcher   Investigates media options and provides recommendations for businesses.

Media services   Group of advertising services that includes media planners, media buyers, and media researcher.

Media-buying service   (See Media buyer.)

Mediator   A neutral third party, with no power to enforce a decision, who meets with the two parties to resolve a dispute without going to court.

Memorandum   A brief document written for interoffice communication.

Mentor   An individual with experience or knowledge in a specific area who provides advice or guidance.

Merchandise   Any products that are bought and sold in business.

Merchandise density   The amount of merchandise displayed or shelved per 1,000 feet.

Merchandise mix   The variety, breadth, and depth of merchandise a store carries.

Merchandise plan   Describes the specific items you acquire to sell in each department at each retail establishment.

Merchant association   Retailers in a shopping center who join together to establish rules regulating the appearance of the stores; they may also share maintenance and security costs.

Merchant credit card service   A financial institution that processes credit card transactions for businesses.

Merger   When two companies that are similar in size join forces.

Message weight   The number of times, including duplication, that an audience is exposed to an advertising message by a specific media vehicle.

Middleman   Any business that helps to distribute a producer's goods to consumers.

Minimum daily balance   Lowest amount in an account during a specified time period, usually a month.

Minutes   A document that provides a brief written summary of a meeting.

Mission statement   A brief description of a company's purpose.

Mixed-use zone   A geographic area that includes residential housing and facilities mixed with commercial businesses.

Model stock plan   List of any merchandise sold by the retailer that is not on the basic stock list.

Modified block style   Format for business letters in which some text starts in the middle of a line.

Money market account   A savings vehicle that earns a higher interest rate than a savings account.

Mortgage agreement   A legally binding contract in which the borrower agrees to give the creditor the deed to the property offered as collateral if the borrower is not able to repay the loan.

Mutual ownership   Depositors and borrowers in a thrift.

N

NAICS code   A standard method of categorizing businesses.

Navigation   Moving between pages on a single web site or between web sites.

Needs   Items humans can't live without.

Negligent   Occurs when an individual or business did not take proper care or exhibited careless behavior.

Negotiate   The process of dealing with another party to reach an agreement.

Neighborhood business district   An unplanned business area that is usually located on a major road near a residential area.

Neighborhood center   A small shopping center that meets the basic product and service needs of a neighborhood.

Net pay   The amount an employee receives after all deductions are taken from wages.

Net worth   The portion of a company's assets owned by the business's owners.

Networking   The exchange of information and services among individuals and businesses.

Night depository box   Allows for deposits to be made to a financial institution after it has closed for the day.

Noise   Anything that distorts or slows the message transfer in a communication process.

Non-binding arbitration   An arbitrator recommends a solution but has no authority to force disputing parties to agree.

Non-competition clause   Prevents a seller from opening a similar business within a specific geographic area.

Non-directive interview   Flexible interview format; does not follow a rigid agenda.

Nondisclosure agreement   A contract in which the individuals promise to protect the confidentiality of any secret information that is revealed during business transactions or employment.

Noneconomic damages   Any loss that can't be measured by a dollar amount.

Nonexempt   A classification of employee who performs manual or intellectual labor but is not required to exercise discretion or independent judgment.

Nonprofit business   Established to raise funds for a specific cause such as medical research, homeless children, or literacy programs.

Nonuser   A consumer who has never used a product or service.

Notary public   A licensed public officer who certifies that writings are authentic.

O

Objective and task method   A method of determining an advertising budget that recognizes and uses the relationship between what a business wants to accomplish and the amount it wants to spend.

Obligee   Customer who a surety company will pay if a bonded service isn't completed.

Occupational Safety and Health Administration (OSHA)   Government agency established to prevent work-related injuries, illnesses, and deaths.

Officer   Supervises the day-to-day administration and management tasks and hires managers and other employees to manage and complete the tasks associated with a corporation's business purpose.

One-way exclusive dealing   An arrangement between a supplier and retailer wherein a supplier gives a retailer exclusive rights to sell a product in a specific area, but the retailer does not do anything for the supplier.

Online store   A web site that enables consumers to purchase products on the Internet.

Open-ended credit   Credit that can be used repeatedly until the consumer reaches a credit limit.

Operating agreement   A legal document that describes the rights and responsibilities of each member in an LLC.

Operating expenses   Ongoing and recurrent expenses involved in operating a business.

Operating line of credit   A source of business financing that provides a limited line of credit to a business for a specific time period.

Opportunity cost   A potential benefit sacrificed by pursuing an alternative.

Organizational chart   A graphic representation of the hierarchy of a company's managers and employees.

Outline   A listing of the primary parts of a document.

Outsourcing   Paying an outside company to perform a specific business activity.

Overtime   Hours worked beyond the standard schedule.

Owner's equity   The difference between total assets and total liabilities; the business owner's share of the assets of the business.

P

Palming off   Practice of deceitful diversion of patronage when a retailer buys merchandise from one manufacturer, but places the label of a more popular manufacturer on the products.

Paraphrase   Express the same information in different words.

Partnership   A business owned by two or more individuals that has not been incorporated.

Partnership agreement   A legal document that describes the rights and responsibilities of each partner in a partnership.

Part-time   Employees who work fewer than 35 hours per week.

Pass-through taxation   Business profit is treated as personal income for a sole proprietor.

Patent   A government-issued protection that grants property rights to an inventor, for a limited time, thereby preventing others from making, using, offering for sale, or selling the invention in the United States or importing the invention from another country.

Patterned interview   Interview format that is rigid and inflexible.

Payroll   List of employees entitled to receive pay.

Payroll records   Documents that identify amounts paid to employees and withheld from paychecks.

Peak   The end of an expansion phase in a business cycle.

Penalty APR   The interest rate that goes into effect for all future payments if a credit card holder is late making a payment.

Percentage of sales method   Basing a current advertising budget on a percentage of last year's sales or a percentage of the sales the business expects to make this year.

Perceptual positioning strategy   Marketing that emphasizes emotional or subjective opinions about a product.

Performance review   A process that enables an employee and supervisor to discuss and evaluate the employee's job performance.

Perks   Minor benefits of employment.

Permit bond   A bond that guarantees that a business will comply with local codes that apply to a specific situation.

Personal selling   Direct communication between a sales representative and a consumer when the intention of the communication is a purchase.

Personnel density   The number of store employees per 1,000 square feet of retail space.

Petty cash   A small supply of cash, usually around $100, used to pay small expenses.

Physical positioning strategy   Marketing strategy that emphasizes the objective physical characteristics of a product.

Plant patent   Protects inventions or discoveries and asexual reproduction of any distinct and new variety of plant.

Point of indifference   A boundary between two cities at which customers will shop in either city.

Point-of-purchase advertising   Advertising that includes signs, banners, flags, and special merchandise displays.

Positioning   The process of making a product different from other products in the consumer's mind.

Positioning theme   A central motivating idea that creates a focus for marketing activities and helps a business make internal decisions that create substance for a customers.

Predatory pricing   The practice of charging different prices in different locations to eliminate competition.

Premium   Items that are free or cost less with the purchase of another item.

Press release   A statement prepared for distribution to the media.

Price line   Assigning one of several standard prices to products categorized by cost and quality.

Primary research   Gathering information directly from a source for a specific purpose.

Principal   Amount borrowed in a loan.

Private corporation   A business that does not trade its shares publicly. Trading/selling of shares is governed by the corporation.

Private sector   Workers not employed by a local, state, or federal government office or agency.

Probation   Trial period when an employee is subject to testing and evaluation to determine fitness for a position.

Producers   The members of a production team who create the desired effects for a radio or television commercial.

Product liability   Insurance that provides some assistance when a consumer makes a claim against a company.

Production scheduling   Identifies the steps in a manufacturing process, the time required to complete each step, and the sequence of the steps.

Production services   Producers and production assistants who bring images and words to life for radio and television commercials.

Profit   Results when the amount of money coming into your business is larger than the amount leaving your business.

Profit and loss statement   A summary of a company's earnings and expenses over a specified period of time.

Promissory note   A legal contract in which one party agrees to repay a debt.

Promotional discount   Discount offered by suppliers to retailers that perform an advertising or promotional service for the supplier.

Prop   Physical items used to illustrate or emphasize a particular point.

Proposal   A document, or bid, created to respond to a Request for a Proposal (RFP) that describes how the supplier can fill the listed requirements.

Prospecting   The process of identifying potential customers.

Prototype   A full-size functional model of an invention.

Psychographics   Describes a market segmentation method that concentrates on the consumer's activities, interests, and opinions.

Public accommodation   A private business that provides goods or services to the public.

Public accountant   A consultant often used by small businesses to perform accounting tasks.

Public corporation   A company owned by its stockholders who trade its shares, also called stock, publicly on a stock market.

Public relations   The business function that works with the media.

Publicity   Information about a company's activities that are covered by the news media without payment.

Punitive damages   Damages awarded to punish a business proven to have manufactured and distributed a product even though it knew the product was dangerous.

Purchase order   A legally binding offer sent to a supplier to buy products or services upon specific terms and conditions.

Q

Qualification   Requirements an applicant must meet to be considered for a specific position.

Quantity discount   The dollar amount based on the quantity of merchandise purchased that is subtracted from the list price.

R

Range   The maximum distance a consumer will travel to buy a product.

Raw material   Matter that can be converted by manufacturing or processing into new and useful products.

Reach   The percentage of the target audience that is exposed to an advertisement in the specified time period.

Reasonable accommodation   Any modification to a job or work environment that will enable a qualified applicant or employee with a disability to apply for or hold a position.

Rebate   A return of a portion of the purchase price from the manufacturer to the purchaser.

Recall   Public call for the return of a defective or contaminated product.

Receiver   The person in a communication process who decodes a sender's message.

Recession   A period of significant decline in trade, employment, and income.

Reconciliation   Process to verify the match between a bank statement and a company's records.

Referral   A testimony of the supplier's good business practices.

Regional center   A shopping center that contains retailers who sell products such as general merchandise, clothing, and furniture.

Registered agent   An individual who acts as point of contact for a corporation.

Repetitive production   Performing the same simple manufacturing activity over and over.

Replacement cost   The cost to replace an item.

Repositioning   Starting subsequent marketing and branding cycles of a product at square one.

Request for a Proposal   A document that describes a task or project to be completed by a vendor. It sets guidelines to complete the project and criteria to evaluate the work performed.

Researcher   A person who collects data by studying advertising results and target audiences.

Residential zone   A geographic area that includes areas that provide housing, public services, and facilities for the residential population.

Resignation   Employees choose to leave a job.

Resources   Natural sources of materials or wealth.

Responsibility   Completing a task and answering to another individual for it.

Restructuring   Assigning new responsibilities to existing employees.

Résumé   Summary of an individual's qualifications, education, and experience.

Retail   The sale of goods or services directly to the final customer.

Retail price   Amount a customer pays for an item, excluding discounts.

Retraction   Public withdrawal of false statements, admitting that they were not true.

Risk level   Identifies the probability of losing the money, time, or materials invested in the business.

Ritual   A formalized act or series of acts that are performed frequently.

Rough layout   An early step in the design of an advertisement in which preliminary or rough versions of photos, graphics, and text are used to demonstrate the concept.

S

Salary   Fixed amount every week or two weeks, regardless of minor variations in the number of hours worked each week.

Salary range   Minimum and maximum amount an employee can be paid for performing a job.

Sales promotion   The use of incentives to increase the brand value for consumers or distributors.

Sales tax returns   Forms that document the sales taxes collected and paid to state or local government.

Sampling   The practice of giving away samples of a product or service to persuade consumers to buy the product or service.

Scarcity   A condition that occurs when consumers want more than the available resources can support.

Search time   The amount of time a consumer spends finding products or services he or she wants.

Seasonal discount   Discount given by suppliers to retailers that take delivery of products during the off-season.

Seasonal goods   Merchandise that are popular only during certain times of the year.

Seasonal service   Useful labor that does not produce a tangible product and is popular only during certain times of the year.

Secondary business district   An unplanned business area that grows around a major intersection.

Secondary research   Information that was previously gathered in published sources.

Secure socket layer (SSL)   Data encryption method that protects data, such as online payment information, transferred between an Internet host and the browser.

Securities and Exchange Commission (SEC)   Government agency that protects investors by educating consumers and regulating the disclosure of information by public companies.

Self-employment taxes   Contributions to the social security and Medicare programs.

Seller's permit   Permit required by some states for businesses that sell or lease tangible property.

Sender   Originator of a message.

Service   Useful labor that does not produce a tangible product.

Servicemark   A symbol used to identify the source of a service and distinguish it from any other service that may be similar.

Settle accounts   Process of submitting credit card receipts to a financial institution that aren't submitted automatically.

Share of voice method   When a company spends more than its competition so consumers become more aware of the company's product than its competitor's product.

Shareholder   Individuals who own shares of a corporation.

Shopping cart   Software program incorporated into a web site to collect and record purchasing information.

Shopping center   A shopping district owned, planned, and managed by a single individual or business.

Shrinkage   The loss of products to a business due to shoplifting.

Signature   Stored data including text and graphics that can be placed automatically at the end of all e-mail messages.

Skill   The ability to use knowledge effectively, often as a result of experience.

Slander   A false spoken statement that injures the reputation of a business.

Slogan   A catchphrase meant to help consumers remember a brand name.

Small claims court   Court where limited civil claims are prosecuted without formal legal representation.

Social class   A group that shares the same economic or social status.

Social entrepreneur   Individual who establishes nonprofit businesses.

Software piracy   Unauthorized copying of software.

Sole proprietorship   A business owned by a single individual that is not registered with a state as any other form of business.

Staple goods   Merchandise that are constantly demanded by customers.

Staple service   Useful labor that does not produce a tangible product but is constantly demanded by customers.

Start-up costs   Any amount paid for creating a business before it begins operating.

Statement   Document identifying transactions in an account.

Stationery   The paper on which company documents are printed.

Stock turn rate   The number of times the average stock is sold during the year.

Stockkeeping unit (SKU)   Merchandise classifications based on the characteristics of the merchandise such as type, material, color, price, size, or brand.

Stop payment   Instructions to a financial institution to refuse payment when a specific draft or check is presented.

Storyboard   A series of sketches that show the sequential visual scenes and the matching text for a commercial.

Strategic objective   A goal that a business plans to achieve in three to five years.

Strict liability   Assigns liability without requiring any evidence of negligence.

Structure   Defines the sequence in which the content appears in a document.

Substantiate   Proof that what a business says in its advertising claims about a product's quality, safety, or performance are true.

Super-regional center   Shopping center that has more than 750,000 square feet available to be leased.

Supervisor   Individual who manages other employees.

Surety company   Company that issues bonds.

Sweep account   Savings account to which cash balances are transferred from other accounts in order to earn higher interest rates.

Sweepstakes   Determining winners by chance without judging.

Swipe   Process of passing a credit card through a piece of equipment that reads the information on a card's magnetic strip.

Switcher   A consumer who switches from brand to brand.

Synergy   Interaction that creates a total effect greater than the sum of the individual parts.

T

Tactical objective   Short-term goals necessary to reach a strategic objective.

Target segment   A subgroup of a market that is chosen to be the focus of a marketing and advertising campaign.

Task group   Individuals from several departments who work together to complete a single task.

Tax return   A form that reports an individual's or a company's tax liability to federal, state, and local governments.

Telecommute   Work performed at home via electronic link-up with an employer.

Teleprompter   A device that displays a magnified electronic script in front of a public speaker.

Term   Length of time money in a certificate of deposit account is retained by a financial institution.

Term loan   Loan for property improvements, expansion, and changes that provide long-term benefits.

Termination for cause   Terminating an employee because his or her behavior seriously violates company policy or creates significant jeopardy for the company or its employees.

Territorial restrictions   Restrictions placed on a retailer by a supplier, which limit the geographic area in which a retailer can resell the supplier's merchandise.

Third party   Checks written to a business, individual, or government agency other than your business or an employee.

Threshold   Defines the minimum demand for a product or service that must exist in an area to maintain a store's existence.

Thrift   Full-service savings and loan associations that maintain a high percentage of their loans in real estate.

Thumbnail   Shows a general idea of where items in an advertisement will be placed and is one-fourth the size of the proposed advertisement.

Top-of-the-mind awareness   Identifies the leading brands in a specific product category by asking a consumer to name brands in that category.

Trade discount   When a buyer performs wholesale or retail services for a supplier.

Trade magazine   Publications that contain information about a specific industry or interest.

Trademark   A symbol used to identify the source of a physical product and distinguish it from any other products that may be similar. *See also* Servicemark.

Traffic manager   Coordinates the action between creative services and media services and ensures that ads are ready for the media placement deadline.

Train-the-trainer   One employee is trained by an outside resource, then teaches the information to others in the company.

Transaction clearinghouse   Verifies credit card information and validates the customer's credit line.

Trough   The end of a contraction phase in a business cycle.

Two-way exclusive dealing   Illegal arrangement between a supplier and a retailer that gives a retailer exclusive rights to sell a product in a specific area for which the retailer offers to do something for the supplier.

Tying arrangement   A supplier with a strong product forces a retailer to buy a weak product before allowing the retailer to buy the strong product.

U

Undue hardship   The difficulty or expense of providing accommodations for a disabled employee.

Uniform Resource Locator (URL)   Identifies the address for a specific web page.

Unique Selling Proposition (USP) philosophy   Technique to highlight some unique aspect of a product to separate it from all other like products in the mind of the consumer.

Unique visitor   An individual who views a web site.

User license   Permission to use a software program.

User positioning   A marketing plan that focuses on the user, rather than on any aspect of the product.

Utility   An item's usefulness.

Utility patent   Based on the functionality of the product, a utility patent is appropriate for inventions or discoveries of a new and useful process, machine, article of manufacture, or compositions of matter, or any new useful improvement of these items.

V

Value   The worth, utility, or importance of an item.

Venture capital firm   A business that invests in small, emerging companies in exchange for a percentage of ownership.

Videoconference   A broadcast of a live or recorded presentation; it can be transmitted over the Internet to separate locations at the same time.

Virus   A program hidden in a message or attachment that performs an undesirable act.

Visual learner   A person who learns best by seeing how something is done.

Voluntary termination   *See* Resignation.

Voucher   Documents the transaction when money is disbursed from the petty cash fund.

W

Wages   Payment based on the number of hours worked or pieces produced.

Walk-in   People seeking employment who show up without a previous appointment.

Wants   Items one would like to have but can live without.

Warranty   A guarantee of the integrity of a product that usually ensures the buyer that the business will take responsibility for repair or replacement of defective parts or the entire product.

Web hosting   A company that provides electronic storage space for individuals and businesses.

Whistle-blower   An individual who reports unsafe or hazardous working conditions to OSHA.

White space   Areas of an advertisement containing no text or graphics. Used to help focus attention on important elements.

Wholesaler   Middleman that buys directly from a producer and sells to retailers or large commercial users.

Wire transfer   Instructs an institution to pay a specific amount to an individual or business.

Work for hire   Work performed by an employee in the course of normal business; often used in determining copyright ownership.

Workers' compensation insurance   Pays medical and disability benefits when a worker is injured according to a state-approved formula.

Wrongful death   Death caused by the fault of another or from a defective product.

Z

Zoning ordinances   Laws that regulate the use of private land by limiting development and business activities within specific geographic areas.

INDEX